Stanley Gibbons
Commonwealth

Northern Caribbean, Bahamas & Bermuda

3rd edition 2013

STANLEY GIBBONS LTD
London and Ringwood

By Appointment to
Her Majesty The Queen
Stanley Gibbons Ltd
London
Philatelists

Published by Stanley Gibbons Ltd
Editorial, Publications Sales Offices
and Distribution Centre:
7 Parkside, Christchurch Road, Ringwood,
Hants BH24 3SH

© Stanley Gibbons Ltd 2013

Copyright Notice

The contents of this Catalogue, including the numbering system and illustrations, are fully protected by copyright. No part of this publication may be reproduced, stored in a retrieval system, or transmitted in any form or by any means, electronic, mechanical, photocopying, recording or otherwise, without the prior permission of Stanley Gibbons Limited. Requests for such permission should be addressed to the Catalogue Editor. This Catalogue is sold on condition that it is not, by way of trade or otherwise, lent, re-sold, hired out, circulated or otherwise disposed of other than in its complete, original and unaltered form and without a similar condition including this condition being imposed on the subsequent purchaser.

British Library Cataloguing in
Publication Data.
A catalogue record for this book is available
from the British Library.

Errors and omissions excepted
the colour reproduction of stamps is only as
accurate as the printing process will allow.

ISBN-10: 0-85259-877-7
ISBN-13: 978-0-85259-877-1

Item No. 2980-13

Printed by
Stephens & George, Wales

Contents

Stanley Gibbons Holdings Plc	iv
Complete lists of parts	v
General Philatelic Information	vi
Prices	vi
Guarantee	vii
Condition Guide	ix
The Catalogue in General	x
Contacting the editor	x
Technical matters	xi
Acknowledgements	xxi
Abbreviations	xxii
Features Listing	xxiii
International Philatelic Glossary	xxv
Bahamas	1
Stamp Booklets	40
Special Delivery Stamps	40
Bermuda	42
Stamp Booklets	71
Express Letter Stamps	71
Postal Fiscal	71
Cayman Islands	72
Stamp Booklets	99
Jamaica	102
Stamp Booklets	138
Postal Fiscals	138
Official Stamps	139
Telegraph Stamps	139
Turks and Caicos Islands	140
Turks Islands	140
Turks and Caicos Islands	142
Stamp Booklets	180
Caicos Islands	180
Stamp Booklet	182

Stanley Gibbons Holdings Plc

Stanley Gibbons Limited, Stanley Gibbons Auctions
399 Strand, London WC2R 0LX
Tel: +44 (0)207 836 8444
Fax: +44 (0)207 836 7342
E-mail: help@stanleygibbons.com
Website: www.stanleygibbons.com
for all departments, Auction and Specialist Stamp Departments.

Open Monday–Friday 9.30 a.m. to 5 p.m.
Shop. Open Monday–Friday 9 a.m. to 5.30 p.m. and Saturday 9.30 a.m. to 5.30 p.m.

Stanley Gibbons Publications Gibbons Stamp Monthly and Philatelic Exporter
7 Parkside, Christchurch Road, Ringwood, Hampshire BH24 3SH.
Tel: +44 (0)1425 472363
Fax: +44 (0)1425 470247
E-mail: help@stanleygibbons.com
Publications Mail Order.
FREEPHONE 0800 611622

Monday–Friday 8.30 a.m. to 5 p.m.

Stanley Gibbons (Guernsey) Limited
18–20 Le Bordage, St Peter Port, Guernsey GY1 1DE.
Tel: +44 (0)1481 708270
Fax: +44 (0)1481 708279
E-mail: investment@stanleygibbons.com

Stanley Gibbons (Jersey) Limited
18 Hill Street, St Helier, Jersey, Channel Islands JE2 4UA.
Tel: +44 (0)1534 766711
Fax: +44 (0)1534 766177
E-mail: investment@stanleygibbons.com

Stanley Gibbons (Asia) Limited
Level 10
Central Building
1-3 Pedder Street
Hong Kong
Tel: +852 3975 2988
E-mail: ganandappa@stanleygibbons.com

Benham Collectibles Limited
Unit K, Concept Court,
Shearway Business Park
Folkestone Kent CT19 4RG
E-mail: benham@benham.com

Fraser's
(a division of Stanley Gibbons Ltd)
399 Strand, London WC2R 0LX
Autographs, photographs, letters and documents
Tel: +44 (0)207 836 8444
Fax: +44 (0)207 836 7342
E-mail: sales@frasersautographs.com
Website: www.frasersautographs.com

Monday–Friday 9 a.m. to 5.30 p.m. and Saturday 10 a.m. to 4 p.m.

Stanley Gibbons Publications Overseas Representation
Stanley Gibbons Publications are represented overseas by the following

Australia Renniks Publications PTY LTD
Unit 3 37-39 Green Street,
Banksmeadow, NSW 2019, Australia
Tel: +612 9695 7055
Website: www.renniks.com

Canada Unitrade Associates
99 Floral Parkway, Toronto, Ontario M6L 2C4, Canada
Tel: +1 416 242 5900
Website: www.unitradeassoc.com

Germany Schaubek Verlag Leipzig
Am Glaeschen 23, D-04420
Markranstaedt, Germany
Tel: +49 34 205 67823
Website: www.schaubek.de

Italy Ernesto Marini S.R.L.
V. Struppa, 300, Genova, 16165, Italy
Tel: +3901 0247-3530
Website: www.ernestomarini.it

Japan Japan Philatelic
PO Box 2, Suginami-Minami, Tokyo 168-8081, Japan
Tel: +81 3330 41641
Website: www.yushu.co.jp

Netherlands also covers Belgium Denmark, Finland & France
Uitgeverij Davo BV
PO Box 411, Ak Deventer, 7400 Netherlands
Tel: +315 7050 2700
Website: www.davo.nl

New Zealand House of Stamps
PO Box 12, Paraparaumu, New Zealand
Tel: +61 6364 8270
Website: www.houseofstamps.co.nz

New Zealand Philatelic Distributors
PO Box 863
15 Mount Edgecumbe Street
New Plymouth 4615, New Zealand
Tel: +6 46 758 65 68
Website: www.stampcollecta.com

Norway SKANFIL A/S
SPANAV. 52 / BOKS 2030
N-5504 HAUGESUND, Norway
Tel: +47-52703940
E-mail: magne@skanfil.no

Singapore C S Philatelic Agency
Peninsula Shopping Centre #04-29
3 Coleman Street, 179804, Singapore
Tel: +65 6337-1859
Website: www.cs.com.sg

South Africa Peter Bale Philatelics
P O Box 3719, Honeydew, 2040, South Africa
Tel: +27 11 462 2463
Tel: +27 82 330 3925
E-mail: balep@iafrica.com

Sweden Chr Winther Sorensen AB
Box 43, S-310 20 Knaered, Sweden
Tel: +46 43050743
Website: www.collectia.se

USA Regency Superior Ltd
229 North Euclid Avenue
Saint Louis, Missouri 63108, USA

PO Box 8277, St Louis,
MO 63156-8277, USA
Toll Free Tel: (800) 782-0066
Tel: (314) 361-5699
Website: www.RegencySuperior.com
Email: info@regencysuperior.com

Stanley Gibbons Stamp Catalogues

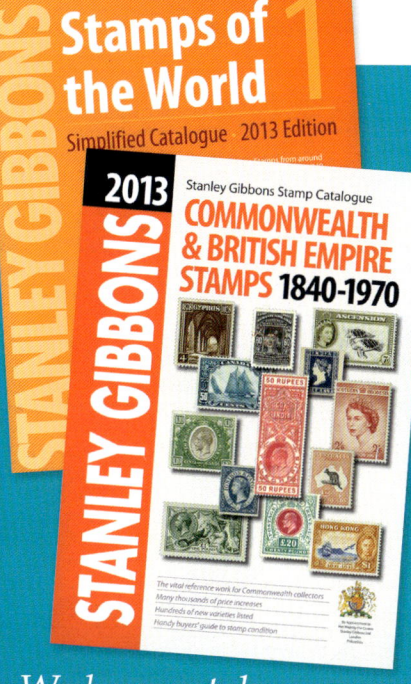

1 Commonwealth & British Empire Stamps 1840–1970 (115th edition, 2013)

Commonwealth Country Catalogues

Australia & Dependencies (8th Edition, 2013)
Bangladesh, Pakistan & Sri Lanka (2nd edition, 2010)
Belize, Guyana, Trinidad & Tobago (1st edition, 2009)
Brunei, Malaysia & Singapore (2nd edition, 2009)
Canada (4th edition, 2011)
Central Africa (2nd edition, 2008)
Cyprus, Gibraltar & Malta (3rd edition, 2011)
East Africa with Egypt & Sudan (2nd edition, 2010)
Eastern Pacific (2nd edition, 2011)
Falkland Islands (5th edition, 2012)
Hong Kong (4th edition, 2013)
India (including Convention & Feudatory States) (4th edition, 2013)
Indian Ocean (2nd edition, 2012)
Ireland (4th edition, 2011)
Leeward Islands (2nd edition, 2012)
New Zealand (3rd edition, 2011)
Northern Caribbean, Bahamas & Bermuda (3rd edition, 2013)
St. Helena & Dependencies (4th edition, 2011)
Southern Africa (2nd edition, 2008)
Southern & Central Africa (1st edition, 2011)
West Africa (2nd edition, 2012)
Western Pacific (2nd edition, 2009)
Windward Islands & Barbados (2nd edition, 2012)

Stamps of the World 2013

Volume 1 Abu Dhabi – Charkhari
Volume 2 Chile – Georgia
Volume 3 German Commands – Jasdan
Volume 4 Jersey – New Republic
Volume 5 New South Wales – Singapore
Volume 6 Sirmoor – Zululand

We also produce a range of thematic catalogues for use with Stamps of the World.

Great Britain Catalogues

Collect British Stamps (64th edition, 2013)
Great Britain Concise Stamp Catalogue (28th edition, 2013)
Collect Channel Islands & Isle of Man (28th edition, 2013)

Great Britain Specialised

Volume 1 Queen Victoria (16th edition, 2012)
Volume 2 King Edward VII to King George VI (13th edition, 2009)
Volume 3 Queen Elizabeth II Pre-decimal issues (12th edition, 2011)
Volume 4 Queen Elizabeth II Decimal Definitive Issues – Part 1 (10th edition, 2008)

Queen Elizabeth II Decimal Definitive Issues – Part 2 (10th edition, 2010)

Foreign Countries

2   *Austria & Hungary* (7th edition, 2009)
3   *Balkans* (5th edition, 2009)
4   *Benelux* (6th edition, 2010)
5   *Czech Republic, Slovakia & Poland* (7th edition, 2012)
6   *France* (7th edition, 2010)
7   *Germany* (10th edition, 2012)
8   *Italy & Switzerland* (7th edition, 2009)
9   *Portugal & Spain* (6th edition, 2011)
10 *Russia* (6th edition, 2008)
11 *Scandinavia* (7th edition, 2013)
12 *Africa since Independence A-E* (2nd edition, 1983)
13 *Africa since Independence F-M* (1st edition, 1981)
14 *Africa since Independence N-Z* (1st edition, 1981)
15 *Central America* (3rd edition, 2007)
16 *Central Asia* (4th edition, 2006)
17 *China* (9th edition, 2012)
18 *Japan & Korea* (5th edition, 2008)
19 *Middle East* (7th edition, 2009)
20 *South America* (4th edition, 2008)
21 *South-East Asia* (5th edition, 2012)
22 *United States of America* (7th edition, 2010)

We have catalogues to suit every aspect of stamp collecting

Our catalogues cover stamps issued from across the globe - from the Penny Black to the latest issues. Whether you're a specialist in a certain reign or a thematic collector, we should have something to suit your needs. All catalogues include the famous SG numbering system, making it as easy as possible to find the stamp you're looking for.

To order, call **01425 472 363** or for our full range of catalogues, visit **www.stanleygibbons.com**

STANLEY GIBBONS
Est 1856

Stanley Gibbons
7 Parkside, Christchurch Road, Ringwood, Hants, BH24 3SH
+44 (0)1425 472 363
www.stanleygibbons.com

Information and Guidelines

General Philatelic Information and Guidelines to the Scope of Stanley Gibbons Commonwealth Catalogues

These notes reflect current practice in compiling the Stanley Gibbons Commonwealth Catalogues.

The Stanley Gibbons Stamp Catalogue has a very long history and the vast quantity of information it contains has been carefully built up by successive generations through the work of countless individuals. Philately is never static and the Catalogue has evolved and developed over the years. These notes relate to the current criteria upon which a stamp may be listed or priced. These criteria have developed over time and may have differed somewhat in the early years of this catalogue. These notes are not intended to suggest that we plan to make wholesale changes to the listing of classic issues in order to bring them into line with today's listing policy, they are designed to inform catalogue users as to the policies currently in operation.

PRICES

The prices quoted in this Catalogue are the estimated selling prices of Stanley Gibbons Ltd at the time of publication. They are, unless it is specifically stated otherwise, for examples in fine condition for the issue concerned. Superb examples are worth more; those of a lower quality considerably less.

All prices are subject to change without prior notice and Stanley Gibbons Ltd may from time to time offer stamps below catalogue price. Individual low value stamps sold at 399 Strand are liable to an additional handling charge. Purchasers of new issues should note the prices charged for them contain an element for the service rendered and so may exceed the prices shown when the stamps are subsequently catalogued. Postage and handling charges are extra.

No guarantee is given to supply all stamps priced, since it is not possible to keep every catalogued item in stock. Commemorative issues may, at times, only be available in complete sets and not as individual values.

Quotation of prices. The prices in the left-hand column are for unused stamps and those in the right-hand column are for used.

A dagger (†) denotes that the item listed does not exist in that condition and a blank, or dash, that it exists, or may exist, but we are unable to quote a price.

Prices are expressed in pounds and pence sterling. One pound comprises 100 pence (£1 = 100p).

The method of notation is as follows: pence in numerals (e.g. 10 denotes ten pence); pounds and pence, up to £100, in numerals (e.g. 4.25 denotes four pounds and twenty-five pence); prices above £100 are expressed in whole pounds with the '£' sign shown.

Unused stamps. Great Britain and Commonwealth: the prices for unused stamps of Queen Victoria to King George V are for lightly hinged examples. Unused prices for King Edward VIII, King George VI and Queen Elizabeth issues are for unmounted mint.

Some stamps from the King George VI period are often difficult to find in unmounted mint condition. In such instances we would expect that collectors would need to pay a high proportion of the price quoted to obtain mounted mint examples. Generally speaking lightly mounted mint stamps from this reign, issued before 1945, are in considerable demand.

Used stamps. The used prices are normally for stamps postally used but may be for stamps cancelled-to-order where this practice exists.

A pen-cancellation on early issues can sometimes correctly denote postal use. Instances are individually noted in the Catalogue in explanation of the used price given.

Prices quoted for bisects on cover or large piece are for those dated during the period officially authorised.

Stamps not sold unused to the public (e.g. some official stamps) are priced used only.

The use of 'unified' designs, that is stamps inscribed for both postal and fiscal purposes, results in a number of stamps of very high face value. In some instances these may not have been primarily intended for postal purposes, but if they are so inscribed we include them. We only price such items used, however, where there is evidence of normal postal usage.

Cover prices. To assist collectors, cover prices are quoted for issues up to 1945 at the beginning of each country.

The system gives a general guide in the form of a factor by which the corresponding used price of the basic loose stamp should be multiplied when found in fine average condition on cover.

Care is needed in applying the factors and they relate to a cover which bears a single of the denomination listed; if more than one denomination is present the most highly priced attracts the multiplier and the remainder are priced at the simple figure for used singles in arriving at a total.

The cover should be of non-philatelic origin; bearing the correct postal rate for the period and distance involved and cancelled with the markings normal to the offices concerned. Purely philatelic items have a cover value only slightly greater than the catalogue value for the corresponding used stamps. This applies generally to those high-value stamps used philatelically rather than in the normal course of commerce. Low-value stamps, e.g. ¼d. and ½d., are desirable when used as a single rate on cover and merit an increase in 'multiplier' value.

First day covers in the period up to 1945 are not within the scope of the system and the multiplier should not be used. As a special category of philatelic usage, with wide variations in valuation according to scarcity, they require separate treatment.

Oversized covers, difficult to accommodate on an album page, should be reckoned as worth little more than the corresponding value of the used stamps. The condition of a cover also affects its value. Except for 'wreck covers', serious damage or soiling reduce the value where the postal markings and stamps are ordinary ones. Conversely, visual appeal adds to the value and this can include freshness of appearance, important addresses, old-fashioned but legible handwriting, historic town-names, etc.

The multipliers are a base on which further value would be added to take account of the cover's postal historical importance in demonstrating such things as unusual, scarce or emergency cancels, interesting routes, significant postal markings, combination usage, the development of postal rates, and so on.

Minimum price. The minimum catalogue price quoted is 10p. For individual stamps prices between 10p. and 95p. are provided as a guide for catalogue users. The lowest price charged for individual stamps or sets purchased from Stanley Gibbons Ltd is £1

Set prices. Set prices are generally for one of each value, excluding shades and varieties, but including major colour changes. Where there are alternative shades, etc., the cheapest is usually included. The number of stamps in the set is always stated for clarity. The prices for sets containing *se-tenant* pieces are based on the prices quoted for such combinations, and not on those for the individual stamps.

Varieties. Where plate or cylinder varieties are priced in used condition the price quoted is for a fine used example with the cancellation well clear of the listed flaw.

Specimen stamps. The pricing of these items is explained under that heading.

Stamp booklets. Prices are for complete assembled booklets in fine condition with those issued before 1945 showing normal wear and tear. Incomplete booklets and those which have been 'exploded' will, in general, be worth less than the figure quoted.

Repricing. Collectors will be aware that the market factors of supply and demand directly influence the prices quoted in this Catalogue. Whatever the scarcity of a particular stamp, if there is no one in the market who wishes to buy it cannot be expected to achieve a high price. Conversely, the same item actively sought by numerous potential buyers may cause the price to rise.

All the prices in this Catalogue are examined during the preparation of each new edition by the expert staff of Stanley Gibbons and repriced as necessary. They take many factors into account, including supply and demand, and are in close touch with the international stamp market and the auction world.

Commonwealth cover prices and advice on postal history material originally provided by Edward B Proud.

GUARANTEE

All stamps are guaranteed originals in the following terms:

If not as described, and returned by the purchaser, we undertake to refund the price paid to us in the original transaction. If any stamp is certified as genuine by the Expert Committee of the Royal Philatelic Society, London, or by BPA Expertising Ltd, the purchaser shall not be entitled to make any claim against us for any error, omission or mistake in such certificate.

Consumers' statutory rights are not affected by the above guarantee.

The recognised Expert Committees in this country are those of the Royal Philatelic Society, 41 Devonshire Place, London W1G, 6JY, and BPA Expertising Ltd, PO Box 1141, Guildford, Surrey GU5 0WR. They do not undertake valuations under any circumstances and fees are payable for their services.

Information and Guidelines

MARGINS ON IMPERFORATE STAMPS

| Superb | Very fine | Fine | Average | Poor |

GUM

| Unmounted | Very lightly mounted | Lightly mounted | Mounted/large part original gum (o.g.). | Heavily mounted small part o.g. |

CENTRING

| Superb | Very fine | Fine | Average | Poor |

CANCELLATIONS

| Superb | Very fine | Fine | Average | Poor |

| Superb | Very fine |

| Fine | Average | Poor |

viii

Information and Guidelines

CONDITION GUIDE
To assist collectors in assessing the true value of items they are considering buying or in reviewing stamps already in their collections, we now offer a more detailed guide to the condition of stamps on which this catalogue's prices are based.

For a stamp to be described as 'Fine', it should be sound in all respects, without creases, bends, wrinkles, pin holes, thins or tears. If perforated, all perforation 'teeth' should be intact, it should not suffer from fading, rubbing or toning and it should be of clean, fresh appearance.

Margins on imperforate stamps: These should be even on all sides and should be at least as wide as half the distance between that stamp and the next. To have one or more margins of less than this width, would normally preclude a stamp from being described as 'Fine'. Some early stamps were positioned very close together on the printing plate and in such cases 'Fine' margins would necessarily be narrow. On the other hand, some plates were laid down to give a substantial gap between individual stamps and in such cases margins would be expected to be much wider.

An 'average' four-margin example would have a narrower margin on one or more sides and should be priced accordingly, while a stamp with wider, yet even, margins than 'Fine' would merit the description 'Very Fine' or 'Superb' and, if available, would command a price in excess of that quoted in the catalogue.

Gum: Since the prices for stamps of King Edward VIII, King George VI and Queen Elizabeth are for 'unmounted' or 'never hinged' mint, even stamps from these reigns which have been very lightly mounted should be available at a discount from catalogue price, the more obvious the hinge marks, the greater the discount.

Catalogue prices for stamps issued prior to King Edward VIII's reign are for mounted mint, so unmounted examples would be worth a premium. Hinge marks on 20th century stamps should not be too obtrusive, and should be at least in the lightly mounted category. For 19th century stamps more obvious hinging would be acceptable, but stamps should still carry a large part of their original gum—'Large part o.g.'—in order to be described as 'Fine'.

Centring: Ideally, the stamp's image should appear in the exact centre of the perforated area, giving equal margins on all sides. 'Fine' centring would be close to this ideal with any deviation having an effect on the value of the stamp. As in the case of the margins on imperforate stamps, it should be borne in mind that the space between some early stamps was very narrow, so it was very difficult to achieve accurate perforation, especially when the technology was in its infancy. Thus, poor centring would have a less damaging effect on the value of a 19th century stamp than on a 20th century example, but the premium put on a perfectly centred specimen would be greater.

Cancellations: Early cancellation devices were designed to 'obliterate' the stamp in order to prevent it being reused and this is still an important objective for today's postal administrations. Stamp collectors, on the other hand, prefer postmarks to be lightly applied, clear, and to leave as much as possible of the design visible. Dated, circular cancellations have long been 'the postmark of choice', but the definition of a 'Fine' cancellation will depend upon the types of cancellation in use at the time a stamp was current—it is clearly illogical to seek a circular datestamp on a Penny Black.

'Fine', by definition, will be superior to 'Average', so, in terms of cancellation quality, if one begins by identifying what 'Average' looks like, then one will be half way to identifying 'Fine'. The illustrations will give some guidance on mid-19th century and mid-20th century cancellations of Great Britain, but types of cancellation in general use in each country and in each period will determine the appearance of 'Fine'.

As for the factors discussed above, anything less than 'Fine' will result in a downgrading of the stamp concerned, while a very fine or superb cancellation will be worth a premium.

Combining the factors: To merit the description 'Fine', a stamp should be fine in every respect, but a small deficiency in one area might be made up for in another by a factor meriting an 'Extremely Fine' description.

Some early issues are so seldom found in what would normally be considered to be 'Fine' condition, the catalogue prices are for a slightly lower grade, with 'Fine' examples being worth a premium. In such cases a note to this effect is given in the catalogue, while elsewhere premiums are given for well-centred, lightly cancelled examples.

Stamps graded at less than fine remain collectable and, in the case of more highly priced stamps, will continue to hold a value. Nevertheless, buyers should always bear condition in mind.

The Catalogue in General

Contents. The Catalogue is confined to adhesive postage stamps, including miniature sheets. For particular categories the rules are:
(a) Revenue (fiscal) stamps are listed only where they have been expressly authorised for postal duty.
(b) Stamps issued only precancelled are included, but normally issued stamps available additionally with precancel have no separate precancel listing unless the face value is changed.
(c) Stamps prepared for use but not issued, hitherto accorded full listing, are nowadays foot-noted with a price (where possible).
(d) Bisects (trisects, etc.) are only listed where such usage was officially authorised.
(e) Stamps issued only on first day covers or in presentation packs and not available separately are not listed but may be priced in a footnote.
(f) New printings are only included in this Catalogue where they show a major philatelic variety, such as a change in shade, watermark or paper. Stamps which exist with or without imprint dates are listed separately; changes in imprint dates are mentioned in footnotes.
(g) Official and unofficial reprints are dealt with by footnote.
(h) Stamps from imperforate printings of modern issues which occur perforated are covered by footnotes, but are listed where widely available for postal use.

Exclusions. The following are excluded:
(a) non-postal revenue or fiscal stamps;
(b) postage stamps used fiscally (although prices are now given for some fiscally used high values);
(c) local carriage labels and private local issues;
(d) bogus or phantom stamps;
(e) railway or airline letter fee stamps, bus or road transport company labels or the stamps of private postal companies operating under licence from the national authority;
(f) cut-outs;
(g) all types of non-postal labels and souvenirs;
(h) documentary labels for the postal service, e.g. registration, recorded delivery, air-mail etiquettes, etc.;
(i) privately applied embellishments to official issues and privately commissioned items generally;
(j) stamps for training postal officers.

Full listing. 'Full listing' confers our recognition and implies allotting a catalogue number and (wherever possible) a price quotation.

In judging status for inclusion in the catalogue broad considerations are applied to stamps. They must be issued by a legitimate postal authority, recognised by the government concerned, and must be adhesives valid for proper postal use in the class of service for which they are inscribed. Stamps, with the exception of such categories as postage dues and officials, must be available to the general public, at face value, in reasonable quantities without any artificial restrictions being imposed on their distribution.

For errors and varieties the criterion is legitimate (albeit inadvertent) sale through a postal administration in the normal course of business. Details of provenance are always important; printers' waste and deliberately manufactured material are excluded.

Certificates. In assessing unlisted items due weight is given to Certificates from recognised Expert Committees and, where appropriate, we will usually ask to see them.

Date of issue. Where local issue dates differ from dates of release by agencies, 'date of issue' is the local date. Fortuitous stray usage before the officially intended date is disregarded in listing.

Catalogue numbers. Stamps of each country are catalogued chronologically by date of issue. Subsidiary classes are placed at the end of the country, as separate lists, with a distinguishing letter prefix to the catalogue number, e.g. D for postage due, O for official and E for express delivery stamps.

The catalogue number appears in the extreme left-column. The boldface Type numbers in the next column are merely cross-references to illustrations.

Once published in the Catalogue, numbers are changed as little as possible; really serious renumbering is reserved for the occasions when a complete country or an entire issue is being rewritten. The edition first affected includes cross-reference tables of old and new numbers.

Our catalogue numbers are universally recognised in specifying stamps and as a hallmark of status.

Illustrations. Stamps are illustrated at three-quarters linear size. Stamps not illustrated are the same size and format as the value shown, unless otherwise indicated. Stamps issued only as miniature sheets have the stamp alone illustrated but sheet size is also quoted. Overprints, surcharges, watermarks and postmarks are normally actual size. Illustrations of varieties are often enlarged to show the detail. Stamp booklet covers are illustrated half-size, unless otherwise indicated.

Designers. Designers' names are quoted where known, though space precludes naming every individual concerned in the production of a set. In particular, photographers supplying material are usually named only where they also make an active contribution in the design stage; posed photographs of reigning monarchs are, however, an exception to this rule.

CONTACTING THE CATALOGUE EDITOR

The editor is always interested in hearing from people who have new information which will improve or correct the Catalogue. As a general rule he must see and examine the actual stamps before they can be considered for listing; photographs or photocopies are insufficient evidence.

Submissions should be made in writing to the Catalogue Editor, Stanley Gibbons Publications at the Ringwood office. The cost of return postage for items submitted is appreciated, and this should include the registration fee if required.

Where information is solicited purely for the benefit of the enquirer, the editor cannot undertake to reply if the answer is already contained in these published notes or if return postage is omitted. Written communications are greatly preferred to enquiries by telephone or e-mail and the editor regrets that he or his staff cannot see personal callers without a prior appointment being made. Correspondence may be subject to delay during the production period of each new edition.

The editor welcomes close contact with study circles and is interested, too, in finding reliable local correspondents who will verify and supplement official information in countries where this is deficient.

We regret we do not give opinions as to the genuineness of stamps, nor do we identify stamps or number them by our Catalogue.

TECHNICAL MATTERS

The meanings of the technical terms used in the catalogue will be found in our *Philatelic Terms Illustrated*.

References below to (more specialised) listings are to be taken to indicate, as appropriate, the Stanley Gibbons *Great Britain Specialised Catalogue* in five volumes or the *Great Britain Concise Catalogue*.

1. Printing

Printing errors. Errors in printing are of major interest to the Catalogue. Authenticated items meriting consideration would include: background, centre or frame inverted or omitted; centre or subject transposed; error of colour; error or omission of value; double prints and impressions; printed both sides; and so on. Designs *tête-bêche*, whether intentionally or by accident, are listable. *Se-tenant* arrangements of stamps are recognised in the listings or footnotes. Gutter pairs (a pair of stamps separated by blank margin) are not included in this volume. Colours only partially omitted are not listed. Stamps with embossing omitted are reserved for our more specialised listings.

Printing varieties. Listing is accorded to major changes in the printing base which lead to completely new types. In recess-printing this could be a design re-engraved; in photogravure or photolithography a screen altered in whole or in part. It can also encompass flat-bed and rotary printing if the results are readily distinguishable.

To be considered at all, varieties must be constant.

Early stamps, produced by primitive methods, were prone to numerous imperfections; the lists reflect this, recognising re-entries, retouches, broken frames, misshapen letters, and so on. Printing technology has, however, radically improved over the years, during which time photogravure and lithography have become predominant. Varieties nowadays are more in the nature of flaws and these, being too specialised for this general catalogue, are almost always outside the scope.

In no catalogue, however, do we list such items as: dry prints, kiss prints, doctor-blade flaws, colour shifts or registration flaws (unless they lead to the complete omission of a colour from an individual stamp), lithographic ring flaws, and so on. Neither do we recognise fortuitous happenings like paper creases or confetti flaws.

Overprints (and surcharges). Overprints of different types qualify for separate listing. These include overprints in different colours; overprints from different printing processes such as litho and typo; overprints in totally different typefaces, etc. Major errors in machine-printed overprints are important and listable. They include: overprint inverted or omitted; overprint double (treble, etc.); overprint diagonal; overprint double, one inverted; pairs with one overprint omitted, e.g. from a radical shift to an adjoining stamp; error of colour; error of type fount; letters inverted or omitted, etc. If the overprint is handstamped, few of these would qualify and a distinction is drawn. We continue, however, to list pairs of stamps where one has a handstamped overprint and the other has not.

Varieties occurring in overprints will often take the form of broken letters, slight differences in spacing, rising spaces, etc. Only the most important would be considered for listing or footnote mention.

Sheet positions. If space permits we quote sheet positions of listed varieties and authenticated data is solicited for this purpose.

De La Rue plates. The Catalogue classifies the general plates used by De La Rue for printing British Colonial stamps as follows:

VICTORIAN KEY TYPE

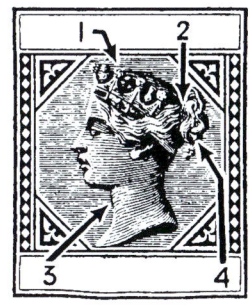

Die I

1. The ball of decoration on the second point of the crown appears as a dark mass of lines.
2. Dark vertical shading separates the front hair from the bun.
3. The vertical line of colour outlining the front of the throat stops at the sixth line of shading on the neck.
4. The white space in the coil of the hair above the curl is roughly the shape of a pin's head.

Die II

1. There are very few lines of colour in the ball and it appears almost white.
2. A white vertical strand of hair appears in place of the dark shading.
3. The line stops at the eighth line of shading.

The Catalogue in General

4. The white space is oblong, with a line of colour partially dividing it at the left end.

Plates numbered 1 and 2 are both Die I. Plates 3 and 4 are Die II.

GEORGIAN KEY TYPE

Die I

A. The second (thick) line below the name of the country is cut slanting, conforming roughly to the shape of the crown on each side.
B. The labels of solid colour bearing the words "POSTAGE" and "& REVENUE" are square at the inner top corners.
C. There is a projecting "bud" on the outer spiral of the ornament in each of the lower corners.

Die II

A. The second line is cut vertically on each side of the crown.
B. The labels curve inwards at the top.
C. There is no "bud" in this position.

Unless otherwise stated in the lists, all stamps with watermark Multiple Crown CA (w **8**) are Die I while those with watermark Multiple Crown Script CA (w **9**) are Die II. The Georgian Die II was introduced in April 1921 and was used for Plates 10 to 22 and 26 to 28. Plates 23 to 25 were made from Die I by mistake.

2. Paper

All stamps listed are deemed to be on (ordinary) paper of the wove type and white in colour; only departures from this are normally mentioned.

Types. Where classification so requires we distinguish such other types of paper as, for example, vertically and horizontally laid; wove and laid bâtonné; card(board); carton; cartridge; glazed; granite; native; pelure; porous; quadrillé; ribbed; rice; and silk thread.

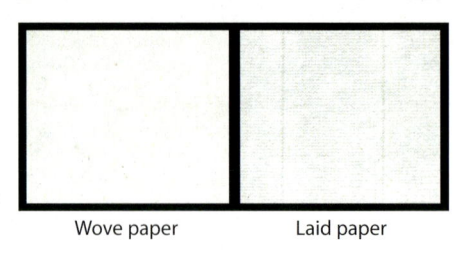

Wove paper   Laid paper

Granite paper   Quadrillé paper

Burelé band

The various makeshifts for normal paper are listed as appropriate. The varieties of double paper and joined paper are recognised. The security device of a printed burelé band on the back of a stamp, as in early Queensland, qualifies for listing.

Descriptive terms. The fact that a paper is handmade (and thus probably of uneven thickness) is mentioned where necessary. Such descriptive terms as "hard" and "soft"; "smooth" and "rough"; "thick", "medium" and "thin" are applied where there is philatelic merit in classifying papers.

Coloured, very white and toned papers. A coloured paper is one that is coloured right through (front and back of the stamp). In the Catalogue the colour of the paper is given in italics, thus:

black/*rose* = black design on rose paper.

Papers have been made specially white in recent years by, for example, a very heavy coating of chalk. We do not classify shades of whiteness of paper as distinct varieties. There does exist, however, a type of paper from early days called toned. This is off-white, often brownish or buffish, but it cannot be assigned any definite colour. A toning effect brought on by climate, incorrect storage or gum staining is disregarded here, as this was not the state of the paper when issued.

"Ordinary" and "Chalk-surfaced" papers. The availability of many postage stamps for revenue purposes made necessary some safeguard against the illegitimate re-use of stamps with removable cancellations. This was at first secured by using fugitive inks and later by printing on paper surfaced by coatings containing either chalk or china clay, both of which made it difficult to remove any form of obliteration without damaging the stamp design.

This catalogue lists these chalk-surfaced paper varieties from their introduction in 1905. Where no indication is given, the paper is "ordinary".

The "traditional" method of indentifying chalk-surfaced papers has been that, when touched with a silver wire, a black mark is left on the paper, and the listings in this catalogue are based on that test. However, the test itself is now largely discredited, for, although the mark can be removed by a soft rubber, some damage to the stamp will result from its use.

The difference between chalk-surfaced and pre-war ordinary papers is fairly clear: chalk-surfaced papers being smoother to the touch and showing a characteristic sheen when light is reflected off their surface. Under good magnification tiny bubbles or pock marks can be seen on the surface of the stamp and at the tips of the perforations the surfacing appears "broken". Traces of paper fibres are evident on the surface of ordinary paper and the ink shows a degree of absorption into it.

Initial chalk-surfaced paper printings by De La Rue had a thinner coating than subsequently became the norm. The characteristics described above are less pronounced in these printings.

During and after the Second World War, substitute papers replaced the chalk-surfaced papers, these do not react to the silver test and are therefore classed as "ordinary", although differentiating them without recourse to it is more difficult, for, although the characteristics of the chalk-surfaced paper remained the same, some of the ordinary papers appear much smoother than earlier papers and many do not show the watermark clearly. Experience is the only solution to identifying these, and comparison with stamps whose paper type is without question will be of great help.

Another type of paper, known as "thin striated" was used only for the Bahamas 1s. and 5s. (Nos. 155a, 156a, 171 and 174) and for several stamps of the Malayan states. Hitherto these have been described as "chalk-surfaced" since they gave some reaction to the silver test, but they are much thinner than usual chalk-surfaced papers, with the watermark showing clearly. Stamps on this paper show a slightly 'ribbed' effect when the stamp is held up to the light. Again, comparison with a known striated paper stamp, such as the 1941 Straits Settlements Die II 2c. orange (No. 294) will prove invaluable in separating these papers.

Glazed paper. In 1969 the Crown Agents introduced a new general-purpose paper for use in conjunction with all current printing processes. It generally has a marked glossy surface but the degree varies according to the process used, being more marked in recess-printing stamps. As it does not respond to the silver test this presents a further test where previous printings were on chalky paper. A change of paper to the glazed variety merits separate listing.

Green and yellow papers. Issues of the First World War and immediate postwar period occur on green and yellow papers and these are given separate Catalogue listing. The original coloured papers (coloured throughout) gave way to surface-coloured papers, the stamps having "white backs"; other stamps show one colour on the front and a different one at the back. Because of the numerous variations a grouping of colours is adopted as follows:

Yellow papers
(1) The original *yellow* paper (throughout), usually bright in colour. The gum is often sparse, of harsh consistency and dull-looking. Used 1912–1920.
(2) The *white-backs*. Used 1913–1914.
(3) A bright lemon paper. The colour must have a pronounced greenish tinge, different from the "yellow" in (1). As a rule, the gum on stamps using this lemon paper is plentiful, smooth and shiny, and the watermark shows distinctly. Care is needed with stamps printed in green on yellow paper (1) as it may appear that the paper is this lemon. Used 1914–1916.
(4) An experimental *orange-buff* paper. The colour must have a distinct brownish tinge. It is not to be confused with a muddy yellow (1) nor the misleading appearance (on the surface) of stamps printed in red on yellow paper where an engraved plate has been insufficiently wiped. Used 1918–1921.
(5) An experimental *buff* paper. This lacks the brownish tinge of (4) and the brightness of the yellow shades. The gum is shiny when compared with the matt type used on (4). Used 1919–1920.
(6) A *pale yellow* paper that has a creamy tone to the yellow. Used from 1920 onwards.

Green papers
(7) The original "green" paper, varying considerably through shades of blue-green and yellow-green, the front and back sometimes differing. Used 1912–1916.
(8) The *white backs*. Used 1913–1914.
(9) A paper blue-green on the surface with *pale olive* back. The back must be markedly paler than the front and this and the pronounced olive tinge to the back distinguish it from (7). Used 1916–1920.
(10) Paper with a vivid green surface, commonly called *emerald-green*; it has the olive back of (9). Used 1920.
(11) Paper with *emerald-green* both back and front. Used from 1920 onwards.

3. Perforation and Rouletting
Perforation gauge. The gauge of a perforation is the number of holes in a length of 2 cm. For correct classification the size of the holes (large or small) may need to be distinguished; in a few cases the actual number of holes on each edge of the stamp needs to be quoted.

Measurement. The Gibbons *Instanta* gauge is the standard for measuring perforations. The stamp is viewed against a dark background with the transparent gauge put on top of it. Though the gauge measures to decimal accuracy, perforations read from it are generally quoted in the Catalogue to the nearest half. For example:
 Just over perf 12¾ to just under 13¼ = perf 13
 Perf 13¼ exactly, rounded up   = perf 13½
 Just over perf 13¼ to just under 13¾ = perf 13½
 Perf 13¾ exactly, rounded up   = perf 14
However, where classification depends on it, actual quarter-perforations are quoted.

Notation. Where no perforation is quoted for an issue it is imperforate. Perforations are usually abbreviated (and spoken) as follows, though sometimes they may be spelled out for clarity. This notation for rectangular stamps (the majority) applies to diamond shapes if "top" is read as the edge to the top right.
P 14: perforated alike on all sides (read: "perf 14").
P 14×15: the first figure refers to top and bottom, the second to left and right sides (read: "perf 14 by 15"). This is a compound perforation. For an upright triangular stamp the first figure refers to the two sloping sides and second to the base. In inverted

triangulars the base is first and the second figure to the sloping sides.

- P 14–15: perforation measuring anything between 14 and 15: the holes are irregularly spaced, thus the gauge may vary along a single line or even along a single edge of the stamp (read: "perf 14 to 15").
- P 14 *irregular*: perforated 14 from a worn perforator, giving badly aligned holes irregularly spaced (read: "irregular perf 14").
- P *comp(ound)* 14×15: two gauges in use but not necessarily on opposite sides of the stamp. It could be one side in one gauge and three in the other; or two adjacent sides with the same gauge. (Read: "perf compound of 14 and 15".) For three gauges or more, abbreviated as "P 12, 14½, 15 *or compound*" for example.
- P 14, 14½: perforated approximately 14¼ (read: "perf 14 or 14½"). It does *not* mean two stamps, one perf 14 and the other perf 14½. This obsolescent notation is gradually being replaced in the Catalogue.

Imperf: imperforate (not perforated)
Imperf×P 14: imperforate at top ad bottom and perf 14 at sides.
P 14×*imperf*: perf 14 at top and bottom and imperforate at sides.

Such headings as "P 13×14 (*vert*) and P 14×13 (*horiz*)" indicate which perforations apply to which stamp format—vertical or horizontal.

Some stamps are additionally perforated so that a label or tab is detachable; others have been perforated for use as two halves. Listings are normally for whole stamps, unless stated otherwise.

Imperf×perf

Other terms. Perforation almost always gives circular holes; where other shapes have been used they are specified, e.g. square holes; lozenge perf. Interrupted perfs are brought about by the omission of pins at regular intervals. Perforations merely simulated by being printed as part of the design are of course ignored. With few exceptions, privately applied perforations are not listed.

In the 19th century perforations are often described as clean cut (clean, sharply incised holes), intermediate or rough (rough holes, imperfectly cut, often the result of blunt pins).

Perforation errors and varieties. Authenticated errors, where a stamp normally perforated is accidentally issued imperforate, are listed provided no traces of perforation (blind holes or indentations) remain. They must be provided as pairs, both stamps wholly imperforate, and are only priced in that form.

Stamps imperforate between stamp and sheet margin are not listed in this catalogue, but such errors on Great Britain stamps will be found in the *Great Britain Specialised Catalogue*.

Pairs described as "imperforate between" have the line of perforations between the two stamps omitted.

Imperf between (horiz pair): a horizontal pair of stamps with perfs all around the edges but none between the stamps.

Imperf between (vert pair): a vertical pair of stamps with perfs all around the edges but none between the stamps.

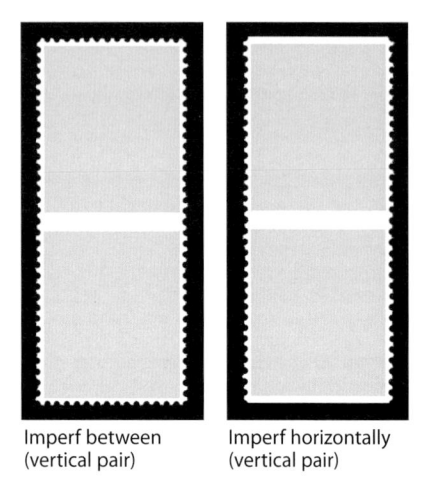

Imperf between (vertical pair)   Imperf horizontally (vertical pair)

Where several of the rows have escaped perforation the resulting varieties are listable. Thus:

Imperf vert (horiz pair): a horizontal pair of stamps perforated top and bottom; all three vertical directions are imperf—the two outer edges and between the stamps.

Imperf horiz (vert pair): a vertical pair perforated at left and right edges; all three horizontal directions are imperf—the top, bottom and between the stamps.

Straight edges. Large sheets cut up before issue to post offices can cause stamps with straight edges, i.e. imperf on one side or on two sides at right angles. They are not usually listable in this condition and are worth less than corresponding stamps properly perforated all round. This does not, however, apply to certain stamps, mainly from coils and booklets, where straight edges on various sides are the manufacturing norm affecting every stamp. The listings and notes make clear which sides are correctly imperf.

Malfunction. Varieties of double, misplaced or partial perforation caused by error or machine malfunction are not listable, neither are freaks, such as perforations placed diagonally from paper folds, nor missing holes caused by broken pins.

Types of perforating. Where necessary for classification, perforation types are distinguished.
These include:

Line perforation from one line of pins punching single rows of holes at a time.
Comb perforation from pins disposed across the sheet in comb formation, punching out holes at three sides of the stamp a row at a time.
Harrow perforation applied to a whole pane or sheet at one stroke.
Rotary perforation from toothed wheels operating across a sheet, then crosswise.
Sewing machine perforation. The resultant condition,

clean-cut or rough, is distinguished where required.

Pin-perforation is the commonly applied term for pin-roulette in which, instead of being punched out, round holes are pricked by sharp-pointed pins and no paper is removed.

Mixed perforation occurs when stamps with defective perforations are re-perforated in a different gauge.

Punctured stamps. Perforation holes can be punched into the face of the stamp. Patterns of small holes, often in the shape of initial letters, are privately applied devices against pilferage. These (perfins) are outside the scope except for Australia, Canada, Cape of Good Hope, Papua and Sudan where they were used as official stamps by the national administration. Identification devices, when officially inspired, are listed or noted; they can be shapes, or letters or words formed from holes, sometimes converting one class of stamp into another.

Rouletting. In rouletting the paper is cut, for ease of separation, but none is removed. The gauge is measured, when needed, as for perforations. Traditional French terms descriptive of the type of cut are often used and types include:

Arc roulette (percé en arc). Cuts are minute, spaced arcs, each roughly a semicircle.

Cross roulette (percé en croix). Cuts are tiny diagonal crosses.

Line roulette (percé en ligne or en ligne droite). Short straight cuts parallel to the frame of the stamp. The commonest basic roulette. Where not further described, "roulette" means this type.

Rouletted in colour or coloured roulette (percé en lignes colorées or en lignes de coleur). Cuts with coloured edges, arising from notched rule inked simultaneously with the printing plate.

Saw-tooth roulette (percé en scie). Cuts applied zigzag fashion to resemble the teeth of a saw.

Serpentine roulette (percé en serpentin). Cuts as sharply wavy lines.

Zigzag roulette (percé en zigzags). Short straight cuts at angles in alternate directions, producing sharp points on separation. US usage favours "serrate(d) roulette" for this type.

Pin-roulette (originally *percé en points* and now *perforés trous d'epingle*) is commonly called pin-perforation in English.

4. Gum

All stamps listed are assumed to have gum of some kind; if they were issued without gum this is stated. Original gum (o.g.) means that which was present on the stamp as issued to the public. Deleterious climates and the presence of certain chemicals can cause gum to crack and, with early stamps, even make the paper deteriorate. Unscrupulous fakers are adept in removing it and regumming the stamp to meet the unreasoning demand often made for "full o.g." in cases where such a thing is virtually impossible.

The gum normally used on stamps has been gum arabic until the late 1960s when synthetic adhesives were introduced. Harrison and Sons Ltd for instance use *polyvinyl alcohol,* known to philatelists as PVA. This is almost invisible except for a slight yellowish tinge which was incorporated to make it possible to see that the stamps have been gummed. It has advantages in hot countries, as stamps do not curl and sheets are less likely to stick together. Gum arabic and PVA are not distinguished in the lists except that where a stamp exists with both forms this is indicated in footnotes. Our more specialised catalogues provide separate listing of gums for Great Britain.

Self-adhesive stamps are issued on backing paper, from which they are peeled before affixing to mail. Unused examples are priced as for backing paper intact, in which condition they are recommended to be kept. Used examples are best collected on cover or on piece.

5. Watermarks

Stamps are on unwatermarked paper except where the heading to the set says otherwise.

Detection. Watermarks are detected for Catalogue description by one of four methods: (1) holding stamps to the light; (2) laying stamps face down on a dark background; (3) adding a few drops of petroleum ether 40/60 to the stamp laid face down in a watermark tray; (4) by use of the Stanley Gibbons Detectamark, or other equipment, which work by revealing the thinning of the paper at the watermark. (Note that petroleum ether is highly inflammable in use and can damage photogravure stamps.)

Listable types. Stamps occurring on both watermarked and unwatermarked papers are different types and both receive full listing.

Single watermarks (devices occurring once on every stamp) can be modified in size and shape as between different issues; the types are noted but not usually separately listed. Fortuitous absence of watermark from a single stamp or its gross displacement would not be listable.

To overcome registration difficulties the device may be repeated at close intervals *(a multiple watermark),* single stamps thus showing parts of several devices. Similarly, a *large sheet watermark* (or *all-over watermark*) covering numerous stamps can be used. We give informative notes and illustrations for them. The designs may be such that numbers of stamps in the sheet automatically lack watermark: this is not a listable variety. Multiple and all-over watermarks sometimes undergo modifications, but if the various types are difficult to distinguish from single stamps notes are given but not separate listings.

Papermakers' watermarks are noted where known but not listed separately, since most stamps in the sheet will lack them. Sheet watermarks which are nothing more than officially adopted papermakers' watermarks are, however, given normal listing.

Marginal watermarks, falling outside the pane of stamps, are ignored except where misplacement caused the adjoining row to be affected, in which case they may be footnoted.

Watermark errors and varieties. Watermark errors are recognised as of major importance. They comprise stamps intended to be on unwatermarked paper but issued watermarked by mistake, or stamps printed on paper with the wrong watermark. Varieties showing letters omitted from the watermark are also included, but broken or deformed bits on the dandy roll are not listed unless they represent repairs.

Watermark positions. The diagram shows how watermark position is described in the Catalogue. Paper has a side intended for printing and watermarks are usually impressed so that they read normally when looked through from that printed side. However, since philatelists customarily detect watermarks by looking at the back of the stamp the watermark diagram also makes clear what is actually seen.

xv

The Catalogue in General

w **10**
V over Crown

w **11**
Crown over A

Resuming the general types, two watermarks found in issues of several Australian States are: w **10**, *V over Crown*, and w **11**, *Crown over A*.

w **12**
Multiple St. Edward's Crown Block CA

w **13**
Multiple PTM

The *Multiple St. Edward's Crown Block CA* watermark, w **12**, was introduced in 1957 and besides the change in the Crown (from that used in Multiple Crown Script CA, w **9**) the letters reverted to block capitals. The new watermark began to appear sideways in 1966 and these stamps are generally listed as separate sets.

The watermark w **13**, *Multiple PTM*, was introduced for new Malaysian issues in November 1961.

w **14**
Multiple Crown CA Diagonal

By 1974 the two dandy-rolls the "upright" and the "sideways" for w **12** were wearing out; the Crown Agents therefore discontinued using the sideways watermark one and retained the other only as a stand-by. A new dandy-roll with the pattern of w **14**, *Multiple Crown CA Diagonal*, was introduced and first saw use with some Churchill Centenary issues.

The new watermark had the design arranged in gradually spiralling rows. It is improved in design to allow smooth passage over the paper (the gaps between letters and rows had caused jolts in previous dandy-rolls) and the sharp corners and angles, where fibres used to accumulate, have been eliminated by rounding.

This watermark had no "normal" sideways position amongst the different printers using it. To avoid confusion our more specialised listings do not rely on such terms as "sideways inverted" but describe the direction in which the watermark points.

w **15**
Multiple POST OFFICE

During 1981 w **15**, *Multiple POST OFFICE* was introduced for certain issues prepared by Philatelists Ltd, acting for various countries in the Indian Ocean, Pacific and West Indies.

w **16**
Multiple Crown Script CA Diagonal

A new Crown Agents watermark was introduced during 1985, w **16**, *Multiple Crown Script CA Diagonal*. This was very similar to the previous w **14**, but showed "CA" in script rather than block letters. It was first used on the omnibus series of stamps commemorating the Life and Times of Queen Elizabeth the Queen Mother.

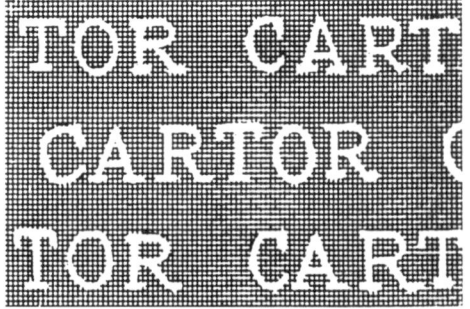

w **17**
Multiple CARTOR

Watermark w **17**, *Multiple CARTOR*, was used from 1985 for issues printed by this French firm for countries which did not normally use the Crown Agents watermark.

xviii

w **18**

In 2008, following the closure of the Crown Agents Stamp Bureau, a new Multiple Crowns watermark, w **18** was introduced

In recent years the use of watermarks has, to a small extent, been superseded by fluorescent security markings. These are often more visible from the reverse of the stamp (Cook Islands from 1970 onwards), but have occurred printed over the design (Hong Kong Nos. 415/30). In 1982 the Crown Agents introduced a new stock paper, without watermark, known as "C-Kurity" on which a fluorescent pattern of blue rosettes is visible on the reverse, beneath the gum. This paper was used for issues from Gambia and Norfolk Island.

6. Colours

Stamps in two or three colours have these named in order of appearance, from the centre moving outwards. Four colours or more are usually listed as multicoloured.

In compound colour names the second is the predominant one, thus:

orange-red = a red tending towards orange;
red-orange = an orange containing more red than usual.

Standard colours used. The 200 colours most used for stamp identification are given in the Stanley Gibbons Stamp Colour Key. The Catalogue has used the Stamp Colour Key as standard for describing new issues for some years. The names are also introduced as lists are rewritten, though exceptions are made for those early issues where traditional names have become universally established.

Determining colours. When comparing actual stamps with colour samples in the Stamp Colour Key, view in a good north daylight (or its best substitute; fluorescent "colour matching" light). Sunshine is not recommended. Choose a solid portion of the stamp design; if available, marginal markings such as solid bars of colour or colour check dots are helpful. Shading lines in the design can be misleading as they appear lighter than solid colour. Postmarked portions of a stamp appear darker than normal. If more than one colour is present, mask off the extraneous ones as the eye tends to mix them.

Errors of colour. Major colour errors in stamps or overprints which qualify for listing are: wrong colours; one colour inverted in relation to the rest; albinos (colourless impressions), where these have Expert Committee certificates; colours completely omitted, but only on unused stamps (if found on used stamps the information is footnoted) and with good credentials, missing colours being frequently faked.

Colours only partially omitted are not recognised, Colour shifts, however spectacular, are not listed.

Shades. Shades in philately refer to variations in the intensity of a colour or the presence of differing amounts of other colours. They are particularly significant when they can be linked to specific printings. In general, shades need to be quite marked to fall within the scope of this Catalogue; it does not favour nowadays listing the often numerous shades of a stamp, but chooses a single applicable colour name which will indicate particular groups of outstanding shades. Furthermore, the listings refer to colours as issued; they may deteriorate into something different through the passage of time.

Modern colour printing by lithography is prone to marked differences of shade, even within a single run, and variations can occur within the same sheet. Such shades are not listed.

Aniline colours. An aniline colour meant originally one derived from coal-tar; it now refers more widely to colour of a particular brightness suffused on the surface of a stamp and showing through clearly on the back.

Colours of overprints and surcharges. All overprints and surcharges are in black unless stated otherwise in the heading or after the description of the stamp.

7. Specimen Stamps

Originally, stamps overprinted SPECIMEN were circulated to postmasters or kept in official records, but after the establishment of the Universal Postal Union supplies were sent to Berne for distribution to the postal administrations of member countries.

During the period 1884 to 1928 most of the stamps of British Crown Colonies required for this purpose were overprinted SPECIMEN in various shapes and sizes by their printers from typeset formes. Some locally produced provisionals were handstamped locally, as were sets prepared for presentation. From 1928 stamps were punched with holes forming the word SPECIMEN, each firm of printers using a different machine or machines. From 1948 the stamps supplied for UPU distribution were no longer punctured.

Stamps of some other Commonwealth territories were overprinted or handstamped locally, while stamps of Great Britain and those overprinted for use in overseas postal agencies (mostly of the higher denominations) bore SPECIMEN overprints and handstamps applied by the Inland Revenue or the Post Office.

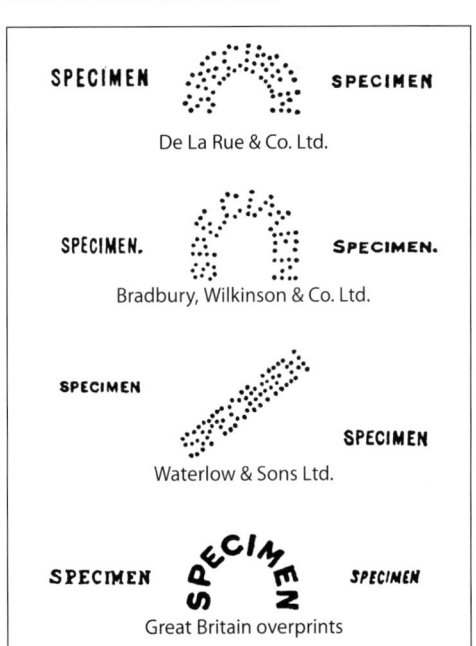

De La Rue & Co. Ltd.

Bradbury, Wilkinson & Co. Ltd.

Waterlow & Sons Ltd.

Great Britain overprints

Some of the commoner types of overprints or punctures are illustrated here. Collectors are warned that dangerous forgeries of the punctured type exist.

The *Stanley Gibbons Commonwealth Catalogues* record those Specimen overprints or perforations intended for distribution by the UPU to member countries. In addition the Specimen overprints of Australia and its dependent territories, which were sold to collectors by the Post Office, are also included.

Various Perkins Bacon issues exist obliterated with a "CANCELLED" within an oval of bars handstamp.

Perkins Bacon "CANCELLED" Handstamp

This was applied to six examples of those issues available in 1861 which were then given to members of Sir Rowland Hill's family. 75 different stamps (including four from Chile) are recorded with this handstamp although others may possibly exist. The unauthorised gift of these "CANCELLED" stamps to the Hill family was a major factor in the loss of the Agent General for the Crown Colonies (the forerunner of the Crown Agents) contracts by Perkins Bacon in the following year. Where examples of these scarce items are known to be in private hands the catalogue provides a price.

For full details of these stamps see *CANCELLED by Perkins Bacon* by Peter Jaffé (published by Spink in 1998).

All other Specimens are outside the scope of this volume.

Specimens are not quoted in Great Britain as they are fully listed in the Stanley Gibbons *Great Britain Specialised Catalogue*.

In specifying type of specimen for individual high-value stamps, "H/S" means handstamped, "Optd" is overprinted and "Perf" is punctured. Some sets occur mixed, e.g. "Optd/Perf". If unspecified, the type is apparent from the date or it is the same as for the lower values quoted as a set.

Prices. Prices for stamps up to £1 are quoted in sets; higher values are priced singly. Where specimens exist in more than one type the price quoted is for the cheapest. Specimen stamps have rarely survived even as pairs; these and strips of three, four or five are worth considerably more than singles.

8. Luminescence

Machines which sort mail electronically have been introduced in recent years. In consequence some countries have issued stamps on fluorescent or phosphorescent papers, while others have marked their stamps with phosphor bands.

The various papers can only be distinguished by ultraviolet lamps emitting particular wavelengths. They are separately listed only when the stamps have some other means of distinguishing them, visible without the use of these lamps. Where this is not so, the papers are recorded in footnotes or headings.

For this catalogue we do not consider it appropriate that collectors be compelled to have the use of an ultraviolet lamp before being able to identify stamps by our listings. Some experience will also be found necessary in interpreting the results given by ultraviolet. Collectors using the lamps, nevertheless, should exercise great care in their use as exposure to their light is potentially dangerous to the eyes.

Phosphor bands are listable, since they are visible to the naked eye (by holding stamps at an angle to the light and looking along them, the bands appear dark). Stamps existing with or without phosphor bands or with differing numbers of bands are given separate listings. Varieties such as double bands, bands omitted, misplaced or printed on the back are not listed.

Detailed descriptions appear at appropriate places in the listings in explanation of luminescent papers; see, for example, Australia above No. 363, Canada above Nos. 472 and 611, Cook Is. above 249, etc.

For Great Britain, where since 1959 phosphors have played a prominent and intricate part in stamp issues, the main notes above Nos. 599 and 723 should be studied, as well as the footnotes to individual listings where appropriate. In general the classification is as follows.

Stamps with phosphor bands are those where a separate cylinder applies the phosphor after the stamps are printed. Issues with "all-over" phosphor have the "band" covering the entire stamp. Parts of the stamp covered by phosphor bands, or the entire surface for "all-over" phosphor versions, appear matt. Stamps on phosphorised paper have the phosphor added to the paper coating before the stamps are printed. Issues on this paper have a completely shiny surface.

Further particularisation of phosphor – their methods of printing and the colours they exhibit under ultraviolet – is outside the scope. The more specialised listings should be consulted for this information.

9. Coil Stamps

Stamps issued only in coil form are given full listing. If stamps are issued in both sheets and coils the coil stamps are listed separately only where there is some feature (e.g. perforation or watermark sideways) by which singles can be distinguished. Coil stamps containing different stamps *se-tenant* are also listed.

Coil join pairs are too random and too easily faked to permit of listing; similarly ignored are coil stamps which have accidentally suffered an extra row of perforations from the claw mechanism in a malfunctioning vending machine.

10. Stamp Booklets

Stamp booklets are now listed in this catalogue.

Single stamps from booklets are listed if they are distinguishable in some way (such as watermark or perforation) from similar sheet stamps.

Booklet panes are listed where they contain stamps of different denominations *se-tenant*, where stamp-size labels are included, or where such panes are otherwise identifiable. Booklet panes are placed in the listing under the lowest denomination present.

Particular perforations (straight edges) are covered by appropriate notes.

11. Miniature Sheets and Sheetlets

We distinguish between "miniature sheets" and "sheetlets" and this affects the catalogue numbering. An item in sheet form that is postally valid, containing a single stamp, pair, block or set of stamps, with wide, inscribed and/or decorative margins, is a miniature sheet if it is sold at post offices as an indivisible entity. As such the Catalogue allots a single MS number and describes what stamps make it up. The sheetlet or small sheet differs in that the individual stamps are intended to be purchased separately for postal purposes. For sheetlets, all the component postage stamps are numbered individually and the composition explained in a footnote. Note that the definitions refer to post office sale—not how items may be subsequently offered by stamp dealers.

12. Forgeries and Fakes

Forgeries. Where space permits, notes are considered if they can give a concise description that will permit unequivocal detection of a forgery. Generalised warnings, lacking detail, are not nowadays inserted, since their value to the collector is problematic.

Forged cancellations have also been applied to genuine stamps. This catalogue includes notes regarding those manufactured by "Madame Joseph", together with the cancellation dates known to exist. It should be remembered that these dates also exist as genuine cancellations.

For full details of these see *Madame Joseph Forged Postmarks* by Derek Worboys (published by the Royal Philatelic Society London and the British Philatelic Trust in 1994) or *Madame Joseph Revisited* by Brian Cartwright (published by the Royal Philatelic Society London in 2005).

Fakes. Unwitting fakes are numerous, particularly "new shades" which are colour changelings brought about by exposure to sunlight, soaking in water contaminated with dyes from adherent paper, contact with oil and dirt from a pocketbook, and so on. Fraudulent operators, in addition, can offer to arrange: removal of hinge marks; repairs of thins on white or coloured papers; replacement of missing margins or perforations; reperforating in true or false gauges; removal of fiscal cancellations; rejoining of severed pairs, strips and blocks; and (a major hazard) regumming. Collectors can only be urged to purchase from reputable sources and to insist upon Expert Committee certification where there is any kind of doubt.

The Catalogue can consider footnotes about fakes where these are specific enough to assist in detection.

ACKNOWLEDGEMENTS

We are grateful to individual collectors, members of the philatelic trade and specialist societies and study circles for their assistance in improving and extending the Stanley Gibbons range of catalogues. The addresses of societies and study circles relevant to this volume are:

British West Indies Study Circle
Membership Secretary: Steve Jarvis
5 Redbridge Drive, Andover SP10 2LF

British Caribbean Philatelic Study Group
Overseas Director: David Druett
Pennymead Auctions, 1 Brewerton Street
Knaresborough, North Yorkshire, HG5 8AZ

Bermuda Collectors Society
Secretary: John Pare
405 Perimeter St, Mt Horeb, Wisconsin 52572, USA

Abbreviations

Printers

A.B.N. Co.	American Bank Note Co, New York.
B.A.B.N.	British American Bank Note Co. Ottawa
B.D.T.	B.D.T. International Security Printing Ltd, Dublin, Ireland
B.W.	Bradbury Wilkinson & Co, Ltd.
Cartor	Cartor S.A., La Loupe, France
C.B.N.	Canadian Bank Note Co, Ottawa.
Continental	Continental Bank Note Co. B.N. Co.
Courvoisier	Imprimerie Courvoisier S.A., La-Chaux-de-Fonds, Switzerland.
D.L.R.	De La Rue & Co, Ltd, London.
Enschedé	Joh. Enschedé en Zonen, Haarlem, Netherlands.
Format	Format International Security Printers Ltd., London
Harrison	Harrison & Sons, Ltd. London
J.W.	John Waddington Security Print Ltd., Leeds
P.B.	Perkins Bacon Ltd, London.
Questa	Questa Colour Security Printers Ltd, London
Walsall	Walsall Security Printers Ltd
Waterlow	Waterlow & Sons, Ltd, London.

General Abbreviations

Alph	Alphabet
Anniv	Anniversary
Comp	Compound (perforation)
Des	Designer; designed
Diag	Diagonal; diagonally
Eng	Engraver; engraved
F.C.	Fiscal Cancellation
H/S	Handstamped
Horiz	Horizontal; horizontally
Imp, Imperf	Imperforate
Inscr	Inscribed
L	Left
Litho	Lithographed
mm	Millimetres
MS	Miniature sheet
N.Y.	New York
Opt(d)	Overprint(ed)
P or P-c	Pen-cancelled
P, Pf or Perf	Perforated
Photo	Photogravure
Pl	Plate
Pr	Pair
Ptd	Printed
Ptg	Printing
R	Right
R.	Row
Recess	Recess-printed
Roto	Rotogravure
Roul	Rouletted
S	Specimen (overprint)
Surch	Surcharge(d)
T.C.	Telegraph Cancellation
T	Type
Typo	Typographed
Un	Unused
Us	Used
Vert	Vertical; vertically
W or wmk	Watermark
Wmk s	Watermark sideways

(†) = Does not exist
(–) (or blank price column) = Exists, or may exist, but no market price is known.
/ between colours means "on" and the colour following is that of the paper on which the stamp is printed.

Colours of Stamps
Bl (blue); blk (black); brn (brown); car, carm (carmine); choc (chocolate); clar (claret); emer (emerald); grn (green); ind (indigo); mag (magenta); mar (maroon); mult (multicoloured); mve (mauve); ol (olive); orge (orange); pk (pink); pur (purple); scar (scarlet); sep (sepia); turq (turquoise); ultram (ultramarine); verm (vermilion); vio (violet); yell (yellow).

Colour of Overprints and Surcharges
(B.) = blue, (Blk.) = black, (Br.) = brown, (C.) = carmine, (G.) = green, (Mag.) = magenta, (Mve.) = mauve, (Ol.) = olive, (O.) = orange, (P.) = purple, (Pk.) = pink, (R.) = red, (Sil.) = silver, (V.) = violet, (Vm.) or (Verm.) = vermilion, (W.) = white, (Y.) = yellow.

Arabic Numerals
As in the case of European figures, the details of the Arabic numerals vary in different stamp designs, but they should be readily recognised with the aid of this illustration.

٠ ١ ٢ ٣ ٤ ٥ ٦ ٧ ٨ ٩
0 1 2 3 4 5 6 7 8 9

Features Listing

An at-a-glance guide to what's in the Stanley Gibbons catalogues

Area	Feature	Collect British Stamps	Stamps of the World	Thematic Catalogues	Stamps and country and British Empire Commonwealth catalogues	Comprehensive Catalogue, Parts 1-22 (including	Great Britain Concise	Specialised catalogues
General	SG number	√	√	√		√	√	√
General	Specialised Catalogue number							√
General	Year of issue of first stamp in design	√	√	√		√	√	√
General	Exact date of issue of each design					√	√	
General	Face value information	√	√	√		√	√	√
General	Historical and geographical information	√	√	√		√	√	√
General	General currency information, including dates used	√	√	√		√	√	√
General	Country name	√	√	√		√	√	√
General	Booklet panes					√	√	√
General	Coil stamps					√		√
General	First Day Covers	√					√	√
General	Brief footnotes on key areas of note	√	√	√		√	√	√
General	Detailed footnotes on key areas of note					√	√	√
General	Extra background information					√	√	√
General	Miniature sheet information (including size in mm)	√	√	√		√	√	√
General	Sheetlets					√		
General	Stamp booklets					√	√	√
General	Perkins Bacon "Cancelled"					√		
General	PHQ Cards	√					√	√
General	Post Office Label Sheets						√	
General	Post Office Yearbooks	√					√	√
General	Presentation and Souvenir Packs	√					√	√
General	Se-tenant pairs	√				√	√	√
General	Watermark details - errors, varieties, positions					√	√	√
General	Watermark illustrations	√				√	√	√
General	Watermark types	√				√	√	√
General	Forgeries noted					√		√
General	Surcharges and overprint information	√	√	√		√	√	√
Design and Description	Colour description, simplified		√	√				
Design and Description	Colour description, extended	√				√	√	√
Design and Description	Set design summary information	√	√	√		√	√	√
Design and Description	Designer name					√	√	√
Design and Description	Short design description	√	√	√		√	√	√

xxiii

Features Listing

Area	Feature	Collect British Stamps	Stamps of the World	Thematic Catalogues	Comprehensive Catalogue, Parts 1-22 (including Commonwealth and British Empire Stamps and country catalogues)	Great Britain Concise	Specialised catalogues
Design and Description	Shade varieties					√	√ √
Design and Description	Type number	√	√		√	√	√
Illustrations	Multiple stamps from set illustrated	√			√	√	√
Illustrations	A Stamp from each set illustrated in full colour (where possible, otherwise mono)	√	√	√	√	√	√
Price	Catalogue used price	√	√	√	√	√	√
Price	Catalogue unused price	√	√	√	√	√	√
Price	Price - booklet panes				√	√	√
Price	Price - shade varieties				√	√	√
Price	On cover and on piece price				√	√	√
Price	Detailed GB pricing breakdown	√			√	√	√
Print and Paper	Basic printing process information	√	√	√	√	√	√
Print and Paper	Detailed printing process information, e.g. Mill sheets				√		√
Print and Paper	Paper information				√		√
Print and Paper	Detailed perforation information	√			√	√	√
Print and Paper	Details of research findings relating to printing processes and history						√
Print and Paper	Paper colour	√	√		√	√	√
Print and Paper	Paper description to aid identification				√	√	√
Print and Paper	Paper type				√	√	√
Print and Paper	Ordinary or chalk-surfaced paper				√	√	√
Print and Paper	Embossing omitted note						√
Print and Paper	Essays, Die Proofs, Plate Descriptions and Proofs, Colour Trials information						√
Print and Paper	Glazed paper				√	√	√
Print and Paper	Gum details				√		√
Print and Paper	Luminescence/Phosphor bands - general coverage	√			√	√	√
Print and Paper	Luminescence/Phosphor bands - specialised coverage						√
Print and Paper	Overprints and surcharges - including colour information	√	√	√	√	√	√
Print and Paper	Perforation/Imperforate information	√	√		√	√	√
Print and Paper	Perforation errors and varieties				√	√	√
Print and Paper	Print quantities				√		√
Print and Paper	Printing errors				√	√	√
Print and Paper	Printing flaws						√
Print and Paper	Printing varieties				√	√	√
Print and Paper	Punctured stamps - where official				√		
Print and Paper	Sheet positions				√	√	√
Print and Paper	Specialised plate number information						√
Print and Paper	Specimen overprints (only for Commonwealth & GB)				√	√	√
Print and Paper	Underprints					√	√
Print and Paper	Visible Plate numbers	√			√	√	√
Print and Paper	Yellow and Green paper listings				√		√
Index	Design index	√			√	√	

International Philatelic Glossary

English	French	German	Spanish	Italian
Agate	Agate	Achat	Agata	Agata
Air stamp	Timbre de la poste aérienne	Flugpostmarke	Sello de correo aéreo	Francobollo per posta aerea
Apple Green	Vert-pomme	Apfelgrün	Verde manzana	Verde mela
Barred	Annulé par barres	Balkenentwertung	Anulado con barras	Sbarrato
Bisected	Timbre coupé	Halbiert	Partido en dos	Frazionato
Bistre	Bistre	Bister	Bistre	Bistro
Bistre-brown	Brun-bistre	Bisterbraun	Castaño bistre	Bruno-bistro
Black	Noir	Schwarz	Negro	Nero
Blackish Brown	Brun-noir	Schwärzlichbraun	Castaño negruzco	Bruno nerastro
Blackish Green	Vert foncé	Schwärzlichgrün	Verde negruzco	Verde nerastro
Blackish Olive	Olive foncé	Schwärzlicholiv	Oliva negruzco	Oliva nerastro
Block of four	Bloc de quatre	Viererblock	Bloque de cuatro	Bloco di quattro
Blue	Bleu	Blau	Azul	Azzurro
Blue-green	Vert-bleu	Blaugrün	Verde azul	Verde azzurro
Bluish Violet	Violet bleuâtre	Bläulichviolett	Violeta azulado	Violtto azzurrastro
Booklet	Carnet	Heft	Cuadernillo	Libretto
Bright Blue	Bleu vif	Lebhaftblau	Azul vivo	Azzurro vivo
Bright Green	Vert vif	Lebhaftgrün	Verde vivo	Verde vivo
Bright Purple	Mauve vif	Lebhaftpurpur	Púrpura vivo	Porpora vivo
Bronze Green	Vert-bronze	Bronzegrün	Verde bronce	Verde bronzo
Brown	Brun	Braun	Castaño	Bruno
Brown-lake	Carmin-brun	Braunlack	Laca castaño	Lacca bruno
Brown-purple	Pourpre-brun	Braunpurpur	Púrpura castaño	Porpora bruno
Brown-red	Rouge-brun	Braunrot	Rojo castaño	Rosso bruno
Buff	Chamois	Sämisch	Anteado	Camoscio
Cancellation	Oblitération	Entwertung	Cancelación	Annullamento
Cancelled	Annulé	Gestempelt	Cancelado	Annullato
Carmine	Carmin	Karmin	Carmín	Carminio
Carmine-red	Rouge-carmin	Karminrot	Rojo carmín	Rosso carminio
Centred	Centré	Zentriert	Centrado	Centrato
Cerise	Rouge-cerise	Kirschrot	Color de ceresa	Color Ciliegia
Chalk-surfaced paper	Papier couché	Kreidepapier	Papel estucado	Carta gessata
Chalky Blue	Bleu terne	Kreideblau	Azul turbio	Azzurro smorto
Charity stamp	Timbre de bienfaisance	Wohltätigkeitsmarke	Sello de beneficenza	Francobollo di beneficenza
Chestnut	Marron	Kastanienbraun	Castaño rojo	Marrone
Chocolate	Chocolat	Schokolade	Chocolate	Cioccolato
Cinnamon	Cannelle	Zimtbraun	Canela	Cannella
Claret	Grenat	Weinrot	Rojo vinoso	Vinaccia
Cobalt	Cobalt	Kobalt	Cobalto	Cobalto
Colour	Couleur	Farbe	Color	Colore
Comb-perforation	Dentelure en peigne	Kammzähnung, Reihenzähnung	Dentado de peine	Dentellatura e pettine
Commemorative stamp	Timbre commémoratif	Gedenkmarke	Sello conmemorativo	Francobollo commemorativo
Crimson	Cramoisi	Karmesin	Carmesí	Cremisi
Deep Blue	Blue foncé	Dunkelblau	Azul oscuro	Azzurro scuro
Deep bluish Green	Vert-bleu foncé	Dunkelbläulichgrün	Verde azulado oscuro	Verde azzurro scuro

International Philatelic Glossary

English	French	German	Spanish	Italian
Design	Dessin	Markenbild	Diseño	Disegno
Die	Matrice	Urstempel. Type, Platte	Cuño	Conio, Matrice
Double	Double	Doppelt	Doble	Doppio
Drab	Olive terne	Trüboliv	Oliva turbio	Oliva smorto
Dull Green	Vert terne	Trübgrün	Verde turbio	Verde smorto
Dull purple	Mauve terne	Trübpurpur	Púrpura turbio	Porpora smorto
Embossing	Impression en relief	Prägedruck	Impresión en relieve	Impressione a relievo
Emerald	Vert-eméraude	Smaragdgrün	Esmeralda	Smeraldo
Engraved	Gravé	Graviert	Grabado	Inciso
Error	Erreur	Fehler, Fehldruck	Error	Errore
Essay	Essai	Probedruck	Ensayo	Saggio
Express letter stamp	Timbre pour lettres par exprès	Eilmarke	Sello de urgencia	Francobollo per espresso
Fiscal stamp	Timbre fiscal	Stempelmarke	Sello fiscal	Francobollo fiscale
Flesh	Chair	Fleischfarben	Carne	Carnicino
Forgery	Faux, Falsification	Fälschung	Falsificación	Falso, Falsificazione
Frame	Cadre	Rahmen	Marco	Cornice
Granite paper	Papier avec fragments de fils de soie	Faserpapier	Papel con filamentos	Carto con fili di seta
Green	Vert	Grün	Verde	Verde
Greenish Blue	Bleu verdâtre	Grünlichblau	Azul verdoso	Azzurro verdastro
Greenish Yellow	Jaune-vert	Grünlichgelb	Amarillo verdoso	Giallo verdastro
Grey	Gris	Grau	Gris	Grigio
Grey-blue	Bleu-gris	Graublau	Azul gris	Azzurro grigio
Grey-green	Vert gris	Graugrün	Verde gris	Verde grigio
Gum	Gomme	Gummi	Goma	Gomma
Gutter	Interpanneau	Zwischensteg	Espacio blanco entre dos grupos	Ponte
Imperforate	Non-dentelé	Geschnitten	Sin dentar	Non dentellato
Indigo	Indigo	Indigo	Azul indigo	Indaco
Inscription	Inscription	Inschrift	Inscripción	Dicitura
Inverted	Renversé	Kopfstehend	Invertido	Capovolto
Issue	Émission	Ausgabe	Emisión	Emissione
Laid	Vergé	Gestreift	Listado	Vergato
Lake	Lie de vin	Lackfarbe	Laca	Lacca
Lake-brown	Brun-carmin	Lackbraun	Castaño laca	Bruno lacca
Lavender	Bleu-lavande	Lavendel	Color de alhucema	Lavanda
Lemon	Jaune-citron	Zitrongelb	Limón	Limone
Light Blue	Bleu clair	Hellblau	Azul claro	Azzurro chiaro
Lilac	Lilas	Lila	Lila	Lilla
Line perforation	Dentelure en lignes	Linienzähnung	Dentado en linea	Dentellatura lineare
Lithography	Lithographie	Steindruck	Litografía	Litografia
Local	Timbre de poste locale	Lokalpostmarke	Emisión local	Emissione locale
Lozenge roulette	Percé en losanges	Rautenförmiger Durchstich	Picadura en rombos	Perforazione a losanghe
Magenta	Magenta	Magentarot	Magenta	Magenta
Margin	Marge	Rand	Borde	Margine
Maroon	Marron pourpré	Dunkelrotpurpur	Púrpura rojo oscuro	Marrone rossastro
Mauve	Mauve	Malvenfarbe	Malva	Malva
Multicoloured	Polychrome	Mehrfarbig	Multicolores	Policromo
Myrtle Green	Vert myrte	Myrtengrün	Verde mirto	Verde mirto
New Blue	Bleu ciel vif	Neublau	Azul nuevo	Azzurro nuovo
Newspaper stamp	Timbre pour journaux	Zeitungsmarke	Sello para periódicos	Francobollo per giornali

International Philatelic Glossary

English	French	German	Spanish	Italian
Obliteration	Oblitération	Abstempelung	Matasello	Annullamento
Obsolete	Hors (de) cours	Ausser Kurs	Fuera de curso	Fuori corso
Ochre	Ocre	Ocker	Ocre	Ocra
Official stamp	Timbre de service	Dienstmarke	Sello de servicio	Francobollo di
Olive-brown	Brun-olive	Olivbraun	Castaño oliva	Bruno oliva
Olive-green	Vert-olive	Olivgrün	Verde oliva	Verde oliva
Olive-grey	Gris-olive	Olivgrau	Gris oliva	Grigio oliva
Olive-yellow	Jaune-olive	Olivgelb	Amarillo oliva	Giallo oliva
Orange	Orange	Orange	Naranja	Arancio
Orange-brown	Brun-orange	Orangebraun	Castaño naranja	Bruno arancio
Orange-red	Rouge-orange	Orangerot	Rojo naranja	Rosso arancio
Orange-yellow	Jaune-orange	Orangegelb	Amarillo naranja	Giallo arancio
Overprint	Surcharge	Aufdruck	Sobrecarga	Soprastampa
Pair	Paire	Paar	Pareja	Coppia
Pale	Pâle	Blass	Pálido	Pallido
Pane	Panneau	Gruppe	Grupo	Gruppo
Paper	Papier	Papier	Papel	Carta
Parcel post stamp	Timbre pour colis postaux	Paketmarke	Sello para paquete postal	Francobollo per pacchi postali
Pen-cancelled	Oblitéré à plume	Federzugentwertung	Cancelado a pluma	Annullato a penna
Percé en arc	Percé en arc	Bogenförmiger Durchstich	Picadura en forma de arco	Perforazione ad arco
Percé en scie	Percé en scie	Bogenförmiger Durchstich	Picado en sierra	Foratura a sega
Perforated	Dentelé	Gezähnt	Dentado	Dentellato
Perforation	Dentelure	Zähnung	Dentar	Dentellatura
Photogravure	Photogravure, Heliogravure	Rastertiefdruck	Fotograbado	Rotocalco
Pin perforation	Percé en points	In Punkten durchstochen	Horadado con alfileres	Perforato a punti
Plate	Planche	Platte	Plancha	Lastra, Tavola
Plum	Prune	Pflaumenfarbe	Color de ciruela	Prugna
Postage Due stamp	Timbre-taxe	Portomarke	Sello de tasa	Segnatasse
Postage stamp	Timbre-poste	Briefmarke, Freimarke, Postmarke	Sello de correos	Francobollo postale
Postal fiscal stamp	Timbre fiscal-postal	Stempelmarke als Postmarke verwendet	Sello fiscal-postal	Fiscale postale
Postmark	Oblitération postale	Poststempel	Matasello	Bollo
Printing	Impression, Tirage	Druck	Impresión	Stampa, Tiratura
Proof	Épreuve	Druckprobe	Prueba de impresión	Prova
Provisionals	Timbres provisoires	Provisorische Marken. Provisorien	Provisionales	Provvisori
Prussian Blue	Bleu de Prusse	Preussischblau	Azul de Prusia	Azzurro di Prussia
Purple	Pourpre	Purpur	Púrpura	Porpora
Purple-brown	Brun-pourpre	Purpurbraun	Castaño púrpura	Bruno porpora
Recess-printing	Impression en taille douce	Tiefdruck	Grabado	Incisione
Red	Rouge	Rot	Rojo	Rosso
Red-brown	Brun-rouge	Rotbraun	Castaño rojizo	Bruno rosso
Reddish Lilac	Lilas rougeâtre	Rötlichlila	Lila rojizo	Lilla rossastro
Reddish Purple	Poupre-rouge	Rötlichpurpur	Púrpura rojizo	Porpora rossastro
Reddish Violet	Violet rougeâtre	Rötlichviolett	Violeta rojizo	Violetto rossastro
Red-orange	Orange rougeâtre	Rotorange	Naranja rojizo	Arancio rosso
Registration stamp	Timbre pour lettre chargée (recommandée)	Einschreibemarke	Sello de certificado	Francobollo per raccomandate lettere
Reprint	Réimpression	Neudruck	Reimpresión	Ristampa
Reversed	Retourné	Umgekehrt	Invertido	Rovesciato

xxvii

International Philatelic Glossary

English	French	German	Spanish	Italian
Rose	Rose	Rosa	Rosa	Rosa
Rose-red	Rouge rosé	Rosarot	Rojo rosado	Rosso rosa
Rosine	Rose vif	Lebhaftrosa	Rosa vivo	Rosa vivo
Roulette	Percage	Durchstich	Picadura	Foratura
Rouletted	Percé	Durchstochen	Picado	Forato
Royal Blue	Bleu-roi	Königblau	Azul real	Azzurro reale
Sage green	Vert-sauge	Salbeigrün	Verde salvia	Verde salvia
Salmon	Saumon	Lachs	Salmón	Salmone
Scarlet	Écarlate	Scharlach	Escarlata	Scarlatto
Sepia	Sépia	Sepia	Sepia	Seppia
Serpentine roulette	Percé en serpentin	Schlangenliniger Durchstich	Picado a serpentina	Perforazione a serpentina
Shade	Nuance	Tönung	Tono	Gradazione de colore
Sheet	Feuille	Bogen	Hoja	Foglio
Slate	Ardoise	Schiefer	Pizarra	Ardesia
Slate-blue	Bleu-ardoise	Schieferblau	Azul pizarra	Azzurro ardesia
Slate-green	Vert-ardoise	Schiefergrün	Verde pizarra	Verde ardesia
Slate-lilac	Lilas-gris	Schierferlila	Lila pizarra	Lilla ardesia
Slate-purple	Mauve-gris	Schieferpurpur	Púrpura pizarra	Porpora ardesia
Slate-violet	Violet-gris	Schieferviolett	Violeta pizarra	Violetto ardesia
Special delivery stamp	Timbre pour exprès	Eilmarke	Sello de urgencia	Francobollo per espressi
Specimen	Spécimen	Muster	Muestra	Saggio
Steel Blue	Bleu acier	Stahlblau	Azul acero	Azzurro acciaio
Strip	Bande	Streifen	Tira	Striscia
Surcharge	Surcharge	Aufdruck	Sobrecarga	Soprastampa
Tête-bêche	Tête-bêche	Kehrdruck	Tête-bêche	Tête-bêche
Tinted paper	Papier teinté	Getöntes Papier	Papel coloreado	Carta tinta
Too-late stamp	Timbre pour lettres en retard	Verspätungsmarke	Sello para cartas retardadas	Francobollo per le lettere in ritardo
Turquoise-blue	Bleu-turquoise	Türkisblau	Azul turquesa	Azzurro turchese
Turquoise-green	Vert-turquoise	Türkisgrün	Verde turquesa	Verde turchese
Typography	Typographie	Buchdruck	Tipografia	Tipografia
Ultramarine	Outremer	Ultramarin	Ultramar	Oltremare
Unused	Neuf	Ungebraucht	Nuevo	Nuovo
Used	Oblitéré, Usé	Gebraucht	Usado	Usato
Venetian Red	Rouge-brun terne	Venezianischrot	Rojo veneciano	Rosso veneziano
Vermilion	Vermillon	Zinnober	Cinabrio	Vermiglione
Violet	Violet	Violett	Violeta	Violetto
Violet-blue	Bleu-violet	Violettblau	Azul violeta	Azzurro violetto
Watermark	Filigrane	Wasserzeichen	Filigrana	Filigrana
Watermark sideways	Filigrane couché	Wasserzeichen liegend	Filigrana acostado	Filigrana coricata
Wove paper	Papier ordinaire, Papier uni	Einfaches Papier	Papel avitelado	Carta unita
Yellow	Jaune	Gelb	Amarillo	Giallo
Yellow-brown	Brun-jaune	Gelbbraun	Castaño amarillo	Bruno giallo
Yellow-green	Vert-jaune	Gelbgrün	Verde amarillo	Verde giallo
Yellow-olive	Olive-jaunâtre	Gelboliv	Oliva amarillo	Oliva giallastro
Yellow-orange	Orange jaunâtre	Gelborange	Naranja amarillo	Arancio giallastro
Zig-zag roulette	Percé en zigzag	Sägezahnartiger Durchstich	Picado en zigzag	Perforazione a zigzag

About Us

Our History
Edward Stanley Gibbons started trading postage stamps in his father's chemist shop in 1856. Since then we have been at the forefront of stamp collecting for over 150 years. We hold the Royal Warrant, offer unsurpassed expertise and quality and provide collectors with the peace of mind of a certificate of authenticity on all of our stamps. If you think of stamp collecting, you think of Stanley Gibbons and we are proud to uphold that tradition for you.

399 Strand
Our world famous stamp shop is a collector's paradise, with all of our latest catalogues, albums and accessories and, of course, our unrivalled stockholding of postage stamps.

www.stanleygibbons.com   shop@stanleygibbons.com   +44 (0)20 7836 8444

Specialist Stamp Sales
For the collector that appreciates the value of collecting the highest quality examples, Stanley Gibbons is the only choice. Our extensive range is unrivalled in terms of quality and quantity, with specialist stamps available from all over the world.

www.stanleygibbons.com/stamps   shop@stanleygibbons.com   +44 (0)20 7836 8444

Stanley Gibbons Auctions and Valuations
Sell your collection or individual rare items through our prestigious public auctions or our regular postal auctions and benefit from the excellent prices being realised at auction currently. We also provide an unparalleled valuation service.

www.stanleygibbons.com/auctions   auctions@stanleygibbons.com   +44 (0)20 7836 8444

Stanley Gibbons Publications
One of the world's first stamp catalogues was printed by Stanley Gibbons in 1865 and we haven't looked back since! Our catalogues are trusted worldwide as the industry standard and we print countless titles each year. We also publish consumer and trade magazines, Gibbons Stamp Monthly and Philatelic Exporter to bring you news, views and insights into all things philatelic. Never miss an issue by subscribing today and benefit from exclusive subscriber offers each month.

www.stanleygibbons.com   orders@stanleygibbons.com   +44 (0)1425 472 363

Stanley Gibbons Investments
The Stanley Gibbons Investment Department offers a unique range of investment propositions that have consistently outperformed more traditional forms of investment. You can own your very own piece of history. Whether it is the Penny Black, a Victoria Cross or an official royal document signed by the Queen of England in the 16th century, we have something to amaze you and potentially offer you excellent investment returns.

www.stanleygibbons.com/investment   investment@stanleygibbons.com   +44 (0)1481 708 270

Fraser's Autographs
Autographs, manuscripts and memorabilia from Henry VIII to current day. We have over 60,000 items in stock, including movie stars, musicians, sport stars, historical figures and royalty. Fraser's is the UK's market leading autograph dealer and has been dealing in high quality autographed material since 1978.

www.frasersautographs.com   sales@frasersautographs.com   +44 (0)20 7557 4404

stanleygibbons.com
Our website offers the complete philatelic service. Whether you are looking to buy stamps, invest, read news articles, browse our online stamp catalogue or find new issues, you are just one click away from anything you desire in the world of stamp collecting at stanleygibbons.com. Happy browsing!

www.stanleygibbons.com

Stanley Gibbons
399 Strand

BY APPOINTMENT TO
HER MAJESTY THE QUEEN
STANLEY GIBBONS LTD
LONDON
PHILATELISTS

Looking for a reason to visit London?
We can give you 3 million...

At 399 Strand - Stanley Gibbons' flagship stamp shop – you can choose from over 3 million stamps, from mixed packets and kiloware to rare investment grade items worth hundreds of thousands of pounds. In fact, you can find pretty much everything you could ever need...

Specialist stamps
Get complete peace of mind on all your purchases by viewing stamps before you buy. Andrew Mansi is on hand to give you advice on specialist stamps from Great Britain and the Commonwealth.

Accessories
Visit 399 Strand, where you can buy all your albums and accessories over the counter and try them before you buy. Stephen Bowyer will advise you on the accessories that are right for you and if we haven't got what you need in stock, we'll mail it to you free of charge.

New issues
It's not all about £16,000 Prussian Blues. We're delighted to offer you a complete range of "normal stuff" with our over the counter new issue service managed by our friendly shop staff who will give you an unrivalled personal service.

It may surprise you, but you will find new issues from a range of countries at 399, including Great Britain, Jersey, Guernsey, Isle of Man, Australia, New Zealand, Canada, USA, China, Israel, French Antarctic Territory, British Antarctic Territory and Falklands.

So why not pop in next time you're in London and see what you can find? We'd be delighted to see you.

Please contact Wayne Elliott - shop@stanleygibbons.com
399 Strand opening hours **Mon-Fri 9am-5pm Sat 9:30am-5pm Sun Closed**

Est 1856
STANLEY GIBBONS

Stanley Gibbons
399 Strand, London, WC2R 0LX
+44 (0)20 7836 8444
www.stanleygibbons.com

Bahamas

The British Post Office at Nassau was established during the early days of the West Indies packet system, and was certainly operating by 1733. The first known local postmark dates from 1802.

The crowned-circle handstamp No. CC1 was issued in 1846 and was generally replaced, for the public mails, by various stamps of Great Britain in 1858.

Local mail deliveries were rudimentary until 1859 when Nos. 1/2 were issued by the colonial authorities for interisland mails. Examples used for this purpose are usually cancelled in manuscript or with a "27" postmark. The "local" 1d. stamp became valid for overseas mails in May, 1860, when the colonial authorities took over this service from the British G.P.O.

CC 2   **"A05"**

NASSAU
CROWNED-CIRCLE HANDSTAMPS

CC1   CC **2** BAHAMAS (Nassau) (18.5.1846) (R.) *Price on cover*   £2250

No. CC1 was later struck in black and used as an Official Paid mark between July 1899 and September 1935. Handstamps as Types CC **1** and CC **3** (only three known) struck in black were used for the same purpose from 1933 until 1953; but it is believed that these were never employed during the pre-stamp period. *Price on cover from £50.*

Stamps of GREAT BRITAIN cancelled "A 05".

1858–60
Z1	1d. rose-red (1857), perf 14	£2250
Z2	2d. blue (1858) (Plate Nos. 7, 8)	£1300
Z3	4d. rose (1857)	£450
Z3*a*	6d. purple (1854), embossed	£5000
Z4	6d. lilac (1856)	£350
Z5	1s. green (1856)	£2500

PRICES FOR STAMPS ON COVER TO 1945	
No. 1	from × 10
No. 2	—
Nos. 3/6	from × 8
No. 7	—
Nos. 8/11	from × 10
Nos. 12/15	from × 4
Nos. 16/19*a*	from × 6
Nos. 20/5	from × 15
Nos. 26/8	from × 4
No. 29	—
Nos. 30/2	from × 15
No. 33	from × 30
Nos. 35/7	from × 6
Nos. 38/9	from × 10
No. 39*b*	from × 30
No. 40	from × 50
No. 41	from × 6
No. 42	from × 15
No. 43	from × 5
Nos. 44/*a*	from × 10
No. 45	from × 40
Nos. 47/57	from × 4
Nos. 58/89	from × 2
Nos. 90/130	from × 3
Nos. 131/2	from × 10
Nos. 141/5	from × 4
Nos. 146/8	from × 6
Nos. 149/57	from × 3
Nos. 158/60	from × 4
No. 161	from × 8
Nos. 162/75	from × 5
Nos. S1/3	from × 20

CROWN COLONY

1 **2** **3**

(Eng and recess P.B.)

1859 (10 June)–**60**. No wmk. Imperf.

(a) Thick, opaque paper
1	**1**	1d. reddish lake *(shades)*	£5000	£2250

(b) Thin paper
| 2 | **1** | 1d. dull lake (4.60) | 65·00 | £1500 |

No. 1, the printing on thick opaque paper, is very rare in unused condition. Unused remainders, on medium to thick, but slightly transparent, paper are worth about £250.

Collectors are warned against false postmarks upon the remainder stamps of 1d., imperf, on thick paper.

1860 (Oct). No wmk. Clean-cut perf 14 to 16.
3	**1**	1d. lake (H/S "CANCELLED" in oval £8500)	£5500	£750

For notes on "CANCELLED" examples see Catalogue Introduction. Examples with this handstamp on No. 3 are imperforate horizontally.

1861 (June)–**62**. No wmk.

(a) Rough perf 14 to 16
4	**1**	1d. lake	£650	£325
5	**2**	4d. dull rose (Dec, 1861)	£1400	£400
		a. Imperf between (pair)	£35000	
6		6d. grey-lilac (Dec, 1861)	£4250	£600
		a. Pale dull lilac	£3250	£500

(b) P 11 to 12½ (1862)
7	**1**	1d. lake	£2250	

No. 7 was a perforation trial on a new machine at Perkins, Bacon. It was not sent out to the Colony and is also known part perforated.

(Recess D.L.R.)

1862. No wmk.*

(a) P 11½, 12
8	**1**	1d. carmine-lake	£1000	£190
9		1d. lake	£1600	£275
10	**2**	4d. dull rose	£3750	£425
11		6d. lavender-grey	£11000	£500

(b) P 11½, 12, compound with 11
12	**1**	1d. carmine-lake	£2250	£850
13		1d. lake	£2500	£950
14	**2**	4d. dull rose	£21000	£2000
15		6d. lavender-grey	£21000	£1900

(c) P 13
16	**1**	1d. lake	£900	£170
17		1d. brown-lake	£750	£140
18	**2**	4d. dull rose	£2750	£375
19		6d. lavender-grey	£3250	£475
		a. Lilac	£2750	£450

*Stamps exist with part of papermaker's sheet wmk ("T. H. SAUNDERS" and date).

1863–77. Wmk Crown CC.

(a) P 12½
20	**1**	1d. brown-lake	£100	70·00
		w. Wmk inverted	£180	£110
		x. Wmk reversed		
		y. Wmk inverted and reversed	—	£170
21		1d. carmine-lake	£120	70·00
		w. Wmk inverted	£180	95·00
		x. Wmk reversed	£130	70·00
22		1d. carmine-lake (aniline)	£150	75·00
		w. Wmk inverted	£225	
		x. Wmk reversed		
23		1d. rose-red	70·00	45·00
		w. Wmk inverted	£130	
		x. Wmk reversed	70·00	45·00
24		1d. red	70·00	45·00
		w. Wmk inverted		
		x. Wmk reversed	—	45·00
25		1d. vermilion	75·00	45·00
		w. Wmk inverted	£120	80·00
		x. Wmk reversed	75·00	45·00
		y. Wmk inverted and reversed	£180	£100
26	**2**	4d. bright rose	£300	60·00
		w. Wmk inverted	—	£225
		x. Wmk reversed	—	80·00
27		4d. dull rose	£400	60·00
		w. Wmk inverted	—	£225
		x. Wmk reversed	£375	60·00
		y. Wmk inverted and reversed	£950	£225
28		4d. brownish rose (*wmk reversed*)	£475	80·00

BAHAMAS

		w. Wmk inverted	—	£250
29		6d. rose-lilac	—	£2250
		w. Wmk inverted	£6500	
30		6d. lilac (*shades*)	£425	75·00
		w. Wmk inverted	—	£225
		x. Wmk reversed		
31		6d. deep violet	£160	60·00
		w. Wmk inverted	£600	£225
		x. Wmk reversed	£180	65·00
		y. Wmk inverted and reversed		
32		6d. violet (aniline)	£250	90·00
		x. Wmk reversed	£250	95·00

(b) P 14

33	1	1d. scarlet-vermilion (1877)	70·00	15·00
		x. Wmk reversed	80·00	23·00
34		1d. scarlet (or scarlet-vermilion) (aniline)	£1000	
		x. Wmk reversed		
35	2	4d. bright rose (1876)	£400	40·00
		w. Wmk inverted	£900	£225
36		4d. dull rose	£1500	40·00
		w. Wmk inverted		
37		4d. rose-lake	£450	40·00

No. 29 is believed to be the shade of the first printing only and should not be confused with other lilac shades of the 6d.

No. 34 is not known postally used, although manuscript fiscal cancellations on this shade do exist.

(Typo D.L.R.)

1863–**80**. Wmk Crown CC.

(a) P 12½

38	3	1s. green (1865)	£2750	£300

(b) P 14

39	3	1s. deep green	£400	50·00
		aw. Wmk inverted		
		b. Green	£120	30·00
		ba. Thick paper (1880)	8·00	9·50
		bw. Wmk inverted (thick paper)	—	£150

1882 (Mar). Wmk Crown CA.

(a) P 12

40	1	1d. scarlet-vermilion	60·00	14·00
		x. Wmk reversed	—	65·00
41	2	4d. rose	£550	45·00

(b) P 14

42	1	1d. scarlet-vermilion	£475	60·00
		x. Wmk reversed	£600	
43	2	4d. rose	£850	60·00
		x. Wmk reversed	£950	70·00

1882 (Mar)–**98**. Wmk Crown CA. P 14.

44	3	1s. green	50·00	14·00
44*a*		1s. blue-green (1898)	38·00	40·00

FOURPENCE
(4)

1883. No. 31 surch with T **4**.

45	2	4d. on 6d. deep violet	£550	£400
		a. Surch inverted	£18000	£10000
		x. Wmk reversed	£600	£450

Type **4** was applied by handstamp and occurs in various positions. Caution is needed in buying Nos. 45/x.

2½d. Sloping "2" (R. 10/6)   **6d.** Malformed "E"

(Typo D.L.R.)

1884–**90**. Wmk Crown CA. P 14.

47	5	1d. pale rose	85·00	14·00
48		1d. carmine-rose	7·50	2·00
49		1d. bright carmine (aniline)	4·00	5·50
50		2½d. dull blue (1888)	85·00	18·00
51		2½d. blue	48·00	8·00
		a. Sloping "2"	£450	£120
52		2½d. ultramarine	11·00	1·75
		a. Sloping "2"	£160	70·00
		s. Optd "SPECIMEN"	65·00	
		w. Wmk inverted	£225	£110
53		4d. deep yellow	9·50	4·00
54		6d. mauve (1890)	6·00	35·00
		a. Malformed "E" (R. 6/6)	£200	£400
		s. Optd "SPECIMEN"	65·00	
56		5s. sage-green	85·00	95·00
57		£1 Venetian red	£275	£225
47/57 Set of 6			£350	£325

Examples of Nos. 54/7 are known showing a forged Bahamas postmark dated "AU 29 94".

6 Queen's Staircase, Nassau   **7**   **8**

(Recess D.L.R.)

1901 (23 Sept)–**03**. Wmk Crown CC. P 14.

58	6	1d. black and red	15·00	2·00
		w. Wmk inverted	£160	£160
		y. Wmk inverted and reversed	£275	
59		5d. black and orange (1.03)	8·50	50·00
		x. Wmk reversed	£275	
		y. Wmk inverted and reversed	£200	£325
60		2s. black and blue (1.03)	29·00	60·00
		x. Wmk reversed	£400	
61		3s. black and green (1.03)	50·00	65·00
		w. Wmk inverted	£120	£130
		y. Wmk inverted and reversed		
58/61 Set of 4			90·00	£160
58s/61s Optd "SPECIMEN" Set of 4			£150	

For stamps in this design, but with Mult Crown CA or Mult Script CA watermarks see Nos. 75/80 and 111/14.

(Typo D.L.R.)

1902 (18 Dec)–**10**. Wmk Crown CA. P 14.

62	7	1d. carmine	1·50	1·50
63		2½d. ultramarine	8·00	1·25
		a. Sloping "2"	£250	£120
64		4d. orange	15·00	60·00
65		4d. deep yellow (3.10)	27·00	75·00
66		6d. brown	6·00	28·00
		a. Malformed "E" (R. 6/6)	£170	£300
67		1s. grey-black and carmine	22·00	55·00
68		1s. brownish grey and carmine (6.07)	22·00	55·00
69		5s. dull purple and blue	75·00	95·00
70		£1 green and black	£300	£350
62/70 Set of 7			£375	£550
62s/70s Optd "SPECIMEN" Set of 7			£300	

Examples of most values are known showing a forged Nassau postmark dated "2 MAR 10".

1906 (Apr)–**11**. Wmk Mult Crown CA. P 14.

71	7	½d. pale green (5.06)	5·00	3·25
		s. Optd "SPECIMEN"	55·00	
72		1d. carmine-rose	26·00	1·25
73		2½d. ultramarine (4.07)	27·00	26·00
		a. Sloping "2"	£350	£400
		w. Wmk inverted	£160	£160
74		6d. bistre-brown (8.11)	17·00	48·00
		a. Malformed "E" (R. 6/6)	£275	£475
71/4 Set of 4			65·00	70·00

1911 (Feb)–**19**. Wmk Mult Crown CA. P 14.

75	6	1d. black and red	23·00	2·75
		a. Grey-black and scarlet (1916)	4·75	2·75
		b. Grey-black & deep carmine-red (1919)	10·00	7·00
76		3d. purple/yellow (thin paper) (18.5.17)	5·50	40·00
		a. Reddish pur/buff (thick paper) (1.19)	7·00	9·00
		s. Optd "SPECIMEN"	50·00	
		x. Wmk reversed	†	£475
77		3d. black and brown (23.3.19)	2·75	2·25
		s. Optd "SPECIMEN"	50·00	
		w. Wmk inverted		
		x. Wmk reversed	†	£475
78		5d. black and mauve (18.5.17)	3·50	5·50
		s. Optd "SPECIMEN"	50·00	
79		2s. black and blue (11.16)	32·00	55·00
		w. Wmk inverted	£475	
80		3s. black and green (8.17)	70·00	55·00
		w. Wmk inverted	£325	£325
		y. Wmk inverted and reversed	£160	£150
75/80 Set of 6			£100	£110

(Typo D.L.R.)

1912–**19**. Wmk Mult Crown CA. Chalk-surfaced paper (1s. to £1). P 14.

81	8	½d. green	80	12·00
		a. Yellow-green	2·75	17·00

82		1d. carmine (aniline)	3·50	30
		a. Deep rose	8·00	2·25
		b. Rose	11·00	3·00
		w. Wmk inverted	£325	£130
		y. Wmk inverted and reversed	†	£325
83		2d. grey (1919)	2·25	3·00
84		2½d. ultramarine	4·75	32·00
		a. Deep dull blue	18·00	42·00
		b. Sloping "2"	£275	£425
85		4d. orange-yellow	5·50	24·00
		a. Yellow	2·50	20·00
86		6d. bistre-brown	1·75	7·00
		a. Malformed "E" (R. 6/6)	£130	£225
87		1s. grey-black and carmine	1·75	9·00
		a. Jet-black and carmine	14·00	22·00
88		5s. dull purple and blue	40·00	70·00
		a. Pale dull purple and deep blue	55·00	80·00
89		£1 dull green and black	£190	£325
		a. Green and black	£250	£350
81/9 Set of 9			£225	£425
81s/9s Optd "SPECIMEN" Set of 9			£325	

1.1.17. WAR TAX
(9)   (10)

1917 (18 May). No. 75b optd with T **9** in red by D.L.R.

90	6	1d. grey-black and deep carmine-red	40	2·00
		a. Long stroke to "7" (R. 4/6)	40·00	75·00
		s. Optd "SPECIMEN"	65·00	

It was originally intended to issue No. 90 on 1 January 1917, but the stamps were not received in the Bahamas until May. Half the proceeds from their sale were donated to the British Red Cross Society.

1918 (21 Feb–10 July). Nos. 75/6, 81/2 and 87 optd at Nassau with T **10**.

91	8	½d. green	12·00	48·00
92		1d. carmine (aniline)	1·00	50
		w. Wmk inverted	£300	
		x. Wmk reversed	£375	
93	6	1d. black and red (10 July)	3·75	8·50
		a. Opt double, one inverted	£850	
		b. Opt double	£1700	£1800
		c. Opt inverted	£1500	£1600
		x. Wmk reversed	£350	
94		3d. purple/yellow (thin paper)	2·50	2·25
		a. Opt double	£1600	£1700
		b. Opt inverted	£1100	£1200
		c. "W" of "WAR" inserted by hand	£4750	
95	8	1s. grey-black and carmine	£110	£150
91/5 Set of 5			£120	£190

No. 93 was only on sale for ten days.
No. 94c occurred on R. 1/1 of one sheet, the original "W" having been omitted as a result of a paper fold.
Examples of Nos. 91/2 with overprint inverted, and of Nos. 91/2 and 95 with overprint double, are now considered to be forgeries.

WAR TAX   WAR TAX   WAR CHARITY 3.6.18.
(11)   (12)   (13)

1918 (20 July). Optd by D.L.R. in London with T **11** or **12** (3d).

96	8	½d. green	1·75	1·75
		w. Wmk inverted		
		x. Wmk reversed		
97		1d. carmine	3·50	35
		a. Wmk sideways	£250	
		w. Wmk inverted		
		y. Wmk inverted and reversed	£325	
98	6	3d. purple/yellow	1·00	1·50
		w. Wmk inverted	£160	
		x. Wmk reversed	£190	
99	8	1s. grey-black and carmine (R.)	11·00	5·00
96/9 Set of 4			15·00	7·75
96s/9s Optd "SPECIMEN" Set of 4			£170	

1919 (21 Mar). No. 77 optd with T **12** by D.L.R.

100	6	3d. black and brown	1·00	5·00
		a. "C" and "A" missing from wmk	£1800	
		s. Optd "SPECIMEN"	50·00	
		w. Wmk inverted	70·00	

No. 100a shows the "C" omitted from one impression and the "A" missing from the next one to the right (as seen from the front of the stamp). The "C" is badly distorted in the second watermark.

1919 (1 Jan). No. 75b optd with T **13** by D.L.R.

101	6	1d. grey-black and deep carmine-red (R.)	30	2·50
		a. Opt double	£2000	
		s. Optd "SPECIMEN"	55·00	
		w. Wmk inverted	75·00	
		x. Wmk reversed	80·00	90·00
		y. Wmk inverted and reversed	£150	

The date is that originally fixed for the issue of the stamp. The year 1918 was also the bicentenary of the appointment of the first Royal governor.

WAR   WAR   TAX   TAX
(14)   (15)

1919 (14 July).

(a) Optd with T **14** by D.L.R.

102	8	½d. green (R.)	30	1·25
103		1d. carmine	1·50	1·50
104	—	1s. grey-black and carmine (R.)	27·00	55·00

(b) No. 77 optd with T **15**

105	6	3d. black and brown	1·00	8·00
		w. Wmk inverted	65·00	
		ws. Ditto. Optd "SPECIMEN"	90·00	
		x. Wmk reversed	70·00	
		y. Wmk inverted and reversed	£120	
102/5 Set of 4			27·00	60·00
102s/5s Optd "SPECIMEN" Set of 4			£170	

16   17 Great Seal of the Bahamas.

(Recess D.L.R.)

1920 (1 Mar). Peace Celebration. Wmk Mult Crown CA (sideways*). P 14.

106	16	½d. green	1·00	5·50
		a. "A" of "CA" missing from wmk	£800	
		x. Wmk sideways reversed	£325	£325
107		1d. carmine	2·75	1·00
		a. "A" of "CA" missing from wmk	†	£600
		x. Wmk sideways reversed	£375	
		y. Wmk Crown to right of CA and reversed	£375	
108		2d. slate-grey	2·75	7·50
		a. "C" of "CA" missing from wmk	£850	
109		3d. deep brown	2·75	9·00
		a. "C" of "CA" missing from wmk	£900	
		w. Wmk Crown to right of CA	£275	
110		1s. deep myrtle-green	15·00	38·00
		a. Substituted crown in wmk	£1700	
		b. "C" of "CA" missing from wmk	£1700	
		x. Wmk sideways reversed	£600	
106/10 Set of 5			22·00	55·00
106s/10s Optd "SPECIMEN" Set of 5			£170	

*The normal sideways watermark shows Crown to left of CA, as seen from the back of the stamp.
For illustration of the substituted watermark crown see Catalogue Introduction.

1921 (29 Mar)–**29**. Wmk Script CA. P 14.

111	6	1d. grey and rose-red	3·50	3·50
		x. Wmk reversed	£325	
112		5d. black and purple (8.29)	3·75	45·00
113		2s. black and blue (11.22)	22·00	70·00
114		3s. black and green (9.24)	55·00	70·00
111/14 Set of 4			75·00	£130
111s/14s Optd or Perf (5d.) "SPECIMEN" Set of 4			£200	

Examples of all values are known showing a forged Nassau postmark dated "2 MAR 10".

½d. Elongated "E" (left pane R. 9/6)

BAHAMAS

1921 (8 Sept)–**37**. Wmk Mult Script CA. Chalk-surfaced paper (3d., 1s., 5s., £1). P 14.

115	8	½d. green (1924)		50	40
		a. Elongated "E"		80·00	85·00
116		1d. carmine		1·00	15
117		1½d. brown-red (1934)		13·00	1·00
118		2d. grey (1927)		1·50	2·25
119		2½d. ultramarine (1922)		1·00	2·25
		y. Wmk inverted and reversed		†	£750
120		3d. purple/*pale yellow* (1931)		6·50	16·00
		a. *Purple/orange-yellow* (1937)		10·00	23·00
121		4d. orange-yellow (1924)		1·50	2·75
122		6d. bistre-brown (1922)		70	1·25
		a. Malformed "E" (R.6/6)		£100	£140
123		1s. black and carmine (1926)		6·00	5·50
124		5s. dull purple and blue (1924)		42·00	65·00
125		£1 green and black (1926)		£170	£350
115/25 *Set of 11*				£200	£400
115s/25s Optd or Perf (1½d., 3d.) "SPECIMEN" *Set of 11*				£500	

(Recess B.W.)

1930 (2 Jan). Tercentenary of Colony. Wmk Mult Script CA. P 12.

126	17	1d. black and scarlet		3·50	2·75
127		3d. black and deep brown		5·50	15·00
128		5d. black and deep purple		5·50	15·00
129		2s. black and deep blue		18·00	50·00
130		3s. black and green		48·00	85·00
126/30 *Set of 5*				70·00	£150
126s/30s Perf "SPECIMEN" *Set of 5*				£170	

18

18a Windsor Castle

(Recess B.W.)

1931 (14 July)–**46**. Wmk Mult Script CA. P 12.

131	18	2s. slate-purple and deep ultramarine		27·00	35·00
		a. *Slate-purple and indigo* (9.42)		£100	50·00
		b. *Brownish black and indigo* (13.4.43)		15·00	9·00
		c. *Brownish black and steel-blue* (6.44)		19·00	3·50
132		3s. slate-purple and myrtle-green		38·00	32·00
		a. *Brownish black and green* (13.4.43)		13·00	4·50
		ab. "A" of "CA" missing from wmk.		£1700	
		b. *Brownish black and myrtle-green* (1.10.46)		8·00	8·50
131s/2s Perf "SPECIMEN" *Set of 2*				95·00	

Most of the stamps from the September 1942 printing (No. 131*a* and further stocks of the 3s. similar to No. 132) were used for the 1942 "LANDFALL" overprints.

Diagonal line by turret (Plate 2A R. 10/1 and 10/2)

Dot to left of chapel (Plate 2B R. 8/3)

Dot by flagstaff (Plate 4 R. 8/4)

Dash by turret (Plate 4 R. 3/6)

1935 (6 May). Silver Jubilee. Wmk Mult Script CA. P 13½×14.

141	**18a**	1½d. deep blue and carmine		1·00	3·50
		h. Dot by flagstaff		£120	£200
		i. Dash by turret		£300	
142		2½d. brown and deep blue		5·00	9·50
		f. Diagonal line by turret		£180	£250
		g. Dot to left of chapel		£350	
143		6d. light blue and olive-green		7·00	15·00
		g. Dot to left of chapel		£225	£300
		h. Dot by flagstaff		£350	
144		1s. slate and purple		7·00	14·00
		h. Dot by flagstaff		£325	£400
		i. Dash by turret		£450	£550
141/4 *Set of 4*				18·00	38·00
141s/4s Perf "SPECIMEN" *Set of 4*				£140	

19 Greater Flamingos in flight

(Recess Waterlow)

1935 (22 May). Wmk Mult Script CA. P 12½.

145	19	8d. ultramarine and scarlet		8·50	3·25
		s. Perf "SPECIMEN"		75·00	

19a King George VI and Queen Elizabeth

20 King George VI

(Des and recess D.L.R.)

1937 (12 May). Coronation. Wmk Mult Script CA. P 14.

146	19a	½d. green		15	15
147		1½d. yellow-brown		40	1·10
148		2½d. bright blue		55	1·10
146/8 *Set of 3*				1·00	2·10
146s/8s Perf "Specimen" *Set of 3*				£120	

½d. Accent flaw (right pane R. 1/5) (1938 ptg only)

2d. Short "T" in "TWO" (right pane R. 3/6) (Retouched on No. 152*c*, although bottom of letter is still pointed)

3d. "RENCE" flaw (Right pane R. 9/3. Later corrected.

(Typo D.L.R.)

1938 (11 Mar)–**52**. Wmk Mult Script CA. Chalk-surfaced paper (1s. to £1). P 14.

149	20	½d. green		2·75	1·25
		a. Elongated "E"		£180	
		b. Accent flaw		£500	
		c. *Bluish green* (11.9.42)		3·75	3·50
		ca. Elongated "E"		£225	
		d. *Myrtle-green* (11.12.46)		10·00	11·00
		da. Elongated "E"		£400	
149*e*		½d. brown-purple (18.2.52)		1·00	3·75
		ea. Error. Crown missing		£14000	
		eb. Error. St Edward's Crown		£4000	£3000
		ec. Elongated "E"		£170	£275
150		1d. carmine		8·50	2·00
150*a*		1d. olive-grey (17.9.41)		3·50	3·50
		ab. *Pale slate* (11.9.42)		60	70
151		1½d. red-brown (19.4.38)		1·50	1·25
		a. *Pale red-brown* (19.4.48)		9·00	2·75
152		2d. pale slate (19.4.38)		19·00	3·50
		a. Short "T"		£850	£375
152*b*		2d. scarlet (17.9.41)		1·00	65

4

BAHAMAS

	ba. Short "T"		£140	£120
	bb. "TWO PENCE" printed double		†	£15000
	bc. Dull rose-red (19.4.48)		6·00	3·25
152c	2d. green (1.5.51)		2·00	80
153	2½d. ultramarine		3·25	1·50
153a	2½d. violet (1.7.43)		1·25	1·25
	ab. "2½ PENNY" printed double		£5000	
154	3d. violet (19.4.38)		16·00	3·00
154a	3d. blue (4.43)		2·50	1·25
	aa. "RENCE" flaw		£3500	
	ab. Bright ultramarine (19.4.48)		7·50	6·00
154b	3d. scarlet (1.2.52)		2·25	3·25
154c	10d. yellow-orange (18.11.46)		2·50	20
155	1s. grey-black and carmine (thick paper) (15.9.38)		30·00	6·50
	a. Brownish grey and scarlet (thin striated paper) (4.42)		£800	£100
	b. Ordinary paper. Black and carmine (9.42)		27·00	7·00
	c. Ordinary paper. Grey-black and bright crimson (6.3.44)		19·00	75
	d. Pale brownish grey and crimson (19.4.48)		18·00	1·50
156	5s. lilac & blue (thick paper) (19.4.38)		£170	£100
	a. Dull rose-lilac and blue (thin striated paper) (4.42)		£4250	£700
	b. Ordinary paper. Purple and blue (9.42)		38·00	25·00
	c. Ordinary paper. Dull mauve and deep blue (11.46)		£120	70·00
	d. Brown-purple and deep bright blue (19.4.48)		42·00	19·00
	e. Red-purple and deep bright blue (8.51)		24·00	24·00
157	£1 deep grey-green and black (thick paper) (15.9.38)		£250	£150
	a. Ordinary paper. Blue-green and black (13.4.43)		60·00	55·00
	b. Ordinary paper. Grey-green and black (3.44)		£200	£140
149/57a Set of 17			£150	85·00
149s/57s Perf "SPECIMEN" Set of 14			£600	

Nos. 149/50a exist in coils, constructed from normal sheets.

No. 149eb occurs on a row in the watermark in which the crowns and letters "CA" alternate.

The thick chalk-surfaced paper, used for the initial printing of the 1s., 5s. and £1, was usually toned and had streaky gum. The April 1942 printing for the 1s. and 5s., which was mostly used for the "LANDFALL" overprints, was on thin striated paper. Printings of the three values between September 1942 and November 1946 were on a thick, smooth, opaque ordinary paper.

21 Sea Garden, Nassau

22 Fort Charlotte

23 Greater Flamingos in flight

(24) 3d.

(Recess Waterlow)

1938 (1 July). Wmk Mult Script CA. P 12½.

158	21	4d. light blue and red-orange	1·25	1·00
159	22	6d. olive-green and light blue	1·25	1·00
160	23	8d. ultramarine and scarlet	16·00	3·50
158/60 Set of 3			17·00	5·00
158s/60s Perf "SPECIMEN" Set of 3			£140	

1940 (28 Nov). No. 153 surcharged with T **24** by The Nassau Guardian.

161	20	3d. on 2½d. blue	1·50	3·00

1492 LANDFALL OF COLUMBUS 1942

(25)

25a Houses of Parliament, London

Broken "OF" and "US" (R.2/6, late printing)

1942 (12 Oct). 450th Anniv of Landing of Columbus in New World. Optd as T **25** by The Nassau Guardian.

162	20	½d. bluish green	30	60
		a. Elongated "E"	75·00	
		b. Opt double	£2250	
		c. Accent flaw	£600	
163		1d. pale slate	30	60
164		1½d. red-brown	40	60
165		2d. scarlet	50	65
		a. Short "T"	£130	
166		2½d. ultramarine	50	65
167		3d. ultramarine	30	65
		a. "RENCE" flaw	£3500	
168	21	4d. light blue and red-orange	40	90
		a. "COIUMBUS" (R. 5/2)	£1100	£1300
169	22	6d. olive-green and light blue	40	1·75
		a. "COIUMBUS" (R. 5/2)	£1100	£1400
170	23	8d. ultramarine and scarlet	3·50	70
		a. "COIUMBUS" (R. 5/2)	£12000	£4000
171	20	1s. brownish grey and scarlet (thin striated paper)	12·00	5·00
		a. Ordinary paper. Black and carmine	12·00	15·00
		b. Ordinary paper. Grey-black and bright crimson	23·00	14·00
		c. Broken "OF" and "US"	£300	
172	18	2s. slate-purple and indigo	20·00	28·00
		a. Brownish black and indigo	8·50	10·00
		b. Brownish black and steel-blue	40·00	35·00
		c. Stop after "COLUMBUS" (R. 2/12)	£5000	£5000
173		3s. slate-purple and myrtle-green	9·00	6·50
		a. Brownish black and green	55·00	50·00
		b. Stop after "COLUMBUS" (R. 2/12)	£2500	
174	20	5s. reddish lilac and blue (thin striated paper)	50·00	22·00
		a. Ordinary paper. Purple and blue	23·00	14·00
		b. Broken "OF" and "US"	£650	
175		£1 deep grey-green & blk (thick paper)	80·00	£130
		a. Ordinary paper. Grey-green & black	30·00	25·00
		b. Broken "OF" and "US"	£900	
162/75a Set of 14			80·00	60·00
162s/75s Perf "SPECIMEN" Set of 14			£550	

These stamps replaced the definitive series for a period of six months. Initially stocks of existing printings were used, but when further supplies were required for overprinting a number of new printings were produced, some of which, including the new colour of the 3d., did not appear without overprint until much later.

No. 167 perforated "SPECIMEN" is known with the overprint double. (Price, £850).

(Des and recess D.L.R.)

1946 (11 Nov). Victory. Wmk Mult Script CA. P 13½×14.

176	25a	1½d. brown	10	60
177		3d. blue	10	60
176s/7s Perf "Specimen" Set of 2			90·00	

26 Infant Welfare Clinic

27 Agriculture (combine harvester)

28 Sisal

29 Straw work

BAHAMAS

30 Dairy farm
31 Fishing fleet 
32 Hatchet Bay, Eleuthera 
33 Tuna fishing 
34 Paradise Beach 
35 Modern hotels 
36 Yacht racing 
37 Watersports—skiing 
38 Shipbuilding 
39 Transportation 
40 Salt production 
41 Parliament buildings 

(Recess C.B.N.)

1948 (11 Oct). Tercentenary of Settlement of Island of Eleuthera. T **26/41**. P 12.

178	**26**	½d. orange	40	1·75
179	**27**	1d. sage-green	40	35
180	**28**	1½d. yellow	40	80
181	**29**	2d. scarlet	40	40
182	**30**	2½d. brown-lake	70	75
183	**31**	3d. ultramarine	2·50	85
184	**32**	4d. black	60	70
185	**33**	6d. emerald-green	2·50	80
186	**34**	8d. violet	1·25	70
187	**35**	10d. carmine	1·25	35
188	**36**	1s. sepia	3·00	50
189	**37**	2s. magenta	5·00	8·50
190	**38**	3s. blue	13·00	8·50
191	**39**	5s. mauve	20·00	5·50
192	**40**	10s. grey	17·00	13·00
193	**41**	£1 vermilion	17·00	17·00
178/93 Set of 16			75·00	55·00

For a full range of Stanley Gibbons catalogues, please visit www.stanleygibbons.com

41a King George VI and Queen Elizabeth
41b 

(Des and photo Waterlow (T **41a**) Design recess; name typo B.W. (T **41b**))

1948 (1 Dec). Royal Silver Wedding. Wmk Mult Script CA.
194 **41a** 1½d. red-brown (P 14×15) 20 25
195 **41b** £1 slate-green (P 11½×11) 45·00 32·00

1948 (1 Dec). Royal Silver Wedding. As Nos. 112/13 of Antigua.
194 1½d. red-brown 20 25
195 £1 slate-green 45·00 32·00

41c Hermes, Globe and Forms of Transport
41d Hemispheres, Jet-powered Vickers Viking airliner and Steamer 
41e Hermes and Globe 
41f UPU Monument 

(Recess Waterlow (T **41c**, **41f**). Designs recess; name typo B.W. (T **41d**, **41e**))

1949 (10 Oct). 75th Anniv of Universal Postal Union. Wmk Mult Script CA.
196 **41c** 2½d. violet (P 13½-14) 35 75
197 **41d** 3d. deep blue (P 11×11½) 2·25 3·50
198 **41e** 6d. greenish blue (P 11×11½) 55 3·25
199 **41f** 1s. carmine (P 13½-14) 55 75
196/9 Set of 4 3·25 7·50

41g Queen Elizabeth II

(Des and eng B.W. Recess D.L.R.)

1953 (3 June). Coronation. Wmk Mult Script CA. P 13½×14.
200 **41g** 6d. black and pale blue 1·75 60

42 Infant Welfare Clinic
43 Queen Elizabeth II 

(Recess B.W.)

1954 (1 Jan)–**63**. Designs previously used for King George VI issue, but bicoloured with portrait of Queen Elizabeth II as in T **42**, and commemorative inscr omitted. Wmk Mult Script CA. P 11×11½.
201 **42** ½d. black and red-orange 10 1·50

6

BAHAMAS

202	27	1d. olive-green and brown	10	30
203	32	1½d. blue and black	15	80
204	29	2d. yellow-brown and myrtle-green	15	30
		a. Yellow-brn & dp myrtle-grn (23.1.62)	11·00	12·00
205	31	3d. black and carmine-red	65	1·25
206	37	4d. turquoise-green and deep reddish purple	30	30
		a. Turq-blue and dp reddish pur (23.1.62)	24·00	23·00
207	30	5d. red-brown and deep bright blue	1·40	2·25
208	39	6d. light blue and black	2·25	20
		w. Wmk inverted	—	£900
209	34	8d. black and reddish lilac	70	40
		a. Black and deep reddish lilac (21.11.56)	7·00	2·75
210	35	10d. black and ultramarine	30	10
		a. Black and deep ultramarine (8.1.63)	8·50	2·75
211	36	1s. ultramarine and olive-brown	1·75	10
		a. Ultramarine and dp ol-sepia (19.2.58)	7·50	1·00
212	28	2s. orange-brown and black	3·00	70
		a. Chestnut and black (19.2.58)	17·00	2·00
213	38	2s.6d. black and deep blue	3·50	2·00
214	33	5s. bright emerald and orange	22·00	75
		a. Brt emerald & reddish orange (14.1.59)	85·00	10·00
215	40	10s. black and slate-black	35·00	2·50
216	41	£1 slate-black and violet	29·00	7·00
201/16 Set of 16			90·00	18·00

Nos. 201/2, 205, 208 and 211 exist in coils, constructed from normal sheets.

See also No. 246.

(Recess Waterlow)

1959 (10 June). Centenary of First Bahamas Postage Stamp. W w **12**. P 13½.

217	43	1d. black and scarlet	50	20
218		2d. black and blue-green	50	1·00
219		6d. black and blue	60	40
220		10d. black and chocolate	60	1·00
217/20 Set of 4			2·00	2·40

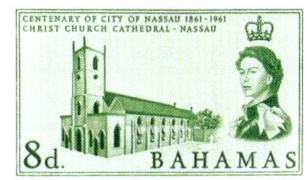

44 Christ Church Cathedral

(Photo Enschedé)

1962 (30 Jan). Nassau Centenary. T **44** and similar horiz design. P 14×13.

221		8d. green	65	55
222		10d. bluish violet	65	25

Design:—10d. Nassau Public Library.

45 Protein Foods

BAHAMAS TALKS 1962

(**46**)

(Des M. Goaman. Photo Harrison)

1963 (4 June). Freedom from Hunger. W w **12**. P 14×14½.

223	45	8d. sepia	40	40
		a. Name and value omitted	£1100	£2000

1963 (15 July). Bahamas Talks, 1962. Nos. 209/10 optd with T **46**.

224		8d. black and reddish lilac	65	75
225		10d. black and deep ultramarine	65	75

46a Red Cross Emblem

NEW CONSTITUTION 1964

(**47**)

(Des V. Whiteley. Litho B.W.)

1963 (2 Sept). Red Cross Centenary. W w **12**. P 13½.

226	46a	1d. red and black	50	75
227		10d. red and blue	1·75	2·50

SELF GOVERNMENT

1964 (7 Jan). New Constitution. As Nos. 201/16 but W w **12**, optd with T **47**, by B.W.

228		½d. black and red-orange	15	1·50
229		1d. olive-green and brown	15	15
230		1½d. blue and black	70	1·50
231		2d. yellow-brown and deep myrtle-green	15	20
232		3d. black and carmine-red	2·00	1·75
233		4d. turquoise-blue and deep reddish purple	70	55
234		5d. red-brown and deep bright blue	70	1·50
235		6d. light blue and black	3·25	30
236		8d. black and reddish lilac	70	30
237		10d. black and deep ultramarine	30	15
238		1s. ultramarine and olive-brown	1·50	15
239		2s. chestnut and black	2·00	1·75
240		2s.6d. black and deep blue	3·00	2·75
241		5s. bright emerald and orange	7·00	3·25
242		10s. black and slate-black	7·00	5·50
243		£1 slate-black and violet	7·50	25·00
228/43 Set of 16			32·00	42·00

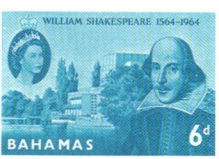

47a Shakespeare and Memorial Theatre, Stratford-upon-Avon

(Des R. Granger Barrett. Photo Harrison)

1964 (23 April). 400th Birth Anniv of William Shakespeare. W w **12**. P 14×14½.

244	47a	6d. turquoise	30	10
		w. Wmk inverted	65·00	

(**48**)

1964 (1 Oct). Olympic Games, Tokyo. As No. 211 but W w **12**, surch with T **48**.

245		8d. on 1s. ultramarine and olive-brown	45	15

1964 (6 Oct). As No. 204a, but wmk w **12**.

246		2d. yellow-brown and deep myrtle-green	1·00	30

49 Colony's Badge

50 Out Island regatta

51 Hospital

52 High School

53 Greater Flamingo

54 RMS *Queen Elizabeth*

55 "Development"

7

BAHAMAS

56 Yachting
57 Public square 
58 Sea Gardens 
59 Old cannons at Fort Charlotte 
60 Sikorsky S-38 flying boat, 1929 and Boeing 707 airliner 
61 Williamson Film Project, 1914 and Undersea Post Office, 1939 
62 Queen or Pink Conch 
63 Columbus's flagship 

(Queen's portrait by Anthony Buckley. Litho and recess (portrait and "BAHAMAS") B.W.)

1965 (7 Jan–14 Sept). Horiz designs as T **49/63**. W w **12**. P 13½.

247	49	½d. multicoloured	15	2·25
248	50	1d. slate, light blue and orange	50	1·00
249	51	1½d. rose-red, green and brown	15	3·75
250	52	2d. slate, green and turquoise-blue	15	10
251	53	3d. red, light blue and purple	4·50	20
252	54	4d. green, blue and orange-brown	5·00	3·50
253	55	6d. dull green, light blue and rose	1·25	10
254	56	8d. reddish purple, light blue and bronze green	50	30
255	57	10d. orange-brown, green and violet	25	10
256	58	1s. red, yellow, turquoise-blue and deep emerald	1·00	20
		a. Red, yellow, dull blue & emerald (14.9.65)	75	10
257	59	2s. brown, light blue and emerald	1·00	1·25
258	60	2s.6d. yellow-olive, blue and carmine	2·50	3·00
259	61	5s. orange-brown, ultramarine and green	2·75	1·00
260	62	10s. rose, blue and chocolate	16·00	3·50
261	63	£1 chestnut, blue and rose-red	21·00	11·00
247/261 Set of 15			50·00	27·00

Nos. 247/8, 251, 253 and 256 exist in coils, constructed from normal sheets.

63a I.T.U. Emblem

(Des M. Goaman. Litho Enschedé)

1965 (17 May). I.T.U Centenary. W w **12**. P 11×11½.

262	63a	1d. light emerald and orange	15	10
		w. Wmk inverted	£100	
263		2s. purple and yellow-olive	65	45
		w. Wmk inverted	16·00	

1965 (12 July). No. 254 surch with T **64**.

| 264 | | 9d. on 8d. reddish purple, light blue and bronze-green | 30 | 15 |

64a I.C.Y. Emblem

(Des V. Whiteley. Litho Harrison)

1965 (25 Oct). International Co-operation Year. W w **12**. P 14½.

265	64a	½d. reddish purple and turquoise-green	10	1·10
266		1s. deep bluish green and lavender	30	40

64b Sir Winston Churchill, and St. Paul's Cathedral in Wartime
64c Queen Elizabeth II and Duke of Edinburgh 

(Des Jennifer Toombs. Photo Harrison)

1966 (24 Jan). Churchill Commemoration. W w **12**. P 14.

267	64b	½d. new blue	10	75
		w. Wmk inverted	60·00	
268		2d. deep green	50	30
269		10d. brown	85	85
270		1s. bluish violet	85	1·40
267/70 Set of 4			2·00	3·00

(Des H. Baxter. Litho B.W.)

1966 (4 Feb). Royal Visit. W w **12**. P 11×12.

271	64c	6d. black and ultramarine	1·00	50
272		1s. black and magenta	1·25	1·25

(New Currency. 100 cents = 1 Bahamas dollar)

(65)   (66)

1966 (25 May). Decimal Currency. Nos. 247/61 variously surch as T **55/6**, by B.W.

273		1c. on ½d. multicoloured	10	30
274		2c. on 1d. slate, light blue and orange	75	30
275		3c. on 2d. slate, green and turquoise-blue	10	10
276		4c. on 3d. red, light blue and purple	2·00	20
277		5c. on 4d. green, blue and orange-brown	2·00	3·00
		a. Surch omitted (vert strip of 10)	£3250	
278		8c. on 6d. dull green, light blue and rose	20	20
279		10c. on 8d. reddish purple, light blue and bronze-green	30	75
280		11c. on 1½d. rose-red, green and brown	15	30
281		12c. on 10d. orange-brown, green and violet	15	10
282		15c. on 1s. multicoloured	25	10
283		22c. on 2s. brown, light blue and emerald	60	1·25
284		50c. on 2s.6d. yellow-olive, blue and carmine	1·00	1·40
285		$1 on 5s. orange-brown, ultram and green	1·75	1·50
286		$2 on 10s. rose, blue and chocolate	7·50	4·50
287		$3 on £1 chestnut, blue and rose-red	7·50	4·50
273/287 Set of 15			22·00	16·00

The above were made on new printings, some of which vary slightly in shade, and in No. 273 the shield appears as vermilion and green instead of carmine and blue-green due to a different combination of the printing colours.

No. 277a. One sheet exists and the stamp can be distinguished from No. 252 when in a vertical strip of ten as these were printed in sheets of 100 whereas No. 252 was printed in sheets of 60 (six rows of ten across).

66a Footballer's Legs, Ball and Jules Rimet Cup

BAHAMAS

(Des V. Whiteley. Litho Harrison)
1966 (1 July). World Cup Football Championship. W w **12** (sideways). P 14.
288	**66a**	8c. violet, yellow-green, lake and yellow-brown	35	15
289		15c. chocolate, blue-green, lake and yellow-brown	40	25

66b W.H.O. Building

(Des M. Goaman. Litho Harrison)
1966 (20 Sept). Inauguration of W.H.O. Headquarters, Geneva. W w **12** (sideways). P 14.
290	**66b**	11c. black, yellow-green and light blue	50	90
291		15c. black, light purple and yellow-brown	50	50

66c "Education"

66d "Science"

66e "Culture"

(Des Jennifer Toombs. Litho Harrison)
1966 (1 Dec). 20th Anniv of U.N.E.S.C.O. W w **12** (sideways). P 14.
292	**66c**	3c. slate-violet, red, yellow and orange	10	10
293	**66d**	15c. orange-yellow, violet and deep olive	35	20
294	**66e**	$1 black, bright purple and orange	1·10	2·00
292/4	Set of 3		1·40	2·00

67 Oceanic
68 Conch Shell

(Portrait by Anthony Buckley. Litho and recess (portrait, "BAHAMAS" and value), B.W.)
1967 (25 May)–**71**. As T **49**/**63** and additional design (T **67**) but values in decimal currency, as T **68** and colours changed. Toned paper. W w **12**. P 13½.
295	**49**	1c. multicoloured (as ½d.)	10	3·25
		a. Whiter paper (1970)	45	3·25
296	**50**	2c. slate, light blue & deep emerald (as 1d.)	50	60
		a. Whiter paper (1970)	1·40	9·00
297	**52**	3c. slate, green and violet (as 2d.)	10	10
		a. Whiter paper (1970)	42·00	5·00
298	**53**	4c. red, light blue and ultramarine (as 3d.)	4·75	50
		a. Whiter paper (9.70*)	12·00	18·00
299	**67**	5c. black, greenish blue and purple	1·00	3·50
		a. Whiter paper (1970)	2·25	8·50
300	**55**	8c. dull green, light blue and sepia (as 6d.)	2·75	10
		a. Whiter paper (1970)	£160	20·00
301	**56**	10c. reddish purple, greenish blue & carmine (as 8d.)	30	70
		a. Whiter paper (1970)	1·00	4·00
302	**51**	11c. rose-red, green and blue (as 1½d.)	25	80
		a. Whiter paper (1970)	1·00	2·50
303	**57**	12c. orange-brown green and olive (as 10d.)	25	10
		a. Whiter paper (4.71)	12·00	29·00
304	**58**	15c. red, yellow, turquoise-blue and carmine (as 1s.)	55	10
		a. Whiter paper (1970)	£250	26·00
305	**59**	22c. brown, new blue and rose-red (as 2s.)	70	65
		a. Whiter paper (1970)	1·50	9·00
306	**60**	50c. yellow-olive, new blue and emerald (as 2s.6d.)	2·75	1·00
		a. Whiter paper (1970)	2·25	6·00
307	**61**	$1 orange-brown ultramarine and slate-purple (as 5s.)	2·00	60
		a. Whiter paper (4.71)	20·00	80·00
308	**68**	$2 multicoloured	13·00	3·00
		a. Whiter paper (4.71)	32·00	90·00
309	**63**	$3 chestnut, new blue and purple (as £1)	3·75	2·00
		a. Whiter paper (4.71)	32·00	90·00
295/309	Set of 15		29·00	15·00
295a/309a	Set of 15 (whiter paper)		£500	£350

*This is the earliest known date recorded in the Bahamas.

The 3c. has the value at right instead of at left as on No. 250.

The 1970–71 printings on whiter paper were released as needed, the 12c., $1, $2 and $3 only a week or two before the issue was withdrawn. Due to the marked difference in paper and the use of some new plates there are marked differences in shade in nearly all values.

69 Bahamas Crest

(Des R. Granger Barrett. Photo Enschedé)
1967 (1 Sept). Diamond Jubilee of World Scouting. T **69** and similar horiz design. Multicoloured. W w **12** (sideways*). P 14×13.
310		3c. Type **69**	35	15
		w. Wmk Crown to left of CA	42·00	
311		15c. Scout badge	40	15

*The normal sideways watermark shows Crown to right of CA, *as seen from the back of the stamp.*

71 Globe and Emblem
74 Golf

(Des R. Granger Barrett, Litho D.L.R)
1968 (13 May). Human Rights Year. T **71** and similar horiz designs. Multicoloured. W w **12** (sideways*). P 14×13½.
312		3c. Type **71**	10	10
313		12c. Scales of Justice and emblem	20	10
314		$1 Bahamas Crest and emblem	70	80
312/14	Set of 3		90	85

*The normal sideways watermark shows Crown to right of CA on the 12c. and Crown to left of CA on the others, *each when seen from the back of the stamp.*

(Litho B.W.)
1968 (20 Aug). Tourism. T **74** and similar vert designs. Multicoloured. P 13.
315		5c. Type **74**	1·75	1·75
316		11c. Yachting	1·25	50

BAHAMAS

317	15c. Horse-racing	1·75	55
318	50c. Water-skiing	2·50	7·00
315/18	Set of 4	6·50	8·75

78 Racing Yacht and Olympic Monument

(Photo Harrison)

1968 (29 Sept). Olympic Games, Mexico City. T **78** and similar horiz designs. No wmk. P 14½×13½.

319	5c. red-brown, orange-yellow and blue-green	40	75
320	11c. multicoloured	40	25
321	50c. multicoloured	60	1·25
322	$1 olive-grey, greenish blue and violet	2·00	2·25
319/22	Set of 4	3·00	4·00

Designs:—11c. Long-jumping and Olympic Monument; 50c. Running and Olympic Monument; $1 Type **78**.

It is understood that the above were released by the Philatelic Agency in the U.S.A. on 1st September.

81 Legislative Building

(Des J. Cooter, Litho Format)

1968 (1 Nov). 14th Commonwealth Parliamentary Conference. T **81** and similar multicoloured designs. P 14.

323	3c. Type **81**	10	30
324	10c. Bahamas Mace and Westminster Clock Tower (vert)	15	30
325	12c. Local straw market (vert)	15	25
326	15c. Horse-drawn Surrey	20	35
323/6	Set of 4	55	1·20

85 Obverse and reverse of $100 Gold Coin

(Recess D.L.R.)

1968 (2 Dec). Gold Coins commemorating the first General Election under the New Constitution. T **85** and similar "boomerang" shaped designs. P 13½.

327	3c. red/gold	40	40
328	12c. blue-green/gold	45	50
329	15c. dull purple/gold	50	60
330	$1 black/gold	1·25	4·50
327/30	Set of 4	2·40	5·50

Designs:—12c. Obverse and reverse of $50 gold coin; 15c. Obverse and reverse of $20 gold coin; $1 Obverse and reverse of $10 gold coin.

89 First Flight Postcard of 1919

90 Sikorsky S-38 Flying Boat of 1929

(Des V. Whiteley. Litho Format)

1969 (30 Jan). 50th Anniv of Bahamas Airmail Service. P 14.

| 331 | **89** | 12c. multicoloured | 50 | 50 |
| 332 | **90** | 15c. multicoloured | 60 | 1·75 |

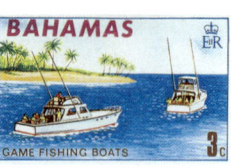

91 Game-fishing Boats

92 "The Adoration of the Shepherds" (Louis le Nain)

(Des J. Cooter. Litho Format)

1969 (26 Aug). Tourism. One Millionth Visitor to Bahamas. T **91** and similar horiz designs. Multicoloured. W w **12** (sideways). P 14½.

333	3c. Type **91**	25	10
334	11c. Paradise Beach	35	15
335	12c. "Sunfish" sailing boats	35	15
336	15c. Rawson Square and Parade	45	25
333/6	Set of 4	1·25	60
MS337	130×96 mm. Nos. 333/6	2·75	4·00

(Des G. Drummond. Litho D.L.R.)

1969 (15 Oct). Christmas. T **92** and similar vert designs. W w **12**. P 12.

338	3c. Type **92**	20	20
339	11c. "The Adoration of the Shepherds" (Poussin)	30	30
340	12c. "The Adoration of the Kings" (Gerard David)	30	20
341	15c. "The Adoration of the Kings" (Vincenzo Foppa)	30	65
338/41	Set of 4	1·00	1·25

93 Badge of Girl Guides

(Des Mrs. R. Sands. Litho Harrison)

1970 (23 Feb). Girl Guides Diamond Jubilee. T **93** and similar designs. Multicoloured. W w **12**. P 14½.

342	3c. Type **93**	30	30
	w. Wmk inverted		
343	12c. Badge of Brownies	45	40
344	15c. Badge of Rangers	50	50
	w. Wmk inverted	17·00	
342/4	Set of 3	1·10	1·10

94 U.P.U. Headquarters and Emblem

(Des L. Curtis, Litho J.W.)

1970 (20 May). New U.P.U. Headquarters Building. W w **12** (sideways). P 14.

| 345 | **94** | 3c. multicoloured | 10 | 40 |
| 346 | | 15c. multicoloured | 20 | 60 |

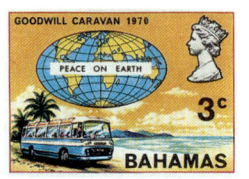

95 Coach and Globe

BAHAMAS

(Des G. Drummond. Litho B.W.)

1970 (14 July). "Goodwill Caravan". T **95** and similar horiz designs. Multicoloured. W w **12** (sideways*). P 13½×13.

347	3c. Type **95**	85	20
	w. Wmk Crown to right of CA		
348	11c. Diesel train and globe	1·60	60
349	12c. *Canberra* (liner), yacht and globe	1·60	60
	w. Wmk Crown to right of CA	3·50	
350	15c. B.A.C. One Eleven airliner and globe	1·60	1·75
347/50 Set of 4		5·00	2·75
MS351 165×125 mm. Nos. 347/50		9·50	17·00

*The normal sideways watermark shows Crown to left of CA, *as seen from the back of the stamp*.

96 Nurse, Patients and Greater Flamingo

97 "The Nativity" (detail, Pittoni)

(Photo Harrison)

1970 (1 Sept). Centenary of British Red Cross. T **96** and similar horiz design. Multicoloured. W w **12** (sideways*). P 14½.

352	3c. Type **96**	1·00	50
	a. Gold ("EIIR", etc) omitted	£700	
	w. Wmk Crown to right of CA	42·00	
353	15c. Hospital and Blue Marlin	1·00	1·75

*The normal sideways watermark shows Crown to left of CA, *as seen from the back of the stamp*.

(Des G. Drummond. Litho D.L.R.)

1970 (3 Nov). Christmas. T **97** and similar vert designs. Multicoloured. W w **12**. P 13.

354	3c. Type **97**	15	15
355	11c. "The Holy Family" (detail, Anton Raphael Mengs)	20	25
356	12c. "The Adoration of the Shepherds" (detail, Giorgione)	20	20
357	15c. "The Adoration of the Shepherds" (detail, School of Seville)	30	75
354/7 Set of 4		75	1·25
MS358 114×140 mm. Nos. 354/7 plus two labels		1·40	4·25

98 International Airport

99 Snowflake

(Des Mrs. W. Wasile. Litho Format)

1971 (27 Apr–Sept). Multicoloured designs as T **98**. W w **12** (sideways on $1 to $3). P 14½×14 (1 to 50c.) or 14×14½ ($1 to $3).

359	1c. Type **98**	10	30
360	2c. Breadfruit	15	35
361	3c. Straw market	15	30
362	4c. Hawksbill turtle	1·75	11·00
363	5c. Nassau Grouper	60	60
364	6c. As 4c. (21.9.71)	45	1·25
365	7c. Hibiscus (21.9.71)	2·00	5·00
366	8c. Yellow Elder	60	1·50
	w. Wmk inverted		
367	10c. Bahamian sponge boat	55	30
368	11c. Greater Flamingos	2·50	3·25
	w. Wmk inverted	14·00	
369	12c. As 7c.	2·00	3·00
370	15c. Bonefish	55	55
	w. Wmk inverted		
371	18c. Royal Poinciana (21.9.71)	65	65
	w. Wmk inverted		
372	22c. As 18c.	2·75	16·00
373	50c. Post Office, Nassau	1·40	1·75
374	$1 Pineapple (*vert*)	7·00	2·00
375	$2 Crawfish (*vert*)	4·00	4·00
376	$3 Junkanoo (*vert*)	3·50	10·00
359/76 Set of 18		27·00	55·00

See also Nos. 395/400, 460/73 and 518/25.

(Litho (15c. additionally die-stamped in gold) Walsall)

1971 (19 Oct). Christmas. T **99** and similar horiz designs. W w **12**. P 14×14½.

377	3c. deep reddish purple, orange and gold	10	10
378	11c. light ultramarine and gold	20	15
	w. Wmk inverted	1·00	
379	15c. multicoloured	20	20
380	18c. bluish green, royal blue and gold	25	25
377/80 Set of 4		65	60
MS381 126×95 mm. Nos. 377/80. P 15		1·25	1·50

Designs:—11c. "Peace on Earth" (doves); 15c. Arms of Bahamas and holly; 18c. Starlit lagoon.

100 High jumping

(Des J. W. Litho B.W.)

1972 (11 July). Olympic Games, Munich. T **100** and similar horiz designs. Multicoloured. W w **12**. P 13½.

382	10c. Type **100**	35	60
383	11c. Cycling	1·75	75
384	15c. Running	60	75
385	18c. Sailing	95	1·25
382/5 Set of 4		3·25	3·00
MS386 127×95 mm. Nos. 382/5		3·25	3·00

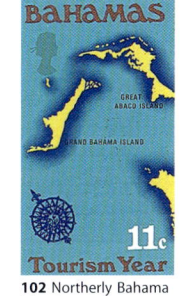

101 Shepherd

102 Northerly Bahama Islands

(Des Jennifer Toombs. Litho (15c. additionally embossed) J.W.)

1972 (3 Oct). Christmas. T **101** and similar vert designs. Multicoloured. W w **12** (sideways on 6 and 20c.). P 14.

387	3c. Type **101**	10	10
388	6c. Bells	10	10
389	15c. Holly and Cross	15	20
390	20c. Poinsettia	25	45
387/90 Set of 4		50	70
MS391 108×140 mm. Nos. 387/90 (wmk sideways)		80	3·00

(Des M. Shamir. Litho Format)

1972 (1 Nov). Tourism Year of the Americas. Sheet 133×105 mm, containing T **102** and similar vert designs. P 15.

MS392 11, 15, 18 and 50c. multicoloured ... 4·00 3·25

The four designs are printed horizontally *se-tenant* in **MS**392, forming a composite map design of the Bahamas.

103 Mace and Galleon

(Des (from photograph by D. Groves) and photo Harrison)

1972 (13 Nov). Royal Silver Wedding. Multicoloured; background colour given. W w **12**. P 14×14½.

393	**103**	11c. rose	15	15
		w. Wmk inverted	85·00	

11

BAHAMAS

394	18c. bluish violet	15	20
	w. Wmk inverted		1·50

1972 (23 Nov)–**73**. As Nos. 363, 366 and 373/6 but W w **12** (sideways* on 5 to 50c. and upright on $1 to $3).

395	5c. Nassau Grouper	13·00	3·00
396	8c. Yellow Elder (25.7.73)	50·00	
	w. Wmk Crown to left of CA	2·75	2·00
397	50c. Post Office, Nassau (25.7.73)	1·50	2·50
	w. Wmk Crown to left of CA	2·75	
398	$1 Pineapple (25.7.73)	1·50	4·00
399	$2 Crawfish (25.7.73)	1·50	6·00
400	$3 Junkanoo (1973)	2·25	14·00
395/400	Set of 6	20·00	28·00

*The normal sideways watermark shows Crown to right of CA *as seen on the back of the stamp.*

Nos. 401/9 are vacant.

104 Weather Satellite

(Des C. Abbott. Litho Questa)

1973 (3 Apr). I.M.O./W.M.O. Centenary. T **104** and similar horiz design. Multicoloured. W w **12**. P 14.

410	15c. Type **104**	50	25
411	18c. Weather radar	60	35

INDEPENDENT

105 C. A. Bain (national hero)

106 "The Virgin in Prayer" (Sassoferrato)

(Des PAD Studio. Litho Questa)

1973 (10 July–1 Aug). Independence. T **105** and similar vert designs. Multicoloured. W w **12** (sideways). P 14½×14.

412	3c. Type **105**	10	10
413	11c. Coat of arms	15	10
414	15c. Bahamas flag	20	15
415	$1 Governor-General, M. B. Butler (1 Aug)	65	1·00
412/15	Set of 4	1·00	1·10
MS416	86×121 mm. Nos. 412/15 (1 Aug)	2·00	2·00

(Des C. Abbott. Litho Format)

1973 (16 Oct). Christmas. T **106** and similar vert designs. Multicoloured. W w **12** (sideways*). P 14.

417	3c. Type **106**	10	10
418	11c. "Virgin and Child with St. John" (Filipino Lippi)	15	15
419	15c. "A Choir of Angels" (Simon Marmion)	15	15
420	18c. "The Two Trinities" (Murillo)	25	25
417/20	Set of 4	60	55
MS421	120×99 mm. Nos. 417/20	1·75	1·40
	w. Wmk Crown to right of CA	3·25	

*The normal sideways watermark shows Crown to left of CA, *as seen from the back of the stamp.*

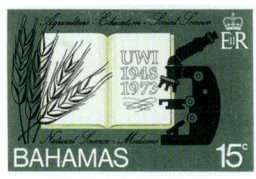

107 "Agriculture and Sciences"

(Des C. Abbott. Litho Questa)

1974 (5 Feb). 25th Anniv of University of West Indies. T **107** and similar horiz design. Multicoloured. W w **12**. P 13½.

422	15c. Type **107**	20	25
423	18c. "Arts, Engineering and General Studies"	25	30

108 U.P.U. Monument, Berne

(Des P. Powell. Litho Questa)

1974 (23 Apr). Centenary of Universal Postal Union. Designs as T **108** showing different arrangements of the U.P.U. Monument. W w **12** (upright on 3c., 14c. and MS428; sideways on others). P 14.

424	**108**	3c. multicoloured	10	15
425	–	13c. multicoloured (*vert*)	20	25
426	–	14c. multicoloured	20	30
427	–	18c. multicoloured (*vert*)	25	40
424/7	Set of 4		65	1·00
MS428	128×95 mm. Nos. 424/7		80	1·60
	w. Wmk inverted		£190	

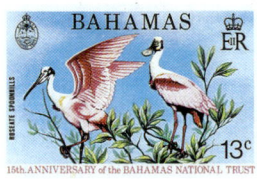

109 Roseate Spoonbills

(Des G. Drummond. Litho Questa)

1974 (10 Sept). 15th Anniv of Bahamas National Trust. T **109** and similar horiz designs. Multicoloured. W w **12** (sideways). P 13½.

429	13c. Type **109**	1·40	90
430	14c. White-crowned Pigeon	1·40	65
431	21c. White-tailed Tropic Birds	1·75	1·00
432	36c. Cuban Amazon	1·75	4·50
429/32	Set of 4	5·50	6·25
MS433	123×120 mm. Nos. 429/32	8·00	12·00

110 "The Holy Family" (Jacques de Stella)

(Des J. W. Litho Enschedé)

1974 (29 Oct). Christmas. T **110** and similar horiz designs. Multicoloured. W w **12** (sideways). P 13×13½.

434	8c. Type **110**	10	10
435	10c. "Madonna and Child" (16th-cent Brescian School)	15	15
436	12c. "Virgin and Child with St. John the Baptist and St. Catherine" (Previtali)	15	15
437	21c. "Virgin and Child with Angels" (Previtali)	25	30
434/7	Set of 4	60	60
MS438	126×105 mm. Nos. 434/7	1·00	1·40

111 *Anteos maerula*

(Des PAD Studio. Litho D.L.R.)

1975 (4 Feb). Butterflies. T **111** and similar horiz designs. Multicoloured. W w **12**. P 14×13½.

439	3c. Type **111**	25	15
440	14c. *Eurema nicippe*	80	50

BAHAMAS

441	18c. *Papilio andraemon*	95	65
442	21c. *Euptoieta hegesia*	1·10	85
	w. Wmk inverted	55·00	
439/42 Set of 4		2·75	2·00
MS443 119×94 mm. Nos. 439/42		7·50	6·50

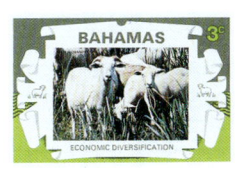

112 Sheep Husbandry

113 Rowena Rand (evangelist)

(Des Daphne Padden. Litho Questa)

1975 (27 May). Economic Diversification. T **112** and similar multicoloured designs. P 14.

444	3c. Type **112**	10	10
445	14c. Electric-reel fishing (*vert*)	20	15
446	18c. Farming	25	20
447	21c. Oil Refinery (*vert*)	80	35
444/7 Set of 4		1·25	65
MS448 127×94 mm. Nos. 444/7		1·25	1·50

(Des Jennifer Toombs. Litho Questa)

1975 (22 July). International Women's Year. T **113** and similar vert design. W w **14**. P 14.

449	14c. bistre-brown, lt turquoise-blue & ultram	20	50
450	18c. lemon, bright yellow-green and sepia	25	75

Design:—18c. I.W.Y. symbol and Harvest symbol.

114 "Adoration of the Shepherds" (Perugino)

(Des Jennifer Toombs. Litho J.W.)

1975 (2 Dec). Christmas. T **114** and similar horiz design. Multicoloured. W w **14** (sideways). P 13.

451	3c. Type **114**	15	60
452	8c. "Adoration of the Magi" (Ghirlandaio)	20	10
453	18c. As 8c.	55	90
454	21c. Type **114**	60	95
451/4 Set of 4		1·40	2·25
MS455 142×107 mm. Nos. 451/4. P 13½		2·25	4·50

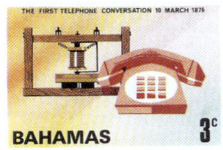

115 Telephones, 1876 and 1976

(Des G. Vasarbelyi. Litho D.L.R.)

1976 (23 Mar). Telephone Centenary. T **115** and similar horiz designs. Multicoloured. W w **14** (sideways*). P 14.

456	3c. Type **115**	20	50
	w. Wmk Crown to right of CA	2·25	
457	16c. Radio-telephone link, Deleporte	40	50
	w. Wmk Crown to right of CA		
458	21c. Alexander Graham Bell	50	65
	w. Wmk Crown to right of CA	70·00	
459	25c. Satellite	60	1·00
	w. Wmk Crown to right of CA	2·75	
456/9 Set of 4		1·50	2·40

*The normal sideways watermark shows Crown to left of CA, as seen from the back of the stamp.

1976 (30 May)–79. Designs as Nos. 359/63, 365/7 and 373/6 (some with new face values). W w **14** (sideways on $1 to $3). *Ordinary paper*.

460	1c. Type **98** (1.11.76)	1·75	3·00
	a. Chalk-surfaced paper (1979)	18·00	19·00
461	2c. Breadfruit	2·00	30
462	3c. Straw market (1.11.76)	2·25	3·50
	a. Chalk-surfaced paper (1979)	60	60
463	5c. Nassau Grouper (1.11.76)	4·00	3·50
	a. Chalk-surfaced paper (1979)	70	70
464	8c. Yellow Elder	9·50	30
465	10c. Bahamian sponge boat	1·50	30
466	16c. As 7c. (2.11.76)	1·25	35
	a. Chalk-surfaced paper (1979)	70	80
	aw. Wmk inverted	20·00	
467	21c. As 2c. (2.11.76)	2·50	1·50
	a. Chalk-surfaced paper (1979)	80	1·25
	aw. Wmk inverted	20·00	
468	25c. As 4c. (2.11.76)	90	40
	a. Chalk-surfaced paper (1979)	90	2·00
	aw. Wmk inverted	20·00	
469	40c. As 10c. (2.11.76)	8·00	75
470	50c. Post Office, Nassau	1·50	1·75
471	$1 Pineapple	1·50	2·50
472	$2 Crawfish (2.5.76)	2·00	7·00
	a. Chalk-surfaced paper (1979)	10·00	27·00
473	$3 Junkanoo (1.11.76)	1·50	9·50
460/73 Set of 14		35·00	32·00
460a/72a Set of 7		29·00	45·00

No. 474 is vacant.

116 Map of North America

(Des and litho Walsall)

1976 (1 June). Bicentenary of American Revolution. T **116** and similar horiz design. Multicoloured. W w **14** (sideways*). P 14.

475	16c. Type **116**	30	30
476	$1 John Murray, Earl of Dunmore	1·50	1·75
MS477 127×100 mm. No. 476×4		6·00	7·50
	w. Wmk Crown to right of CA	19·00	

*The normal sideways watermark shows Crown to left of CA, as seen from the back of the stamp.

117 Cycling

118 "Virgin and Child" (detail, Lippi)

(Des J.W. Litho Questa)

1976 (13 July). Olympic Games, Montreal. T **117** and similar vert designs. W w **14**. P 14.

478	8c. magenta, blue and pale cobalt	1·60	20
479	16c. orange, brown and pale cobalt	35	30
480	25c. blue, deep magenta and pale cobalt	45	50
481	40c. brown, orange and pale cobalt	55	1·60
478/81 Set of 4		2·75	2·40
MS482 100×126 mm. Nos. 478/81		3·00	3·25

Designs:—16c. Jumping; 25c. Sailing; 40c. Boxing.

(Des G. Drummond. Litho Questa)

1976 (5 Oct). Christmas. T **118** and similar vert designs. Multicoloured. W w **14**. P 14.

483	3c. Type **118**	10	10
484	21c. "Adoration of the Shepherds" (School of Seville)	30	15
485	25c. "Adoration of the Kings" (detail, Foppa)	30	20
486	40c. "Virgin and Child" (detail, Vivarini)	40	40
483/6 Set of 4		1·00	75
MS487 107×127 mm. Nos. 483/6		1·00	2·00

BAHAMAS

119 Queen beneath Cloth of Gold Canopy

(Des G. Vasarhelyi. Litho Cartor)

1977 (7 Feb). Silver Jubilee. T **119** and similar horiz designs. Multicoloured. W w **14** sideways* (**MS**492). No wmk (others). P 12.

488	8c. Type **119**	10	10
489	16c. Crowning	15	15
490	21c. Taking the Oath	15	15
491	40c. Queen with sceptre and orb	25	30
488/91 Set of 4		60	60
MS492 122×90 mm. Nos. 488/91		80	1·25

*The sideways watermark shows Crown to the right of CA, as seen form the back of the stamp.

120 Featherduster

(Des BG Studio. Litho J.W.)

1977 (24 May). Marine Life. T **120** and similar designs. Multicoloured. W w **14** (sideways). P 13½.

493	3c. Type **120**	40	15
494	8c. Porkfish and cave	60	20
495	16c. Elkhorn Coral	70	40
496	21c. Soft Coral and sponge	80	55
493/6 Set of 4		2·25	1·10
MS497 119×93 mm. Nos. 493/6. P 14½		2·75	4·50

121 Scouts around Campfire and Home-made Shower

(Des Harrison. Litho J.W.)

1977 (27 Sept). Sixth Caribbean Scout Jamboree. T **121** and similar horiz design. Multicoloured. W w **14** (sideways). P 13½.

498	16c. Type **121**	75	30
499	21c. Boating scenes	85	35

One used example of No. 498 is known with the mauve (face value and inscription) omitted.

(**122**)

123 Virgin and Child

1977 (19 Oct). Royal Visit. As Nos. 488/92, but W w **14** (sideways*), optd with T **122**.

500	8c. Type **119**	15	10
501	16c. The Crowning	20	15
	w. Wmk Crown to right of CA	70	
502	21c. Taking the Oath	25	25
503	40c. Queen with sceptre and orb	30	40
500/3 Set of 4		80	75
MS504 122×90 mm. Nos. 500/3		1·25	1·50

	w. Wmk Crown to right of CA	2·25	

*The normal sideways watermark shows Crown to right of CA on 8, 21, 40c.; to left on 16c. and miniature sheet; all as seen from the back of the stamp.

(Des and litho J.W.)

1977 (25 Oct). Christmas. T **123** and similar vert designs. Multicoloured. W w **14**. P 13½.

505	3c. Type **123**	10	10
506	16c. The Magi	30	25
507	21c. Nativity scene	30	40
508	25c. The Magi and star	40	45
505/8 Set of 4		1·00	1·10
MS509 136×74 mm. Nos. 505/8. P 14		1·00	1·75

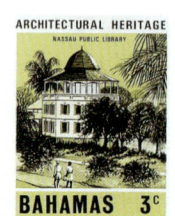

124 Public Library, Nassau (Colonial)

(Des G. Drummond. Litho Questa)

1978 (28 Mar). Architectural Heritage. T **124** and similar vert designs. W w **14**. P 14½×14.

510	3c. black and apple-green	10	10
511	8c. black and pale greenish blue	15	10
512	16c. black and mauve	20	20
513	18c. black and salmon-pink	25	30
510/13 Set of 4		60	65
MS514 91×91 mm. Nos. 510/13		70	1·60

Designs:—8c. St Matthew's Church (Gothic); 16c. Government House (Colonial); 18c. Hermitage, Cat Island (Spanish).

125 Sceptre, St. Edward's Crown and Orb

126 Coat of Arms within Wreath and Three Ships

(Des BG Studio. Litho Enschedé)

1978 (27 June). 25th Anniv of Coronation. T **125** and similar vert design. Multicoloured. W w **14**. P 14×13½.

515	16c. Type **125**	15	10
516	$1 Queen in Coronation regalia	50	65
MS517 147×96 mm. Nos. 515/16		1·25	1·00
	w. Wmk inverted	10·00	

1978 (1 June). As Nos. 359/76, but no Wmk.

518	1c. Type **98**	65	3·25
519	5c. Nassau Grouper	1·00	1·00
520	16c. Hibiscus	1·25	2·00
521	25c. Hawksbill Turtle	8·50	1·75
522	50c. Post Office, Nassau	2·50	3·50
523	$1 Pineapple	2·50	3·00
524	$2 Crawfish	4·50	8·00
525	$3 Junkanoo	4·50	8·00
518/25 Set of 8		23·00	27·00

Nos. 526/31 are vacant.

(Des Jennifer Toombs. Litho Questa)

1978 (14 Nov). Christmas. T **126** and similar horiz design. W w **14** (sideways). P 14×14½.

532	5c. gold, bright crimson and bright rose	15	10
533	21c. gold, deep ultramarine and violet-blue	30	25
MS534 95×95 mm. Nos. 532/3		1·75	5·50

Design:—21c. Three angels with trumpets.

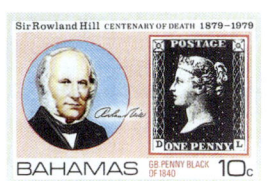

127 Child reaching for Adult

128 Sir Rowland Hill and Penny Black

(Litho J.W.)

1979 (15 May). International Year of the Child. T **127** and similar vert designs. Multicoloured. W w **14**. P 13.

535	5c. Type **127**	20	15
536	16c. Boys playing leap-frog	40	45
537	21c. Girls skipping	50	60
538	25c. Bricks with I.Y.C. emblem	50	75
535/8 Set of 4		1·40	1·75
MS539 101×125 mm. Nos. 535/8. P 14		1·40	3·25

(Des J. Cooter. Litho Format)

1979 (14 Aug). Death Centenary of Sir Rowland Hill. T **128** and similar horiz designs. Multicoloured. W w **14** (sideways). P 13½×14.

540	10c. Type **128**	30	10
541	21c. Printing press, 1840 and 6d. stamp of 1862	40	30
542	25c. Great Britain 6d. stamp of 1856 with "A 05" (Nassau) cancellation and Two-penny blue	40	50
543	40c. Early mailboat and 1d. stamp of 1859	45	70
540/3 Set of 4		1·40	1·40
MS544 115×80 mm. Nos. 540/3		2·00	3·25

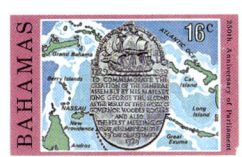

129 Commemorative Plaque and Map of Bahamas

(Des G. Drummond. Litho Secura, Singapore)

1979 (27 Sept). 250th Anniv of Parliament. T **129** and similar horiz designs. Multicoloured. W w **14** (sideways*). P 13½.

545	16c. Type **129**	35	10
	w. Wmk Crown to right of CA	45	
546	21c. Parliament Buildings	40	15
	w. Wmk Crown to right of CA	50	
547	25c. Legislative Chamber	40	15
	w. Wmk Crown to right of CA	55	
548	$1 Senate Chamber	80	1·00
	w. Wmk Crown to right of CA	1·40	
545/8 Set of 4		1·75	1·25
MS549 116×89 mm. Nos. 545/8 (Wmk upright)		2·50	3·75
	w. Wmk inverted	2·50	

The normal sideways watermark shows Crown to left of CA, *as seen from the back of the stamp.*

130 Goombay Carnival Headdress

131 Landfall of Columbus, 1492

(Des BG Studio. Litho J.W.)

1979 (6 Nov). Christmas. T **130** and similar vert designs showing Goombay Carnival headdresses. W w **14**. P 13.

550	5c. multicoloured	10	10
551	10c. multicoloured	15	10
552	16c. multicoloured	20	10
553	21c. multicoloured	20	20
554	25c. multicoloured	25	20
	w. Wmk inverted	3·50	
555	40c. multicoloured	30	45
550/5 Set of 6		1·00	1·00
MS556 50×88 mm. Nos. 550/5 (Wmk sideways). P 13½		2·00	3·00

(Des J.W. Litho Format)

1980 (9 July). Horiz designs as T **131**. Multicoloured. W w **14**. P 14½.

557	1c. Type **131**	1·25	2·50
558	3c. Blackbeard the Pirate, 1718	30	2·50
559	5c. Eleutheran Adventurers (Articles and Orders, 1647)	30	1·25
560	10c. Ceremonial mace	20	40
	w. Wmk inverted	40·00	8·00
561	12c. The Loyalists, 1783–88 (Colonel Andrew Deveaux)	30	2·50
562	15c. Slave trading, Vendue House	5·50	1·25
	w. Wmk inverted	60·00	
563	16c. Wrecking in the 1800's	1·75	1·25
564	18c. Blockade running (American Civil War)	2·50	2·50
565	21c. Bootlegging, 1919–29	60	2·50
	a. "BAHAMAS" omitted	£600	
	w. Wmk inverted	60·00	60·00
566	25c. Pineapple cultivation	40	2·50
567	40c. Sponge clipping	70	1·50
568	50c. Tourist development	75	1·50
569	$1 Modern agriculture	75	4·25
570	$2 Modern air and sea transport	4·25	5·50
571	$3 Banking in the Bahamas (Central Bank)	1·25	4·00
572	$5 Independence, 10 July 1973 (Prince of Wales and Prime Minister L. O. Pindling)	1·50	6·00
557/72 Set of 16		19·00	38·00

No. 565a comes from a sheet showing a major shift of the orange colour so that stamps in the bottom horizontal row are without "BAHAMAS".

See also Nos. 720/6 for stamps watermarked w **16**.

132 Virgin and Child

(Des B. Malone. Litho Walsall)

1980 (28 Oct). Christmas. Straw-work. T **132** and similar vert designs. Multicoloured. W w **14**. P 14½×14.

573	5c. Type **132**	10	10
574	21c. Three Kings	25	10
575	25c. Angel	25	15
576	$1 Christmas Tree	75	85
573/6 Set of 4		1·25	1·00
MS577 168×105 mm. Nos. 573/6		1·25	2·25

133 Disabled Person with Walking-stick

(Des and litho Walsall)

1981 (10 Feb). International Year for Disabled Persons. T **133** and similar horiz design. Multicoloured. W w **14** (sideways). P 14½×14.

578	5c. Type **133**	10	10
579	$1 Disabled person in wheelchair	1·25	1·25
MS580 120×60 mm. Nos. 578/9		1·40	2·50

134 Grand Bahama Tracking Site

135 Prince Charles and Lady Diana Spencer

BAHAMAS

(Litho Enschedé)

1981 (21 Apr). Space Exploration. T **134** and similar multicoloured designs. W w **14** (sideways* on 10 and 25c.). P 13½.
581	10c. Type **134**	30	15
582	20c. Satellite view of Bahamas (vert)	60	50
	w. Wmk inverted	23·00	
583	25c. Satellite view of Eleuthera	65	60
	w. Wmk Crown to right of CA	1·60	
584	50c. Satellite view of Andros and New Providence (vert)	1·00	1·25
581/4 Set of 4		2·25	2·25
MS585 115×99 mm. Nos. 581/4 (Wmk sideways)		2·25	2·25

*The normal sideways watermark shows Crown to left of CA, as seen from the back of the stamp.

(Des C. Abbott. Litho Questa)

1981 (22 July). Royal Wedding. T **135** and similar horiz design. Multicoloured. W w **14** (sideways*). P 14×14½.
586	30c. Type **135**	1·50	30
587	$2 Prince Charles and Prime Minister Pindling	1·50	1·25
MS588 142×120 mm. Nos. 586/7		5·00	1·25
	a. Upper stamp in miniature sheet imperf on 3 sides	£750	
	w. Wmk Crown to right of CA	30·00	

*The normal sideways watermark shows Crown to left of CA, as seen from the back of the stamp.

No. **MS**588a shows the upper stamp in the miniature sheet perforated at foot only.

136 Bahama Pintail

(Des Walsall. Litho Questa)

1981 (25 Aug). Wildlife (1st series). Birds. T **136** and similar horiz designs. Multicoloured. W w **14** (sideways). P 14.
589	5c. Type **136**	1·25	60
590	20c. Reddish Egret	1·75	60
591	25c. Brown Booby	1·75	65
592	$1 Black-billed Whistling Duck	3·50	7·50
589/92 Set of 4		7·50	8·50
MS593 100×74 mm. Nos. 589/92		8·50	8·50

See also Nos. 626/30, 653/7 and 690/4.

(**137**)

1981 (21 Sept). Commonwealth Finance Ministers' Meeting. Nos. 559/60, 566 and 568 optd with T **137**.
594	5c. Eleutheran Adventurers (Articles and Orders, 1647)	15	15
	a. Opt inverted	40·00	
595	10c. Ceremonial mace	20	20
	w. Wmk inverted	5·00	
596	25c. Pineapple cultivation	50	60
597	50c. Tourist development	85	1·50
594/7 Set of 4		1·50	2·25

138 Poultry  **139** Father Christmas

(Des L. McCombie. Litho J.W.)

1981 (16 Oct). World Food Day. T **138** and similar horiz designs. Multicoloured. W w **14** (sideways). P 13.
598	5c. Type **138**	20	10
599	20c. Sheep	35	35
600	30c. Lobsters	45	50
601	50c. Pigs	75	1·50
598/601 Set of 4		1·60	2·25
MS602 115×63 mm. Nos. 598/601. P 14		1·50	3·25

(Des local artists. Litho Format)

1981 (24 Nov). Christmas. T **139** and similar vert designs. Multicoloured. W w **14**. P 13½×14.
603	5c. Type **139**	55	85
	a. Sheetlet of 9. Nos. 603/11	5·50	8·00
604	5c. Mother and child	55	85
605	5c. St. Nicholas, Holland	55	85
606	25c. Lussibruden, Sweden	70	95
607	25c. Mother and child (*different*)	70	95
608	25c. King Wenceslas, Czechoslovakia	70	95
609	30c. Mother with child on knee	70	95
610	30c. Mother carrying child	70	95
611	$1 Christkindl Angel, Germany	1·00	1·50
603/11 Set of 9		5·50	8·00

Nos. 603/11 were printed together, *se-tenant*, in a sheetlet of 9.

140 Robert Koch

141 Male Flamingo (*Phoenicopterus ruber*)

(Des A. Theobald. Litho Harrison)

1982 (3 Feb). Centenary of Discovery of Tubercle Bacillus by Robert Koch. T **140** and similar horiz designs. W w **14** (sideways). P 14.
612	5c. black, red-brown and rose-lilac	75	50
613	16c. black, drab and dull orange	1·40	50
614	21c. multicoloured	1·60	55
615	$1 multicoloured	3·00	7·50
612/15 Set of 4		6·00	8·25
MS616 94×97 mm. Nos. 612/15. P 14½		6·00	7·50

Designs:—16c. Stylized infected person; 21c. Early and modern microscopes; $1 Mantoux test.

(Des N. Arlott. Litho Questa)

1982 (28 Apr). Greater Flamingos T **141** and similar vert designs. Multicoloured. W w **14**. P 14×13½.
617	25c. Type **141**	1·60	1·00
	a. Horiz strip of 5. Nos. 617/21	7·00	4·50
618	25c. Female	1·60	1·00
619	25c. Female with nestling	1·60	1·00
620	25c. Juvenile	1·60	1·00
621	25c. Immature bird	1·60	1·00
617/21 Set of 5		7·00	4·50

Nos. 617/21 were printed together, *se-tenant*, in horizontal strips of 5 throughout the sheet, forming a composite design.

142 Lady Diana Spencer at Ascot, June 1981

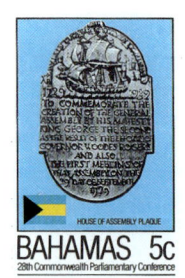

143 House of Assembly Plaque

(Des C. Abbott. Litho Format)

1982 (1 July). 21st Birthday of Princess of Wales. T **142** and similar vert designs. Multicoloured. W w **14**. P 13½×14 (16c.,$1) or 13½ (others).
622	16c. Bahamas coat of arms	20	10
	a. Perf 13½	1·00	1·50

623	25c. Type **142**		45	15
624	40c. Bride and Earl Spencer arriving at St. Paul's		60	20
	w. Wmk inverted		12·00	
625	$1 Formal portrait		1·00	1·25
622/5 Set of 4			2·00	1·40

(Des Walsall. Litho Questa)

1982 (18 Aug). Wildlife (2nd series). Mammals. Horiz designs as T **136**. Multicoloured. W w **14** (sideways). P 14.

626	10c. Buffy Flower Bat		1·00	15
627	16c. Bahaman Hutia		1·25	25
628	21c. Common Racoon		1·50	55
629	$1 Common Dolphin		3·00	1·90
626/9 Set of 4			6·00	2·50
MS630 115×76 mm. Nos. 626/9			6·00	3·50

(Des and litho Walsall)

1982 (16 Oct). 28th Commonwealth Parliamentary Association Conference. T **143** and similar vert designs. Multicoloured. W w **14**. P 14×13½.

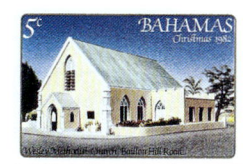

631	5c. Type **143**		15	10
632	25c. Association coat of arms		50	35
633	40c. Coat of arms		80	60
634	50c. House of Assembly		1·10	75
631/4 Set of 4			2·25	1·60

144 Wesley Methodist Church, Baillou Hill Road

(Des Jennifer Toombs. Litho Format)

1982 (3 Nov). Christmas. Churches. T **144** and similar horiz designs. Multicoloured. W w **14** (sideways). P 14.

635	5c. Type **144**		10	20
636	12c. Centreville Seventh Day Adventist Church		15	20
637	15c. The Church of God of Prophecy, East Street		15	30
638	21c. Bethel Baptist Church, Meeting Street		15	30
639	25c. St. Francis Xavier Catholic Church, Highbury Park		15	50
640	$1 Holy Cross Anglican Church, Highbury Park		60	3·00
635/40 Set of 6			1·10	4·00

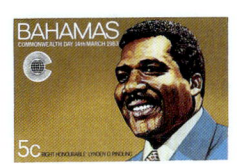

145 Prime Minister Lynden O. Pindling

(Des Walsall. Litho Questa)

1983 (14 Mar). Commonwealth Day T **145** and similar horiz designs. Multicoloured. W w **14** (sideways). P 14.

641	5c. Type **145**		10	10
642	25c. Bahamian and Commonwealth flags		50	40
643	35c. Map showing position of Bahamas		50	50
644	$1 Ocean liner		1·10	1·40
641/4 Set of 4			2·00	2·25

═══ **20**c ═══

(**146**)

1983 (5 Apr). Nos. 562/5 surch as T **146**.

645	20c. on 15c. Slave trading, Vendue House		50	35
646	31c. on 21c. Bootlegging, 1919–29		60	55
	w. Wmk inverted		2·25	
647	35c. on 16c. Wrecking in the 1800's		70	60
648	80c. on 18c. Blockade running (American Civil War)		80	1·40
	w. Wmk inverted		8·50	
645/8 Set of 4			2·40	2·50

147 Customs Officers and Queen Elizabeth 2 (liner)

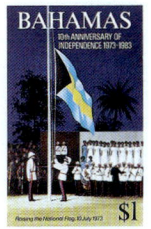

148 Raising the National Flag

(Des Walsall. Litho Harrison)

1983 (31 May). 30th Anniv of Customs Co-operation Council. T **147** and similar vert design. Multicoloured. W w **14**. P 13½×13.

649	31c. Type **147**		1·50	45
650	$1 Customs officers and Lockheed Jet Star 1 airliner		3·50	2·75

(Des L. Curtis. Litho Questa)

1983 (6 July). 10th Anniv of Independence. W w **14**. P 14.

651	**148**	$1 multicoloured	1·00	1·40
MS652 105×65 mm. No. 651. P 12			1·00	1·40

(Des F. Solomon, adapted N. Arlott. Litho Harrison)

1983 (24 Aug). Wildlife (3rd series). Butterflies. Horiz designs as T **136**. W w **14** (sideways). P 14½×14.

653	5c. multicoloured		1·25	20
654	25c. multicoloured		2·00	40
655	31c. black, bistre-yellow and bright rose-red		2·00	55
656	50c. multicoloured		2·00	85
653/6 Set of 4			6·50	1·75
MS657 120×80 mm. Nos. 653/6			6·50	6·00
a. Perf 14			3·50	6·50

Designs:—5c. *Atalopedes carteri*; 25c. *Ascia monuste*; 31c. *Phoebis agarithe*; 50c. *Dryas julia*.

No. **MS**657a was perforated by Questa, the remainder of the issue by Harrison.

149 "Loyalist Dreams"

(Des A. Lowe; adapted C. Abbott. Litho Questa)

1983 (28 Sept). Bicentenary of Arrival of American Loyalists in the Bahamas. T **149** and similar multicoloured designs. W w **14** (sideways on 31c., 35c.). P 14.

658	5c. Type **149**		10	10
659	31c. New Plymouth, Abaco (*horiz*)		30	50
660	35c. New Plymouth Hotel (*horiz*)		40	70
661	50c. "Island Hope"		45	90
658/61 Set of 4			1·10	2·00
MS662 111×76 mm. Nos. 658/61. Wmk sideways			1·25	2·50

150 Consolidated PBY-5 Catalina

(Des and litho Harrison)

1983 (13 Oct). Air Bicentenary of Manned Flight. T **150** and similar horiz designs. Multicoloured. W w **14** (sideways). P 14.

663	10c. Type **150**		55	15
664	25c. Avro Type 688 Tudor IV		75	30
665	31c. Avro Type 691 Lancastrian		85	45

BAHAMAS

666	35c. Consolidated Commodore	1·00	50
663/6	*Set of 4*	2·75	1·25

For these stamps without the Manned Flight logo see Nos. 699/702 (W w **14** (sideways) and 752/3 (W w **16** (sideways)).

151 "Christmas Bells" (Monica Pinder)

152 1861 4d. Stamp

(Des local children, adapted G. Vasarhelyi. Litho Walsall)

1983 (1 Nov). Christmas. Children's Paintings. T **151** and similar multicoloured designs. W w **14** (sideways on 31c. and 50c.). P 14.

667	5c. Type **151**	15	10
668	20c. "Flamingo" (Cory Bullard)	35	30
669	25c. "Yellow Hibiscus with Christmas Candle" (Monique Bailey)...	45	40
670	31c. "Santa goes a Sailing" (Sabrina Seiler) (*horiz*)	55	45
671	35c. "Silhouette scene with Palm Trees" (James Blake)	60	50
672	50c. "Silhouette scene with Pelicans" (Erik Russell) (*horiz*)	70	70
667/72	*Set of 6*	2·50	2·25

(Des D. Miller. Litho Format)

1984 (22 Feb). 125th Anniv of First Bahamas Postage Stamp. T **152** and similar vert design. Multicoloured. W w **14**. P 14.

673	5c. Type **152**	25	10
674	$1 1859 1d. stamp	1·75	1·50

153 *Trent I* (paddle steamer)

(Des L. Curtis. Litho Questa)

1984 (25 Apr). 250th Anniv of "Lloyd's List" (newspaper). T **153** and similar vert designs. Multicoloured. W w **14**. P 14½×14.

675	5c. Type **153**	50	10
676	31c. *Orinoco II* (mailship), 1886...........................	1·00	60
677	35c. Cruise liners in Nassau harbour	1·10	75
678	50c. *Oropesa* (container ship)	1·40	1·60
675/8	*Set of 4*	3·50	2·75

154 Running

(Des McCombie Skinner Studio. Litho Questa)

1984 (20 June). Olympic Games, Los Angeles. T **154** and similar horiz designs. W w **14** (sideways). P 14×14½.

679	5c. green, black and gold.......................................	15	20
680	25c. new blue, black and gold	50	50
681	31c. brown-lake, black and gold.............................	55	60
682	$1 sepia, black and gold.......................................	6·00	7·00
679/82	*Set of 4*	6·50	7·50
MS683	115×80 mm. Nos. 679/82	6·50	8·00

Designs:—25c. Shot-putting; 31c. Boxing; $1 Basketball.

155 Bahamas and Caribbean Community Flags

156 Bahama Woodstar

(Des McCombie Skinner Studio. Litho Questa)

1984 (4 July). 5th Conference of Caribbean Community Heads of Government. W w **14**. P 14.

684	**155** 50c. multicoloured	1·00	1·00

(Des N. Arlott. Litho Questa)

1984 (15 Aug). 25th Anniv of National Trust. T **156** and similar vert designs. Multicoloured. W w **14**. P 14.

685	31c. Type **156**...	3·75	3·75
	a. Horiz strip of 5. Nos. 685/9	16·00	16·00
686	31c. Belted Kingfishers, Greater Flamingos and *Eleutherodactylus planirostris* (frog)........	3·75	3·75
687	31c. Black-necked Stilts, Greater Flamingos and *Phoebis sennae* (butterfly)	3·75	3·75
688	31c. *Urbanus proteus* (butterfly) and *Chelonia mydas* (turtle)	3·75	3·75
689	31c. Osprey and Greater Flamingos	3·75	3·75
685/9	*Set of 5*	16·00	16·00

Nos. 685/9 were printed together, *se-tenant*, in horizontal strips of 5 throughout the sheet, forming a composite design.

(Des N. Arlott. Litho Questa)

1984 (18 Sept). Wildlife (4th series). Reptiles and Amphibians. Horiz designs as T **136**. W w **14** (sideways). P 14.

690	5c. Allen's Cay Iguana	85	20
691	25c. Curly-tailed Lizard	1·75	60
692	35c. Greenhouse Frog	2·00	85
693	50c. Atlantic Green Turtle	2·25	3·50
690/3	*Set of 4*	6·25	4·75
MS694	112×82 mm. Nos. 690/3	6·25	7·50

157 "The Holy Virgin with Jesus and Johannes" (19th-century porcelain plaque after Titian)

158 Brownie Emblem and Queen or Pink Conch

(Des D. Slater. Litho J.W.)

1984 (7 Nov). Christmas. Religious Paintings. T **157** and similar vert designs. Multicoloured. W w **14**. P 13½.

695	5c. Type **157**..	30	10
696	31c. "Madonna with Child in Tropical Landscape" (aquarelle, Anais Colin)	1·00	60
	w. Wmk inverted	1·00	
697	35c. "The Holy Virgin with the Child" (miniature on ivory, Elena Caula)	1·25	65
695/7	*Set of 3*	2·25	1·25
MS698	116×76 mm. Nos. 695/7. P 14	2·50	4·25

1985 (2 Jan). Air. As Nos. 663/6, but without Manned Flight logo. W w **14** (sideways*). P 14.

699	10c. Type **150**...	80	50
700	25c. Avro Type 688 Tudor IV	95	50
	w. Wmk Crown to right of CA	40·00	
701	31c. Avro Type 691 Lancastrian.............................	95	60
	w. Wmk Crown to right of CA	20·00	
702	35c. Consolidated Commodore	1·40	1·10
699/702	*Set of 4*	3·50	2·40

*The normal sideways watermark shows Crown to left of CA, *as seen from the back of the stamp*.

See also Nos. 752/3 for stamps watermarked w **16** (sideways).

18

BAHAMAS

(Des Berta Dallen Sands. Litho Walsall)

1985 (22 Feb). International Youth Year. 75th Anniv of Girl Guide Movement. T **158** and similar horiz designs. Multicoloured. W w **14** (sideways). P 14.

703	5c. Type **158**	60	50
704	25c. Tents and coconut palm	1·25	1·00
705	31c. Guide salute and Greater Flamingos	1·90	1·50
706	35c. Ranger emblem and marlin	1·90	1·50
703/6 Set of 4		5·00	4·00
MS707 95×74 mm. Nos. 703/6		5·50	7·50

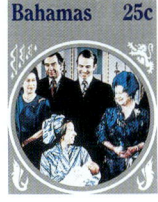

159 Killdeer

160 The Queen Mother at the Christening of Peter Phillips, 1977

(Des Josephine Martin. Litho Walsall)

1985 (24 Apr). Birth Bicentenary of John J. Audubon (ornithologist). T **159** and similar multicoloured designs. W w **14** (sideways on 5c., $1). P 14.

708	5c. Type **159**	1·00	60
709	31c. Mourning Dove (*vert*)	2·25	60
710	35c. "Mourning Dove" (John J. Audubon) (*vert*)	2·25	65
711	$1 "Killdeer" (John J. Audubon)	4·00	4·50
708/11 Set of 4		8·50	5·50

(Des A. Theobald ($1.25), C. Abbott (others). Litho Questa)

1985 (7 June). Life and Times of Queen Elizabeth the Queen Mother. T **160** and similar vert designs. Multicoloured. W w **16**. P 14½×14.

712	5c. Visiting Auckland, New Zealand, 1927	45	20
713	25c. Type **160**	70	40
714	35c. The Queen Mother attending church	75	55
	w. Wmk inverted	80	
715	50c. With Prince Henry at his christening (from photo by Lord Snowdon)	1·50	2·00
712/15 Set of 4		3·00	2·75
MS716 91×73 mm. $1.25, In horse-drawn carriage, Sark. Wmk sideways		2·75	1·90

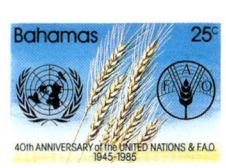

161 Ears of Wheat and Emblems

162 Queen Elizabeth II

(Des A. Theobald. Litho Questa)

1985 (26 Aug). 40th Anniv of United Nations and F.A.O. (Food and Agriculture Organization). W w **16** (sideways). P 14.

| 717 | **161** 25c. multicoloured | 1·25 | 70 |

(Des L. Curtis. Litho Walsall)

1985 (16 Oct). Commonwealth Heads of Government Meeting, Nassau. T **162** and similar vert design. Multicoloured. W w **16**. P 14½.

718	31c. Type **162**	3·00	3·75
	w. Wmk inverted	18·00	
719	35c. Bahamas Prime Minister's flag and Commonwealth emblem	3·00	3·75
	w. Wmk inverted	18·00	

1985 (6 Nov). As Nos. 557/8, 560 and 566, but W w **16**. P 14½.

720	1c. Type **131**	2·50	5·50
721	3c. Blackbeard the Pirate, 1718	3·00	6·00
723	10c. Ceremonial mace	3·00	1·75
726	25c. Pineapple cultivation	7·00	6·50
720/6 Set of 4		14·00	18·00

163 "Grandma's Christmas Bouquet" (Alton Roland Lowe)

163a Princess Elizabeth aged One, 1927

(Des D. Miller. Litho J.W.)

1985 (12 Nov). Christmas. Paintings by Alton Roland Lowe. T **163** and similar multicoloured designs. W w **16** (sideways on 5, 35c.). P 13×13½ (5, 35c.) or 13½×13 (others).

736	5c. Type **163**	60	40
737	25c. "Junkanoo Romeo and Juliet" (*vert*)	1·50	1·00
738	31c. "Bunce Gal" (*vert*)	1·75	1·50
739	35c. "Home for Christmas"	1·75	3·25
736/9 Set of 4		5·00	5·50
MS740 110×68 mm. Nos. 736/9. Wmk sideways. P 14		2·75	3·25

(Des A. Theobald. Litho Harrison)

1986 (21 Apr). 60th Birthday of Queen Elizabeth II. T **163a** and similar vert designs. W w **16** (sideways on 5, 35c.). P 14½×14.

741	10c. Type **163a**	15	15
742	25c. The Coronation, 1953	30	30
	w. Wmk inverted	6·00	
743	35c. Queen making speech at Commonwealth Banquet, Bahamas, 1985	35	40
744	40c. In Djakova, Yugoslavia, 1972	35	45
	w. Wmk inverted	8·00	
745	$1 At Crown Agents Head Office, London 1983	80	1·40
741/5 Set of 5		1·75	2·40

164 1980 1c. and 18c. Definitive Stamps

164a Prince Andrew and Miss Sarah Ferguson

(Des G. Drummond. Litho Walsall)

1986 (19 May). "Ameripex '86" International Stamp Exhibition, Chicago. T **164** and similar designs. W w **16** (sideways on 5 to 50c.). P 14.

746	5c. multicoloured	85	50
747	25c. multicoloured	2·00	50
748	31c. multicoloured	2·25	60
749	50c. multicoloured	3·00	5·00
750	$1 black, emerald and pale blue	3·25	6·00
746/50 Set of 5		10·00	11·00
MS751 80×80 mm. No. 750		4·00	4·00

Designs: *Horiz* (showing Bahamas stamps)—25c. 1969 50th Anniversary of Bahamas Airmail Service pair; 31c. 1976 Bicentenary of American Revolution 16c.; 50c. 1981 Space Exploration miniature sheet. *Vert*—$1 Statue of Liberty.

Nos. 750/1 also commemorate the Centenary of the Statue of Liberty.

1986 (17 June). Air. As Nos. 699/700, but W w **16** (sideways). P 14.

752	10c. Type **150**	2·50	1·00
753	25c. Avro Type 688 Tudor IV	2·75	1·75

(Des D. Miller. Litho Walsall)

1986 (23 July). Royal Wedding. T **164a** and similar square design. W w **16**. P 14½×14.

756	10c. Type **164a**	20	20
757	$1 Prince Andrew	1·25	2·10

165 Rock Beauty (juvenile)

19

BAHAMAS

(Des Harrison Studio. Litho Questa)

1986 (5 Aug)–**90**. Fishes. T **165** and similar horiz designs. Multicoloured. W w **16**. P 14.

A. Without imprint date at foot.

758A	5c. Type **165**	75	75
759A	10c. Stoplight Parrotfish	80	1·00
760A	15c. Jackknife-fish	1·50	1·50
761A	20c. Flamefish	1·25	1·25
762A	25c. Peppermint Basslet ("Swissguard Basslet")	1·50	1·50
763A	30c. Spot-finned Butterflyfish	1·10	1·10
764A	35c. Queen Triggerfish	1·10	2·75
765A	40c. Four-eyed Butterflyfish	1·50	1·25
766A	45c. Royal Gramma ("Fairy Basslet")	1·50	1·25
767A	50c. Queen Angelfish	2·00	3·75
768A	60c. Blue Chromis	3·50	4·00
769A	$1 Spanish Hogfish	3·50	4·00
770A	$2 Harlequin Bass	8·00	9·00
771A	$3 Black-barred Soldierfish	6·00	7·00
772A	$5 Cherub Angelfish ("Pygmy Angelfish")	6·50	8·00
773A	$10 Red Hind (2.1.87)	20·00	27·00
758A/73A Set of 16		55·00	65·00

B. With imprint date

759B	10c. Stoplight Parrotfish (8.90)	1·00	3·00
762B	25c. Peppermint Basslet ("Swissguard Basslet") (8.90)	1·50	3·00
765B	40c. Four-eyed Butterflyfish (15.8.88)	1·10	1·60
766B	45c. Royal Gramma ("Fairy Basslet") (8.90)	1·60	3·50
767B	50c. Queen Angelfish (8.90)	3·00	3·50
769B	$1 Spanish Hogfish (15.8.88)	4·50	3·00
770B	$2 Harlequin Bass (15.8.88)	14·00	9·50
771B	$3 Black-barred Soldierfish (8.90)	5·00	14·00
772B	$5 Cherub Angelfish ("Pygmy Angelfish") (8.90)	6·50	15·00
759B/72B Set of 9		35·00	50·00

Imprint dates: "1988", Nos. 765B, 769B/70B; "1990", Nos. 759B, 762B, 765B/7B, 769B, 771B/2B.

For those designs watermarked w **14** see Nos. 791/9.

166 Christ Church Cathedral, Nassau, 1861

(Des L. Curtis. Litho Walsall)

1986 (16 Sept). 125th Anniv of City of Nassau, Diocese and Cathedral. T **166** and similar vert design. Multicoloured. W w **16**. P 14½×14.

774	10c. Type **166**	30	20
775	40c. Christ Church Cathedral, 1986	70	80
MS776 75×100 mm. Nos. 774/5		4·25	6·50

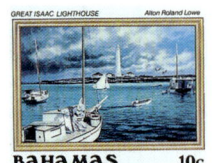

167 Man and Boy looking at Crib   **168** Great Isaac Lighthouse

(Des Jennifer Toombs. Litho Questa)

1986 (4 Nov). Christmas. International Peace Year. T **167** and similar horiz designs. Multicoloured. W w **16** (sideways). P 14.

777	10c. Type **167**	35	20
778	40c. Mary and Joseph journeying to Bethlehem	85	75
779	45c. Children praying and Star of Bethlehem	95	1·00
780	50c. Children exchanging gifts	1·00	2·50
777/80 Set of 4		2·75	4·00
MS781 95×90 mm. Nos. 777/80		8·50	11·00

(Des A. Lowe, adapted L. Curtis. Litho Walsall)

1987 (31 Mar). Lighthouses. T **168** and similar horiz designs. Multicoloured. W w **16** (sideways). P 14×14½.

782	10c. Type **168**	3·00	85
783	40c. Bird Rock Lighthouse	6·00	1·75
784	45c. Castle Island Lighthouse	6·00	2·00
785	$1 "Hole in the Wall" Lighthouse	9·00	12·00
782/5 Set of 4		22·00	15·00

169 Anne Bonney   **170** Boeing 737

(Des D. and Jane Hartley. Litho Questa)

1987 (2 June). Pirates and Privateers of the Caribbean. T **169** and similar vert designs. Multicoloured. W w **16**. P 14½.

786	10c. Type **169**	4·00	1·50
787	40c. Edward Teach ("Blackbeard")	7·00	4·00
788	45c. Captain Edward England	7·00	4·00
789	50c. Captain Woodes Rogers	7·50	8·00
786/9 Set of 4		23·00	16·00
MS790 75×95 mm. $1.25, Map of Bahamas and colonial coat of arms		14·00	7·50

1987 (25 June). As Nos. 758/60 and 765/70, but W w **14**. With imprint date. P 14.

791	5c. Type **165**	1·50	3·00
792	10c. Stoplight Parrotfish	1·25	1·00
793	15c. Jackknife-fish	2·00	3·00
794	40c. Four-eyed Butterflyfish	2·00	3·50
795	45c. Royal Gramma	2·25	3·00
796	50c. Queen Angelfish	3·00	3·50
797	60c. Blue Chromis	2·25	6·00
798	$1 Spanish Hogfish	2·50	7·00
799	$2 Harlequin Bass	3·00	9·50
791/9 Set of 9		18·00	35·00

Imprint dates: "1987", Nos. 791/9; "1988", No. 792; "1989", No. 791.

(Des A. Theobald. Litho Questa)

1987 (7 July). Air. Aircraft. T **170** and similar horiz designs. Multicoloured. W w **16**. P 14.

800	15c. Type **170**	3·50	1·50
801	40c. Boeing 757-200	4·50	2·25
802	45c. Airbus Industrie A300B4-200	4·50	2·25
803	50c. Boeing 747-200	5·00	4·50
800/3 Set of 4		16·00	9·50

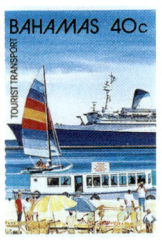

171 Norway (liner) and Catamaran   **172** Cattleyopsis lindenii

(Des A. Theobald. Litho Questa)

1987 (26 Aug). Tourist Transport. T **171** and similar vert designs. Multicoloured. W w **16**. P 14.

804	40c. Type **171**	2·25	2·25
	a. Horiz strip of 5. Nos. 804/8	10·00	10·00
805	40c. Liners and speedboat	2·25	2·25
806	40c. Game fishing boat and cruising yacht	2·25	2·25
807	40c. Game fishing boat and racing yachts	2·25	2·25
808	40c. Fishing boat and schooner	2·25	2·25
809	40c. Hawker Siddeley H.S.748 airliner	2·25	2·25
	a. Horiz strip of 5. Nos. 809/13	10·00	10·00
810	40c. Boeing 737 and Boeing 727-200 airliners	2·25	2·25
811	40c. Beech 200 Super King Air aircraft and radio beacon	2·25	2·25
812	40c. Aircraft and Nassau control tower	2·25	2·25

20

BAHAMAS

813	40c. Helicopter and parked aircraft	2·25	2·25
804/13 Set of 10		20·00	20·00

Nos. 804/8 and 809/13 were each printed together, se-tenant, in horizontal strips of 5 throughout the sheets, each strip forming a composite design.

(Des. A. Lowe; adapted L. Curtis. Litho Questa)

1987 (20 Oct). Christmas. Orchids. T **172** and similar horiz designs. Multicoloured. W w **16** (sideways). P 14×14½.

814	10c. Type **172**	1·75	60
815	40c. *Encyclia lucayana*	3·00	1·50
816	45c. *Encyclia hodgeana*	3·00	1·50
817	50c. *Encyclia lleidae*	3·00	3·00
814/17 Set of 4		9·50	6·00
MS818 120×92 mm. Nos. 814/17		12·00	13·00

173 King Ferdinand and Queen Isabella of Spain

174 Whistling Ducks in Flight

(Des L. Curtis. Litho Format)

1988 (24 Feb). 500th Anniv of Discovery of America by Columbus (1992) (1st issue). T **173** and similar vert designs. Multicoloured. W w **14**. P 14×14½.

819	10c. Type **173**	85	60
820	40c. Columbus before Talavera Committee	1·75	1·75
821	45c. Lucayan village	1·90	1·90
822	50c. Lucayan potters	2·00	3·50
819/22 Set of 4		6·00	7·00
MS823 65×50 mm. $1.50, Map of Antilles, c. 1500. Wmk sideways		6·00	3·75

See also Nos. 844/8, 870/4, 908/12, 933/7 and **MS**946.

(Des W. Oliver. Litho Walsall)

1988 (29 Apr). Black-billed Whistling Duck. T **174** and similar horiz designs. Multicoloured. W w **14** (sideways). P 14×14½.

824	5c. Type **174**	2·25	1·75
825	10c. Whistling Duck in reeds	2·25	1·75
826	20c. Pair with brood	4·00	2·75
827	45c. Pair wading	6·00	3·25
824/7 Set of 4		13·00	8·50

175 Grantstown Cabin, c. 1820

(Des N. Shewring. Litho B.D.T.)

1988 (9 Aug). 150th Anniv of Abolition of Slavery. T **175** and similar horiz design. Multicoloured. W w **14** (sideways). P 13½.

828	10c. Type **175**	50	30
829	40c. Basket-making, Grantstown	1·25	95

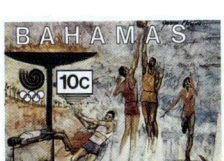

176 Olympic Flame, High Jumping, Hammer throwing, Basketball and Gymnastics

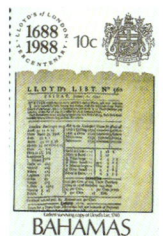

176a Lloyds List of 1740

(Des D. Miller. Litho Walsall)

1988 (30 Aug). Olympic Games, Seoul. T **176** and similar horiz designs taken from painting by James Martin. Multicoloured. W w **16** (sideways). P 14.

830	10c. Type **176**	90	50
831	40c. Athletics, archery, swimming, long jumping, weightlifting and boxing	90	60
832	45c. Javelin throwing, gymnastics, hurdling and shotput	90	60
833	$1 Athletics, hurdling, gymnastics and cycling	3·50	5·00
830/3 Set of 4		5·50	6·00
MS834 113×85 mm. Nos. 830/3. W w **14** (sideways)		6·00	3·25

(Des O. Bell and D. Miller (40c.), E. Nisbet and D. Miller ($1), D. Miller (others). Litho Format)

1988 (4 Oct). 300th Anniv of Lloyd's of London. T **176a** and similar multicoloured designs. W w **14** (sideways on 40, 45c.). P 14.

835	10c. Type **176a**	30	20
836	40c. Freeport Harbour (*horiz*)	2·00	60
837	45c. Space shuttle over Bahamas (*horiz*)	2·00	60
838	$1 *Yarmouth Castle* (freighter) on fire	3·50	3·00
835/8 Set of 4		7·00	4·00

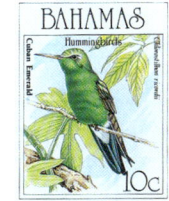

177 "Oh Little Town of Bethlehem"

178 Cuban Emerald

(Des Josephine Martin. Litho Questa)

1988 (21 Nov). Christmas. Carols. T **177** and similar vert designs. Multicoloured. W w **16**. P 14½×14.

839	10c. Type **177**	55	30
840	40c. "Little Donkey"	1·50	75
841	45c. "Silent Night"	1·50	90
842	50c. "Hark the Herald Angels Sing"	1·60	2·25
839/42 Set of 4		4·75	3·75
MS843 88×108 mm. Nos. 839/42. W w **14**		2·75	2·75

(Des A. Lowe (50c.), L. Curtis (others). Litho Questa)

1989 (25 Jan). 500th Anniv of Discovery of America by Columbus (1992) (2nd issue). Vert designs as T **173**. Multicoloured. W w **16**. P 14½×14.

844	10c. Columbus drawing chart	2·25	85
845	40c. Types of caravel	3·25	1·75
846	45c. Early navigational instruments	3·25	1·75
847	50c. Arawak artefacts	3·25	5·00
844/7 Set of 4		11·00	8·50
MS848 64×64 mm. $1.50, Caravel under construction (from 15th-cent Nuremburg Chronicles)		2·50	2·50

(Des N. Shewring. Litho Questa)

1989 (29 Mar). Hummingbirds. T **178** and similar vert designs. Multicoloured. W w **16**. P 14½×14.

849	10c. Type **178**	1·75	1·25
850	40c. Ruby-throated Hummingbird	3·00	2·00
851	45c. Bahama Woodstar	3·00	2·00
852	50c. Rufous Hummingbird	3·25	4·50
849/52 Set of 4		10·00	8·75

179 Teaching Water Safety

(Des S. Noon. Litho Questa)

1989 (31 May). 125th Anniv of International Red Cross. T **179** and similar horiz designs. Multicoloured. W w **16** (sideways). P 14×14½.

853	10c. Type **179**	1·75	50
854	$1 Henri Dunant (founder) and Battle of Solferino	3·75	5·50

BAHAMAS

179a "Apollo 8" Communications Station, Grand Bahama

180 Church of the Nativity, Bethlehem

(Des A. Theobald ($2), D. Miller (others). Litho Questa)

1989 (20 July). 20th Anniv of First Manned Landing on Moon. T **179a** and similar multicoloured designs. W w **16** (sideways on 40, 45c.). P 14×13½ (10c., $1) or 14 (others).

855	10c. Type **179a**	1·25	50
856	40c. Crew of "Apollo 8" (30×30 mm)	2·00	90
857	45c. "Apollo 8" emblem (30×30 mm)	2·00	90
858	$1 The Earth seen from "Apollo 8"	2·75	5·00
855/8	Set of 4	7·25	6·50
MS859	100×83 mm. $2 "Apollo 11" astronauts in training, Manned Spacecraft Centre, Houston. P 14×13½	5·00	6·00

(Des E. Weishoff. Litho Questa)

1989 (16 Oct). Christmas. Churches of the Holy Land. T **180** and similar vert designs. Multicoloured. W w **14**. P 14½×14.

860	10c. Type **180**	1·50	30
861	40c. Basilica of the Annunciation, Nazareth	2·50	70
862	45c. Tabgha Church, Galilee	2·50	70
863	$1 Church of the Holy Sepulchre, Jerusalem	4·50	7·00
860/3	Set of 4	10·00	8·00
MS864	92×109 mm. Nos. 860/3. Wmk sideways	10·00	11·00

181 1974 U.P.U. Centenary 13c. Stamp and Globe

(Des J. Sayer. Litho Questa)

1989 (17 Nov). "World Stamp Expo '89" International Stamp Exhibition, Washington. T **181** and similar multicoloured designs. W w **16** (sideways). P 14.

865	10c. Type **181**	70	40
866	40c. 1970 New U.P.U. Headquarters Building 3c. and building	1·40	85
867	45c. 1986 "Ameripex '86" $1 and Capitol, Washington	1·40	90
868	$1 1949 75th anniversary of U.P.U. 2½d. and Boeing 737 airliner	5·50	7·00
865/8	Set of 4	8·00	8·25
MS869	107×80 mm. $2 Map showing route of Columbus, 1492 (30×38 mm). P 14½	10·00	14·00

(Des A. Lowe (50c.), L. Curtis (others). Litho Questa)

1990 (24 Jan). 500th Anniversary of Discovery of America by Columbus (1992) (3rd issue). Vert designs as T **173**. Multicoloured. W w **14**. P 14½×14.

870	10c. Launching caravel	1·75	80
871	40c. Provisioning ship	2·75	2·00
872	45c. Shortening sail	2·75	2·00
873	50c. Lucayan fishermen	2·75	4·00
870/3	Set of 4	9·00	8·00
MS874	70×61 mm. $1.50, Departure of Columbus, 1492	5·50	7·00

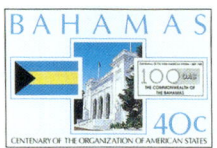

182 Bahamas Flag, O.A.S. Headquarters and Centenary Logo

(Des O. Bell. Litho Questa)

1990 (14 Mar). Centenary of Organization of American States. W w **16** (sideways). P 14.

875	**182**	40c. multicoloured	2·00	2·25

183 Supermarine Spitfire Mk I *Bahamas I*

(Des A. Theobald. Litho Questa)

1990 (3 May). "Stamp World London 90" International Stamp Exhibition, London. Presentation Fighter Aircraft. Sheet 107×78 mm. containing T **183** and similar horiz design. Multicoloured. W w **16** (sideways). P 14.

MS876 $1 Type **183**; $1 Hawker Hurricane Mk IIc *Bahamas V* .... 10·00 8·50

184 Teacher with Boy

(Des G. Vasarhelyi. Litho Questa)

1990 (27 June). International Literacy Year. T **184** and similar horiz designs. Multicoloured. W w **16** (sideways). P 14.

877	10c. Type **184**	1·00	50
878	40c. Three boys in class	1·75	1·25
879	50c. Teacher and children with books	1·75	5·00
877/9	Set of 3	4·00	4·00

184a "Queen Elizabeth 1940" (Sir Gerald Kelly)

184b Queen Elizabeth at Garden Party, France, 1938

(Des D. Miller. Litho Questa)

1990 (4 Aug). 90th Birthday of Queen Elizabeth the Queen Mother. W w **16**. P 14×15 (40c.) or 14½ ($1.50).

880	**184a**	40c. multicoloured	1·50	50
881	**184b**	$1.50 brownish black and ochre	2·75	6·00

185 Cuban Amazon preening

186 The Annunciation

(Des N. Arlott. Litho Questa)

1990 (26 Sept). Cuban Amazon (Bahamian Parrot). T **185** and similar vert designs. Multicoloured. W w **14**. P 14.

882	10c. Type **185**	1·25	85
883	40c. Pair in flight	2·25	1·50
884	45c. Cuban Amazon's head	2·25	1·50
885	50c. Perched on branch	2·50	3·75
882/5	Set of 4	7·50	7·00
MS886	73×63 mm. $1.50, Feeding on berries	8·00	10·00

BAHAMAS

(Des Jennifer Toombs. Litho B.D.T.)

1990 (5 Nov). Christmas. T **186** and similar vert designs. Multicoloured. W w **14**. P 14×13½.
887	10c. Type **186**..	65	50
888	40c. The Nativity..................................	1·25	70
889	45c. Angel appearing to Shepherds.........	1·25	70
890	$1 The three Kings................................	3·00	6·00
887/90 Set of 4...		5·50	7·00
MS891 94×110 mm. Nos. 887/90........................		14·00	14·00

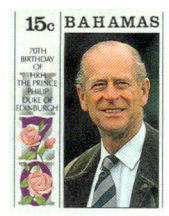

187 Green Heron   **187a** Prince Philip

(Des N. Arlott. Litho Questa)

1991 (4 Feb–1 July). Birds. T **187** and similar vert designs. Multicoloured. W w **16** (sideways). "1991" *imprint date*. P 14.
892	5c. Type **187**..	80	1·50
893	10c. Turkey Vulture................................	1·50	2·25
894	15c. Osprey...	3·00	80
895	20c. Clapper Rail...................................	1·00	80
896	25c. Royal Tern.....................................	1·75	1·25
897	30c. Key West Quail Dove.......................	1·75	1·25
898	40c. Smooth-billed Ani..........................	1·75	55
899	45c. Burrowing Owl...............................	3·00	80
900	50c. Hairy Woodpecker..........................	2·50	80
901	55c. Mangrove Cuckoo..........................	2·75	1·25
902	60c. Bahama Mockingbird......................	2·50	1·75
903	70c. Red-winged Blackbird.....................	2·50	1·75
904	$1 Thick-billed Vireo.............................	3·00	1·50
905	$2 Bahama Yellowthroat........................	6·00	7·00
906	$5 Stripe-headed Tanager.....................	11·00	14·00
907	$10 Greater Antillean Bullfinch (1 July)....	16·00	18·00
892/907 Set of 16..		55·00	50·00

For these designs watermarked w **14** (sideways) see Nos. 975/88.

(Des A. Lowe (55c.), L. Curtis (others). Litho Questa)

1991 (9 Apr). 500th Anniv of Discovery of America by Columbus (1992) (4th issue). Vert designs as T **173**. Multicoloured. W w **16**. P 14½×14.
908	15c. Columbus navigating by stars............	1·75	85
909	40c. Fleet in mid-Atlantic.......................	2·50	2·25
910	55c. Lucayan family worshipping at night...	2·50	2·50
911	60c. Map of First Voyage.......................	3·25	5·00
908/11 Set of 4...		9·00	9·75
MS912 56×61 mm. $1.50, *Pinta's* look-out sighting land..		6·00	7·00

(Des D. Miller. Litho Questa)

1991 (17 June). 65th Birthday of Queen Elizabeth II and 70th Birthday of Prince Philip. T **187a** and similar vert design. Multicoloured. W w **16** (sideways). P 14½×14.
913	15c. Type **187a**....................................	1·00	1·50
	a. Horiz pair. Nos. 913/14 separated by label..	2·75	3·50
914	$1 Queen Elizabeth II............................	1·75	2·00

Nos. 913/14 were printed together, *se-tenant*, in sheetlets of 10 (2x5) with designs alternating and the vertical rows separated by inscribed labels.

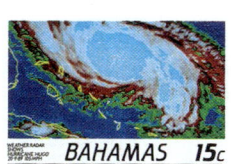

188 Radar Plot of Hurricane Hugo   **189** The Annunciation

(Des A. Theobald. Litho B.D.T)

1991 (28 Aug). International Decade for Natural Disaster Reduction. T **188** and similar horiz designs. Multicoloured. W w **16** (sideways). P 14.
915	15c. Type **188**......................................	1·50	65
916	40c. Diagram of hurricane.....................	2·00	1·50
917	55c. Flooding caused by Hurricane David, 1979...	2·25	2·25
918	60c. U.S. Dept of Commerce weather reconnaissance Lockheed WP-3D Orion	3·00	4·00
915/18 Set of 4...		8·00	7·50

(Des Jennifer Toombs. Litho B.D.T.)

1991 (28 Oct). Christmas. T **189** and similar vert designs. Multicoloured. W w **14**. P 14.
919	15c. Type **189**......................................	1·25	30
920	55c. Mary and Joseph travelling to Bethlehem..	2·25	1·00
921	60c. Angel appearing to the shepherds....	2·25	1·50
922	$1 Adoration of the Kings.....................	3·75	4·50
919/22 Set of 4...		8·50	7·00
MS923 92×108 mm. Nos. 919/22......................		10·00	11·00

190 First Progressive Liberal Party Cabinet

(Des G. Vasarhelyi. Litho B.D.T.)

1992 (10 Jan). 25th Anniv of Majority Rule. T **190** and similar multicoloured designs. W w **14** (sideways on 15c. and 40c.). P 14.
924	15c. Type **190**......................................	75	40
925	40c. Signing of Independence Constitution..	1·60	1·10
926	55c. Prince of Wales handing over Constitutional Instrument (*vert*)...............	1·75	1·50
927	60c. First Bahamian Governor-General, Sir Milo Butler (*vert*).....................................	2·00	3·50
924/7 Set of 4...		5·50	6·00

190a Queen Elizabeth with Bouquet

(Des D. Miller. Litho Questa ($1), B.D.T. (others))

1992 (6 Feb). 40th Anniv of Queen Elizabeth II's Accession. T **143** and similar horiz designs. Multicoloured. W w **14** (sideways). P 14.
928	15c. Type **143**......................................	60	30
929	40c. Queen Elizabeth with flags..............	1·10	70
930	55c. Queen Elizabeth at display..............	1·10	90
931	60c. Three portraits of Queen Elizabeth...	1·25	1·50
932	$1 Queen Elizabeth II............................	1·50	2·50
928/32 Set of 5...		5·00	5·50

(Des A. Lowe and L. Curtis. Litho Questa)

1992 (17 Mar). 500th Anniv of Discovery of America by Columbus (5th issue). Vert designs as T **173**. Multicoloured. W w **16**. P 14½×14.
933	15c. Lucayans sighting fleet...................	2·00	1·00
934	40c. *Santa Maria* and dolphins...............	2·75	1·75
935	55c. Lucayan canoes approaching ships..	2·75	2·25
936	60c. Columbus giving thanks for landfall..	3·25	4·25
933/6 Set of 4..		9·75	8·25
MS937 61×57 mm. $1.50, Children at Columbus Monument...		3·50	6·00

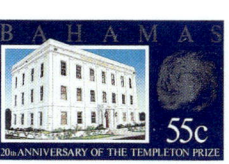

191 Templeton, Galbraith and Hanaberger Ltd Building   **192** Pole Vaulting

(Des O. Bell. Litho Questa)

1992 (22 Apr). 20th Anniv of Templeton Prize for Religion. W w **16** (sideways). P 14½.
938	**191** 55c. multicoloured.........................	1·50	1·75

23

BAHAMAS

(Des O. Bell. Litho Questa)

1992 (2 June). Olympic Games, Barcelona. T **192** and similar vert designs. Multicoloured. W w **14**. P 14½.

939	15c. Type **192**..	60	50
940	40c. Javelin...	1·00	90
941	55c. Hurdling..	1·10	1·25
942	60c. Basketball...	7·00	5·00
939/42 *Set of 4*...		8·75	7·00
MS943 70×50 mm. $2 Sailing.............................		7·50	9·00

193 Arid Landscape and Starving Child

194 Mary visiting Elizabeth

(Des Jennifer Toombs. Litho Enschedé)

1992 (11 Aug). International Conference on Nutrition. T **193** and similar horiz design. Multicoloured. W w **14** (sideways). P 14½×13½.

944	15c. Type **193**..	1·25	75
945	55c. Seedling, cornfield and child................	2·00	2·00

(Des L. Curtis. Litho B.D.T.)

1992 (12 Oct). 500th Anniv of Discovery of America by Columbus (6th issue). Sheet 65×65 mm, containing vert design as T **173**. Multicoloured. W w **16**. P 13½.

MS946 $2 Columbus landing in Bahamas .... 7·50 8·00

(Des Jennifer Toombs. Litho B.D.T.)

1992 (2 Nov). Christmas. T **194** and similar vert designs. Multicoloured. W w **14**. P 14×13½.

947	15c. Type **194**..	40	20
948	55c. The Nativity..	1·10	1·00
949	60c. Angel and Shepherds...........................	1·25	1·50
950	70c. Wise Men and star...............................	1·40	2·50
947/50 *Set of 4*...		3·75	4·75
MS951 95×110 mm. Nos. 947/50............................		7·50	8·50

HURRICANE RELIEF + $1

(**195**)

196 Flags of Bahamas and U.S.A. with Agricultural Worker

1992 (16 Nov). Hurricane Relief. No. **MS**876 showing each stamp surch with T **195**.

MS952 $1 + $1 Type **183**; $1 + $1 Hawker Hurricane MkIIc *Bahamas V*.. 12·00 15·00

(Des Lorraine Cox, adapted D. Miller. Litho Questa)

1993 (16 Mar). 50th Anniv of The Contract (U.S.A.–Bahamas farm labour programme). T **196** and similar horiz designs, each including national flags. Multicoloured. W w **16** (sideways). P 14×14½.

953	15c. Type **196**..	1·75	70
954	55c. Onions..	2·25	1·50
955	60c. Citrus fruit...	2·50	2·50
956	70c. Apples..	2·75	3·25
953/6 *Set of 4*...		8·25	7·00

(Des A. Theobald. Litho Questa)

1993 (1 Apr). 75th Anniv of Royal Air Force. T **196a** and similar horiz designs. Multicoloured. W w **14** (sideways). P 14.

957	15c. Type **196a**..	1·75	85
958	40c. Gloster Gladiator I...............................	2·25	1·00
959	55c. De Havilland D.H.100 Vampire F.3......	2·50	1·75
960	70c. English Electric Lightning F.3..............	3·00	5·00
957/60 *Set of 4*...		8·50	9·50
MS961 110×77 mm. 60c. Avro Shackleton M.R.2; 60c. Fairey Battle; 60c. Douglas Boston III; 60c. De Havilland D.H.9a..		8·75	7·75

197 1978 Coronation Anniversary Stamps

198 *Lignum vitae* (national tree)

(Des D. Miller. Litho Enschedé)

1993 (2 June). 40th Anniv of Coronation. T **197** and similar horiz designs. Multicoloured. W w **14** (sideways). P 13½.

962	15c. Type **197**..	70	50
963	55c. Two examples of 1953 Coronation stamp.	1·75	1·75
964	60c. 1977 Silver Jubilee 8c. and 16c. stamps......	1·75	2·00
965	70c. 1977 Silver Jubilee 21c. and 40c. stamps ...	2·00	2·75
962/5 *Set of 4*...		5·50	6·25

(Des N. Shewring. Litho B.D.T.)

1993 (8 July). 20th Anniv of Independence. T **198** and similar vert designs. Multicoloured. W w **14**. P 14.

966	15c. Type **198**..	30	20
967	55c. Yellow Elder (national flower)..............	90	90
968	60c. Blue Marlin (national fish)....................	1·25	1·25
969	70c. Greater Flamingo (national bird)..........	2·00	3·00
966/9 *Set of 4*...		4·00	4·75

199 Cordia

200 The Annunciation

(Des D. Miller and A. Lowe. Litho B.D.T.)

1993 (8 Sept). Environment Protection (1st series). Wildflowers. T **199** and similar vert designs. Multicoloured. W w **14**. P 13½.

970	15c. Type **199**..	1·50	50
971	55c. Seaside Morning Glory........................	3·00	1·25
972	60c. Poinciana...	3·25	2·25
973	70c. Spider Lily..	3·75	4·50
970/3 *Set of 4*...		10·50	7·75

See also Nos. 1017/22, 1035/9, 1084/8, 1121/4, 1149/54 and 1193/7.

1993 (23 Sept)–**95**. As Nos. 893/4, 896/8, 901 and 906, but W w **14** (sideways). *With imprint date*. P 14.

975	10c. Turkey Vulture.....................................	4·00	1·75
976	15c. Osprey (4.95).......................................	1·00	1·00
978	25c. Royal Tern...	1·00	70
979	30c. Key West Quail Dove...........................	6·50	1·25
980	40c. Smooth-billed Ani (31.12.93)...............	1·25	1·75
983	55c. Mangrove Cuckoo................................	2·00	1·00
988	$5 Stripe-headed Tanager...........................	6·50	9·00
975/88 *Set of 7*...		20·00	15·00

Imprint dates: "1993", Nos. 975, 978/80, 983, 988; "1995", Nos. 976, 978, 980, 983, 988.

(Des Jennifer Toombs. Litho B.D.T.)

1993 (1 Nov). Christmas. T **200** and similar vert designs. Multicoloured. W w **14**. P 13½.

990	15c. Type **200**..	75	50
991	55c. Angel and shepherds............................	2·25	1·75
992	60c. Holy family..	2·25	2·00
993	70c. Three Kings...	2·75	3·75
990/3 *Set of 4*...		7·25	7·25
MS994 86×106 mm. $1 Virgin Mary with Child		5·50	7·50

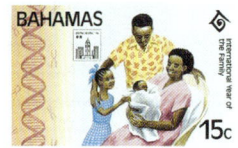

201 Family

BAHAMAS

(Des Jennifer Toombs. Litho B.D.T.)

1994 (18 Feb). "Hong Kong '94" International Stamp Exhibition. International Year of the Family. T **201** and similar horiz designs. Multicoloured. W w **16** (sideways). P 13½.

995	15c. Type **201**	1·50	40
996	55c. Children doing homework	2·50	1·25
997	60c. Grandfather and grandson fishing	2·75	1·75
998	70c. Grandmother teaching grandchildren the Lord's Prayer	3·25	5·00
995/8 Set of 4		9·00	7·50

202 Flags of Bahamas and Great Britain

(Des D. Miller. Litho B.D.T.)

1994 (7 Mar). Royal Visit. T **202** and similar vert designs. Multicoloured. W w **14**. P 13½.

999	15c. Type **202**	1·50	50
1000	55c. Royal Yacht *Britannia*	2·75	1·75
1001	60c. Queen Elizabeth II	2·75	1·75
1002	70c. Queen Elizabeth and Prince Philip	2·75	4·50
999/1002 Set of 4		8·75	7·75

203 Yachts

204 Logo and Bahamas 1968 Olympic Games Stamps

(Des D. Miller and A. Lowe. Litho B.D.T.)

1994 (27 Apr). 40th Anniv of National Family Island Regatta. T **203** and similar multicoloured designs. W w **14** (sideways). P 13½.

1003	15c. Type **203**	80	40
1004	55c. Dinghies racing	1·75	1·25
1005	60c. Working boats	1·75	1·75
1006	70c. Sailing sloop	2·25	4·00
1003/6 Set of 4		6·00	6·75
MS1007 76×54 mm. $2 Launching sloop (*vert*). Wmk upright		8·00	9·00

(Des D. Miller. Litho Enschedé)

1994 (31 May). Centenary of International Olympic Committee. T **204** and similar multicoloured designs. W w **14** (sideways on 55c. and 70c.). P 13½.

1008	15c. Type **204**	1·75	50
1009	55c. 1976 Olympic Games stamps (*vert*)	2·75	1·25
1010	60c. 1984 Olympic Games stamps	2·75	2·25
1011	70c. 1992 Olympic Games stamps (*vert*)	3·00	4·50
1008/11 Set of 4		9·25	7·75

205 Star of Order

206 *Calpodes ethlius* and Canna

(Des D. Miller. Litho Enschedé)

1994 (5 July). First Recipients of Order of the Caribbean Community. Sheet 90×69 mm. W w **14**. P 13×14.

MS1012 **205** $2 multicoloured	5·50	6·50

(Des R. Watton. Litho Walsall)

1994 (16 Aug). Butterflies and Flowers. T **206** and similar vert designs. Multicoloured. W w **14**. P 14.

1013	15c. Type **206**	1·10	55
1014	55c. *Phoebis sennae* and Cassia	2·00	1·50
1015	60c. *Anartia jatrophae* and Passion Flower	2·25	2·25
1016	70c. *Battus devilliersi* and Calico Flower	2·25	3·00
1013/16 Set of 4		7·00	6·50

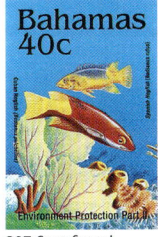

207 Spot-finned Hogfish and Spanish Hogfish

208 Angel

(Des A. Robinson. Litho Enschedé)

1994 (13 Sept). Environment Protection (2nd series). Marine Life. T **207** and similar vert designs. Multicoloured. W w **14**. P 13×14½.

1017	40c. Type **207**	1·00	1·25
	a. Horiz strip of 5. Nos. 1017/21	4·50	5·50
1018	40c. Tomate and Long-spined Squirrelfish	1·00	1·25
1019	40c. French Angelfish	1·00	1·25
1020	40c. Queen Angelfish	1·00	1·25
1021	40c. Rock Beauty	1·00	1·25
1017/21 Set of 5		4·50	5·50
MS1022 57×55 mm. $2 Rock Beauty, Queen Angelfish and windsurfer		6·00	7·00

Nos. 1017/21 were printed together, *se-tenant*, in horizontal strips of 5 throughout the sheet with the backgrounds forming a composite design.

(Des Jennifer Toombs. Litho B.D.T.)

1994 (31 Oct). Christmas. T **208** and similar multicoloured designs. W w **16** (sideways). P 14.

1023	15c. Type **208**	30	30
1024	55c. Holy Family	90	1·10
1025	60c. Shepherds	1·10	1·40
1026	70c. Wise Men	1·25	2·50
1023/6 Set of 4		3·25	4·75
MS1027 73×85 mm. $2 Jesus in manger. Wmk upright		3·50	5·00

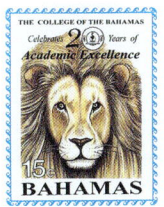

209 Lion and Emblem

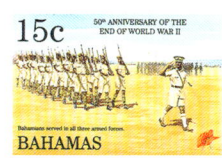

209a Bahamian Infantry drilling

(Des D. Miller. Litho Enschedé)

1995 (8 Feb). 20th Anniv of the College of the Bahamas. T **209** and similar vert design. Multicoloured. W w **14**. P 14×13½.

1028	15c. Type **209**	30	30
1029	70c. Queen Elizabeth II and College building	1·25	1·75

(Des R. Watton. Litho Cartor (Nos. 1030/3) or Questa (No. **MS**1034))

1995 (8 May). 50th Anniv of End of Second World War. T **209a** and similar multicoloured designs. W w **14** (sideways). P 13½.

1030	15c. Type **209a**	75	50
1031	55c. Consolidated PBY-5A Catalina flying boat	2·00	1·25
1032	60c. Bahamian women in naval operations room	2·00	2·25
1033	70c. Consolidated B-24 Liberator bomber	2·50	3·75
1030/3 Set of 4		6·50	7·00
MS1034 75×85 mm. $2 Reverse of 1939–45 War Medal (*vert*). Wmk upright. P 14		2·50	4·00

25

BAHAMAS

210 Kirtland's Warbler on Nest

211 Eleuthera Cliffs

(Des N. Arlott. Litho Cartor)

1995 (7 June). Environment Protection (3rd series). Endangered Species. Kirtlands Warbler. T **210** and similar vert designs. Multicoloured. W w **14**. P 13½.

1035	15c. Type **210**	55	75
	w. Wmk inverted	55	75
	wa. Strip of 4. Nos. 1035/8	2·00	2·75
1036	15c. Singing on branch	55	75
	w. Wmk inverted	55	75
1037	25c. Feeding chicks	55	75
	w. Wmk inverted	55	75
1038	25c. Catching insects	55	75
	w. Wmk inverted	55	75
1035/8 Set of 4		2·00	2·75
MS1039 73×67 mm. $2 On branch. Wmk sideways. P 13		7·50	8·50

Nos. 1035/8 were issued in sheets of 50 of each design and Nos. 1035w/8w in sheets of 16 (4×4) containing horizontal and vertical se-tenant strips.

No. **MS**1039 does not show the W.W.F. Panda emblem.

(Des D. Miller. Litho Questa)

1995 (18 July). Tourism. T **211** and similar horiz designs. Multicoloured. W w **16** (sideways). P 14½.

1040	15c. Type **211**	1·50	50
1041	55c. Clarence Town, Long Island	2·50	1·25
1042	60c. Albert Lowe Museum	2·75	2·00
1043	70c. Yachts	3·00	5·00
1040/3 Set of 4		8·75	8·25

212 Pigs and Chick

(Des Jennifer Toombs. Litho Cartor)

1995 (5 Sept). 50th Anniv of Food and Agriculture Organization. T **212** and similar horiz designs. Multicoloured. W w **14** (sideways). P 13½×13.

1044	15c. Type **212**	1·50	50
1045	55c. Seedling and hand holding seed	2·00	1·10
1046	60c. Family with fruit and vegetables	2·50	2·25
1047	70c. Fishes and crustaceans	3·50	4·50
1044/7 Set of 4		8·50	7·50

213 Sikorsky S-55 Helicopter, Sinai, 1957

(Des A. Theobald. Litho B.D.T.)

1995 (24 Oct). 50th Anniv of United Nations. T **213** and similar horiz designs. Multicoloured. W w **16** (sideways). P 14.

1048	15c. Type **213**	70	50
1049	55c. Ferret armoured car, Sinai, 1957	1·25	1·25
1050	60c. Fokker F.27 Friendship (airliner), Cambodia, 1991-93	1·50	2·00
1051	70c. Lockheed C-130 Hercules (transport)	1·60	2·75
1048/51 Set of 4		4·50	6·00

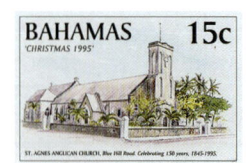

214 St. Agnes Anglican Church

(Des R. Watton. Litho B.D.T.)

1995 (17 Nov). Christmas. Churches. T **214** and similar horiz designs. Multicoloured. W w **16** (sideways). P 14.

1052	15c. Type **214**	30	25
1053	55c. Church of God, East Street	90	90
1054	60c. Sacred Heart Roman Catholic Church	95	1·25
1055	70c. Salem Union Baptist Church	1·10	1·75
1052/5 Set of 4		3·00	3·75

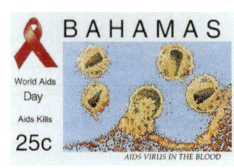

215 Microscopic View of AIDS Virus

(Des N. Shewring. Litho B.D.T.)

1995 (1 Dec). World AIDS Day. T **215** and similar horiz design. Multicoloured. W w **14** (sideways). P 14.

1056	25c. Type **215**	60	50
1057	70c. Research into AIDS	1·00	1·50

216 Sunrise Tellin

(Des D. Miller. Litho Questa)

1996 (2 Jan–1 July). Sea Shells. T **216** and similar horiz designs. Multicoloured. "1996" imprint date. W w **14** (sideways). P 14.

1058	5c. Type **216**	50	1·50
1059	10c. Queen Conch	55	1·50
1060	15c. Angular Triton	75	55
1061	20c. True Tulip	1·00	1·00
1062	25c. Reticulated Cowrie-helmet	1·00	80
1063	30c. Sand Dollar	1·25	80
1063a	35c. As 30c.	1·50	80
1064	40c. Lace Short-frond Murex	1·50	80
1065	45c. Inflated Sea Biscuit	1·75	80
1066	50c. West Indian Top Shell	1·75	1·00
1067	55c. Spiny Oyster	1·75	1·00
1068	60c. King Helmet	1·75	1·25
1068a	65c. As 45c.	2·50	1·25
1069	70c. Lion's Paw	2·00	1·50
1069a	80c. As 55c.	2·50	1·50
1070	$1 Crown Cone	3·00	2·25
1071	$2 Atlantic Partridge Tun	4·50	5·50
1072	$5 Wide-mouthed Purpura	9·00	13·00
1073	$10 Atlantic Trumpet Triton (1 July)	25·00	24·00
1058/73 Set of 16		50·00	50·00

For 70c. in miniature sheet with "1997" imprint date see No. **MS**1097 and for the $1 with inverted watermark and "1997" imprint date No. **MS**1096.

For these designs with watermark w **14** (upright) and "1997" imprint date see Nos. 1098/1113.

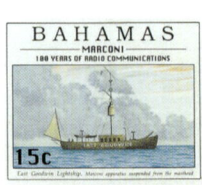

217 East Goodwin Lightship with Marconi Apparatus on Mast

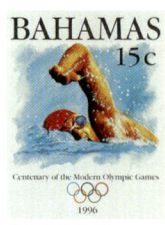

218 Swimming

BAHAMAS

(Des N. Shewring. Litho B.D.T.)

1996 (2 Apr). Centenary of Radio. T **217** and similar horiz designs. Multicoloured. W w **14** (sideways). P 13½×14.
1074	15c. Type **217**...	1·75	80
1075	55c. Newspaper headline concerning Dr. Crippen...	2·50	1·25
1076	60c. *Philadelphia* (liner) and first readable transatlantic message...........................	2·50	2·00
1077	70c. Guglielmo Marconi and *Elettra* (yacht)...	2·75	3·50
1074/7 *Set of 4*...		8·50	6·75
MS1078 80×47 mm. $2 *Titanic* and *Carpathia* (liners)....		8·50	8·50

(Des S. Noon. Litho B.D.T.)

1996 (25 June). Centenary of Modern Olympic Games. T **218** and similar vert designs. Multicoloured. W w **16**. P 14×13½.
1079	15c. Type **218**...	40	35
1080	55c. Running...	90	90
1081	60c. Basketball...	2·00	1·75
1082	70c. Long jumping.....................................	1·40	2·50
1079/82 *Set of 4*...		4·25	5·00
MS1083 73×68 mm. $2 Javelin throwing...........................		3·00	4·00

219 Green Anole **220** The Annunciation

(Des Doreen McGuiness. Litho Questa)

1996 (3 Sept). Environment Protection (4th series). Reptiles. T **219** and similar vert designs. Multicoloured. W w **16**. P 14.
1084	15c. Type **219**...	55	50
1085	55c. Little Bahama Bank Boa.....................	1·10	1·00
1086	60c. Inagua Freshwater Turtle...................	1·50	1·75
1087	70c. Acklins Rock Iguana...........................	1·75	2·75
1084/7 *Set of 4*...		4·50	5·50
MS1088 85×105 mm. Nos. 1084/7..		5·50	6·50

(Des Jennifer Toombs. Litho B.D.T.)

1996 (4 Nov). Christmas. T **220** and similar vert designs. Multicoloured. W w **14**. P 14.
1089	15c. Type **220**...	1·25	40
1090	55c. Joseph and Mary travelling to Bethlehem...	2·50	1·00
1091	60c. Shepherds and Angel.........................	2·50	1·50
1092	70c. Adoration of the Magi........................	2·75	4·00
1089/92 *Set of 4*...		8·00	6·25
MS1093 70×87 mm. $2 Presentation in the Temple.......		4·00	4·50

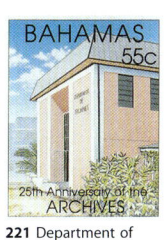

221 Department of Archives Building **221a** Queen Elizabeth II in Bonn, 1992

(Des N. Shewring. Litho Questa)

1996 (9 Dec). 25th Anniv of Archives Department. T **221** and similar horiz design showing Archives Building. W w **16**. P 14½×14.
1094	**221**	55c. multicoloured...........................	1·50	1·00
MS1095 83×54 mm. $2 multicoloured. Wmk sideways. P 14...			4·75	6·50

(Des D. Miller. Litho Questa)

1997 (3 Feb). "HONG KONG '97" International Stamp Exhibition. Sheet 130×90 mm, containing design as No. 1070 but with "1997" imprint date. Multicoloured. W w **14** (inverted). P 14.
MS1096 $1 Crown Cone.. 3·25 3·50

(Des D. Miller. Litho Walsall)

1997 (20 June). Return of Hong Kong to China. Sheet 130×90 mm containing design as No. 1069, but with "1997" imprint date.
MS1097 70c. Lion's Paw... 2·00 2·50

1997 (1 July)–**99**. As Nos. 1058/73, but W w **14** (upright). *With imprint date.* P 14.
1098	5c. Type **216** (22.9.97)............................	75	1·50
1099	10c. Queen Conch (22.9.97).....................	50	1·50
1100	15c. Angular Triton (22.9.97).....................	75	25
1101	20c. True Tulip (22.9.97)............................	70	45
1102	25c. Reticulated Cowrie-helmet (22.9.97)........	1·00	40
1103	30c. Sand Dollar (22.9.97).........................	2·00	1·25
1103*a*	35c. As 30c. (29.7.99)............................	3·25	75
1104	40c. Lace Short-frond Murex (22.9.97).....	1·50	70
1105	45c. Inflated Sea Biscuit (22.9.97)............	1·75	1·40
1106	50c. West Indian Top Shell (22.9.97).........	1·75	85
1107	55c. Spiny Oyster (22.9.97).......................	2·25	1·40
1108	60c. King Helmet (22.9.97)........................	2·25	1·00
1108*a*	65c. As 45c. (29.7.99)............................	4·00	1·25
1109	70c. Lion's Paw (22.9.97)...........................	3·00	1·50
1109*a*	80c. As 55c. (29.7.99)............................	4·50	2·00
1110	$1 Crown Cone......................................	3·25	2·00
1111	$2 Atlantic Partridge Tun.......................	5·00	5·00
1112	$5 Wide-mouthed Purpura...................	11·00	13·00
1113	$10 Atlantic Trumpet Triton...................	18·00	18·00
1098/113 *Set of 19*...		60·00	50·00

Imprint dates: "1997", Nos. 1098/103, 1104/8, 1110/13; "1999", Nos. 1098/102, 1103*a*/4, 1106, 1108/*a*, 1109*a*/13; "2000", Nos. 1098, 1100, 1102, 1106, 1108, 1109, 1111. "2001", Nos. 1100, 1102, 1106, 1108*a*, 1110, 1111.

(Des N. Shewring (No. **MS**1120), D. Miller (others). Litho Questa (No. **MS**1120) or Cartor (others))

1997 (9 July). Golden Wedding of Queen Elizabeth and Prince Philip. T **221a** and similar multicoloured designs. W w **14**. P 13.
1114	50c. Type **221a**...	2·00	2·25
	a. Horiz pair. Nos. 1114/15.................	4·00	4·50
1115	50c. Prince Philip and Prince Charles at Trooping the Colour...........................	2·00	2·25
1116	60c. Prince Philip......................................	2·00	2·25
	a. Horiz pair. Nos. 1116/17.................	4·00	4·50
1117	60c. Queen at Trooping the Colour.........	2·00	2·25
1118	70c. Queen Elizabeth and Prince Philip at polo, 1970...	2·00	2·25
	a. Horiz pair. Nos. 1118/19.................	4·00	4·50
1119	70c. Prince Charles playing polo.............	2·00	2·25
1114/19 *Set of 6*...		11·00	12·00
MS1120 110×70 mm. $2 Queen Elizabeth and Prince Philip in landau (*horiz*). W w **14** (sideways). P 14×14½..			6·50	7·00

Nos. 1114/15, 1116/17 and 1118/19 were each printed together, *se-tenant*, in horizontal pairs throughout the sheets with the backgrounds forming composite designs.

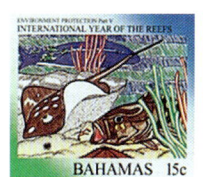

222 Underwater Scene

(Des D. Miller. Litho Questa)

1997 (3 Sept). Environment Protection (5th series). International Year of the Reefs. T **222** and similar horiz designs showing different children's paintings of underwater scenes. W w **16** (sideways). P 14½.
1121	15c. multicoloured...................................	1·25	60
1122	55c. multicoloured...................................	2·25	1·00
1123	60c. multicoloured...................................	2·25	1·75
1124	70c. multicoloured...................................	2·50	3·00
1121/4 *Set of 4*...		7·50	5·75

223 Angel **223a** Diana, Princess of Wales

BAHAMAS

(Des Jennifer Toombs. Litho Cartor)

1997 (4 Nov). Christmas. T **223** and similar vert designs. Multicoloured. W w **14** (inverted). P 13×13½.

1125	15c. Type **223**..	1·50	40
1126	55c. Mary and Baby Jesus	2·25	80
1127	60c. Shepherd	2·25	1·25
1128	70c. King	2·75	3·75
1125/8 Set of 4...		8·00	5·50
MS1129 74×94 mm. $2 Baby Jesus wrapped in swaddling-bands. Wmk upright		8·00	8·50

(Des D. Miller. Litho Questa)

1998 (31 Mar). Diana, Princess of Wales Commemoration. T **223a** and similar vert designs. Multicoloured. W w **16** (No. 1130). P 14½×14.

| 1130 | 15c. Type **223a**... | 50 | 50 |
| MS1131 145×70 mm. 15c. As No. 1130; 55c. Wearing striped jacket, 1983; 60c. In evening dress, 1983; 70c. Meeting crowds, 1993. W w **14** (sideways) .... | | 2·00 | 2·75 |

223b Handley Page Hyderabad

(Des A. Theobald. Litho Enschedé)

1998 (1 Apr). 80th Anniv of the Royal Air Force. T **223b** and similar horiz designs. Multicoloured. W w **14** (sideways*). P 13½×14.

1132	15c. Type **223b**...	55	40
1133	55c. Hawker Demon...................................	1·00	85
1134	60c. Gloster Meteor F.8.............................	1·10	1·25
1135	70c. Lockheed Neptune MR.1.................	1·40	2·25
1132/5 Set of 4...		3·50	4·25
MS1136 110×76 mm. 50c. Sopwith Camel; 50c. Short 184 (seaplane); 50c. Supermarine Spitfire PR.19; 50c. North American Mitchell III		4·00	4·25

*The normal sideways watermark shows Crown to left of CA on Nos. 1132/5 and Crown to right of CA on No. **MS**1136, both as seen from the back of the stamp.

224 Newsletters

(Des D. Miller. Litho Questa)

1998 (15 Apr). 50th Anniv of Organisation of American States. T **224** and similar horiz design. Multicoloured. W w **14** (sideways). P 13½×14.

| 1137 | 15c. Type **224**.. | 30 | 30 |
| 1138 | 55c. Headquarters building and flags, Washington .... | 70 | 80 |

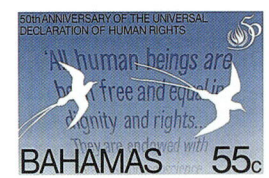

225 Start of Declaration and Tropic Birds

(Des D. Miller. Litho Questa)

1998 (15 Apr). 50th Anniv of Universal Declaration of Human Rights. W w **14** (sideways). P 13½×14.

| 1139 | **225** | 55c. bright blue and black........................ | 1·75 | 1·00 |

226 University Arms and Graduates

(Des D. Miller. Litho Questa)

1998 (15 Apr). 50th Anniv of University of the West Indies. W w **14** (sideways). P 13½×14.

| 1140 | **226** | 55c. multicoloured... | 1·50 | 1·00 |

227 Supreme Court Building

(Des D. Miller. Litho Cartor)

1998 (9 July). 25th Anniv of Independence. T **227** and similar horiz designs. Multicoloured. W w **14** (sideways). P 13½.

1141	15c. Type **227**..	1·00	50
1142	55c. Nassau Library.....................................	1·75	1·00
1143	60c. Government House	1·90	1·50
1144	70c. Gregory Arch...	2·00	3·00
1141/4 Set of 4...		6·00	5·50
MS1145 70×55 mm. $2 Island Regatta, George Town ...		3·50	5·00

228 *Disney Magic* (cruise liner) at Night

(Des N. Shewring. Litho Questa)

1998 (1 Aug). Disney Cruise Line's Castaway Coy Holiday Development. T **228** and similar horiz design. Multicoloured. W w **14** (sideways). P 14.

1146	55c. Type **228**..	2·00	2·00
	a. Pair. Nos. 1146/7...............................	4·00	4·00
	b. Booklet pane. Nos. 1146/7, each × 5 with margins all round............................	18·00	
1147	55c. *Disney Magic* by day............................	2·00	2·00

Nos. 1146/7 were printed together, *se-tenant*, in horizontal and vertical pairs throughout the sheet.

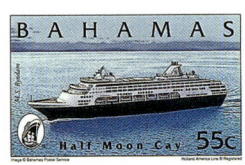

229 *Ryndam* (cruise liner)

(Des N. Shewring. Litho Cartor)

1998 (19 Aug). Holland America Line's Half Moon Cay Holiday Development. W w **14** (sideways). P 13½×13.

| 1148 | **229** | 55c. multicoloured... | 2·75 | 1·25 |

230 Barrel Pink Rose    **231** The Annunciation

(Des D. Miller. Litho B.D.T.)

1998 (8 Sept). Environment Protection (6th series). Roses. T **230** and similar horiz designs. Multicoloured. W w **14** (sideways). P 14.

1149	55c. Type **230**..	1·50	1·60
	a. Booklet pane. Nos. 1149/53, each × 2 with margins all round............................	12·00	
1150	55c. Yellow Cream..	1·50	1·60
1151	55c. Seven Sisters...	1·50	1·60
1152	55c. Big Red..	1·50	1·60
1153	55c. Island Beauty	1·50	1·60
1149/53 Set of 5...		6·75	7·25
MS1154 100×70 mm. No. 1153..		1·50	1·75

28

BAHAMAS

(Des Jennifer Toombs. Litho Questa)

1998 (10 Nov). Christmas. T **231** and similar horiz designs. Multicoloured. W w **16** (sideways). P 14½.
1155	15c. Type **231**	50	30
1156	55c. Shepherds	1·00	70
1157	60c. Three Kings	1·25	1·10
1158	70c. The Flight into Egypt	1·50	2·75
1155/8 Set of 4		3·25	4·25
MS1159 87×67 mm. $2 The Nativity		3·00	4·00

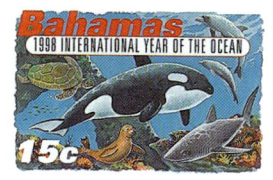

232 Killer Whale and other Marine Life

(Des B. Dare. Litho Questa)

1998 (24 Nov). International Year of the Ocean. T **232** and similar horiz design. Multicoloured. W w **14** (sideways). P 13½×14.
1160	15c. Type **232**	65	50
1161	55c. Tropical fish	85	90

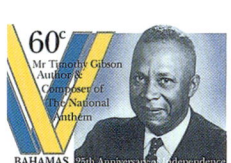

233 Timothy Gibson (composer)
234 Head of Greater Flamingo and Chick

(Des D. Miller. Litho Cartor)

1998 (10 Dec). 25th Anniv of "March on Bahamaland" (national anthem). W w **14** (sideways). P 13½.
1162	**233**	60c. multicoloured	1·00	1·25

(Des A. Robinson. Litho Questa)

1999 (9 Feb). 40th Anniv of National Trust (1st issue). Inagua National Park. T **234** and similar vert designs. Multicoloured. W w **16**. P 14.
1163	55c. Type **234**	1·50	1·60
	a. Horiz strip of 5. Nos. 1163/7	6·75	7·25
1164	55c. Pair with two chicks	1·50	1·60
1165	55c. Greater Flamingos asleep or stretching wings	1·50	1·60
1166	55c. Greater Flamingos feeding	1·50	1·60
1167	55c. Greater Flamingos in flight	1·50	1·60
1163/7 Set of 5		6·75	7·25

Nos. 1163/7 were printed together, *se-tenant*, in horizontal strips of 5 throughout the sheet with the backgrounds forming a composite design. See also Nos. 1173/7, 1198/1202 and 1207/11.

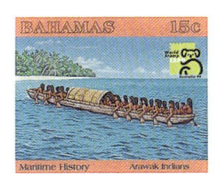

235 Arawak Indian Canoe

(Des D. Miller. Litho Questa)

1999 (9 Mar). "Australia. '99" World Stamp Exhibition, Melbourne. Maritime History. T **235** and similar horiz designs. Multicoloured. W w **14** (sideways). P 14½.
1168	15c. Type **235**	55	30
1169	55c. *Santa Maria* (Columbus), 1492	2·25	1·40
1170	60c. *Queen Anne's Revenge* (Blackbeard), 1716	2·25	1·75
1171	70c. *The Banshee* (Confederate paddle steamer) running blockade	2·50	3·50
1168/71 Set of 4		6·75	6·25
MS1172 110×66 mm. $2 Firing on American ships, 1776		5·50	5·50

(Des A. Robinson. Litho Questa)

1999 (6 Apr). 40th Anniv of National Trust (2nd issue). Exuma Cays Land and Sea Park. Vert designs as T **234**. Multicoloured. W w **16**. P 14.
1173	55c. Dolphin	1·60	1·75
	a. Horiz strip of 5. Nos. 1173/7	7·25	8·00
1174	55c. Angelfish and Parrotfish	1·60	1·75
1175	55c. Queen Triggerfish	1·60	1·75
1176	55c. Turtle	1·60	1·75
1177	55c. Lobster	1·60	1·75
1173/7 Set of 5		7·25	8·00

Nos. 1173/7 were printed together, *se-tenant*, in horizontal strips of 5 throughout the sheet, with the backgrounds forming a composite design.

236 Society Headquarters Building

(Des N. Shewring. Litho Cartor)

1999 (9 June). 40th Anniv of Bahamas Historical Society. W w **14** (sideways). P 13.
1178	**236**	$1 multicoloured	1·50	2·25

236a Constructing Ascent Module
236b Visiting Herts Hospital, 1940

(Des J. Batchelor (65c.), N. Shewring (others). Litho Walsall)

1999 (20 July). 30th Anniv of First Manned Landing on Moon. T **236a** and similar multicoloured designs. W w **16**. P 14×13½.
1179	15c. Type **236a**	45	40
1180	65c. Diagram of command and service module	1·25	1·25
1181	70c. Lunar module descending	1·25	1·75
1182	80c. Lunar module preparing to dock with service module	1·25	2·50
1179/82 Set of 4		3·75	5·50
MS1183 90×80 mm. $2 Earth as seen from Moon (*circular, 40 mm diam.*). Wmk sideways. P 14		3·25	4·25

(Des D. Miller. Litho Cartor)

1999 (24 Aug). "Queen Elizabeth the Queen Mother's Century". T **236b** and similar horiz designs. W w **14** (sideways). P 13½.
1184	15c. Type **236b**	60	35
1185	65c. With Princess Elizabeth, Hyde Park, 1944	1·50	1·00
1186	70c. With Prince Andrew, 1997	1·50	1·50
1187	80c. With Irish Guards' mascot, 1997	1·50	1·75
1184/7 Set of 4		4·50	4·25
MS1188 145×70 mm. $2 Lady Elizabeth Bowes-Lyon with her brother David, 1904, and England World Cup team celebrating, 1966. W w **16** (sideways)		4·50	5·00

237 *Delaware* (American mail ship), 1880

(Des J. Batchelor. Litho Cartor)

1999 (7 Sept). 125th Anniv of Universal Postal Union. Ships. T **237** and similar horiz designs. Multicoloured. W w **16** (sideways). P 13½.
1189	15c. Type **237**	1·50	50
1190	65c. *Atlantis* (liner), 1923	2·50	1·25

29

BAHAMAS

1191	70c. *Queen of Bermuda* (liner), 1937	2·50	2·25
1192	80c. U.S.S. *Saufley* (destroyer), 1943	3·00	3·25
1189/92 Set of 4		8·50	6·50

238 "Turtle Pond" (Green Turtle)

239 Man on Elephant Float

(Des D. Miller. Litho B.D.T.)

1999 (21 Sept). Environment Protection (7th series). Marine Life Paintings by Ricardo Knowles. T **238** and similar horiz designs. Multicoloured. W w **14** (sideways). P 13½×14.

1193	15c. Type **238**	50	35
1194	65c. "Turtle Cliff" (Loggerhead Turtle)	1·25	1·00
1195	70c. "Barracuda"	1·40	1·40
1196	80c. "Coral Reef"	1·50	2·25
1193/6 Set of 4		4·25	4·50
MS1197 90×75 mm. $2 "Atlantic Bottle-nosed Dolphins"		4·50	5·50

The 65c. is inscribed "GREEN TURTLES" in error.

(Des A. Robinson. Litho Walsall)

1999 (8 Oct). 40th Anniv of National Trust (3rd issue). Birds. Vert designs as T **234**. Multicoloured. W w **16**. P 14.

1198	65c. Gull	1·75	1·75
	a. Horiz strip of 5. Nos. 1198/1202	8·00	8·00
1199	65c. Heron	1·75	1·75
1200	65c. Hummingbird	1·75	1·75
1201	65c. Duck	1·75	1·75
1202	65c. Parrot	1·75	1·75
1198/1202 Set of 5		8·00	8·00

Nos. 1198/1202 were printed together, se-tenant, in horizontal strips of 5 throughout the sheet with the backgrounds forming a composite design.

(Des C. Fernander, adapted D. Miller. Litho Walsall)

1999 (25 Oct). Christmas. Junkanoo Festival. T **239** and similar vert designs. Multicoloured. W w **14**. P 14½×14.

1203	15c. Type **239**	50	30
1204	65c. Man in winged costume	1·00	1·00
1205	70c. Man in feathered mask	1·25	1·25
1206	80c. Man blowing conch shell	1·50	2·00
1203/6 Set of 4		3·75	4·00

(Des A. Robinson. Litho Walsall)

1999 (30 Nov). 40th Anniv of National Trust (4th issue). Flora and Fauna. Vert designs as T **234**. Multicoloured. W w **16**. P 14.

1207	65c. Foxglove	2·25	2·25
	a. Horiz strip of 5. Nos. 1207/11	10·00	10·00
1208	65c. Vole	2·25	2·25
1209	65c. Hummingbird	2·25	2·25
1210	65c. Lizard	2·25	2·25
1211	65c. Red Hibiscus	2·25	2·25
1207/11 Set of 5		10·00	10·00

Nos. 1207/11 were printed together, se-tenant, in horizontal strips of 5 throughout the sheet with the backgrounds forming a composite design.

240 New Plymouth

(Des D. Miller. Litho Cartor)

2000 (25 Jan). Historic Fishing Villages. T **240** and similar horiz designs. Multicoloured. W w **14** (sideways). P 13½×13.

1212	15c. Type **240**	1·25	40
1213	65c. Cherokee Sound	2·25	1·00
1214	70c. Hope Town	2·50	2·00
1215	80c. Spanish Wells	2·75	3·25
1212/15 Set of 4		8·00	6·00

241 Gold Medal Winning Bahamas Women's Relay Team

(Des N. Shewring. Litho Questa)

2000 (22 Feb). "The Golden Girls" (winners of 4×100 metre Relay at I.A.A.F. World Track and Field Championships '99, Spain. Sheet 100×55 mm. W w **14** (sideways). P 14½.

MS1216 **241** $2 multicoloured ... 3·00 3·75

242 Prickly Pear

243 Re-arming and Re-fuelling Spitfire

(Des A. Lowe. Litho Questa)

2000 (2 May). Medicinal Plants. T **242** and similar horiz designs. Multicoloured. W w **14** (sideways). P 14½.

1217	15c. Type **242**	35	30
1218	65c. Buttercup	1·25	1·25
1219	70c. Shepherd's Needle	1·25	1·50
1220	80c. Five Fingers	1·40	2·25
1217/20 Set of 4		3·75	4·75

(Des J. Batchelor. Litho Cartor)

2000 (15 May). "The Stamp Show 2000" International Stamp Exhibition, London. 60th Anniv of Battle of Britain. T **243** and similar horiz designs. Multicoloured. W w **14** (sideways). P 13½.

1221	15c. Type **243**	70	45
1222	65c. Sqdn. Ldr. Stanford-Tuck's Hurricane Mk.I	1·40	1·40
1223	70c. Dogfight between Spitfires and Heinkel IIIs	1·60	1·75
1224	80c. Flight of Spitfires attacking	1·60	2·25
1221/4 Set of 4		4·75	5·25
MS1225 90×70 mm. $2 Presentation Spitfire *Bahamas*.		3·50	4·00

244 Teachers' and Salaried Workers' Co-operative Credit Union Building

(Des N. Shewring. Litho Questa)

2000 (27 June). Co-operatives Movement in Bahamas. Sheet 90×50 mm. W w **14** (sideways). P 14.

MS1226 **244** $2 multicoloured ... 3·50 4·25

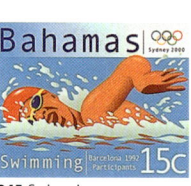

245 Swimming

246 *Encyclia cochleata*

(Des B. Dare. Litho Questa)

2000 (17 July). Olympic Games, Sydney. T **245** and similar horiz designs, each inscribed with details of previous Bahamian participation. Multicoloured. W w **14** (sideways). P 14½.

1227	15c. Type **245**	50	30
1228	65c. Triple jump	1·40	1·25
1229	70c. Women's 4×100m relay	1·40	1·40

BAHAMAS

1230	80c. Sailing	1·50	2·25
1227/30	Set of 4	4·25	4·75

(Litho Questa)

2000 (7 Nov). Christmas. Orchids. T **246** and similar vert designs. Multicoloured. W w **14** (inverted). P 14½.

1231	15c. Type **246**	85	30
1232	65c. *Encyclia plicata*	1·75	1·40
1233	70c. *Bletia purpurea*	1·90	1·75
1234	80c. *Encyclea gracilis*	2·25	2·50
1231/4	Set of 4	6·00	5·50

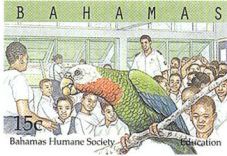

247 Parrot and Primary School Class

(Des N. Shewring. Litho Questa)

2000 (12 Dec). Bahamas Humane Society. T **247** and similar horiz designs. Multicoloured. W w **14** (sideways). P 14.

1235	15c. Type **247**	1·75	50
1236	65c. Cat and Society stall	2·75	1·40
1237	70c. Dogs and veterinary surgery	3·25	2·75
1238	80c. Goat and animal rescue van	3·25	4·00
1235/8	Set of 4	10·00	7·75

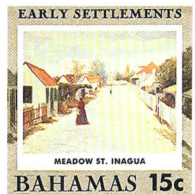

248 "Meadow Street, Inagua"

(Litho Questa)

2001 (6 Feb). Early Settlements. Paintings by Ricardo Knowles. T **248** and similar horiz designs. Multicoloured. W w **14** (sideways). P 14.

1239	15c. Type **248**	40	30
1240	65c. "Bain Town"	1·25	1·00
1241	70c. "Hope Town, Abaco"	1·40	1·40
1242	80c. "Blue Hills"	1·50	2·25
1239/42	Set of 4	4·00	4·50

249 Lynden Pindling presenting Independence Constitution, 1972

250 "Cocoaplum"

(Des A. Robinson. Litho Questa)

2001 (22 Mar). Sir Lynden Pindling (former Prime Minister) Commemoration. T **249** and similar horiz design. Multicoloured. W w **14** (sideways). P 14½.

1243	15c. Type **249** (I)	50	40
	a. Type II (6 Aug)	1·10	65
1244	65c. Sir Lynden Pindling with Bahamas flag	1·40	1·50

Two types of 15c.: I. Incorrectly dated "10th July, 1972". II. Correctly dated "10th July 1973".

(Litho Questa)

2001 (15 May). Edible Wild Fruits. Paintings by Alton Roland Lowe. T **250** and similar horiz designs. Multicoloured. W w **14** (sideways). P 14×14½.

1245	15c. Type **250**	35	25
1246	65c. "Guana Berry"	1·25	1·10
1247	70c. "Mastic"	1·25	1·25
1248	80c. "Seagrape"	1·50	2·25
1245/8	Set of 4	4·00	4·25

251 Reddish Egret

(Des A. Robinson. Litho Questa)

2001 (2 July). Birds and their Eggs. T **251** and similar horiz designs. Multicoloured. W w **14**. P 14.

1249	5c. Type **251**	75	1·50
1250	10c. Purple Gallinule	75	1·50
1251	15c. Antillean Nighthawk	1·00	55
1252	20c. Wilson's Plover	1·25	1·00
1253	25c. Killdeer	1·25	70
1254	30c. Bahama Woodstar	1·40	1·00
1255	40c. Bahama Swallow	1·40	1·25
1256	50c. Bahama Mockingbird	1·75	1·25
1257	60c. Black-cowled Oriole	2·00	1·50
1258	65c. Great Lizard Cuckoo	2·00	1·25
1259	70c. Audubon's Shearwater	2·25	1·50
1260	80c. Grey Kingbird	2·25	1·50
1261	$1 Bananaquit	3·25	3·00
1262	$2 Yellow Warbler	6·00	6·00
1263	$5 Greater Antillean Bullfinch	13·00	14·00
1264	$10 Roseate Spoonbill	22·00	24·00
1249/64	Set of 16	55·00	55·00

On 21 March 2002 Nos. 1252/3, 1255 and 1264 were reprinted with an imprint date of 2002. On 15 October 2002 there was a further printing of No. 1253 also showing an imprint date of 2002.

252 H.M.S. *Norfolk* (cruiser), 1933    **253** "Adoration of the Shepherds"

(Des J. Batchelor. Litho Questa)

2001 (21 Aug). Royal Navy Ships connected to Bahamas. T **252** and similar horiz designs. Multicoloured. W w **14** (sideways). P 14.

1265	15c. Type **252**	1·50	50
1266	25c. H.M.S. *Scarborough* (sloop), 1930s	1·75	70
1267	50c. H.M.S. *Bahamas* (frigate), 1944	2·25	1·75
1268	65c. H.M.S. *Battleaxe* (frigate), 1979	2·50	1·75
1269	70c. H.M.S. *Invincible* (aircraft carrier), 1997	2·50	2·25
1270	80c. H.M.S. *Norfolk* (frigate), 2000	2·50	3·00
1265/70	Set of 6	11·50	9·00

(Litho Questa)

2001 (6 Nov). Christmas. Paintings by Rubens. T **253** and similar vert designs. Multicoloured. W w **14**. P 14.

1271	15c. Type **253**	55	25
1272	65c. "Adoration of the Magi"(with Van Dyck)	1·40	1·10
1273	70c. "Holy Virgin in Wreath of Flowers" (with Breughel)	1·50	1·40
1274	80c. "Holy Virgin adored by Angels"	1·60	2·00
1271/4	Set of 4	4·50	4·25

253a Princess Elizabeth 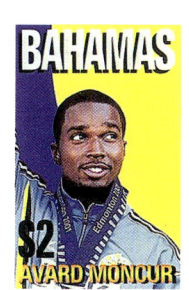   **254** Avard Moncur (athlete)

31

BAHAMAS

(Des A. Robinson. Litho Questa)

2002 (6 Feb). Golden Jubilee. T **253a** and similar designs. W w **14** (sideways). P 14½.

1275	15c. brownish black, light emerald and gold	45	25
1276	65c. multicoloured	1·25	1·00
1277	70c. multicoloured	1·40	1·50
1278	80c. multicoloured	1·40	2·00
1275/8 *Set of 4*		4·00	4·25
MS1279 162×95 mm. Nos. 1275/8 and $2 multicoloured. P 13½ ($2) or 14½ (others)		6·50	6·50

Designs: *Horiz*—65c. Queen Elizabeth in Bonn, 1992; 70c. Queen Elizabeth with Prince Edward, 1965; 80c. Queen Elizabeth at Sandringham, 1996. *Vert* (38×51 *mm*)—$2 Queen Elizabeth after Annigoni. Designs as Nos. 1275/8 in No. **MS**1279 omit the gold frame around each stamp and the "Golden Jubilee 1952–2002" inscription.

(Litho Questa)

2002 (16 Apr). Award of BAAA Most Outstanding Male Athlete Title to Avard Moncur. Sheet 65×98 mm. W w **14**. P 14×13½.

MS1280 254 $2 multicoloured		3·25	3·75

255 Statue of Liberty with U.S. and Bahamas Flags

(Des A. Robinson. Litho Questa)

2002 (14 May). In Remembrance. Victims of Terrorist Attacks on U.S.A. (11 September 2001). W w **14** (sideways). P 14.

1281	**255**	$1 multicoloured	3·00	3·00

(Des A. Lowe. Litho Walsall)

2002 (2 July). Medicinal Plants (2nd series). Horiz designs as T **242**. Multicoloured. W w **14** (sideways). P 14×14½.

1282	15c. Wild Sage	50	35
1283	65c. Seaside Maho	1·40	1·10
1284	70c. Sea Ox-eye	1·50	1·60
1285	80c. Mexican Poppy	1·50	2·00
1282/5 *Set of 4*		4·50	4·50

255a Queen Elizabeth at American Red Cross Club, London, 1944

256 Rice Bird and Rice

(Des A. Robinson. Litho Questa)

2002 (5 Aug). Queen Elizabeth the Queen Mother Commemoration. T **255a** and similar vert designs. W w **14**. P 14½×14.

1286	15c. blackish brown, gold and purple	75	40
1287	65c. multicoloured	1·75	1·50
MS1288 145×70 mm. 70c. black and gold; 80c. multicoloured. Wmk sideways		3·75	3·75

Designs:—65c. Queen Mother at Remembrance Service, 1989; 70c. Queen Elizabeth, 1944; 80c. Queen Mother at Cheltenham Races, 2000. Designs in No. **MS**1288 omit the "1900–2002" inscription and the coloured frame.

(Litho BDT)

2002 (1 Oct). Illustrations from The Natural History of Carolina, Florida and the Bahama Islands by Mark Catesby (1747). T **256** and similar square designs. Multicoloured. W w **14** (sideways). P 14.

1289	15c. Type **256**	85	45
1290	25c. Alligator and Red Mangrove	1·00	60
1291	50c. Parrot Fish	1·40	1·10
1292	65c. Ilathera Duck and Sea Oxeye	1·75	1·50
1293	70c. Flamingo and Gorgonian Coral	1·90	2·00
1294	80c. Crested Bittern and Inkberry	2·00	2·25
1289/94 *Set of 6*		8·00	7·00

257 "While Shepherds watched their Flocks"

(Des O. Bell. Litho Questa)

2002 (29 Oct). Christmas. Scenes from Carols. T **257** and similar horiz designs. Multicoloured. W w **14** (sideways). P 14×14½.

1295	15c. Type **257**	60	25
1296	65c. "We Three Kings"	1·40	1·10
1297	70c. "Once in Royal David's City"	1·50	1·50
1298	80c. "I saw Three Ships"	1·60	2·25
1295/8 *Set of 4*		4·50	4·50

258 Flamingo on Nest

259 Captain Edward Teach ("Blackbeard")

(Litho Enschede)

2003 (18 Feb). Wetlands (1st series). Inagua National Park Flamingos. T **258** and similar horiz designs. Multicoloured. W w **14** (sideways). P 14.

1299	15c. Type **258**	70	45
1300	25c. Flock of flamingos feeding	95	65
1301	50c. Group of flamingos	1·50	1·10
1302	65c. Group of flamingos walking	1·75	1·50
1303	70c. Flamingos taking-off	1·90	1·90
1304	80c. Flamingos in flight	2·00	2·25
1299/304 *Set of 6*		8·00	7·00

See also Nos. 1336/41.

(Des A. Dominguez. Litho Enschede)

2003 (25 Mar). Pirates. T **259** and similar vert designs. Multicoloured. W w **14**. P 14.

1305	15c. Type **259**	85	45
1306	25c. Captain "Calico Jack" Rackham	1·25	65
1307	50c. Anne Bonney	2·00	1·40
1308	65c. Captain Woodes Rogers	2·25	1·75
1309	70c. Sir John Hawkins	2·25	2·25
1310	80c. Captain Bartholomew Roberts ("Black Bart")	2·50	2·50
1305/10 *Set of 6*		10·00	8·00

Nos. 1305/10 were printed in separate small sheets of 10 with illustrated margins.

260 Dinghies

260a Piper Cub

(Des D. Miller. Litho BDT)

2003 (23 Apr). 50th Anniv of Family Island Regatta. T **260** and similar vert designs. Multicoloured. W w **14**. P 13½.

1311	15c. Type **260**	75	40
1312	65c. *New Courageous* (racing sloop)	2·00	1·50
1313	70c. *New Susan Chase* (racing sloop)	2·25	2·00
1314	80c. *Tida Wave* (racing sloop)	2·40	2·75
1311/14 *Set of 4*		6·75	6·00

BAHAMAS

(Des A. Robinson. Litho DLR)

2003 (2 June). 50th Anniv of Coronation. Horiz designs as T **320** of Jamaica. Multicoloured. W w **14** (sideways). P 14×14½.
1315	65c. Queen with crown, orb and sceptre	1·50	1·40
1316	80c. Royal family on Buckingham Palace balcony	2·00	2·25
MS1317	95×115 mm. 15c. As No. 1315; 70c. As No. 1316	2·25	2·50

Nos. 1315/16 have scarlet frame; stamps from **MS**1317 have no frame and country name in mauve panel.

(Des A. Lowe. Litho Enschedé)

2003 (8 July). Medicinal Plants (3rd series). Horiz designs as T **242**. W w **14** (sideways). P 13½×14.
1318	15c. Asystasia	40	25
1319	65c. Cassia	1·40	1·25
1320	70c. Lignum Vitae	1·50	1·60
1321	80c. Snowberry	1·60	2·00
1318/21	Set of 4	4·50	4·50

(Des J. Batchelor. Litho Enschedé)

2003 (16 Sept). Centenary of Powered Flight. T **260a** and similar horiz designs. Multicoloured. W w **14** (sideways). P 13½×14.
1322	15c. Type **260a**	90	60
1323	25c. De Havilland Tiger Moth	1·25	90
1324	50c. Lockheed SR-71A Blackbird	1·75	1·60
1325	65c. Supermarine S6B	2·00	1·90
1326	70c. North American P-51D Mustang "Miss America"	2·00	2·00
1327	80c. Douglas DC-3 Dakota	2·25	2·50
1322/7	Set of 6	9·00	8·50

Nos. 1322/7 were each printed in sheets of 20 containing vertical rows of stamps alternated with rows of illustrated half stamp-size labels.

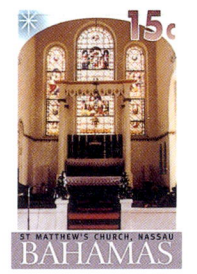

261 Interior with Stained Glass Window

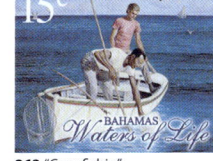

262 "Crawfishin"

(Litho BDT)

2003 (28 Oct). Christmas. St. Matthew's Church, Nassau. T **261** and similar multicoloured designs. W w **14** (sideways on horiz designs). P 15×14 (vert) or 14×15 (horiz).
1328	15c. Type **261**	60	25
1329	65c. Church interior (horiz)	1·50	1·10
1330	70c. St. Matthew's Church (horiz)	1·75	1·60
1331	80c. Church tower	2·00	2·00
1328/31	Set of 4	5·25	4·50

(Des D. Miller. Litho BDT)

2003 (24 Nov). "Waters of Life". Paintings by Alton Lowe. T **262** and similar horiz designs. Multicoloured. W w **14** (sideways). P 13½×14.
1332	15c. Type **262**	75	30
1333	65c. "Summer"	1·75	1·25
1334	70c. "The Whelkers"	2·00	1·75
1335	80c. "Annual Visit"	2·25	2·25
1332/5	Set of 4	6·00	5·00

263 Egrets on Dead Tree

(Des R. Watton. Litho BDT)

2004 (24 Feb). Wetlands (2nd series). Harrold and Wilson Ponds, New Providence Island. T **263** and similar horiz designs. Multicoloured. W w **14** (sideways). P 13½×14.
1336	15c. Type **263**	60	40
1337	25c. Green-backed Heron and duck	80	65
1338	50c. Birdwatchers in canoes	1·50	1·40
1339	65c. Egret and Bahama Pintail ducks	1·75	1·60
1340	70c. Egret and Louisiana heron	2·00	2·00
1341	80c. Birdwatchers with binoculars and telescope	2·25	2·75
1336/41	Set of 6	8·00	8·00

264 Methodist Church, Cupid's Cay, Governor's Harbour

(Des N. Shewring. Litho BDT)

2004 (27 Apr). 300th Birth Anniv of John Wesley (founder of Methodist Church) (2003). T **264** and similar multicoloured designs. W w **14** (inverted on 50c., 80c., sideways on others). P 13½.
1342	15c. Type **264**	70	40
1343	25c. Church, Grants Town, Nassau	90	55
1344	50c. Wooden Chapel, Marsh Harbour (vert)	1·60	1·50
1345	65c. Ebeneezer Methodist Church	1·90	1·75
1346	70c. Trinity Methodist Church	2·25	2·50
1346a	80c. Portrait by Antonius Roberts (vert)	2·50	3·00
1342/6	Set of 6	9·00	8·75

265 Cattleya

266 Elbow Reef Lighthouse

(Des A. R. Lowe. Litho BDT)

2004 (25 May). Bicentenary of the Royal Horticultural Society. T **265** and similar horiz designs. Multicoloured. W w **14** (sideways). P 14.
1347	15c. Type **265**	90	50
1348	65c. Hibiscus	1·40	1·10
1349	70c. Canna	1·50	1·60
1350	80c. Thunbergia	2·00	2·25
1347/50	Set of 4	5·25	4·75

(Des J. Batchelor. Litho BDT)

2004 (6 July). Lighthouses (1st series). T **266** and similar vert designs. Multicoloured. W w **14**. P 14.
1351	15c. Type **266**	1·00	50
1352	50c. Great Stirrup	1·75	1·25
1353	65c. Great Isaac	2·00	1·50
1354	70c. Hole in the Wall	2·25	2·00
1355	80c. Hog Island	2·50	2·50
1351/5	Set of 5	8·50	7·00

See also Nos. 1396/1400.

267 Boxing

268 "Anticipation"

(Des J. Vasarhelyi. Litho Cartor)

2004 (24 Aug). Olympic Games, Athens. T **267** and similar vert designs. Multicoloured. W w **14**. P 13½.
1356	15c. Type **267**	50	30
1357	50c. Swimming	1·25	1·10
1358	65c. Tennis	1·40	1·40

BAHAMAS

| 1359 | 70c. Relay racing | 1·40 | 1·75 |
| 1356/9 | Set of 4 | 4·00 | 4·00 |

2004 (14 Sept). As No. 1253 but W w **14** (sideways). "2004" imprint date. P 14.

| 1359a | 25c. Killdeer | 1·25 | 75 |

(Litho BDT)

2004 (26 Oct). Christmas. Junkanoo Festival. T **268** and similar multicoloured designs. W w **14** sideways (horiz) or inverted (vert). P 14.

1360	15c. Type **268**	40	20
1361	25c. "First Time"	50	25
1362	50c. "On The Move" (vert)	1·00	60
1363	65c. "I'm Ready" (vert)	1·10	1·00
1364	70c. "Trumpet Player" (vert)	1·25	1·40
1365	80c. "Drummer Boy" (vert)	1·40	1·60
1360/5	Set of 6	5·00	4·75

269 RMS *Mauretania*

(Des Anthony Theobald. Litho Enschedé)

2004 (7 Dec). Merchant Ships. T **269** and similar horiz designs. Multicoloured. W w **14** (sideways). P 13×13½.

1366	15c. Type **269**	80	45
1367	25c. MV *Adonia*	1·10	65
1368	50c. MS *Royal Princess*	1·75	1·40
1369	65c. SS *Queen of Nassau*	1·90	1·50
1370	70c. RMS *Transvaal Castle*	2·00	2·00
1371	80c. SS *Norway*	2·25	2·50
1366/71	Set of 6	9·00	7·75

(Des A. Lowe. Litho BDT)

2005 (8 Feb). Medicinal Plants (4th series). Horiz designs as T **242**. Multicoloured. W w **14** (sideways). P 14.

1372	15c. Aloe Vera	35	25
1373	25c. Red Stopper	45	35
1374	50c. Blue Flower	80	80
1375	65c. Bay Lavender	1·10	1·25
1372/5	Set of 4	2·40	2·40

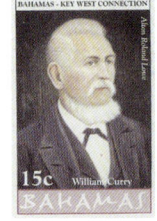

270 Commando Squadron   **271** William Curry

(Litho BDT)

2005 (29 Mar). 25th Anniv of the Royal Bahamas Defence Force. T **270** and similar horiz designs. Multicoloured. W w **14** (sideways). P 14.

1376	15c. Type **270**	60	40
1377	25c. HMBS *Abaco*	85	55
1378	50c. HMBS *Bahamas*	1·60	1·25
1379	65c. Officers and marines in uniform	1·75	1·75
1376/9	Set of 4	4·25	3·50

(Des J. Batchelor. Litho Cartor)

2005 (29 Apr). Bicentenary of Battle of Trafalgar. Multicoloured. (except **MS**1386) designs as T **336** of Jamaica. W w **14** (sideways* on 50, 65, 80c.) or no wmk (70c.). P 13½.

1380	15c. Tower Sea Service pistols, 1801 RN pattern (vert)	60	40
1381	25c. Royal Marine, 1805 (vert)	80	55
1382	50c. HMS *Boreas* off Bahamas, 1787	1·50	1·25
1383	65c. "Death of Nelson" (A. W. Devis)	1·60	1·40
1384	70c. HMS *Victory*	2·00	2·00
1385	80c. *Achille* surrendering to HMS *Polyphemus*	2·00	2·25
1380/5	Set of 6	7·75	7·00

MS1386 120×78 mm. $1 Admiral Collingwood (brownish black, black and brownish grey) (vert); $1 HMS *Polyphemus* (vert). Wmk inverted | 8·00 | 8·50

*No. 1382/3 shows the top of the crown pointing left, but No. 1385 shows the top of the crown pointing to the right, as seen from the back of the stamp. Nos. 1380/5 were each printed in sheetlets of 6 with illustrated margins. No. 1384 contains traces of powdered wood from HMS *Victory*.

(Des A. Lowe. Litho BDT)

2005 (17 May). Abaco—Key West Connections. T **271** and similar multicoloured designs. W w **14** (sideways on 25, 65c.). P 14½×14 (vert) or 14×14½ (horiz).

1387	15c. Type **271**	45	35
1388	25c. Captain John Bartlum's House (horiz)	60	50
1389	50c. Captain John Bartlum	1·25	1·25
1390	65c. Captain Tuggy Roberts' House (horiz)	1·50	1·75
1387/90	Set of 4	3·50	3·50

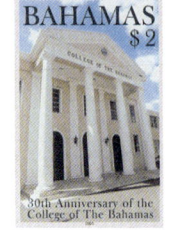

272 Flags of EU and Bahamas and Map   **273** College Entrance, Nassau

(Des D. Miller. Litho BDT)

2005 (1 June). 50th Anniv of First Europa Stamp. T **272** and similar horiz designs, all showing flags of EU and Bahamas, outline Map of Western Europe and different seascapes. Multicoloured. P 14×14½.

1391	15c. Type **272**	45	45
1392	25c. Seascape with bands of thin high cloud	65	65
1393	50c. Seascape with small island	1·25	1·40
1394	$5 Seascape with clouds	9·00	11·00
1391/4	Set of 4	10·00	12·00
MS1395	120×77 mm. Nos. 1391/4	10·00	12·00

Nos. 1391/4 were each printed in small sheets of 4.

(Des J. Batchelor. Litho BDT)

2005 (6 July). Lighthouses (2nd series). Vert designs as T **266**. Multicoloured. W w **14**. P 14.

1396	15c. Bird Rock	90	50
1397	50c. Castle Island	2·00	1·25
1398	65c. San Salvador	2·25	1·50
1399	70c. Great Inagua	2·50	2·50
1400	80c. Cay Lobos	2·75	3·00
1396/400	Set of 5	9·50	8·00

(Des A. Robinson. Litho BDT)

2005 (18 Aug). Pope John Paul II Commemoration. Vert design as T **338** of Jamaica. W w **14** (inverted). P 14½×14.

| 1401 | $1 multicoloured | 2·75 | 2·75 |

No. 1401 was printed in sheetlets of eight stamps with an enlarged illustrated right margin.

(Litho BDT)

2005 (11 Oct). 30th Anniv of the College of the Bahamas. Sheet 81×88 mm. W w **14**. P 14.

| **MS**1402 | **273** $2 multicoloured | 3·25 | 3·75 |

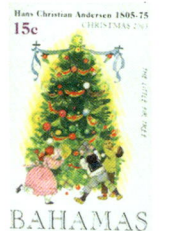

273a The Little Fir Tree   **274** Bahama Nuthatch

(Des V. Ambrus. Litho Enschedé)

2005 (8 Nov). Christmas. Birth Bicentenary of Hans Christian Andersen (writer). T **273a** and similar vert designs. Multicoloured. W w **14**. P 14.

| 1403 | 15c. Type **273a** | 30 | 20 |
| 1404 | 25c. The Princess and the Pea | 45 | 35 |

1405	50c. The Tin Soldier	90	90
1406	65c. Thumbelina	1·10	1·25
1403/6	Set of 4	2·50	2·40

(Des A. Harris. Litho BDT)

2006 (28 Mar). BirdLife International. Bahama Nuthatch (*Sitta insularis*). T **274** and similar horiz designs. Multicoloured. W w **14** (sideways). P 14.

1407	15c. Type **274**.	90	50
1408	25c. On thick branch (facing left)	1·40	70
1409	50c. On tree trunk (facing right)	2·00	1·40
1410	65c. On thin branch among pine needles	2·25	1·60
1411	70c. Nuthatch seen from underside	2·50	2·50
1412	80c. On tree trunk near hole (facing left)	2·75	3·00
1407/12	Set of 6	10·50	8·75
MS1413	170×85 mm. Nos. 1407/12	10·50	10·50

The stamps within No. **MS**1413 form a composite design showing nuthatches in Caribbean pine trees.

274a Princess Elizabeth

(Litho BDT)

2006 (21 Apr). 80th Birthday of Queen Elizabeth II. T **274a** and similar horiz designs. Multicoloured. W w **14** (sideways). P 14.

1414	15c. Type **274a**	70	35
1415	25c. Queen Elizabeth II, c. 1952	1·00	55
1416	50c. Wearing blue feathered hat	1·75	1·40
1417	65c. Wearing hat with brim raised at one side	2·00	2·00
1414/17	Set of 4	5·00	3·75
MS1418	144×75 mm. $1.50 As No. 1415; $1.50 As No. 1416	8·00	8·00

275 H. R. (Rusty) Bethel (Manager, ZNS Radio 1945–70)

(Des D. Bain. Litho BDT)

2006 (26 May). 70th Anniv of Broadcasting in the Bahamas. T **275** and similar horiz designs. Multicoloured. W w **14** (sideways). P 14.

1419	15c. Type **275**	55	30
1420	25c. New Broadcasting Corporation of the Bahamas logo	75	40
1421	50c. National Headquarters of Broadcasting Corporation of the Bahamas	1·25	1·00
1422	65c. ZNS Nassau Radio stations building	1·50	1·25
1423	70c. Radio mast and map of Bahamas	1·75	1·75
1424	80c. "ZNS Radio" (70th anniv) and microphone	1·75	2·00
1419/24	Set of 6	6·75	6·00

276 Amaryllis (*Hippeastrum puniceum*)

(Litho BDT)

2006 (3 July). Flowers of the Bahamas. Paintings by Alton Roland Lowe. T **276** and similar horiz designs. Multicoloured. W w **14** (sideways). P 14.

1425	5c. Type **276**	50	75
1426	10c. *Barleria cristata*	55	1·00
1427	25c. Desert rose (*Adenium obesum*)	40	20
1428	35c. Poor man's orchid (*Bauhinia* sp.)	55	25
1429	40c. Frangipani (*Plumeria* sp.)	1·25	65
1430	55c. Herald's trumpet (*Beaumontia grandiflora*)	1·75	1·25
1431	65c. Oleander (*Nerium oleander*)	1·90	1·25
1432	75c. Bird of Paradise (*Strelitzia reginae*)	2·00	1·50
1433	80c. *Plumbago capensis*	2·00	1·60
1434	90c. Rose (*Rosa* sp.)	2·50	2·00
1435	$1 Rubber vine (*Cryptostegia madagascariensis*)	2·75	2·25
1436	$2 Star of Bethlehem (*Jatropha integerrima*)	5·50	5·50
1437	$5 Angel's trumpet (*Brugmansia suaveolens*)	13·00	15·00
1438	$10 Wine lily (*Crinum* sp.)	24·00	26·00
1425/38	Set of 14	50·00	50·00

Nos. 1425/6 were reprinted in March 2007 with 2007 imprint date.
Nos. 1435/8 were reprinted in 2008 with 2008 imprint date.

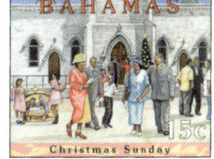

277 *Centrosema virginianum* (blue pea)

278 Christmas Sunday

(Des D. Miller. Litho Lowe-Martin, Canada)

2006 (31 Oct). Wild Flowering Vines. Paintings by Alton Roland Lowe. T **277** and similar horiz designs. Multicoloured. W w **14** (sideways). P 12½×13½.

1439	15c. Type **277**	60	35
1440	50c. *Urechites lutea* (allamanda)	1·40	1·00
1441	65c. *Ipomoea indica* (morning glory)	1·50	1·40
1442	70c. *Ipomoea microdactyla* (sky vine)	1·75	2·00
1439/42	Set of 4	4·75	4·25

(Des N. Shewring. Litho Lowe-Martin, Canada)

2006 (28 Nov). Christmas. T **278** and similar horiz designs. Multicoloured. W w **14**. P 13.

1443	15c. Type **278**	40	25
1444	25c. Christmas dinner	60	30
1445	50c. Bay Street shopping	1·00	1·00
1446	65c. Boxing Day Junkanoo	1·25	1·00
1447	70c. Watch Night service	1·40	1·60
1448	80c. New Year's Day Junkanoo	1·50	2·25
1443/8	Set of 6	5·50	5·75

279 Blainville's Beaked Whale

280 Princess Elizabeth and Lt. Philip Mountbatten, 1949

(Des J. Pointer. Litho BDT)

2007 (23 Jan). Endangered Species. Blainville's Beaked Whale (*Mesoplodon densirostris*). T **279** and similar horiz designs. Multicoloured. W w **14** (sideways, sideways inverted on 25c.). P 14.

1449	15c. Type **279**	60	40
	a. Strip of 4. Nos. 1449 and 1450w/52	3·75	4·00
1450	25c. Three whales	80	60
	w. Wmk top of letters to left	80	60
1451	50c. Whale just beneath surface	1·40	1·25
1452	60c. Two whales	1·50	1·40
1449/52	Set of 4	3·75	3·25

Nos. 1449/52 were printed together, *se-tenant*, in horizontal and vertical strips of four in sheets of 16, and also in separate sheets.
On No. 1450, the 25c. stamps from separate sheets, the sideways watermark has the tops of the letters CA pointing to the right, *as seen from the back of the stamp*. All the other stamps, from *se-tenant* sheetlets or separate sheets, have the tops of the letters CA pointing to the left, when seen from the back of the stamp.

(Litho BDT)

2007 (1 June). Diamond Wedding of Queen Elizabeth II and Prince Philip. T **280** and similar vert designs. Multicoloured. W w **14**. P 14.

1453	15c. Type **280**	50	25
1454	25c. Princess Elizabeth riding in carriage on her wedding day, 1949	75	45
1455	50c. Princess Elizabeth and Prince Philip waving from balcony on wedding day, 1949	1·40	1·25

BAHAMAS

1456	65c. Princess Elizabeth, Prince Philip and Queen Mary	1·60	1·75
1453/6 Set of 4		3·75	3·25

MS1457 125×85 mm. $5 Wedding portrait (42×56 *mm*). Wmk sideways.............. 11·00 12·00

Nos. 1453/6 were each printed in sheetlets of six stamps with enlarged illustrated margins.

281 Bahamas Scouts at Church Service

282 Scouts repairing Causeway ("Service")

(Des Andrew Robinson. Litho BDT)

2007 (9 July). Centenary of Scouting. T **281** and similar multicoloured designs. W w **14** (sideways). P 14.

1458	15c. Type **281**	70	40
1459	25c. Scout in adventure playground	90	55
1460	50c. Scout barbecue	1·50	1·25
1461	65c. Bahamas girl scouts on parade	1·75	1·75
1458/61 Set of 4		4·25	3·50

MS1462 90×65 mm. 70c. Scouts playing ball (*vert*); 80c. Lord Baden-Powell (*vert*). Wmk upright.............. 2·50 3·00

(Des Derek Miller. Litho Lowe Martin Group, Canada)

2007 (18 Sept). 20th Anniv of Governor-General's Youth Award. T **282** and similar square designs. Multicoloured. W w **14** (sideways). P 12½×12½.

1463	15c. Type **282**	30	20
1464	25c. Painting ("Skills")	45	30
1465	50c. Kayaking ("Physical Recreation")	90	90
1466	65c. Hiking ("Adventurous Journey")	1·25	1·25
1467	70c. Conch shell emblem	1·50	2·00
1463/7 Set of 5		4·00	4·25

283 Flower Decoration

284 Choir

(Litho BDT)

2007 (13 Nov). Christmas. Tree Decorations. T **283** and similar vert designs. Multicoloured. W w **14**. P 14.

1468	15c. Type **283**	25	15
1469	25c. Sea shells decoration	40	25
1470	50c. Sea shells decoration (*different*)	90	70
1471	65c. Bow and sea shells decoration	1·25	90
1472	70c. Gold woven decoration	1·40	1·50
1473	80c. "Angel" made from sea shells	1·60	1·50
1468/73 Set of 6		5·25	5·00

(Litho Lowe-Martin, Canada)

2007 (13 Dec). 300th Birth Anniv of Charles Wesley. T **284** and similar multicoloured designs. W w **14** (sideways). P 12½×13.

1474	15c. Type **284**	40	25
1475	50c. Charles and John Wesley (evangelists) (*vert*)	1·00	80
1476	65c. Revd. Charles Wesley and "Hymns and Sacred Poems" (*vert*)	1·25	1·25
1477	70c. Harbour Island Methodist Church (*horiz*)	1·50	1·75
1474/7 Set of 4		3·75	3·50

285 *Heliconius charitonius* (zebra longwing)

(Des Derek Miller. Litho BDT)

2008 (18 Feb). Bahamas Butterflies. T **285** and similar horiz designs. Multicoloured. W w **14** (sideways). P 14.

1478	15c. Type **285**	50	30
1479	25c. *Dryas julia carteri* (Julia)	70	45
1480	50c. *Phoebis sennae* (cloudless sulphur)	1·40	1·10
1481	65c. *Danaus gilippus berenice* (The Queen)	1·60	1·25
1482	70c. *Urbanus proteus* (long-tailed skipper)	1·75	2·00
1483	80c. *Dione vanillae insularis* (Gulf fritillary)	2·00	2·50
1478/83 Set of 6		7·00	7·00

MS1484 170×75 mm. Nos. 1478/83.............. 7·50 8·00

286 His Majesty's Independant Company

287 Athlete breaking Finish Tape

(Des Ross Watton. Litho BDT)

2008 (20 Mar). Military Uniforms. T **286** and similar vert designs. Multicoloured. W w **14**. P 14.

1485	15c. Type **286**	50	30
1486	25c. 47th Regiment of Foot	70	45
1487	50c. 99th Regiment of Foot	1·40	1·25
1488	65c. Royal Artillery	1·50	1·50
1489	70c. Black Garrison Companies	1·75	2·00
1485/9 Set of 5		5·25	5·00

Nos. 1485/9 were each printed in sheetlets of six stamps with enlarged illustrated margins.

(Des Richard Allen. Litho BDT)

2008 (30 Apr). Olympic Games, Beijing. T **287** and similar square designs. Multicoloured. W w **14** (sideways). P 13½.

1490	15c. Type **287**	40	25
1491	50c. High jump	1·25	1·00
1492	65c. Javelin thrower	1·50	1·50
1493	70c. Triple jump	1·75	2·00
1490/3 Set of 4		4·50	4·25

(Litho BDT)

2008 (Aug)–**2009**. As Nos. 1425/38 but W w **18** (sideways). P 14.

1494	5c. Type **276**	15	20
1495	10c. *Barleria cristata*	25	20
1495a	15c. Yesterday, today and tomorrow (*Brunfelsia solanaceae*) (2009)	30	15
1496	40c. Frangipani (*Plumeria sp.*)	95	50
1497	55c. Herald's trumpet (*Beaumontia grandiflora*)	1·40	90
1498	65c. Oleander (*Nerium oleander*)	1·60	1·00
1499	75c. Bird of Paradise (*Strelitzia reginae*)	1·75	1·10
1500	80c. *Plumbago capensis*	2·00	1·25
1501	90c. Rose (*Rosa* sp.)	2·25	1·40
1502	$1 Rubber vine (*Cryptostegia madagascariensis*)	2·40	1·50
1503	$2 Star of Bethlehem (*Jatropha integerrima*)	4·50	4·25
1504	$5 Angel's trumpet (*Brugmansia suaveolens*)	12·00	13·00
1505	$10 Wine lily (*Crinum* sp.)	22·00	24·00
1494/505 Set of 12		48·00	45·00

Imprint dates: "2008", Nos. 1494/5, 1496/505; "2009", Nos. 1494/5a.

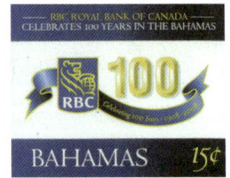

288 Centenary Emblem

(Des Trevaugh Neely. Litho Lowe-Martin)

2008 (22 Sept). Centenary of the Royal Bank of Canada in the Bahamas. T **288** and similar horiz designs. Multicoloured. W w **18** (sideways). P 12½×13.

1506	15c. Type **288**	50	30
1507	25c. Regional Head Office	65	45
1508	50c. Main Branch, Bay Street, Nassau, early 1900s	1·40	1·00

1509	65c.	Artist's rendering of new Carmichael Road Branch, Nassau	1·60	1·75
1510	70c.	Ross McDonald, Head of Caribbean Banking, and Nathaniel Beneby Jr., Vice President and Country Head	1·75	2·25
1506/10 Set of 5			5·50	5·25

289 Launch of Space Shuttle Discovery in STS-26 "Return to Flight" Mission

290 The Three Kings worshipping Jesus

(Litho Enschedé)

2008 (1 Oct). 50th Anniv of NASA. T **289** and similar horiz designs. Multicoloured. W w **14** (sideways). P 13½.

1511	15c.	Type **289**	50	30
1512	25c.	Apollo 16 Command and Service Module over the Moon, 1972	70	45
1513	50c.	*Skylab 3*, 1973	1·40	1·00
1514	65c.	Hubble Space Telescope	1·60	1·50
1515	70c.	Gasses in the Swan Nebula	1·75	1·90
1516	80c.	Star forming region in the Carina Nebula	2·00	2·25
1511/16 Set of 6			7·25	6·75

(Litho Lowe-Martin)

2008 (11 Nov). Christmas. Book Illustrations by Leonhard Diefenbach from "The First Christmas for Our Dear Little Ones" by Rosa Mulholland. T **290** and similar horiz designs. Multicoloured. W w **18** (sideways). P 12½×13.

1517	15c.	Type **290**	45	15
1518	50c.	The Three Kings at the court of King Herod	1·25	80
1519	65c.	Shepherds telling the news of the birth of Jesus	1·60	1·50
1520	70c.	The shepherds visit the Baby Jesus	1·75	2·00
1517/20 Set of 4			4·50	4·00

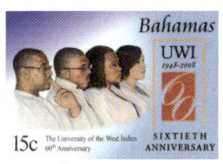

291 Students

(Des Derek Miller. Litho Lowe-Martin)

2008 (25 Nov). 60th Anniv of the University of the West Indies. T **291** and similar horiz designs. Multicoloured. W w **18** (sideways). P 12½×13.

1521	15c.	Type **291**	30	20
1522	25c.	Plaque marking Bahamas Clinical Training Programme becoming part of University of the West Indies, 2007	50	40
1523	65c.	Scroll	1·60	1·75
1521/3 Set of 3			2·25	2·10

292 Battle of Lexington, 1775

(Litho Lowe-Martin)

2008 (9 Dec). 225th Anniv of the Treaty of Paris (recognising US Independence). T **292** and similar horiz designs. Multicoloured. W w **18** (sideways). P 12½×13.

1524	15c.	Type **292**	60	40
1525	50c.	Washington crossing the Delaware, 1776	1·50	1·25
1526	65c.	American signatories of Treaty of Paris, 1783 (Benjamin West)	1·75	1·75
1527	70c.	Detail of Treaty of Paris showing signatures	2·00	2·25
1524/7 Set of 4			5·25	5·00

293 Bahamas Oriole (*Icterus northropi*)

294 Peony

(Des Nick Shewring. Litho Enschedé)

2009 (6 Jan). Endangered Species–Resident Breeders. T **293** and similar vert designs. Multicoloured. W w **14**. P 13½.

1528	15c.	Type **293**	75	40
1529	50c.	Rose throated parrot (*Amazona leucocephala bahamensis*)	1·75	1·25
1530	65c.	Great lizard cuckoo (*Saurothera merlini bahamensis*)	2·00	1·75
1531	70c.	Audubon's shearwater (*Puffinus lherminieri*)	2·25	2·25
1528/31 Set of 4			6·00	5·00

2009 (10 Apr). China 2009 World Stamp Exhibition and Peony Festival, Luoyang. Sheet 180×110 mm. Multicoloured; colours of right-hand borders given. Litho. P 13.

MS1532 Type **294**×8 (colours of right-hand borders cream, white, pale pink, pale blue, pale flesh, pale green, pale yellow and pale azure) .... 9·00 10·00

295 "Tripod"

(Des Alton Roland Lowe. Litho Lowe-Martin)

2009 (1 May). Potcake Dogs. T **295** and similar horiz designs. Multicoloured. W w **18** (sideways). P 12½×13.

1533	15c.	Type **295**	70	40
1534	50c.	"Amigo"	1·75	1·25
1535	65c.	"Turtle"	2·00	1·75
1536	70c.	"Oreo"	2·25	2·50
1533/6 Set of 4			6·00	5·50

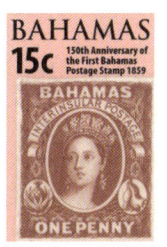

296 Bahamas 1859 1d. Stamp

296a Hawker Sea Hurricane

(Litho Lowe-Martin Group, Canada)

2009 (26 May). 150th Anniv of the First Bahamas Stamp. T **296** and similar vert designs. Multicoloured, background colour given. W w **18**. P 13.

1537	**296**	15c. pink	70	70
		a. Block of 4. Nos. 1537/40	2·50	2·50
1538		15c. azure	70	70
1539		15c. dull green	70	70
1540		15c. dull reddish lilac	70	70
1537/40 Set of 4			2·50	2·50
MS1541 130×100 mm. Nos. 1537/40			2·50	2·50

Nos. 1537/40 were printed together, *se-tenant*, as blocks of four stamps in sheets of 40.

(Des Tim O'Brien. Litho BDT)

2009 (16 June). Centenary of Naval Aviation. T **296a** and similar horiz designs. Multicoloured. W w **18** (sideways). P 14.

1542	15c.	Type **296a**	65	40
1543	65c.	Hawker Sea Fury	2·00	1·75
1544	70c.	Fairey Gannet	2·25	2·25

BAHAMAS

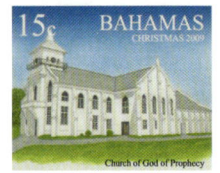

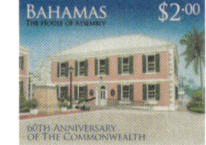

1545	80c. De Havilland Sea Vampire		2·50	2·75
1542/5 *Set of 4*			6·75	6·25

MS1546 110×70 mm. $2 Aircraft on deck of merchant aircraft carrier MV *Empire MacKendrick* .... 6·50 6·50

Nos. 1542/5 were each printed in sheetlets of eight stamps with a central label and enlarged illustrated bottom margins.

297 East Street Tabernacle of Church of God of Prophecy

298 The House of Assembly

(Des Derek Miller. Litho BDT)

2009 (18 Nov). Christmas. Churches. T **297** and similar horiz designs. Multicoloured. W w **18** (sideways). P 13½.

1547	15c. Type **297**	35	15
1548	25c. The Mission Baptist Church	50	30
1549	50c. Grant's Town Seventh-Day Adventist Church	95	65
1550	65c. Wesley Methodist Church, Harbour Island	1·50	1·40
1551	70c. St. Francis Xavier Cathedral	1·60	1·75
1552	80c. St. Ambrose Anglican Church	1·75	2·25
1547/52 *Set of 6*		6·00	6·00

(Des Derek Miller. Litho BDT)

2009 (24 Nov). 60th Anniv of the Commonwealth. Sheet 120×85 mm. W w **18** (sideways). P 13½.

MS1553 **298** $2 multicoloured .... 4·50 5·00

299 Dolphin and Whale

300 Winston Churchill

(Des Tito Baldwin. Litho Lowe-Martin Group)

2010 (3 Mar). Friends of the Environment. T **299** and similar horiz designs. Multicoloured. W w **18** (sideways). P 13.

1554	15c. Type **299**	35	15
1555	50c. Parrot and island map	1·00	75
1556	65c. Lizard and turtle	1·50	1·25
1557	70c. Bird and tree	1·60	2·00
1554/7 *Set of 4*		4·00	3·75

(Litho)

2010 (18 June). 70th Anniv of the Battle of Britain. T **300** and similar vert designs showing different portraits of Churchill and quotations from his speeches. Multicoloured. W w **18** (inverted on **MS**1563a). P 13.

1558	15c. Type **300** ("...we shall never surrender...")	55	25
1559	25c. ...the Battle of Britain is about to begin..	75	35
1560	50c. "...never in the field of human conflict was so much owed by so many to so few..."	1·25	90
1561	65c. ...this was their finest hour	1·75	1·50
1562	70c. ...upon this battle depends the survival of Christian civilization	2·00	2·25
1563	80c. ...we shall fight on the beaches	2·25	2·75
1558/63 *Set of 6*		7·75	7·25

MS1563*a* 110×70 mm. $2 Sir Douglas Bader .... 6·50 6·50

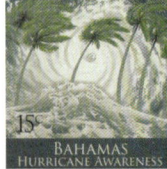

301 Palm Trees in High Wind

302 Cruise Ship and Fireworks

(Litho Lowe-Martin)

2010 (28 Sept). Hurricane Awareness. T **301** and similar square designs. Multicoloured. W w **18** (sideways). P 12½×13.

1564	15c. Type **301**	80	40
1565	50c. Map tracking hurricane across Bahamas	1·60	1·40
1566	65c. Reconnaissance aircraft flying through storm to measure intensity	2·25	2·25
1567	70c. Hurricane and NEMA (National Emergency Management Agency) logo	2·75	3·00
1564/7 *Set of 4*		6·75	6·25

(Des Andrew Robinson. Litho B.D.T)

2010 (10 Nov). Christmas. 'Tourist Winter Escapes'. T **302** and similar horiz designs. Multicoloured. P 14.

1568	15c. Type **302**	75	40
1569	50c. Atlantis Hotel, Paradise Island and fireworks	1·75	1·25
1570	65c. Aircraft tailfin and fireworks	2·25	1·75
1571	70c. Fort Fincastle and Water Tower and fireworks	2·75	2·25
1568/71 *Set of 4*		6·75	6·00

303 The Annual Heart Ball

(Des Andrew Robinson. Litho BDT)

2011 (12 Feb). 50th Anniv of the Sir Victor Sassoon Heart Foundation. T **303** and similar horiz designs. Multicoloured. P 14.

1572	15c. Type **303**	75	55
1573	50c. Doctor with young child	1·75	1·50
1574	65c. Doctor and young girl	2·25	2·25
1575	70c. Sir Victor Sassoon	2·75	3·00
1572/5 *Set of 4*		6·75	6·50

303a Queen Elizabeth II, Balmoral 6 February 1982

(Litho BDT)

2011 (23 Mar). Queen Elizabeth II and Prince Philip. 'A Lifetime of Service'. T **303a** and similar diamond-shaped designs. Multicoloured. P 13½.

1576	15c. Type **303a**	75	50
1577	50c. Queen Elizabeth II and Prince Philip, Windsor Castle, June 1959	1·75	1·40
1578	65c. Queen Elizabeth II and Prince Philip, Thames Valley University, London, 20 February 2009	2·25	1·90
1579	70c. Queen Elizabeth II and Prince Philip, Westminster Abbey, 8 March 2010	2·50	2·50
1580	$1 Queen Elizabeth II and Prince Philip, Buckingham Palace, 19 July 1957	4·00	4·25
1581	$2 Prince Philip, Balmoral, 6 February 1982	6·50	7·00
1576/81 *Set of 6*		16·00	16·00

MS1582 175×164 mm. Nos. 1576/81 and three stamp-size labels .... 16·00 16·00

MS1583 110×70 mm. $2.50 Queen Elizabeth II and Prince Philip, Sandringham House, Norfolk, 1992 .... 8·00 8·00

Nos. 1576/81 were printed in separate sheetlets of eight stamps.

No. **MS**1583 forms a diamond shape but with the left, right and top corners removed.

304 Prince William and Miss Catherine Middleton at Friend's Wedding, Austria, September 2008

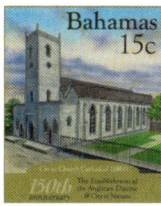

305 Christ Church Cathedral

(Des Andrew Robinson. Litho BDT)

2011 (21 June). Royal Wedding. T **304** and similar multicoloured designs. P 15×14 (**MS**1587) or 14 (others).
1584	15c. Type **304**...	60	25
1585	50c. Engagement photograph, St. James's Palace, London, November 2010..................	1·75	1·50
1586	65c. Kissing on Buckingham Palace balcony after wedding..	2·25	2·50
1584/6 Set of 3...		4·25	3·75
MS1587 94×64 mm. $5 Wedding in Westminster Abbey (vert)..		16·00	16·00

(Des Robin Carter. Litho Lowe-Martin)

2011 (12 Sept). 150th Anniv of the Anglican Diocese and City of Nassau. T **305** and similar vert designs. Multicoloured. P 12½×13.
1588	15c. Type **305**...	75	50
1589	50c. Rawson Square, 1861............................	1·75	1·40
1590	65c. Government House, 1861.....................	2·25	1·90
1591	70c. Bay Street, 1861...................................	2·50	2·50
1592	$1 Dr. Charles Caulfield (first Bishop of Nassau), 1862..	4·00	4·00
1593	$2 Royal Governor Charles Bayley, 1857–64	6·50	7·50
1588/93 Set of 6..		16·00	16·00

306 Angel Gabriel appearing to Mary

307 Common Sea Fan (*Gorgonia ventalina*)

(Des Victor Ambrus. Litho Cartor)

2011 (17 Nov). Christmas. Angels. T **306** and similar vert designs. Multicoloured. P 13½.
1594	15c. Type **306**..	75	30
1595	25c. Angel watching over Mary and Joseph on journey to Bethlehem............................	1·10	35
1596	50c. Angel guiding Wise Men.........................	1·75	1·25
1597	65c. Angel watching over Infant Jesus in manger...	2·25	2·00
1598	70c. Angel appearing to Shepherds.................	2·50	2·75
1599	80c. Angel watching over Mary and Infant Jesus...	2·75	3·25
1594/9 Set of 6...		10·00	9·00

(Des Andrew Robinson. Litho Cartor)

2012 (3 Jan). Marine Life. T **307** and similar horiz designs. Multicoloured. P 13½.
1600	5c. Type **307**..	25	25
1601	10c. Christmas tree worm (*Spirobranchus giganteus*)..	35	35
1602	15c. Elkhorn coral (*Acropora palmata*)............	65	35
1603	20c. Cushion sea star (*Oreaster reticulatus*).....	75	40
1604	25c. Queen conch (*Strombus gigas*)...............	90	40
1605	30c. Hawksbill turtle (*Eretmochelys imbricata*)	1·00	55
1606	40c. Green moray eel (*Gymnothorax funebris*)	1·25	65
1607	50c. Bonefish (*Albula vulpes*)...........................	1·50	80
1608	60c. Spider crab (*Mithrax spinosissimus*).......	1·75	1·10
1609	65c. Spiny lobster (*Panulirus argus*)................	1·90	1·10
1610	70c. Nassau grouper (*Epinephelus striatus*)....	2·25	1·25
1611	80c. Yellowtail snapper (*Ocyurus chrysurus*)...	2·75	2·50
1612	$1 Great barracuda (*Sphyraena barracuda*)..	3·75	3·25
1613	$2 Spotted eagle ray (*Aetobatus narinari*)....	6·50	6·00
1614	$5 Caribbean reef shark (*Carcharhinus perezi*)	14·00	15·00
1615	$10 Bottlenose dolphin (*Tursiops truncatus*) .	26·00	28·00
1600/15 Set of 16...		55·00	55·00

308 Caribbean Flamingo

309 Boxer and Houses of Parliament

(Des Owen Bell. Litho BDT)

2012 (21 Mar). Endangered Species. Caribbean Flamingo (*Phoenicopterus ruber*). T **308** and similar vert designs. Multicoloured. P 14.
1616	15c. Type **308**..	75	30
	a. Without white border..........................	75	60
	b. Strip of 4. Nos. 1616a/19a.................	7·25	7·25
1617	50c. Chick and egg...	1·75	1·25
	a. Without white border..........................	1·75	1·50
1618	65c. Two flamingos feeding............................	2·50	2·25
	a. Without white border..........................	2·50	2·50
1619	70c. Three flamingos in foreground................	3·00	3·25
	a. Without white border..........................	3·00	3·50
1616/19 Set of 4...		7·25	6·25
MS1620 90×70 mm. $5 Flamingos on beach..............		16·00	16·00

Nos. 1616/19 have white borders to the designs and were printed in separate sheets of ten stamps.

Nos. 1616a/19a have no white borders to the designs which extend to the perforations. They were printed together, *se-tenant*, as horizontal and vertical strips of five stamps in sheetlets of 16.

(Des Andrew Robinson. Litho Cartor)

2012 (26 June). Olympic Games, London. Olympic Sports and London Landmarks. T **309** and similar vert designs. Multicoloured. P 13½×13.
1621	15c. Type **309**..	75	30
1622	50c. High jump and Nelson's Column	1·75	1·25
1623	65c. Swimmer at start and Tower Bridge	2·25	2·00
1624	70c. Running athlete and Main Olympic Stadium..	2·50	2·75
1621/4 Set of 4...		6·50	5·75

310 Prince Harry at Thanksgiving Service, Christ Church Cathedral, Nassau

311 Mary Ingraham

(Des Andrew Robinson. Litho BDT)

2012 (16 Aug). Diamond Jubilee and Visit of Prince Harry, March 2012. T **310** and similar vert designs. Multicoloured. P 14.
1625	15c. Type **310**..	75	30
1626	50c. Prince Harry visiting Harbour Island, Eleuthera...	1·75	1·25
1627	65c. Prince Harry at Youth Rally, Thomas A. Robinson National Stadium, Nassau..	2·25	2·00
1628	70c. Queen Elizabeth II..................................	2·50	2·75
1625/8 Set of 4...		6·50	5·75

(Des Andrew Robinson. Litho BDT)

2012 (10 Oct). 50th Anniv of Women's Suffrage. Campaigners for Women's Suffrage. T **311** and similar vert designs. Multicoloured. P 14.
1629	15c. Type **311**..	75	30
1630	25c. Georgianna Symonette............................	1·10	65
1631	50c. Mabel Walker...	1·75	1·25
1632	65c. Eugenia Lockhart	2·25	2·00
1633	70c. Dame Alberta Isaacs...............................	2·50	2·75
1634	80c. Dr. Doris Johnson...................................	2·75	3·25
1629/34 Set of 6...		10·00	9·00

BAHAMAS

312 The Annunciation    **313** Queen Victoria

(Des Andrew Robinson. Litho BDT)

2012 (1 Nov). Christmas. T **312** and similar square designs. Multicoloured. P 13.

1635	15c. Type **312**	65	55
1636	25c. Joseph and Mary find no room at the inn in Bethlehem	80	65
1637	50c. The Nativity	1·50	1·25
1638	65c. An Angel appears to the Shepherds	2·10	1·90
1639	70c. Three Wise Men carrying gifts of gold, frankincense and myrrh	2·50	2·75
1640	80c. Flight into Egypt	2·75	3·25
1635/40 Set of 6		9·25	9·25

(Litho BDT)

2013 (6 Feb). 60th Anniv of Coronation. 'A Celebration of Coronation Commemoratives'. T **313** and similar multicoloured designs. P 14 (1641/5) or 15×14 (**MS**1646).

1641	65c. Type **313**	2·10	1·90
1642	70c. Coronation of King Edward VII and Queen Alexandra, 1902	2·50	2·25
1643	80c. King George V and Queen Mary	2·75	2·50
1644	$1 King George VI and Queen Elizabeth's tour of Canada and USA, 1939 (souvenir)	3·00	3·00
1645	$2 Crown, shamrock, thistle, daffodil, poppy and Union flag (souvenir of Coronation of Queen Elizabeth II)	6·00	7·00
1641/5 Set of 5		15·00	15·00
MS1646 110×70 mm. $3 Queen Elizabeth II, c. 1953 (32×48 mm)		8·00	7·50

Nos. 1641/5 were printed in separate sheets of eight stamps and a central stamp-size label, all with enlarged illustrated margins.

314 Sir William Murphy (Governor of the Bahamas) presenting Colonial Police Medal for Gallantry to Constable Fred Neville Seymour, 10 June 1948

(Litho BDT)

2013 (15 May). 120th Anniv of Royal Bahamas Police Force Band. T **314** and similar horiz designs. Multicoloured. P 14.

1647	15c. Type **314**	65	55
1648	25c. Royal Bahamas Police Force Band performing as Queen Elizabeth II boards Royal Yacht *Britannia*, 1975	75	65
1649	50c. Royal Bahamas Police Force Band performing	1·50	1·25
1650	65c. Royal Bahamas Police Force Band and Atlantis Resort	2·10	1·90
1651	70c. Close-up of drum being played	2·50	2·25
1652	80c. Royal Bahamas Police Force Band marching down road	2·75	2·50
1647/52 Set of 6		9·50	8·50

315 Constitutional Conference, 1972

(Litho BDT)

2013 (8 July). 40th Anniv of Independence. T **315** and similar horiz designs. Multicoloured. P 14.

1653	15c. Type **315**	65	55
1654	25c. Sir Milo Butler, first Governor General	75	65
1655	50c. Arms and Sir Lynden Pindling, first Prime Minister	1·50	1·25
1656	65c. Fenrick Sturrup, David Tucker, Edward Williams, Austin Smith and patrol vessel HMBS *Flamingo*	2·10	1·90
1657	70c. Rhodes scholars Christian Campbell, Desiree Cox and Myron Rolle	2·50	2·25
1653/7 Set of 5		7·00	6·00

STAMP BOOKLETS

1938. Black on pink cover with map and "BAHAMAS ISLES OF JUNE" on reverse. Stapled.

SB1	2s. booklet containing twelve 1d. (No. 150) in blocks of 6 and eight 1½d. (No. 151) in folded block of 8	£11000

1961. (15 Aug). Brown-purple cover (3s.) or green cover (6s.) Stitched.

SB2	3s. booklet containing eight each of 1d., 1½d. and 2d. (Nos. 202/4) in blocks of 4	28·00
SB3	6s. booklet containing four of each of 4d., 6d. and 8d. (Nos. 206, 208/9) in blocks of 4	35·00

1965. (23 Mar). Pink cover (3s.) or green cover (6s.).

SB4	3s. booklet containing eight each of 1d., 1½d. and 2d. (Nos. 248/50) in blocks of 4	19·00
SB5	6s. booklet containing four each of 4d., 6d. and 8d. (Nos. 252/4) in blocks of 4	19·00

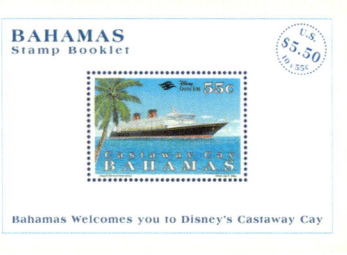

B **1**

1998 (1 Aug). Disney Cruise Line's Castaway Cay Holiday Development. Folded card cover, 100×67 mm, as Type B **1**. Pane attached by selvedge.

SB6	$5.50 booklet containing pane No. 1146b	18·00

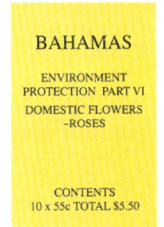

B **2** (*Illustration reduced. Actual size* 137×70 *mm*)

1998 (8 Sept). Environment Protection (6th issue). Roses. Folded card cover as Type B **2**. Pane attached by selvedge.

SB7	$5.50 booklet containing pane No. 1149a	12·00

SPECIAL DELIVERY STAMPS

SPECIAL DELIVERY

(S **1**)

1916 (1 May). No. 59 optd with Type S **1** by The Nassau Guardian.

S1	**6**	5d. black and orange	7·00	42·00
		a. Opt double	£800	£1200
		b. Opt double, one inverted	£950	£1300
		c. Opt inverted	£1300	£1400
		d. Pair, one without opt	£27000	£35000
		x. Wmk reversed	£750	

No. S1 was issued as a result of a reciprocal arrangement between the Bahamas and Canadian Post Offices, whereby the application of a special delivery stamp from the country of destination would ensure special treatment on arrival. Canadian special delivery stamps were supplied to the Bahamas Post Office, but, there being no equivalent in Bahamas, the current 5d. definitive was overprinted "SPECIAL DELIVERY" and sent to Canada.

There were three printings from similar settings of 30 (6×5), and each sheet had to pass through the press twice. The first printing of 600 was on sale from March 1916 at four post offices in Canada; Ottawa, Toronto, Westmount (Montreal) and Winnipeg; and was used in combination with Canadian stamps and cancelled in Canada. Towards the end of 1916, however, the Canadian authorities decided to leave the Bahamas stamps to be cancelled on arrival in Nassau.

The second printing of 6000 was released in February 1917 and the third, estimated to be 1200 to 1800, in March the same year. They were both on sale only in the Bahamas. In August 1917 the Canadian Post Office became aware of the later printings and ordered all remaining stocks at the four offices in Canada to be sold off, bringing the facility to an end.

It is not possible to identify the three printings with certainty without plating both the basic stamp and the overprint. The first printing was applied to stamps from vignette plate 1 only, while the second and third were applied to stamps from both plate 1 and plate 2. In general, the word "SPECIAL" is further to the right in relation to "DELIVERY" in the second printing than the first or third, but this alone should not be considered conclusive.

Our prices for No. S1 are for the second printing and any stamps which can be positively identified as being from the first or third would be worth about ten times (first) or four times (third) as much, either unused or used. Examples on cover, posted at one of the four eligible Canadian offices and with the special delivery stamp cancelled in Canada, are very scarce.

All the errors appear to be from the second printing.

SPECIAL DELIVERY	SPECIAL DELIVERY
(S 2)	(S 3)

1917 (2 July). As No. 59, but Wmk Mult Crown CA. Optd with Type S 2 by D.L.R.
S2   6   5d. black and orange 60   10·00
             s. Optd "SPECIMEN"............................. 70·00

1918. No. 78 optd with Type S 3 by D.L.R.
S3   6   5d. black and mauve (R.) 40   4·00
             s. Optd "SPECIMEN"............................. 70·00

Nos. S2/3 were only on sale in the Bahamas.

Bermuda

The first internal postal system for Bermuda was organised by Joseph Stockdale, the proprietor of the *Bermuda Gazette*, in January 1784. This service competed with that of the colonial post office, set up in May 1812, until 1818.

Control of the overseas postal services passed to the British G.P.O. in 1818. The internal delivery system was discontinued between 1821 and 1830. The overseas posts became a colonial responsibility in September 1859.

CROWNED-CIRCLE HANDSTAMPS

CC1	CC **1**	ST. GEORGES BERMUDA (R.) (1.8.1845)	
		Price on cover	£8500
CC2		IRELAND ISLE BERMUDA (R.) (1.8.1845)	
		Price on cover	£7500
CC3		HAMILTON BERMUDA (R.) (13.11.1846)	
		Price on cover	£4000

For Nos. CC1 and CC3 used as adhesive Postmasters' Stamps see Nos. O7 and O6.

PRICES FOR STAMPS ON COVER TO 1945

Nos.	
Nos. 1/11	from × 5
Nos. 12/17	from × 10
Nos. 19/29a	from × 8
Nos. 30/a	from × 10
Nos. 31/4	from × 4
Nos. 34/55	from × 3
Nos. 56/8	from × 10
Nos. 59/76	from × 4
Nos. 76a/93	from × 3
Nos. 94/7	from × 4
Nos. 98/106	from × 3
Nos. 107/15	from × 4
Nos. 116/21	from × 5
No. 122	from × 20

COLONY

1848–61. Postmasters' Stamps. Adhesives prepared and issued by the postmasters at Hamilton and St. Georges. Dated as given in brackets.

(a) By W. B. Perot at Hamilton

O1	O **1**	1d. black/*bluish grey* (1848)	—	£170000
O2		1d. black/*bluish grey* (1849)	—	£200000
O3		1d. red/*thick white* (1853)	—	£150000
O4		1d. red/*bluish wove* (1854)	—	£375000
O5		1d. red/*bluish wove* (1856)	—	£225000
O6	O **2**	(1d.) carmine-red/*bluish laid* (1861)	£130000	£95000

*(b) By J. H. Thies at St. Georges. As Type O **2** but inscr "ST. GEORGES"*

O7	—	(1d.) carmine-red/*buff* (1860)	†	£85000

Stamps of Type O **1** bear manuscript value and signature, the dates being those shown on the eleven known examples. The stamps are distributed between the dates as follows: 1848 three examples, 1849 two examples, 1853 three examples, 1854 two examples, 1856 one example.

It is believed that the franking value of Nos. O6/7 was 1d., although this is not shown on the actual stamps. Four examples are known of this type used from Hamilton, from March 1861 (and one unused), and five used from St. Georges between July 1860 and January 1863, both issues being cancelled by pen.

Prices shown reflect our estimation of value based on known copies. For instance of the two copies known of No. O4, one is in the Royal collection and the other is on entire.

It is possible that a fourth postmaster's provisional was used by Robert Ward at Hamilton in late 1862 when two examples of Type O **2** on laid paper are known cancelled by blue crayon.

(Typo D.L.R.)

1865–1903. Wmk Crown CC.

(a) P 14

1	**1**	1d. rose-red (25.9.65)	£100	1·25
		a. Imperf	£50000	£27000
		w. Wmk inverted	£500	£190
2		1d. pale rose	£140	7·50
		w. Wmk inverted	£550	£250
3	**2**	2d. dull blue (14.3.66)	£450	32·00
		w. Wmk inverted	£1500	£600
4		2d. bright blue (1877)	£475	21·00
		w. Wmk inverted	£1500	£600
5	**3**	3d. yellow-buff (10.3.73)	£475	65·00
		aw. Wmk inverted	£1300	£300
		ax. Wmk reversed	£2000	£1000
5b		3d. orange (1875)	£2000	£160
6	**4**	6d. dull purple (25.9.65)	£1000	75·00
		w. Wmk inverted	—	£1400
7		6d. dull mauve (2.7.74)	23·00	12·00
		w. Wmk inverted	£160	£225
8	**5**	1s. green (25.9.65)	£350	70·00
		w. Wmk inverted	£900	£350

(b) P 14×12½

10	**3**	3d. yellow-buff (12.81)	£180	60·00
10a	**4**	6d. bright mauve (1903)	16·00	22·00
		w. Wmk inverted	£1200	£1300
11	**5**	1s. green (11.93)	16·00	£120
		a. Imperf between (vert strip of 3)	£12000	
		w. Wmk inverted	£1100	

No. 11a occurs from Rows 8, 9, and 10 of four panes, possibly from a single sheet. Some of the stamps have become partially separated. One *used* vertical pair is known (*Price* £12000).

Although they arrived in Bermuda in March 1880, stamps perforated 14×12½ were not issued until the dates given above.

1874 (12 Mar–19 May). Nos. 1 and 8 surch diagonally.

*(a) With T **6** ("P" and "R" different type)*

12	**1**	3d. on 1d. rose-red	£18000	
13	**5**	3d. on 1s. green	£2500	£850

*(b) With T **6a** ("P" same type as "R")*

13b	**5**	3d. on 1s. green	£2000	£800

*(c) With T **7** (19 May)*

14	**5**	3d. on 1s. green	£1500	£650

The 3d. on 1d. was a trial surcharge which was not regularly issued, though a few examples were postally used before 1879. Nos. 13, 13b and 14, being handstamped, are found with double or partial double surcharges.

(Surch by Queens Printer, Donald McPhee Lee)

1875 (March–May). Surch with T **8**.

15	**2**	1d. on 2d. (No. 3) (23 Apr)	£700	£375
		a. No stop after "Penny"	£25000	£13000
16	**3**	1d. on 3d. (No. 5) (8 May)	£450	£350
17	**5**	1d. on 1s. (No. 8) (11 Mar)	£500	£250
		a. Surch inverted	—	£50000
		b. No stop after "Penny"	£40000	£18000

It is emphasised that the prices quoted for Nos. 12/17 are for fine examples. The many stamps from these provisional issues which are in inferior condition are worth much less.

BERMUDA

(Typo D.L.R.)

1880 (25 Mar). Wmk Crown CC. P 14.

19	9	½d. stone	7·50	4·75
		w. Wmk inverted	£110	£200
		y. Wmk inverted and reversed	£2000	
20	10	4d. orange-red	18·00	1·75
		w. Wmk inverted	—	£1500
		x. Wmk reversed		

(Typo D.L.R.)

1883–1904. Wmk Crown CA. P 14.

21	9	½d. dull green (10.92)	7·50	4·50
21a		½d. deep grey-green (1893)	4·50	80
22	1	1d. dull rose (12.83)	£170	4·75
		w. Wmk inverted	£650	£375
23		1d. rose-red	90·00	3·25
		w. Wmk inverted	—	£375
24		1d. carmine-rose (3.86)	60·00	1·00
		w. Wmk inverted	—	£375
24a		1d. aniline carmine (1889)	17·00	20
		aw. Wmk inverted	£400	£190
25	2	2d. blue (12.86)	70·00	7·00
		x. Wmk reversed	†	£1100
26		2d. aniline purple (7.93)	16·00	5·00
26a		2d. brown purple (1898)	4·75	2·00
27	11	2½d. deep ultramarine (10.11.84)	24·00	3·75
		aw. Wmk inverted	£800	£275
27b		2½d. pale ultramarine	16·00	40
		bw. Wmk inverted	—	£225
28	3	3d. grey (20.1.86)	23·00	9·50
28a	10	4d. orange-brown (18.1.04)	35·00	60·00
		ax. Wmk reversed	£500	£700
29	5	1s. yellow-brown (1893)	22·00	21·00
		ax. Wmk reversed	£1600	£1000
29b		1s. olive-brown	14·00	21·00
		bx. Wmk reversed	£1600	£1100
21/9b Set of 8			£170	90·00
21s, 26s & 29s Optd "SPECIMEN" Set of 3			£375	

1893 PROVISIONAL POSTCARD. Following the reduction of the overseas postcard rate to 1d. in 1893 existing stocks of postal stationery postcards, including some from the September 1880 issue franked with Nos. 19 and 22, were surcharged "One Penny". This surcharge was applied by the *Royal Gazette* press. It is generally believed that an individual in the Post Office acquired all the examples showing Nos. 19 and 22, but provisional postcards are known used to Europe or locally. *Price from* £600 *unused,* £1600 *used*.

ONE FARTHING
(12)   13 Dry Dock    14

1901. As Nos. 29/a but colour changed, surch with T **12** by D.L.R.

30	5	¼d. on 1s. dull grey (11.1.01)	5·00	75
		as. Optd "SPECIMEN"	80·00	
30b		¼d. on 1s. bluish grey (18.3.01)	5·50	1·25
		ba. "F" in "FARTHING" inserted by handstamp	£7500	£9000

Nine examples of No. 30ba are known, seven unused (one being in the Royal Collection) and two used (one on postcard). It would appear that the "F" in position one of an unspecified horizontal row was damaged and an additional impression of the letter was then inserted by a separate handstamp.

(Typo D.L.R.)

1902 (Nov)–**03**. Wmk Crown CA. P 14.

31	13	½d. black and green (12.03)	13·00	3·75
32		1d. brown and carmine	8·00	10
33		3d. magenta and sage-green (9.03)	5·00	2·25
31/3 Set of 3			23·00	5·50
31s/3s Optd "SPECIMEN" Set of 3			£150	

1906–10. Wmk Mult Crown CA. P 14.

34	13	¼d. brown and violet (9.08)	1·75	1·50
35		½d. black and green (12.06)	19·00	65
36		½d. green (3.09)	21·00	4·25
37		1d. brown and carmine (4.06)	38·00	20
		w. Wmk inverted	£650	£350
38		1d. red (5.08)	22·00	10
39		2d. grey and orange (10.07)	7·50	10·00
40		2½d. brown and ultramarine (12.06)	28·00	7·00
41		2½d. blue (14.2.10)	24·00	9·50
42		4d. blue and chocolate (11.09)	3·00	16·00
34/42 Set of 9			£150	45·00
34s, 36s, 38s/42s Optd "SPECIMEN" Set of 7			£400	

(Recess D.L.R.)

1910–25. Wmk Mult Crown CA. P 14.

44	14	¼d. brown (26.3.12)	1·75	2·50
		a. Pale brown	2·00	1·50
45		½d. green (4.6.10)	3·25	25
		a. Deep green (1918)	15·00	1·25
		x. Wmk reversed	£700	£500
46		1d. red (I) (15.10.10)	20·00	30
		a. Rose-red (1916)	26·00	30
		b. Carmine (12.19)	60·00	8·00
		w. Wmk inverted	£700	£500
		x. Wmk reversed	£1000	£750
		y. Wmk inverted and reversed	£750	£750
47		2d. grey (1.13)	5·00	19·00
48		2½d. blue (27.3.12)	3·50	60
		w. Wmk inverted	£550	£550
		x. Wmk reversed	—	£550
		y. Wmk inverted and reversed	£425	£325
49		3d. purple/*yellow* (1.13)	3·00	6·00
49a		4d. red/*yellow* (1.9.19)	14·00	15·00
50		6d. purple (26.3.12)	19·00	20·00
		a. Pale claret (2.6.24)	11·00	8·50
51		1s. black/*green* (26.3.12)	6·00	4·50
		a. Jet black/*olive* (1925)	5·50	21·00
		ax. Wmk reversed	£1600	
44/51 Set of 9			60·00	50·00
44s/51s Optd "SPECIMEN" Set of 9			£450	

Nos. 44 to 51a are comb-perforated 13.8×14 or 14. No. 45 exists also line-perforated 14 probably from the printing dispatched to Bermuda on 13 March 1911.

See also Nos. 77/87a.

15

HIGH VALUE KEY TYPES. The reign of King Edward VII saw the appearance of the first in a new series of "key type" designs, initially for Nyasaland, to be used for high value denominations where a smaller design was felt to be inappropriate. The system was extended during the reign of King George V, using the portrait as Bermuda Type **15**, to cover Bermuda, Ceylon, Leeward Islands, Malaya — Straits Settlements, Malta and Nyasaland. A number of these territories continued to use the key type concept for high value King George VI stamps and one, Leeward Islands, for stamps of Queen Elizabeth II.

In each instance the King George V issues were printed in sheets of 60 (12×5) on various coloured papers. The system utilised a common "head" plate used with individual "duty" plates which printed the territory name and face value.

Many of the major plate flaws on the King George V head plate occur in different states, having been repaired and then damaged once again, perhaps on several occasions. Later printings of R. 1/12 show additional damage to the crown and upper scrolls. The prices quoted in the listings are for examples approximately as illustrated.

Break in scroll (R. 1/12)    Broken crown and scroll (R. 2/12)

Stay up to date with all things philatelic.
Subscribe to **Gibbons Stamp Monthly** –
The UK's number one stamp magazine

43

BERMUDA

Nick in top right scroll (R. 3/12) (Some printings from 1920 onwards show attempts at repair)

Break through scroll (R. 1/9. Ptgs from June 1929. Some show attempts at repair)

Break in lines below left scroll (R. 4/9. Ptgs from May 1920)

Damaged leaf at bottom right (R. 5/6. Ptgs from April 1918)

Gash in fruit and leaf (R. 5/12. Ptgs from November 1928)

(Typo D.L.R)

1918 (1 Apr)–**22**. Wmk Mult Crown CA. Chalk-surfaced paper. P 14.

51b	15	2s. purple and blue/*blue* (19.6.20)	21·00	55·00
		ba. Break in scroll	£275	
		bb. Broken crown and scroll	£225	
		bc. Nick in top right scroll	£275	
		be. Break in lines below left scroll	£275	£400
		bf. Damaged leaf at bottom right	£275	
		bx. Wmk reversed	£2000	£2500
52		2s.6d. black and red/*blue*	35·00	80·00
		a. Break in scroll	£325	£400
52b		4s. black and carmine (19.6.20)	60·00	£160
		ba. Break in scroll	£300	£650
		bb. Broken crown and scroll	£300	£650
		bc. Nick in top right scroll	£325	£650
		be. Break in lines below left scroll	£350	£650
		bf. Damaged leaf at bottom right	£350	
53		5s. deep green and deep red/*yellow*	75·00	£140
		a. Break in scroll	£425	
		c. Nick in top right scroll	£425	£550
		d. Green and carmine-red/*pale yellow* (1920)	60·00	£120
		da. Break in scroll	£375	£550
		db. Broken crown and scroll	£375	£550
		de. Break in lines below left scroll	£400	
		df. Damaged leaf at bottom right	£400	
		dw. Wmk inverted	£450	£550
		dx. Wmk reversed	£4500	
		dy. Wmk inverted and reversed	£4250	
54		10s. green and carmine/*pale bluish green*	£180	£350
		a. Break in scroll	£750	
		c. Green and red/*pale bluish green* (10.22)	£275	£425
		ca. Break in scroll	£950	
		cb. Broken crown and scroll	£950	
		ce. Break in lines below left scroll	£1000	
		cf. Damaged leaf at bottom right	£1000	
		cw. Wmk inverted	†	—
55		£1 purple and black/*red*	£325	£550
		a. Break in scroll	£850	
		b. Broken crown and scroll	£1000	
		c. Nick in top right scroll	£1000	
		d. Break through scroll	£2000	
		e. Break in lines below left scroll	£1500	
		f. Damaged leaf at bottom right	£1200	
		g. Gash in fruit and leaf	£2000	
		w. Wmk inverted	£1900	£2500
51b/5 Set of 6			£600	£1100
51bs/5s Optd "SPECIMEN" Set of 6			£850	

Beware of cleaned copies of the 10s. with faked postmarks. Examples of Nos. 51b/5 are known showing a forged Hamilton double ring postmark dated "22 JAN 13".

See also Nos. 88/93.

WAR TAX (16)   WAR TAX (17)

1918 (4 May). Nos. 46 and 46a optd with T **16** by the Bermuda Press.

56	14	1d. red	50	1·25
		a. Rose-red	1·00	2·00
		ay. Wmk inverted and reversed	†	£2000

1920 (5 Feb). No. 46b optd with T **17** by the Bermuda Press.

58	14	1d. carmine	3·25	3·00

The War Tax stamps represented a compulsory levy on letters to Great Britain and often Empire Countries in addition to normal postal fees until 31 Dec 1920. Subsequently they were valid for ordinary postage.

18   **19**

(Des by the Governor (Gen. Sir James Willcocks). Typo D.L.R.)

1920 (11 Nov)–**21**. Tercentenary of Representative Institutions (1st issue). Chalk-surfaced paper (3d. to 1s.). P 14.

(a) Wmk Mult Crown CA (sideways*) (19.1.21)

59	18	¼d. brown	3·50	27·00
		a. "C" of "CA" missing from wmk	£800	
		b. "A" of "CA" missing from wmk	£800	
		w. Wmk Crown to right of CA	£300	£350
		x. Wmk sideways reversed	£350	£450
		y. Wmk sideways inverted and reversed	£450	£600
60		½d. green	9·50	18·00
		a. "C" of "CA" missing from wmk	£1100	
		b. "A" of "CA" missing from wmk	£1300	
		w. Wmk Crown to right of CA	£450	£500
		x. Wmk sideways reversed	£475	£500
		y. Wmk sideways inverted and reversed	£550	£550
61		2d. grey	17·00	55·00
		a. "C" of "CA" missing from wmk	£1100	
		w. Wmk Crown to right of CA	£650	
		y. Wmk sideways inverted and reversed	£850	£900
62		3d. dull and deep purple/*pale yellow*	12·00	55·00
		w. Wmk Crown to right of CA	£1000	
		x. Wmk sideways reversed	£1100	£1100
63		4d. black and red/*pale yellow*	12·00	40·00
		a. "C" of "CA" missing from wmk	£1700	
		x. Wmk sideways reversed	£850	
64		1s. black/*blue-green*	17·00	48·00

(b) Wmk Mult Script CA (sideways*)

65	18	1d. carmine	4·50	30
		w. Wmk Crown to right of CA	†	£750
		y. Wmk sideways inverted and reversed	†	£750
66		2½d. bright blue	19·00	20·00
67		6d. dull and bright purple (19.1.21)	29·00	95·00
59/67 Set of 9			£110	£325
59s/67s Optd "SPECIMEN" Set of 9			£375	

*The normal sideways watermark shows Crown to left of CA, *as seen from the back of the stamp.*

BERMUDA

(Des H. J. Dale. Recess D.L.R.)
1921 (12 May). Tercentenary of Representative Institutions (2nd issue). P 14.

(a) Wmk Mult Crown CA (sideways*)

68	**19**	2d. slate-grey	11·00	50·00
		a. "C" of "CA" missing from wmk.	£1000	£1000
		w. Wmk Crown to left of CA	£700	
69		2½d. bright ultramarine	14·00	6·00
		a. "C" of "CA" missing from wmk.	£1000	
		b. "A" of "CA" missing from wmk.	£1000	
		w. Wmk Crown to left of CA	—	£900
		x. Wmk sideways reversed	£1100	£700
70		3d. purple/*pale yellow*	5·50	18·00
		w. Wmk Crown to left of CA		
71		4d. red/*pale yellow*	32·00	30·00
		x. Wmk sideways reversed	£275	£425
72		6d. purple	19·00	65·00
		a. "C" of "CA" missing from wmk.	£1300	
		b. "A" of "CA" missing from wmk.	£1400	
		c. Substituted crown in wmk	†	£2500
73		1s. black/*green*	25·00	65·00

(b) Wmk Mult Script CA (sideways*)

74	**19**	¼d. brown	4·25	3·75
		w. Wmk Crown to left of CA	£550	£550
		x. Wmk sideways reversed	£750	£650
		y. Wmk sideways inverted and reversed	—	£750
75		½d. green	3·50	8·50
		w. Wmk Crown to left of CA	£250	£325
		x. Wmk sideways reversed	£650	
		y. Wmk sideways inverted and reversed	£475	
		ys. Optd "SPECIMEN"	£160	
76		1d. deep carmine	9·00	35
		a. "C" of "CA" missing from wmk.	£750	
		w. Wmk Crown to left of CA	£700	£600
		x. Wmk sideways reversed	£500	£650
		y. Wmk sideways inverted and reversed	£1000	£700
68/76 *Set of 9*			95·00	£225
68s/76s Optd "SPECIMEN" *Set of 9*			£350	

*The normal sideways watermark shows Crown to right of CA, *as seen from the back of the stamp.*

For illustration of the substituted watermark crown see Catalogue Introduction.

Examples of most values of Nos. 59/76 are known showing part strikes of the forged Hamilton postmark mentioned below Nos. 51b/5.

Three Types of the 1d.

I. Scroll at top left very weak and figure "1" has pointed serifs.
II. Scroll weak. "1" has square serifs and "1d" is heavy.
III. Redrawn. Scroll is completed by a strong line and "1" is thinner with long square serifs.

Two Types of the 2½d.

I. Short, thick figures, especially of the "1", small "d".
II. Figures taller and thinner, "d" larger.

1922–34. Wmk Mult Script CA. P 14.

77	**14**	¼d. brown (7.28)	1·50	3·00
77a		½d. green (11.22)	1·50	15
		aw. Wmk inverted	£750	£475
		ax. Wmk reversed	£750	£475
78		1d. scarlet (I) (11.22)	17·00	60
		a. Carmine (7.24)	18·00	60
		bx. Wmk reversed	£550	£500
78c		1d. carmine (II) (12.25)	55·00	7·50
		d. Scarlet (8.27)	28·00	3·25
79		1d. scarlet (III) (10.28)	14·00	30
		a. Carmine-lake (1934)	25·00	2·25
79b		1½d. red-brown (27.3.34)	10·00	35
80		2d. grey (12.23)	1·50	1·50
		x. Wmk reversed	75·00	
81		2½d. pale sage-green (12.22)	3·25	1·50
		a. Deep sage-green (1924)	3·25	1·50
		aw. Wmk inverted	—	£500
		ax. Wmk reversed	£750	£500
		ay. Wmk inverted and reversed	£750	£500
82		2½d. ultramarine (I) (1.12.26)	5·00	50
		aw. Wmk inverted	£275	£300
82b		2½d. ultramarine (II) (3.32)	1·75	70
83		3d. ultramarine (12.24)	19·00	26·00
		w. Wmk inverted	£160	£200
84		3d. purple/*yellow* (10.26)	4·00	1·00
85		4d. red/*yellow* (8.24)	2·25	1·00
		x. Wmk reversed	£425	£550
86		6d. purple (8.24)	1·50	80
87		1s. black/*emerald* (10.27)	8·00	9·00
		a. Brownish black/*yellow-green* (1934)	35·00	50·00
77/87 *Set of 12*			65·00	40·00
77s/87s Optd or Perf (1½d.) "SPECIMEN" *Set of 12*			£600	

Both comb and line perforations occur on Nos. 77/87a.

Detailed gauges are as follows:

13.7×13.9 comb	—	Nos. 77a, 78/a, 80, 81/a, 83, 84, 85, 86, 87
13.75 line	—	Nos. 77a, 77, 78c/d, 79/a, 79b, 80, 82, 82b, 84, 85, 86, 87/a
13.75×14 line	—	Nos. 77a, 78c/d, 79b, 80, 82b, 86, 87a
14×13.75 line	—	Nos. 79/a
14 line	—	Nos. 81/a

Breaks in scrolls at right (R. 1/3. Ptgs of 12s.6d. from July 1932)

1924–32. Wmk Mult Script CA. Chalk-surfaced paper. P 14.

88	**15**	2s. purple and bright blue/*pale blue* (1.9.27)	50·00	75·00
		a. Break in scroll	£250	
		b. Broken crown and scroll	£250	
		c. Nick in top right scroll	£275	
		e. Break in lines below left scroll	£275	
		f. Damaged leaf at bottom right	£275	
		g. Purple and blue/*grey-blue* (1931)	65·00	85·00
		ga. Break in scroll	£300	£500
		gb. Broken crown and scroll	£300	
		gd. Break through scroll	£350	£550
		ge. Break in lines below left scroll	£350	
		gf. Damaged leaf at bottom right	£350	
		gg. Gash in fruit and leaf	£350	
89		2s.6d. black and carmine/*pale blue* (4.27)	60·00	£100
		a. Break in scroll	£300	
		b. Broken crown and scroll	£300	
		e. Break in lines below left scroll	£350	
		f. Damaged leaf at bottom right	£350	
		g. Black and red/*blue to deep blue* (6.29)	75·00	£110
		ga. Break in scroll	£350	
		gb. Broken crown and scroll	£350	
		gd. Break through scroll	£400	
		ge. Break in lines below left scroll	£400	
		gf. Damaged leaf at bottom right	£400	
		gg. Gash in fruit and leaf	£400	
		h. Grey-black and pale orange-vermilion/*grey-blue* (3.30)	£2750	£2750
		ha. Break in scroll	£5500	
		hb. Broken crown and scroll	£5500	
		hd. Break through scroll	£5500	
		he. Break in lines below left scroll	£5500	
		hf. Damaged leaf at bottom right	£5500	
		hg. Gash in fruit and leaf	£5500	
		i. Black and carmine-red/*deep grey-blue* (8.30)	£100	£140
		ia. Break in scroll	£500	
		ib. Broken crown and scroll	£500	
		id. Break through scroll	£600	
		ie. Break in lines below left scroll	£600	
		if. Damaged leaf at bottom right	£600	
		ig. Gash in fruit and leaf	£600	

BERMUDA

	j. Black and scarlet-vermilion/dp bl (9.31)		90·00	£130
	ja. Break in scroll		£450	
	jb. Broken crown and scroll		£450	
	jc. Nick in top right scroll		£500	£600
	jd. Break through scroll		£550	
	je. Break in lines below left scroll		£550	
	jf. Damaged leaf at bottom right		£550	
	jg. Gash in fruit and leaf		£550	
	k. Black & brt orange-vermilion/deep blue (8.32)		£3250	£3000
	kb. Broken crown and scroll		£6000	
	kc. Nick in top right scroll		£6000	
	kd. Break through scroll		£6000	
	ke. Break in lines below left scroll		£6000	
	kf. Damaged leaf at bottom right		£6000	
	kg. Gash in fruit and leaf		£6000	
92	10s. green and red/*pale emerald* (12.24)		£140	£250
	a. Break in scroll		£750	£1000
	b. Broken crown and scroll		£700	£1000
	e. Break in lines below left scroll		£800	
	f. Damaged leaf at bottom right		£800	
	g. Green and red/*deep emerald* (1930)		£150	£275
	ga. Break in scroll		£750	
	gb. Broken crown and scroll		£700	£900
	gc. Nick in top right scroll		£750	
	gd. Break through scroll		£850	£1000
	ge. Break in lines below left scroll		£850	
	gf. Damaged leaf at bottom right		£750	
	gg. Gash in fruit and leaf		£750	
93	12s.6d. grey and orange (8.32)		£250	£375
	a. Break in scroll		£700	£900
	b. Broken crown and scroll		£750	£950
	c. Nick in top right scroll		£800	£950
	d. Break through scroll		£900	
	e. Break in lines below left scroll		£900	
	f. Damaged leaf at bottom right		£800	
	g. Gash in fruit and leaf		£800	
	h. Break in scrolls at right		£900	
	i. Error. Ordinary paper			
88/93 Set of 4			£450	£700
88s/93s Optd or Perf (12s.6d) "SPECIMEN" Set of 4			£550	

The true No. 89*h* is the only stamp on grey-blue paper, other deeper orange-vermilion shades exist on different papers. No. 89k was despatched to Bermuda in July/August 1932, but is not known used before 1937.

Beware of fiscally used 2s.6d. 10s. and 12s.6d. stamps cleaned and bearing faked postmarks. Large quantities were used for a "head tax" levied on travellers leaving the country.

For 12s.6d. design inscribed "Revenue" at both sides see No. F1 under POSTAL FISCAL.

Damaged turret (Plate "1" R. 5/6)

Kite and vertical log (Plate "2A" R. 10/6)

Kite and horizontal log (Plate "2B" R. 10/6)

Bird by turret (Plate "7" R. 1/5)

1935 (6 May). Silver Jubilee. As Nos. 141/4 of Bahamas, but ptd by Waterlow. P 11×12.

94	1d. deep blue and scarlet	1·00	2·25
	j. Damaged turret	£700	
	m. "Bird" by turret	£190	£225
95	1½d. ultramarine and grey	1·00	3·50
	m. "Bird" by turret	£200	£275
96	2½d. brown and deep blue	1·50	2·50
	m. "Bird" by turret	£275	£325
97	1s. slate and purple	22·00	50·00
	k. Kite and vertical log	£275	£400
	l. Kite and horizontal log	£600	£750
94/7 Set of 4		23·00	50·00
94s/7s Perf "Specimen" Set of 4		£225	

20 Red Hole, Paget

21 South Shore

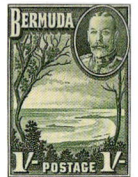

22 *Lucie* (yacht)

23 Grape Bay, Paget Parish

24 Point House, Warwick Parish

25 Gardener's Cottage, Par-la-Ville, Hamilton

(Recess B.W.)

1936 (14 Apr)–**47**. T **12**. Wmk Mult Script CA (sideways on horiz designs).

98	**20**	½d. bright green	10	10
99	**21**	1d. black and scarlet	65	30
100		1½d. black and chocolate	1·00	50
101	**22**	2d. black and pale blue	5·00	1·50
102	**23**	2½d. light and deep blue	1·00	25
103	**24**	3d. black and scarlet	4·50	2·75
104	**25**	6d. carmine-lake and violet	80	10
		a. Claret and dull violet (6.47)	6·50	2·75
105	**23**	1s. green	15·00	19·00
106	**20**	1s.6d. brown	50	10
98/106 Set of 9			25·00	22·00
98s/106s Perf "SPECIMEN" Set of 9			£325	

All are line-perf 11.9, except printings of the 6d. from July 1951 onwards, which are comb-perf 11.9×11.75.

1937 (14 May). Coronation. As Nos. 146/8 of Bahamas, but printed by D.L.R. P 14.

107	1d. scarlet	90	1·50
108	1½d. yellow-brown	60	1·75
109	2½d. bright blue	70	1·75
107/9 Set of 3		2·00	4·50
107s/9s Perf "SPECIMEN" Set of 3		£225	

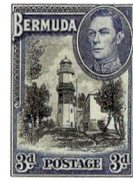

26 Ships in Hamilton Harbour

27 St. David's Lighthouse

28 White-tailed Tropic Bird, Arms of Bermuda and Native Flower
29 King George VI 

(Des Miss Higginbotham (T **28**). Recess B.W.)

1938 (20 Jan)–**52**. T **22**, T **23** (but with portrait of King George VI) and T **26** to **28**. Wmk Mult Script CA. P 12.

110	**26**	1d. black and red (*a*) (*b*)	2·75	20
111		1½d. deep blue and purple-brown (*a*)		
		(*b*)	11·00	1·50
		a. Blue and brown (3.43)	15·00	7·00
		b. lt blue & purple-brn (*a*) (*b*) (9.45)	2·25	2·00
		ba. "A" of "CA" missing from wmk	£1800	
112	**22**	2d. light blue and sepia (*a*)	50·00	10·00
112*a*		2d. ultramarine and scarlet (*a*) (*b*)		
		(8.11.40)	3·25	2·25
113	**23**	2½d. light and deep blue (*a*)	11·00	1·25
113*a*		2½d. lt blue & sepia-black (*a*)		
		(18.12.41)	5·00	5·00
		b. Pale blue & sepia-black (*a*) (3.43)	4·00	3·50
		c. Bright blue and deep sepia-black		
		(23.9.52)	6·00	8·00
114	**27**	3d. black and rose-red (*a*)	42·00	6·00
114*a*		3d. black & deep blue (*a*) (*b*)		
		(16.7.41)	2·50	40
114*b*	**28**	7½d. black, blue & brt grn (*a*)		
		(18.12.41)	11·00	4·50
		c. Black, blue & yellow-grn (*a*) (3.43)	8·00	2·75
115	**23**	1s. green (*a*) (*b*)	2·00	50
		a. Bluish green (*b*) (20.6.52)	10·00	7·50

Perforations. Two different perforating machines were used on the various printings of these stamps: (*a*) the original 11.9 line perforation; (*b*) 11.9×11.75 comb perforation, introduced in July 1950. These perforations occur as indicated above.

Shading omitted from top right scroll (R. 1/1. March 1943 ptgs of 2s. and £1)

Lower right scroll with broken tail (R. 2/10. Line perforated printings only)

Broken top right scroll (R. 5/11. Line perforated ptgs only. A retouched state of the flaw is visible in later ptgs up to March 1943)

Broken lower right scroll (R. 5/12. Occurs on printings made between May 1941 and March 1943)

Gash in chin (R. 2/5. Ptgs between May 1941 and March 1943)

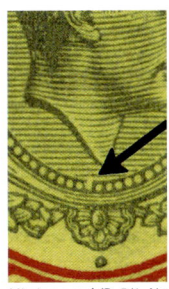

Missing pearl (R. 5/1, Nov 1945 ptg of 5s. only)

"ER" joined (R. 1/2. Occurs in its complete state on 1938 ptg only. Subsequent ptgs show it incomplete)

Damaged left value tablet (R. 1/11. Part of 1951 ptg only)

(Typo D.L.R.)

1938 (20 Jan)–**53**. T **29**. Wmk Mult Crown CA (£1) or Mult Script CA (others). Chalk-surfaced paper. P 14 (comb).

116		2s. deep purple and ultramarine/*grey-blue*.	£110	18·00
		a. Deep reddish purple and ultram/grey-blue (21.11.40)*	£350	48·00
		b. Perf 14¼ line. Deep purple and ultram/grey-blue (14.11.41)*	£350	£100
		bc. Lower right scroll with broken tail	£3750	£1700
		bd. Broken top right scroll	£1900	£850
		be. Broken lower right scroll	£1900	£850
		bf. Gash in chin	£2500	£1200
		c. Ordinary paper. Pur & bl/dp bl (7.6.42)	11·00	1·50
		ce. Broken lower right scroll	£225	£110
		cf. Gash in chin	£325	£140
		d. Ordinary paper. Purple and deep blue/pale blue (5.3.43)	14·00	1·75
		db. Shading omitted from top right scroll	£2000	£2000
		de. Broken lower right scroll	£700	£700
		df. Gash in chin	£850	£850
		e. Perf 13. Ordinary paper. Dull purple and blue/pale blue (15.2.50)	14·00	17·00
		f. Perf 13. Ordinary paper. Reddish purple and blue/pale blue (10.10.50)	15·00	29·00
117		2s.6d. black and red/*grey-blue*	70·00	14·00
		a. Perf 14¼ line. Black and red/grey-blue (21.2.42)*	£600	£120
		ac. Lower right scroll with broken tail	£4000	£1800
		ad. Broken top right scroll	£2500	£1000
		ae. Broken lower right scroll	£2500	£1000
		af. Gash in chin	£3000	£1400
		b. Ordinary paper. Black and red/pale blue (5.3.43)	22·00	12·00
		be. Broken lower right scroll	£650	£600
		bf. Gash in chin	£850	£700
		c. Perf 13. Ordinary paper. Black and orange-red/pale blue (10.10.50)	17·00	11·00
		d. Perf 13. Ordinary paper. Black and red/pale blue (18.6.52)	16·00	22·00
118		5s. green and red/*yellow*	£150	42·00
		a. Pale green & red/yellow (14.3.39)*	£375	85·00
		b. Perf 14¼ line. Dull yellow-green and red/yellow (11.10.42)*	£300	40·00
		bc. Lower right scroll with broken tail	£3250	£1100
		bd. Broken top right scroll	£1300	£550
		be. Broken lower right scroll	£1300	£550
		bf. Gash in chin	£1600	£750
		c. Ordinary paper. Bronze-green & carmine-red/pale yellow (5.42)*	£1400	£170
		ce. Broken lower right scroll	£8500	£2750

47

BERMUDA

	cf. Gash in chin..................................	£9000	£2750
	d. Ordinary paper. *Pale bluish green and carmine-red/pale yellow* (5.3.43).........	£100	50.00
	de. Broken lower right scroll.................	£1100	£800
	df. Gash in chin....................................	£1200	£800
	e. Ordinary paper. *Green and red/pale yellow* (5.45)*.....................................	50.00	27.00
	ea. Missing pearl...................................	£1000	
	f. Perf 13. Ordinary paper. *Yellow-green and red/pale yellow* (15.2.50)..........	35.00	30.00
	g. Perf 13. *Green and scarlet/yellow (chalk-surfaced)* (10.10.50).........	60.00	75.00
119	10s. green and deep lake/*pale emerald*....	£450	£325
	a. *Bluish green & deep red/green* (8.39)*....	£225	£130
	b. Perf 14¼ line. Ordinary paper. *Yellow green and carmine/green* (1942)*.........	£550	£130
	bc. Lower right scroll with broken tail......	£4750	£2250
	bd. Broken top right scroll.....................	£2500	£1300
	be. Broken lower right scroll.................	£2500	£1300
	bf. Gash in chin....................................	£3250	£1400
	c. Ordinary paper. *Yellowish green and deep carmine-red/green* (5.3.43)........	70.00	65.00
	ce. Broken lower right scroll.................	£2750	
	cf. Gash in chin....................................	£2750	
	d. Ordinary paper. *Deep green and dull red/green (emerald back)* (11.12.46).....	85.00	70.00
	e. Perf 13. Ordinary paper. *Green and vermilion/green* (19.9.51)................	48.00	50.00
	f. Perf 13. Ordinary paper. *Green and dull red/green* (16.4.53).........................	50.00	65.00
120	12s.6d. deep grey and brownish orange.......	£550	£450
	a. *Grey and brownish orange (shades)*.......	£225	75.00
	b. *Grey and pale orange* (9.11.40)*........	£110	55.00
	c. Ordinary paper (2.3.44)*..................	£120	70.00
	ce. Broken lower right scroll.................	£2250	£2500
	cf. Gash in chin....................................	£2500	
	d. Ordinary paper. *Grey and yell†* (17.9.47)*.....................................	£700	£500
	e. Perf 13. *Grey and pale orange (chalk surfaced)* (10.10.50).........................	£100	85.00
121	£1 purple and black/*red*.......................	£275	£100
	a. "ER" joined.....................................	£1100	£600
	b. *Pale purple & black/pale red* (13.5.43)*....	90.00	75.00
	ba. "ER" joined.....................................	£700	£600
	be. Broken lower right scroll.................	£2000	£1500
	bf. Gash in chin....................................	£2250	£1700
	c. *Dp reddish pur and blk/pale red* (5.3.43)*	60.00	75.00
	ca. "ER" joined.....................................	£650	£700
	cb. Shading omitted from top right scroll.....	£4000	
	ce. Broken lower right scroll.................	£1800	
	cf. Gash in chin....................................	£2000	
	d. Perf 13. *Violet & black/scarlet* (7.12.51).....	55.00	85.00
	da. Damaged left value tablet................	£4500	
	e. Perf 13. *Brt violet & blk/scar* (10.12.52).....	£180	£275
110/21d Set of 16..		£350	£225
110s/21s Perf "SPECIMEN" *Set of 16*...................		£2000	

Following extensive damage to their printing works on 29 December 1940 much of De La Rue's work was transferred to other firms operating under their supervision. It is understood that Williams Lea & Co produced those new printings ordered for the Bermuda high value stamps during 1941. The first batch of these printings showed the emergency use, by Williams Lea, of a 14¼ line perforating machine (exact gauge 14.15) instead of the comb perforation (exact gauge 13.9×13.8).

Dates marked * are those of earliest known use.

In No. 116c the coloured surfacing of the paper is mottled with white specks sometimes accompanied by very close horizontal lines. In Nos. 116d, 117b and 118c/d the surfacing is the same colour as the back, sometimes applied in widely spaced horizontal lines giving the appearance of laid paper.

†No. 120d is the so-called "lemon" shade.

HALF PENNY

X   X
30

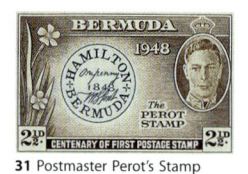

31 Postmaster Perot's Stamp

1940 (20 Dec). No. 110 surch with T **30** by *Royal Gazette*, Hamilton.
122   **26**   ½d. on 1d. black and red (*shades*)............ 1·25   3·25
    The spacing between "PENNY" and "X" varies from 12½ mm to 14 mm.

1946 (6 Nov). Victory. As Nos. 176/7 of Bahamas.
123   1½d. brown 15   15
124   3d. blue 40   65
123s/4s Perf "SPECIMEN" *Set of 2*............................ £160

1948 (1 Dec). Royal Silver Wedding. As Nos. 194/5 of Bahamas.
125   1½d. red-brown 30   50
126   £1 carmine .... 45·00   55·00

                               (Recess B.W.)

1949 (11 Apr). Centenary of Postmaster Perot's Stamp. Wmk Mult Script CA. P 13½.
127   **31**   2½d. blue and brown 35   35
128   3d. black and blue 35   15
129   6d. violet and green 40   15
127/9 *Set of 3* .... 1·00   60

1949 (10 Oct). 75th Anniv of Universal Postal Union. As Nos. 196/9 of Bahamas.
130   2½d. blue-black 30   2·00
    a. "C" of "CA" missing from watermark........ £1200
131   3d. deep blue .... 1·75   1·25
132   6d. purple 40   75
133   1s. blue-green 40   1·50
130/3 *Set of 4* .... 2·50   2·50

1953 (4 June). Coronation. As No. 200 of Bahamas, but ptd by B. W.
134   1½d. black and blue .... 1·25   40

32 Easter Lilies    **33** Postmaster Perot's stamp

34 Easter Lily    **35** *Victory II* (racing dinghy)

36 Sir George Somers and *Sea Venture*    **37** Map of Bermuda

38 *Sea Venture* (galleon), coin and Perot stamp    **39** White-tailed Tropic Bird

40 Early Bermudan coinage    **41** Arms of St. Georges

42 Warwick Fort    **43** 1 tog coin

44 Obverse and reverse of 1 tog coin

45 Arms of Bermuda

Die I "Sandy's"   Die II "Sandys"

(Des C. Deakins (½d., 3d., 1s.3d., 5s.), J. Berry (1d., 1½d., 2½d., 4d., 1s.), B. Brown (2d., 6d., 8d.), D. Haig (4½d., 9d.), Pamela Braley-Smith (2s.6d.) and E. C. Leslie (10s.) Recess (except £1, centre typo), B.W.)

1953 (9 Nov)–**62**. W **T 32/45**. Wmk Mult Script CA. P 13½.

135	32	½d. olive-green	1·00	4·50
		a. Yellow-olive (19.5.54)	40	2·25
136	33	1d. black and red	2·00	50
		a. Black and deep red (19.5.54)	6·50	1·25
137	34	1½d. green	30	10
138	35	2d. ultramarine and brown-red	50	40
139	36	2½d. rose-red	2·00	50
140	37	3d. deep purple (I)	30	10
140a		3d. deep purple (II) (2.1.57)	1·00	20
141	33	4d. black and bright blue	55	1·75
142	38	4½d. emerald	1·50	1·00
143	39	6d. black and deep turquoise	6·50	60
143a		8d. black and red (16.5.55)	3·25	30
143b	38	9d. violet (6.1.58)	12·00	2·50
144	40	1s. orange	50	15
145	37	1s.3d. blue (I)	3·75	30
		a. Greenish blue (21.9.54)	12·00	1·50
145b		1s.3d. blue (II) (2.1.57)	7·00	50
		bc. Bright blue (14.8.62)	24·00	8·50
146	41	2s. brown	4·00	85
147	42	2s.6d. scarlet	10·00	45
148	43	5s. carmine	22·00	85
149	44	10s. deep ultramarine	19·00	9·00
		a. Ultramarine (13.2.57)	80·00	19·00
150	45	£1 brown, blue, red, grn and bronze-grn	45·00	21·00
135/150 Set of 18			£120	38·00

Nos. 136, 138 and 143 exist in coils, constructed from normal sheets.

1953 (26 Nov). Royal Visit. As No. 143 but inscr "ROYAL VISIT 1953" in top left corner.

151		6d. black and deep turquoise	1·00	20

Three Power Talks **Three Power Talks**
December, 1953. **December, 1953.**
(**46**) (**46a**)

First setting (Type **46**). First line 24½ mm long.
Second setting (Type **46a**). First line 25¼ mm long.

1953 (8 Dec). Three Power Talks. Nos. 140 and 145 optd with T **46** by Royal Gazette, Hamilton.

152	37	3d. deep purple (Type **46**) (B.)	20	10
		a. Optd with Type **46a**	1·75	30
153		1s.3d. blue (Type **46**) (R.)	20	10
		a. Optd with Type **46a**	6·50	6·00

50TH ANNIVERSARY U S — BERMUDA OCEAN RACE 1956
(**47**)

48 Perot's Post Office

1956 (22 June). 50th Anniv of United States–Bermuda Yacht Race. Nos. 143a and 145a optd with T **47** by the Bermuda Press.

154		8d. black and red (Bk.)	30	45
155		1s.3d. greenish blue (R.)	30	55

(Des W. Harrington. Recess B.W.)

1959 (1 Jan). Wmk Mult Script CA. P 13½.

156	48	6d. black and deep mauve	1·50	15

49 Arms of King James I and Queen Elizabeth II

(Des W. Harrington. Recess; arms litho D.L.R.)

1959 (29 July). 350th Anniv of First Settlement. Arms, red, yellow and blue; frame colours below. W w **12**. P 13.

157	49	1½d. grey-blue	35	10
158		3d. drab-grey	40	50
159		4d. reddish purple	45	55
160		8d. slate-violet	45	15
161		9d. olive-green	45	1·25
162		1s.3d. brown	45	30
157/162 Set of 6			2·25	2·50

50 The Old Rectory, St. George's, *circa* 1730

51 Church of St. Peter, St. George's

52 Government House, 1892

53 The Cathedral, Hamilton, 1894

54 H.M. Dockyard, 1811

55 Perot's Post Office, 1848

56 G.P.O Hamilton, 1869

57 Library, Par-la-Ville

58 Bermuda cottage, *circa* 1705

59 Christ Church, Warwick, 1719

BERMUDA

60 City Hall Hamilton, 1960
61 Town of St. George 
62 Bermuda house, circa 1710 
63 Bermuda house, early 18th century 
64 Colonial Secretariat, 1833 
65 Old Post Office, Somerset, 1890 
66 The House of Assembly, 1815 
5s. Top loop of "P" of "Postage" broken. (Pl. 1A-1A, R. 1/1). Corrected on No. 246 

(Des W. Harrington. Photo Harrison)

1962 (26 Oct)–**68**. T **50/66**. W w **12** (upright). P 12½.

163	50	1d. reddish purple, black and orange...	10	75
		w. Wmk inverted	—	£750
164	51	2d. lilac, indigo, yellow and green	1·00	35
		a. Lilac omitted	£1000	£1000
		b. Green omitted	†	£7500
		c. Imperf (pair)	£2250	
		d. Pale lilac, indigo, yell and grn (22.10.68)	5·50	3·50
		w. Wmk inverted	—	£300
165	52	3d. yellow-brown and light blue	10	10
166	53	4d. red-brown and magenta	20	40
167	54	5d. grey-blue and rose	75	3·00
168	55	6d. grey-blue, emerald and light blue..	30	30
		w. Wmk inverted	£180	£200
169	56	8d. bright blue, bright green and orange	30	35
170	57	9d. light blue and brown	30	60
170a	58	10d. violet and ochre (8.2.65)	15·00	1·50
		aw. Wmk inverted	£1500	£1100
171	59	1s. black, emerald, bright blue and orange	30	10
172	60	1s.3d. lake, grey and bistre	75	15
		w. Wmk inverted	†	£2500
173	58	1s.6d. violet and ochre	75	1·00
174	61	2s. red-brown and orange	3·00	1·25
175	62	2s.3d. bistre-brown and yellow-green	1·00	7·00
176	63	2s.6d. bistre-brn, bluish grn & olive-yell	55	50
177	64	5s. brown-purple and blue-green	1·25	1·50
		a. Broken "P"	32·00	
		w. Wmk inverted	£250	£250
178	65	10s. magenta, deep bluish green and buff	5·00	7·00
		w. Wmk inverted	£600	£700
179	66	£1 black, yellow-olive and yellow-orange	14·00	14·00
163/79 Set of 18			40·00	35·00

Three examples of No. 164b are known, all used on piece. The 3d. value with the yellow-brown omitted, previously No. 165a, is no longer listed as this is believed to be a dry print. All reported examples show traces of the yellow-brown.

See also Nos. 195/200 and 246a.

1963 (4 June). Freedom from Hunger. As No. 223 of Bahamas.
180 1s.3d. sepia 60 40

1963 (2 Sept). Red Cross Centenary. As Nos. 226/7 of Bahamas.
181 3d. red and black 50 25
182 1s.3d. red and blue .... 1·00 2·50

67 Tsotsi in the Bundu (Finn class dinghy)

(Des V. Whiteley. Photo D.L.R.)

1964 (28 Sept). Olympic Games, Tokyo. W w **12**. P 14×13½.
183 **67** 3d. red, violet and blue 10 10

1965 (17 May). I.T.U. Centenary. As Nos. 262/3 of Bahamas.
184 3d. light blue and emerald 35 25
185 2s. yellow and ultramarine .... 65 1·50

68 Scout Badge and St. Edward's Crown

(Des W. Harrington. Photo Harrison)

1965 (24 July). 50th Anniv of Bermuda Boy Scouts Association. W w **12**. P 12½.
186 **68** 2s. multicoloured 50 50
            w. Wmk inverted .... 55·00 65·00

1965 (25 Oct). International Co-operation Year. As Nos. 265/6 of Bahamas.
187 4d. reddish purple and turquoise-green 40 20
188 2s.6d. deep bluish green and lavender 60 80

1966 (24 Jan). Churchill Commemoration. As Nos. 267/70 of Bahamas.
189 3d. new blue 30 20
190 6d. deep green .... 70 1·00
191 10d. brown .... 1·00 75
192 1s.3d. bluish violet .... 1·25 2·50
189/92 Set of 4 .... 3·00 4·00

1966 (1 July). World Cup Football Championship. As Nos. 288/9 of Bahamas.
193 10d. violet, yellow-green, lake and yellow-brn .... 1·00 15
194 2s.6d. chocolate, blue-grn, lake & yell-brn .... 1·25 1·25

1966 (25 Oct)–**69**. Designs as Nos. 164, 167 (1s.6d.), 169, 170a/1 and 174 but W w **12** (sideways*).
195 51 2d. lilac, indigo, yellow and green (20.5.69) .... 6·50 8·00
         w. Wmk Crown to right of CA .... — £350
196 56 8d. brt blue, brt green and orange ...... 50 1·50
197 58 10d. violet and ochre (1.11.66) 75 60
         w. Wmk Crown to right of CA £1300 £1300
198 59 1s. black, emerald, brt bl and orge (14.2.67) .... 70 1·40
199 54 1s.6d. grey-blue and rose (1.11.66) .... 1·00 30
         w. Wmk Crown to right of CA £110 £120
200 61 2s. red-brown and orange .... 1·00 60
195/200 Set of 6 .... 9·50 11·00

*The normal sideways watermark shows Crown to left of CA, *as seen from the back of the stamp*.

The 2d. value exists with PVA gum only, and the 8d. exists with PVA gum as well as gum arabic.

1966 (1 Dec). 20th Anniv of U.N.E.S.C.O. As Nos. 292/4 of Bahamas.
201 4d. slate-violet, red, yellow and orange 45 15
202 1s.3d. orange-yellow, violet and deep olive 75 50
203 2s. black, bright purple and orange .... 1·00 1·10
201/3 Set of 3 .... 2·00 1·60

BERMUDA

69 G.P.O. Building

(Des G. Vasarhelyi. Photo Harrison)

1967 (23 June). Opening of New General Post Office, Hamilton. W w **12**. P 14½.

204	**69**	3d. multicoloured	10	10
205		1s. multicoloured	15	10
206		1s.6d. multicoloured	30	25
207		2s.6d. multicoloured	35	70
204/7 Set of 4			75	1·00

70 *Mercury* (cable ship) and Chain Links

(Des V. Whiteley. Photo Harrison)

1967 (14 Sept). Inauguration of Bermuda–Tortola Telephone Service. T **70** and similar horiz designs. Multicoloured. W w **12**. P 14½×14.

208		3d. Type **70**	15	10
209		1s. Map, telephone and microphone	25	10
210		1s.6d. Telecommunications media	25	25
211		2s.6d. *Mercury* (cable ship) and marine fauna	40	70
208/11 Set of 4			1·00	1·00

74 Human Rights Emblem and Doves

(Des M. Farrar Bell. Litho Harrison)

1968 (1 Feb). Human Rights Year. W w **12**. P 14×14½.

212	**74**	3d. indigo, blue and dull green	10	10
213		1s. yellow-brown, blue and light blue	10	10
214		1s.6d. black, blue and rose	10	15
215		2s.6d. grey-green, blue and yellow	15	25
212/15 Set of 4			30	55

REPRESENTATIVE GOVERNMENT

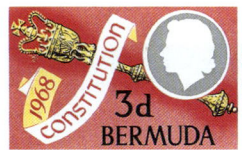

75 Mace and Queen's Profile

(Des R. Granger Barrett. Photo Harrison)

1968 (1 July). New Constitution. T **75** and similar horiz design. W w **12**. P 14.

216	**75**	3d. multicoloured	10	10
217		1s. multicoloured	10	10
218		1s.6d. greenish yellow, black and turq-bl.	10	20
219		2s.6d. lilac, black and orange-yellow	15	75
216/19 Set of 4			30	1·00

Design:—1s.6d., 2s.6d. Houses of Parliament and House of Assembly, Bermuda.

77 Football, Athletics and Yachting

(Des V. Whiteley. Photo Harrison)

1968 (24 Sept). Olympic Games, Mexico. W w **12**. P 12½.

220	**77**	3d. multicoloured	15	10
		a. Red-brown ("BERMUDA" and value) omitted	£4750	£5000
221		1s. multicoloured	25	10
222		1s.6d. multicoloured	50	30
223		2s.6d. multicoloured	50	1·40
220/3 Set of 4			1·25	1·75

78 Brownie and Guide    **80** Emerald-studded Gold Cross and Seaweed

(Des Harrison. Litho Format)

1969 (17 Feb). 50th Anniv of Bermuda Girl Guides. P 14.

224	**78**	3d. multicoloured	10	10
225		1s. multicoloured	20	10
226		– 1s.6d. multicoloured	25	40
227		– 2s.6d. multicoloured	35	1·40
224/7 Set of 4			80	1·75

Design:—1s.6d., 2s.6d. Guides and badge.

(Des K. Giles adapted by V. Whiteley. Photo Harrison)

1969 (29 Sept). Underwater Treasure. T **80** and similar vert design. Multicoloured. W w **12** (sideways). P 14½×14.

228		4d. Type **80**	20	10
229		1s.3d. Emerald-studded gold cross and seabed	35	15
		a. Green (jewels) omitted		
230		2s. Type **80**	45	90
231		2s.6d. As 1s.3d.	45	1·75
228/31 Set of 4			1·25	2·50

(New Currency. 100 cents = 1 Bermuda dollar)

1c

(**82**) Tall "2" (Pl 1A. R. 2/2) **2c**

1970 (6 Feb). Decimal Currency. As Nos. 163, 165/6, 168, 170, 172, 175/9 and 195/200 surch as T **82**. W w **12** (sideways* on 2, 5, 10, 12, 15, 18, 24, 30, 60c., $1.20 and $2.40).

232		1c. on 1d. reddish purple, black and orange	10	1·75
		w. Wmk inverted	50·00	50·00
233		2c. on 2d. lilac, indigo, yellow and green	10	10
		a. Lilac omitted	£1000	
		b. Vert pair, one without surch	£7500	
		c. Tall "2"	10·00	
		dw. Wmk Crown to right of CA	£120	£150
		e. Wmk upright (No. 164)	2·50	5·50
		ea. Tall "2"	35·00	
		f. Wmk upright (No. 164*d*)	5·00	6·50
		fa. Tall "2"	55·00	
234		3c. on 3d. yellow-brown and light blue	10	30
235		4c. on 4d. red-brown and magenta (Br.)	10	10
236		5c. on 8d. bright blue, brt green and orange	15	2·25
237		6c. on 6d. grey-blue, emerald & light blue	15	1·75
		a. Horiz pair, one with albino surch, the other with albino bar	£5000	
		w. Wmk inverted	£325	£190

51

BERMUDA

238	9c. on 9d. light blue and brown (Br.)	30	2·75
239	10c. on 10d. violet and ochre	30	25
240	12c. on 1s. black, emerald, brt blue and orge..	30	1·25
241	15c. on 1s.3d. lake, grey and bistre	2·00	1·75
242	18c. on 1s.6d. grey-blue and rose	80	65
243	24c. on 2s. red-brown and orange	85	4·00
	w. Wmk Crown to right of CA	£140	£200
244	30c. on 2s.6d. bistre-brown, bluish green and olive-yellow	1·00	3·00
245	36c. on 2s.3d. bistre-brown & yellow-green	1·75	8·00
246	60c. on 5s. brown-purple and blue-green	2·25	4·00
	a. Surch omitted †	£1500	
247	$1.20 on 10s. mag, dp bluish green and buff	5·50	12·00
248	$2.40 on £1 black, yellow-olive and yellow-orange	6·50	15·00
232/48	Set of 17	20·00	50·00

*The normal sideways watermark shows Crown to left of CA, *as seen from the back of the stamp.*

†No. 246a differs from the normal No. 177 by its watermark, which is sideways, and its gum, which is PVA.

83 Spathiphyllum

(Des W. Harrington. Photo D.L.R.)

1970 (6 July)–**75**. Flowers. Multicoloured designs as T **83**. W w **12** (sideways on horiz designs). P 14.

249	1c. Type **83**	10	20
250	2c. Bottlebrush	20	25
251	3c. Oleander (*vert*)	15	10
252	4c. Bermudiana	15	10
253	5c. Poinsettia	2·50	20
254	6c. Hibiscus	30	30
255	9c. Cereus	20	45
256	10c. Bougainvillea (*vert*)	20	15
257	12c. Jacaranda	60	60
258	15c. Passion-Flower	90	1·00
258a	17c. As 15c. (2.6.75)	2·75	5·00
259	18c. Coralita	2·25	1·00
259a	20c. As 18c. (2.6.75)	2·75	4·00
260	24c. Morning Glory	1·50	5·00
260a	25c. As 24c. (2.6.75)	2·75	4·50
261	30c. Tecoma	1·00	1·00
262	36c. Angel's Trumpet	1·25	1·75
262a	40c. As 36c. (2.6.75)	2·75	5·50
263	60c. Plumbago	1·75	1·25
263a	$1 As 60c. (2.6.75)	3·25	6·50
264	$1.20 Bird of Paradise flower	2·25	1·25
264a	$2 As $1.20 (2.6.75)	9·00	10·00
265	$2.40 Chalice Cup	4·50	1·50
265a	$3 As $2.40 (2.6.75)	11·00	11·00
249/65a	Set of 24	48·00	50·00

See also Nos. 303/6 and 340/1.

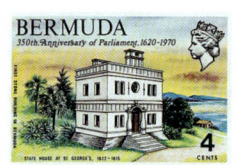

84 The State House, St. George's

(Des G. Drummond. Litho Questa)

1970 (12 Oct). 350th Anniv of Bermuda Parliament. T **84** and similar horiz designs. Multicoloured. W w **12** (sideways). P 14.

266	4c. Type **84**	10	10
267	15c. The Sessions House, Hamilton	30	20
268	18c. St. Peter's Church, St. George's	30	25
269	24c. Town Hall, Hamilton	40	1·00
266/9	Set of 4	1·00	1·40
MS270	131×95 mm. Nos. 266/9	1·10	1·50

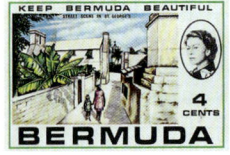

85 Street Scene, St. George's

86 Building of the *Deliverance*

(Des G. Drummond. Litho Questa)

1971 (8 Feb). "Keep Bermuda. Beautiful". T **85** and similar horiz designs. Multicoloured. W w **12** (sideways). P 14.

271	4c. Type **85**	20	10
272	15c. Horseshoe Bay	65	65
273	18c. Gibb's Hill Lighthouse	1·50	2·25
274	24c. Hamilton Harbour	1·25	2·50
271/274	Set of 4	3·25	5·00

(Des E. Amos. Adapted C. Abbott. Litho Questa)

1971 (10 May). Voyage of the "Deliverance". T **86** and similar multicoloured designs. W w **12** (sideways on 4c. and 24c.). P 14.

275	4c. Type **86**	60	20
276	15c. *Deliverance* and *Patience* at Jamestown	1·50	1·75
277	18c. Wreck of the *Sea Venture*	1·50	2·25
278	24c. *Deliverance* and *Patience* on the high seas	1·75	2·50
275/278	Set of 4	4·75	6·00

The 15c. and 18c. are vert designs.

87 Green overlooking Ocean View

HEATH - NIXON DECEMBER 1971

(**88**)

(Des G. Drummond. Litho D.L.R.)

1971 (1 Nov). Golfing in Bermuda. T **87** and similar horiz designs. Multicoloured. W w **12** (sideways*). P 13.

279	4c. Type **87**	70	10
	w. Wmk Crown to right of CA	55·00	55·00
280	15c. Golfers at Port Royal	1·25	65
281	18c. Castle Harbour	1·25	1·00
	w. Wmk Crown to right of CA	3·50	
282	24c. Belmont	1·50	2·00
279/282	Set of 4	4·25	3·25

*The normal sideways watermark shows Crown to left of CA, *as seen from the back of the stamp.*

1971 (20 Dec). Anglo-American Talks. Nos. 252, 258, 259 and 260 optd with T **88** by Format.

283	4c. Bermudiana	10	10
284	15c. Passion Flower	10	20
285	18c. Coralita	15	65
286	24c. Morning Glory	20	1·00
283/286	Set of 4	50	1·75

89 Bonefish

(Des Maynard Reece. Litho B.W.)

1972 (21 Aug). World Fishing Records. T **89** and similar horiz designs. Multicoloured. W w **12**. P 13½×14.

287	4c. Type **89**	30	10
288	15c. Wahoo	30	50
289	18c. Yellow-finned Tuna	35	75
290	24c. Greater Amberjack	40	1·25
287/290	Set of 4	1·25	2·25

90 "Admiralty Oar" and Mace

(Des (from photograph by D. Groves) and photo Harrison)

1972 (20 Nov). Royal Silver Wedding. Multicoloured; background colour given. W w **12**. P 14×14½.

291	**90**	4c. bright bluish violet	15	10
292		15c. rose-carmine	15	50
		w. Wmk inverted	2·00	3·00

BERMUDA

91 Palmetto

91a Princess Anne and Captain Mark Phillips

(Des Jennifer Toombs. Litho J.W.)

1973 (3 Sept). Tree Planting Year. T **91** and similar vert designs. Multicoloured. W w **12** (sideways). P 14.

293	4c. Type **91**	25	10
294	15c. Olivewood Bark	65	75
	a. Brown (Queen's head and value) omitted	£2250	
295	18c. Bermuda Cedar	70	1·25
296	24c. Mahogany	75	1·60
293/296	Set of 4	2·10	3·25

(Des PAD Studio. Litho Questa)

1973 (21 Nov*). Royal Wedding. Centre multicoloured. W w **12** (sideways). P 13½.

297	**91a**	15c. bright mauve	15	15
298		18c. steel blue	15	15

*This is the local date of issue. The Crown Agents released the stamps on the 14 November.

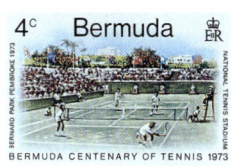

92 Bernard Park, Pembroke, 1973

(Des J.W. Litho Questa)

1973 (17 Dec). Lawn Tennis Centenary. T **92** and similar horiz designs. Multicoloured. W w **12**. P 14.

299	4c. Type **92**	30	10
300	15c. Clermont Court, 1873	40	65
301	18c. Leamington Spa Court, 1872	45	1·75
302	24c. Staten Island Courts, 1874	50	2·00
299/302	Set of 4	1·50	4·00

1974 (13 June)–**76**. As Nos. 253/4, 257 and 261, but W w **12** (upright).

303	5c. Poinsettia	90	1·00
304	6c. Hibiscus	9·50	14·00
305	12c. Jacaranda	1·75	5·50
	w. Wmk inverted	75·00	
306	30c. Tecoma (11.6.76)	7·00	8·00
303/306	Set of 4	17·00	26·00

Nos. 307/19 are vacant.

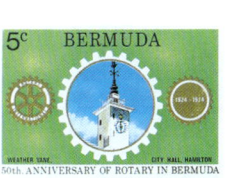

93 Weather Vane, City Hall

94 Jack of Clubs and "good bridge hand"

(Des G. Drummond. Litho Questa)

1974 (24 June). 50th Anniv of Rotary in Bermuda. T **93** and similar horiz designs. Multicoloured. W w **12** (sideways). P 14.

320	5c. Type **93**	15	10
321	17c. St. Peter's Church, St. George's	45	35
322	20c. Somerset Bridge	50	1·50
323	25c. Map of Bermuda, 1626	60	2·25
320/323	Set of 4	1·50	3·75

(Des J.W. Litho Format)

1975 (27 Jan). World Bridge Championships, Bermuda. T **94** and similar vert designs. Multicoloured. W w **12**. P 14.

324	5c. Type **94**	20	10
325	17c. Queen of Diamonds and Bermuda Bowl	35	50
326	20c. King of Hearts and Bermuda Bowl	40	1·75
327	25c. Ace of Spades and Bermuda Bowl	40	2·50
324/327	Set of 4	1·25	4·25

95 Queen Elizabeth II and the Duke of Edinburgh

(Des and photo Harrison)

1975 (17 Feb). Royal Visit. W w **14**. P 14×14½.

328	**95**	17c. multicoloured	60	65
329		20c. multicoloured	65	2·10

96 Short S.23 Flying Boat *Cavalier*, 1937

97 Supporters of American Army raiding Royal Magazine

(Des R. Granger Barrett. Litho Questa)

1975 (28 Apr). 50th Anniv of Air-mail Service to Bermuda. T **96** and similar horiz designs. Multicoloured. W w **14** (sideways). P 14.

330	5c. Type **96**	40	10
331	17c. U.S.N. airship *Los Angeles*, 1925	1·25	85
332	20c. Lockheed L.049 Constellation, 1946	1·40	2·75
333	25c. Boeing 747-100, 1970	1·50	3·50
330/333	Set of 4	4·00	6·50
MS334	128×85 mm. Nos. 330/3	11·00	15·00

(Des J. Cooter. Litho J. W.)

1975 (27 Oct). Bicentenary of Gunpowder Plot, St George's. T **97** and similar horiz designs. Multicoloured. W w **14** (sideways*). P 13×13½.

335	5c. Type **97**	15	10
336	17c. Setting off for raid	30	40
337	20c. Loading gunpowder aboard American ship	35	1·40
338	25c. Gunpowder on beach	35	1·50
	w. Wmk Crown to left of CA	90·00	
335/338	Set of 4	1·00	3·00
MS339	165×138 mm. Nos. 335/8. P 14 (*sold for* 75c.)	2·75	7·00

*The normal sideways watermark shows Crown to right of CA, *as seen from the back of the stamp*.

1975 (8 Dec)–**76**. As Nos. 250 and 254, but W w **14** (sideways).

340	2c. Bottlebrush	85	4·00
341	6c. Hibiscus (11.6.76)	6·00	8·50

Nos. 342/56 are vacant.

98 Launching *Ready* (bathysphere)

99 Christian Radich (cadet ship)

(Des G. Drummond. Litho Questa)

1976 (29 Mar). 50th Anniv of Bermuda Biological Station. T **98** and similar multicoloured designs. W w **14** (sideways on 17 and 20c.). P 14.

357	5c. Type **98**	30	10

53

BERMUDA

358	17c. View from the sea (*horiz*)	60	60
359	20c. H.M.S. *Challenger*, 1873 (*horiz*)	65	2·25
360	25c. Beebe's bathysphere descent, 1934	70	3·00
357/360 Set of 4		2·00	5·50

(Des R. Granger Barrett. Litho J.W.)

1976 (15 June). Tall Ships Race, 1976. T **99** and similar horiz designs. Multicoloured. W w **12** (sideways). P 13.

361	5c. Type **99**	75	20
362	12c. *Juan Sebastian de Elcano* (Spanish cadet schooner)	80	2·25
363	17c. *Eagle* (U.S. coastguard cadet ship)	80	1·50
364	20c. *Sir Winston Churchill* (cadet schooner)	80	1·75
365	40c. *Kruzenshtern* (Russian cadet barque)	1·00	2·75
366	$1 *Cutty Sark* trophy	1·25	7·00
361/366 Set of 6		4·75	14·00

100 Silver Trophy and Club Flags
101 Royal Visit, 1975 

(Des C. Abbott. Litho Questa)

1976 (16 Aug). 75th Anniv of the St. George's v. Somerset Cricket Cup Match. T **100** and similar horiz designs. Multicoloured. W w **14** (sideways*). P 14½×14.

367	5c. Type **100**	30	10
	w. Wmk Crown to right of CA		
368	17c. Badge and Pavilion, St. George's Club	50	65
369	20c. Badge and Pavilion, Somerset Club	65	2·75
370	25c. Somerset playing field	1·00	3·75
367/370 Set of 4		2·25	6·50

*The normal sideways watermark shows Crown to left of CA, *as seen from the back of the stamp.*

(Des Harrison. Litho Walsall)

1977 (7 Feb). Silver Jubilee. T **101** and similar vert designs. Multicoloured. W w **14**. P 13½.

371	5c. Type **101**	10	10
	w. Wmk inverted	£120	80·00
372	20c. St. Edward's Crown	15	20
373	$1 Queen in Chair of Estate	40	1·25
371/373 Set of 3		55	1·40

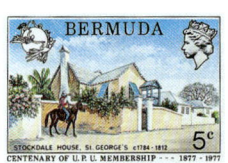

102 Stockdale House, St. George's 1784–1812

(Des G. Drummond. Litho J.W.)

1977 (20 June). Centenary of U.P.U. Membership. T **102** and similar horiz designs. Multicoloured. W w **14** (sideways). P 13.

374	5c. Type **102**	15	10
375	15c. Perot Post Office and stamp	25	50
376	17c. St. George's P.O. circa 1860	25	50
377	20c. Old G.P.O., Hamilton, circa 1935	30	60
378	40c. New G.P.O., Hamilton, 1967	45	1·10
374/378 Set of 5		1·25	2·50

103 17th-Century Ship approaching Castle Island

(Des R. Granger-Barrett. Litho Questa)

1977 (26 Sept). Piloting. T **103** and similar horiz designs. Multicoloured. W w **14** (sideways). P 13½.

379	5c. Type **103**	50	10
380	15c. Pilot leaving ship, 1795	70	60
381	17c. Pilots rowing out to paddle-steamer	80	60
382	20c. Pilot gigs and brig *Harvest Queen*	85	2·25
383	40c. Modern pilot cutter and R.M.S. *Queen Elizabeth 2*	1·60	3·75
379/383 Set of 5		4·00	6·50

104 Great Seal of Queen Elizabeth I
105 White-tailed Tropic Bird 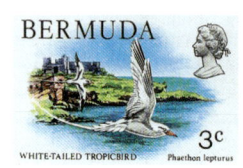

(Des BG Studio. Litho Questa)

1978 (28 Aug). 25th Anniv of Coronation. T **104** and similar vert designs. Multicoloured. W w **14**. P 14×13½.

384	8c. Type **104**	10	10
385	50c. Great Seal of Queen Elizabeth II	30	30
386	$1 Queen Elizabeth II	60	75
384/386 Set of 3		80	1·00

(Des G. Drummond. Photo Harrison)

1978 (15 Nov)–**83**. Wildlife. Horiz designs as T **105**. Multicoloured. W w **14** (sideways* on 8, 15, 20, 40c. and $1). P 14×14½ (4, 5c., $2, $3, $5) or 14 (others).

387	3c. Type **105**	2·50	2·50
	aw. Wmk inverted	29·00	
	b. Perf 14×14½ (3.8.83)†	2·75	3·00
	bw. Wmk inverted	£250	
388	4c. White-eyed Vireo	3·00	3·00
	w. Wmk inverted	95·00	
389	5c. Eastern Bluebird	1·25	1·75
	w. Wmk inverted	85·00	35·00
390	7c. Whistling Frog (19.2.79)	50	1·50
391	8c. Common Cardinal	1·25	55
392	10c. Spiny Lobster (19.2.79)	20	10
393	12c. Land Crab (19.2.79)	30	70
394	15c. Lizard (Skink) (19.2.79)	30	15
395	20c. Four-eyed Butterflyfish (12.3.79)	30	30
	w. Wmk Crown to right of CA	1·00	1·25
396	25c. Red Hind (12.3.79)	30	20
	a. Greenish blue omitted	£4750	
397	30c. *Danaus plexippus* (butterfly) (19.2.79)	2·25	2·50
398	40c. Rock Beauty (12.3.79)	50	1·75
399	50c. Banded Butterflyfish (12.3.79)	55	1·50
400	$1 Blue Angelfish (12.3.79)	3·00	1·75
	w. Wmk Crown to right of CA	£325	
401	$2 Humpback Whale (12.3.79)	2·00	2·25
402	$3 Green Turtle (19.2.79)	2·50	2·50
403	$5 Cahow	5·00	5·00
387/403 Set of 17		23·00	25·00

*The normal sideways watermark shows Crown to left of CA, *as seen from the back of the stamp.*

†Earliest known postmark date.

106 Map by Sir George Somers, 1609
107 Policeman and Policewoman

BERMUDA

(Des J. Cooter. Litho Questa)

1979 (14 May). Antique Maps. T **106** and similar multicoloured designs. W w **14** (sideways on 8, 15, 25 and 50c.). P 14×13½ (20c.) or 13½×14 (others).

404	8c. Type **106**.	15	10
405	15c. Map by John Seller, 1685	20	15
406	20c. Map by H. Moll, 1729-40 (vert)	25	25
407	25c. Map by Desbruslins, 1740	30	30
408	50c. Map by Speed, 1626	45	80
404/408	Set of 5	1·25	1·40

(Des L. Curtis. Litho Questa)

1979 (26 Nov). Centenary of Police Force. T **107** and similar multicoloured designs. W w **14** (sideways on 20 and 25c.). P 14.

409	8c. Type **107**.	30	10
	w. Wmk inverted	12·00	5·50
410	20c. Policeman directing traffic (horiz)	50	55
411	25c. Blue Heron (police launch) (horiz)	60	65
412	50c. Police car and motorcycle	80	1·50
409/412	Set of 4	2·00	2·50

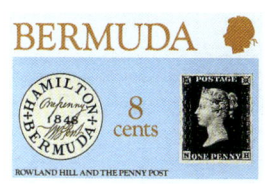

108 1848 1d. "Perot" and Penny Black Stamps

(Des J.W. Litho Enschedé)

1980 (25 Feb). Death Centenary of Sir Rowland Hill (1979). T **108** and similar horiz designs. Multicoloured. W w **14** (sideways). P 13×13½.

413	8c. Type **108**	20	10
414	20c. 1848 1d. "Perot" stamp and Sir Rowland Hill	30	25
415	25c. 1848 1d. "Perot" stamp and early letter	30	30
416	50c. 1848 1d. "Perot" stamp and "Paid 1" cancellation	35	1·00
413/416	Set of 4	1·00	1·50

109 Lockheed L-1011 TriStar 500 Airliner approaching Bermuda

110 Gina Swainson with Rose

(Des R. Granger Barrett. Litho Harrison)

1980 (6 May). "London 1980" International Stamp Exhibition. Mail-carrying Transport. T **109** and similar horiz designs. Multicoloured. W w **14** (sideways*). P 13×13½.

417	25c. Type **109**	30	15
418	50c. Orduna I (liner) in Grassy Bay	45	35
	w. Wmk Crown to right of CA	55·00	
419	$1 Delta (screw steamer) at St George's Harbour	85	1·10
420	$2 Lord Sidmouth (sailing packet) in Old Ship Channel, St. George's	1·40	2·25
417/420	Set of 4	2·75	3·50

*The normal sideways watermark shows Crown to left of CA, as seen from the back of the stamp.

(Des Walsall. Litho Questa)

1980 (8 May). "Miss World 1979-80" (Gina Swainson) Commemoration. T **110** and similar vert designs. Multicoloured. W w **14**. P 14×13½.

421	8c. Type **110**	15	10
422	20c. After crowning ceremony	20	20
423	50c. On Peacock Throne at "Welcome Home" party	35	35
424	$1 In Bermuda carriage	70	90
421/424	Set of 4	1·25	1·40

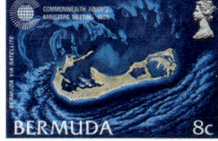

111 Queen Elizabeth the Queen Mother

112 Bermuda from Satellite

(Des and litho Harrison)

1980 (4 Aug). 80th Birthday of Queen Elizabeth the Queen Mother. W w **14** (sideways). P 14.

425	**111**	25c. multicoloured	30	1·00

(Des L. Curtis. Litho Questa)

1980 (24 Sept). Commonwealth Finance Ministers Meeting. T **112** and similar horiz designs. Multicoloured. W w **14** (sideways*). P 14.

426	8c. Type **112**	10	10
427	20c. "Camden"	20	40
428	25c. Princess Hotel, Hamilton	20	50
	w. Wmk Crown to right of CA	£110	
429	50c. Government House	35	1·50
426/429	Set of 4	75	2·25

*The normal sideways watermark shows Crown to left of CA, as seen from the back of the stamp.

113 Kitchen, 18th-century

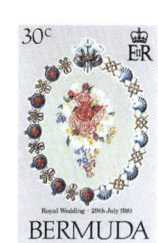

114 Wedding Bouquet from Bermuda

(Des J.W. Litho Questa)

1981 (21 May). Heritage Week. T **113** and similar horiz designs. Multicoloured. W w **14** (sideways*). P 14.

430	8c. Type **113**	15	10
	w. Wmk Crown to right of CA	10·00	6·00
431	25c. Gathering Easter lilies, 20th-century	20	35
432	30c. Fishing, 20th-century	30	50
433	40c. Stone cutting, 19th-century	30	80
	w. Wmk Crown to right of CA	1·50	2·75
434	50c. Onion shipping, 19th-century	50	90
435	$1 Privateering, 17th-century	1·10	2·50
430/435	Set of 6	2·25	4·75

*The normal sideways watermark shows Crown to left of CA, as seen from the back of the stamp.

(Des J.W. Litho Questa)

1981 (22 July). Royal Wedding. T **114** and similar vert designs. Multicoloured. W w **14**. P 14.

436	30c. Type **114**	20	20
437	50c. Prince Charles as Royal Navy Commander	35	40
438	$1 Prince Charles and Lady Diana Spencer	55	80
436/438	Set of 3	1·00	1·25

115 "Service", Hamilton

116 Lightbourne's Cone (Conus lightbourni)

(Des L. Curtis. Litho Questa)

1981 (28 Sept). 25th Anniv of Duke of Edinburgh Award Scheme. T **115** and similar vert designs. Multicoloured. W w **14**. P 14.

439	10c. Type **115**	15	10
440	25c. "Outward Bound", Paget Island	20	20

55

BERMUDA

441	30c. "Expedition", St. David's Island	20	30
442	$1 Duke of Edinburgh	55	1·25
439/442	Set of 4	1·00	1·75

(Des Walsall. Litho Questa)

1982 (22 Apr). Sea-shells. T **116** and similar horiz designs. Multicoloured. W w **14** (sideways). P 14.

443	10c. Type **116**	30	10
444	25c. Finlay's Frog Shell (*Bursa finlayi*)	55	55
445	30c. Royal Bonnet (*Sconsia striata*)	60	60
446	$1 Lightbourne's Murex (*Murex lightbourni*)	1·75	3·25
443/446	Set of 4	2·75	4·00

117 Regimental Colours and Colour Party

118 Charles Fort

(Des G. Drummond. Litho Questa)

1982 (17 June). Bermuda Regiment. T **117** and similar horiz designs. Multicoloured. W w **14** (sideways). P 14.

447	10c. Type **117**	60	10
448	25c. Queen's Birthday Parade	80	80
449	30c. Governor inspecting Guard of Honour	1·10	1·40
450	40c. Beating the Retreat	1·25	1·75
451	50c. Ceremonial gunners	1·25	2·00
452	$1 Guard of Honour, Royal visit, 1975	1·75	3·50
447/452	Set of 6	6·00	8·50

(Des L. Curtis. Litho Questa)

1982 (18 Nov). Historic Bermuda Forts. T **118** and similar multicoloured designs. W w **14** (sideways on 30c. and $1). P 14.

453	10c. Type **118**	20	20
454	25c. Pembroke Fort	50	85
455	30c. Southampton Fort (*horiz*)	60	1·25
456	$1 Smiths Fort and Pagets Fort (*horiz*)	1·75	4·50
453/456	Set of 4	2·75	6·00

119 Arms of Sir Edwin Sandys

120 Early Fitted Dinghy

(Des Harrison. Litho J.W.)

1983 (14 Apr). Coats of Arms (1st series). T **119** and similar vert designs. Multicoloured. W w **14**. P 13.

457	10c. Type **119**	45	15
458	25c. Arms of the Bermuda Company	1·10	1·00
459	50c. Arms of William Herbert, Earl of Pembroke	1·90	3·75
460	$1 Arms of Sir George Somers	2·50	6·50
457/460	Set of 4	5·50	10·00

See also Nos. 482/5 and 499/502.

(Des L. Curtis. Litho Harrison)

1983 (23 June). Fitted Dinghies. T **120** and similar vert designs. W w **14** (sideways). P 14.

461	12c. Type **120**	45	15
462	30c. Modern dinghy inshore	60	75
463	40c. Early dinghy (*different*)	70	90
464	$1 Modern dinghy with red and white spinnaker	1·40	3·25
461/464	Set of 4	2·75	4·50

121 Curtiss N-9 Seaplane (first flight over Bermuda)

122 Joseph Stockdale

(Des A. Theobald. Litho Walsall)

1983 (13 Oct). Bicentenary of Manned Flight. T **121** and similar horiz designs. Multicoloured. W w **14** (sideways). P 14.

465	12c. Type **121**	60	20
466	30c. Stinson Pilot Radio seaplane (First completed flight between U.S.A. and Bermuda)	1·25	1·25
467	40c. Short S.23 flying boat *Cavalier* (First scheduled passenger flight)	1·50	1·75
468	$1 U.S.N. *Los Angeles* (airship) moored to U.S.S. *Patoka*	2·75	5·00
465/468	Set of 4	5·50	7·50

(Des L. Curtis. Litho Harrison)

1984 (26 Jan). Bicentenary of Bermuda's First Newspaper and Postal Service. T **122** and similar multicoloured designs. W w **14** (sideways)* on 40c. and $1). P 14.

469	12c. Type **122**	25	15
470	30c. *The Bermuda Gazette*	45	80
471	40c. Stockdale's postal service (*horiz*)	60	1·10
	w. Wmk Crown to right of CA	£100	£100
472	$1 *Lady Hammond* (mail boat) (*horiz*)	2·00	3·25
469/472	Set of 4	3·00	4·75

*The normal sideways watermark shows Crown to left of CA, *as seen from the back of the stamp.*

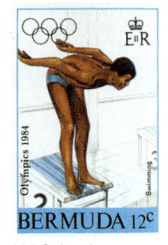

123 Sir Thomas Gates and Sir George Somers

124 Swimming

(Des R. Granger Barrett. Litho Walsall)

1984 (3 May). 375th Anniv of First Settlement. T **123** and similar horiz designs. Multicoloured. W w **14** (sideways). P 14.

473	12c. Type **123**	20	15
474	30c. Jamestown, Virginia	50	1·25
475	40c. Wreck of *Sea Venture*	90	1·25
476	$1 Fleet leaving Plymouth, Devon	2·00	6·00
473/476	Set of 4	3·25	7·75
MS477	130×73 mm. Nos. 474 and 476	3·75	10·00

(Des C. Collins. Litho J.W.)

1984 (19 July). Olympic Games, Los Angeles. T **124** and similar multicoloured designs. W w **14** (sideways on 30c., $1). P 14.

478	12c. Type **124**	40	15
479	30c. Track and field events (*horiz*)	70	75
480	40c. Equestrian competition	1·10	1·25
481	$1 Sailing (*horiz*)	2·00	5·50
478/481	Set of 4	3·75	7·00

(Des Harrison. Litho J.W.)

1984 (27 Sept). Coats of Arms (2nd series). Vert designs as T **119**. Multicoloured. W w **14**. P 13.

482	12c. Arms of Henry Wriothesley, Earl of Southampton	50	15
483	30c. Arms of Sir Thomas Smith	1·00	85
	w. Wmk inverted	1·50	
484	40c. Arms of William Cavendish, Earl of Devonshire	1·25	1·50
485	$1 Town arms of St. George	2·75	4·50
482/485	Set of 4	5·00	6·00

56

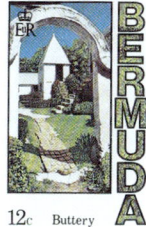

125 Buttery    **126** Osprey

(Des D. Miller. Litho Walsall)

1985 (24 Jan). Bermuda Architecture. T **125** and similar multicoloured designs. W w **14** (inverted on 12c, $1.50, sideways on 30c, 40c.). P 13½×13 (12c, $1.50) or 13×13½ (30c, 40c.).

486	12c. Type **125**..	35	15
487	30c. Limestone rooftops (*horiz*)...............	80	70
488	40c. Chimneys (*horiz*)................................	95	1·00
489	$1.50 Entrance archway...............................	2·50	4·25
486/489 Set of 4		4·25	5·50

(Des D. Miller. Litho Walsall)

1985 (28 Mar). Birth Bicentenary of John J. Audubon (ornithologist). T **126** and similar multicoloured designs showing original drawings. W w **14** (sideways on 40c.). P 14.

490	12c. Type **126**..	2·00	65
491	30c. Yellow-crowned Night Heron............	2·00	95
492	40c. Great Egret (*horiz*).............................	2·25	1·25
493	$1.50 Eastern Bluebird...............................	3·75	6·50
490/493 Set of 4		9·00	8·50

127 The Queen Mother with Grandchildren, 1980

(Des A. Theobald ($1), C. Abbott (others). Litho Questa)

1985 (7 June). Life and Times of Queen Elizabeth the Queen Mother. T **127** and similar vert designs. Multicoloured. W w **16**. P 14½×14.

494	12c. Queen Consort, 1937...........................	35	15
	w. Wmk inverted		
495	30c. Type **127**...	60	50
	w. Wmk inverted	1·75	
496	40c. At Clarence House on 83rd birthday...	70	60
497	$1.50 With Prince Henry at his christening (from photo by Lord Snowdon)................	2·00	2·75
494/497 Set of 4		2·75	3·50
MS498 91×73 mm. $1 With Prince Charles at 80th birthday celebrations. Wmk sideways......................		3·75	3·50

(Des Harrison. Litho J.W.)

1985 (19 Sept). Coats of Arms (3rd series). Vert designs as T **119**. Multicoloured. W w **14**. P 13×13½.

499	12c. Hamilton...	75	15
500	30c. Paget..	1·40	80
501	40c. Warwick..	1·60	1·40
502	$1.50 City of Hamilton................................	3·75	4·25
499/502 Set of 4		6·75	6·00

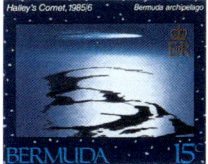

128 Halley's Comet and Bermuda Archipelago

(Des Jennifer Toombs. Litho Walsall)

1985 (21 Nov). Appearance of Halley's Comet. T **128** and similar horiz designs. Multicoloured. W w **16** (sideways). P 14×14½.

503	15c. Type **128**..	85	25
504	40c. Halley's Comet, A.D. 684 (from Nuremberg Chronicles, 1493)................	1·60	1·75
505	50c. "Halley's Comet, 1531" (from Peter Apian woodcut, 1532).....................................	1·90	2·50
506	$1.50 "Halley's Comet, 1759" (Samuel Scott).....	3·50	6·50
503/506 Set of 4		7·00	10·00

129 *Constellation* (Schooner), 1943

(Des L. Curtis. Litho Questa)

1986 (16 Jan)–**90**. Ships Wrecked on Bermuda. T **129** and similar horiz designs. Multicoloured. W w **16** (sideways*). P 14.

A. Without imprint date at foot

507A	3c. Type **129**...	70	2·25
508A	5c. *Early Riser* (pilot boat), 1876.................	20	20
509A	7c. *Madiana* (steamer), 1903 (20.3.86)........	65	2·75
510A	10c. *Curlew* (sail/steamer), 1856..................	30	30
511A	12c. *Warwick* (galleon), 1619.......................	60	80
	w. Wmk Crown to right of CA....................	£120	30·00
512A	15c. H.M.S. *Vixen* (gunboat), 1890 (18.9.86)..	40	60
512cA	18c. As 7c. (22.9.88)....................................	8·00	4·25
513A	20c. *San Pedro* (Spanish galleon), 1594 (20.3.86)...	1·10	80
514A	25c. *Alert* (fishing sloop), 1877 (18.9.86).....	60	3·00
515A	40c. *North Carolina* (barque), 1880 (18.9.86)..	65	1·25
516A	50c. *Mark Antonie* (Spanish privateer), 1777 (18.9.86)...	1·50	3·25
517A	60c. *Mary Celestia* (Confederate paddle-steamer), 1864 (20.3.86).........................	1·50	1·75
517cA	70c. *Caesar* (brig), 1818 (27.10.88).............	8·50	6·50
518A	$1 *L'Herminie* (French frigate), 1839 (18.9.86)...	4·00	4·50
519A	$1.50 As 70c. (20.3.86)..................................	4·50	6·50
520A	$2 *Lord Amherst* (transport), 1778 (20.3.86)...	5·00	8·00
521A	$3 *Minerva* (sailing ship), 1849 (20.3.86).....	5·50	9·00
522A	$5 *Caraquet* (cargo liner), 1923 (18.9.86)....	4·50	11·00
523A	$8 H.M.S. *Pallas* (frigate), 1783.................	5·50	14·00
507A/523A Set of 19		48·00	70·00

B. With imprint date

507B	3c. Type **129** (1.8.90)................................	1·75	3·50
513B	20c. *San Pedro* (Spanish galleon), 1594 (1.8.90)...	4·00	4·00
518B	$1 *L'Herminie* (French frigate), 1839 (7.89)..	1·50	2·00
520B	$2 *Lord Amherst* (transport), 1778 (7.89).....	2·50	6·50
521B	$3 *Minerva* (sailing ship), 1849 (7.89)..........	4·25	9·50
507B/521B Set of 5		12·50	23·00

*The normal sideways watermark shows Crown to left of CA, *as seen from the back of the stamp*.

It is reported that the vessel depicted on the 70c. is the *Wolf* and not the *Caesar*.

Imprint dates: "1989", Nos. 518B, 520B/1B; "1990", Nos. 507B, 513B.

No. 523A shows "BERMUDA" printed in yellow fluorescent ink as a security marking.

For some of these designs watermarked w **14** (sideways) see Nos. 664/78.

129a Princess Elizabeth aged three, 1929 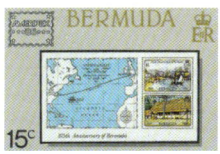   **129b** 1984 375th Anniv of Settlement miniature sheet

(Des A. Theobald. Litho Harrison)

1986 (21 Apr). 60th Birthday of Queen Elizabeth II. T **129a** and similar vert designs. Multicoloured. W w **16**. P 14½×14.

524	15c. Type **129a**..	45	30
	w. Wmk inverted.......................................	29·00	18·00

BERMUDA

525	40c. With Earl of Rosebery at Oaks May Meeting, Epsom, 1954................	80	60
526	50c. With Duke of Edinburgh, Bermuda, 1975	80	75
527	60c. At British Embassy, Paris, 1972................	90	90
528	$1.50 At Crown Agents Head Office, London, 1983................	2·00	2·50
524/528 Set of 5		4·50	4·50

(Des G. Drummond. Litho Walsall)

1986 (22 May). "Ameripex '86" International Stamp Exhibition, Chicago. T **129b** and similar horiz designs. Multicoloured. W w **16** (sideways). P 14.

529	15c. Type **129b**................	1·50	30
530	40c. 1973 Lawn Tennis Centenary 24c.......	2·25	70
531	50c. 1983 Bicentenary of Manned Flight 12c................	2·25	1·00
532	$1 1976 Tall Ships Race 17c................	3·75	3·00
529/532 Set of 4		7·50	7·50
MS533 80×80 mm. $1.50, Statue of Liberty and *Monarch of Bermuda*		8·75	8·00

No. **MS**533 also commemorates the Centenary of the Statue of Liberty.

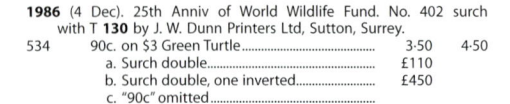

90c

(130)

1986 (4 Dec). 25th Anniv of World Wildlife Fund. No. 402 surch with T **130** by J. W. Dunn Printers Ltd, Sutton, Surrey.

534	90c. on $3 Green Turtle................	3·50	4·50
	a. Surch double................	£110	
	b. Surch double, one inverted................	£450	
	c. "90c" omitted................		

131 Train in Front Street, Hamilton, 1940

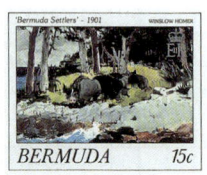

132 "Bermuda Settlers", 1901

(Des A. Theobald. Litho Walsall)

1987 (22 Jan). Transport (1st series). Bermuda Railway. T **131** and similar horiz designs. Multicoloured. W w **16** (sideways). P 14.

535	15c. Type **131**................	2·00	25
536	40c. Train crossing Springfield Trestle........	2·50	90
537	50c. "St. George Special" at Bailey's Bay Station................	2·50	1·50
538	$1.50 Boat train at St. George................	4·00	6·25
535/538 Set of 4		10·00	8·00

See also Nos. 557/60, 574/7 and 624/9.

(Des L. Curtis. Litho Walsall)

1987 (30 Apr). Bermuda Paintings (1st series). Works by Winslow Homer. T **132** and similar horiz designs. Multicoloured. W w **16** (sideways). P 14×14½.

(a) Sheet stamps (No. 541 with a buff frame)

539	15c. Type **132**................	60	25
540	30c. "Bermuda", 1900................	85	45
541	40c. "Bermuda Landscape", 1901................	95	55
542	50c. "Inland Water", 1901................	1·10	70
543	$1.50 "Salt Kettle", 1899................	2·50	2·50
539/543 Set of 5		5·50	4·00

(b) Booklet stamps, each with grey frame

544	40c. Type **132**................	1·00	1·75
	a. Booklet pane. Nos. 544/8, each×2.......	9·00	
545	40c. As No. 540................	1·00	1·75
546	40c. As No. 541................	1·00	1·75
547	40c. As No. 542................	1·00	1·75
548	40c. As No. 543................	1·00	1·75
544/548 Set of 5		4·50	8·00

See also Nos. 607/10 and 630/3.

133 Sikorsky S-42B Flying Boat *Bermuda Clipper* of Pan Am

134 19th-century Wagon carrying Telephone Poles

(Des A. Theobald. Litho Walsall)

1987 (18 June). 50th Anniv of Inauguration of Bermuda–U.S.A. Air Service. T **133** and similar horiz designs. Multicoloured. W w **16** (sideways). P 14.

549	15c. Type **133**................	2·00	15
550	40c. Short S.23 flying boat *Cavalier* of Imperial Airways................	3·00	70
551	50c. *Bermuda Clipper* in flight over signpost..	3·25	80
552	$1.50 *Cavalier* on apron and *Bermuda Clipper* in flight................	6·00	3·50
549/552 Set of 4		13·00	4·75

(Des L. Curtis. Litho B.D.T.)

1987 (1 Oct). Centenary of Bermuda Telephone Company. T **134** and similar horiz designs. Multicoloured. W w **16** (sideways). P 14×13½.

553	15c. Type **134**................	75	15
554	40c. Early telephone exchange................	1·40	60
555	50c. Early and modem telephones................	1·75	70
556	$1.50 Communications satellite orbiting Earth................	2·75	5·75
553/556 Set of 4		6·00	6·50

135 Mail Wagon, *c.* 1869

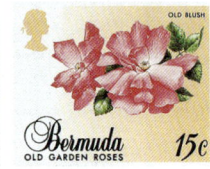

136 "Old Blush"

(Des O. Bell. Litho Questa)

1988 (3 Mar). Transport (2nd series). Horse-drawn Carts and Wagons. T **135** and similar horiz designs. Multicoloured. W w **16** (sideways). P 14.

557	15c. Type **135**................	25	15
558	40c. Open cart, *c.* 1823................	55	55
559	50c. Closed cart, *c.* 1823................	65	70
560	$1.50 Two-wheeled wagon, *c.* 1930........	2·00	3·25
557/560 Set of 4		3·00	4·25

(Des R. Gorringe. Litho B.D.T.)

1988 (21 Apr). Old Garden Roses (1st series). T **136** and similar multicoloured designs. W w **14** (sideways on horiz designs). P 14×13½ (vert) or 13½×14 (horiz).

561	15c. Type **136**................	85	25
562	30c. "Anna Olivier"................	1·25	45
563	40c. *Rosa chinensis semperflorens* (vert)........	1·40	85
564	50c. "Archduke Charles"................	1·50	1·25
565	$1.50 *Rosa chinensis viridiflora* (vert)........	3·00	6·50
561/565 Set of 5		7·25	8·50

See also Nos. 584/8 and, for these designs with the royal cypher instead of the Queen's head, Nos. 589/98, and 683/6.

136a Loss of H.M.S. *Lutine* (frigate), 1799

137 Devonshire Parish Militia, 1812

(Des D. Miller (18c.), E. Nisbet and D. Miller (others). Litho Questa)

1988 (13 Oct). 300th Anniv of Lloyd's of London. Multicoloured. W w **16** (sideways* on 50, 60c.). P 14.

566	18c. Type **136a**................	85	25
	w. Wmk inverted................	10·00	
567	50c. *Sentinel* (cable ship) (horiz)................	1·60	65
	w. Wmk Crown to right of CA................	23·00	
568	60c. *Bermuda* (liner), Hamilton, 1931 (horiz)..	1·75	75
	w. Wmk Crown to right of CA................	14·00	
569	$2 Loss of H.M.S. *Valerian* (sloop) in hurricane, 1926................	3·00	4·50
566/569 Set of 4		6·50	5·50

*The normal sideways watermark shows Crown to left of CA, *as seen from the back of the stamp.*

58

BERMUDA

(Des A. Barbosa. Litho Harrison)

1988 (10 Nov). Military Uniforms. T **137** and similar vert designs. Multicoloured. W w **14**. P 14½.
570	18c. Type **137**	1·50	25
571	50c. 71st (Highland) Regiment, 1831–34	2·00	1·10
572	60c. Cameron Highlanders, 1942	2·25	1·25
573	$2 Troop of horse, 1774	4·75	8·50
570/573 Set of 4		9·50	10·00

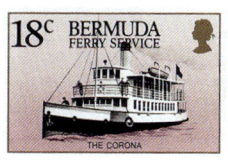

138 *Corona* (ferry)    **139** Morgan's Island

(Des C. Abbott, adapted L. Curtis. Litho Questa)

1989 (16 Feb). Transport (3rd series). Ferry Services. T **138** and similar horiz designs. Multicoloured. W w **16** (sideways). P 14.
574	18c. Type **138**	35	25
575	50c. Rowing boat ferry	75	65
576	60c. St. George's barge ferry	85	75
577	$2 *Laconia*	2·50	4·50
574/577 Set of 4		4·00	5·50

(Des A. Theobald. Litho Questa)

1989 (11 May). 150 Years of Photography. T **139** and similar horiz designs. Multicoloured. W w **14** (sideways). P 14×14½.
578	18c. Type **139**	85	25
579	30c. Front Street, Hamilton	1·10	45
580	50c. Waterfront, Front Street, Hamilton	1·60	1·25
581	60c. Crow Lane from Hamilton Harbour	1·75	1·40
582	70c. Shipbuilding, Hamilton Harbour	1·90	2·50
583	$1 Dockyard	2·25	3·50
578/583 Set of 6		8·50	8·50

(Des R. Gorringe. Litho B.D.T.)

1989 (13 July). Old Garden Roses (2nd series). Multicoloured designs as T **136**. W w **14** (sideways on 50, 60c. and $1.50). P 14×13½ (18, 30c.) or 13½×14 (others).
584	18c. "Agrippina" (*vert*)	90	25
585	30c. "Smiths Parish" (*vert*)	1·25	60
586	50c. "Champney's Pink Cluster"	1·75	1·40
587	60c. "Rosette Delizy"	1·75	1·60
588	$1.50 *Rosa bracteata*	2·75	6·75
584/588 Set of 5		7·50	9·50

For these designs with the royal cypher instead of the Queen's head, see Nos. 589/98.

1989 (13 July). Old Garden Roses (3rd series). Designs as Nos. 561/5 and 584/8 but with royal cypher at top left instead of Queen's head. Multicoloured. W w **14** (sideways on horiz, inverted on vert designs). P 13½.
589	50c. As No. 565 (*vert*)	1·75	2·50
	a. Booklet pane. Nos. 589/98	16·00	22·00
590	50c. As No. 563	1·75	2·50
591	50c. Type **136**	1·75	2·50
592	50c. As No. 562	1·75	2·50
593	50c. As No. 564	1·75	2·50
594	50c. As No. 585 (*vert*)	1·75	2·50
595	50c. As No. 584 (*vert*)	1·75	2·50
596	50c. As No. 586	1·75	2·50
597	50c. As No. 587	1·75	2·50
598	50c. As No. 588	1·75	2·50
589/598 Set of 10		16·00	22·00

Nos. 589/98 were only issued in $5 stamp booklets in which the pane has margins on three sides.

140 Main Library, Hamilton    **141** 1865 1d. Rose

(Des O. Bell. Litho B.D.T.)

1989 (5 Oct). 150th Anniv of Bermuda Library. T **140** and similar horiz designs. Multicoloured. W w **14** (sideways). P 13½×14.
599	18c. Type **140**	60	25
600	50c. The Old Rectory, St. George's	1·25	65
601	60c. Somerset Library, Springfield	1·25	85
602	$2 Cabinet Building, Hamilton	3·25	5·50
599/602 Set of 4		5·50	6·50

(Des D. Miller. Litho Questa)

1989 (3 Nov). Commonwealth Postal Conference. T **141** and similar vert designs. Multicoloured. W w **16**. P 14.
603	18c. brownish grey, brown-rose & brt scar	1·50	25
604	50c. brownish grey, slate-bl & pale grey-bl	2·00	75
605	60c. brownish grey, dull purple and purple	2·25	1·25
606	$2 brownish grey, dull green & brt emer	3·75	6·00
603/606 Set of 4		8·50	7·50

Designs:—50c. 1866 2d. blue; 60c. 1865 6d. purple; $2 1865 1s. green.

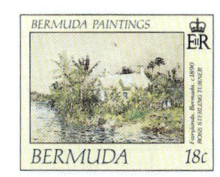

142 "Fairylands, *c.* 1890" (Ross Turner)    (**143**)

(Des L. Curtis. Litho B.D.T.)

1990 (19 Apr). Bermuda. Paintings (2nd series). T **142** and similar horiz designs. Multicoloured. W w **16** (sideways). P 13½.
607	18c. Type **142**	75	25
608	50c. "Shinebone Alley, *c.* 1953" (Ogden Pleissner)	1·25	1·25
609	60c. "Salt Kettle, 1916" (Prosper Senat)	1·25	1·50
610	$2 "St. George's, 1934" (Jack Bush)	3·25	7·00
607/610 Set of 4		6·00	9·00

1990 (3 May). "Stamp World London 90" International Stamp Exhibition, London. Nos. 603/6 optd with T **143**.
611	18c. brownish grey, brown-rose & brt scar	1·25	25
612	50c. brownish grey, slate-bl & pale grey-bl	1·75	1·50
613	60c. brownish grey, dull purple and purple	2·00	1·75
614	$2 brownish grey, dull green & brt emer	3·50	6·00
611/614 Set of 4		7·75	8·50

144   **145** The Halifax and Bermudas Cable Company Office, Hamilton

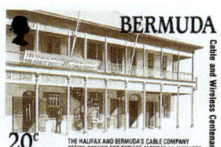

1990 (13 Aug). Nos. 511A, 516A and 519A surch as T **144**.
615	30c. on 12c. *Warwick* (galleon), 1619	1·75	1·50
616	55c. on 50c. *Mark Antonie* (Spanish privateer), 1777	2·25	2·50
617	80c. on $1.50 *Caesar* (brig), 1818	2·50	5·00
615/617 Set of 3		6·00	8·00

(Des C. Abbott. Litho Harrison)

1990 (18 Oct). Centenary of Cable and Wireless in Bermuda. T **145** and similar horiz designs. P 14.
618	20c. light brown and black	70	25
619	55c. light brown and black	2·00	1·25
620	70c. multicoloured	2·00	2·75
621	$2 multicoloured	4·75	8·00
618/621 Set of 4		8·50	11·00

Designs—55c. *Westmeath* (cable ship), 1890, 70c. Wireless transmitter station, St. George's, 1928; $2 *Sir Eric Sharp* (cable ship).

BUSH - MAJOR
16 MARCH 1991

(**146**)

1991 (16 Mar). President Bush–Prime Minister Major Talks, Bermuda. Nos. 618/19 optd with T **146** by Island Press.
622	**145**	20c. light brown and black	2·00	1·50
623	–	55c. light brown and black	3·00	3·50

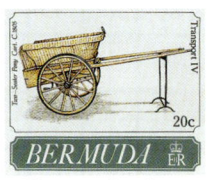

BERMUDA

147 Two-seater Pony Cart, 1805

(Des N. Shering. Litho Walsall)

1991 (21 Mar). Transport (4th series). Horse-drawn Carriages. T **147** and similar horiz designs. Multicoloured. W w **14** (sideways). P 14½.

624	20c. Type **147**	80	30
625	30c. Varnished rockaway, 1830	90	60
626	55c. Vis-a-Vis victoria, 1895	1·60	1·10
627	70c. Semi-formal phaeton, 1900	2·25	2·50
628	80c. Pony runabout, 1905	2·50	3·75
629	$1 Ladies phaeton, 1910	2·75	4·50
624/629 Set of 6		9·75	11·50

148 "Bermuda, 1916" (Prosper Senat)

148a Prince Philip in tropical naval uniform

(Des L. Curtis. Litho Questa)

1991 (16 May). Bermuda Paintings (3rd series). T **148** and similar multicoloured designs. W w **14** (sideways on 55c., $2). P 13½×14 (20, 70c.) or 14×13½ (55c., $2).

630	20c. Type **148**	1·00	30
631	55c. "Bermuda Cottage", 1930 (Frank Allison) (horiz)	2·00	1·40
632	70c. "Old Maid's Lane", 1934 (Jack Bush)	2·50	3·25
633	$2 "St. George's", 1953 (Ogden Pleissner) (horiz)	5·00	8·50
630/633 Set of 4		9·50	12·00

(Des D. Miller. Litho Questa)

1991 (20 June). 65th Birthday of Queen Elizabeth II and 70th Birthday of Prince Philip. T **148a** and similar vert designs. Multicoloured. W w **16** (sideways). P 14½×14.

634	55c. Type **148a**	1·25	1·75
	a. Horiz pair. Nos. 634/5 separated by label	2·50	3·50
635	70c. Queen Elizabeth II in Bermuda	1·25	1·75

Nos. 634/5 were printed together in a similar sheet format to Nos. 913/14 of Bahamas.

149 H.M.S. *Argonaut* (cruiser) in Floating Dock

149a Old fort on beach

(Des N. Shewring. Litho Walsall)

1991 (19 Sept). 50th Anniv of Second World War. T **149** and similar horiz designs. Multicoloured. W w **14** (sideways). P 14.

636	20c. Type **149**	1·50	40
637	55c. Kindley Airfield	2·25	1·40
638	70c. Boeing 314A flying boat and map of Atlantic route	2·75	3·25
639	$2 Censored trans-Atlantic mail	4·50	8·50
636/639 Set of 4		10·00	12·00

(Des D. Miller. Litho Questa ($1), B.D.T. (others))

1992 (6 Feb). 40th Anniv of Queen Elizabeth II's Accession. T **149a** and similar horiz designs. Multicoloured. W w **14** (sideways). P 14.

640	20c. Type **149a**	60	30
641	30c. Public gardens	75	55
642	55c. Cottage garden	1·25	90
643	70c. Beach and hotels	1·60	2·25
644	$1 Queen Elizabeth II	1·90	2·75
640/644 Set of 5		5·50	6·00

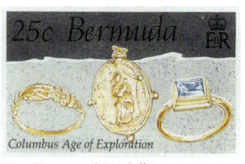

150 Rings and Medallion

(Des N. Shewring. Litho Enschedé)

1992 (23 July). 500th Anniv of Discovery of America by Columbus. Spanish Artifacts. T **150** and similar horiz designs. Multicoloured. W w **14** (sideways). P 13½.

645	25c. Type **150**	1·25	35
646	35c. Ink wells	1·40	75
647	60c. Gold ornaments	2·25	2·00
648	75c. Bishop buttons and crucifix	2·50	3·25
649	85c. Earrings and pearl buttons	2·75	3·75
650	$1 Jug and bowls	3·00	4·25
645/650 Set of 6		12·00	13·00

151 "Wreck of *Sea Venture*"

152 German Shepherd

(Des D. Miller. Litho Questa)

1992 (24 Sept). Stained Glass Windows. T **151** and similar horiz designs. Multicoloured. W w **14** (sideways). P 13½×14.

651	25c. Type **151**	1·75	40
652	60c. "Birds in tree"	3·00	2·00
653	75c. "St. Francis feeding bird"	3·50	3·00
654	$2 "Shells"	7·50	11·00
651/654 Set of 4		14·00	15·00

(Des Jacqueline Murray-Hall, adapted D. Miller. Litho Enschedé)

1992 (12 Nov). 7th World Congress of Kennel Clubs. T **152** and similar multicoloured designs. W w **14** (sideways on 25, 35c.). P 13½.

655	25c. Type **152**	1·50	40
656	35c. Irish Setter	1·75	70
657	60c. Whippet (*vert*)	2·50	2·25
658	75c. Border Terrier (*vert*)	2·50	3·25
659	85c. Pomeranian (*vert*)	3·00	4·25
660	$1 Schipperke (*vert*)	3·00	4·75
655/660 Set of 6		13·00	14·00

1993 (25 Feb). As Nos. 510, 512, 513/14, 517 and 522/3, but W w **14** (sideways). With "1992" imprint date. P 14.

664	10c. Curlew (sail/steamer), 1856	1·75	2·00
665	15c. H.M.S. *Vixen* (gunboat), 1890	2·50	2·00
667	20c. *San Pedro* (Spanish galleon), 1594	2·50	2·00
668	25c. *Alert* (fishing sloop), 1877	2·50	60
672	60c. *Mary Celestia* (Confederate paddle steamer), 1864	5·50	1·75
677	$5 *Caraquet* (cargo liner), 1923	12·00	12·00
678	$8 H.M.S. *Pallas* (frigate), 1788	18·00	20·00
664/678 Set of 7		40·00	35·00

No. 678 does not have the fluorescent security marking present on the previous printing, No. 523A.

153 Policeman, Cyclist and Liner

154 "Duchesse de Brabant" and Bee

(Des adapted D. Miller. Litho Questa.)

1993 (25 Feb). Tourism Posters by Adolph Treidler. T **153** and similar vert designs. Multicoloured. W w **14**. P 14.

679	25c. Type **153**	2·25	80
680	60c. Seaside golf course	3·00	2·75
681	75c. Deserted beach	2·50	2·75
682	$2 Dancers in evening dress and liner	4·50	7·00
679/682 Set of 4		11·00	12·00

(Des D. Miller. Litho Questa)

1993 (1 Apr). Garden Roses (4th series). W w **16** (sideways). P 14.

683	**154** 10c. multicoloured	75	1·40
	a. Booklet pane. Nos. 683×2 and 685×3 with margins all round	8·50	
	b. Pane. No. 683×10 with margins all round	6·50	
684	25c. multicoloured	75	60
	a. Booklet pane. No. 684×5 with margins all round	3·25	
685	50c. multicoloured	2·75	4·00
686	60c. multicoloured	1·25	1·75
	a. Booklet pane. No. 686×5 with margins all round	5·50	
683/686 Set of 4		4·75	7·00

The 10c. was available as a loose pane of 10 and from $2.95 stamp booklets which also contained the 25c. and 50c. values. The 25c. was also issued, together with the 60c., in $4.25 booklets.

154a Consolidated PBY-5 Catalina

(Des A. Theobald. Litho Questa)

1993 (1 Apr). 75th Anniv of Royal Air Force. T **154a** and similar horiz designs. Multicoloured. W w **14** (sideways). P 14.

687	25c. Type **154a**	85	35
688	60c. Supermarine Spitfire Mk IX	2·00	2·00
689	75c. Bristol Type 156 Beaufighter MkX	2·25	2·25
690	$2 Handley Page Halifax Mk III	3·75	6·00
687/690 Set of 4		8·00	9·50

155 Hamilton from the Sea

(Des R. Baxter and Sheila Semos (25c.), N. Shewring and Sheila Semos (others). Litho Questa)

1993 (16 Sept). Bicentenary of Hamilton. T **155** and similar horiz designs. Multicoloured. W w **14** (sideways). P 14½.

691	25c. Type **155**	1·25	35
692	60c. Waterfront	2·25	2·00
693	75c. Barrel warehouse	2·25	2·50
694	$2 Sailing ships off Hamilton	6·00	8·00
691/694 Set of 4		10·50	11·50

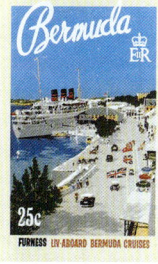

156 *Queen of Bermuda* (liner) at Hamilton

157 Queen Elizabeth II in Bermuda

(Des adapted D. Miller. Litho B.D.T.)

1994 (20 Jan). 75th Anniv of Furness Line's Bermuda Cruises. T **156** and similar multicoloured designs showing Adolph Treidler posters. W w **16** (sideways on 60c. and 75c.). P 15×14 (vert) or 14×15 (horiz).

695	25c. Type **156**	65	35
696	60c. *Queen of Bermuda* entering port (*horiz*)	1·50	1·60
697	75c. *Queen of Bermuda* and *Ocean Monarch* (liners) (*horiz*)	1·60	1·90
698	$2 Passengers on promenade deck at night	3·50	6·50
695/698 Set of 4		6·50	9·25

The vessel depicted on the 60c. was incorrectly identified as the *Queen of Bermuda* on the original, 1930s, travel poster.

(Des D. Miller. Litho Enschedé)

1994 (9 Mar). Royal Visit. T **157** and similar vert designs. Multicoloured. W w **14**. P 14.

699	25c. Type **157**	1·00	35
700	60c. Queen Elizabeth and Prince Philip in open carriage	2·50	1·75
701	75c. Royal Yacht *Britannia*	5·50	3·50
699/701 Set of 3		8·00	5·00

158 Peach

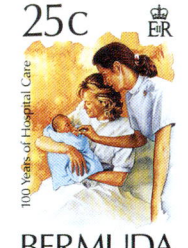

159 Nurse with Mother and Baby

(Des Christine Phillips-Watlington and D. Miller. Litho Questa)

1994 (14 July)–**96**. Flowering Fruits. T **158** and similar multicoloured designs. W w **14** (sideways on horiz designs). P 14.

A. Without imprint date

702A	5c. Type **158**	30	30
703A	7c. Fig	40	1·75
704A	10c. Calabash (*vert*) (6.10.94)	35	35
705A	15c. Natal Plum	40	40
706A	18c. Locust and Wild Honey (23.3.95)	4·50	3·75
707A	20c. Pomegranate	50	50
708A	25c. Mulberry (*vert*) (6.10.94)	60	35
709A	35c. Grape (6.10.94)	70	55
710A	55c. Orange (*vert*) (6.10.94)	1·00	80
711A	60c. Surinam Cherry (23.3.95)	3·00	2·00
712A	75c. Loquat (23.3.95)	2·00	1·50
713A	90c. Sugar Apple (23.3.95)	2·75	2·50
714A	$1 Prickly Pear (*vert*) (6.10.94)	1·75	1·75
715A	$2 Paw Paw (23.3.95)	5·50	6·50
716A	$3 Bay Grape (23.3.95)	6·00	7·50
717A	$5 Banana (*vert*) (6.10.94)	7·50	8·00
718A	$8 Lemon	11·00	12·00
702A/718A Set of 17		42·00	45·00

B. Imprint date ("1996") at foot (1.9.96)

706B	18c. Locust and Wild Honey	1·50	1·50

The Queen's head on the stamps from the first instalment, 5, 7, 15, 20c., and $8, is smaller than on the remainder of the issue.

For some of these designs watermarked w **16** (sideways on horiz designs) and with imprint date see Nos. 792/804.

(Des S. Noon. Litho Enschedé)

1994 (15 Sept). Centenary of Hospital Care. T **159** and similar vert designs. Multicoloured. W w **14**. P 15×14.

719	25c. Type **159**	1·00	35
720	60c. Patient on dialysis machine	2·00	1·90
721	75c. Casualty on emergency trolley	2·25	2·25
722	$2 Elderly patient in wheelchair with physiotherapists	4·75	7·00
719/722 Set of 4		9·00	10·50

160 Gombey Dancers

BERMUDA

(Des Jennifer Toombs. Litho Enschedé)

1994 (10 Nov). Cultural Heritage (1st series). T **160** and similar horiz designs. Multicoloured. W w **14** (sideways). P 14×15.
723	25c. Type **160**...	75	35
724	60c. Christmas carol singers....................	1·40	1·50
725	75c. Marching band..................................	2·50	2·00
726	$2 National Dance Group performers...........	4·75	7·50
723/726 Set of 4		8·50	10·00

See also Nos. 731/4.

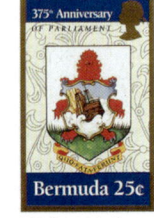

161 Bermuda 1970 Flower 1c. Stamps and 1c. Coin

162 Bermuda Coat of Arms

(Des D. Miller. Litho Enschedé)

1995 (6 Feb). 25th Anniv of Decimal Currency. T **161** and similar horiz designs. Multicoloured. W w **14** (sideways). P 13½×14.
727	25c. Type **161**...	75	35
728	60c. 1970 5c. stamps and coin	1·40	1·50
729	75c. 1970 10c. stamps and coin	1·75	2·00
730	$2 1970 25c. stamps and coin	4·50	6·50
727/730 Set of 4		7·50	9·25

(Des Jennifer Toombs. Litho Enschedé)

1995 (30 May). Cultural Heritage (2nd series). Horiz designs as T **160**. Multicoloured. W w **14** (sideways). P 14×15.
731	25c. Kite flying	75	35
732	60c. Majorettes	1·50	1·50
733	75c. Portuguese dancers	1·75	2·00
734	$2 Floral float	4·00	6·00
731/734 Set of 4		7·25	9·00

(Des Sheila Semas. Litho Enschedé)

1995 (3 Nov). 375th Anniv of Bermuda Parliament. W w **14**. P 14×13½.
735	**162**	25c. multicoloured	1·25	35
736		$1 multicoloured	2·50	3·25

For design as No. 736, but inscr "Commonwealth Finance Ministers Meeting" see No. 765.

163 U.S. Navy Ordnance Island Submarine Base

164 Triple Jump

(Des R. Walton. Litho Walsall)

1995 (4 Dec). Military Bases. T **163** and similar horiz designs. Multicoloured. W w **14** (sideways). P 14.
737	20c. Type **163**...	90	60
738	25c. Royal Naval Dockyard	90	35
739	60c. U.S.A.F. Fort Bell and Kindley Field	1·75	1·25
740	75c. R.A.F. Darrell's Island flying boat base.....	2·00	2·00
741	90c. U.S. Navy operating base	2·25	3·00
742	$1 Canadian Forces Communications Station, Daniel's Head..........................	2·25	3·00
737/742 Set of 6		9·00	9·25

(Des S. Noon. Litho B.D.T.)

1996 (21 May). Olympic Games, Atlanta. T **164** and similar vert designs. Multicoloured. W w **16**. P 14.
743	25c. Type **164**...	70	35
744	30c. Cycling	3·50	1·00
745	65c. Yachting	2·00	1·00
746	80c. Show jumping	2·00	3·00
743/746 Set of 4		7·50	5·50

165 Jetty and Islets, Hamilton

166 Somerset Express Mail Cart, c. 1900

(Des D. Miller. Litho Walsall)

1996 (21 May). Panoramic Paintings of Hamilton (Nos. 747/51) and St. George's (Nos. 752/6) by E. J. Holland. T **165** and similar horiz designs. Multicoloured. W w **14** (sideways). P 14×14½.
747	60c. Type **165**...	1·75	2·25
	a. Booklet pane. Nos. 747/56, with margins all round	16·00	20·00
748	60c. End of island and buildings	1·75	2·25
749	60c. Yachts and hotel	1·75	2·25
750	60c. Islet, hotel and cathedral.................	1·75	2·25
751	60c. Cliff and houses by shore.................	1·75	2·25
752	60c. Islet and end of main island	1·75	2·25
753	60c. Yacht and houses on hillside	1·75	2·25
754	60c. Yacht and St. George's Hotel on hilltop..	1·75	2·25
755	60c. Shoreline and fishing boats	1·75	2·25
756	60c. Entrance to harbour channel...........	1·75	2·25
747/756 Set of 10		16·00	20·00

Nos. 747/56 were only available from $6 stamp booklets containing a pane of 10 (5×2) (No. 747a) showing the Hamilton panorama above that of St. George's.

(Des B. Dare. Litho Enschedé)

1996 (7 June). "CAPEX '96" International Stamp Exhibition, Toronto. Local Transport. T **166** and similar horiz designs. Multicoloured. W w **14** (sideways). P 13½×14.
757	25c. Type **166**...	1·25	35
758	60c. Victoria carriage and railcar, 1930s.........	2·75	1·75
759	75c. First bus, 1946	2·75	2·00
760	$2 Sightseeing bus, c. 1947	5·00	7·50
757/760 Set of 4		10·50	10·50

167 Hog Fish Beacon

168 Waterville

(Des N. Shewring. Litho Enschedé)

1996 (15 Aug). Lighthouses. T **167** and similar vert designs. Multicoloured. W w **14** (inverted on $2). P 14×13½.
761	30c. Type **167**...	1·75	50
762	65c. Gibbs Hill Lighthouse	2·25	1·25
763	80c. St. David's Lighthouse	2·75	2·00
764	$2 North Rock Beacon	4·75	7·00
	w. Wmk upright		
761/764 Set of 4		10·50	9·75

(Litho Enschedé)

1996 (24 Sept). Commonwealth Finance Ministers' Meeting. As No. 736, but inscr "Commonwealth Finance Ministers Meeting" at top and with wider gold frame. W w **14**. P 14×13½.
765	$1 multicoloured	2·50	3·00

(Des D. Miller. Litho Walsall)

1996 (28 Nov). Architectural Heritage. T **168** and similar horiz designs. Multicoloured. W w **16** (sideways). P 14.
766	30c. Type **168**...	1·25	45
767	65c. Bridge House	1·60	1·50
768	80c. Fannie Fox's Cottage	2·00	2·00
769	$2.50 Palmetto House	4·25	7·00
766/769 Set of 4		8·00	10·00

(Des N. Shewring. Litho Walsall)

1997 (12 Feb). "HONG KONG '97" International Stamp Exhibition. Designs as Nos. 761/4, but incorporating "HONG KONG'97" logo and with one value changed. W w **14**. P 14.
770	30c. As Type **167**......................................	2·25	65

771	65c. Gibbs Hill Lighthouse		3·00	1·50
772	80c. St. David's Lighthouse		3·25	2·25
773	$2.50 North Rock Beacon		6·00	10·00
770/773	Set of 4		13·00	13·00

The 65c. and 80c. also show "c. 1900" added to the inscription at foot.

169 White-tailed Tropic Bird

170 Queen Elizabeth II with Crowd

(Des N. Arlott. Litho B.D.T.)

1997 (17 Apr). Bird Conservation. T **169** and similar multicoloured designs. W w **16** (sideways on 30c., $2.50). P 14.

774	30c. Type **169**		75	50
775	60c. White-tailed Tropic Bird and chick (vert)		1·50	1·25
776	80c. Cahow and chick (vert)		2·00	2·00
777	$2.50 Cahow		4·00	6·50
774/777	Set of 4		7·50	9·25

For these designs, redrawn with larger inscriptions and different face values, including the W.W.F. panda emblem see Nos. 852/6.

(Des D. Miller. Litho Questa)

1997 (9 Oct). Golden Wedding of Queen Elizabeth and Prince Philip. T **170** and similar horiz design. Multicoloured. W w **14** (sideways). P 14½.

778	30c. Type **170**		50	40
779	$2 Queen Elizabeth and Prince Philip		3·25	4·50
MS780	90×56 mm. Nos. 778/9		3·75	4·50

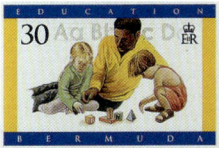

171 Father playing with Children

172 "Fox's Cottage, St. David's" (Ethel Tucker)

(Litho Questa)

1997 (18 Dec). Education. T **171** and similar horiz designs. Multicoloured. W w **14** (sideways). P 14.

781	30c. Type **171**		60	40
782	40c. Teacher and children with map		70	55
	a. Imperf (pair)			
783	60c. Boys holding sports trophy		95	1·25
784	65c. Pupils outside Berkeley Institute		1·00	1·25
785	80c. Scientific experiments		1·40	2·00
786	90c. New graduates		1·60	2·50
781/786	Set of 6		5·50	7·25

(Des D. Miller. Litho Questa)

1998 (31 Mar). Diana, Princess of Wales Commemoration. Sheet, 145×70 mm, containing vert designs. Multicoloured. W w **14** (sideways). P 14½×14.

MS787	30c. Wearing black hat, 1983; 40c. Wearing floral dress; 65c. Wearing blue evening dress, 1996; 80c. Carrying bouquets, 1993 (sold at $2.15+25c. charity premium)		2·25	3·75

(Litho Enschedé)

1998 (4 June). Paintings by Catherine and Ethel Tucker. T **172** and similar horiz designs. Multicoloured. W w **14** (sideways). P 13½×14.

788	30c. Type **172**		1·25	40
789	40c. "East Side, Somerset"		1·40	70
790	65c. "Long Bay Road, Somerset"		2·25	1·25
791	$2 "Flatts Village"		5·00	7·50
788/791	Set of 4		9·00	9·00

1998 (9 July). As Nos. 702/18, but with W w **16** (sideways on horiz designs) and with imprint date ("1998"). P 14.

792	5c. Peach		50	1·50
795	15c. Natal Plum		75	60
796	18c. Locust and Wild Honey		80	60
797	20c. Pomegranate		80	75
798	25c. Mulberry (vert)		80	75
802	75c. Loquat		2·25	1·75
803	90c. Sugar Apple		2·50	2·50
804	$1 Prickly Pear (vert)		2·75	3·75
792/804	Set of 8		10·00	11·00

The Queen's head on the 5, 15 and 20c. has been redrawn to the larger size used for the other values.

173 Horse and Carriage

(Des J. Semos. Litho Walsall)

1998 (24 Sept). Hospitality in Bermuda. T **173** and similar horiz designs. Multicoloured. W w **16** (sideways). P 14½.

809	25c. Type **173**		1·25	40
810	30c. Golf club desk		1·75	75
811	65c. Chambermaid preparing room		1·50	1·25
812	75c. Kitchen staff under training		1·50	2·00
813	80c. Waiter at beach hotel		1·75	2·25
814	90c. Nightclub bar		2·00	3·00
809/814	Set of 6		8·75	8·75

174 Agave attenuata

175 "Lizard with Fairy Lights" (Claire Critchley)

(Des Harris and Mitchell Associates. Litho Questa)

1998 (15 Oct). Centenary of Botanical Gardens. T **174** and similar horiz designs. W w **14** (sideways). P 14.

815	30c. Type **174**		1·25	40
816	65c. Bermuda Palmetto Tree		2·25	90
817	$1 Banyan Tree		2·75	2·75
818	$2 Cedar Tree		4·00	7·00
815/818	Set of 4		9·25	10·00

(Litho B.D.T.)

1998 (26 Nov). Christmas. Children's Paintings. T **175** and similar multicoloured design. W w **14** (sideways on 40c.). P 14.

819	25c. Type **175**		1·25	35
820	40c. "Christmas stairway" (Cameron Bowling) (horiz)		1·50	1·25

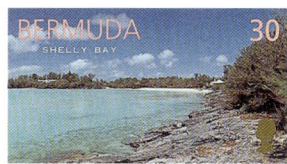

176 Shelly Bay

(Des Sheila Semos. Litho Walsall)

1999 (29 Apr). Bermuda Beaches. T **176** and similar horiz designs. Multicoloured. W w **14** (sideways). P 13×13½.

821	30c. Type **176**		90	40
822	60c. Catherine's Bay		1·25	1·00
823	65c. Jobson's Cove		1·40	1·10
824	$2 Warwick Long Bay		3·75	6·50
821/824	Set of 4		6·50	8·00

177 Tracking Station

178 Theodolite and Map, 1901

BERMUDA

(Des D. Miller. Litho Walsall (No. **MS**829), Cartor (others))

1999 (21 July). 30th Anniv of First Manned Landing on Moon. T **177** and similar multicoloured designs. W w **14** (sideways on 30c., 75c.). P. 13.

825	30c. Type **177**	1·00	40
826	60c. Mission launch (*vert*)	1·50	90
827	75c. Aerial view of tracking station, Bermuda	1·75	1·25
828	$2 Astronaut on Moon (*vert*)	3·75	6·00
825/828	Set of 4	7·25	7·75

MS829 90×80 mm. 65c. Earth as seen from Moon (*circular, 40 mm diam*). W w **16** (sideways). P. 14. .... 3·25 4·00

(Litho Questa)

1999 (26 Aug). Centenary of First Digital Map of Bermuda. T **178** and similar horiz designs. W w **14** (sideways). P. 14.

830	30c. multicoloured	1·50	40
831	65c. black, stone and silver	2·25	1·50
832	80c. multicoloured	2·75	2·50
833	$1 multicoloured	2·75	4·00
830/833	Set of 4	8·25	7·50

Designs:—65c. Street map, 1901; 80c. Street plan and aerial photograph, 1999; $1 Satellite and Bermuda from Space, 1999.

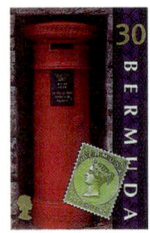

179 Victorian Pillar Box and Bermuda 1865 1s. Stamp

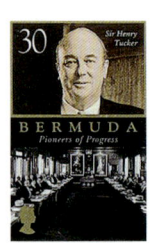

180 Sir Henry Tucker and Meeting of House of Assembly

(Litho Questa)

1999 (7 Oct). Bermuda Postal History. T **179** and similar vert designs. W w **14**. Multicoloured. P. 14.

834	30c. Type **179**	1·00	40
835	75c. King George V pillar box and 1920 2s. stamp	2·25	1·50
836	95c. King George VI wall box and 1938 3d. stamp	2·50	3·25
837	$1 Queen Elizabeth II pillar box and 1953 Coronation 1½d. stamp	2·50	3·25
834/837	Set of 4	7·50	7·75

(Des Sheila Scows. Litho Cartor)

2000 (1 May). Pioneers of Progress. T **180** and similar vert designs. Each sepia, black and gold. W w **14**. P 13½.

838	30c. Type **180**	1·10	1·25
	a. Strip of 3. Nos. 838/40	3·00	3·25
839	30c. Gladys Morrell and suffragettes	1·10	1·25
840	30c. Dr. E. F. Gordon and workers	1·10	1·25
838/840	Set of 3	3·00	3·25

Nos. 838/40 were printed together, *se-tenant*, in horizontal and vertical strips of 3 throughout the sheet.

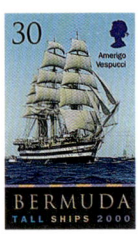

181 *Amerigo Vespucci* (full-rigged ship)

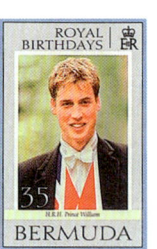

182 Prince William

(Des Sheila Semos. Litho Questa)

2000 (23 May). Tall Ships Race. T **181** and similar vert designs. Multicoloured. W w **14**. P. 14.

841	30c. Type **181**	1·50	50
842	60c. *Europa* (barque)	2·00	1·50
843	80c. *Juan Sebastian de Elcareo* (schooner)	2·25	3·00
841/843	Set of 3	5·25	4·50

(Litho Questa)

2000 (7 Aug). Royal Birthdays. T **182** and similar vert designs. Multicoloured. W w **14**. P. 14.

844	35c. Type **182**	1·50	55
845	40c. Duke of York	1·50	65
846	50c. Princess Royal	1·60	1·10
847	70c. Princess Margaret	2·00	2·75
848	$1 Queen Elizabeth the Queen Mother	2·50	3·50
844/848	Set of 5	8·25	7·75

MS849 160×90 mm. Nos. 844/8 .... 9·00 9·50

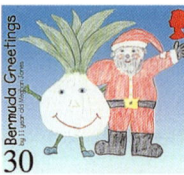

183 Santa Claus with Smiling Vegetable (Meghan Jones)

184 King's Castle

(Adapted Sheila Semos. Litho B.D.T.)

2000 (26 Sept). Christmas. Children's Paintings. T **183** and similar horiz design. Multicoloured. W w **16** (sideways). P 13½.

850	30c. Type **183**	1·00	45
851	45c. Christmas tree and presents (Carlita Lodge)	1·25	80

(Des. N. Arlott. Litho Questa)

2001 (1 Feb). Endangered Species. Bird Conservation. Designs as Nos. 774/7, but with different face values, inscriptions redrawn and W.W.F. panda emblem added. Multicoloured. W w **14** (sideways on horiz designs). P. 14.

852	15c. As Type **169**	1·00	1·25
853	15c. Cahow	1·00	1·25
854	20c. White-tailed Tropic Bird with chick (*vert*)	1·00	1·25
855	20c. Cahow with chick (*vert*)	1·00	1·25
852/855	Set of 4	3·50	4·50

MS856 200×190 mm. Nos. 852/5 each×4. Wmk sideways .... 12·00 14·00

The two designs for each value were printed as separate panes of 25 in combined sheets of 50.

No. **MS**856, which includes the "HONG KONG 2001" logo on the margin, contains two separate blocks of 8 showing the two designs of each value *se-tenant*, both horizontally and vertically.

(Des Sheila Semos. Litho Questa)

2001 (1 May). Historic Buildings, St. George's. T **184** and similar horiz designs. Multicoloured. W w **14** (sideways). P 13½.

857	35c. Type **184**	1·10	55
858	50c. Bridge House	1·50	75
859	55c. Whitehall	1·60	1·00
860	70c. Fort Cunningham	1·90	2·25
861	85c. St. Peter's Church	2·50	3·25
862	95c. Water Street	2·50	3·25
857/862	Set of 6	10·00	10·00

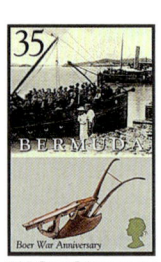

185 Boer War Prisoners on Boat and Plough

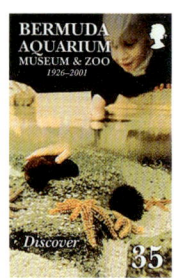

186 Girl touching Underwater Environment

(Des Sheila Semos. Litho Questa)

2001 (28 June). Centenary of Anglo-Boer War. T **185** and similar vert designs. Multicoloured. W w **14**. P. 14.

863	35c. Type **185**	85	55
864	50c. Prisoners in shelter and boot	1·10	75
865	70c. Elderly Boer with children and jewellery	1·60	1·75
866	95c. Bermuda residents and illustrated envelope of 1902	2·00	3·00
863/866	Set of 4	5·00	5·50

BERMUDA

(Des J. Semos. Litho BDT)

2001 (9 Aug). 75th Anniv of Bermuda Aquarium. T **186** and similar multicoloured designs. W w **14** (sideways on horiz designs). P 15×14 (vert) or 14×15 (horiz).

867	35c. Type **186**	90	55
868	50c. Museum exhibits (*horiz*)	1·25	75
869	55c. Feeding giant tortoise (*horiz*)	1·25	95
870	70c. Aquarium building (*horiz*)	1·75	1·75
871	80c. Lesson from inside tank	1·75	2·25
872	95c. Turtle	2·25	3·00
867/872	Set of 6	8·25	8·25

187 "Fishing Boats" (Charles Lloyd Tucker)

(Des Sheila Semos. Litho BDT)

2001 (9 Oct). Paintings of Charles Lloyd Tucker. T **187** and similar horiz designs. Multicoloured. W w **14**. P 14×14½.

873	35c. Type **187**	1·40	55
874	70c. "Bandstand and City Hall, Hamilton"	2·00	1·50
875	85c. "Hamilton Harbour"	2·25	2·50
876	$1 "Train in Front Street, Hamilton"	3·00	4·25
873/876	Set of 4	8·00	8·00

187a Princess Elizabeth with Corgi

(Des A. Robinson. Litho Questa)

2002 (6 Feb). Golden Jubilee. W w **14** (sideways). P 14½.

877	10c. brownish black, bluish violet and gold	60	60
878	35c. multicoloured	1·50	1·10
879	70c. brownish black, bluish violet and gold	2·00	1·60
880	85c. multicoloured	2·25	2·25
877/880	Set of 4	5·75	5·00
MS881	162×95 mm. Nos. 877/80 and $1 multicoloured. P 13½ ($1) or 14½ (others)	7·00	7·50

Designs: *Horiz*—10c. Type **187a**; 35c. Queen Elizabeth in evening dress, 1965; 70c. Queen Elizabeth in car, 1952; 85c. Queen Elizabeth on Merseyside, 1991. *Vert* (38×51 *mm*)—$2 Queen Elizabeth after Annigoni. Designs as Nos. 877/80 in No. **MS**881 omit the gold frame around each stamp and the "Golden Jubilee 1952–2002" inscription.

188 Fantasy Cave

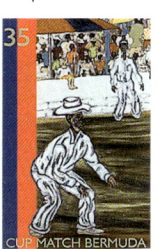

189 Fielder and Somerset Club Colours

(Des Sheila Semos. Litho Questa)

2002 (1 May). Caves. T **188** and similar horiz designs. Multicoloured. W w **14** (sideways). P 14.

882	35c. Type **188**	1·60	55
883	70c. Crystal Cave	2·25	1·75
884	80c. Prospero's Cave	2·50	2·75
885	$1 Cathedral Cave	3·00	4·50
882/885	Set of 4	8·50	8·50

(Des Sheila Semos. Litho Questa)

2002 (4 July). Centenary of Bermuda Cup Cricket Match. T **189** and similar multicoloured designs. W w **14**. P 14.

886	35c. Type **189**	1·50	1·50
887	35c. Batsman and wicketkeeper with St. George's Club colours	1·50	1·50
MS888	110×85 mm. $1 Batsman (48×31 mm). Wmk sideways. P 13½×14	3·50	4·00

189a Duchess of York

190 Slit Worm-shell

(Des A. Robinson. Litho Questa)

2002 (5 Aug). Queen Elizabeth the Queen Mother Commemoration. T **189a** and similar vert designs. W w **14**. P 14×14½.

889	30c. sepia, gold and purple	1·00	45
890	$1.25 multicoloured	2·50	3·00
MS891	145×70 mm. Nos. 889/90. Wmk sideways. P 14½×14	4·50	4·75

Designs:—30c. Type **189a**, 1923; $1.25 Queen Mother on her birthday, 1995. Designs as Nos. 889/90 in No. **MS**891 omit the "1900–2002" inscription and the coloured frame.

(Litho Questa)

2002 (10 Sept)–**03**. Shells. T **190** and similar vert designs. Multicoloured. W w **14** (sideways on horiz designs). P 14.

A. Printed in litho by Questa. Without imprinted date

892A	5c. Type **190**	15	30
893A	10c. Netted Olive	20	40
894A	20c. Angular Triton (*horiz*) (23.1.03)	50	60
895A	25c. Frog Shell (*horiz*) (20.3.03)	60	60
896A	30c. Colourful Atlantic Moon (*horiz*) (20.3.03)	70	65
897A	35c. Noble Wentletrap	1·00	45
898A	40c. Atlantic Trumpet Triton (*horiz*) (23.1.03)	1·00	55
899A	45c. Zigzag Scallop	1·10	55
900A	50c. Bermuda Cone	1·25	65
901A	75c. Very Distorted Distorsio (*horiz*) (20.3.03)	2·00	1·10
902A	80c. Purple Sea Snail (*horiz*) (23.1.03)	2·25	1·40
903A	90c. Flame Helmet (*horiz*) (23.1.03)	2·25	1·75
904A	$1 Scotch Bonnet (*horiz*) (20.3.03)	2·50	2·00
905A	$2 Gold Mouth Triton (*horiz*) (20.3.03)	4·75	4·25
906A	$3 Bermuda's Slit Shell (*horiz*) (23.1.03)	6·50	6·00
907A	$4 Reticulated Cowrie-helmet (*horiz*) (23.1.03)	7·50	8·00
908A	$5 Dennison's Morum (*horiz*) (20.3.03)	8·50	9·50
909A	$8 Sunrise Tellin	13·00	16·00
892/909	Set of 18	50·00	50·00

B. Printed in lithograph by Enschedé. With imprint date "2008"

| 897B | 35c. Noble Wentletrap (30.1.2008) | 1·00 | 60 |

191 Dove of Peace

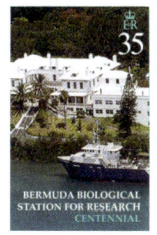

192 Research Station and *Weatherbird II* (research ship)

(Litho Walsall)

2002 (7 Nov). World Peace Day. T **191** and similar vert design showing dove. W w **14**. P 14½.

910	35c. multicoloured	1·25	50
911	70c. multicoloured	2·00	2·25

(Des Advantage. Litho Questa)

2003 (4 Feb). Centenary of Bermuda Biological Research Station. T **192** and similar multicoloured designs. W w **14** (sideways on horiz designs). P 14.

912	35c. Type **192**	1·50	50
913	70c. Spotfin Butterflyfish (*horiz*)	2·50	1·75

BERMUDA

914	85c. Collecting coral (*horiz*)	2·75	3·00
915	$1 Krill	3·25	3·75
912/915 Set of 4		9·00	8·00

193 Costume Dolls

193a Queen in Coronation Coach

(Des Advantage. Litho DLR)

2003 (15 May). Heritage "Made in Bermuda" (1st series). T **193** and similar vert designs. Multicoloured. W w **14**. P 14½×14.

916	35c. Type **193**	1·00	40
917	70c. Model sailing ship	1·75	1·40
918	80c. Abstract sculpture in wood	2·00	2·25
919	$1 Silverware	2·50	3·00
916/919 Set of 4		6·50	6·25

See also Nos. 934/7 and 952/5.

(Des A. Robinson. Litho DLR)

2003 (2 June). 50th Anniv of Coronation. T **193a** and similar horiz designs. Multicoloured. W w **14** (sideways). P 14×14½.

920	35c. Type **193a**	75	40
921	70c. Queen in Coronation chair, flanked by bishops of Durham and Bath & Wells	1·25	1·50
MS922 95×115 mm. $1.25 As 35c.; $2 As 70c.		5·50	6·50

Nos. 920/1 have scarlet frame; stamps from **MS**922 have no frame and country name in mauve panel.

(Litho De La Rue)

2003 (4 July). 30th Anniv of CARICOM. Nos. 886/7 additionally inscr "30th Anniversary CARICOM" vertically in white at left of stamp.

923	35c. Type **189**	1·50	1·25
924	35c. Batsman and wicketkeeper with St. George's Club colours	1·50	1·25

194 Red Poinsettias

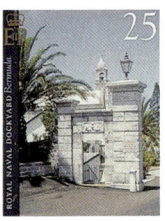

195 Gateway

(Des Advantage. Litho DLR)

2003 (9 Oct). Christmas Greetings. Poinsettias. T **194** and similar vert designs. Multicoloured. W w **14**. P 14½×14.

925	30c. Type **194**	75	35
926	45c. White poinsettias	1·10	55
927	80c. Pink poinsettias	2·00	2·75
925/927 Set of 3		3·50	3·25

(Des Advantage. Litho Enschedé)

2004 (19 Feb). Royal Naval Dockyard, Bermuda. T **195** and similar vert designs. Multicoloured. W w **14**. P 14×13½.

928	25c. Type **195**	65	50
929	35c. Fountain and Clock Tower	90	80
930	70c. Waterside seat and Clock Tower	1·75	1·50
931	85c. Marina	1·90	2·25
932	95c. Window in ramparts	2·25	2·75
933	$1 Boats moored at pontoon and Clocktower Centre	2·40	3·25
928/933 Set of 6		9·00	10·00

(Des Sheila Semos. Litho Enschede)

2004 (15 May). Heritage "Made in Bermuda" (2nd series). Vert designs as T **193**. Multicoloured. W w **14**. P 13½.

934	35c. Carver chair	65	45
935	70c. Ceramic jug and plate	1·10	90
936	80c. Glass fish and glass plate with shell design	1·25	1·40
937	$1.25 Quilt	1·75	2·50
934/937 Set of 4		4·25	4·75

196 Bluefin Tuna

197 Yellow *Oncydium* Orchids

(Des D. Miller. Litho BDT)

2004 (19 Aug). Endangered Species. Bluefin Tuna. T **196** and similar horiz designs. Multicoloured. W w **14** (sideways). P 14.

938	10c. Type **196**	30	50
	a. Strip of 4. Nos. 938/41	4·75	4·75
939	35c. Five bluefin tuna	85	85
940	85c. Bluefin tuna near surface of water	1·90	1·90
941	$1.10 Bluefin tuna swimming left	2·25	2·50
938/941 Set of 4		4·75	4·75

Nos. 938/41 were printed together, *se-tenant*, as horizontal and vertical strips of four stamps in sheets of 16, and also in seperate sheets of 50 (2 panes of 25).

(Des Sheila Semos. Litho Enschedé)

2004 (18 Nov). 50th Anniv of the Orchid Society. T **197** and similar vert designs. Multicoloured. W w **14**. P 14.

942	35c. Type **197**	1·10	55
943	45c. *Encyclia radiate*	1·25	65
944	85c. Purple and white orchids	2·50	2·50
945	$1.10 *Paphiopedilum spicerianum*	3·00	3·25
942/945 Set of 4		7·00	6·25

198 1940 Map of Bermuda and Compass

(Des Sheila Semos. Litho Enschedé)

2005 (13 Jan). 500th Anniv of Discovery of Bermuda by Juan de Bermudez (Spanish navigator). T **198** and similar horiz designs. Multicoloured. W w **14** (sideways). P 14×15.

946	25c. Type **198**	1·50	65
947	35c.18 46 map and sextant	1·75	65
948	70c. 1764 map and box compass	2·75	1·75
949	$1.10 1692 map and telescope	4·00	4·50
950	$1.25 1548 map and callipers	4·00	5·00
946/950 Set of 5		12·50	11·00
MS951 115×95 mm. $5 Aerial view of Bermuda		16·00	17·00

(Des Advantage. Litho Enschedé)

2005 (19 May). Heritage "Made in Bermuda" (3rd series). Vert designs as T **193**. Multicoloured. W w **14**. P 14.

952	35c. Picture of Bermuda Gombey dancers	80	45
953	70c. Papier-maché sculpture of parrotfish on tube coral	1·50	1·40
954	85c. Stained glass picture of lion and lamb	2·00	2·50
955	$1 Earrings and pendant of silver, pearls and garnets	2·25	3·00
952/955 Set of 4		6·00	6·50

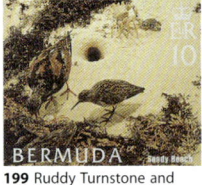

198a H.M.S. *Victory*

199 Ruddy Turnstone and Semipalmated Sandpiper

(Des J. Batchelor. Litho Cartor)

2005 (23 June). Bicentenary of Battle of Trafalgar. T **198a** and similar horiz designs. Multicoloured. No wmk (10c.) or W w **14** (sideways) (others). P 13½.

956	10c. Type **198a**	80	80

957	35c. H.M.S. *Pickle* under construction in Bermuda		1·50	60
958	70c. H.M.S. *Pickle* picking up survivors from burning *Achille*		2·00	2·00
959	85c. H.M.S. *Pickle* racing back to England with news of victory		2·25	2·75
956/959 Set of 4			6·00	5·50

No. 956 contains traces of powdered wood from HMS *Victory*.

(Des Sheila Semos. Litho Enschedé)

2005 (18 Aug). Bermuda Habitats. T **199** and similar horiz designs showing scenes from dioramas in Bermuda Natural History Museum. Multicoloured. W w **14** (sideways). P 14.

960	10c. Type **199**	75	80
961	25c. Least Bittern in reeds	1·40	60
962	35c. White-tailed Tropic Bird	1·60	50
963	70c. Eastern Bluebird	2·25	1·75
964	85c. Saw-whet Owl	2·75	3·00
965	$1 Yellow-crowned Night Heron	3·00	3·50
960/965 Set of 6		10·50	9·00

200 Christmas Tree with Lights
201 Man working on Overhead Power Cables

(Des Advantage. Litho BDT)

2005 (27 Oct). Christmas Greetings. Festival of Lights. T **200** and similar horiz designs. Multicoloured. W w **14** (sideways (30c.), sideways inverted (others)). P 14.

966	30c. Type **200**	60	50
967	45c. Dolphin	80	60
968	80c. Snowman	1·50	2·00
966/968 Set of 3		2·50	2·75

(Des Advantage. Litho Cartor)

2006 (13 Jan). Centenary of the Bermuda Electric Light Company Ltd. T **201** and similar horiz designs. Multicoloured. W w **14** (sideways (35c.), sideways inverted (others)). P 13½.

969	35c. Type **201**	80	45
970	70c. Engineer, power lines and vehicle	1·60	1·40
971	85c. Power plant	2·00	2·50
972	$1 Office block	2·25	3·00
969/972 Set of 4		6·00	6·50

201a Princess Elizabeth with Corgi
202 Map of Bermuda, 1747

(Litho BDT)

2006 (21 Apr). 80th Birthday of Queen Elizabeth II. T **201a** and similar horiz designs. Multicoloured. W w **14** (sideways). P 14.

973	35p. Type **201a**	1·40	60
974	70p. Queen wearing tiara (black/white photo)	2·00	1·40
975	85p. Wearing tiara and drop earrings (colour photo)	2·25	2·25
976	$1.25 Wearing blue hat	3·25	4·00
973/976 Set of 4		8·00	7·50
MS977 144×75 mm. $1.25 As No. 974; $2 As No. 975		7·50	8·50

(Des Advantage. Litho Enschede)

2006 (27 May). Washington 2006 International Stamp Exhibition. W w **14** (inverted). P 14×13½.

978	**202** $1.10 multicoloured	2·50	2·75
MS979 82×65 mm. No. 978		2·50	2·75

(Des Sheila Semos. Litho Cartor)

2006 (22 June). Heritage "Made in Bermuda" (4th series). Vert designs as T **193**. Multicoloured. W w **14** (inverted on 70c.). P 13.

980	35c. Bees, honeycomb and honey	1·40	55
981	70c. "Stonecutters" (detail) (Sharon Wilson)	2·00	1·50
982	85c. "I've Caught Some Whoppers" (sculpture) by Desmond Fountain	2·50	2·75
983	$1.25 Flower and perfume (Bermuda Perfumery)	3·50	4·00
980/983 Set of 4		8·50	8·00

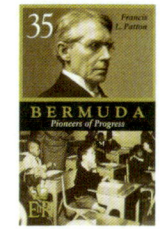

203 Advent Wreath
204 Francis L. Patton

(Des Sheila Semos. Litho Enschedé)

2006 (12 Oct). Christmas. Greetings. Advent Wreaths. T **203** and similar vert designs showing different advent wreaths. W w **14** (inverted). P 14.

984	30c. multicoloured	1·00	50
985	35c. multicoloured	1·10	30
986	45c. multicoloured	1·40	50
987	80c. multicoloured	2·75	3·00
984/987 Set of 4		5·50	4·75

(Des AdVantage. Litho Cartor)

2007 (15 Feb). Pioneers of Progress (2nd series). Educators. T **204** and similar vert designs. Multicoloured. W w **14**. P 13½.

988	35c. Type **204**	75	85
989	35c. Adele Tucker	75	85
990	35c. Edith and Matilda Crawford	75	85
991	35c. Millie Neversen	75	85
992	35c. May Francis	75	85
988/992 Set of 5		3·25	3·75

205 Hull under Construction at Rockport, Maine, USA

(Des Sheila Semos. Litho Cartor)

2007 (17 May). *Spirit of Bermuda*. T **205** and similar horiz designs showing the sail training schooner. Multicoloured. W w **14** (sideways (35c.), sideways inverted (others)). P 13½.

993	10c. Type **205**	60	60
994	35c. Close-up view	1·25	40
995	70c. *Spirit of Bermuda* at sea	2·00	1·25
996	85c. Off coast of Bermuda	2·25	2·00
997	$1.10 At Hamilton, Bermuda	2·50	2·75
998	$1.25 *Spirit of Bermuda* seen from stern	2·75	3·25
993/998 Set of 6		10·00	9·25

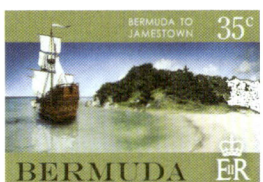

206 *Deliverance* off Building Bay

(Des Sheila Semos. Litho Cartor)

2007 (21 June). 400th Anniv of Jamestown, Virginia, USA. Voyage of the *Deliverance* from Bermuda to Jamestown, 1610. T **206** and similar horiz design. Multicoloured. W w **14** (sideways (35c.), sideways inverted ($1.10)). P 12½.

999	35c. Type **206**	1·75	75
1000	$1.10 *Deliverance* sailing from Building Bay, St. George's, Bermuda	4·00	4·50

BERMUDA

206a Bishop's Own Cubs, Government House, 22 February 1930

(Des Andrew Robinson. Litho BDT)

2007 (23 Aug). Centenary of World Scouting. T **206a** and similar horiz designs. Multicoloured. W w **14** (sideways). P 14.
1001	35c. Type **206a**	1·00	40
1002	70c. Lord Baden-Powell inspecting the Cubs, Hamilton, February 1930	1·75	1·40
1003	85c. Scout parade, Front Street, Hamilton, 25 February 1930	2·00	2·25
1004	$1.10 Dance of Kaa, Government House, 25 February 1930	2·25	2·50
1001/1004	*Set of 4*	6·25	6·00

MS1005 90×65 mm. $1.25 Bermuda Scouts emblem; $2 Lord Baden-Powell inspecting the Cubs, Hamilton, February 1930 (both vert) .... 7·00 8·00

207 "Celeste & Al Harris"   **208** Perot Stamp, 1848

(Litho Enschedé)

2008 (19 Mar). Bermuda Calypso Music. T **207** and similar horiz designs showing album covers. Multicoloured. W w **14** (sideways). P 14.
1006	35c. Type **207**	1·00	40
1007	70c. "Bermuda Calypsos"	1·75	1·40
1008	85c. "Calypso Varieties from Bermuda"	2·00	2·25
1009	$1.10 "The Talbot Brothers of Bermuda"	2·25	2·50
1006/1009	*Set of 4*	6·25	6·00

(Litho Enschedé)

2008 (23 Apr). 160th Anniv of the Perot Stamp (stamps prepared and issued by W. B. Perot, postmaster at Hamilton). W w **14**. P 14.
1010	**208**	35c. light reddish brown and black	1·25	55
1011		70c. slate-blue and black	2·25	1·60
1012		85c. olive-sepia and black	2·75	2·75
1013		$1.25 silver and black	4·00	4·50
1010/1013		*Set of 4*	9·25	8·50

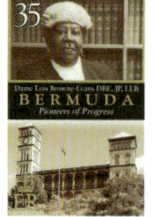

209 Deep Bay, West Pembroke   **210** Dame Lois Browne-Evans

(Litho BDT)

2008 (1 May). Bermuda Scenes. T **209** and similar horiz designs. Multicoloured. Self-adhesive. P 12×12½.
1014	(35c.) Type **209**	1·25	1·00
	a. Booklet pane. No. 1014×10	11·00	
1015	(70c.) Spanish Point Park	1·60	1·75
	a. Booklet pane. No. 1015×10	14·50	
1016	(85c.) Flatts Inlet	1·75	2·00
	a. Booklet pane. No. 1016×10	16·00	
1017	(95c.) Tucker's Town Bay	1·90	2·50
	a. Booklet pane. No. 1017×10	17·00	
1014/1017	*Set of 4*	6·00	6·50

Nos. 1014/17 were only available in separate booklets, Nos. SB8/11.
No. 1014 is inscribed "Postage Paid Local", No. 1015 "Postage Paid Zone 1", No. 1016 "Postage Paid Zone 2" and No. 1017 "Postage Paid Zone 3".

(Des DCI, Bermuda. Litho Cartor)

2008 (11 June). Pioneers of Progress (3rd series). T **210** and similar vert designs. Multicoloured. W w **14**. P 13½.
1018	35c. Type **210** (barrister and PLP leader 1968–72, 1976–85)	1·25	1·25
1019	35c. Dr. Pauulu Roosevelt Brown Kamarakafego (civil rights campaigner and rural technologist)	1·25	1·25

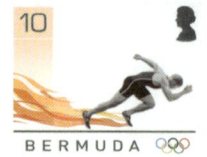

211 Sprinter at Start   **212** Reindeer Lights outside Houses

(Des Sheila Semos. Litho Lowe-Martin, Canada)

2008 (23 July). Olympic Games, Beijing. T **211** and similar horiz designs. Multicoloured. W w **14** (sideways). P 12½×13.
1020	10c. Type **211**	60	60
1021	35c. Swimmer diving from start	1·40	40
1022	70c. Horse and rider jumping	2·50	2·25
1023	85c. Yachting	2·75	3·25
1020/1023	*Set of 4*	6·50	6·00

(Des DCI Bermuda. Litho Enschedé)

2008 (1 Oct). Christmas. Greetings. T **212** and similar horiz designs showing Christmas lights. Multicoloured. W w **18** (sideways). P 13½.
1024	30c. Type **212**	70	40
1025	35c. Lights on balcony and across street	75	35
1026	45c. Horse and carriage and street lamp lights on roof	1·00	45
1027	80c. Single storey house with lights around roof and verandah and in garden	1·60	2·25
1024/1027	*Set of 4*	3·50	3·00

213 Hamilton in 1930s and Modern Photographs

(Des DCI Bermuda. Litho Enschedé)

2009 (22 Jan). 400th Anniv of Settlement of Bermuda. T **213** and similar horiz designs, each showing scene from past and modern photograph . Multicoloured. W w **18** (sideways). P 12½.
1028	35c. Type **213**	1·10	50
1029	70c. St. George's in 1830s painting by Thomas Driver and modern photograph	2·00	1·60
1030	85c. Flatts Village in 1797 watercolour by Capt. George Tobin and modern photograph	2·50	2·50
1031	$1.25 17th-century map and aerial photograph of Bermuda	3·75	4·75
1028/1031	*Set of 4*	8·50	8·50

214 Aerial View of Cooper's Island

(Litho Lowe-Martin)

2009 (16 Apr). International Year of Astronomy. 40th Anniv of First Moon Landing. T **214** and similar multicoloured designs. W w **18** (inverted). P 13.
1032	35c. Type **214**	1·00	45
1033	70c. Tracking Station, Cooper's Island	2·00	1·50
1034	85c. Apollo 11 Lunar Landing Module, 1969	2·25	2·25

BERMUDA

1035	95c. STS 126, 2008	2·50	2·75
1036	$1.25 International Space Station	3·25	3·75
1032/1036	Set of 5	10·00	9·50

MS1037 100×80 mm. $1.10 Lunar Landing Module on Moon (39×59 mm). Wmk sideways .... 2·75 3·25

Nos. 1032/6 were printed in separate sheets of six stamps with enlarged illustrated margins.

215 Winner and Trophy

(Des Leslie Todd. Litho BDT)

2009 (21 May). Centenary of Bermuda Marathon Derby. T **215** and similar horiz designs. W w **18** (sideways). P 14.

1038	**215**	35c. black, brown-red and brown	85	35
1039	–	70c. black, orange-yellow and brown	1·50	1·40
1040	–	85c. black, orange-yellow and brown	1·90	2·00
1041	–	$1.10 black, brown-red and brown	2·25	3·00
1038/1041	Set of 4		6·00	6·00

Designs: 70c. Winner with trophy (different); 85c. Runners and motorcycle; $1.10 Runners.

216 Concordia

217 "Theatre Boycott, Upstairs Right, 1959" (Robert Barritt)

(Des Jamie McDowell. Litho Cartor)

2009 (11 June). Tall Ships Atlantic Challenge 2009. T **216** and similar multicoloured designs. W w **14** (sideways on 85c., $1.25). P 13½×13 (vert) or 13×13½ (horiz).

1042	35c. Type **216**	1·00	35
1043	70c. *Picton Castle*	1·75	1·25
1044	85c. *Jolie Brise* (horiz)	2·00	1·50
1045	95c. *Tecla*	2·50	2·25
1046	$1.10 *Europa*	2·75	2·75
1047	$1.25 *Etoile* (horiz)	3·25	3·75
1042/1047	Set of 6	12·00	10·50

(Des Sheila Semos. Litho Lowe-Martin Group)

2009 (2 July). 50th Anniv of Theatre Boycott (ended segregation in public buildings). T **217** and similar multicoloured designs. W w **18** (sideways on horiz designs; inverted on vert designs). P 12½.

1048	35c. Type **217**	70	35
1049	70c. "Storm in a Teacup" (Charles Lloyd Tucker) (vert)	1·40	1·25
1050	85c. Bronze statue of boycott leaders by Chesley Trott (vert)	1·75	1·75
1051	$1.25 Scene from documentary "When Voices Rise"	2·75	3·50
1048/1051	Set of 4	6·00	6·25

218 Basket with Berries and Red Bow

219 Guides and Leaders

(Litho Cartor)

2009 (24 Sept). Christmas Greetings. Tree Decorations. T **218** and similar vert designs. Multicoloured. W w **18** (inverted on 85c.). P 14×13½.

1052	30c. Type **218**	60	45
1053	35c. Angel	65	45
1054	70c. Circular basket with red bow	1·25	1·00
1055	85c. Gold bow and tassels	1·60	1·75
1052/1055	Set of 4	3·50	3·25

(Des DeLeon Lottimore. Litho BDT)

2010 (18 Feb). Centenary of Girlguiding. T **219** and similar horiz designs. Multicoloured. W w **18** (sideways). P 14×15.

1056	35c. Type **219**	90	55
1057	70c. Guide camp	1·40	1·25
1058	85c. Parade of guides and brownies	1·75	1·75
1059	$1.10 Guides with carnival float carrying model galleon	2·50	3·00
1056/1059	Set of 4	6·00	6·00

MS1060 127×89 mm. $1.25 1st and 2nd Excelsior Guides (Bermuda's first Black Unit) .... 2·75 3·25

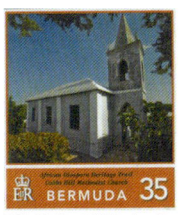

220 Cobbs Hill Methodist Church

221 Lined Seahorse

(Des Marilyn Zuill. Litho Lowe-Martin Group, Canada)

2010 (20 May). African Diaspora Heritage Trail. T **220** and similar vert designs. Multicoloured. W w **18**. P 13×12½.

1061	35c. Type **220**	1·10	60
1062	70c. The Bermudian Heritage Museum	1·75	1·40
1063	85c. St. Peter's Church	2·25	2·25
1064	$1.10 Barr's Bay Park	3·25	3·50
1061/1064	Set of 4	7·50	7·00

(Des Derek Miller. Litho Enschedé)

2010 (17 June). Endangered Species. Lined Seahorse (*Hippocampus erectus*). T **221** and similar vert designs. Multicoloured. W w **18**. P 14.

1065	35c. Type **221**	1·00	60
	a. Strip of 4. Nos. 1065/8	7·50	7·00
1066	70c. Pair of seahorses	1·75	1·40
1067	85c. Pair hiding in seaweed	2·25	2·25
1068	$1.25 Adults and young	3·25	3·50
1065/1068	Set of 4	7·50	7·00

Nos. 1065/8 were printed together, *se-tenant*, as horizontal and vertical strips of four stamps in sheetlets of 16, and also in separate sheets of 50 (2 panes of 25).

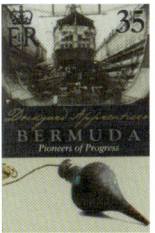

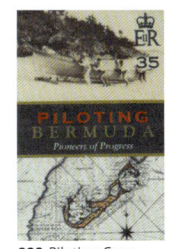

222 HMS *Urgent* in Floating Dock, c.1880

223 Piloting Crew bringing Gig ashore and the Heathers Chart

(Litho BDT)

2010 (23 Sept). Pioneers of Progress (4th series). Dockyard Apprentices. T **222** and similar vert designs. Multicoloured. P 14.

1069	35c. Type **222**	1·00	30
1070	70c. Dockyard Gate and part of dockyard clock	1·75	1·25
1071	85c. George Dixon (senior shipfitter) in front of power saw	2·00	2·25
1072	$1.10 Workmen outside chief constructor's shipfitting shop and tools	3·00	3·50
1069/72	Set of 4	7·00	6·50

69

BERMUDA

(Litho BDT)

2011 (3 Mar). Queen Elizabeth II and Prince Philip "A Lifetime of Service". Diamond-shaped designs as T **303a** of Bahamas. Multicoloured. P 13½.

1073	10c. Queen Elizabeth II, c. 1952	35	35
1074	35c. Queen Elizabeth II and Prince Philip (black and white photo)	1·00	40
1075	70c. Queen Elizabeth II (wearing red) and Prince Philip (in white uniform)	1·75	1·25
1076	85c. Queen Elizabeth II (wearing blue) and Prince Philip	2·25	2·25
1077	$1.10 Princess Elizabeth and Prince Philip (in uniform)	2·50	2·75
1078	$1.25 Prince Philip, c. 1952	2·50	3·00
1073/8 Set of 6		9·00	9·00
MS1079 174×164 mm. Nos. 1073/8 and three stamp-size labels		9·00	9·50
MS1080 110×70 mm. $2.50 Queen Elizabeth II (wearing pale blue) and Prince Philip		5·50	6·00

Nos. 1073/8 was printed in separate sheetlets of eight stamps.
No. **MS**1979 forms a diamond shape with the left, right and top corners removed.

(Des Jackie Aubrey. Litho BDT)

2011 (19 May). Pioneers of Progress (5th series). Piloting. T **223** and similar vert designs. Multicoloured. W w **18**. P 14.

1081	35c. Type **223**	1·00	30
1082	70c. Painting of pilot sloop *Gibbs Hill*	1·75	1·25
1083	85c. Pilot sloop and portrait of pilot Jacob Miners	2·00	2·25
1084	$1.10 Photographs of gig in rough seas and pilot crew at leisure	3·00	3·50
1081/4 Set of 4		7·00	6·50

224 Bermuda Dockyard and Casemates Barracks, 1857

224a Duke and Duchess of Cambridge

(Des Keno K. Simmons. Litho BDT)

2011 (21 July). Casemates Barracks, Bermuda Dockyard. T **224** and similar horiz designs. Multicoloured. W w **18** (sideways). P 14×14½.

1085	35c. Type **224**	1·00	30
1086	70c. Watercolour of western warehouse of Victualling Yard and construction of main Dockyard buildings, 1857	1·75	1·25
1087	85c. Casemates Barracks and Great Eastern Storehouse, late 1850s	2·00	2·25
1088	$1.25 Casemates Barracks complex, late 1800s	3·25	3·75
1085/8 Set of 4		7·25	6·75

(Litho Enschedé)

2011 (1 Sept). Royal Wedding. Sheet 160×91 mm containing multicoloured designs as T **224a**. W w **18** (sideways). P 14.
MS1089 35c. Type **224a**; 70c. Waving from State Landau (*horiz*); 85c. Leaving Buckingham Palace in car with 'JU5T WED' numberplate (*horiz*); $1 Kissing on Buckingham Palace balcony...................... 7·25 7·25

225 Queen Elizabeth II, c. 1955

(Litho BDT)

2012 (6 Feb). Diamond Jubilee. T **225** and similar diamond-shaped designs. Multicoloured. P 13½.

1090	10c. Type **225**	50	50
1091	35c. At State Opening of Parliament, c. 2005	1·25	55
1092	70c. Queen Elizabeth II wearing headscarf, c. 1970	2·00	1·50
1093	85c. Queen Elizabeth II wearing bright pink, c. 2005	2·50	2·25
1094	$1.10 Queen Elizabeth II wearing blue dress, jacket and hat, c. 1955	3·25	3·50
1095	$1.25 Queen Elizabeth II wearing pearl and diamond earrings and necklace, c. 1970	3·75	4·00
1090/5 Set of 6		12·00	11·00
MS1096 174×164 mm.Nos. 1090/5 and three stamp-size labels		12·00	12·00
MS1097 110×70 mm.$2.50 Coronation photograph, 1953		6·00	6·00

Nos. 1090/5 were printed in separate sheetlets of eight stamps.
No. **MS**1096 forms a diamond-shape but with the left, right and top corners removed.

226 William Perot and Cancellation of 1848

(Des Jackie Aubrey. Litho Lowe-Martin Group)

2012 (19 Apr). Bicentenary of Bermuda Postal Service. T **226** and similar horiz designs. Multicoloured. W w **18** (sideways). P 13.

1098	25c. Type **226**	1·25	60
1099	35c. Bermuda Queen Victoria 1d. red stamp and 19th-century mail ferry	1·40	60
1100	70c. Bermuda 1920 Tercentenary of Representative Institutions ½d. stamp and mail carriage, 1920s	2·25	1·75
1101	95c. Bermuda 1940 2d. ultramarine and scarlet yacht stamp and Imperial Airways Cavalier flying boat, 1930s	3·00	3·00
1102	$1.10 Bermuda 1968 2s.6d. Constitution stamp and mail van, 1960s	3·25	3·50
1103	$1.25 Stylised letters ('R-Post 2000s')	3·50	4·00
1098/1103 Set of 6		13·00	12·00

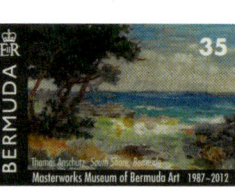

227 South Shore, Bermuda (Thomas Anschutz)

228 Clock Tower

(Litho Enschede)

2012 (12 July). 25th Anniv of Masterworks Museum of Bermuda Art. T **227** and similar multicoloured designs. W w **18** (sideways on horiz designs). P 13½.

1104	35c. Type **227**	1·00	30
1105	70c. St. George's (Ogden Pleissner)	1·75	1·25
1106	80c. *Front Street* (André Biéler)	2·00	2·00
1107	$1.10 *Street Scene, Bermuda (Elliott Street)* (Dorothy Austen Stevens)	2·75	2·75
1108	$1.25 *La Maison du Gouverneur* (Albert Gleizes) (*vert*)	3·00	3·25
1109	$1.65 *The Welcoming Smile* (Frank Small) (*vert*)	4·00	4·50
1104/9 Set of 6		13·00	12·50

(Litho Enschede)

2012 (18 Oct). 400th Anniv of St. Peter's Church, St. George's. T **228** and similar vert designs. Multicoloured. W w **18**. P 13½×13.

1110	35c. Type **228**	75	25
1111	95c. Chandelier and part of roof	2·50	2·00
1112	$1.10 Bronze plaque	2·75	2·50
1113	$1.25 Entrance and steps	3·00	3·50
1110/3 Set of 4		8·00	7·50

70

BERMUDA

STAMP BOOKLETS

1948 (5 Apr–10 May). Pink (No. SB1), or light blue (No. SB2) covers. Stapled.

SB1	5s. booklet containing six 1d., 1½d., 2d., 2½d. and 3d. (Nos. 110, 111b, 112a, 113b, 114a) in blocks of 6 (10 May)		£140
SB2	10s.6d. booklet containing six 3d. and eighteen 6d. (Nos. 114a, 104) in blocks of 6 with twelve air mail labels		£150

WINSLOW HOMER BERMUDIAN WATERCOLOURS

B 1 "Window" Design (*Illustration reduced. Actual size 126×91 mm*)

1987 (30 Apr). Paintings by Winslow Homer. Folded card covers printed in gold. Pane attached by selvedge.
SB3 $4 containing booklet pane of 10 40c. (No. 544a)   9·00

1989 (13 July). Old Garden Roses. Folded card cover, 125×91 mm, as Type B **1**, printed in grey. Pave attached by selvedge.
SB4 $5 containing booklet pane of 10 50c. (No. 589a)   16·00

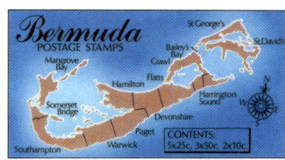

B 2 Map of Bermuda

1993 (1 Apr). Folded card covers, 80×43 mm, as Type B **2** printed in Venetian red, new blue and black. Panes attached by selvedge.
SB5 $2.95 booklet containing panes Nos. 683a and 684a   10·00
SB6 $4.25 booklet containing panes Nos. 684a and 686a   8·00

HAMILTON AND ST. GEORGE'S PANORAMA BOOKLET
BOOKLET CONTENTS: 10 × 60c

B 3 Coats of Arms of Hamilton and St. George's (⅓-size illustration, actual size 130×95 mm)

1996 (21 May). Panoramic Paintings of Hamilton and St George's. Pane attached by selvedge.
SB7 $6 booklet containing pane No. 747a   16·00

B 4 Deep Bay, West Pembroke (*illustration reduced. Actual size 97×63 mm*)

2008 (1 May). Bermuda Scenes. Multicoloured covers as Type B **4**. Self-adhesive.

SB8	($3.50) booklet containing pane No. 1014a (Type B **4**)	11·00
SB9	($7) booklet containing pane No. 1015a (cover showing Spanish Point Park)	14·50
SB10	($8.50) booklet containing pane No. 1016a (cover showing Flatts Inlet)	16·00
SB11	($9.50) booklet containing pane No. 1017a (cover showing Tucker's Town Bay)	17·00

EXPRESS LETTER STAMPS

E **1** Queen Elizabeth II   E **1a**

(Des D. Miller. Litho Enschedé)

1996 (7 Nov). W w **14**. P 14×13½.
E1   E **1** $22 orange and royal blue   30·00   35·00

No. E1 shows the face value, all other inscriptions, the Crown and much of both the inner and the outer frames printed in yellow fluorescent ink as a security marking.

(Litho BDT)

2003 (2 June). W w **14**. P 13½.
E2   E **1a** $25 grey-black, royal blue and violet blue   29·00   30·00

POSTAL FISCAL

1937 (1 Feb). As T **15**, but inscr "REVENUE" at each side. Wmk Mult Script CA. Chalk-surfaced paper. P 14

F1	12s.6d. grey and orange	£1100	£1400
	a. Break in scroll (R. 1/12)	£4250	£6000
	b. Broken crown and scroll (R. 2/12)	£4250	
	d. Break through scroll (R. 1/9)	£4250	
	e. Break in lines below left scroll	£4250	
	f. Damaged leaf at bottom right	£4250	
	g. Gash in fruit and leaf	£4250	
	h. Breaks in scrolls at right (R. 1/3)	£4250	

No. F1 was issued for fiscal purposes towards the end of 1936. Its use as a postage stamp was authorised from 1 February to April 1937. The used price quoted above is for examples postmarked during this period. Later in the same year postmarks with other dates were obtained by favour.

For illustrations of No. F1a/h see above Nos. 51b and 88.

Cayman Islands

The first post office was opened at Georgetown in April 1889. The stamps of Jamaica with the following cancellations were used until 19 February 1901. At some stage, probably around 1891, a supply of the Jamaica 1889 1d., No. 27, was overprinted "CAYMAN ISLANDS", but these stamps were never issued. Two surviving examples are known, one unused and the other cancelled at Richmond in Jamaica.

Types of Jamaica

2   3   4

8   11   13

PRICES OF NOS. Z1/27. These are for a single stamp showing a clear impression of the postmark. Nos. Z1, 2, 6/8, 11/13, 18, 22, 25 and 26 are known used on cover and these are worth considerably more.

GEORGETOWN, GRAND CAYMAN

Z 1

Z 2   Z 3

Stamps of JAMAICA cancelled with Type Z **1** in purple.
1889–94.
Z1	8	½d. yellow-green (No. 16)	£600
Z2	11	1d. purple and mauve (No. 27)	£600
Z2a	2	2d. slate (No. 20a)	£7000
Z3	11	2d. green (No. 28)	£950
Z4		2½d. dull purple and blue (No. 29)	£1300
Z5	4	4d. red-brown (No. 22b)	£4000

Stamps of JAMAICA cancelled with Type Z **2** in purple or black.
1895–98.
Z6	8	½d. yellow-green (No. 16)	£700
Z7	11	1d. purple and mauve (No. 27)	£600
Z8		2½d. dull purple and blue (No. 29)	£1000
Z9	3	3d. sage-green (No 21)	£6000

Stamps of JAMAICA cancelled with Type Z **3**
1898–1901.
Z10	8	½d. yellow-green (No. 16)	£600
		a. Green (No. 16a)	£600
Z11	11	1d. purple and mauve (No. 27)	£600
Z12	13	1d. red (No. 31) (1900)	£650
Z13	11	2½d. dull purple and blue (No. 29)	£850

OFFICIAL STAMPS

Stamps of JAMAICA cancelled with Type Z **1** in purple.
1890–94.
Z14	8	½d. green (No. O1) (opt 17–17½ mm long)	£1400
Z15		½d. green (No. O3) (opt 16 mm long) (1893)	£3500
Z16	11	1d. rose (No. O4)	£1400
Z17		2d. grey (No. O5)	£6000

Stamps of JAMAICA cancelled with Type Z **2** in purple or black.
1895–98.
Z18	8	½d. green (No. O3)	£4000
Z19	11	1d. rose (No. O4)	£6000
Z20		2d. grey (No. O5)	£7000

STAKE BAY, CAYMAN BRAC

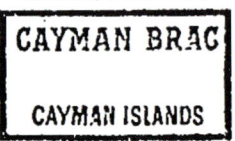

Z **4**

Z **5**

Stamps of JAMAICA cancelled with Type Z **4**.
1898–1900.
Z21	8	½d. yellow-green (No. 16)	£4500
Z22	11	1d. purple and mauve (No. 27)	£4250
Z23		2d. green (No. 28)	£7000
Z24		2½d. dull purple and blue (No. 29)	£4250

Stamps of JAMAICA cancelled with Type Z **5**.
1900–01.
Z25	8	½d. yellow-green (No. 16)	£5000
Z26	11	1d. purple and mauve (No. 27)	£5500
Z27	13	1d. red (No. 31)	£6000
Z28	11	2½d. dull purple and blue (No. 29)	£5500

PRICES FOR STAMPS ON COVER TO 1945	
Nos. 1/2	from × 25
Nos. 3/12	from × 5
Nos. 13/16	from × 4
Nos. 17/19	from × 12
Nos. 25/34	from × 5
Nos. 35/52b	from × 4
Nos. 53/67	from × 5
Nos. 69/83	from × 4
Nos. 84/95	from × 6
Nos. 96/9	from × 5
Nos. 100/11	from × 4
Nos. 112/14	from × 6
Nos. 115/26	from × 2

DEPENDENCY OF JAMAICA

1   2   3

(T **1**/3, **8**/9 and **12**/13 typo D.L.R.)
1900 (1 Nov). Wmk Crown CA. P 14.
| 1 | 1 | ½d. deep green | 19·00 | 26·00 |
| | | a. Pale green | 13·00 | 22·00 |

CAYMAN ISLANDS

2		1d. rose-carmine	14·00	3·75
		a. Pale carmine	19·00	16·00
1s/2s Optd "SPECIMEN" Set of 2				£170

(Dented frame under "A" (R. 1/6 of left pane). (The variety is believed to have occurred at some point between 9 January and 9 April 1902 and is then present on all subsequent printings of the "POSTAGE POSTAGE" design)

1902 (1 Jan)–03. Wmk Crown CA. P 14.

3	2	½d. green (15.9.02)	4·50	27·00
		a. Dented frame		£300
4		1d. carmine (6.3.03)	10·00	10·00
		a. Dented frame	£375	£375
5		2½d. bright blue	10·00	17·00
		a. Dented frame		£425
6		6d. brown	35·00	70·00
		a. Dented frame	£750	£1100
7	3	1s. orange	60·00	£120
		a. Dented frame	£950	£1400
3/7 Set of 5			£100	£225
3s/7s Optd "SPECIMEN" Set of 5			£250	

1905 (Feb–Oct). Wmk Mult Crown CA. P 14.

8	2	½d. green	10·00	14·00
		a. Dented frame	£350	£400
9		1d. carmine (18 Oct)	19·00	17·00
		a. Dented frame	£500	£500
10		2½d. bright blue	10·00	4·75
		a. Dented frame	£375	£350
11		6d. brown	18·00	38·00
		a. Dented frame	£425	£600
12	3	1s. orange	29·00	48·00
		a. Dented frame	£650	
8/12 Set of 5			75·00	£110

1907 (13 Mar). Wmk Mult Crown CA. P 14.

13	3	4d. brown and blue	35·00	60·00
		a. Dented frame	£800	£1000
14	2	6d. olive and rose	40·00	75·00
		a. Dented frame	£800	£1000
15	3	1s. violet and green	60·00	85·00
		a. Dented frame	£950	
16		5s. salmon and green	£200	£325
		a. Dented frame	£5000	£5500
13/16 Set of 4			£300	£475
13s/16s Optd "SPECIMEN" Set of 4			£225	

One Halfpenny. (4) **½D** (5) **1D** (6)

1907 (30 Aug). No. 9 surch at Govt Printing Office, Kingston, with T **4**.

17	2	½d. on 1d. carmine	55·00	85·00
		a. Dented frame	£1000	£1400

1907 (Nov). No. 16 handstamped at Georgetown P.O. with T **5** or **6**.

18	3	½d. on 5s. salmon and green (25 Nov)	£300	£450
		a. Surch inverted		£95000
		b. Surch double	£12000	£11000
		c. Surch double, one inverted		
		d. Surch omitted (in pair with normal)		£95000
		e. Dented frame		£5000
19		1d. on 5s. salmon and green (23 Nov)	£275	£400
		a. Surch double	£22000	
		b. Surch inverted		£140000
		c. Dented frame	£4750	£5000

The ½d. on 5s. may be found with the figures "1" or "2" omitted, owing to defective handstamping.

(8)  (9) **2½D** (10)

1907 (27 Dec)–09. Chalk-surfaced paper (3d. to 10s.). P 14.

(a) Wmk Mult Crown CA

25	8	½d. green	4·25	4·00
26		1d. carmine	1·75	75
27		2½d. ultramarine (30.3.08)	5·50	2·50
28	9	3d. purple/*yellow* (30.3.08)	3·25	2·75
29		4d. black and red/*yellow* (30.3.08)	60·00	80·00
30	8	6d. dull purple and violet purple (2.10.08)	23·00	35·00
		a. Dull and bright purple	32·00	55·00
31	9	1s. black/*green* (5.4.09)	9·00	22·00
32		5s. green and red/*yellow* (30.3.08)	38·00	75·00

(b) Wmk Crown CA (30.3.08)

33	9	1s. black/*green*	65·00	95·00
34	8	10s. green and red/*green*	£180	£250
25/34 Set of 10			£350	£500
25s/30s, 32s/4s Optd "SPECIMEN" Set of 9			£350	

1908 (12 Feb). No. 13 handstamped locally with T **10**.

35	3	2½d. on 4d. brown and blue	£1800	£3500
		a. Surch double	£50000	£30000
		b. Dented frame		£24000

No. 35 should only be purchased when accompanied by an expert committee's certificate or similar form of guarantee.

MANUSCRIPT PROVISIONALS. During May and June 1908 supplies of ½d. and 1d. stamps became exhausted, and the payment of postage was indicated by the postmistress, Miss Gwendolyn Parsons, using a manuscript endorsement. Such endorsements were in use from 12 May to 1 June.

MP1	"(Postage Paid G.A.P.)" (12 May to 1 June)	£6000
MP1*a*	"(Postage Paid G.A.P.)½" (23 May to 1 June)	£8500
MP1*b*	"(Postage Paid G.A.P.)1" (23 May to 1 June)	£7500

In October of the same year there was a further shortage of ¼d. stamps and the manuscript endorsements were again applied by either the new Postmaster, William Graham McCausland or by Miss Parsons who remained as his assistant.

MP2	"Pd ¼d.W.G. McC" (4 to 27 October)	£250
MP2*a*	¼d. Pd. W.G. McC" (14 October)	£1500
MP2*b*	"Pd ¼d.W.G. McC" (6 October)	£2000
MP3	"Paid" (7 October)	£13000
MP4	"Pd ¼d." (8 October)	£8500
MP5	"Paid ¼d/ GAP. asst." (15 October)	£11000

No. MP2 exists in different inks and formats. Nos. MP2 and MP2*a* show the endorsement in two lines, whereas it is in one line on No. MP2*b*.

Manuscript endorsement for the 2½d. rate is also known, but this is thought to have been done by oversight.

A 1d. surcharge on 4d. (No. 29), issued in mid-May, was intended as a revenue stamp and was never authorised for postal use (*price* £250 *un*.). Used examples were either cancelled by favour or passed through the post in error. Exists with surcharge inverted (*price* £2000 *un*.), surcharge double (*price* £2750 *un*.) or surcharge double, both inverted (*price* £3000 *un*.).

11  12  13

1908 (30 June)–09. Wmk Mult Crown CA. Litho. P 14.

38	11	¼d. brown	4·25	50
		a. Grey-brown (2.09)	6·00	1·00
		s. Optd "SPECIMEN"	95·00	

1912 (24 Apr)–20. Die I. Wmk Mult Crown CA. Chalk-surfaced paper (3d. to 10s.). P 14.

40	13	¼d. brown (10.2.13)	1·00	40
41	12	½d. green	2·75	5·00
		w. Wmk inverted	†	£1300
42		1d. red (25.2.13)	3·25	2·50
43	13	2d. pale grey	1·00	10·00
44	12	2½d. bright blue (26.8.14)	6·00	8·50
		a. Deep bright blue (9.11.17)	14·00	25·00
45	13	3d. purple/*yellow* (26.11.14)	15·00	45·00
		a. White back (19.11.13)	3·50	8·00
		b. On lemon (12.3.18)	2·50	18·00
		bs. Optd "SPECIMEN"	70·00	
		c. On orange-buff (1920)	10·00	32·00
		d. On buff (1920)		
		e. On pale yellow (1920)	4·00	30·00
46		4d. black and red/*yellow* (25.2.13)	1·00	10·00
47	12	6d. dull and bright purple (25.2.13)	3·75	7·50
48	13	1s. black/*green* (15.5.16)	3·50	27·00
		as. Optd "SPECIMEN"	65·00	
		b. White back (19.11.13)	3·50	3·50
49		2s. purple and bright blue/*blue*	12·00	65·00
50		3s. green and violet	19·00	75·00

73

CAYMAN ISLANDS

51		5s. green and red/*yellow* (26.8.14)		80·00	£170
52	**12**	10s. deep green and red/*green* (26.11.14)		£140	£250
		as. Optd "SPECIMEN"		£110	
		b. *White back* (19.11.13)		£120	£180
		c. *On blue-green, olive back* (5.10.18)		£110	£250
40/52b Set of 13				£225	£500
40s/4s, 45as, 46s/7s, 48bs, 49s/51s, 52bs Optd "SPECIMEN" Set of 13					£425

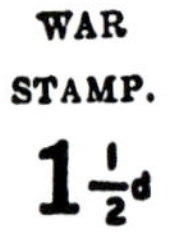

(14)  (15) 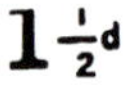 Straight serif (Left-hand pane R. 10/2)

1917 (26 Feb). T **12** surch with T **14** or **15** at Kingston, Jamaica.

53	**14**	1½d. on 2½d. deep blue	18·00	20·00
		a. No fraction bar	£250	£275
		b. Missing stop after "STAMP" (R. 1/4)	£850	
54	**15**	1½d. on 2½d. deep blue	1·75	6·00
		a. No fraction bar	75·00	£140
		b. Straight serif	95·00	£180

On No. 53 "WAR STAMP" and "1½d." were applied separately.

(16) 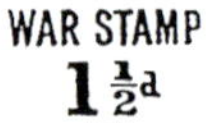 (17)

1917 (4 Sept). T **12** surch with T **16** or **17** by D.L.R.

55	**16**	1½d. on 2½d. deep blue	£750	£2000
56	**17**	1½d. on 2½d. deep blue	30	60
		s. Optd "SPECIMEN"	£120	
		x. Wmk reversed	£160	

De La Rue replaced surcharge Type **16** by Type **17** after only a few sheets as it did not adequately obliterate the original face value. A small quantity, said to be 3½ sheets, of Type **16** was included in the consignment in error.

(17a) 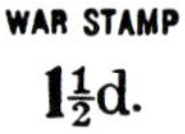 (18)

1919–20. T **12** and **13** (2½d. special printing), optd only, or surch in addition at Kingston (No. 58) or by D.L.R. (others).

57	**17a**	½d. green (4.2.19)	60	2·50
		a. Short opt (right pane R. 10/1)	26·00	
58	**18**	1½d. on 2d. grey (10.3.20)	4·50	7·50
59	**17**	1½d. on 2½d. orange (4.2.19)	80	1·25
57s, 59s Optd "Specimen" Set of 2			£120	

The ½d. stamps on *buff* paper, and later consignments of the 2d. T **13** on *pinkish*, derived their colour from the paper in which they were packed for despatch from England.

No. 57a shows the overprint 2 mm high instead of 2½ mm.

A further surcharge as No. 58, but in red, was prepared in Jamaica during April 1920, but these were not issued.

19

20 King William IV and King George V

1921 (4 Apr)–**26**. P 14.

(a) Wmk Mult Crown CA

60	**19**	3d. purple/*orange-buff*	1·50	8·00
		aw. Wmk inverted	£250	£325
		ay. Wmk inverted and reversed	£160	£200
		b. *Purple/pale yellow*	45·00	60·00
		bw. Wmk inverted	£375	
62		4d. red/*yellow* (1.4.22)	1·00	4·50
63		1s. black/*green*	1·25	9·50
		x. Wmk reversed	£500	
64		5s. yellow-green/*pale yellow*	16·00	70·00
		a. *Deep green/pale yellow*	£100	£160
		b. *Blue-green/pale yellow*	£110	£180
		c. *Deep green/orange-buff* (19.11.21)	£160	£225

67		10s. carmine/*green* (19.11.21)	75·00	£120
60/7 Set of 5			85·00	£190
60s/7s Optd "SPECIMEN" Set of 5				£225

(b) Wmk Mult Script CA

69	**19**	¼d. yellow-brown (1.4.22)	50	1·50
		y. Wmk inverted and reversed	£325	
70		½d. pale grey-green (1.4.22)	50	30
		w. Wmk inverted		
		y. Wmk inverted and reversed		
71		1d. deep carmine-red (1.4.22)	1·40	85
72		1½d. orange-brown	1·75	30
73		2d. slate-grey (1.4.22)	1·75	4·00
74		2½d. bright blue (1.4.22)	50	50
		x. Wmk reversed	£475	
75		3d. purple/*yellow* (29.6.23)	2·50	4·00
		y. Wmk inverted and reversed	£500	
76		4½d. sage-green (29.6.23)	3·50	3·00
77		6d. claret (1.4.22)	5·50	45·00
		a. *Deep claret*	19·00	40·00
79		1s. black/*green* (15.5.25)	9·50	32·00
80		2s. violet/*blue* (1.4.22)	14·00	29·00
81		3s. violet (1.4.22)	23·00	16·00
82		5s. green (15.2.25)	26·00	55·00
83		10s. carmine/*green* (5.9.26)	70·00	£100
69/83 Set of 14			£140	£250
69s/83s Optd "SPECIMEN" Set of 14				£450

An example of the 4d, No. 62, is known with the 'C' missing from the watermark in the top sheet margin.

"A.S.R." PROVISIONAL. On the night of 9/10 November 1932 the Cayman Brac Post Office at Stake Bay, and its contents, was destroyed by a hurricane. Pending the arrival of replacement stamp stocks and cancellation the Postmaster, Mr A. S. Rutty, initialled covers to indicate that postage had been paid. Those destined for overseas addresses additionally received a "Postage Paid" machine postmark in red when they passed through Kingston, Jamaica.

MP6	Endorsed "A.S.R." in manuscript	£11000
MP7	Endorsed "A.S.R." in manuscript and "Postage Paid" machine postmark in red	£16000

These emergency arrangements lasted until 19 December.

(Recess Waterlow)

1932 (5 Dec). Centenary of the "Assembly of Justices and Vestry". Wmk Mult Script CA. P 12½.

84	**20**	¼d. brown	1·50	1·00
		a. "A" of "CA" missing from wmk	£1500	£1500
85		½d. green	2·75	9·50
		a. "A" of "CA" reversed in wmk	£1600	
86		1d. scarlet	2·75	14·00
87		1½d. red-orange	2·75	2·75
		a. "A" of "CA" missing from wmk	£1800	
88		2d. grey	2·75	3·50
89		2½d. ultramarine	2·75	1·50
90		3d. olive-green	7·50	6·00
91		6d. purple	11·00	23·00
92		1s. black and brown	17·00	32·00
93		2s. black and ultramarine	50·00	85·00
94		5s. black and green	£100	£160
95		10s. black and scarlet	£350	£450
84/95 Set of 12			£500	£750
84s/95s Perf "SPECIMEN" Set of 12			£600	

The design of Nos. 92/5 differs slightly from Type **20**.

No. 85a shows one "A" of the watermark reversed so that its head points to right when seen from the back. It is believed that this stamp may also exist with "A" missing.

Examples of all values are known showing a forged George Town postmark dated "DE 31 1932".

21 Cayman Islands

22 Cat Boat

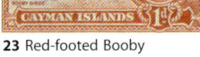

23 Red-footed Booby

24 Queen or Pink Conch Shells

CAYMAN ISLANDS

25 Hawksbill Turtles

(Recess Waterlow)

1935 (1 May). T **21**, **24** and similar designs. Wmk Mult Script CA. P 12½.
96	21	¼d. black and brown	50	1·00
97	22	½d. ultramarine and yellow-green	1·00	1·00
98	23	1d. ultramarine and scarlet	4·00	2·25
99	24	1½d. black and orange	1·50	1·75
100	22	2d. ultramarine and purple	3·75	1·10
101	25	2½d. blue and black	3·25	1·25
102	21	3d. black and olive-green	2·50	3·00
103	25	6d. bright purple and black	8·50	4·00
104	22	1s. black and orange	6·00	6·50
105	23	2s. ultramarine and black	48·00	35·00
106	25	5s. green and black	65·00	65·00
107	24	10s. black and scarlet	£100	£100
96/107 Set of 12			£200	£200
96s/107s Perf "SPECIMEN" Set of 12			£350	

Examples of all values are known showing a forged George Town postmark dated "AU 23 1936".

1935 (6 May). Silver Jubilee. As Nos. 141/4 of Bahamas.
108		½d. black and green	15	1·00
		f. Diagonal line by turret	65·00	90·00
		g. Dot to left of chapel	£150	
		h. Dot by flagstaff	£120	
		i. Dash by turret	£150	
109		2½d. brown and deep blue	6·00	1·00
110		6d. light blue and olive-green	1·50	7·00
		h. Dot by flagstaff	£325	
		i. Dash by turret	£375	
111		1s. slate and purple	12·00	10·00
		h. Dot by flagstaff	£425	£425
		i. Dash by turret	£600	
108/11 Set of 4			17·00	18·00
108s/11s Perf "SPECIMEN" Set of 4			£150	

For illustrations of plate varieties see Bahamas.

1937 (13 May). Coronation Issue. As Nos. 146/8 of Bahamas but printed by B.W. P 11×11½.
112		½d. green	30	1·90
113		1d. carmine	50	20
114		2½d. blue	95	40
112/14 Set of 3			1·60	2·25
112s/14s Perf "SPECIMEN" Set of 3			£150	

26 Beach View
27 Dolphin (fish) (*Coryphaena hippurus*) 
28 Cayman Islands map 
29 Hawksbill Turtles 
30 *Rembro* (schooner) 

(Recess D.L.R. (½d., 2d., 6d., 1s., 10s.), Waterlow (others))

1938 (5 May)–**48**. T **23**/**30**. Wmk Mult Script CA (sideways on ¼d., 1d., 1½d., 2½d., 3d., 2s., 5s.). Various perfs.
115	26	¼d. red-orange (P 12½)	70	55
		a. Perf 13½×12½ (16.7.43)	10	65
116	27	½d. green (P 13×11½)	1·00	55
		a. Perf 14 (16.7.43)	2·50	1·40
		ab. "A" of "CA" missing from wmk	£1700	
117	28	1d. scarlet (P 12½)	30	75
118	26	1½d. black (P 12½)	30	10
119	29	2d. violet (P 11½×13)	3·00	40
		a. Perf 14 (16.7.43)	60	30
120	30	2½d. bright blue (P 12½)	40	20
120a		2½d. orange (P 12½) (25.8.47)	3·50	50
121	28	3d. orange (P 12½)	40	15
121a		3d. bright blue (P 12½) (25.8.47)	3·00	30
122	29	6d. olive-green (P 11½×13)	15·00	4·50
		a. Perf 14 (16.7.43)	3·25	1·25
		b. Brownish olive (P 11½ × 13) (8.7.47)	3·00	1·50
123	27	1s. red-brown (P 13×11½)	6·50	1·50
		a. Perf 14 (16.7.43)	7·00	2·00
		ab. "A" of "CA" missing from wmk	£2500	
124	26	2s. yellow-green (*shades*) (P 12½)	50·00	14·00
		a. Deep green (16.7.43)	25·00	9·00
125	30	5s. carmine-lake (P 12½)	40·00	15·00
		a. Crimson (1948)	75·00	27·00
126	29	10s. chocolate (P 11½×13)	32·00	9·00
		a. Perf 14 (16.7.43)	30·00	9·00
		aw. Wmk inverted		
115/26a Set of 14			£100	35·00
115s/26s Perf "SPECIMEN" Set of 14			£500	

3d. Stop after "1946" (Plate B1 R. 2/1)

1946 (26 Aug). Victory. As Nos. 176/7 of Bahamas.
127		1½d. black	50	40
128		3d. orange-yellow	50	40
		a. Stop after "1946"	30·00	40·00
127s/8s Perf "SPECIMEN" Set of 2			£130	

1948 (29 Nov). Royal Silver Wedding. As Nos. 194/5 of Bahamas.
129		½d. green	10	1·00
130		10s. violet-blue	24·00	30·00

1949 (10 Oct). 75th Anniv of Universal Postal Union. As Nos. 196/9 of Bahamas.
131		2½d. orange	30	1·00
132		3d. deep blue	1·50	2·25
133		6d. olive	60	2·25
134		1s. red-brown	60	50
131/4 Set of 4			2·75	5·50

31 Cat Boat
32 Coconut Grove, Cayman Brac 
33 Green Turtle 
34 Thatch Rope Industry 
35 Cayman Seamen 
36 Map of Cayman Islands 
37 Parrotfish 
38 Bluff, Cayman Brac 

75

CAYMAN ISLANDS

39 Georgetown Harbour
40 Turtle in "crawl" 
41 *Ziroma* (schooner) 
42 Boat-building 
43 Government Offices, Grand Cayman 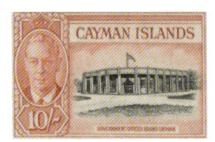

(Recess B.W.)

1950 (2 Oct). T **31/43**. Wmk Mult Script CA. P 11½ × 11.

135	31	¼d. bright blue and pale scarlet	15	60
136	32	½d. reddish violet and emerald-green..	15	1·25
137	33	1d. olive-green and deep blue	60	75
138	34	1½d. green and brown	40	75
139	35	2d. reddish violet and rose-carmine	1·25	1·50
140	36	2½d. turquoise and black	1·25	60
141	37	3d. bright green and light blue	1·40	1·50
142	38	6d. red-brown and blue	2·00	1·25
143	39	9d. scarlet and grey-green	13·00	2·00
144	40	1s. brown and orange	3·25	2·75
145	41	2s. violet and reddish purple	14·00	11·00
146	42	5s. olive-green and violet	24·00	7·00
147	43	10s. black and scarlet	29·00	23·00
135/47	Set of 13		80·00	48·00

44 South Sound Lighthouse, Grand Cayman
45 Queen Elizabeth II 

1953 (2 Mar)–**62**. Designs previously used for King George VI issue but with portrait of Queen Elizabeth II as in T **44/5**. Wmk Mult Script CA. P 11½×11 or 11×11½ (4d., £1).

148	31	¼d. deep bright blue & rose-red (21.2.55)	1·00	50
		a. Bright blue and bright rose-red (5.12.56)	4·00	2·50
149	32	½d. purple and bluish green (7.7.54)	75	50
150	33	1d. brown-olive and indigo (7.7.54)	70	40
151	34	1½d. deep green and red-brown (7.7.54)	60	20
152	35	2d. reddish violet and cerise (2.6.54)	3·00	85
153	36	2½d. turquoise-blue and black (2.6.54)	3·50	80
154	37	3d. bright green and blue (21.2.55)	4·00	60
155	44	4d. black and deep blue	2·00	40
		a. Black and greenish blue (13.10.54)	26·00	24·00
		b. Black and deep bright blue (10.7.62)	15·00	15·00
156	38	6d. lake-brown and deep blue (7.7.54)	1·75	30
157	39	9d. scarlet and bluish green (2.6.54)	7·50	30
158	40	1s. brown and red-orange (21.2.55)	3·75	20
159	41	2s. slate-violet and reddish purple (21.2.55)	13·00	9·00
160	42	5s. olive-green and slate-violet (21.2.55)	15·00	8·00
161	43	10s. black and rose-red (21.2.55)	23·00	8·00
161a	45	£1 blue (6.1.59)	45·00	13·00
148/61a	Set of 15		£110	38·00

1953 (2 June). Coronation. As No. 200 of Bahamas, but printed by B.W.

162		1d. black and emerald	30	2·00

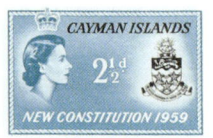

46 Arms of the Cayman Islands

(Photo D.L.R.)

1959 (4 July). New Constitution. Wmk Mult Script CA. P 12.

163	46	2½d. black and light blue	45	2·50
164		1s. black and orange	55	50

CROWN COLONY

47 Cuban Amazon
48 Cat Boat 
49 *Schomburgkia thomsoniana* (orchid) 
50 Map of Cayman Islands 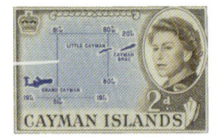
51 Fisherman casting net 
52 West Bay Beach 
53 Green Turtle 
54 *Kirk B* (schooner) 
55 Angler with King Mackerel 
56 Iguana 
57 Swimming pool, Cayman Brac 
58 Water sports 
59 Fort George 

76

CAYMAN ISLANDS

60 Coat of Arms
61 Queen Elizabeth II

(Recess B.W.)

1962 (28 Nov)–**64**. T **47**/**61**. W w **12**. P 11×11½ (vert) or 11½×11 (horiz).

165	**47**	¼d. emerald and red	55	1·00
		a. Emerald and rose (18.2.64)	3·50	4·50
166	**48**	1d. black and yellow-olive	80	20
167	**49**	1½d. yellow and purple	2·75	80
168	**50**	2d. blue and deep brown	1·50	30
169	**51**	2½d. violet and bluish green	85	1·00
170	**52**	3d. bright blue and carmine	30	10
171	**53**	4d. deep green and purple	3·75	60
172	**54**	6d. bluish green and sepia	3·25	30
173	**55**	9d. ultramarine and purple	4·00	40
174	**56**	1s. sepia and rose-red	1·50	10
175	**57**	1s.3d. bluish green and orange-brown	6·50	2·25
176	**58**	1s.9d. deep turquoise and violet	20·00	1·25
177	**59**	5s. plum and deep green	13·00	15·00
178	**60**	10s. olive and blue	22·00	15·00
179	**61**	£1 carmine and black	22·00	28·00
165/79 Set of 15			90·00	60·00

1963 (4 June). Freedom from Hunger. As No. 223 of Bahamas.

180		1s.9d. carmine	30	15

1963 (2 Sept). Red Cross Centenary. As Nos. 226/7 of Bahamas.

181		1d. red and black	30	1·00
182		1s.9d. red and blue	70	1·75

1964 (23 April). 400th Birth Anniv of William Shakespeare. As No. 244 of Bahamas.

183		6d. magenta	20	10

1965 (17 May). I.T.U. Centenary. As Nos. 262/3 of Bahamas.

184		1d. blue and light purple	15	10
185		1s.3d. bright purple and green	55	45

1965 (25 Oct). International Co-operation Year. As Nos. 265/6 of Bahamas.

186		1d. reddish purple and turquoise-green	20	10
187		1s. deep bluish green and lavender	80	25

1966 (24 Jan). Churchill Commemoration. As Nos. 267/70 of Bahamas.

188		¼d. new blue	10	2·25
		w. Wmk inverted	55·00	
189		1d. deep green	60	15
190		1s. brown	1·50	15
		w. Wmk inverted	3·00	4·25
191		1s.9d. bluish violet	1·60	75
188/91 Set of 4			3·25	3·00

1966 (4 Feb). Royal Visit. As Nos. 271/2 of Bahamas.

192		1d. black and ultramarine	75	35
193		1s.9d. black and magenta	2·75	1·50

1966 (1 July). World Cup Football Championships. As Nos. 288/9 of Bahamas.

194		1½d. violet, yellow-green, lake and yellow-brown	25	10
195		1s.9d. chocolate, blue-green, lake and yellow-brown	75	25

1966 (20 Sept). Inauguration of W.H.O. Headquarters, Geneva. As Nos. 290/1 of Bahamas.

196		2d. black, yellow-green and light blue	65	15
197		1s.3d. black, light purple and yellow-brown	1·60	60

62 Telephone and Map

(Des V. Whiteley. Litho Harrison)

1966 (5 Dec). International Telephone Links. W w **12**. P 14½×14.

198	**62**	4d. red, black, greenish blue and olive-green	20	20
199		9d. violet-blue, black, brown-red and light green	20	30

1966 (12 Dec*). 20th Anniv of U.N.E.S.C.O. As Nos. 292/4 of Bahamas.

200		1d. slate-violet, red, yellow and orange	15	10
201		1s.9d. orange-yellow, violet and deep olive	60	10
202		5s. black, bright purple and orange	1·50	70
200/2 Set of 3			2·00	80

*This is the local date of issue; the Crown Agents released the stamps on 1 December.

63 B.A.C. One Eleven 200/400 Airliner over *Ziroma* (Cayman schooner)

(Des V. Whiteley. Photo Harrison)

1966 (17 Dec). Opening of Cayman Jet Service. W w **12**. P 14½.

203	**63**	1s. black, new blue and olive-green	35	30
204		1s.9d. deep purple-brown, ultramarine and emerald	40	35

64 Water-skiing

(Des G. Vasarhelyi. Photo Harrison)

1967 (1 Dec). International Tourist Year. T **64** and similar horiz designs. Multicoloured. W w **12**. P 14½×14.

205		4d. Type **64**	35	10
		a. Gold omitted	£375	£325
206		6d. Skin diving	35	30
207		1s. Sport fishing	35	30
208		1s.9d. Sailing	40	75
205/8 Set of 4			1·25	1·25

A used copy of No. 207 is known with yellow omitted.

68 Former Slaves and Emblem

(Des and photo Harrison)

1968 (3 June). Human Rights Year. W w **12**. P 14½×14.

209	**68**	3d. deep bluish green, black and gold	10	10
		w. Wmk inverted	60	80
210		9d. brown, gold and myrtle-green	10	10
211		5s. ultramarine, gold and myrtle-green	30	90
209/11 Set of 3			40	1·00

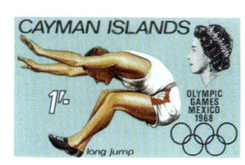

69 Long jumping

(Des R. Granger Barrett. Litho P.B.)

1968 (1 Oct). Olympic Games, Mexico. T **69** and similar multicoloured designs. W w **12**. P 13½.

212		1s. Type **69**	15	10
213		1s.3d. High jumping	20	25
214		2s. Pole vaulting (*vert*)	20	75
212/14 Set of 3			50	1·00

77

CAYMAN ISLANDS

72 "The Adoration of the Shepherds"
(Fabritius)

(Des and photo Harrison)

1968–69. Christmas. T **72** and similar horiz design. Centres multicoloured; country name and frames in gold; value and background in colours given. P 14×14½.

(a) W w **12**. (18.11.68)

215	**72**	¼d. brown	10	20
		a. Gold omitted	£275	
216	–	1d. bluish violet	10	10
217	**72**	6d. bright blue	15	10
218	–	8d. cerise	15	15
219	**72**	1s.3d. bright green	20	25
220	–	2s. grey	25	35

(b) No wmk (8.1.69)

221	**72**	¼d. bright purple	10	20
215/21 Set of 7			80	1·10

Design:—1d., 8d., 2s. "The Adoration of the Shepherds" (Rembrandt).

74 Grand Cayman Thrush

76 Arms of the Cayman Islands

(Des G. Vasarhelyi. Litho Format)

1969 (5 June). Designs as T **74** and T **76** in black, ochre and red (£1) or multicoloured (others). No wmk. P 14.

222	¼d. Type **74**	10	75
223	1d. Brahmin Cattle (*horiz*)	10	10
224	2d. Blowholes on the coast (*horiz*)	10	10
225	2½d. Map of Grand Cayman (*horiz*)	15	10
226	3d. Georgetown scene (*horiz*)	10	10
227	4d. Royal Poinciana (*horiz*)	15	10
228	6d. Cayman Brac and Little Cayman on Chart (*horiz*)	20	10
229	8d. Motor vessels at berth (*horiz*)	25	10
230	1s. Basket-making (*horiz*)	15	10
231	1s.3d. Beach scene (*horiz*)	35	1·00
232	1s.6d. Straw-rope making (*horiz*)	35	1·00
233	2s. Great Barracuda (*horiz*)	1·25	80
234	4s. Government House (*horiz*)	35	80
235	10s. Type **76**	1·00	1·50
236	£1 Queen Elizabeth II (*vert*)	1·25	2·00
222/36 Set of 15		5·00	7·00

1969 (11 Aug). As No. 222, but wmk **12** (sideways).

| 237 | **74** | ¼d. multicoloured | 30 | 65 |

(New Currency. 100 cents = 1 dollar.)

C·DAY
8th September 1969
½c=

(89)

1969 (8 Sept). Decimal Currency. No. 237, and as Nos. 223/36, but wmk w **12** (sideways on horiz designs), surch as T **89**.

238	¼c. on ¼d. Type **74**	10	75
239	1c. on 1d. Brahmin Cattle	10	10
240	2c. on 2d. Blowholes on the coast	10	10
241	3c. on 4d. Royal Poinciana	10	10
242	4c. on 2½d. Map of Grand Cayman	10	10
243	5c. on 6d. Cayman Brac and Little Cayman on Chart	10	10
244	7c. on 8d. Motor vessels at berth	10	10
245	8c. on 3d. Georgetown scene	15	10
246	10c. on 1s. Basket-making	25	10
247	12c. on 1s.3d. Beach scene	35	1·75
248	15c. on 1s.6d. Straw-rope making	45	1·50
249	20c. on 2s. Great Barracuda	1·25	1·75
250	40c. on 4s. Government House	45	85
251	$1 on 10s. Type **76**	1·00	2·50
	w. Wmk inverted	£400	
252	$2 on £1 Queen Elizabeth II	1·50	3·25
238/52 Set of 15		5·00	11·00

90 "Virgin and Child" (Vivarini)

92 "Noli me tangere" (Titian)

(Des adapted by G. Drummond. Photo Harrison)

1969 (14 Nov*). Christmas. Multicoloured; background colours given. W w **12** (sideways on 1, 7 and 20c.). P 14½.

253	**90**	¼c. orange-red	10	10
		w. Wmk inverted	2·75	7·00
254	–	¼c. magenta	10	10
		w. Wmk inverted	2·75	7·00
255	–	¼c. emerald	10	10
		a. Gold frame omitted	£250	
		w. Wmk inverted	1·00	2·00
256	–	¼c. new blue	10	10
		w. Wmk inverted	2·75	7·00
257	–	1c. ultramarine	10	10
258	**90**	5c. orange-red	10	10
259	–	7c. myrtle-green	10	10
260	**90**	12c. emerald	15	15
261	–	20c. brown-purple	20	25
253/61 Set of 9			45	45

Design:—1, 7, 20c. "The Adoration of the Kings" (Gossaert).

*This is the local release date. The Crown Agents released the stamps on 4 November.

(Des L. Curtis. Litho D.L.R.)

1970 (23 Mar). Easter. Paintings multicoloured; frame colours given. P 14.

262	**92**	¼c. carmine-red	10	10
263	–	¼c. deep green	10	10
264	–	¼c. yellow-brown	10	10
265	–	¼c. pale violet	10	10
266	–	10c. chalky blue	35	10
267	–	12c. chestnut	40	10
268	–	40c. plum	55	60
262/8 Set of 7			1·25	75

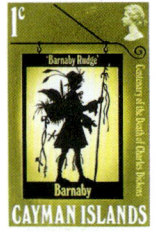

93 Barnaby (*Barnaby Rudge*)

97 Grand Cayman Thrush

(Des Jennifer Toombs. Photo Harrison)

1970 (17 June). Death Centenary of Charles Dickens. T **93** and similar vert designs. W w **12** (sideways*). P 14½×14.

269	1c. black, olive-green and greenish yellow	10	10
	w. Wmk Crown to right of CA	—	2·25
270	12c. black, lake-brown and red	35	10
271	20c. black, ochre-brown and gold	40	10
272	40c. black, bright ultramarine and new blue	45	25
269/72 Set of 4		1·00	50

Designs:—12c. Sairey Gamp (*Martin Chuzzlewit*); 20c. Mr. Micawber and David (*David Copperfield*); 40c. The "Marchioness" (*The Old Curiosity Shop*).

*The normal sideways watermark shows Crown to left of CA, *as seen from the back of the stamp*.

1970 (8 Sept). Decimal Currency. Designs as Nos. 223/37, but with values inscr in decimal currency as T **97**. W w **12** (sideways* on cent values).

273	¼c. Type **97**	65	30
274	1c. Brahmin Cattle	10	10
275	2c. Blowholes on the coast	10	10
276	3c. Royal Poinciana	20	10
277	4c. Map of Grand Cayman	20	10

CAYMAN ISLANDS

278	5c. Cayman Brac and Little Cayman on Chart	35	10
	w. Wmk Crown to right of CA	18·00	
279	7c. Motor vessels at berth	30	10
280	8c. Georgetown scene	30	10
281	10c. Basket-making	30	10
282	12c. Beach scene	90	1·00
283	15c. Straw-rope making	1·25	4·00
284	20c. Great Barracuda	3·25	1·25
285	40c. Government House	85	75
286	$1 Type **76**	1·25	4·75
	w. Wmk inverted	11·00	8·00
287	$2 Queen Elizabeth II	2·00	4·75
273/87 Set of 15		10·50	15·00

*The normal sideways watermark shows Crown to left of CA, as seen from the back of the stamp.

98 The Three Wise Men

(Des G. Drummond. Litho Format)

1970 (8 Oct). Christmas. T **98** and similar horiz design. W w **12** (sideways*). P 14.

288	**98**	¼c. apple-green, grey and emerald	10	10
		w. Wmk Crown to right of CA	5·50	5·50
289	–	1c. black, lemon and turquoise-green	10	10
290	**98**	5c. grey, red-orange and crimson	10	10
291	–	10c. black, lemon and orange-red	10	10
292	**98**	12c. grey, pale turquoise and ultramarine	15	10
293	–	20c. black, lemon and green	20	15
288/93 Set of 6			55	30

Design:—1, 10, 20c. Nativity scene and Globe.
*The normal sideways watermark shows Crown to left of CA, as seen from the back of the stamp.

100 Grand Cayman Terrapin

(Des V. Whiteley. Photo Harrison)

1971 (28 Jan). Turtles. T **100** and similar diamond-shaped designs. W w **12** (sideways*, reading from inscr to "ISLANDS"). P 14½×14.

294	5c. Type **100**	30	25
	w. Wmk Crown to right of CA	22·00	
295	7c. Green Turtle	35	25
	w. Wmk Crown to right of CA	80·00	
296	12c. Hawksbill Turtle	55	30
297	20c. Turtle Farm	1·00	1·40
294/7 Set of 4		2·00	2·00

*The normal sideways watermark shows Crown to left of CA, as seen from the back of the stamp.

101 Dendrophylax fawcettii

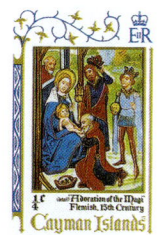

102 "Adoration of the Kings" (French, 15th Cent)

(Des Sylvia Goaman. Litho Questa)

1971 (7 Apr). Orchids. T **101** and similar vert designs. Multicoloured. W w **12**. P 14.

298	¼c. Type **101**	10	1·25
299	2c. Schomburgkia thomsoniana	60	90
300	10c. Vanilla claviculata	2·25	50
301	40c. Oncidium variegatum	4·50	3·50
298/301 Set of 4		6·50	5·50

(Des Jennifer Toombs. Litho Questa)

1971 (15 Oct*). Christmas. T **102** and similar vert designs. Multicoloured. W w **12**. P 14.

302	¼c. Type **102**	10	10
	w. Wmk inverted	2·00	
303	1c. "The Nativity" (Parisian, 14th Cent.)	10	10
304	5c. "Adoration of the Magi" (Burgundian, 15th Cent.)	10	10
305	12c. Type **102**	20	15
306	15c. As 1c.	20	25
307	20c. As 5c.	25	35
302/7 Set of 6		70	80
MS308 113×115 mm. Nos. 302/7		1·25	2·25
	w. Wmk inverted	£275	

*This is the local date of issue. The Crown Agents released the stamps on 27 September.

(Des Anglo Arts Associates. Litho Walsall)

1972 (10 Jan). Co-Axial Telephone Cable. W w **12** (sideways*). P 14.

309	**103**	2c. multicoloured	10	10
310		10c. multicoloured	15	10
		w. Wmk Crown to right of CA	9·00	
311		40c. multicoloured	30	40
		w. Wmk Crown to right of CA	1·00	
309/11 Set of 3			45	45

*The normal sideways watermark shows Crown to left of CA, as seen from the back of the stamp.

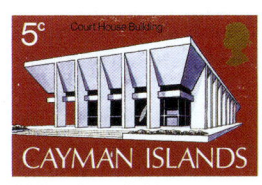

104 Court House Building

(Des C. Abbott. Litho Questa)

1972 (15 Aug). New Government Buildings. T **104** and similar horiz design. Multicoloured. W w **12**. P 13½.

312	5c. Type **104**	10	10
313	15c. Legislative Assembly Building	10	10
314	25c. Type **104**	15	15
315	40c. As 15c.	20	30
312/15 Set of 4		35	45
MS316 121×108 mm. Nos. 312/15		50	2·00
w. Wmk inverted		30·00	

105 Hawksbill Turtle and Queen or Pink Conch

(Des (from photograph by D. Groves) and photo Harrison)

1972 (20 Nov). Royal Silver Wedding. Multicoloured; background colour given. W w **12**. P 14×14½.

317	**105**	12c. deep slate-violet	15	10
318		30c. yellow-olive	15	20
		a. Blue omitted*	£700	
		w. Wmk inverted	2·00	

*The omission of the blue colour results in the Duke's suit appearing sepia instead of deep blue.

106 $1 Coin and Note

79

CAYMAN ISLANDS

(Des and photo D.L.R.)

1973 (15 Jan). First Issue of Currency. T **106** and similar horiz designs. Multicoloured. W w **12** (sideways*). P. 13.

319		3c. Type **106**..	20	10
320		6c. $5 Coin and note............................	20	70
321		15c. $10 Coin and note..........................	60	30
322		25c. $25 Coin and note..........................	80	45
319/22 Set of 4..			1·60	1·10
MS323 128×107 mm. Nos. 319/22.....................			3·50	3·25
		w. Wmk Crown to right of CA................	85·00	

*The normal sideways watermark shows Crown to left of CA, *as seen from the back of the stamp.*

107 "The Way of Sorrow" **108** "The Nativity" (Sforza Book of Hours)

(Des G. Drummond. Litho Questa)

1973 (11 Apr*). Easter. T **107** and similar multicoloured designs showing stained-glass windows. W w **12** (sideways on 10 and 12c.). P 14½.

324		10c. Type **107**..	15	10
325		12c. "Christ Resurrected"........................	20	10
326		20c. "The Last Supper" (*horiz*)............	25	15
327		30c. "Christ on the Cross" (*horiz*)........	30	25
324/7 Set of 4..			80	45
MS328 122×105 mm. Nos. 324/7. Imperf.................			1·00	1·60

*This is the local date of issue; the Crown Agents released the stamps on 15 March.

(Des J. Cooter. Litho Questa)

1973 (2 Oct). Christmas. T **108** and similar vert design. W w **12** (sideways). P 14.

329	**108**	3c. multicoloured................................	10	10
330	–	5c. multicoloured................................	10	10
331	**108**	9c. multicoloured................................	15	10
332	–	12c. multicoloured................................	15	10
333	**108**	15c. multicoloured................................	15	15
334	–	25c. multicoloured................................	20	25
329/34 Set of 6..			65	50

Design:—5, 12, 25c. "The Adoration of the Magi" (Breviary of Queen Isabella).

1973 (14 Nov). Royal Wedding. As Nos. 297/8 of Bermuda. Centre multicoloured. W w **12** (sideways). P 13½.

335		10c. sage-green....................................	10	10
336		30c. bright mauve................................	15	10

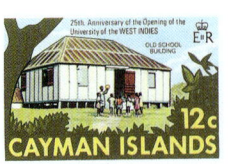

109 White-winged Dove **110** Old School Building

(Des M. Goaman. Litho Walsall)

1974 (2 Jan). Birds (1st series). T **109** and similar vert designs. Multicoloured. W w **12** (sideways). P. 14.

337		3c. Type **109**..	2·00	30
338		10c. Vitelline Warbler............................	2·75	30
339		12c. Antillean Grackle............................	2·75	30
340		20c. West Indian Red-bellied Woodpecker.....	4·25	80
341		30c. Stripe-headed Tanager...................	5·50	1·50
342		50c. Yucatan Vireo................................	7·00	5·50
337/42 Set of 6..			22·00	8·00

See also Nos. 383/8.

(Des PAD Studio. Litho Questa)

1974 (1 May). 25th Anniv of University of West Indies. T **110** and similar horiz designs. Multicoloured. W w **12** (sideways). P 14.

343		12c. Type **110**..	10	10
344		20c. New Comprehensive School............	15	20
345		30c. Creative Arts Centre, Mona............	15	60
343/5 Set of 3..			30	80

111 Hermit Crab and Staghorn Coral

(Des J. W. Litho Kynoch Press)

1974 (1 Aug). Multicoloured designs as T **111** (size 41½×27 mm). W w **12** (sideways on $1 and $2). P. 14.

346		1c. Type **111**..	3·50	1·25
347		3c. Treasure-chest and Lion's Paw........	3·50	75
348		4c. Treasure and Spotted Scorpionfish..	50	70
349		5c. Flintlock pistol and Brain Coral.......	3·00	75
350		6c. Blackbeard and Green Turtle..........	35	2·25
351		9c. Jewelled pomander and Porkfish....	4·00	12·00
352		10c. Spiny Lobster and treasure............	4·50	80
353		12c. Jewelled sword and dagger, and Seafan	35	2·00
354		15c. Cabrit's Murex (*Murex cabritii*) and treasure........	45	1·25
355		20c. Queen or Pink Conch (*Strombus gigas*) and treasure.................	10·00	1·75
356		25c. Hogfish and Treasure.....................	45	70
357		40c. Gold chalice and sea-whip.............	5·00	1·25
358		$1 Coat of arms (*vert*).......................	2·75	3·25
359		$2 Queen Elizabeth II (*vert*)...............	4·00	17·00
346/59 Set of 14..			38·00	42·00

See also Nos. 364/6, 412/19 and 445/52.

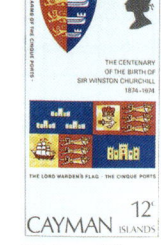

112 Sea Captain and Ship (Shipbuilding) **113** Arms of Cinque Ports and Lord Warden's Flag

(Des G. Vasarhelyi. Litho D.L.R.)

1974 (7 Oct). Local Industries. T **112** and similar horiz designs. Multicoloured. W w **12**. P 14×13½.

360		8c. Type **112**..	30	10
		w. Wmk inverted................................	40	20
361		12c. Thatcher and cottages...................	25	10
		w. Wmk inverted................................	40	30
362		20c. Farmer and plantation...................	25	20
		w. Wmk inverted................................	40	40
360/2 Set of 3..			70	35
MS363 92×132 mm. Nos. 360/2................................			1·50	3·25
		w. Wmk inverted................................	2·25	

1974–75. As Nos. 346/7 and design of 351, but W w **12** (sideways*).

364		1c. Type **111** (29.9.75)......................	4·00	1·50
365		3c. Treasure-chest and Lions-paw (12.11.74)........	4·50	2·00
		w. Wmk Crown to right of CA............	4·50	4·50
366		8c. Jewelled pomander and Porkfish (16.12.74).......	2·50	8·50
364/6 Set of 3..			10·00	11·00

*The normal sideways watermark shows Crown to left of CA, *as seen from the back of the stamp.*
Nos. 367/79 vacant.

(Des P. Powell. Litho D.L.R.)

1974 (30 Nov). Birth Centenary of Sir Winston Churchill. T **113** and similar vert design. Multicoloured. W w **12** (sideways). P 13½×14.

380		12c. Type **113**..	15	10

80

CAYMAN ISLANDS

381	50c. Churchill's coat of arms	45	70
	w. Wmk Crown to right of CA (pair)	38·00	
MS382	98×86 mm. Nos. 380/1	60	1·60

*The normal sideways watermark shows Crown to left of CA on Nos. 380/1 or Crown to right of CA on **MS**382, *as seen from the back of the stamp*.

(Des M. Goaman. Litho Questa)

1975 (1 Jan). Birds (2nd series). Multicoloured designs as T **109**. W w **12** (sideways). P 14.

383	3c. Common Flicker	70	50
384	10c. Black-billed Whistling Duck	1·25	50
385	12c. Yellow Warbler	1·40	65
386	20c. White-bellied Dove	2·00	2·00
387	30c. Magnificent Frigate Bird	3·25	4·25
388	50c. Cuban Amazon	3·75	12·00
	a. Error. Wmk Lesotho W **53** (inverted)	£1200	
383/8 *Set of 6*		11·00	18·00

114 "The Crucifixion"    115 Israel Hands

(Des PAD Studio. Litho D.L.R.)

1975 (24 Mar). Easter. French Pastoral Staffs. T **114** and similar vert design showing "The Crucifixion" (different). Multicoloured. W w **12** (sideways). P 13½×14.

389	**114**	15c. multicoloured	10	20
390	–	35c. multicoloured	20	45
MS391	128×98 mm. Nos. 389/90. W w **12** (upright)		65	2·75
	a. Error. Imperf			

See also Nos. 396/**MS**398.

(Des J.W. Litho Harrison)

1975 (25 July). Pirates. T **115** and similar horiz designs. Multicoloured. W w **12** (sideways*). P 14.

392	10c. Type **115**	35	15
393	12c. John Fenn	35	30
394	20c. Thomas Anstis	60	50
	w. Wmk Crown to right of CA	90·00	
395	30c. Edward Low	65	1·50
392/5 *Set of 4*		1·75	2·25

*The normal sideways watermark shows Crown to left of CA, *as seen from the back of the stamp*.

(Des PAD Studio. Litho Questa)

1975 (30 Oct). Christmas. Vert designs as T **114** showing "Virgin and Child with Angels" (both different). W w **14**. P 14.

396	12c. multicoloured	10	10
397	50c. multicoloured	30	30
MS398	113×85 mm. Nos. 396/7	1·00	3·00

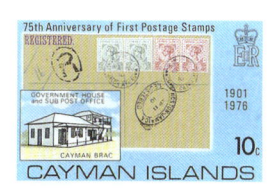

116 Registered Cover, Government House and Sub-Post Office

(Des J. Cooter. Litho Questa)

1976 (12 Mar). 75th Anniv of First Cayman Is. Postage Stamp. T **116** and similar horiz designs. Multicoloured. W w **14** (sideways). P 13½.

399	10c. Type **116**	15	10
400	20c. ½d. stamp and 1890–94 postmark	20	15
401	30c. 1d. stamp and 1908 surcharge	30	25
402	50c. ½d. and 1d. stamps	45	65
399/402 *Set of 4*		1·00	1·00
MS403	117×147 mm. Nos. 399/402	2·00	3·00

117 Seals of Georgia, Delaware and New Hampshire

(Des P. Powell. Litho J.W.)

1976 (29 May). Bicentenary of American Revolution. T **117** and similar horiz designs showing seals of the States given. Multicoloured. W w **14** (sideways). P 13½×14.

404	10c. Type **117**	40	15
405	15c. S. Carolina, New Jersey and Maryland	55	20
406	20c. Virginia, Rhode Is. and Massachusetts	65	25
407	25c. New York, Connecticut and N. Carolina	65	35
408	30c. Pennsylvania seal, Liberty Bell and U.S. Great Seal	70	40
404/8 *Set of 5*		2·75	1·25
MS409	166×124 mm. Nos. 404/8. P 14	4·00	8·50

118 "470" Dinghies 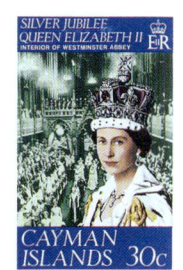   119 Queen Elizabeth II and Westminster Abbey

(Des C. Abbott. Litho D.L.R.)

1976 (16 Aug). Olympic Games, Montreal. T **118** and similar vert design. Multicoloured. W w **14**. P 14.

410	20c. Type **118**	40	10
411	50c. Racing dinghy	70	50

1976 (3 Sept)–**78**. As Nos. 347/9, 352, 355, 358/9 and 366, but W w **14** (upright on $1, inverted on $2, sideways* on others). Chalk-surfaced paper (4, 5c. and $1) or ordinary paper (others).

412	3c. Treasure-chest and Lion's Paw	1·00	4·25
	a. Chalk-surfaced paper (19.10.77)	4·50	4·50
413	4c. Treasure and Spotted Scorpionfish (19.10.77)	1·25	5·00
414	5c. Flintlock pistol and Brain Coral (19.10.77)	6·50	6·50
415	8c. Jewelled pomander and Porkfish	9·50	7·50
	a. Chalk-surfaced paper (19.10.77)	11·00	5·00
416	10c. Spiny Lobster and treasure	4·00	5·00
	a. Chalk-surfaced paper (27.1.78)	3·50	5·00
417	20c. Queen or Pink Conch (*Strombus gigas*) and treasure	3·50	3·00
	a. Chalk-surfaced paper (27.1.78)	3·50	5·00
418	$1 Coat of arms (19.10.77)	6·50	11·00
419	$2 Queen Elizabeth II	8·50	6·50
	a. Chalk-surfaced paper (19.10.77)	9·00	17·00
412/19 *Set of 8*		35·00	42·00

*The normal sideways watermark shows Crown to right of CA on Nos. 416a and 417a, and Crown to left of CA on all other printings of horizontal designs, *all as seen from the back of the stamp*.

(Des BG Studio. Litho Questa)

1977 (7 Feb). Silver Jubilee. T **119** and similar multicoloured designs. W w **14** (sideways on 50c.). P 13½.

427	8c. Prince of Wales' visit, 1973	10	20
	w. Wmk inverted	8·00	
428	30c. Type **119**	15	40
	w. Wmk inverted	30·00	
429	50c. Preparation for the Anointing (*horiz*)	30	75
427/9 *Set of 3*		50	1·25

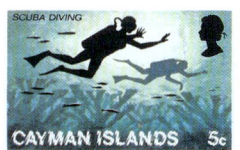

120 Scuba Diving

81

CAYMAN ISLANDS

(Des Jennifer Toombs. Litho J.W.)

1977 (25 July). Tourism. T **120** and similar horiz designs. Multicoloured. W w **14** (sideways). P 13½.

430	5c. Type **120**...	15	10
431	10c. Exploring a wreck.................................	20	10
432	20c. Royal Gramma ("Fairy Basslet") (fish)...	55	20
433	25c. Sergeant Major (fish)............................	65	35
430/3 *Set of 4*...		1·40	60
MS434 146×89 mm. Nos. 430/3. P 14½...........		2·00	4·50

121 *Composia fidelissima* (moth)

(Des J. Cooter. Litho Enschedé)

1977 (2 Dec). Butterflies and Moth. T **121** and similar horiz designs. Multicoloured. W w **14** (sideways). P 14×13.

435	5c. Type **121**..	75	20
436	8c. *Heliconius charithonia*...........................	85	20
437	10c. *Donnas gilippus*...................................	85	20
438	15c. *Agraulis vanillae*..................................	1·25	45
439	20c. *Junonia evarete*...................................	1·25	45
440	30c. *Anartia jatrophae*................................	1·50	70
435/40 *Set of 6*..		5·75	2·00

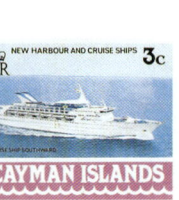

122 *Southward* (liner)  **123** "The Crucifixion" (Dürer)

(Des G. Hutchins. Litho Questa)

1978 (23 Jan). New Harbour and Cruise Ships. T **122** and similar multicoloured designs. W w **14** (sideways* on 3, 5c.). P 14×14½ (3, 5c.) or 14½×14 (others).

441	3c. Type **122**..	40	10
	w. Wmk Crown to right of CA	22·00	
442	5c. *Renaissance* (liner)	40	10
443	30c. New harbour (vert).............................	90	25
444	50c. *Daphne* (liner) (vert)...........................	1·25	65
441/4 *Set of 4*...		2·75	1·00

*The normal sideways watermark shows Crown to left of CA, *as seen from the back of the stamp*.

(Litho Walsall)

1978 (16 Mar)–**80**. Designs as Nos. 346/7, 349, 352, 355 and 357/9 but smaller, 40×26 or 26×40 mm. W w **14** (sideways on 1 to 40c.). Chalk-surfaced paper.

445	1c. Type **111**...	1·00	1·25
446	3c. Treasure-chest and Lion's Paw	80	50
447	5c. Flintlock pistol and Brain Coral (11.12.79)	1·50	2·00
448	10c. Spiny Lobster and treasure (25.5.78)....	1·25	60
449	20c. Queen or Pink Conch (*Strombus gigas*) and treasure (25.5.78)	2·25	1·00
450	40c. Gold chalice and sea-whip (1979*)	13·00	18·00
451	$1 Coat of arms (30.7.80).........................	20·00	5·50
452	$2 Queen Elizabeth II (3.4.80)..................	4·00	20·00
445/52 *Set of 8*...		40·00	45·00

*Supplies of No. 450 were sent to Cayman Islands on 7 May 1979. It is not known when these stamps were first placed on sale.
Nos. 453/8 vacant.

(Des Jennifer Toombs. Litho Cartor)

1978 (20 Mar). Easter and 450th Death Anniv of Dürer. T **123** and similar vert designs. W w **14** (inverted on 20c.). P 12.

459	10c. magenta and black..............................	30	10
	w. Wmk inverted	26·00	
460	15c. yellow and black..................................	40	15
	w. Wmk inverted	24·00	
461	20c. turquoise-green and black.................	50	20
	w. Wmk upright		
462	30c. lilac and black.....................................	60	35

	w. Wmk inverted	3·25	
459/62 *Set of 4*..		1·50	70
MS463 120×108 mm. Nos. 459/62		4·25	6·50
	w. Wmk inverted	6·50	

Designs:—15c. "Christ at Emmaus"; 20c. "The Entry into Jerusalem"; 30c. "Christ washing Peter's Feet".

124 "Explorers" Singing Game 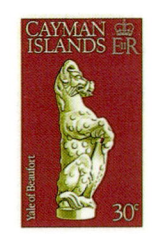   **125** Yale of Beaufort

(Des Walsall. Litho Questa)

1978 (25 Apr). 3rd International Council Meeting of Girls' Brigade. T **124** and similar vert designs. Multicoloured. W w **14**. P 14.

464	3c. Type **124**..	20	10
465	10c. Colour party	25	10
466	20c. Girls and Duke of Edinburgh Award interests	40	20
467	50c. Girls using domestic skills	70	80
464/7 *Set of 4*...		1·40	1·10

(Des C. Abbott. Litho Questa)

1978 (2 June). 25th Anniv of Coronation. T **125** and similar vert designs. P 15.

468	30c. apple-green, deep magenta and silver..	20	25
	a. Sheetlet. Nos. 468/70×2	1·10	1·40
469	30c. multicoloured	20	25
470	30c. apple-green, deep magenta and silver..	20	25
468/70 *Set of 3*		55	65

Designs:—No. 468, Type **125**; No. 469, Queen Elizabeth II; No. 470 Barn Owl.
Nos. 468/70 were printed together in small sheets of 6, containing two *se-tenant* strips of 3, with horizontal gutter margin between.

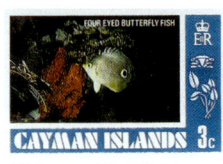

126 Four-eyed Butterflyfish

(Des G. Hutchins, Litho Walsall)

1978 (29 Aug). Fish (1st series). T **126** and similar horiz designs. Multicoloured. W w **14** (sideways). P 14.

471	3c. Type **126**..	25	10
472	5c. Grey Angelfish	30	10
473	10c. Squirrelfish	45	10
474	15c. Queen Parrotfish.................................	60	30
475	20c. Spanish Hogfish	70	35
476	30c. Queen Angelfish	80	50
471/6 *Set of 6*...		2·75	1·25

Examples of the 15c. value inscribed "SERGEANT MAJOR FISH" and 20c. inscribed "PARROT FISH" were prepared, but not issued for postal purposes. See also Nos. 483/8.

127 Lockheed L.18 Lodestar

(Des A. Theobald. Litho Format)

1979 (5 Feb). 25th Anniv of Owen Roberts Airfield. T **127** and similar horiz designs. Multicoloured. W w **14** (sideways). P 14½×14.

477	3c. Type **127**..	30	15
478	5c. Consolidated PBY-5A Catalina................	30	15
479	10c. Vickers Viking 1B.................................	35	15
480	15c. B.A.C. One Eleven 475 on tarmac........	65	25
481	20c. Piper PA-31 Cheyenne II, Bell 47G Trooper helicopter and Hawker Siddeley H.S.125...	75	35

82

482	30c. B.A.C. One Eleven 475 over airfield	1·00	50
477/82 Set of 6		3·00	1·40

128 Trumpetfish

(Des R. Granger Barrett. Litho Questa)

1979 (20 Apr). Fish (2nd series). T **128** and similar horiz designs. Multicoloured. W w **14** (sideways*). P 14.

483	1c. Type **128**	10	10
	w. Wmk Crown to right of CA	35·00	9·00
484	3c. Nassau Grouper	25	10
485	5c. French Angelfish	25	10
	w. Wmk Crown to right of CA	3·50	
486	10c. Schoolmaster Snapper	35	10
487	20c. Banded Butterflyfish	55	25
488	50c. Black-barred Soldierfish	1·00	70
483/8 Set of 6		2·25	1·25

*The normal sideways watermark shows Crown to left of CA, as seen from the back of the stamp.

129 1900 1d. Stamp

(Des J.W. Litho Walsall)

1979 (15 Aug). Death Centenary of Sir Rowland Hill. T **129** and similar horiz designs showing stamps and Sir Rowland Hill. W w **14** (sideways). P 13½.

489	5c. black, rose-carmine and grey-blue	10	10
490	10c. multicoloured	15	10
491	20c. multicoloured	20	25
489/91 Set of 3		30	30
MS492	138×90 mm. 50c. multicoloured	55	65

Designs:—10c. Great Britain 1902 3d.; 20c. 1955 £1 definitive; 50c. 1908 2½d.

130 Holy Family and Angels

(Des G. Vasarhelyi. Litho Secura, Singapore)

1979 (20 Nov). Christmas. T **130** and similar horiz designs. Multicoloured. W w **14** (sideways*). P 13½×13.

493	10c. Type **130**	15	10
	w. Wmk Crown to right of CA	45	
494	20c. Angels appearing before shepherds	25	10
	w. Wmk Crown to right of CA	55	
495	30c. Nativity scene	30	20
	w. Wmk Crown to right of CA	75	
496	40c. Wise men following star	40	30
	w. Wmk Crown to right of CA	1·00	
493/6 Set of 4		1·00	60

*The normal sideways watermark shows Crown to left of CA, as seen from the back of the stamp.

131 Local Rotary Project

(Des Walsall. Litho Secura, Singapore)

1980 (14 Feb). 75th Anniv of Rotary International. T **131** and similar designs in black, bistre-yellow and deep ultramarine. W w **14** (sideways on 20c.). P 13½×13 (20c.) or 13×13½ (others).

497	20c. Type **131**	20	15
498	30c. Paul P. Harris (founder) (vert)	25	20
499	50c. Rotary anniversary emblem (vert)	35	30
	a. Black (Royal cypher, and face value) omitted	£325	
497/9 Set of 3		70	60

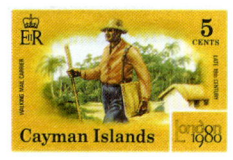

132 Walking Mail Carrier (late 19th-century)

(Des J.W. Litho Walsall)

1980 (6 May). "London 1980" International Stamp Exhibition. T **132** and similar horiz designs. Multicoloured. W w **14** (sideways). P 14.

500	5c. Type **132**	10	10
501	10c. Delivering mail by cat boat (late 19th-century)	15	10
502	15c. Mounted mail carrier (early 20th-century)	20	10
503	30c. Horse-drawn waggonette (early 20th-century)	25	15
504	40c. Postman on bicycle (mid 20th-century)	35	15
505	$1 Motor transport (late 20th-century)	45	55
500/5 Set of 6		1·25	1·00

133 Queen Elizabeth the Queen Mother at the Derby, 1976

134 American Thorny Oyster (*Spondylus americanus*)

(Des and litho Harrison)

1980 (4 Aug). 80th Birthday of Queen Elizabeth the Queen Mother. W w **14** (sideways). P 14.

506	**133**	20c. multicoloured	20	25

(Des J.W. Litho Walsall)

1980 (12 Aug). Shells (1st series). T **134** and similar horiz designs. Multicoloured. W w **14** (sideways). P 14½×14.

507	5c. Type **134**	25	10
508	10c. West Indian Murex (*Murex brevifrons*)	30	10
509	30c. Angular Triton (*Cymatium femorale*)	45	40
510	50c. Caribbean Vase (*Vasum muricatum*)	70	80
507/10 Set of 4		1·50	1·25

See also Nos. 565/8 and 582/5.

135 Lantana

136 Juvenile Tarpon and Fire Sponge

(Des G. Hutchins. Litho Rosenbaum Bros, Vienna)

1980 (21 Oct). Flowers (1st series). T **135** and similar horiz designs. Multicoloured. W w **14** (sideways). P 13½.

511	5c. Type **135**	20	10
512	15c. Bauhinia	25	10
513	30c. Hibiscus Rosa	35	10
514	$1 Milk and Wine Lily	60	90
511/14 Set of 4		1·25	1·10

See also Nos. 541/4.

CAYMAN ISLANDS

(Des G. Drummond. Litho J.W.)

1980 (9 Dec)–**82**. Flora and Fauna of the Mangrove Swamp. Vert designs as T **136**. Multicoloured. W w **14**. P 13½×13.

A. Without imprint date

515A	3c. Type **136**	1·00	2·50
516A	5c. Flat Tree or Mangrove-root Oyster (*Isognomon alatus*)	1·00	1·50
517A	10c. Mangrove Crab	50	1·50
518A	15c. Lizard and *Phyciodes phaon* (butterfly)	1·00	1·75
519A	20c. Louisiana Heron	1·50	2·25
520A	30c. Red Mangrove flower	70	1·00
521A	40c. Red Mangrove seeds	75	1·50
522A	50c. Waterhouse's Leaf-nosed Bat	1·25	1·50
523A	$1 Black-crowned Night Heron	4·50	5·00
524A	$2 Cayman Islands coat of arms	1·25	3·75
525A	$4 Queen Elizabeth II	2·00	4·25
515A/25A	Set of 11	14·00	24·00

B. With imprint date at foot of designs (14.6.82)

515B	3c. Type **136**	5·50	4·00
516B	5c. Flat Tree or Mangrove-root Oyster (*Isognomon alatus*)	1·25	80
517B	10c. Mangrove Crab	1·25	80
518B	15c. Lizard and *Phyciodes phaon* (butterfly)	4·50	1·75
519B	20c. Louisiana Heron	2·50	2·00
520B	30c. Red Mangrove flower	1·50	1·50
521B	40c. Red Mangrove seeds	1·50	1·50
522B	50c. Waterhouse's Leaf-nosed Bat	2·00	2·00
523B	$1 Black-crowned Night Heron	6·00	4·50
524B	$2 Cayman Islands coat of arms	3·75	4·00
525B	$4 Queen Elizabeth II	9·00	11·00
515B/25B	Set of 11	35·00	30·00

Imprint dates: "1982", Nos. 515B/25B; "1984", No. 516B; "1985", Nos. 516B/24B.

For stamps in these designs, but watermark w **16**, see Nos. 626 and 631/2.

137 Eucharist   **138** Wood Slave

(Des Jennifer Toombs. Litho Questa)

1981 (17 Mar). Easter. T **137** and similar vert designs. Multicoloured. W w **14**. P 14.

526	3c. Type **137**	10	10
527	10c. Crown of thorns	10	10
528	20c. Crucifix	15	10
529	$1 Lord Jesus Christ	50	60
526/9	Set of 4	65	70

(Des R. Granger Barrett. Litho Rosenbaum Bros, Vienna)

1981 (16 June). Reptiles and Amphibians. T **138** and similar horiz designs. Multicoloured. W w **14** (sideways*). P 13½.

530	20c. Type **138**	25	20
	w. Wmk Crown to left of CA	70	80
531	30c. Cayman Iguana	30	35
	w. Wmk Crown to left of CA	90	1·00
532	40c. Lion Lizard	40	45
	w. Wmk Crown to left of CA	1·00	1·25
533	50c. Terrapin ("Hickatee")	45	55
	w. Wmk Crown to right of CA	1·25	1·50
530/3	Set of 4	1·25	1·40

*The normal sideways watermark shows Crown to right of CA on Nos. 530/2 and to left on No. 533, *as seen from the back of the stamp.*

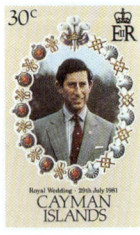

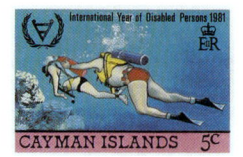

139 Prince Charles   **140** Disabled Scuba Divers

(Des J.W. Litho Walsall)

1981 (22 July). Royal Wedding. T **139** and similar vert designs. Multicoloured. W w **14**. P 14.

534	20c. Wedding bouquet from Cayman Islands	15	10
535	30c. Type **139**	20	10
536	$1 Prince Charles and Lady Diana Spencer	50	75
534/6	Set of 3	75	80

(Des J.W. Litho Walsall)

1981 (29 Sept). International Year for Disabled Persons. T **140** and similar horiz designs. Multicoloured. W w **14** (sideways). P 14.

537	5c. Type **140**	10	10
538	15c. Old School for the Handicapped	25	20
539	20c. New School for the Handicapped	30	25
540	$1 Disabled people in wheelchairs, by the sea	1·25	85
537/40	Set of 4	1·60	1·25

(Des G. Hutchins. Litho Questa)

1981 (20 Oct). Flowers (2nd series). Horiz designs as T **135**. Multicoloured. W w **14** (sideways). P 13½.

541	3c. Bougainvillea	10	10
542	10c. Morning Glory	15	10
543	20c. Wild Amaryllis	25	25
544	$1 Cordia	1·00	1·75
541/4	Set of 4	1·25	2·00

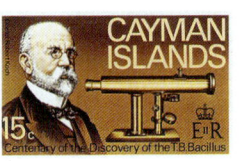

141 Dr. Robert Koch and Microscope   **142** Bride and Groom walking down Aisle

(Des and litho Walsall)

1982 (24 Mar). Centenary of Robert Koch's Discovery of Tubercle Bacillus. T **141** and similar multicoloured designs. W w **14** (sideways on 15c, inverted on 30c). P 14½.

545	15c. Type **141**	25	25
546	30c. Koch looking through microscope (vert)	45	45
547	40c. Microscope (vert)	70	70
548	50c. Dr. Robert Koch (vert)	80	80
545/8	Set of 4	2·00	2·00

(Des Jennifer Toombs. Litho J.W.)

1982 (1 July). 21st Birthday of Princess of Wales. T **142** and similar vert designs. Multicoloured. W w **14**. P 13.

549	20c. Cayman Islands coat of arms	20	25
550	30c. Lady Diana Spencer in London, June 1981	50	45
	w. Wmk inverted	2·00	
551	40c. Type **142**	50	65
552	50c. Formal portrait	1·90	1·00
	w. Wmk inverted	3·00	
549/52	Set of 4	2·75	2·10

143 Pitching Tent   **144** "Madonna and Child with the Infant Baptist"

(Des L. Walker. Litho Questa)

1982 (24 Aug). 75th Anniv of Boy Scout Movement. T **143** and similar horiz designs. Multicoloured. W w **14** (sideways). P 14.

553	3c. Type **143**	15	10
554	20c. Scouts camping	40	40
555	30c. Cub Scouts and Leaders	60	55
556	50c. Boating skills	80	85
553/6	Set of 4	1·75	1·75

84

CAYMAN ISLANDS

(Des PAD Studio. Litho Questa)

1982 (26 Oct). Christmas. Raphael Paintings. T **144** and similar vert designs. Multicoloured. W w **14**. P 14½×14.
557	3c. Type **144**..		10	10
558	10c. "Madonna of the Tower".....................		20	20
	w. Wmk inverted			
559	20c. "Ansidei Madonna".............................		35	35
560	30c. "Madonna and Child"..........................		50	50
	w. Wmk inverted			
557/60 Set of 4..			1·00	1·00

145 Mace

(Des and litho Walsall)

1982 (9 Nov). 150th Anniv of Representative Government. T **145** and similar horiz designs. Multicoloured. W w **14** (sideways). P 14½×14.
561	3c. Type **145**..		10	20
562	10c. Old Courthouse		20	20
563	20c. Commonwealth Parliamentary Association coat of arms		35	45
564	30c. Legislative Assembly building.............		50	90
561/4 Set of 4			1·00	1·60

(Des J.W. Litho Format)

1983 (11 Jan). Shells (2nd series). Horiz designs as T **134**. Multicoloured. W w **14** (sideways). P 13½×13.
565	5c. Colourful Atlantic Moon (*Natica canrena*)		15	30
566	10c. King Helmet (*Cassis tuberosa*).............		25	30
567	20c. Rooster-tail Conch (*Strombus gallus*) ...		30	40
568	$1 Reticulated Cowrie-helmet (*Cypraecassis testiculus*)		50	4·00
565/8 Set of 4			1·10	4·50

146 Legislative Building, Cayman Brac
147 Satellite View of Earth 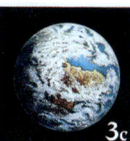

(Des C. Abbott. Litho Questa)

1983 (15 Feb). Royal Visit. T **146** and similar multicoloured designs. W w **14** (sideways on 20c., 30c.). P 14.
569	20c. Type **146**...		45	35
570	30c. Legislative Building, Grand Cayman ...		60	50
571	50c. Duke of Edinburgh (*vert*)....................		1·25	90
572	$1 Queen Elizabeth II (*vert*)		2·00	2·00
569/72 Set of 4			4·00	3·25
MS573 113×94 mm. Nos. 569/72 (wmk sideways)			6·50	4·25

(Des J.W. Litho Questa)

1983 (14 Mar). Commonwealth Day. T **147** and similar horiz designs. Multicoloured. W w **14** (sideways). P 14.
574	3c. Type **147**..		20	15
575	15c. Cayman Islands and Commonwealth flags		75	40
576	20c. Fishing		50	40
577	40c. Portrait of Queen Elizabeth II		75	80
574/7 Set of 4			2·00	1·60

148 MRCU Cessna 188 Ag Wagon Aircraft
149 *Song of Norway* (cruise liner) 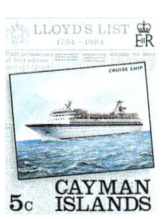

(Des Harrison. Litho Questa)

1983 (10 Oct). Bicentenary of Manned Flight. T **148** and similar horiz designs. Multicoloured. W w **14** (sideways). P 14.
578	3c. Type **148**..		60	50
579	10c. Consolidated PBY-5A Catalina............		65	50
580	20c. Boeing 727-200...................................		1·25	1·50
581	40c. Hawker Siddeley H.S. 748		1·75	3·75
578/81 Set of 4			3·75	5·50

(Des J.W. Litho Questa)

1984 (18 Jan). Shells (3rd series). Horiz designs as T **134**. Multicoloured. W w **14** (sideways). P 14×14½.
582	3c. Florida Moon (*Natica floridana*)		70	40
583	10c. Austin's Cone (*Conus atractus austini*)		80	40
584	30c. Leaning Dwarf Triton (*Colubraria obscura*)		2·25	2·75
585	50c. Filose or Threaded Turban (*Turbo cailletii*)..		2·50	4·25
582/5 Set of 4			5·50	7·00

(Des G. Vasarhelyi and L. Curtis. Litho Questa)

1984 (18 June). 250th Anniv of "Lloyd's List" (newspaper). T **149** and similar vert designs. Multicoloured. W w **14**. P 14½×14.
586	5c. Type **149**..		55	20
587	10c. View of old harbour		55	25
588	25c. Wreck of *Ridgefield* (freighter)............		1·10	1·00
589	50c. *Goldfield* (schooner)		2·00	2·75
586/9 Set of 4			3·75	3·75
MS590 105×75 mm. $1 *Goldfield* (schooner) (*different*).			2·10	2·25

U.P.U. CONGRESS HAMBURG 1984
(**150**) 
151 Snowy Egret

1984 (18 June). Universal Postal Union Congress, Hamburg. No. 589 optd with T **150**.
591	50c. Schooner *Goldfield*.............................		1·50	2·00

(Des Josephine Martin. Litho Questa)

1984 (15 Aug). Birds of the Cayman Islands (1st series). T **151** and similar horiz designs. Multicoloured. W w **14** (sideways). P 14×14½.
592	5c. Type **151**..		1·00	75
593	10c. Bananaquit..		1·00	75
594	35c. Belted Kingfisher		3·25	2·50
595	$1 Brown Booby		6·00	11·00
592/5 Set of 4			10·00	13·50

See also Nos. 627/30.

152 Couple on Beach at Sunset
153 *Schomburgkia thomsoniana* (var. *minor*) 

(Des G. Wilby. Litho Questa)

1984 (17 Oct). Christmas. Local Festivities. T **152** and similar vert designs. Multicoloured. W w **14** (sideways). P 14.
596	5c. Type **152**..		85	1·50
	a. Horiz strip of 4. Nos. 596/9................		3·00	5·50
597	5c. Family and schooner............................		85	1·50
598	5c. Carol singers.......................................		85	1·50
599	5c. East End bonfire..................................		85	1·50
600	25c. Yachts...		1·25	1·50
	a. Horiz strip of 4. Nos. 600/3................		4·50	5·50
601	25c. Father Christmas in power-boat...........		1·25	1·50
602	25c. Children on beach		1·25	1·50
603	25c. Beach party		1·25	1·50
596/603 Set of 8			7·50	11·00
MS604 59×79 mm. $1 As No. 599, but larger, 27×41 mm...			3·50	4·50

Nos. 596/9 and 600/3 were each printed together, *se-tenant*, in horizontal strips of 4 throughout the sheets, the four designs of each value forming a composite picture of a beach scene at night (5c.) or in the daytime (25c.).

85

CAYMAN ISLANDS

(Des Liza Horstman. Litho J.W.)

1985 (13 Mar). Orchids. T **153** and similar vert designs. Multicoloured. W w **14**. P 14×13½.
605	5c. Type **153**	1·00	30
606	10c. *Schomburgkia thomsoniana*	1·00	30
607	25c. *Encyclia plicata*	2·50	1·00
608	50c. *Dendrophylax fawcettii*	3·75	3·00
605/8 Set of 4		7·50	4·25

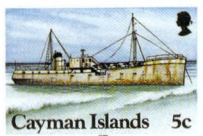

154 Freighter Aground

155 Athletics

(Des Walsall. Litho J.W.)

1985 (22 May). Shipwrecks. T **154** and similar horiz designs. Multicoloured. W w **14** (sideways). P 14.
609	5c. Type **154**	90	50
610	25c. Submerged sailing ship	2·75	1·25
611	35c. Wrecked trawler	3·00	2·50
612	40c. Submerged wreck on its side	3·25	3·50
609/12 Set of 4		9·00	7·00

(Des Harrison. Litho Walsall)

1985 (14 Aug). International Youth Year. T **155** and similar multicoloured designs. W w **14** (sideways on 5c., 15c.). P 14×14½ (5, 15c.) or 14½×14 (others).
613	5c. Type **155**	30	30
614	15c. Students in library	45	40
615	25c. Football (*vert*)	90	55
616	50c. Netball (*vert*)	2·00	3·25
613/6 Set of 4		3·25	4·00

156 Morse Key (1935)

157 Magnificent Frigate Bird

(Des G. Vasarhelyi. Litho Walsall)

1985 (25 Oct). 50th Anniv of Telecommunications System. T **156** and similar vert designs. Multicoloured. W w **16**. P 14.
617	5c. Type **156**	45	70
618	10c. Hand cranked telephone	50	70
	w. Wmk inverted	£150	
619	25c. Tropospheric scatter dish (1966)	1·50	80
	w. Wmk inverted	25·00	
620	50c. Earth station dish aerial (1979)	2·50	5·00
617/20 Set of 4		4·50	6·50

(Des A. Theobald. Litho Format)

1986 (21 Apr). 60th Birthday of Queen Elizabeth II. Vert designs as T **163a** of Bahamas. Multicoloured. W w **16**. P 14×14½.
621	5c. Princess Elizabeth at wedding of Lady May Cambridge, 1931	10	30
622	10c. In Norway, 1955	15	30
623	25c. Queen inspecting Royal Cayman Islands Police, 1983	1·50	75
624	50c. During Gulf tour, 1979	75	2·00
625	$1 At Crown Agents Head Office, London, 1983	1·10	2·75
621/5 Set of 5		3·25	5·50

(Litho J. W.)

1986 (Apr). As No. 516B, but W w **16**. "1986" imprint date. P 13½×13.
626	5c. Mangrove Root Oyster	5·00	6·00

(Des Harrison. Litho Questa)

1986 (21 May). Birds of the Cayman Islands (2nd series). T **157** and similar multicoloured designs. W w **16** (sideways on 10, 40c.). P 14.
627	10c. Type **157**	1·75	1·00
628	25c. Black-billed Whistling Duck (*vert*)	2·25	1·40
629	35c. La Sagra's Flycatcher (*vert*)	2·50	2·50
630	40c. Yellow-faced Grassquit	3·00	5·00
627/30 Set of 4		8·50	9·00

(Litho Questa)

1986 (June). As Nos. 516B/17B, but different printer and W w **16**. "1986" imprint date. P 14.
631	5c. Mangrove Root Oyster	5·00	4·00
632	10c. Mangrove Crab	6·00	4·00

(Des D. Miller. Litho Walsall)

1986 (23 July). Royal Wedding. Square designs as T **164a** of Bahamas. Multicoloured. W w **16**. P 14½×14.
633	5c. Prince Andrew and Miss Sarah Ferguson	40	25
634	50c. Prince Andrew aboard H.M.S. *Brazen*	1·60	2·25

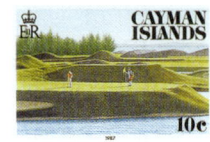

158 Red Coral Shrimp

159 Golf

(Des D. Miller. Litho Walsall)

1986 (15 Sept). Marine Life. T **158** and similar vert designs. Multicoloured. W w **14**. P 13½×13.
635	5c. Type **158**	40	1·00
636	10c. Yellow Crinoid	40	50
637	15c. *Calcinus tibicen* (hermit crab)	35	60
638	20c. Tube dwelling Anemone	35	1·75
639	25c. Christmas Tree Worm	45	2·50
640	35c. Porcupinefish	70	2·75
641	50c. Orangeball Anemone	80	4·50
642	60c. *Astrophyton muricatum* (basket star fish).	3·50	10·00
643	75c. Flamingo Tongue (*Cyphoma gibbosus*)	10·00	12·00
644	$1 *Condylactis gigantea* (sea anemone)	1·10	2·50
645	$2 Diamond Blenny	1·25	5·00
646	$4 Rough File Shell (*Lima scabra*)	2·00	7·00
635/46 Set of 12		19·00	45·00

No. 644 is incorrectly inscribed "Conolylactis gigantea".
Imprint dates: "1986" Nos. 635/46; "1987", Nos. 635/8, 644/6; "1990" Nos. 635/41, 644/5.
For the 10c. value with watermark w **16** see No. 696.

(Des L. Curtis. Litho Walsall)

1987 (26 Jan). Tourism. T **159** and similar horiz designs. Multicoloured. W w **16** (sideways). P 13×13½.
647	10c. Type **159**	2·50	1·25
648	15c. Sailing	2·50	1·25
649	25c. Snorkelling	2·50	1·25
650	35c. Paragliding	2·75	2·00
651	$1 Game fishing	5·50	12·00
647/51 Set of 5		14·00	16·00

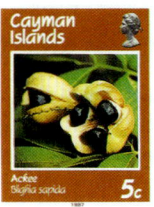

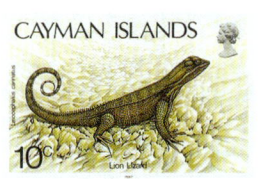

160 Ackee

161 Lion Lizard

(Des Jennifer Toombs. Litho Questa)

1987 (20 May). Cayman Islands Fruits. T **160** and similar vert designs. Multicoloured. W w **16**. P 14½×14.
652	5c. Type **160**	75	1·25
	w. Wmk inverted	14·00	
653	25c. Breadfruit	2·00	55
	w. Wmk inverted	9·00	
654	35c. Pawpaw	2·00	70
655	$1 Soursop	4·50	9·00
652/5 Set of 4		8·25	10·50

(Des I. Loe. Litho Questa)

1987 (26 Aug). Lizards. T **161** and similar horiz designs. Multicoloured. W w **16** (sideways). P 13½×14.
656	10c. Type **161**	2·25	65

657	50c. Iguana		4·50	3·50
658	$1 Anole		5·50	7·00
656/8 Set of 3			11·00	10·00

162 Poinsettia

163 *Hemiargus ammon* and *Strymon martialis*

(Des Annette Robinson. Litho Walsall)

1987 (18 Nov). Flowers. T **162** and similar square designs. Multicoloured. W w **16**. P 14½×14.

659	5c. Type **162**		65	45
660	25c. Periwinkle		1·75	75
661	35c. Yellow Allamanda		1·90	1·10
662	75c. Blood Lily		3·50	4·50
659/62 Set of 4			7·00	6·00

(Des Jane Thatcher. Litho Questa)

1988 (29 Mar). Butterflies. T **163** and similar horiz designs. Multicoloured. W w **16** (sideways). P 14.

663	5c. Type **163**		1·25	65
664	25c. *Phocides pigmalion*		2·50	85
665	50c. *Anaea troglodyta*		4·00	3·75
666	$1 *Papilio andraemon*		5·00	5·00
663/6 Set of 4			11·50	9·25

164 Green Heron

165 Cycling

(Des Jane Thatcher. Litho Walsall)

1988 (27 July). Herons. T **164** and similar vert designs. Multicoloured. W w **16**. P 14.

667	5c. Type **164**		1·25	65
668	25c. Louisiana Heron		2·25	85
669	50c. Yellow-crowned Night Heron		3·00	3·00
670	$1 Little Blue Heron		3·50	4·25
667/70 Set of 4			9·00	8·00

(Des L. Curtis. Litho Walsall)

1988 (21 Sept). Olympic Games, Seoul. T **165** and similar horiz designs. Multicoloured. W w **16** (sideways). P 14×14½.

671	10c. Type **165**		3·00	1·00
672	50c. Cayman Airways Boeing 727 airliner and national team		4·00	3·25
673	$1 "470" dinghy		4·00	4·25
671/3 Set of 3			10·00	7·75
MS674 53×60 mm. $1 Tennis. W w **14** (sideways)			4·00	3·00

166 Princess Alexandra

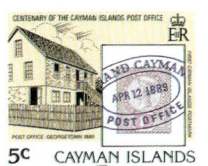

167 Georgetown Post Office and Cayman Postmark on Jamaica 1d., 1889

(Des N. Harvey. Litho B.D.T.)

1988 (1 Nov). Visit of Princess Alexandra. T **166** and similar vert design. Multicoloured. W w **14**. P 15×14.

675	5c. Type **166**		1·75	1·00
676	$1 Princess Alexandra in evening dress		7·50	6·50

(Des L. Curtis. Litho Questa)

1989 (12 Apr). Centenary of Cayman Islands Postal Service. T **167** and similar horiz designs. Multicoloured. W w **16** (sideways). P 14×14½.

677	5c. multicoloured		85	1·00
678	25c. yellowish green, black and new blue		2·00	1·00
679	35c. multicoloured		2·00	1·25
680	$1 multicoloured		8·00	10·50
677/80 Set of 4			11·50	12·50

Designs:—25c. *Orinoco* (mail steamer) and 1900 ½d. stamp; 35c. G.P.O., Grand Cayman and "London 1980" $1 stamp; $1 Cayman Airways B.A.C. One Eleven 200/400 and 1966 1s. Jet Service stamp.

168 Captain Bligh ashore in West Indies

169 Panton House

(Des Jane Hartley. Litho B.D.T.)

1989 (24 May). Captain Bligh's Second Breadfruit Voyage, 1791–93. T **168** and similar vert designs. Multicoloured. W w **16**. P 14.

681	50c. Type **168**		5·00	5·00
	a. Horiz strip of 5. Nos. 681/5		22·00	22·00
682	50c. H.M.S. *Providence* (sloop) at anchor		5·00	5·00
683	50c. Breadfruit in tubs and H.M.S. *Assistant* (transport)		5·00	5·00
684	50c. Sailors moving tubs of breadfruit		5·00	5·00
685	50c. Midshipman and stores		5·00	5·00
681/5 Set of 5			22·00	22·00

Nos. 681/5 were printed together, *se-tenant* as a composite design, in horizontal strips of five throughout the sheet.

(Des S. Conlin. Litho Walsall)

1989 (18 Oct). Architecture. T **169** and similar square designs showing George Town buildings. Multicoloured. W w **14**. P 14½×14.

686	5c. Type **169**		75	1·00
687	10c. Town Hall and Clock Tower		75	1·00
688	25c. Old Court House		1·40	60
689	35c. Elmslie Memorial Church		1·60	75
690	$1 Post Office		3·50	6·50
686/90 Set of 5			7·25	9·00

170 Map of Grand Cayman, 1773, and Surveying Instruments

171 French Angelfish

(Des N. Shewring. Litho Walsall)

1989 (15 Nov). Island Maps and Survey Ships. T **170** and similar horiz designs. Multicoloured. W w **16** (sideways). P 14×14½.

691	5c. Type **170**		2·00	1·50
692	25c. Map of Cayman Islands, 1956, and surveying instruments		4·25	1·25
693	50c. H.M.S. *Mutine*, 1914		6·00	5·50
694	$1 H.M.S. *Vidal*, 1956		9·00	11·00
691/4 Set of 4			19·00	17·00

1990 (Mar). As No. 636, but W w **16**. "1990" imprint date. P 13½×13.

696	10c. Yellow Crinoid		1·75	2·75

CAYMAN ISLANDS

(Des D. Miller. Litho Questa)

1990 (25 Apr). Angelfishes. T **171** and similar horiz designs. Multicoloured. W w **16** (sideways). P 14.

707	10c. Type **171**...	1·25	70
708	25c. Grey Angelfish..................................	2·25	90
709	50c. Queen Angelfish................................	3·50	4·25
710	$1 Rock Beauty..	5·50	8·00
707/10 Set of 4...		11·00	12·50

(Des D. Miller. Litho Questa)

1990 (4 Aug). 90th Birthday of Queen Elizabeth the Queen Mother. Vert designs as T **184a** (50c.) or **184b** of Bahamas. W w **16**. P 14×15 (50c.) or 14½ ($1).

711	50c. multicoloured....................................	1·25	2·25
712	$1 black and blue.....................................	2·75	4·00

Designs:—50c. Silver Wedding photograph, 1948; $1 King George VI and Queen Elizabeth with Winston Churchill, 1940.

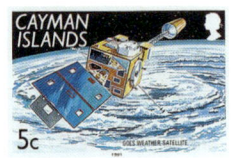

172 *Danaus eresimus*

173 Goes Weather Satellite

(Des G. Drummond. Litho Questa)

1990 (24 Oct). "EXPO '90" International Garden and Greenery Exhibition, Osaka. Butterflies. T **172** and similar horiz designs. Multicoloured. W w **16** (sideways). P 14.

713	5c. Type **172**..	65	60
714	25c. *Brephidium exilis*..............................	1·50	1·10
715	35c. *Phyciodes phaon*...............................	1·75	1·25
716	$1 *Agraulis vanillae*.................................	4·00	6·50
713/16 Set of 4...		7·00	8·50

(Des A. Theobald. Litho Questa)

1991 (8 Aug). International Decade for Natural Disaster Reduction. T **173** and similar horiz designs. Multicoloured. W w **16** (sideways). P 14.

717	5c. Type **173**..	80	70
718	30c. Meteorologist tracking hurricane......	2·00	1·10
719	40c. Damaged buildings............................	2·25	1·25
720	$1 U.S. Dept of Commerce weather reconnaisance Lockheed WP-3D Orion..	5·00	8·50
717/20 Set of 4...		9·00	10·50

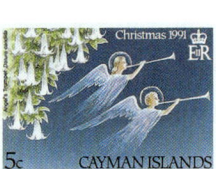

174 Angels and *Datura candida*

175 Coconut Palm

(Des Jennifer Toombs. Litho Questa)

1991 (6 Nov). Christmas. T **174** and similar horiz designs. Multicoloured. W w **16** (sideways). P 14.

721	5c. Type **174**..	80	80
722	30c. Mary and Joseph going to Bethlehem and *Allamanda cathartica*....................	2·00	60
723	40c. Adoration of the Kings and *Euphorbia pulcherrima*.........................	2·25	1·10
724	60c. Holy Family and *Guaiacum officinale*......	3·25	6·50
721/4 Set of 4...		7·50	8·00

(Des D. Miller. Litho Enschedé)

1991 (11 Dec). Island Scenes. T **175** and similar multicoloured designs. W w **14** (sideways on horiz designs). P 12½×13 (vert) or 13×12½ (horiz).

725	5c. Type **175**..	50	50
726	15c. Beach scene (*horiz*)...........................	1·75	50
727	20c. Poincianas in bloom (*horiz*)..............	70	35
728	30c. Blowholes (*horiz*)..............................	1·75	1·00
	a. Silver (inscr and face value) omitted......	£850	
729	40c. Police band (*horiz*)...........................	2·50	1·40
730	50c. *Song of Norway* (liner) at George Town..	2·00	1·40
731	60c. The Bluff, Cayman Brac (*horiz*).........	1·75	2·25
732	80c. Coat of arms.....................................	1·50	2·50
733	90c. View of Hell (*horiz*)..........................	1·60	3·00
734	$1 Game fishing (*horiz*)..........................	3·25	2·50
735	$2 *Nieuw Amsterdam* (1983) and *Holiday* (liners) in harbour........................	8·00	7·50
736	$8 Queen Elizabeth II...............................	16·00	22·00
725/36 Set of 12..		35·00	40·00

Imprint dates: "1991", Nos. 725/36; "1994", No. 725.

(Des D. Miller. Litho Questa ($1), Leigh-Mardon Ltd, Melbourne (others))

1992 (6 Feb). 40th Anniv of Queen Elizabeth II's Accession. Horiz designs as T **187a** of Bahamas. W w **16** (sideways) (30, 40c.) or w **14** (sideways) (others). P 14.

737	5c. Caymans' house.................................	30	30
738	20c. Sunset over islands...........................	1·00	50
739	30c. Beach...	1·10	65
740	40c. Three portraits of Queen Elizabeth....	1·10	1·00
741	$1 Queen Elizabeth II...............................	2·00	3·50
737/41 Set of 5..		5·00	5·50

176 Single Cyclist

177 Woman and Donkey with Panniers

(Des G. Vasarhelyi. Litho Questa)

1992 (5 Aug). Olympic Games, Barcelona. Cycling. T **176** and similar horiz designs. Multicoloured. W w **14** (sideways). P 14.

742	15c. Type **176**..	1·75	65
743	40c. Two cyclists......................................	2·50	1·50
744	60c. Cyclist's legs.....................................	3·00	1·50
745	$1 Two pursuit cyclists.............................	3·75	5·00
742/5 Set of 4...		10·00	9·50

(Des O. Ball. Litho Enschedé)

1992 (21 Oct). Island Heritage. T **177** and similar vert designs. Multicoloured. W w **14**. P 14×13½.

746	5c. Type **177**..	50	60
747	30c. Fisherman weaving net.....................	1·25	85
748	40c. Maypole dancing..............................	1·50	1·10
749	60c. Basket making..................................	2·50	3·50
750	$1 Cooking on caboose............................	3·00	5·00
746/50 Set of 5...		8·00	10·00

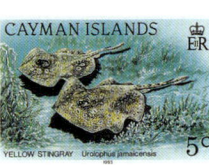

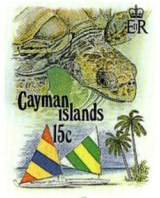

178 Yellow Stingray

179 Turtle and Sailing Dinghies

(Des G. Drummond. Litho Cartor)

1993 (16 June). Rays. T **178** and similar horiz designs. Multicoloured. W w **14** (sideways). P 13½.

751	5c. Type **178**..	70	60
752	30c. Southern Stingray.............................	1·75	1·25
753	40c. Spotted Eagle-ray.............................	2·00	1·50
754	$1 Manta..	4·25	5·50
751/4 Set of 4...		8·00	8·00

(Des D. Miller. Litho B.D.T.)

1993 (30 Sept). Tourism. T **179** and similar vert designs. Multicoloured. W w **14**. P 13½.

755	15c. Type **179**..	1·75	2·00
	a. Horiz strip of 5. Nos. 755/9.................	8·00	9·00
	b. Booklet pane. Nos. 755/64..................	17·00	
756	15c. Tourist boat, fishing launch and scuba diver...	1·75	2·00
757	15c. Golf...	1·75	2·00
758	15c. Tennis..	1·75	2·00
759	15c. Pirates and ship................................	1·75	2·00
760	30c. Liner, tourist launch and yacht..........	2·00	2·25

	a. Horiz strip of 5. Nos. 760/4	9·00	10·00
761	30c. George Town street	2·00	2·25
762	30c. Tourist submarine	2·00	2·25
763	30c. Motor-scooter riders and cyclists	2·00	2·25
764	30c. Cayman Airways Boeing 737 airliners	2·00	2·25
755/64 Set of 10		17·00	19·00

Nos. 755/9 and 760/4 were each printed together, *se-tenant*, in horizontal strips of 5 throughout the sheets. Booklet pane No. 755b contains both *se-tenant* strips as a block of 10 with the horizontal edges of the pane imperforate and margins at left and right.

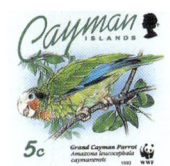

180 Cuban Amazon with Wings spread

181 *Ionopsis utricularioides* and Manger

(Des O. Ball. Litho Leigh-Mardon Ltd, Melbourne)

1993 (29 Oct). Endangered Species. Cuban Amazon ("Grand Cayman Parrot"). T **180** and similar square designs. Multicoloured. W w **14**. P 14.

765	5c. Type **180**	85	1·50
766	5c. On branch with wings folded	85	1·50
767	30c. Head of parrot	2·25	2·50
768	30c. Pair of parrots	2·25	2·50
765/8 Set of 4		5·50	7·25

(Des Jennifer Toombs. Litho B.D.T.)

1993 (6 Dec). Christmas. Orchids. T **181** and similar horiz designs. Multicoloured. W w **16** (sideways). P 13½×14.

769	5c. Type **181**	1·25	75
770	40c. *Encyclia cochleata* and shepherd	2·75	85
771	60c. *Vanilla pompona* and wise men	3·75	4·00
772	$1 *Oncidium caymanense* and Virgin Mary	4·75	7·00
769/72 Set of 4		11·50	11·50

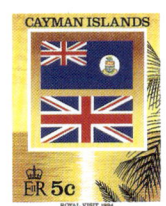

182 Queen Angelfish

183 Flags of Great Britain and Cayman Islands

(Des D. Miller and A. Robinson. Litho Enschedé)

1994 (18 Feb). "Hong Kong '94" International Stamp Exhibition. Reef Life. Sheet 121×85 mm containing T **182** and similar vert designs. Multicoloured. W w **14** (sideways). P 14½×13.

MS773 60c. Type **182**; 60c. Diver with Porkfish and Spot-finned Hogfish; 60c. Rock Beauty and Royal Gramma; 60c. French Angelfish and Banded Butterflyfish .... 8·50 9·50

(Des D. Miller. Litho Questa)

1994 (22 Feb). Royal Visit. T **183** and similar vert designs. Multicoloured. W w **14**. P 14½×14.

774	5c. Type **183**	2·00	1·25
775	15c. Royal Yacht *Britannia*	3·00	1·00
776	30c. Queen Elizabeth II	3·00	1·25
777	$2 Queen Elizabeth and Prince Philip disembarking	9·00	12·00
774/7 Set of 4		15·00	14·00

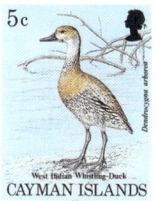

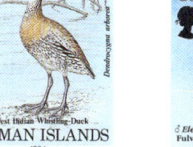

184 Black-billed Whistling Duck

185 *Electrostrymon angelia*

(Des Josephine Martin. Litho Walsall)

1994 (21 Apr). Black-billed Whistling Duck ("West Indian Whistling Duck"). T **184** and similar multicoloured designs. W w **16** (sideways on 15c., 20c.). P 14½.

778	5c. Type **184**	1·50	1·00
779	15c. Duck landing on water (*horiz*)	2·25	75
780	20c. Duck preening (*horiz*)	2·25	80
781	80c. Duck flapping wings	4·50	5·50
782	$1 Adult and duckling	5·00	6·50
778/82 Set of 5		14·00	13·00
MS783 71×45 mm. $1 As No. 782, but including Cayman Islands National Trust symbol		7·00	8·00

(Des K. McGee. Litho Enschedé)

1994 (16 Aug). Butterflies. T **185** and similar vert designs. Multicoloured. W w **14** (sideways). P 13½×14.

784	10c. Type **185**	1·00	1·50
	a. Vert pair. Nos. 784/5	2·00	3·00
785	10c. *Eumaeus atala*	1·00	1·50
786	$1 *Eurema daira*	4·75	5·00
	a. Vert pair. Nos. 786/7	9·50	10·00
787	$1 *Urbanus dorantes*	4·75	5·00
784/7 Set of 4		10·50	11·50

Nos. 784/5 and 786/7 were printed together, *se-tenant*, in vertical pairs throughout the sheets.

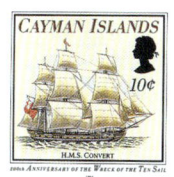

186 H.M.S. *Convert* (frigate)

187 Young Green Turtles

(Des B. Dare. Litho Enschedé)

1994 (12 Oct). Bicentenary of Wreck of Ten Sail off Grand Cayman. T **186** and similar square designs. Multicoloured. W w **14** (sideways). P 13×14.

788	10c. Type **186**	55	55
789	10c. Merchant brig and full-rigged ship	55	55
790	15c. Full-rigged ship near rock	75	50
791	20c. Long boat leaving full-rigged ship	85	55
792	$2 Merchant brig	4·50	7·50
788/92 Set of 5		6·50	8·75

(Des Doreen McGuiness. Litho Questa)

1995 (28 Feb). Sea Turtles. T **187** and similar horiz designs. Multicoloured. W w **16** (sideways). P 14.

793	10c. Type **187**	55	45
794	20c. Kemp's Ridley Turtle	80	55
795	25c. Hawksbill Turtle	90	60
796	30c. Leatherback Turtle	95	70
797	$1.30 Loggerhead Turtle	3·50	4·75
798	$2 Pacific Ridley Turtles	4·50	6·00
793/8 Set of 6		10·00	12·00
MS799 167×94 mm. Nos. 793/8		10·00	11·50

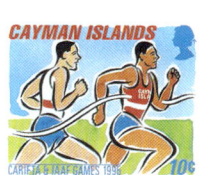

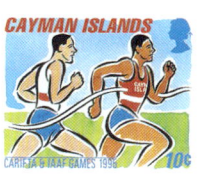

188 Running

189 Queen Elizabeth the Queen Mother

(Des B. Dare. Litho Questa)

1995 (15 Apr). C.A.R.I.F.T.A. and I.A.A.F. Games, George Town. T **188** and similar horiz designs. Multicoloured. W w **14** (sideways). P 14½.

800	10c. Type **188**	60	40
801	20c. High jumping	90	70
802	30c. Javelin throwing	1·25	80
803	$1.30 Yachting	4·25	6·00
800/3 Set of 4		6·25	7·00
MS804 100×70 $2 Athletes with medals		5·50	7·50

CAYMAN ISLANDS

(Des R. Watton. Litho Cartor (Nos. 805/8) or Questa (No. **MS**809))

1995 (8 May). 50th Anniv of End of Second World War. Multicoloured designs as T **209a** of Bahamas. W w **14** (sideways). P 13½.

805	10c. Members of Cayman Home Guard	70	55
806	25c. *Comayagua* (freighter)	1·75	85
807	40c. U-boat *U125*	2·00	1·50
808	$1 U.S. Navy *L-3* airship	3·75	6·00
805/8 *Set of 4*		7·50	8·00
MS809 75×85 mm. $1.30, Reverse of 1939–45 War Medal (*vert*). Wmk upright. P 14		2·00	3·00

(Des N. Shewring. Litho Walsall)

1995 (25 Aug). 95th Birthday of Queen Elizabeth the Queen Mother. Sheet 70×90 mm. W w **14** (sideways). P 14½.

MS810 **189** $4 multicoloured		8·50	9·50

190 Ox and Christ Child    **191** Sea Grape

(Des Doreen McGuiness. Litho Walsall)

1995 (1 Nov). Christmas. Nativity Animals. T **190** and similar vert designs. Multicoloured. W w **14**. P 14×13½.

811	10c. Type **190**	70	30
812	20c. Sheep and lamb	1·25	45
813	30c. Donkey	2·00	60
814	$2 Camels	8·00	10·00
811/14 *Set of 4*		11·00	11·00
MS815 160×75 mm. Nos. 811/14		11·00	11·00

(Des I. Loe. Litho B.D.T.)

1996 (21 Mar). Wild Fruit. T **191** and similar vert designs. Multicoloured. W w **16**. P 14.

816	10c. Type **191**	50	40
817	25c. Guava	1·00	50
818	40c. West Indian Cherry	1·50	80
819	$1 Tamarind	2·75	4·50
816/19 *Set of 4*		5·25	5·50

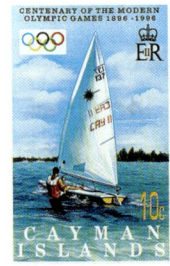

192 "Laser" Dinghy 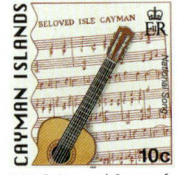   **193** Guitar and Score of National Song

(Des G. Vasarhelyi. Litho Walsall)

1996 (19 June). Centenary of Modern Olympic Games. T **192** and similar vert designs. Multicoloured. W w **14**. P 14×13½.

820	10c. Type **192**	55	40
821	20c. Sailboarding	85	60
822	30c. "Finn" dinghy	1·00	80
823	$2 Running	4·25	7·00
820/3 *Set of 4*		6·00	8·00

(Des N. Shewring. Litho Questa)

1996 (26 Sept). National Identity. T **193** and similar square designs. Multicoloured. W w **14**. P 14.

824	10c. Type **193**	50	60
825	20c. Cayman Airways Boeing 737-200	1·75	60
826	25c. Queen Elizabeth opening Legislative Assembly	1·50	50
827	30c. Seven Mile Beach	1·00	55
828	40c. Scuba diver and Stingrays	1·50	75
829	60c. Children at turtle farm	2·75	1·25
830	80c. Cuban Amazon ("Cayman Parrot") (national bird)	3·75	2·50
831	90c. Silver Thatch Palm (national tree)	2·00	2·50
832	$1 Cayman Islands flag	4·75	3·25
833	$2 Wild Banana Orchid (national flower)	6·50	6·50
834	$4 Cayman Islands coat of arms	10·00	14·00
835	$6 Cayman Islands currency	12·00	17·00
824/35 *Set of 12*		42·00	45·00

Imprint dates: "1996", Nos. 824/35; "1997", No. 824.

For miniature sheet containing No. 830 with "1997" imprint date see No. **MS**840, and for values with watermark sideways Nos. 873/7.

194 "Christmas Time on North Church Street" (Joanne Sibley)   **195** Children accessing Internet

(Des D. Miller. Litho Questa)

1996 (12 Nov). Christmas. Paintings. T **194** and similar square designs. Multicoloured. W w **14** (sideways). P 14.

836	10c. Type **194**	40	30
837	25c. "Gone Fishing" (Lois Brezinsky)	70	50
838	30c. "Claus Encounters" (John Doak)	80	70
839	$2 "A Caymanian Christmas" (Debbie van der Bol)	4·00	6·50
836/9 *Set of 4*		5·50	7·25

(Des D. Miller. Litho Questa)

1997 (3 Feb). "HONG KONG '97" International Stamp Exhibition. Sheet 130×90 mm, containing design as No. 830 with "1997" imprint date. Multicoloured. W w **14** (inverted). P 14.

MS840 80c. Cuban Amazon ("Cayman Parrot")		1·75	2·00

(Des N. Shewring (No. **MS**847), D. Miller (others). Litho Questa (No. **MS**847), B.D.T. (others))

1997 (10 July). Golden Wedding of Queen Elizabeth and Prince Philip. Multicoloured designs as T **221a** of Bahamas. W w **14**. P 13½.

841	10c. Queen Elizabeth	1·10	1·40
	a. Horiz pair. Nos. 841/2	2·10	2·75
842	10c. Prince Philip and Prince Charles at Trooping the Colour	1·10	1·40
843	30c. Prince William horse riding, 1989	1·75	1·90
	a. Horiz pair. Nos. 843/4	3·50	3·75
844	30c. Queen Elizabeth and Prince Philip at Royal Ascot	1·75	1·90
845	40c. Prince Philip at the Brighton Driving Trials	1·90	2·00
	a. Horiz pair. Nos. 845/6	3·75	4·00
846	40c. Queen Elizabeth at Windsor Horse Show, 1993	1·90	2·00
841/6 *Set of 6*		8·50	9·50
MS847 110×70 mm. $1 Queen Elizabeth and Prince Philip in landau (*horiz*). Wmk sideways. P 14×14½		5·50	5·50

Nos. 841/2, 843/4 and 845/6 were each printed together, *se-tenant*, in horizontal pairs throughout the sheets with the backgrounds forming a composite design.

(Des O. Bell. Litho Walsall)

1997 (10 Oct). Telecommunications. T **195** and similar horiz designs. Multicoloured. W w **16** (sideways). P 14×14½.

848	10c. Type **195**	35	25
849	25c. Cable & Wireless cable ship	70	45
850	30c. New area code "345" on children's T-shirts	75	60
851	60c. Satellite dish	1·50	2·50
848/51 *Set of 4*		3·00	3·50

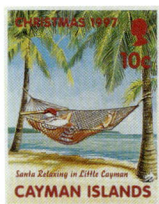

196 Santa in Hammock    **197** West Indian Whistling Duck

CAYMAN ISLANDS

(Des R. Watton. Litho Cartor)

1997 (3 Dec). Christmas. T **196** and similar vert designs. Multicoloured. W w **14**. P 13.

852	10c. Type **196**...	35	25
853	30c. Santa with children on the Bluff.............	65	45
854	40c. Santa playing golf....................................	1·50	80
855	$1 Santa scuba diving.....................................	2·00	3·50
852/5 Set of 4...		4·00	4·50

(Des D. Miller. Litho Questa)

1998 (31 Mar). Diana, Princess of Wales Commemoration. Vert designs as T **223a** of Bahamas. Multicoloured. W w **16** (Nos. 856/7). P 14½×14.

856	10c. Wearing gold earrings, 1997...................	40	30
857	20c. Wearing black hat....................................	70	90
MS858 145×70 mm. 10c. As No. 856; 20c. As No. 857; 40c. With bouquet, 1995; $1 Wearing black and white blouse, 1983. W w **14** (sideways) (sold at $1.70+30c. charity premium)..		2·25	3·25

(Des A. Theobald. Litho B.D.T.)

1998 (1 Apr). 80th Anniv of the Royal Air Force. Horiz designs as T **223b** of Bahamas. Multicoloured. W w **14** (sideways). P 14.

859	10c. Hawker Horsley......................................	60	70
860	20c. Fairey Hendon..	75	80
861	25c. Hawker Siddeley Gnat...........................	85	90
862	30c. Hawker Siddeley Dominie....................	95	1·00
859/62 Set of 4...		2·75	3·00
MS863 110×77 mm. 40c. Airco D.H.9; 60c. Spad 13 Scout; 80c. Airspeed Oxford; $1 Martin Baltimore............		5·50	6·50

(Des N. Shewring. Litho Cartor)

1998 (12 Oct). Birds. T **197** and similar vert designs. Multicoloured. W w **14**. P 13½.

864	10c. Type **197**...	1·25	60
865	20c. Magnificent Frigate Bird........................	1·75	60
866	60c. Red-footed Booby...................................	2·75	3·00
867	$1 Grand Cayman Parrot................................	3·50	4·25
864/7 Set of 4...		8·25	7·75

198 Santa at the Blowholes

199 "They Rolled the Stone Away" (Miss Lassie)

(Des R. Watton. Litho Questa)

1998 (20 Nov). Christmas. T **198** and similar horiz designs. Multicoloured. W w **16** (sideways). P 14½.

868	10c. Type **198**...	30	30
869	30c. Santa diving on wreck of *Capt. Keith Tibbetts*..	75	60
870	40c. Santa at Pedro Castle..............................	90	75
871	60c. Santa arriving on Little Cayman.............	1·75	2·50
868/71 Set of 4...		3·25	3·75

1999 (5 Feb). As Nos. 825, 827 and 829, but W w **14** (sideways). P 14.

873	20c. Cayman Airways Boeing 737-200...........	1·50	75
875	30c. Seven Mile Beach....................................	1·50	75
877	60c. Children at turtle farm............................	3·00	3·50
873/7 Set of 3...		5·50	4·50

Imprint date: "1999", Nos. 873, 875, 877.

(Des D. Miller. Litho Cartor)

1999 (26 Mar). Easter. Paintings by Miss Lassie (Gladwyn Bush). T **199** and similar multicoloured designs. W w **14** (sideways on horiz designs). P 13.

884	10c. Type **199**...	30	35
885	20c. "Ascension" (*vert*)..................................	60	70
886	30c. "The World Praying for Peace"................	75	85
887	40c. "Calvary" (*vert*)......................................	95	1·10
884/7 Set of 4...		2·40	2·75

200 "Cayman House" (Jessica Cranston)

(Adapted D. Miller. Litho Cartor)

1999 (2 June). Vision 2008 Project. Children's Paintings. T **200** and similar horiz designs. Multicoloured. W w **14** (sideways). P 13½.

888	10c. Type **200**...	40	20
889	30c. "Coral Reef" (Sarah Hetley)....................	1·00	55
890	40c. "Fisherman on North Sound" (Sarah Cuff)	1·10	70
891	$2 "Three Fish and a Turtle" (Ryan Martinez)..	4·25	6·50
888/91 Set of 4...		6·00	7·75

200a Photographs of Prince Edward and Miss Sophie Rhys-Jones

201 1969 Christmas ¼c. Stamp

(Des D. Miller. Litho Walsall)

1999 (16 June). Royal Wedding. T **200a** and similar vert design. W w **16**. P 14.

892	10c. Type **200a**...	50	30
893	$2 Engagement photograph.........................	3·75	4·75

(Des J. Batchelor (10c.), N. Shewring (others). Litho Walsall)

1999 (20 July). 30th Anniv of First Manned Landing on Moon. Multicoloured designs as T **236a** of Bahamas. W w **16**. P 14×13½.

894	10c. Coastguard cutter on patrol during launch	45	35
895	25c. Firing of third stage rockets...................	80	60
896	30c. Buzz Aldrin descending to Moon's surface..	85	65
897	60c. Jettisoning of lunar module..................	1·40	2·25
894/7 Set of 4...		3·00	4·00
MS898 90×80 mm. $1.50, Earth as seen from Moon (circular, 40 mm diam). Wmk sideways. P 14.....		3·25	3·50

(Des D. Miller. Litho Cartor)

1999 (18 Aug). "Queen Elizabeth the Queen Mother's Century". Horiz designs as T **236b** of Bahamas. W w **16** (sideways). P 13½.

899	10c. Visiting anti-aircraft battery, London, 1940..	45	40
900	20c. With children on her 94th birthday, 1994..	65	65
901	30c. With Prince Charles and Prince William, 1997..	80	90
902	40c. Reviewing Chelsea Pensioners, 1986.....	90	1·00
899/902 Set of 4...		2·25	2·75
MS903 145×70 mm. $1.50. Duchess of York with Princess Elizabeth, 1926, and Royal Wedding, 1923................		2·50	3·00

(Des D. Miller. Litho Cartor)

1999 (17 Nov). Christmas. T **201** and similar multicoloured designs showing previous Christmas stamps. W w **14** (sideways on $1). P 13½.

904	10c. Type **201**...	40	25
905	30c. 1984 Christmas 5c.................................	70	50
906	40c. 1997 Christmas 10c...............................	85	65
907	$1 1979 Christmas 20c. (*horiz*)....................	1·90	2·50
904/7 Set of 4...		3·00	4·25
MS908 111×100 mm. Nos. 904/7. Wmk upright. P 12.....		3·50	3·50

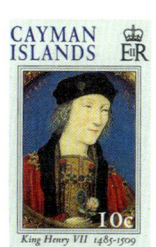

201a King Henry VII

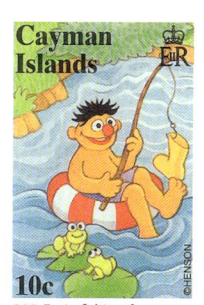

202 Ernie fishing from Rubber Ring

91

CAYMAN ISLANDS

(Des Crown Agents. Litho Walsall)

2000 (29 Feb). "Stamp Show 2000" International Stamp Exhibition, London. Kings and Queens of England. T **201a** and similar vert designs. W w **14**. P 14.

909	10c. Type **201a**	60	70
910	40c. King Henry VIII	1·40	1·75
	a. Sheetlet. Nos. 910/15	7·75	9·50
911	40c. Queen Mary I	1·40	1·75
912	40c. King Charles II	1·40	1·75
913	40c. Queen Anne	1·40	1·75
914	40c. King George IV	1·40	1·75
915	40c. King George V	1·40	1·75
909/15 Set of 7		8·00	10·00

Nos. 910/15 were printed together, *se-tenant*, in sheetlets of 6 with an enlarged illustrated right-hand margin.

(Des Children's Television Workshop. Litho Questa)

2000 (15 Mar). Sesame Street (children's T.V. programme). T **202** and similar vert designs. Multicoloured. W w **14** (inverted on 20c.). P 14½×15.

916	10c. Type **202**	25	35
917	20c. Grover flying	40	50
	a. Sheetlet. Nos. 917/25	3·25	4·00
918	20c. Zoe in airplane	40	50
919	20c. Oscar the Grouch in balloon	40	50
920	20c. The Count on motorbike	40	50
921	20c. Big Bird rollerskating	40	50
922	20c. Cookie Monster heading for Cookie Factory	40	50
923	20c. Type **202**	40	50
924	20c. Bert in rowing boat	40	50
925	20c. Elmo snorkeling	40	50
926	30c. As No. 921	55	55
916/26 Set of 11		4·00	4·75
MS927 139×86 mm. 20c. Elmo with stamps. Wmk inverted		1·00	1·00

Nos. 917/25 were printed together, *se-tenant*, in sheetlets of 9 with the backgrounds forming a composite design.

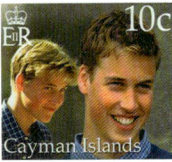

202a Prince William in 1999

203 Green Turtle

(Des A. Robinson. Litho Questa)

2000 (21 June). 18th Birthday of Prince William. T **202a** and similar multicoloured designs. W w **14** (sideways on 30c. and 40c.). P 14½×14 (*horiz*) or 14×14½ (*vert*).

928	10c. Type **202a**	50	40
929	20c. In evening dress, 1997	75	60
930	30c. At Muick Falls, 1997 (*vert*)	90	80
931	40c. In uniform of Parachute Regiment, 1986 (*vert*)	1·25	1·25
928/31 Set of 4		3·00	2·75
MS932 175×95 mm. $1 As baby with toy mouse and Nos. 928/31. Wmk sideways. P 14½		6·50	6·50

(Litho B.D.T.)

2000 (25 Aug). Marine Life. T **203** and similar horiz designs. Multicoloured. W w **16** (sideways). P 14.

933	10c. Type **203**	65	45
934	20c. Queen Angel Fish	1·00	50
935	30c. Sleeping Parrotfish	1·25	65
936	$1 Green Moray Eel	3·75	5·00
933/6 Set of 4		6·00	6·00

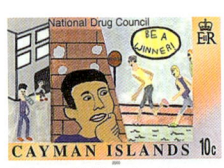

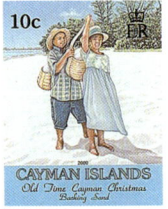

204 Boy thinking about Drugs and Fitness

205 Children on Beach ("Backing Sand")

(Adapted G. Vasarhelyi. Litho B.D.T.)

2000 (27 Sept). National Drugs Council. T **204** and similar horiz designs. Multicoloured. W w **16** (sideways). P 14.

937	10c. Type **204**	60	40
938	15c. Rainbow, sun, clouds and "ez2B Drug Free"	85	40
939	30c. Musicians dancing	1·40	65
940	$2 Hammock between two palm trees	5·00	8·50
937/40 Set of 4		7·00	9·00

(Des N. Shewring. Litho Questa)

2000 (14 Nov). Christmas. Traditional Customs. T **205** and similar vert designs. Multicoloured. W w **14**. P 14½×14.

941	10c. Type **205**	1·00	75
942	30c. Christmas dinner	2·25	80
943	40c. Yard dance	2·50	85
944	60c. Conch shell borders	3·25	4·00
941/4 Set of 4		8·00	5·75

206 Woman on Beach

207 Red Mangrove Cay

(Des Leisel Jobity. Litho B.D.T.)

2001 (8 Mar). United Nations Women's Human Rights Campaign. W w **14**. P 14.

945	**206** 10c. multicoloured	60	60

(Litho Questa)

2001 (21 Apr). Cayman Brac Tourism Project. T **207** and similar multicoloured designs. W w **14** (sideways on horiz designs). P 14.

946	15c. Type **207**	1·25	75
947	20c. Peter's Cave (*vert*)	1·40	1·00
948	25c. Bight Road steps (*vert*)	1·50	1·10
949	30c. Westerly Ponds	1·60	1·10
950	40c. Aerial view of Spot Bay	2·00	1·60
951	60c. The Marshes	3·00	4·00
946/51 Set of 6		9·75	8·50

208 Work of National Council of Voluntary Organisations

(Litho Questa)

2001 (15 Aug). Non-Profit Organisations. T **208** and similar multicoloured designs. W w **14** (sideways on horiz designs). P 14.

952	15c. Type **208**	1·00	75
953	20c. Pet welfare (Cayman Humane Society)	2·25	1·25
954	25c. Stick figures (Red Cross and Red Crescent)	2·25	1·75
955	30c. Pink flowers (Cayman Islands Cancer Society) (*vert*)	2·25	1·75
956	40c. Women's silhouettes and insignia (Lions Club Breast Cancer Awareness Campaign) (*vert*)	2·25	2·00
952/6 Set of 5		9·00	6·75
MS957 145×95 mm. Nos. 952/6. Wmk sideways (sold at $1.80)		10·00	12·00

No. **MS**957 was sold at $1.80 which included a 50c. donation to the featured organisations. Stamps from the miniature sheet have pink margins.

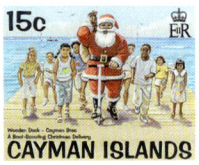

209 Children walking Home

210 Father Christmas on Scooter with Children, Cayman Brac

92

CAYMAN ISLANDS

(Des A. Robinson. Litho Questa)

2001 (29 Sept). Transportation. T **209** and similar multicoloured designs. W w **14** (sideways on horiz designs, inverted on 60c.). P 14×14½ (horiz) or 14½×14 (vert).

958	15c. Type **209**	90	80
959	15c. Boy on donkey	90	80
	a. Perf 14×13½		
960	20c. Bananas by canoe	90	50
	a. Perf 14×13½		
961	25c. Horse and buggy	1·50	55
962	30c. Catboats fishing	1·50	55
963	40c. Schooner	1·75	80
964	60c. Police cyclist (*vert*)	3·25	2·00
965	80c. Lady drivers	2·75	2·00
966	90c. Launching *Cimboco* (motor coaster) (*vert*)	3·50	2·50
967	$1 Amphibian aircraft	4·50	3·75
968	$4 Container ship	11·00	13·00
969	$10 Boeing 767 airliner	24·00	28·00
958/69	*Set of 12*	50·00	50·00

(Des R. Watton. Litho Questa)

2001 (21 Nov). Christmas. T **210** and similar horiz designs. Multicoloured. W w **14** (sideways). P 14×14½.

970	15c. Type **210**	1·00	55
971	30c. Father Christmas on Eagle Ray, Little Cayman	1·40	80
972	40c. Father Christmas in catboat, Grand Cayman	1·60	1·10
973	60c. Father Christmas parasailing over Grand Cayman	2·40	3·50
970/3	*Set of 4*	5·75	5·50

211 Statue of Liberty, U.S. and Cayman Flags

(Des A. Robinson. Litho B.D.T.)

2002 (22 Jan). In Remembrance. Victims of Terrorist Attacks on U.S.A. (11 September 2001). W w **14** (sideways). P 14×15.

974	**211**	$1 multicoloured	3·00	3·50

(Des A. Robinson. Litho Questa)

2002 (6 Feb). Golden Jubilee. Designs as T **253a** of Bahamas. W w **14** (sideways). P 14½.

975	15c. lavender-grey, new blue and gold	50	40
976	20c. multicoloured	65	40
977	30c. grey-black, new blue and gold	80	60
978	80c. multicoloured	2·00	2·25
975/8	*Set of 4*	3·50	3·25

MS979 162×95 mm. Nos. 975/8 and $1 multicoloured. P 13½ ($1) or 14½ (others) ... 7·00 7·00

Designs: Horiz (as Type **253a** of Bahamas)—15c. Princess Elizabeth as young child; 20c. Queen Elizabeth in evening dress, 1976; 30c. Princess Elizabeth and Princess Margaret as Girl Guides, 1942; 80c. Queen Elizabeth at Newbury, 1996. Vert (38×51 *mm*)—$1 Queen Elizabeth after Annigoni. Designs as Nos. 975/8 in No. **MS**979 omit the gold frame around each stamp and the "Golden Jubilee 1952–2002" inscription.

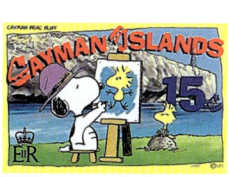

212 Snoopy painting Woodstock at Cayman Brac Bluff

213 Cayman Islands Footballer

(Des O. Bell. Litho BDT)

2002 (9 Mar). "A Cayman Vacation". Peanuts (cartoon characters by Charles Schulz). T **212** and similar horiz designs. Multicoloured. W w **14** (sideways). P 14.

980	15c. Type **212**	75	65
981	20c. Charlie Brown and Sally at Hell Post Office, Grand Cayman	80	65
982	25c. Peppermint Patty and Marcie on beach, Little Cayman	85	75
983	30c. Snoopy as Red Baron and Boeing 737-200 over Grand Cayman	1·10	85
984	40c. Linus and Snoopy at Point of Sand, Little Cayman	1·40	1·10
985	60c. Charlie Brown, playing golf at The Links, Grand Cayman	2·25	3·00
980/5	*Set of 6*	6·50	6·25

MS986 230×160 mm. Nos. 980/5 ... 6·50 7·00

No. **MS**986 is die-cut in the shape of a suitcase.

(Litho BDT)

2002 (30 Apr). World Cup Football Championship, Japan and Korea and 35th Anniv of Cayman Islands Football Association. W w **14**. P 14.

987	**213**	30c. multicoloured	1·50	1·25
988		40c. multicoloured	1·50	1·25

(Des A. Robinson. Litho Questa)

2002 (5 Aug). Queen Elizabeth the Queen Mother Commemoration. Vert designs as T **255a** of Bahamas. W w **14**. P 14×14½ (Nos. 989/90) or 14½×14 (Nos. 991/2).

989	15c. brownish black, gold and purple	80	30
990	30c. multicoloured	1·25	60
991	40c. black, gold and purple	1·50	1·00
992	$1 multicoloured	2·75	3·75
989/92	*Set of 4*	5·75	5·00

MS993 145×70 mm. Nos. 991/2. Wmk sideways. P 14½×14 ... 5·00 6·00

Designs:—15c. Queen Elizabeth at Red Cross and St. John's summer fair, London 1943; 30c. Queen Mother at Royal Caledonian School, Bushey; 40c. Duchess of York in 1936; $1 Queen Mother at film premiere in 1989. Designs in No. **MS**993 omit the "1900–2002" inscription and the coloured frame.

214 Angel Gabriel appearing to Virgin Mary

(Des V. Ambrus. Litho Questa)

2002 (18 Oct). Christmas. T **214** and similar horiz designs. Multicoloured. W w **14** (sideways). P 14.

994	15c. Type **214**	60	55
995	20c. Mary and Joseph travelling to Bethlehem	70	55
996	30c. The Holy Family	85	60
997	40c. Angel appearing to shepherds	1·00	90
998	60c. Three Wise Men	1·60	2·75
994/8	*Set of 5*	4·25	4·75

MS999 234×195 mm. Nos. 994/8 including *se-tenant* labels ... 4·25 5·50

Nos. 994/8 were each printed in sheets of 20, with each horizontal row separated by a row of 42×15 mm inscribed labels. No. **MS**999 has an enlarged upper margin, repeating the design of the 30c., die-cut around the edge of the illustration.

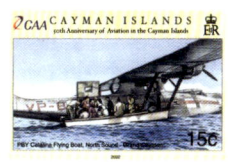

215 Catalina Flying Boat, North Sound, Grand Cayman

(Des N. Shewring. Litho Walsall)

2002 (8 Nov). 50th Anniv of Cayman Islands Aviation. T **215** and similar horiz designs. Multicoloured. W w **14** (sideways). P 14.

1000	15c. Type **215**	1·40	90
1001	20c. Grand Cayman Airport, 1952	1·60	90
1002	25c. Cayman Brac Airways AC50	1·60	1·00
1003	30c. Cayman Airways Boeing 737	1·75	1·00
1004	40c. British Airways Concorde at Grand Cayman, 1984	2·50	1·75
1005	$1.30 Island Air DHC 6 Twin Otter on Little Cayman	6·00	8·50
1000/5	*Set of 6*	13·00	12·50

93

CAYMAN ISLANDS

216 Skipping

(Des R. Watton. Litho BDT)

2003 (27 May). Children's Games. T **216** and similar horiz designs. Multicoloured. W w **14** (sideways). P 13½.
1006	15c. Type **216**	80	70
1007	20c. Maypole dancing	90	70
1008	25c. Gig	1·00	70
1009	30c. Hopscotch	1·10	70
1010	$1 Marbles	3·00	4·50
1006/10 Set of 5		6·00	6·50

(Des A. Robinson. Litho DLR)

2003 (2 June). 50th Anniv of Coronation. Horiz designs as T **320** of Jamaica. Multicoloured. W w **14** (sideways). P 14×14½.
1011	15c. Queen Elizabeth II wearing Imperial State Crown	75	35
1012	$2 Newly crowned Queen flanked by Bishops of Durham and Bath & Wells	4·25	5·00
MS1013 95×115 mm. 20c. As 15c.; $4 As $2		9·00	10·00

Nos. 1011/12 have scarlet frames; stamps from **MS**1013 have no frame and country name in mauve panel.

216a

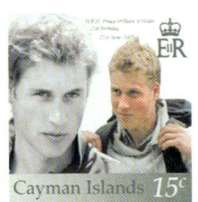

216b Prince William at Tidworth Polo Club, 2002 and on Raleigh International Expedition, 2000

(Litho BDT)

2003 (2 June). W w **14**. P 13½.
1014	**216a** $4 black, dull vermilion and bright reddish violet	8·00	9·00

(Des A. Robinson. Litho DLR)

2003 (21 June). 21st Birthday of Prince William of Wales. Square designs as T **216b**. Multicoloured. W w **14** (sideways on 80c., $1). P 14½.
1015	15c. Type **216b**	70	35
1016	40c. At Golden Jubilee church service, 2002 and Queen Mother's 101st birthday, 2001	1·25	60
1017	80c. At Queen Mother's 101st birthday and at Holyrood House, 2001	2·25	3·00
	a. Horiz pair. Nos. 1017/18	4·50	6·00
1018	$1 At Eton College and at Christmas Day church service in 2000	2·25	3·00
1015/18 Set of 4		5·75	6·25

Nos. 1017/18 were printed together, *se-tenant*, as horizontal pairs in sheets of ten (2×5) with enlarged illustrated left-hand margins.

217 Turtles hatching

218 Bell and "Merry Christmas"

(Des N. Shewring. Litho BDT)

2003 (24 July). 500th Anniv of Discovery of Cayman Islands. T **217** and similar horiz designs. Multicoloured. W w **14** (sideways). P 13½.
1019	15c. Type **217**	1·00	75
1020	20c. Old waterfront, George Town, 1975	1·25	1·00
1021	20c. *Santa Maria* (Columbus) and turtle	1·50	1·00
1022	25c. Nassau Grouper (fish) and corals	1·50	90
1023	30c. *Kirk-B* (Cayman Brac schooner)	1·75	90
1024	40c. George Town harbour	1·75	1·00
1025	60c. Musical instruments	1·75	1·60
1026	80c. Smokewood Tree and Ghost Orchids	2·50	2·50
1027	90c. Little Cayman Baptist Church	2·50	2·75
1028	$1 Loading thatch rope onto *Caymania*	3·00	3·25
1029	$1.30 Children's dance troupe	3·50	4·75
1030	$2 Cayman Parliament in session	4·50	7·00
1019/30 Set of 12		24·00	25·00
MS1031 216×151 mm. Nos. 1019/30		24·00	27·00

(Des A. Robinson. Litho BDT)

2003 (4 Nov). Christmas. T **218** and similar square designs. Multicoloured. W w **14** (sideways). P 13½.
1032	15c. Type **218**	85	65
1033	20c. Christmas wreath and "Celebrate with Family"	95	65
1034	30c. Gold star, angel and "Happy New Year"	1·25	65
1035	40c. Christmas lights and "Happy Holidays"	1·50	75
1036	60c. Poinsettias and "Seasons Greetings"	2·00	3·25
1032/6 Set of 5		6·00	5·50

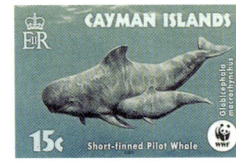

219 Female and Calf

(Des J. Pointer. Litho BDT)

2003 (26 Nov). Endangered Species. Short-finned Pilot Whale. T **219** and similar horiz designs. Multicoloured. W w **14** (sideways). P 14.
1037	15c. Type **219**	1·60	1·25
1038	20c. Four pilot whales	1·75	1·40
1039	30c. Two pilot whales at surface	2·00	1·50
1040	40c. Short-finned Pilot Whale	2·75	2·50
1037/40 Set of 4		7·25	6·00

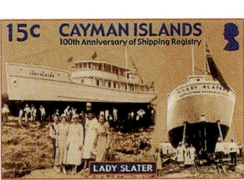

220 *Lady Slater*

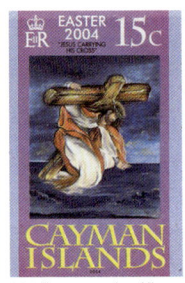

221 "Jesus carrying His Cross" (Carole Mayer)

(Des R. Watton. Litho BDT)

2004 (29 Jan). Centenary of Shipping Registry. T **220** and similar horiz designs. Multicoloured. W w **14** (sideways). P 14×15.
1041	15c. Type **220**	1·50	85
1042	20c. *Seanostrum*	1·60	95
1043	30c. *Kirk Pride*	2·00	1·25
1044	$1 *Boadicea*	6·00	8·00
1041/4 Set of 4		10·00	10·00

(Litho BDT)

2004 (16 Mar). Easter. T **221** and similar vert design. Multicoloured. W w **14** (inverted). P 15×14.
1045	15c. Type **221**	1·00	75
1046	30c. "The Ascension" (Natasha Claire Kozaily)	1·50	1·00

222 Swimming

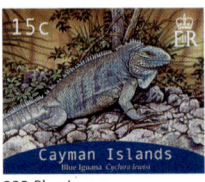

223 Blue Iguana

94

CAYMAN ISLANDS

(Des J. Vasarhelyi. Litho Cartor)

2004 (23 Aug). Olympic Games, Athens. T **222** and similar vert designs. Multicoloured. W w **14**. P 13½.
1047	15c. Type **222**	75	40
1048	40c. Sprinting	1·25	75
1049	60c. Long jump	1·90	1·75
1050	80c. Two Cayman Islands swimmers	2·40	3·50
1047/50 Set of 4		5·75	5·75

(Des N. Shewring. Litho Enschedé)

2004 (26 Oct). Blue Iguana. T **223** and similar horiz designs. Multicoloured. W w **14** (sideways). P 13½×14.
1051	15c. Type **223**	85	70
1052	20c. Baby iguana hatching from egg	95	70
1053	25c. Four iguanas	1·10	75
1054	30c. Baby iguana on finger	1·25	75
1055	40c. Iguana with open mouth	1·50	1·00
1056	90c. Eye of iguana	3·00	4·00
1051/6 Set of 6		7·75	7·00
MS1057 104×58 mm. 60c. Iguana on rock facing right; 80c. Iguana on rock facing left		4·50	5·50

No. **MS**1057 was sold for $1.90, the 50c. premium was donated to the Blue Iguana Recovery Programme.

(Des J. Batchelor. Litho Cartor)

2005 (8 June). Bicentenary of Battle of Trafalgar. Multicoloured designs as T **336** of Jamaica. No wmk (15c.) or W w **14** (sideways on 20, 25, 60c., $2). P 13½.
1058	15c. HMS *Victory*	1·25	90
1059	20c. HMS *Tonnant* tangling into bow of *Algesiras*	1·40	90
1060	25c. Flint cannon lock and linstock	1·40	90
1061	60c. Boatswain's Mate RN	2·00	1·50
1062	$1 Portrait of Admiral Nelson (vert)	2·75	3·25
1063	$2 HMS *Orion* in action against *Intrepide*	6·00	7·50
1058/63 Set of 6		13·00	13·50
MS1064 120×79 mm. 60c. *Pluton* (vert); $2 HMS *Tonnant* (vert)		7·00	8·00

Nos. 1058/63 were each printed in sheetlets of 6 with illustrated margins. No. 1058 contains traces of powdered wood from HMS Victory.

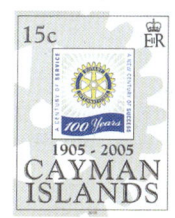

224 Rotary Emblem

(Litho BDT)

2005 (30 June). Centenary of Rotary International. T **224** and similar vert design. W w **14**. P 14.
1065	**224** 15c. multicoloured	70	60
1066	– 30c. ultramarine, black and brownish grey	1·10	1·00

Design: 30c. Polio Plus and Rotary emblems.

225 *Myrmecophila purpurea*

(Des Jennifer Toombs. Litho BDT)

2005 (28 July). Orchids. T **225** and similar multicoloured designs. W w **14** (inverted on 30, 80c., sideways on others). P 14×14½ (horiz) or 14½×14 (vert).
1067	15c. Type **225**	85	70
1068	20c. *Prosthechea boothiana*	90	70
1069	30c. *Tolumnia calochila* (vert)	1·00	70
1070	40c. *Encyclia phoenicia*	1·25	1·00
1071	80c. *Prosthechea cochleata* (vert)	2·25	3·00
1067/71 Set of 5		5·50	5·50
MS1072 80×52 mm. $1.50 *Encyclia kingsii*		4·50	5·50

(Des A. Robinson. Litho BDT)

2005 (18 Aug). Pope John Paul II Commemoration. Vert design as T **338** of Jamaica. W w **14** (inverted). P 14½×14.
1073	30c. multicoloured	1·75	1·25

No. 1073 was printed in sheetlets of eight stamps with an enlarged illustrated right margin.

226 The Queen (butterfly)   **227** Angels

(Litho BDT)

2005 (21 Sept). Butterflies. T **226** and similar horiz designs. Multicoloured.

(a) PVA gum. P 14
1074	15c. Type **226**	70	60
1075	20c. Mexican Fritillary	75	65
1076	25c. Malachite	80	70
1077	30c. Cayman Crescent Spot	85	70
1078	40c. Cloudless Sulphur	1·10	1·00
1079	90c. Swallowtail	2·25	3·50
1074/9 Set of 6		5·75	6·25

(b) Self-adhesive. Size 29×24 mm. P 10×9½
1080	15c. Type **226**	1·00	1·50
	a. Booklet pane. No. 1080×10	9·00	
1081	20c. Mexican Fritillary	1·50	2·25
	a. Booklet pane. No. 1081×6	8·00	
1082	30c. Cayman Crescent Spot	1·10	1·50
	a. Booklet pane. No. 1082×10	10·00	

Nos. 1080/2 were only issued in separate $1.20, $1.50, and $3 booklets, Nos. SB8/10.

(Des N. Shewring. Litho BDT)

2005 (26 Oct). Christmas. T **227** and similar multicoloured designs. W w **14** (sideways on horiz designs). P 13½×15 (vert) or 15×14½ (horiz).
1083	15c. Type **227**	80	40
1084	30c. Three Wise Men (horiz)	1·00	50
1085	40c. Holy Family	1·25	75
1086	60c. Shepherds (horiz)	1·75	2·25
1083/6 Set of 4		4·25	3·50
MS1087 156×106 mm. Nos. 1083/6. P 15		4·00	4·50

228 Wash Wood (*Jacquinia keyensis*)   **229** Hawksbill Turtle

(Des D. Miller. Litho BDT)

2006 (23 Feb). Trees. T **228** and similar vert designs. Multicoloured. W w **14** (sideways). P 13½.
1088	15c. Type **228**	1·00	65
1089	20c. Red mangrove (*Rhizophora mangle*)	1·10	65
1090	30c. Ironwood (*Chionanthus caymanensis*)	1·25	65
1091	60c. West Indian cedar (*Cedrela odorata*)	2·25	1·75
1092	$2 Spanish elm (*Cordia gerascanthus*)	5·00	6·50
1088/92 Set of 5		9·50	9·00

Nos. 1088/92 were printed in separate sheets of 20 with *se-tenant* half stamp-size labels printed with information about how the tree depicted was used.

(Litho BDT)

2006 (21 Apr). 80th Birthday of Queen Elizabeth II. Horiz designs as T **274a** of Bahamas. Multicoloured. W w **14** (sideways). P. 14.
1093	15c. Princess Elizabeth as young child	1·00	50
1094	40c. Queen Elizabeth in uniform, c. 1952	1·75	90
1095	$1 Wearing tiara	2·50	3·00
1096	$2 Wearing white blouse	4·50	5·50
1093/6 Set of 4		8·75	9·00
MS1097 144×75 mm. As Nos. 1094/5, but without white borders		8·00	8·50

(Litho BDT)

2006 (18 July). Cayman's Aquatic Treasures. T **229** and similar multicoloured designs.

*(a) PVA gum. W w **14** (sideways). P 14*
1098	25c. Type **229**	1·25	1·10
1099	25c. Grey angelfish	1·25	1·10

95

CAYMAN ISLANDS

1100	60c. Queen angelfish (vert)	2·25	2·00
1101	75c. Diamond blenny	2·50	2·75
1102	$1 Spotted drum (juvenile) (vert)	3·50	4·00
1098/102 Set of 5		9·75	10·00
MS1103 145×95 mm. As Nos. 1098/102		9·50	10·00

(b) Size 29×24 mm. Self-adhesive. P 10×9½

1104	25c. As Type **229**	1·50	2·00
	a. Booklet pane. No. 1104×10	13·00	
1105	25c. As No. 1099	1·50	2·00
	a. Booklet pane. No. 1105×10	13·00	
1106	60c. As No. 1100	2·00	2·75
	a. Booklet pane. No. 1106×10	18·00	
1107	75c. As No. 1101	2·25	3·00
	a. Booklet pane. No. 1107×10	20·00	

Stamps from **MS**1103 do not have white borders.
Nos. 1104/7 were only issued in separate $2·50, $6 and $7·50 booklets, Nos. SB11/14.

230 Bananaquit    **231** "Faith" and the Three Magi

(Des A. Robinson. Litho Cartor)

2006 (9 Oct). Birds. T **230** and similar horiz designs. Multicoloured. W w **14** (sideways). P 13½.

1108	25c. Type **230**	1·00	50
1109	50c. Vitelline warbler	2·00	1·25
1110	75c. Cuban Amazon ("Grand Cayman Parrot")	2·50	1·75
1111	80c. White-bellied dove ("Caribbean Dove")	2·50	1·75
1112	$1 Caribbean elaenia	3·25	2·25
1113	$1·50 Great red-bellied woodpecker ("West Indian Woodpecker")	5·00	5·00
1114	$1·60 Thick-billed vireo	5·00	5·00
1115	$2 Common flicker ("Northern Flicker")	6·00	6·00
1116	$4 Cuban bullfinch	10·00	11·00
1117	$5 Stripe-headed tanager ("Western spindalis")	11·00	12·00
1118	$10 Loggerhead kingbird	19·00	22·00
1119	$20 Red-legged thrush	32·00	40·00
1108/19 Set of 12		90·00	95·00

(Des Jennifer Toombs. Litho Lowe-Martin, Canada)

2006 (26 Oct). Christmas. T **231** and similar horiz designs. Multicoloured. W w **14** (sideways). P 12½×13.

1120	25c. Type **231**	1·25	45
1121	75c. "Hope" and prophet speaking of the Messiah	2·75	2·00
1122	80c. "Joy" and angel	2·75	2·00
1123	$1 "Love" and Mary with baby Jesus	3·25	4·00
1120/3 Set of 4		9·00	7·75

232 Bananaquit    **233** Brac Reef Dock

(Des Nick Shewring. Litho BDT)

2007 (9 Jan). Birds (2nd series). Designs as Nos. 1108, and 1110/11 but each 30×25 mm with redrawn inscriptions as T **232**. Self-adhesive. P 10.

1124	25c. Type **232**	1·50	2·50
	a. Booklet pane. No. 1124×10	13·00	
1125	75c. Cuban amazon ("GRAND CAYMAN PARROT")	2·50	3·50
	a. Booklet pane. No. 1125×10	22·00	
1126	80c. White-bellied dove ("CARIBBEAN DOVE")	2·50	3·50
	a. Booklet pane. No. 1126×10	22·00	

Nos. 1124/6 were only issued in separate $2·50, $7·50 and $8 stamp booklets, Nos. SB15/17.

(Litho BDT)

2007 (26 June). Cayman Islands Scenes. T **233** and similar multicoloured designs. W w **14** (sideways on horiz designs). P 14.

1127	20c. Type **233**	90	65
1128	25c. Waterfront, Hog Sty Bay, George Town, Grand Cayman	95	65
1129	30c. East End blowholes, Grand Cayman Island (vert)	1·10	65
1130	40c. Man lying in hammock on beach at sunset (vert)	1·25	85
1131	75c. Poinciana flowers	2·25	2·75
1132	$1 Driftwood on shore, Little Cayman Island	2·50	3·50
1127/32 Set of 6		8·00	8·00

(Des Andrew Robinson. Litho BDT)

2007 (9 July). Centenary of Scouting. Multicoloured designs as T **281** of Bahamas. W w **14** (sideways). P 14.

1133	25c. Early Wolf Cubs with their flag	85	60
1134	75c. Modern Cub Scouts after Remembrance Day Parade, 2006	2·25	2·25
1135	80c. Scouts camping	2·25	2·25
1136	$1 Drill team, Remembrance Day Parade, 2005	2·50	3·25
1133/6 Set of 4		7·00	7·50
MS1137 90×65 mm. 50c. Cayman Islands scouts in opening ceremony of 13th Caribbean Scout Jamboree, Jamaica, 2006 (vert); $1·50 Lord Baden-Powell (vert)		4·00	5·00

(Litho BDT)

2007 (12 Sept). Diamond Wedding of Queen Elizabeth II and Duke of Edinburgh. Vert designs as T **280** of Bahamas. Multicoloured. W w **14**. P 14.

1138	50c. Princess Elizabeth alighting from car and Lt. Philip Mountbatten, c. 1949	1·60	1·25
1139	75c. Princess Elizabeth wearing tiara and wedding veil, 1949	2·25	2·25
1140	80c. Queen Elizabeth the Queen Mother and Princesses Elizabeth and Margaret	2·25	2·25
1141	$1 Princess Elizabeth and Duke of Edinburgh in procession down Westminster Abbey aisle on wedding day, 1949	2·50	3·25
1138/41 Set of 4		7·75	8·00
MS1142 125×85 mm. $2 Princess Elizabeth and Lt. Philip Mountbatten, c. 1949 (42×56 mm). Wmk sideways		6·50	6·50

234 Nativity    **235** Beach at Sunset and Turtles ("Hello")

(Litho BDT)

2007 (22 Oct). Christmas. T **234** and similar vert designs showing stained glass windows. Multicoloured. W w **14** (sideways). P 15×14.

1143	25c. Type **234**	75	50
1144	50c. Jesus Christ	1·40	1·00
1145	75c. Jesus with disciples	1·75	1·40
1146	80c. Peace dove	1·75	1·75
1147	$1 The Cross	2·25	2·50
1148	$1·50 Shepherd with lamb	3·25	5·00
1143/8 Set of 6		10·00	11·00

(Des Andrew Robinson. Litho BDT)

2008 (5 Feb). Greetings Stamps. T **235** and similar horiz designs. Multicoloured.

*(a) PVA gum. W w**14** (sideways). P 14*

1149	20c. Type **235**	60	65
	a. Sheetlet. Nos. 1149/54	3·25	3·50
1150	20c. Crossed fingers and horseshoes ("Good Luck")	60	65
1151	20c. Balloons and stars ("Congratulations")	60	65
1152	20c. Invitation and fireworks ("You're Invited")	60	65
1153	20c. Fountain pen and flowers ("Best Wishes")	60	65
1154	20c. Cupid and hearts ("Love")	60	65
1155	25c. Type **235**	60	65
	a. Sheetlet. Nos. 1155/60	3·25	3·50
1156	25c. As No. 1150	60	65
1157	25c. As No. 1151	60	65
1158	25c. As No. 1152	60	65
1159	25c. As No. 1153	60	65
1160	25c. As No. 1154	60	65
1161	50c. Type **235**	1·00	1·25
	a. Sheetlet. Nos. 1161/6	5·50	6·50
1162	50c. As No. 1150	1·00	1·25

1163	50c. As No. 1151		1·00	1·25
1164	50c. As No. 1152		1·00	1·25
1165	50c. As No. 1153		1·00	1·25
1166	50c. As No. 1154		1·00	1·25
1167	75c. Type **235**		1·50	1·60
	a. Sheetlet. Nos. 1167/72		8·00	8·50
1168	75c. As No. 1150		1·50	1·60
1169	75c. As No. 1151		1·50	1·60
1170	75c. As No. 1152		1·50	1·60
1171	75c. As No. 1153		1·50	1·60
1172	75c. As No. 1154		1·50	1·60
1173	80c. Type **235**		1·60	1·75
	a. Sheetlet. Nos. 1173/8		8·50	9·50
1174	80c. As No. 1150		1·60	1·75
1175	80c. As No. 1151		1·60	1·75
1176	80c. As No. 1152		1·60	1·75
1177	80c. As No. 1153		1·60	1·75
1178	80c. As No. 1154		1·60	1·75
1179	$1 Type **235**		1·75	1·90
	a. Sheetlet. Nos. 1179/84		9·50	10·50
1180	$1 As No. 1150		1·75	1·90
1181	$1 As No. 1151		1·75	1·90
1182	$1 As No. 1152		1·75	1·90
1183	$1 As No. 1153		1·75	1·90
1184	$1 As No. 1154		1·75	1·90
1149/84 Set of 36			35·00	38·00

(b) Self-adhesive. Size 30×25 mm. P 10×9½

1185	20c. As Type **235**		55	75
	a. Booklet pane. No. 1185×10		5·00	
1186	25c. As No. 1151		55	75
	a. Booklet pane. No. 1186×10		5·00	
1187	25c. As No. 1152		55	75
	a. Booklet pane. No. 1187×10		5·00	
	b. Champagne and glasses ("You're invited")			
1188	25c. As No. 1154		55	75
	a. Booklet pane. No. 1188×10		5·00	

Nos. 1149/54, 1155/60, 1161/6, 1167/72, 1173/8 and 1179/84 were each printed together, *se-tenant*, in sheetlets of six stamps.

Nos. 1185/8 were only issued in separate $2 or $2.50 booklets, Nos. SB18/21.

The 25c. "You're invited" self-adhesive stamp (No. 1187) originally featured a design showing a "Popping Champagne cork and glasses". This design was rejected and replaced by the "Invitation and fireworks" design. However, examples of the original design were included with those supplies to the Islands and released in error.

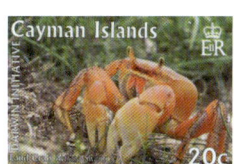

236 Land Crab

(Litho Enschedé)

2008 (9 July). Darwin Initiative. Indigenous Creatures. T **236** and similar multicoloured designs. W w **14** (sideways). P 14.

1189	20c. Type **236**		1·00	75
1190	25c. Dragonfly ("Needlecase")		1·00	75
1191	75c. Little Cayman green anole		2·75	3·00
1192	80c. Cayman Brac ground boa		2·75	3·00
1193	$1 White-shouldered bat		3·25	4·00
1189/93 Set of 5			9·75	10·50
MS1194 110×78 mm. $2 Caribbean reef squid (*vert*). Wmk upright			5·50	6·00

(Des Richard Allen. Litho BDT)

2008 (8 Aug). Olympic Games, Beijing. Square designs as T **287** of Bahamas. Multicoloured. W w **14** (sideways). P 13½.

1195	20c. Swimming – backstroke		1·00	75
1196	25c. Swimming – butterfly		1·00	75
1197	50c. Running		2·00	1·75
1198	75c. Hurdling		3·00	3·50
1195/8 Set of 4			6·25	6·00

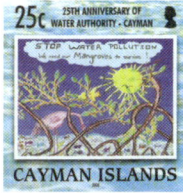

237 "Mangroves and Water" (Shenoweth Holmes)

238 Father Christmas on board Sailing Ship

(Litho Cartor)

2008 (16 Oct). 25th Anniv of Water Authority – Cayman. T **237** and similar square designs showing children's paintings from calendar art competition "I Love My Water". W w **14** (sideways). P 13.

1199	25c. Type **237**		1·00	60
1200	75c. "Rain Drop" (Kristi Ebanks)		2·75	1·90
1201	$2 "Splash of Life" (Jerray Brown)		7·00	8·50
1199/201 Set of 3			9·75	10·00

(Des Derek Miller. Litho BDT)

2008 (12 Nov). Christmas. Unique Transportation. T **238** and similar horiz designs. Multicoloured. W w **14** (sideways). P 14.

1202	25c. Type **238**		1·00	60
1203	75c. Father Christmas with horse and carriage laden with presents		2·75	2·25
1204	80c. Father Christmas in helicopter dropping presents by parachute		2·75	2·25
1205	$1 Father Christmas with racing car		3·25	4·00
1202/5 Set of 4			8·75	8·00

239 Silver Thatch Palm

240 Hammock at Sunset

(Des Nick Shewring. Litho BDT)

2009 (28 Jan). Silver Thatch Palm. T **239** and similar horiz designs. Multicoloured. W w **18** (sideways). P 13½.

1206	25c. Type **239**		1·00	1·25
	a. Horiz strip of 5. Nos. 1206/10		4·50	5·50
1207	25c. Rope strands		1·00	1·25
1208	25c. Twisting the three strands into rope ("Cobbing rope")		1·00	1·25
1209	25c. Basketware ("Thatch products")		1·00	1·25
1210	25c. Traditional home with silver thatch roof		1·00	1·25
1206/10 Set of 5			4·50	5·50

Nos. 1206/10 were printed together, *se-tenant*, in horizontal strips of five stamps, each strip forming a composite design, in sheets of 50 (2 panes of 25).

(Litho Lowe-Martin)

2009 (9 Apr). Cayman Islands Scenes (2nd series). T **240** and similar multicoloured designs.

*(a) PVA gum. W w **18** (inverted on 75c., $1, sideways on others). P 13 (**MS**1217) or 12½ (others)*

1211	20c. Type **240**		80	55
1212	25c. Cayman Islands houses		85	70
1213	75c. Palm trees on beach (*vert*)		2·50	2·25
1214	80c. Cruise ships off Cayman Islands		2·50	2·25
1215	$1 Street with signpost (*vert*)		3·00	3·25
1216	$1.50 Inland landscape of rocks and scrub		4·25	5·50
1211/16 Set of 6			12·50	13·00
MS1217 80×65 mm. $2 Iguana in road, Little Cayman. Wmk sideways			6·00	7·00

(b) Self-adhesive. Size 30×25 mm. P 10×9½

1218	20c. As Type **240**		80	1·25
	a. Booklet pane. No. 1218×10		7·00	
1219	25c. As No. 1212		80	1·25
	a. Booklet pane. No. 1219×10		7·00	

Nos. 1218/19 were only issued in separate $2 or $2.50 booklets, Nos. SB22/3.

(Litho Lowe-Martin)

2009 (20 July). International Year of Astronomy. 40th Anniv of First Moon Landing. Square designs as T **214** of Bermuda. Multicoloured. W w **18** (sideways). P 13.

1220	20c. Mars Rover, 2004		80	55
1221	25c. Space Transportation System 71 launch, 1995		85	70
1222	75c. Hubble Telescope		2·50	2·25
1223	$1 Apollo 11, 1969		3·00	3·25
1224	$1.50 International Space Station		4·50	6·00
1220/4 Set of 5			10·50	11·50
MS1225 100×80 mm. $2 "Hadley Rille" (astronaut Jim Irwin and Lunar Rover) (Alan Bean) (39×59 *mm*). Wmk upright			6·00	7·00

Nos. 1220/4 were printed in separate sheetlets of six stamps with enlarged illustrated margins.

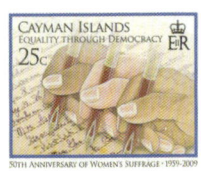

CAYMAN ISLANDS

241 Women's Hands signing Petition

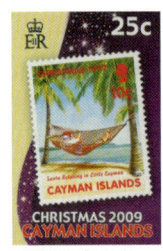

242 10c. Santa in Hammock Stamp

244a Duke and Duchess of Cambridge kissing on Buckingham Palace Balcony

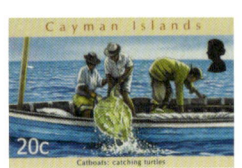

245 Catching Turtles

(Litho BDT)

2009 (23 Sept). 'Equality through Democracy'. 50th Anniv of the Constitution and Women's Suffrage. T **241** and similar horiz designs. Multicoloured. W w **18** (sideways). P 13½.
1226	25c. Type **241**	1·00	1·00
1227	25c. Town Hall, George Town	1·00	1·00
1228	50c. Woman casting vote	1·75	1·75
1226/8 Set of 3		3·25	3·25
MS1229 135×86 mm. Nos. 1226/8		3·25	3·50

(Litho Enschedé)

2009 (22 Oct). Christmas. T **242** and similar vert designs showing 1997 Christmas stamps. Multicoloured. P 14.
1230	25c. Type **242**	75	40
1231	75c. 30c. Santa with children on the Bluff stamp	2·00	2·00
1232	80c. 40c. Santa playing golf	2·25	2·25
1233	$1 $1 Santa scuba diving stamp	3·00	3·50
1230/3 Set of 4		7·25	7·25

243 Hawk-wing Conch (*Strombus raninus*)

244 Brownie, Rainbow and Guide Uniforms

(Des Andrew Robinson. Litho B.D.T)

2010 (30 June). Shells. T **243** and similar multicoloured designs. W w **18** (sideways) (Nos. 1234/9) or inverted (**MS**1240).

(a) Ordinary gum. P 13½
1234	20c. Type **243**	75	50
1235	25c. Ornate scallop (*Chlamys ornata*)	80	50
1236	60c. Chestnut turban (*Turbo castanea*)	2·00	1·50
1237	75c. Beautiful mitre (*Vexillum pulchellum*)	2·25	2·25
1238	80c. Four-toothed nerite (*Nerita versicolor gmelin*)	2·50	2·50
1239	$1.60 White-spotted marginella (*Marginella guttata*)	5·00	6·00
1234/40 Set of 6		12·00	12·00
MS1240 94×64 mm. $3 Queen conch (*Strombus gigas*) Wmk inverted		9·00	10·00

(b) Self-adhesive. As Nos. 1235 and 1237 but size 30×25 mm with redrawn inscriptions and white borders. Die-cut perf 9½
1241	25c. As No. 1235	1·00	1·00
	a. Booklet pane. No. 1241×10	9·00	
1242	75c. As No. 1237	2·25	2·50
	a. Booklet pane. No. 1242×10	20·00	

Nos. 1241/2 were only issued in separate $2.50 or $7.50 booklets, Nos. SB24/5.

(Des Andrew Robinson. Litho Lowe-Martin Group)

2010 (17 Dec). Centenary of Girlguiding. T **244** and similar horiz designs. Multicoloured. W w **18** (sideways). P 12½.
1243	20c. Type **244**	80	60
1244	25c. Camping	90	60
1245	50c. Parade of guides, 1930s	1·75	1·50
1246	80c. Badges of rainbows, brownies and guides	3·25	4·00
1243/6 Set of 4		6·00	6·00

(Litho Enschedé)

2011 (4 Aug). Royal Wedding. T **244a** and similar multicoloured designs. W w **18** (sideways on horiz designs). P 14.
1247	25c. Type **244a**	1·00	50
1248	75c. Duke and Duchess of Cambridge waving from State Landau (*horiz*)	2·75	2·75
1249	80c. Duke and Duchess of Cambridge at Westminster Abbey after wedding ceremony	3·00	3·00
1250	$2 Prince William, Miss Catherine Middleton and her father (*horiz*)	6·50	7·50
1247/50 Set of 4		12·00	12·00

(Des Nick Shewring. Litho BDT)

2011 (31 Aug). Catboats. T **245** and similar horiz designs. Multicoloured.

*(a) Ordinary paper. W w **18** (sideways). P 14*
1251	20c. Type **245**	80	50
1252	25c. Building catboat	90	80
1253	25c. Sailing catboat around Cayman Brac's Bluff	90	80
1254	50c. Catboats racing regatta style	1·75	1·25
1255	$1.60 Unloading cargo from catboats	4·50	5·00
1256	$2 Sewing the sail	5·50	6·50
1251/6 Set of 6		13·00	13·50

(b) Self-adhesive. Size 30×25 mm. Die-cut perf 9½
1257	25c. As No. 1252	90	1·00
	a. Booklet pane. No. 1257×10	8·00	

No. 1257 was only issued in $2.50 booklets, No. SB26.

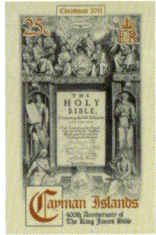

246 King James Bible

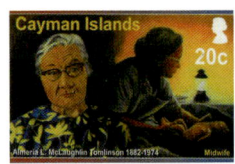

247 Almeria L. McLaughlin Tomlinson (1882–1974) (midwife)

(Des Derek Miller. Litho Lowe-Martin Group)

2011 (8 Nov). Christmas. 400th Anniv of the King James Bible. T **246** and similar vert designs. Multicoloured. W w **18** (inverted). P 12½.
1258	25c. Type **246**	80	35
1259	75c. King James I of Scotland (1566–1625) and VI of England (1603–25)	2·00	1·40
1260	80c. William Tyndale (translator)	2·25	2·00
1261	$1 Printing the King James Bible	2·75	2·75
1262	$1.60 Translators in the Jerusalem Chamber of Westminster Abbey for final editing	5·00	6·00
1258/62 Set of 5		11·50	11·00

(Des Ross Watton. Litho Cartor)

2011 (11 Nov). Pioneers. T **247** and similar horiz designs. Multicoloured. W w **18** (sideways). P 13×13½.
1263	20c. Type **247**	1·00	80
	a. Booklet pane. No. 1263×6 with margins all round	5·50	
1264	25c. Captain Rayal B. Bodden (1885–1976) (shipwright and builder)	1·00	80
	a. Booklet pane. No. 1264×6 with margins all round	5·50	

98

CAYMAN ISLANDS

1265	75c. Irksie Leila Yates (1899–1996) (maternity nurse)	2·00	2·00
	a. Booklet pane. No. 1265×6 with margins all round	11·00	
1266	$1.50 Major Joseph R. Walter (1890–1965) (Inspector of Police)	5·00	6·00
	a. Booklet pane. No. 1266×6 with margins all round	25·00	
1263/6	Set of 4	8·00	8·75

248 Queen Elizabeth II 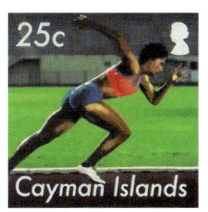   **249** Athlete

(Des Andrew Robinson. Litho BDT)

2012 (12 June). Diamond Jubilee. T **248** and similar horiz designs. Multicoloured.

(a) Ordinary paper. W w 18 (sideways). P 14

1267	25c. Type **248**	1·00	45
1268	80c. Queen Elizabeth II wearing pink hat, c. 1970	2·50	2·00
1269	$1 Queen Elizabeth II on walkabout through crowd, c. 2000	2·75	2·75
1270	$1.50 Coronation of Queen Elizabeth II, 1953	4·75	5·50
1267/70	Set of 4	10·00	9·75

(b) Self-adhesive. Size 30×25 mm. Die-cut perf 9½

1271	25c. As Type **248**	1·00	1·00
	a. Booklet pane. No. 1271×10	9·00	

No. 1271 is as Type **248** but with the face value at bottom right and the inscription 'Diamond Jubilee 1952 - 2012' at centre right.
No. 1271 was issued in $2.50 stamp booklets, No. SB31.

(Des Andrew Robinson. Litho BDT)

2012 (2 Aug). Olympic Games, London. T **249** and similar horiz designs. Multicoloured. W w **18** (sideways). P 13.

1272	25c. Type **249**	80	45
1273	50c. Hurdler	1·75	1·00
1274	75c. Swimmer (butterfly)	2·25	2·00
1275	80c. Two athletes sprinting at finish	2·50	2·25
1276	$1.60 Swimming (front crawl)	4·75	6·00
1272/6	Set of 5	11·00	10·50

250 Patrol Boats

(Des Nick Shewring. Litho BDT)

2012 (30 Aug). Emergency Services. T **250** and similar horiz designs. Multicoloured.

(a) Ordinary gum. W w 18 (sideways). P 14

1277	20c. Type **250**	1·25	65
1278	25c. Ambulance Service	1·25	65
1279	75c. Fire Department	3·00	2·00
1280	$1.50 9-1-1 Public Safety Communications	4·50	5·00
1281	$2 Police Helicopter	6·50	7·50
1277/81	Set of 5	14·50	14·00

(b) Self-adhesive. Size 30×25 mm. Die-cut perf 9½

1282	25c. As No. 1278	1·25	1·25
	a. Booklet pane. No. 1282×10	11·00	
1283	75c. As No. 1279	2·75	3·25
	a. Booklet pane. No. 1283×10	23·00	

No. 1278 has the inscription 'Ambulance Service' along the right-hand edge of the stamp reading downwards, but No. 1282 has it reading upwards. No. 1283 has the inscription 'Fire Department' along the left-hand edge of the stamp starting at the bottom left corner instead of above the face value.
Nos. 1282/3 come from $2.50 or $7.50 booklets, Nos. SB32/3.

251 Stoplight Parrotfish (*Sparisoma viride*)

(Des Andrew Robinson. Litho BDT)

2012 (9 Oct). Marine Life. T **251** and similar horiz designs. Multicoloured.

(a) Ordinary paper. W w 18 (sideways). P 14

1284	25c. Type **251**	1·00	50
1285	50c. Green Sea Turtle (*Chelonia mydas*)	1·75	80
1286	75c. Common Sea Fan (*Gorgonia ventalina*) and Yellow Tube Sponge (*Aplysina fistularis*)	2·25	1·00
1287	80c. Upside-down Jellyfish (*Cassiopea xamachana*)	2·25	1·25
1288	$1 Yellowtail Damselfish (*Microspathodon chrysurus*)	2·50	2·00
1289	$1.50 Spotted Trunkfish (*Lactophrys bicaudalis*)	3·50	3·50
1290	$1.60 Caribbean Spiny Lobster (*Panulirus argus*)	3·75	3·75
1291	$2 Giant Barrel Sponge (*Xestospongia muta*)	4·50	4·50
1292	$4 Caribbean Reef Shark (*Carcharhinus perezii*)	9·00	10·00
1293	$5 Great Barracuda (*Sphyraena barracuda*)	10·00	11·00
1294	$10 Southern Stingray (*Dasyatis americana*)	20·00	21·00
1295	$20 West Indian Spider Crab (*Mithrax spinosissimus*)	38·00	42·00
1284/95	Set of 12	90·00	90·00
MS1296	No. 1288×4	10·00	10·00

(b) Self-adhesive. Size 30×25 mm. Die-cut perf 14×15

1297	25c. As Type **251**	1·00	1·00
	a. Booklet pane. No. 1297×10	9·00	
1298	75c. As No. 1286	2·25	2·50
	a. Booklet pane. No. 1298×10	19·00	
1299	80c. As No. 1287	2·25	2·50
	a. Booklet pane. No. 1299×10	19·00	

Nos. 1297/9 were issued in $2.50, $7.50 or $8 booklets, Nos. SB34/6.

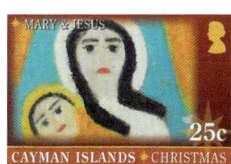

252 Mary and Jesus

(Litho BDT)

2012 (6 Nov). Christmas. Paintings by Gladwyn K. Bush (Miss Lassie). T **252** and similar horiz designs. Multicoloured. P 14.

1300	25c. Type **252**	1·00	40
1301	75c. His Name is Jesus	2·25	1·40
1302	80c. Every Knee shall Bow	2·25	1·75
1303	$1 Nativity	2·50	3·00
1300/3	Set of 4	7·25	6·00

Nos. 1300/03 were each printed in sheets of 16 (2 panes 2×8), each stamp *se-tenant* with a label showing a verse from the Bible.

STAMP BOOKLETS

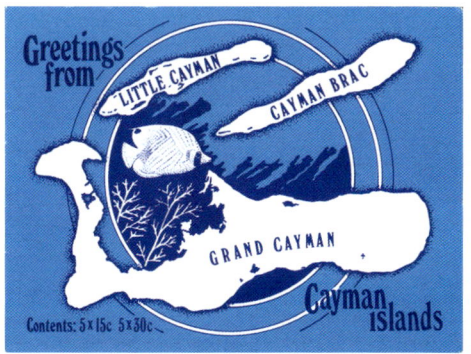

B **1**

CAYMAN ISLANDS

1993 (30 Sept). Tourism. Deep ultramarine and bright greenish blue cover, 104×76 mm, as Type B **1**. Pane attached by selvedge.
SB1 $2.25 booklet containing pane of five 15c. and five 30c. (No. 755b)... 17·00

B **2**

1994 (12 Oct). Bicentenary of Wreck of Ten Sail off Grand Cayman. Multicoloured covers, 120×64 mm, as Type B **2**. Stamps attached by selvedge.
SB2 $1 booklet containing block of ten 10c. stamps (No. 788) .... 5·00
SB3 $1.50 booklet containing block of ten 15c. stamps (No. 790) .... 6·50
SB4 $2 booklet containing block of ten 20c. stamps (No. 791) .... 7·50

B **3**

1996 (26 Sept). National Identity. Multicoloured covers, 113×65 mm, as Type B **3** illustrating stamp design enclosed. Stamps attached by selvedge.
SB5 $1 booklet containing block of ten 10c. stamps (No. 824) .... 5·00
SB6 $3 booklet containing block of ten 30c. stamps (No. 827) .... 9·00
SB7 $4 booklet containing block of ten 40c. stamps (No. 828) .... 10·00

B **4** Mexican Fritillary

2005 (21 Sept). Butterflies. Multicoloured covers, 103×60 mm, as Type B **4**. Self-adhesive.
SB8 $1.20 booklet containing pane of six 210c. stamps (No. 1081a) (Type B **4**)................................ 8·00
SB9 $1.50 booklet containing pane of ten 15c. stamps (No. 1080a) (cover showing The Queen butterfly) ...... 9·00
SB10 $3 booklet containing block of ten 30c. stamps (No. 1082a) (cover showing Cayman Crescent Spot)... 10·00

B **5** Hawksbill Turtle

2006 (18 July). Cayman's Aquatic Treasures. Multicoloured covers, 104×60 mm, as Type B **5**. Self-adhesive.
SB11 $2.50 booklet containing pane of ten 25c. (No. 1104a) (Type B **5**) .... 13·00
SB12 $2.50 booklet containing pane of ten 25c. (No. 1105a) (cover showing grey angelfish)................ 13·00
SB13 $6 booklet containing pane of ten 60c. (No. 1106a) (cover showing queen angelfish)............... 18·00
SB14 $7.50 booklet containing pane of ten 75c. (No. 1107a) (cover showing diamond blenny)............. 20·00

B **6** Bananaquit

2007 (9 Jan). Birds. Multicoloured covers, 103×60 mm, as Type B **6**. Self-adhesive.
SB15 $2.50 booklet containing pane of ten 25c. (No. 1124a) (Type B **6**) .... 13·00
SB16 $7.50 booklet containing pane of ten 75c. (No. 1125a) (cover showing Cuban amazon).................. 22·00
SB17 $8 booklet containing pane of ten 80c. (No. 1126a) (cover showing white-bellied dove)........ 22·00

B **7** Beach at Sunset and Turtles ("Hello")

2008 (5 Feb). Greetings Stamps. Multicoloured covers, 103×60 mm, as Type B **7**. Self-adhesive.
SB18 $2 booklet containing pane of ten 20c. (No. 1185a) (Type B **7**) .... 5·00
SB19 $2.50 booklet containing pane of ten 25c. (No. 1186a) ("Congratulations" cover) .... 5·00
SB20 $2.50 booklet containing pane of ten 25c. (No. 1187a) ("You're invited" cover) .... 5·00
SB21 $2.50 booklet containing pane of ten 25c. (No. 1188a) ("Love" cover) .... 5·00

CAYMAN ISLANDS

B **8** Hammock at Sunset

2009 (9 Apr). Cayman Islands Scenes. Multicoloured covers, 103×61 mm, as Type B **8**. Self-adhesive.
SB22 $2 booklet containing pane of ten 20c. (No. 1218a) (Type B **8**) .... 7·00
SB23 $2.50 booklet containing pane of ten 25c. (No. 1219a) (cover showing palm tree and pier) .... 7·00

B **9** Ornate Scallop

2010 (30 Jun). Shells. Multicoloured covers, 103×60 mm, as Type B **9**. Self-adhesive.
SB24 $2.50 booklet containing pane of ten 25c. (No. 1241a) .... 9·00
SB25 $7.50 booklet containing pane of ten 75c. (No. 1242a) (cover showing beautiful mitre) .... 20·00

B **10** Building Catboat

2011 (31 Aug). Catboats. Multicoloured cover, 103×60 mm, as Type B **10**. Self-adhesive.
SB26 $2.50 booklet containing pane of ten 25c. (No. 1257a) .... 8·00

B **11** Union Jack and Arms of Cayman Islands

2011 (11 Nov). Pioneers. Multicoloured covers, 176×92 mm, as Type B **11**. Booklet contains text and illustrations on interleaving pages. Stitched.
SB27 $1.20 booklet containing pane of six 20c. (No. 1263a) . 5·50

SB28 $1.50 booklet containing pane of six 25c. (No. 1264a) . 5·50
SB29 $4.50 booklet containing pane of six 75c. (No. 1265a) . 11·00
SB30 $9 booklet containing pane of six $1.50 (No. 1266a) .... 25·00

B **12** Queen Elizabeth II

2012 (12 Jun). Diamond Jubilee. Multicoloured cover, 104×60 mm, as Type B **12**. Self-adhesive.
SB31 $2.50 booklet containing pane of ten 25c. (No. 1271a)   9·00

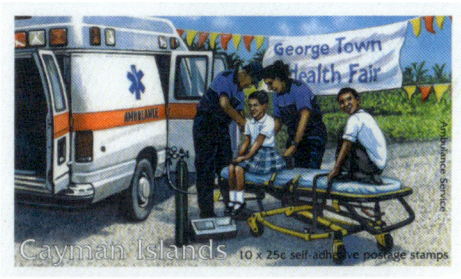

B **13** Ambulance Service

2012 (30 Aug). Emergency Services. Multicoloured covers, 104×61 mm, as Type B **13**. Self-adhesive.
SB32 $2.50 booklet containing pane of ten 25c. (No. 1282a) (Type B **13**) .... 11·00
SB33 $7.50 booklet containing pane of ten 75c. (No. 1283a) (cover showing Fire Department) .... 23·00

B **14** Stoplight Parrotfish (*Sparisoma viride*)

2012 (9 Oct). Marine Life. Multicoloured covers, 103×61 mm, as Type B **14**. Self-adhesive.
SB34 $2.50 booklet containing pane of ten 25c. (No. 1297a) (Type B **14**) .... 9·00
SB35 $7.50 booklet containing pane of ten 75c. (No. 1298a) (cover showing Common Sea Fan and Yellow Tube Sponge) .... 19·00
SB36 $8 booklet containing pane of ten 80c. (No. 1299a) (cover showing Upside-down Jellyfish) .... 19·00

Jamaica

Records show that the first local Postmaster for Jamaica on a regular basis was appointed as early as 1671, although a reasonably organised service did not evolve until 1687–8. In the early years of the 18th century overseas mail was carried by the British packets, but between 1704 and 1711 this service was run on a commercial basis by Edmund Dummer. Following the collapse of the Dummer scheme Jamaica was virtually without a Post Office until 1720 and it was not until 1755 that overseas mail was again carried by British packets.

Stamps of Great Britain were used in Jamaica from 8 May 1858, initially on overseas mail only, but their use was extended to mail sent to Jamaican addresses from 1 February 1859. The island assumed responsibility for the postal service on 1 August 1860 and the use of Great Britain stamps then ceased.

KINGSTON

Z 1

Stamps of GREAT BRITAIN cancelled "A 01" as Type Z **1**.

1858–60.

Z1	1d. rose-red (1857), *perf 16*	£800
Z2	1d. rose-red (1857), *perf 14*	£100
Z4	4d. rose-carmine *or* rose (1857)	80·00
Z5	6d. lilac (1856)	80·00
Z6	1s. green (1856)	£400

Z 2

Stamps of GREAT BRITAIN cancelled "A 01" as Type Z **2**.

1859–60.

Z7	1d. rose-red (1857), *perf 14*	£375
Z9	4d. rose-carmine *or* rose (1857)	85·00
Z10	6d. lilac (1856)	85·00
Z11	1s. green (1856)	£800

Z 3

Stamps of GREAT BRITAIN cancelled "A 01" as Type Z **3**.

1859–60.

Z12	1d. rose-red (1857), *perf 14*	£550
Z14	4d. rose-carmine *or* rose (1857)	£375
	a. Thick *glazed* paper	£650
Z15	6d. lilac (1856)	£375
Z16	1s. green (1856)	

Cancellation "A 01" was later used by the London, Foreign Branch Office.

OTHER JAMAICA POST OFFICES

British stamps were issued to several District post offices between 8 May 1858 and 1 March 1859 (i.e. before the Obliterators A 27—A 78 were issued). These can only be distinguished (off the cover) when they have the Town's date-stamp on them. They are worth about three times the price of those with an obliteration number.

Stamps of GREAT BRITAIN cancelled "A 27" to "A 78" as Type Z **1**.

1859–60.

"A 27". ALEXANDRIA

Z17	1d. rose-red (1857), *perf 14*	£1000
Z17a	2d. blue (1855) Large Crown, *perf 14* (Plate 6)	£1800
Z18	4d. rose (1857)	£400
Z19	6d. lilac (1856)	£750

"A 28". ANNOTTO BAY

Z20	1d. rose-red (1857), *perf 14*	£550
Z21	4d. rose (1857)	£225
Z22	6d. lilac (1856)	£450

"A 29". BATH

Z23	1d. rose-red (1857), *perf 14*	£350
Z24	4d. rose (1857)	£225
Z25	6d. lilac (1856)	£650

"A 30". BLACK RIVER

Z26	1d. rose-red (1857), *perf 14*	£350
Z27	4d. rose (1857)	£170
Z28	6d. lilac (1856)	£300

"A 31". BROWN'S TOWN

Z29	1d. rose-red (1857), *perf 14*	£450
Z30	4d. rose (1857)	£400
Z31	6d. lilac (1856)	£400

"A 32". BUFF BAY

Z32	1d. rose-red (1857), *perf 14*	£400
Z33	4d. rose (1857)	£325
Z34	6d. lilac (1856)	£300

"A 33". CHAPELTON

Z35	1d. rose-red (1857), *perf 14*	£400
Z36	4d. rose (1857)	£275
Z37	6d. lilac (1856)	£375

"A 34". CLAREMONT

Z38	1d. rose-red (1857), *perf 14*	£650
Z39	4d. rose (1857)	£325
Z40	6d. lilac (1856)	£375

"A 35". CLARENDON

Z41	1d. rose-red (1857), *perf 14*	£475
Z42	4d. rose (1857)	£250
Z43	6d. lilac (1856)	£400

"A 36". DRY HARBOUR

Z44	1d. rose-red (1857), *perf 14*	£750
Z45	4d. rose (1857)	£500
Z46	6d. lilac (1856)	£450

"A 37". DUNCANS

Z47	1d. rose-red (1857), *perf 14*	£800
Z48	4d. rose (1857)	£650
Z49	6d. lilac (1856)	£475

"A 38". EWARTON

A 38 was allocated to EWARTON but this office was closed towards the end of 1858 before the postmark arrived. A 38 was re-issued to Falmouth in 1862.

"A 39". FALMOUTH

Z53	1d. rose-red (1857), *perf 14*	£250
Z54	4d. rose (1857)	£140
Z55	6d. lilac (1856)	£150
Z56	1s. green (1856)	£1400

"A 40". FLINT RIVER

Z57	1d. rose-red (1857), *perf 14*	£425
Z58	4d. rose (1857)	£300
Z59	6d. lilac (1856)	£350
Z60	1s. green (1856)	£1400

"A 41". GAYLE

Z61	1d. rose-red (1857), *perf 14*	£750
Z62	4d. rose (1857)	£250
Z63	6d. lilac (1856)	£325
Z64	1s. green (1856)	£900

"A 42". GOLDEN SPRING

Z65	1d. rose-red (1857), *perf 14*	£550
Z66	4d. rose (1857)	£425
Z67	6d. lilac (1856)	£700
Z68	1s. green (1856)	£1300

"A 43". GORDON TOWN

Z69	1d. rose-red (1857), *perf 14*	
Z70	4d. rose (1857)	
Z71	6d. lilac (1856)	£800

"A 44". GOSHEN

Z72	1d. rose-red (1857), *perf 14*	£300
Z73	4d. rose (1857)	£275
Z74	6d. lilac (1856)	£150

"A 45". GRANGE HILL

Z75	1d. rose-red (1857), *perf 14*	£375
Z76	4d. rose (1857)	£130
Z77	6d. lilac (1856)	£160
Z77a	1s. green (1856)	£1300

JAMAICA

"A 46". GREEN ISLAND
Z78	1d. rose-red (1857), perf 14	£500
Z79	4d. rose (1857)	£325
Z80	6d. lilac (1856)	£450
Z81	1s. green (1856)	£1300

"A 47". HIGHGATE
Z82	1d. rose-red (1857), perf 14	£350
Z83	4d. rose (1857)	£250
Z84	6d. lilac (1856)	£425

"A 48". HOPE BAY
Z85	1d. rose-red (1857), perf 14	£750
Z86	4d. rose (1857)	£350
Z87	6d. lilac (1856)	£750

"A 49". LILLIPUT
Z88	1d. rose-red (1857), perf 14	£325
Z89	4d. rose (1857)	£350
Z90	6d. lilac (1856)	£190

"A 50". LITTLE RIVER
A 50 was allocated for use at LITTLE RIVER but this office was closed late in 1858, before the obliterator could be issued. Issued to Malvern in 1862.

"A 51". LUCEA
Z91	1d. rose-red (1857), perf 14	£475
Z92	4d. rose (1857)	£160
Z93	6d. lilac (1856)	£350

"A 52". MANCHIONEAL
Z94	1d. rose-red (1857), perf 14	£550
Z95	4d. rose (1857)	£350
Z96	6d. lilac (1856)	£600

"A 53". MANDEVILLE
Z97	1d. rose-red (1857), perf 14	£325
Z98	4d. rose (1857)	£140
Z99	6d. lilac (1856)	£300

"A 54". MAY HILL
Z100	1d. rose-red (1857), perf 14	£225
Z101	4d. rose (1857)	£200
Z102	6d. lilac (1856)	£140
Z102a	1s. green (1856)	£1800

"A 55". MILE GULLY
Z103	1d. rose-red (1857), perf 14	£450
Z104	4d. rose (1857)	£375
Z105	6d. lilac (1856)	£375

"A 56". MONEAGUE
Z106	1d. rose-red (1857), perf 14	£425
Z107	4d. rose (1857)	£400
Z108	6d. lilac (1856)	£750

"A 57". MONTEGO BAY
Z109	1d. rose-red (1857), perf 14	£350
Z110	4d. rose (1857)	£110
Z111	6d. lilac (1856)	£130
Z112	1s. green (1856)	£1200

"A 58". MONTPELIER
Z113	1d. rose-red (1857), perf 14	
Z114	4d. rose (1857)	
Z115	6d. lilac (1856)	£1200

"A 59". MORANT BAY
Z116	1d. rose-red (1857), perf 14	£600
Z117	4d. rose (1857)	£140
Z118	6d. lilac (1856)	£160

"A 60". OCHO RIOS
Z119	1d. rose-red (1857), perf 14	£1200
Z120	4d. rose (1857)	£190
Z121	6d. lilac (1856)	£400

"A 61". OLD HARBOUR
Z122	1d. rose-red (1857), perf 14	£350
Z123	4d. rose (1857)	£250
Z124	6d. lilac (1856)	£300

"A 62". PLANTAIN GARDEN RIVER
Z125	1d. rose-red (1857), perf 14	£300
Z126	4d. rose (1857)	£190
Z127	6d. lilac (1856)	£300

"A 63". PEAR TREE GROVE
No genuine specimen of A 63 has been found on a British stamp.

"A 64". PORT ANTONIO
Z131	1d. rose-red (1857), perf 14	£600
Z132	4d. rose (1857)	£400
Z133	6d. lilac (1856)	£425

"A 65". PORT MORANT
Z134	1d. rose-red (1857), perf 14	£425
Z135	4d. rose (1857)	£200
Z136	6d. lilac (1856)	£400

"A 66". PORT MARIA
Z137	1d. rose-red (1857), perf 14	£375
Z138	4d. rose (1857)	£160
Z139	6d. lilac (1856)	£425

"A 67". PORT ROYAL
Z140	1d. rose-red (1857), perf 14	£600
Z140a	2d. blue (1858) (plate 9)	£2750
Z141	4d. rose (1857)	£650
Z142	6d. lilac (1856)	£600

"A 68". PORUS
Z143	1d. rose-red (1857), perf 14	£400
Z144	4d. rose (1857)	£180
Z145	6d. lilac (1856)	£550

"A 69". RAMBLE
Z146	1d. rose-red (1857), perf 14	£350
Z147	4d. rose (1857)	£325
	a. Thick glazed paper	£600
Z149	6d. lilac (1856)	£450

"A 70". RIO BUENO
Z150	1d. rose-red (1857), perf 14	£425
Z151	4d. rose (1857)	£325
Z152	6d. lilac (1856)	£250

"A 71". RODNEY HALL
Z153	1d. rose-red (1857), perf 14	£325
Z154	4d. rose (1857)	£200
Z155	6d. lilac (1856)	£250

"A 72". ST. DAVID
Z156	1d. rose-red (1857), perf 14	£400
Z157	4d. rose (1857)	£550
Z158	6d. lilac (1856)	

"A 73". ST. ANN'S BAY
Z159	1d. rose-red (1857), perf 14	£350
Z160	4d. rose (1857)	£180
Z161	6d. lilac (1856)	£300
Z161a	1s. green (1856)	£1600

"A 74". SALT GUT
Z162	1d. rose-red (1857), perf 14	£425
Z163	4d. rose (1857)	£275
Z164	6d. lilac (1856)	£375

"A 75". SAVANNAH-LA-MAR
Z165	1d. rose-red (1857), perf 14	£190
Z166	4d. rose (1857)	£140
Z167	6d. lilac (1856)	£300
Z168	1s. green (1856)	£1200

"A 76". SPANISH TOWN
Z169	1d. rose-red (1857), perf 14	£200
Z170	4d. rose (1857)	£120
Z171	6d. lilac (1856)	£190
Z172	1s. green (1856)	£950

"A 77". STEWART TOWN
Z173	1d. rose-red (1857), perf 14	£650
Z174	4d. rose (1857)	£475
Z175	6d. lilac (1856)	£375

"A 78". VERE
Z176	1d. rose-red (1857), perf 14	£475
Z177	4d. rose (1857)	£190
Z178	6d. lilac (1856)	£140
Z179	1s. green (1856)	£1400

PRICES FOR STAMPS ON COVER
Nos. 1/6	from × 4
Nos. 7/15	from × 6
Nos. 16/26	from × 8
Nos. 27/9	from × 6
No. 30	from × 5
Nos. 31/2	from × 15
Nos. 33/6	from × 5
Nos. 37/56	from × 3
No. 57	from × 4
Nos. 58/67	from × 3
Nos. 68/77	from × 6
Nos. 78/89	from × 3
Nos. 90/103	from × 4
Nos. 104/7	from × 5
Nos. 108/17	from × 3
Nos. 118/20	from × 5

JAMAICA

PRICES FOR STAMPS ON COVER		
Nos.	121/33a	from × 4
Nos.	134/40	from × 8
Nos.	F1/9	from × 3
Nos.	O1/5	from × 3

CROWN COLONY

PRINTERS. Until 1923, all the stamps of Jamaica were typographed by De La Rue & Co, Ltd, London, *unless otherwise stated*.

The official dates of issue are given, where known, but where definite information is not available the dates are those of earliest known use, etc.

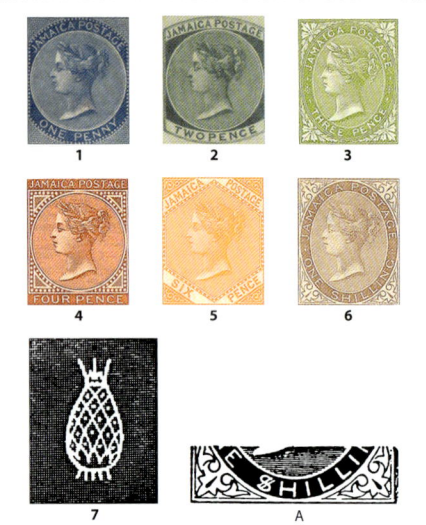

1860 (23 Nov)–**70**. W **7**. P 14.

1	1	1d. pale blue	65·00	15·00
		a. Pale greenish blue	95·00	21·00
		b. Blue	65·00	12·00
		c. Deep blue (1865)	£130	35·00
		d. Bisected (½d.) (20.11.61) (on cover)	†	£650
		w. Wmk inverted	£160	50·00
2	2	2d. rose	£200	55·00
		a. Deep rose	£160	55·00
		w. Wmk inverted	—	90·00
3	3	3d. green (10.9.63)	£140	25·00
		w. Wmk inverted	£180	48·00
4	4	4d. brown-orange	£250	50·00
		a. Red-orange	£225	22·00
		w. Wmk inverted	—	—
5	5	6d. dull lilac	£180	22·00
		a. Grey-purple	£275	35·00
		b. Deep purple (1870)	£800	55·00
		w. Wmk inverted	—	£100
6	6	1s. yellow-brown	£475	25·00
		a. Purple-brown (1862)	£550	23·00
		b. Dull brown (1868)	£190	27·00
		c. "$" for "S" in "SHILLING" (A)	£2750	£600
		w. Wmk inverted	—	75·00

The diagonal bisection of the 1d. was authorised by a P.O. notice dated 20 November 1861 to pay the ½d. rate for newspapers or book post. Examples are only of value when on original envelope or wrapper. The authority was withdrawn as from 1 December 1872. Fakes are frequently met with. Other bisections were unauthorised.

The so-called "dollar variety" of the 1s. occurs once in each sheet of stamps in all shades and in later colours, etc, on the second stamp in the second row of the left upper pane. The prices quoted above are for the dull brown shade, the prices for the other shades being proportionate to their normal value.

All values except the 3d. are known imperf, mint only.

There are two types of watermark in the 3d. and 1s., one being short and squat and the other elongated.

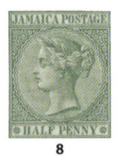

1870–83. Wmk Crown CC.

(a) P 14

7	8	½d. claret (29.10.72)	19·00	3·50
		a. Deep claret (1883)	24·00	5·50
		w. Wmk inverted	—	55·00
8	1	1d. blue (4.73)	95·00	75
		a. Deep blue	£100	1·50
		w. Wmk inverted	£190	38·00
9	2	2d. rose (4.70)	£100	70
		a. Deep rose	£110	1·00
		w. Wmk inverted	£160	38·00
10	3	3d. green (1.3.70)	£140	8·50
		w. Wmk inverted	—	90·00
11	4	4d. brown-orange (1872)	£300	12·00
		a. Red-orange (1883)	£400	6·00
		w. Wmk inverted	—	85·00
12	5	6d. mauve (10.3.71)	90·00	5·50
		w. Wmk inverted	—	65·00
13	6	1s. dull brown (*to* deep) (23.2.73)	25·00	8·50
		a. "$" for "S" in "SHILLING" (A)	£1300	£600
		w. Wmk inverted	—	90·00

(b) P 12½

14	9	2s. Venetian red (27.8.75)	45·00	27·00
		w. Wmk inverted	70·00	75·00
15	10	5s. lilac (27.8.75)	£110	£160
		w. Wmk inverted	£140	£200
7/15 Set of 9			£850	£190

The ½d., 1d., 4d., 2s. and 5s. are known imperforate.

1883–97. Wmk Crown CA. P 14.

16	8	½d. yellow-green (2.85)	8·50	1·50
		a. Green	2·50	10
		w. Wmk inverted	—	42·00
		x. Wmk reversed	—	90·00
17	1	1d. blue (1884)	£325	7·00
		w. Wmk inverted		†
18		1d. rose (*to* deep) (3.3.85)	80·00	2·00
		a. Carmine (1886)	65·00	60
		w. Wmk inverted	—	60·00
19	2	2d. rose (*to* deep) (17.3.84)	£225	4·75
		w. Wmk inverted	—	80·00
20		2d. grey (1885)	£150	8·00
		a. Slate (1886)	£100	65
		w. Wmk inverted	—	40·00
21	3	3d. sage-green (11.86)	4·00	1·25
		a. Pale olive-green	2·50	2·00
22	4	4d. red-orange* (9.3.83)	£425	22·00
		aw. Wmk inverted		
		b. Red-brown (shades) (1885)	2·00	35
		bw. Wmk inverted	95·00	40·00
23	5	6d. deep yellow (4.10.90)	35·00	8·00
		a. Orange-yellow	5·00	3·50
24	6	1s. brown (*to* deep) (3.97)	8·50	6·00
		a. "$" for "S" in "SHILLING" (A)	£800	£500
		b. Chocolate	16·00	12·00
25	9	2s. Venetian red (2.97)	30·00	28·00
26	10	5s. lilac (2.97)	65·00	90·00
16/26 Set of 11			£750	£130
16s, 18s, 20s/3s Optd "SPECIMEN" Set of 6			£700	

*No. 22 is the same colour as No. 11a.

The 1d. carmine, 2d. slate, and 2s. are known imperf. All values to the 6d. inclusive are known perf 12. These are proofs.

1889 (8 Mar)–**91**. Value tablet in second colour. Wmk Crown CA. P 14.

27	11	1d. purple and mauve	9·00	20
		w. Wmk inverted	—	45·00
28		2d. green	35·00	5·00
		a. Deep green (brown gum)	20·00	7·50
		aw. Wmk inverted	80·00	
29		2½d. dull purple and blue (25.2.91)	8·00	50
			£120	
27/9 Set of 3			32·00	5·00
27s/9s Optd "SPECIMEN" Set of 3			£150	

A very wide range of shades may be found in the 1d. The headplate was printed in many shades of purple, and the duty plate in various shades of mauve and purple and also in carmine, etc. There are fewer shades for the other values and they are not so pronounced.

1d. stamps with the duty plate in blue are colour changelings.

1890 (4 June)–**91**. No. 22b surch with T **12** by C. Vendyres, Kingston.

30	4	2½d. on 4d. red-brown	38·00	16·00
		a. Spacing between lines of surch 1½ mm (2.91)	48·00	20·00
		b. Surch double	£325	£225
		c. "PFNNY" for "PENNY"	85·00	65·00

104

JAMAICA

		ca. Ditto and broken "K" for "Y"	£150	£110
		w. Wmk inverted	95·00	45·00

This provisional was issued pending receipt of No. 29 which is listed above for convenience of reference.

Three settings exist. (1) Ten varieties arranged in a single vertical row and repeated six times in the pane. (2) Twelve varieties, in two horizontal rows of six, repeated five times, alternate rows show 1 and 1½ mm spacing between lines of surcharge. (3) Three varieties, arranged horizontally and repeated twenty times. All these settings can be reconstructed by examination of the spacing and relative position of the words of the surcharge and of the broken letters, etc, which are numerous.

A variety reading "PFNNK", with the "K" unbroken, is a forgery.

Surcharges misplaced either horizontally or vertically are met with, the normal position being central at the foot of the stamp with "HALF-PENNY" covering the old value.

13 Llandovery Falls, Jamaica (photo by Dr. J. Johnston)

14 Arms of Jamaica

(Recess D.L.R.)

1900 (1 May)–**01**. Wmk Crown CC (sideways*). P 14.

31	13	1d. red	10·00	20
		w. Wmk Crown to left of CC	10·00	50
		x. Wmk reversed	—	70·00
		y. Wmk sideways inverted and reversed		
32		1d. slate-black and red (25.9.01)	9·00	20
		a. Blued paper	£110	£100
		b. Imperf between (vert pair)	£22000	
		w. Wmk Crown to left of CC	23·00	11·00
		x. Wmk reversed	—	70·00
		y. Wmk sideways inverted and reversed		

31s/2s Optd "SPECIMEN" Set of 2 .... £140

*The normal sideways wmk shows Crown to right of CC, *as seen from the back of the stamp.*

Many shades exist of both centre and frame of the bi-coloured 1d. which was, of course, printed from two plates and the design shows minor differences from that of the 1d. red which was printed from a single plate.

1903 (16 Nov)–**04**. Wmk Crown CA. P 14.

33	14	½d. grey and dull green	1·50	30
		a. "SER.ET" for "SERVIET"	40·00	45·00
		w. Wmk inverted	35·00	38·00
34		1d. grey and carmine (24.2.04)	4·00	10
		a. "SER.ET" for "SERVIET"	32·00	35·00
35		2½d. grey and ultramarine	7·50	30
		a. "SER.ET" for "SERVIET"	65·00	75·00
36		5d. grey and yellow (1.3.04)	15·00	23·00
		a. "SER.ET" for "SERVIET"	£800	£1000
		w. Wmk inverted	£140	

33/6 Set of 4 .... 25·00 23·00
33s/6s Optd "SPECIMEN" Set of 4 .... 95·00

The "SER.ET" variety occurs on R. 4/2 of the left upper pane. It was corrected by De La Rue in July 1905, following the printing of Nos. 37 and 43.

The centres of the above and later bi-coloured stamps in the Arms type vary in colour from grey to grey-black.

15 Arms type redrawn

16 Arms type redrawn

1905–11. Wmk Mult Crown CA. P 14.

(a) Arms types. Chalk-surfaced paper

37	14	½d. grey and dull green (20.11.05)	3·00	20
		a. "SER.ET" for "SERVIET"	26·00	40·00
		w. Wmk inverted		
38	15	½d. yell-grn (*ordinary paper*) (8.11.06)	11·00	50
		aw. Wmk inverted	†	£150
		b. Dull green	3·00	20
		c. Deep green	4·75	20
39	14	1d. grey and carmine (20.11.05)	18·00	1·75
		w. Wmk inverted	—	£130
40	16	1d. carmine (*ordinary paper*) (1.10.09)	1·50	10
		w. Wmk inverted	60·00	
41	14	2½d. grey and ultramarine (12.11.07)	4·75	7·00
42		2½d. pale ultramarine (*ordinary paper*) (21.9.10)	4·75	1·25
43		5d. grey and orange-yellow (24.4.07)	2·50	1·75
			65·00	75·00
		a. "SER.ET" for "SERVIET"	£1400	£1600
44		6d. dull and bright purple (18.8.11)	14·00	18·00
45		5s. grey and violet (11.05)	55·00	55·00

37/45 Set of 9 .... £150 £140
38s, 40s, 42s, 44s/5s Optd "SPECIMEN" Set of 5 .... £200

See note below No. 36 concerning grey centres.

(b) Queen Victoria types. Ordinary paper

46	3	3d. olive-green (3.8.05)	9·00	4·50
		a. Sage-green (1907)	6·50	3·00
47		3d. purple/yellow (10.3.10)	7·50	3·50
		a. Chalk-surfaced paper. *Pale purple/yellow* (11.7.10)	2·00	1·50
		aw. Wmk inverted	55·00	60·00
48	4	4d. red-brown (6.6.08)	75·00	75·00
49		4d. black/yellow (*chalk-surfaced paper*) (21.9.10)	12·00	55·00
50		4d. red/yellow (3.10.11)	1·50	5·50
51	5	6d. dull orange (27.6.06)	15·00	25·00
		a. *Golden yellow* (9.09)	32·00	65·00
52		6d. lilac (19.11.09)	29·00	60·00
		a. Chalk-surfaced paper. *Purple* (7.10)	10·00	28·00
53	6	1s. brown (11.06)	23·00	45·00
		a. *Deep brown*	35·00	60·00
		b. "$" for "S" in "SHILLING" (A)	£1300	£1400
54		1s. black/green (*chalk-surfaced paper*) (21.9.10)	9·50	8·50
		a. "$" for "S" in "SHILLING" (A)	£950	£1200
55	9	2s. Venetian red (11.08)	£120	£160
56		2s. pur/bl (*chalk-surfaced paper*) (21.9.10)	11·00	6·00

46/56 Set of 11 .... £250 £350
47s, 49s, 50s, 52s, 54s, 56s Optd "SPECIMEN" Set of 6 .... £300

No. 38 exists in coils constructed from normal sheets.

17

18

(T **17/18** typo D.L.R.)

1911 (3 Feb). Wmk Mult Crown CA. P 14.

57	17	2d. grey	7·00	13·00
		s. Optd "SPECIMEN"	60·00	

1912–20. Wmk Mult Crown CA. Chalk-surfaced paper (3d. to 5s.). P 14.

58	18	1d. carmine-red (5.12.12)	1·50	10
		a. Scarlet (1916)	7·50	70
59		1½d. brown-orange (13.7.16)	1·25	40
		a. Yellow-orange	17·00	
		b. Wmk sideways	†	£1700
		w. Wmk inverted	†	£200
60		2d. grey (2.8.12)	2·00	1·75
		a. Slate-grey	3·00	3·00
61		2½d. blue (13.2.13)	1·50	15
		a. Deep bright blue	65	1·00
62		3d. purple/yellow (6.3.12)	50	45
		a. White back (2.4.13)	55	40
		b. On lemon (25.9.16)	3·75	1·50
		bs. Optd "SPECIMEN"	32·00	
		w. Wmk inverted		
63		4d. black and red/yellow (4.4.13)	50	2·75
		a. White back (7.5.14)	75	3·25
		b. On lemon (1916)	23·00	19·00
		bs. Optd "SPECIMEN"	32·00	
		c. On pale yellow (1919)	22·00	15·00
64		6d. dull and bright purple (14.11.12)	4·50	10·00
		a. Dull purple and bright mauve (1915)	1·00	1·00
		b. Dull purple & bright magenta (1920)	6·00	2·25
65		1s. black/green (2.8.12)	2·25	2·00
		a. White back (4.1.15)	4·50	4·75
		b. On blue-green, olive back (1920)	3·00	8·50
66		2s. purple and bright blue/blue (10.1.19)	23·00	32·00
67		5s. green and red (5.9.19)	80·00	£100
		a. On pale yellow (1920)	£110	£120
		b. On orange-buff (1920)	£180	£200

58/67 Set of 10 .... £100 £120
58s/67s Optd "SPECIMEN" Set of 10 .... £225

No. 58 exists in coils constructed from normal sheets.

The paper of No. 67 is a bright yellow and the gum rough and dull. No. 67*a* is on practically the normal creamy "pale yellow" paper, and the gum is smooth and shiny. The paper of No. 67*b* approaches the "coffee" colour of the true "orange-buff", and the colours of both head and frame are paler, the latter being of a carmine tone.

For the ½d. and 6d. with Script wmk see Nos. 92/3.

105

JAMAICA

RED CROSS LABELS. A voluntary organization, the Jamaica War Stamp League later the Jamaica Patriotic Stamp League, was founded in November 1915 by Mr. Lewis Ashenheim, a Kingston solicitor. The aims of the League were to support the British Red Cross, collect funds for the purchase of aircraft for the Royal Flying Corps and the relief of Polish Jews.

One fund-raising method used was the sale, from 1 December 1915, of ½d. charity labels. These labels, which were available from post offices, depicted a bi-plane above a cross and were printed in red by Dennison Manufacturing Company, Framingham, U.S.A., the stamps being perforated 12 except for those along the edges of the sheet which have one side imperforate.

From 22 December 1915 supplies of the labels were overprinted "JAMAICA" in red, the colour of this overprint being changed to black from 15 January 1916. Copies sold from 11 March 1916 carried an additional "Half-Penny" surcharge, also in black.

Such labels had no postal validity when used by the general public, but, by special order of the Governor, were accepted for the payment of postage on the League's official mail. To obtain this concession the envelopes were to be inscribed "Red Cross Business" or "Jamaica Patriotic Stamp League" and the labels used endorsed with Mr. Ashenheim's signature. Such covers are rare.

	WAR STAMP. (19)	WAR STAMP. (20)	WAR STAMP. (21)

(T **19/21** optd Govt Printing Office, Kingston)

1916 (1 Apr–Sept). Optd with T **19**.

68	15	½d. yellow-green	20	35
		a. No stop after "STAMP" (R. 18/2)	16·00	27·00
		b. Opt double	£140	£160
		c. Opt inverted	£130	£150
		d. Space between "W" and "A" (R. 20/1)	19·00	32·00
		e. Blue-green	10	60
		ea. No stop after "STAMP" (R. 3/11 or 11/1)	15·00	29·00
		eb. Space between "W" and "A" (R. 20/1)	18·00	40·00
		w. Wmk inverted		
69	18	3d. purple/yellow (white back)	28·00	45·00
		a. On lemon (6.16)	2·25	22·00
		ab. No stop after "STAMP" (R. 8/6 or 9/6)	38·00	£100
		b. On pale yellow (9.16)	16·00	£100

Minor varieties: ½d. (i) Small "P"; (ii) "WARISTAMP" (raised quad between words); (iii) Two stops after "STAMP". 3d. "WARISTAMP". There were several settings of the overprint used for each value. Where two positions are quoted for a variety these did not occur on the same sheet.

NOTE. The above and succeeding stamps with "WAR STAMP" overprint were issued for payment of a special war tax on letters and postcards or on parcels. Ordinary unoverprinted stamps could also be used for this purpose.

1916 (Sept–Dec). Optd with T **20**.

70	15	½d. blue-green (shades) (2.10.16)	10	30
		a. No stop after "STAMP" (R. 5/7)	18·00	50·00
		b. Opt omitted (in pair with normal)	£5500	£4750
		c. "R" inserted by hand (R. 1/10)	£1800	£1500
		w. Wmk inverted	65·00	
71	18	1½d. orange (1.9.16)	10	15
		aa. Wmk sideways	†	£2000
		a. No stop after "STAMP" (R. 4/12, 8/6, 10/10, 11/1, 18/12, 19/12)	5·00	7·50
		b. "S" in "STAMP" omitted (R. 6/12) (Dec)	£180	£190
		c. "S" inserted by hand	£425	
		d. "R" in "WAR" omitted (R. 1/10)	£3250	£3000
		e. "R" inserted by hand (R. 1/10)	£1500	£1200
		f. Inverted "d" for "P"	£200	£160
		w. Wmk inverted	17·00	16·00
72		3d. purple/lemon (2.10.16)	6·50	1·00
		aa. Opt inverted	£325	
		a. No stop after "STAMP" (R. 5/7)	65·00	70·00
		b. "S" in "STAMP" omitted (R. 6/12) (Dec)	£850	£850
		c. "S" inserted by hand	£200	£200
		e. On yellow (12.16)	13·00	10·00
		ea. "S" in "STAMP" omitted (R. 6/12)	£1000	£1000
		eb. "S" inserted by hand	£425	£375

Nos. 70c, 71c, 71e, 72c and 72eb show the missing "R" or "S" inserted by handstamp. The 3d. is known with this "S" handstamp inverted or double.

Minor varieties, such as raised quads, small stop, double stop, spaced letters and letters of different sizes, also exist in this overprint. The setting was altered several times.

1917 (March). Optd with T **21**.

73	15	½d. blue-green (shades) (25.3.17)	1·75	30
		a. No stop after "STAMP" (R. 2/5, 8/11, 8/12)	16·00	27·00
		b. Stop inserted and "P" impressed a second time (R. 7/6)	£250	
		c. Optd on back only	£250	
		d. Opt inverted	24·00	55·00
74	18	1½d. orange (3.3.17)	20	10
		aa. Wmk sideways	†	£1700
		a. No stop after "STAMP" (R. 2/5, 8/11, 8/12)	3·00	18·00
		b. Stop inserted and "P" impressed a second time (R. 7/6)	£250	
		c. Opt double	80·00	85·00
		d. Opt inverted	80·00	75·00
		e. "WAP STAMP" (R. 6/2)		
		w. Wmk inverted	16·00	21·00
75		3d. purple/yellow (3.3.17)	2·00	1·40
		a. No stop after "STAMP" (R. 2/5, 8/11, 8/12)	25·00	50·00
		b. Stop inserted and "P" impressed a second time (R. 7/6)	£225	
		c. Opt inverted	£140	£180
		d. Opt sideways (reading up)	£400	
		da. Opt omitted (in horiz pair with No. 75d)	£3750	

Examples of No. 75d. exist showing parts of two or more overprints.

No. 75da shows the left-hand stamp as No. 75d and the right-hand stamp without overprint.

There are numerous minor varieties in this overprint with the setting being altered several times.

WAR STAMP
(22)

1919 (4 Oct)–**20**. Optd with T **22** in red by D.L.R.

76	15	½d. green	20	15
77	18	3d. purple/yellow	14·00	3·25
		a. Short opt (right pane R. 10/1)		
		b. Pale purple/buff (3.1.20)	5·00	1·25
		c. Deep purple/buff (1920)	14·00	8·00
76s/7s Optd "SPECIMEN" Set of 2			85·00	

We list the most distinct variations in the 3d. The buff tone of the paper varies considerably in depth.

No. 77a shows the overprint 2 mm high instead of 2½ mm. The variety was corrected after the first overprinting. It is not found on the ½d.

23 Jamaica Exhibition, 1891

24 Arawak Woman preparing Cassava

25 War Contingent embarking, 1915

26 King's House, Spanish Town

Re-entry. Nos. 80a, 93a

The greater part of the design is re-entered, the hull showing in very solid colour and the people appear very blurred. There are also minor re-entries on stamps above (R. 7/4 and 6/4).

106

JAMAICA

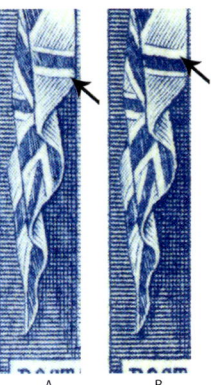

27 Return of War Contingent, 1919
A   B

28 Landing of Columbus, 1494 
29 Cathedral, Spanish Town 
30 Statue of Queen Victoria, Kingston

31 Admiral Rodney Memorial, Spanish Town 
32 Sir Charles Metcalfe Statue, Kingston 
33 Jamaican scenery

34

(Typo (½d., 1d.), recess (others) D.L.R.)

1919–21. T **23/34**. Wmk Mult Crown CA (sideways* on 1d., 1½d. and 10s.). Chalk-surfaced paper (½d., 1d.). P 14.

78	23	½d. green and olive-green (12.11.20)	1·00	1·00
		w. Wmk inverted		
		x. Wmk reversed		
		y. Wmk inverted and reversed		
79	24	1d. carmine and orange (3.10.21)	1·75	1·75
		w. Wmk Crown to left of CA		
80	25	1½d. green (shades) (4.7.19)	40	1·00
		a. Major re-entry (R. 8/4)	£100	
		b. "C" of "CA" missing from wmk.	†	£325
		c. "A" of "CA" missing from wmk.	£425	£350
		w. Wmk Crown to left of CA	32·00	38·00
		x. Wmk reversed	—	85·00
		y. Wmk sideways inverted and reversed	95·00	75·00
81	26	2d. indigo and green (18.2.21)	1·00	4·00
		w. Wmk inverted	50·00	
		y. Wmk inverted and reversed	55·00	
82	27	2½d. deep blue and blue (A) (18.2.21)	13·00	3·00
		a. Blue-black and deep blue	1·50	1·75
		b. "C" of "CA" missing from wmk.	£300	£250
		c. "A" of "CA" missing from wmk.	£275	
		w. Wmk inverted	32·00	
		x. Wmk reversed	50·00	
		y. Wmk inverted and reversed	50·00	
83	28	3d. myrtle-green and blue (8.4.21)	4·50	2·50
		w. Wmk inverted	45·00	48·00
		x. Wmk reversed	†	£150
84	29	4d. brown and deep green (21.1.21)	2·50	9·00
		w. Wmk inverted		
		x. Wmk reversed		
85	30	1s. orange-yell & red-orge (10.12.20)	3·75	5·50
		a. Frame inverted	£38000	£25000
		b. "C" of "CA" missing from wmk.	£600	
		c. "A" of "CA" missing from wmk.	£650	
		w. Wmk inverted	†	£120
		x. Wmk reversed	†	£300
86	31	2s. light blue and brown (10.12.20)	9·00	29·00
		b. "C" of "CA" missing from wmk.	£650	
		c. "A" of "CA" missing from wmk.		
		w. Wmk inverted	42·00	60·00
		x. Wmk reversed		
		y. Wmk inverted and reversed	£140	
87	32	3s. violet-blue and orange (10.12.20)	23·00	£120
88	33	5s. blue and yellow-orange (15.4.21)	60·00	90·00
		a. Blue and pale dull orange	50·00	80·00
		w. Wmk inverted		
		x. Wmk reversed		
89	34	10s. myrtle-green (6.5.20)	80·00	£150
78/89 Set of 12			£160	£350
78s/89s Optd "SPECIMEN" Set of 12			£300	

*The normal sideways wmk on Nos. 79/80 shows Crown to right of CA, as seen from the back of the stamp.

The 2½d. of the above series showed the Union Jack at left, incorrectly, as indicated in illustration A. In the issue on paper with Script wmk the design was corrected (Illustration B).

An example of No. 80 has been reported with the "A" inverted to the left of and above its normal position.

The "C" omitted variety has been reported on an example of No. 88 overprinted "SPECIMEN".

34a "Abolition of Slavery" 1st August 1838

Prepared for use but not issued

1921. Recess. P 14.

(a) Wmk Mult Crown CA

90	34a	6d. red and dull blue-green	£60000	
		s. Optd "SPECIMEN"	£800	
		xs. Ditto, wmk reversed	£1200	

(b) Wmk Mult Script CA (Sideways)

91		6d. red and dull blue-green	£35000	
		s. Optd "SPECIMEN"	£800	

The 6d. stamps were prepared and sent out to Jamaica, but for political reasons were not issued, and the stocks destroyed. "SPECIMEN" examples of both watermarks were distributed by the UPU in the normal way, but only one example of No. 90 and four examples of No. 91 exist in private hands without opt.

"Bow" flaw (R. 18/12)

1921 (21 Oct)–**27**. Wmk Mult Script CA. Chalk-surfaced paper (6d.). P 14.

92	18	½d. green (3.11.27)	3·00	10
		a. Bow flaw	85·00	30·00
93		6d. dull purple and bright magenta	16·00	4·00
92s/3s Optd "SPECIMEN" Set of 2			95·00	

35 "POSTAGE & REVENUE" added
36 "Port Royal in 1853" (A. Duperly)

JAMAICA

(Printing as before; the 6d. recess-printed)
1921–29. As Nos. 78/89. Wmk Mult Script CA (sideways* on 1d. and 1½d.). Chalk-surfaced paper (½d., 1d.). P 14.

94	23	½d. green and olive-green (5.2.22)	50	50
		a. Green and deep olive-green	30	50
		w. Wmk inverted	45·00	45·00
95	35	1d. carmine and orange (5.12.22)	1·50	10
		w. Wmk Crown to right of CA	2·75	10
		x. Wmk reversed	—	85·00
96	25	1½d. green (shades) (2.2.21)	2·75	45
		a. Major re-entry (R. 8/4)	£120	
		w. Wmk Crown to left of CA	—	32·00
		x. Wmk reversed	42·00	42·00
		y. Wmk sideways inverted and reversed	—	80·00
97	26	2d. indigo and green (4.11.21)	7·50	80
		a. Indigo and grey-green (1925)	12·00	1·00
		w. Wmk inverted	†	
98	27	2½d. deep blue and blue (B) (4.11.21)	5·50	1·75
		a. Dull blue and blue (B)	6·00	60
		w. Wmk inverted	40·00	40·00
		x. Wmk reversed		
		y. Wmk inverted and reversed		
99	28	3d. myrtle-green and blue (6.3.22)	4·50	70
		a. Green and pale blue	2·75	20
		w. Wmk inverted		
		x. Wmk reversed		
100	29	4d. brown and deep green (5.12.21)	1·25	30
		a. Chocolate and dull green	1·25	30
		w. Wmk inverted	45·00	
		x. Wmk reversed	70·00	
101	36	6d. black and blue (5.12.22)	14·00	1·50
		a. Grey and dull blue	13·00	1·00
102	30	1s. orange and red-orange (4.11.21)	1·75	80
		a. Orange-yellow and brown-orange	1·75	65
		w. Wmk inverted		
		x. Wmk reversed	—	£200
103	31	2s. light blue and brown (5.2.22)	3·25	65
		w. Wmk inverted	40·00	40·00
104	32	3s. violet-blue and orange (23.8.21)	17·00	9·00
105	33	5s. blue and yellow-brown (8.11.23)	30·00	25·00
		a. Blue and pale dull orange	75·00	80·00
		b. Blue and yellow-orange (1927)	38·00	23·00
		c. Blue and pale bistre-brown (1929)	38·00	22·00
		w. Wmk inverted		
		x. Wmk reversed	—	£325
106	34	10s. myrtle-green (3.22)	55·00	70·00
94/106	Set of 13		£120	95·00
94s/106s Optd "SPECIMEN" Set of 13			£300	

*The normal sideways wmk shows Crown to left of CA on No. 95 or Crown to right of CA on No. 96, *both as seen from the back of the stamp*.
The frame of No. 105*a* is the same colour as that of No. 88*a*.

The designs of all values of the pictorial series, with the exception of the 5s. and 10s. (which originated from the Governor, Sir Leslie Probyn), were selected by Mr. F. C. Cundall, F.S.A. The 1d. and 5s. were drawn by Miss Cundall, the 3d. by Mrs. Cundall, and the 10s. by De La Rue & Co. The 6d. is from a lithograph. The other designs are from photographs, the frames of all being the work of Miss Cundall and Miss Wood.

37    **38**    **39**

(Centres from photos by Miss V. F. Taylor. Frames des F. C. Cundall, F.S.A., and drawn by Miss Cundall. Recess B.W.)
1923 (1 Nov). Child Welfare. Wmk Mult Script CA. P 12.

107	37	½d. +½d. black and green	1·00	5·50
107b	38	1d. +½d. black and scarlet	3·00	11·00
107c	39	2½d. +½d. black and blue	20·00	19·00
107/7c Set of 3			22·00	32·00
107as/7cs Optd "SPECIMEN" Set of 3			£140	

Sold at a premium of ½d. for the Child Welfare League, these stamps were on sale annually from 1 November to 31 January, until 31 January 1927, when their sale ceased, the remainders being destroyed on 21 February 1927.

40    **41**    **42**

Die I    Die II

(Recess D.L.R.)
1929–32. Wmk Mult Script CA. P 14.

108	40	1d. scarlet (Die I) (15.3.29)	13·00	20
		a. Die II (1932)	13·00	10
109	41	1½d. chocolate (18.1.29)	7·50	15
110	42	9d. maroon (5.3.29)	7·50	1·00
108/10 Set of 3			25·00	1·10
108s/10s Perf "SPECIMEN" Set of 3			£110	

In Die I the shading below JAMAICA is formed of thickened parallel lines, and in Die II of diagonal cross-hatching.

43 Coco Palms at Don Christopher's Cove 
44 Wag Water River, St. Andrew

45 Priestman's River, Portland

(Dies eng and recess Waterlow)
1932. Wmk Mult Script CA (sideways on 2d. and 2½d.). P 12½.

111	43	2d. black and green (4.11.32)	32·00	3·50
		a. Imperf between (vert pair)	£14000	
112	44	2½d. turquoise-blue and ultram (5.3.32)	6·50	1·50
		a. Imperf between (vert pair)	£23000	£23000
113	45	6d. grey-black and purple (4.2.32)	32·00	4·75
111/13 Set of 3			65·00	8·75
111s/13s Perf "SPECIMEN" Set of 3			£120	

Extra flagstaff (Plate "1" R. 9/11)
Short extra flagstaff (Plate "2" R. 2/1) 
Lightning conductor (Plate "3" R. 2/5) 

Flagstaff on right-hand turret (Plate "5" R. 7/1)
Double Flagstaff (Plate "6" R. 5/2) 

1935 (6 May). Silver Jubilee. As Nos. 141/4 of Bahamas, but ptd by B.W. P 11×12.

114		1d. deep blue and scarlet	50	15
		b. Short extra flagstaff	£1500	
		d. Flagstaff on right-hand turret	£140	£160
		e. Double flagstaff	£140	£160

JAMAICA

115	1½d. ultramarine and grey-black	60	1·50
	a. Extra flagstaff	90·00	£130
	b. Short extra flagstaff	£130	£160
	c. Lightning conductor	£110	£140
116	6d. green and indigo	12·00	20·00
	a. Extra flagstaff	£200	£275
	b. Short extra flagstaff	£350	
	c. Lightning conductor	£250	
117	1s. slate and purple	8·00	17·00
	a. Extra flagstaff	£250	£325
	b. Short extra flagstaff	40·00	
	c. Lightning conductor	£300	
114/17 Set of 4		19·00	35·00
114s/17s Perf "SPECIMEN" Set of 4		£110	

1937 (12 May). Coronation. As Nos. 146/8 of Bahamas, but printed by D.L.R. P 14.

118	1d. scarlet	30	15
119	1½d. grey-black	65	30
120	2½d. bright blue	1·00	70
118/20 Set of 3		1·75	1·00
118s/20s Perf "SPECIMEN" Set of 3		£100	

46 King George VI 
47 Coco Palms at Don Christopher's Cove 
47a Wag Water River, St. Andrew 
48 Bananas 
49 Citrus Grove 
49a Priestman's River, Portland 
50 Kingston Harbour 
51 Sugar Industry 
52 Bamboo Walk 
52a Jamaican scenery 
53 King George VI 
53a Tobacco Growing and Cigar Making

2d. Extra branch (Centre plate (1) with frame Pl (1) to 7, R. 6/1)

2d. Fishing rod (Centre plate (1) with frame Pl (1) to 7, R. 6/10)

6d. "Exhaust pipe" variety (Centre plate (1), R. 6/1)

1s. Repaired chimney (Centre plate 1, R. 11/1)

(Recess D.L.R. (T **48**, 5s. and 10s.), Waterlow (others))

1938 (10 Oct)–**52**. T **46**/**53a** and as Nos. 88, 112/13, but with inset portrait of King George VI, as in T **49**. Wmk Mult Script CA. P 13½×14 (½d., 1d., 1½d.), 14 (5s., 10s.) or 12½ (others).

121	**46**	½d. blue-green	1·75	10
		a. Wmk sideways	†	£7000
121b		½d. orange (25.10.51)	2·75	30
122		1d. scarlet	1·25	10
122a		1d. blue-green (25.10.51)	3·50	10
123		1½d. brown	1·25	10
124	**47**	2d. grey and green (10.12.38)	1·25	1·00
		a. Extra branch	45·00	27·00
		b. Fishing rod	45·00	27·00
		c. Perf 13×13½ (1939)	2·75	50
		cb. "C" of "CA" missing from wmk	£1500	
		d. Perf 12½×13 (1951)	1·25	10
125	**47a**	2½d. greenish blue and ultram (10.12.38)	8·00	2·50
126	**48**	3d. ultramarine and green (10.12.38)	1·00	1·50
		a. "A" of "CA" missing from wmk	£1500	
126b		3d. greenish blue and ultram (15.8.49)	4·50	1·25
126c		3d. green and scarlet (1.7.52)	5·50	30
127	**49**	4d. brown and green (10.12.38)	1·00	10
128	**49a**	6d. grey and purple (10.12.38)	8·50	30
		aa. "Exhaust pipe"	£250	50·00
		a. Perf 13½×13 (10.10.50)	2·25	10

109

JAMAICA

129	50	9d. lake (10.12.38)	1·00	50
		a. "A" of "CA" missing from wmk	£1600	
130	51	1s. green and purple-brown (10.12.38)	13·00	20
		a. Repaired chimney	£650	£110
		b. "A" of "CA" missing from wmk	†	
131	52	2s. blue and chocolate (10.12.38)	35·00	1·00
132	52a	5s. slate-blue and yellow-orange (10.12.38)	15·00	3·75
		a. Perf 14, line (1941)	£6500	£250
		b. Perf 13 (24.10.49)	10·00	3·00
		ba. Blue and orange (10.10.50)	10·00	3·00
133	53	10s. myrtle-green (10.12.38)	11·00	10·00
		aa. Perf 13 (10.10.50)	18·00	7·00
133a	53a	£1 chocolate and violet (15.8.49)	60·00	38·00
121/33a Set of 18			£150	50·00
121s/33s Perf "SPECIMEN" Set of 13			£350	

No. 130a occurred in conjunction with Frame plate 2 on printings between 1942 and 1951.

No. 132a shows the emergency use of a line perforation machine, giving an irregular gauge of 14–14.15, after the De La Rue works were damaged in December 1940. The normal comb measures 13.8×13.7.

Nos. 121 and 122 exist in coils constructed from normal sheets.

SELF-GOVERNMENT

54 Courthouse, Falmouth

55 King Charles II and King George VI

56 Institute of Jamaica

57 House of Assembly

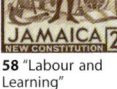

58 "Labour and Learning"

59 Scroll, flag and King George VI

(Recess Waterlow)

1945 (20 Aug)–**46**. New Constitution. T **54/9**. Wmk Mult Script CA. P 12½.

134	54	1½d. sepia	30	30
		a. Perf 12½×13 (1946)	10·00	1·75
135	55	2d. green	14·00	1·00
		a. Perf 12½×13 (1945)	30	50
136	56	3d. ultramarine	30	50
		a. Perf 13 (1946)	3·25	2·75
137	57	4½d. slate	60	30
		a. Perf 13 (1946)	4·50	4·75
138	58	2s. red-brown	1·25	50
139	59	5s. indigo	3·50	1·00
140	55	10s. green	3·00	2·25
134/40 Set of 7			8·25	4·75
134s/40s Perf "SPECIMEN" Set of 7			£200	

1946 (14 Oct). Victory. As Nos. 176/7 of Bahamas. P 13½×14.

141		1½d. purple-brown	2·50	10
		a. Perf 13½	65	4·50
142		3d. blue	7·00	3·00
		a. Perf 13½	65	8·00
141s/2s Perf "SPECIMEN" Set of 2			90·00	

1948 (1 Dec). Royal Silver Wedding. As Nos. 194/5 of Bahamas.

143		1½d. red-brown (P 14×15)	30	10
144		£1 scarlet (P 11½×11)	28·00	75·00

1949 (10 Oct). 75th Anniv of Universal Postal Union. As Nos. 196/9 of Bahamas.

| 145 | | 1½d. red-brown (P 13½–14) | 20 | 15 |

146		2d. deep blue-green (P 11×11½)	1·25	5·25
147		3d. deep blue (P 11×11½)	50	1·50
148		6d. purple (P 13½–14)	50	2·50
145/8 Set of 4			2·25	8·50

59a Arms of University

59b Princess Alice

(Recess Waterlow)

1951 (16 Feb). Inauguration of B.W.I. University College. Wmk Mult Script CA. P 14×14½.

149	59a	2d. black and red-brown	30	50
150	59b	6d. grey-black and purple	70	30

60 Scout Badge and Map of Caribbean

61 Scout Badge and Map of Jamaica

(Des. C. D'Souza. Litho B.W.)

1952 (5 Mar). First Caribbean Scout Jamboree. Wmk Mult Script CA. P 13½×13 (2d.) or 13×13½ (6d.).

151	60	2d. blue, apple-green and black	30	10
152	61	6d. yellow-green, carmine-red and black	70	60

1953 (2 June). Coronation. As No. 200 of Bahamas. P 13½×13.

| 153 | | 2d. black and deep yellow-green | 1·50 | 10 |

62 Coco Palms at Don Christopher's Cove

(Recess Waterlow)

1953 (25 Nov). Royal Visit. Wmk Mult Script CA. P 12½×13.

| 154 | 62 | 2d. grey-black and green | 55 | 10 |

63 HMS *Britannia* (ship of the line) at Port Royal

64 Old Montego Bay

65 Old Kingston

66 Proclamation of Abolition of Slavery, 1838

JAMAICA

(Recess D.L.R.)
1955 (10 May). Tercentenary Issue. T **63/6**. Wmk Mult Script CA. P 12½.

155	63	2d. black and olive-green	85	10
156	64	2½d. black and deep bright blue	15	35
157	65	3d. black and claret	15	30
158	66	6d. black and carmine-red	30	20
155/8		Set of 4	1·25	80

67 Coconut Palms
68 Sugar Cane
69 Pineapples

70 Bananas
71 Mahoe
72 Breadfruit

73 Ackee
74 Streamertail

75 Blue Mountain Peak
76 Royal Botanic Gardens, Hope

77 Rafting on the Rio Grande
78 Fort Charles

79 Arms of Jamaica
80 Arms of Jamaica

(Recess B.W. (T **79/80**), D.L.R. (others))
1956 (1 May)–58. T **67/80**. Wmk Mult Script CA. P 13 (½d. to 6d.), 13½ (8d. to 2s.) or 11½ (3s. to £1).

159	67	½d. black and deep orange-red	10	10
160	68	1d. black and emerald	10	10
161	69	2d. black and carmine-red (2.8.56)	15	10
162	70	2½d. black and deep bright blue (2.8.56)	75	50
163	71	3d. emerald and red-brown (17.12.56)	20	10
164	72	4d. bronze-green and blue (17.12.56)	30	10
		w. Wmk inverted	£180	£120
165	73	5d. scarlet and bronze-green (17.12.56)	30	2·50
166	74	6d. black and deep rose-red (3.9.56)	3·25	10
167	75	8d. ultramarine and red-orange (15.11.56)	2·00	10
168	76	1s. yellow-green and blue (15.11.56)	2·00	10
169	77	1s.6d. ultram and reddish purple (15.11.56)	1·00	10
170	78	2s. blue and bronze-green (15.11.56)	15·00	3·25
		a. *Grey-blue and bronze-green* (24.4.58)	25·00	3·50
171	79	3s. black and blue (2.8.56)	3·00	3·50
172		5s. black and carmine-red (15.8.56)	4·00	7·50
173	80	10s. black and blue-green (15.8.56)	35·00	22·00
174		£1 black and purple (15.8.56)	35·00	22·00
159/74		Set of 16	90·00	55·00

An earlier £1 value, in the design of No. 133*a* but showing the portrait of Queen Elizabeth II, was prepared, but not issued.

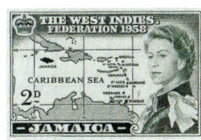

80a Federation Map

(Recess B.W.)
1958 (22 Apr). Inauguration of British Caribbean Federation. W w **12**. P 11½×11.

175	80a	2d. deep green	70	10
176		5d. blue	1·10	3·50
177		6d. scarlet	1·25	40
175/7		Set of 3	2·75	3·50

81 Bristol 175 Britannia 312 flying over *City of Berlin*, 1860
83 1s. Stamps of 1860 and 1956

82 Postal mule-cart and motor-van

(Recess Waterlow)
1960 (4 Jan). Stamp Centenary. T **81/83** and similar design. W w **12**. P 13×13½ (1s.) or 13½×14 (others).

178	81	2d. blue and reddish purple	75	10
179	82	6d. carmine and olive-green	75	50
180	83	1s. red-brown, yellow-green and blue	75	55
178/80		Set of 3	2·00	1·00

INDEPENDENT

INDEPENDENCE (84)
INDEPENDENCE 1962 (85)

86 Military Bugler and Map

(Des V. Whiteley. Photo D.L.R. (2, 4d., 1s.6d., 5s.))
1962 (8 Aug)–63. Independence.

*(a) Nos. 159/60, 162, 171, 173/4 optd as T **84** and Nos. 163, 165/8, 170 optd with T **85***

181	67	½d. black and deep orange-red	10	1·00
182	68	1d. black and emerald	10	10
183	70	2½d. black and deep bright blue	15	1·00
184	71	3d. emerald and red-brown	15	10
185	73	5d. scarlet and bronze-green	25	60
186	74	6d. black and deep rose-red	2·75	10
187	75	8d. ultramarine and red-orge (opt at upper left)	20	10
		a. Opt at lower left (17.9.63?)	1·25	30
188	76	1s. yellow-green and blue	20	10

111

JAMAICA

189	**78**	2s. blue and bronze-green	1·00	1·50
		a. Dp blue and dp bronze-green (20.8.63)	14·00	6·00
190	**79**	3s. black and blue	1·00	1·50
191	**80**	10s. black and blue-green	4·25	4·25
192		£1 black and purple	4·25	5·50

(b) Horiz designs as T **86**. *W w* **12**. *P* 13

193		2d. multicoloured	2·25	10
194		4d. multicoloured	1·50	10
195		1s.6d. black and red	5·50	85
196		5s. multicoloured	10·00	6·50
181/96 *Set of 16*			30·00	21·00

Designs:—2, 4d. Type **86**; 1s.6d. Gordon House and banner; 5s. Map, factories and fruit.
For these overprints on stamps watermarked w **12** see Nos. 205/13.

89 Kingston Seal, Weightlifting, Boxing, Football and Cycling

93 Farmer and Crops

(Photo Harrison)

1962 (11 Aug). Ninth Central American and Caribbean Games, Kingston. T **89** and similar horiz designs. W w **12**. P 14½×14.

197		1d. sepia and carmine-red	20	10
198		6d. sepia and greenish blue	20	10
199		8d. sepia and bistre	20	10
200		2s. multicoloured	30	90
197/200 *Set of 4*			80	1·00

Designs:—6d. Kingston seal, diving, sailing, swimming and water polo; 8d. Kingston seal, pole-vaulting, javelin throwing, discus throwing, relay-racing and hurdling; 2s. Kingston coat of arms and athlete.
An imperf miniature sheet exists, but this was never available at face value or at any post office.

(Des M. Goaman. Litho D.L.R.)

1963 (4 June). Freedom from Hunger. P 12½.

201	**93**	1d. multicoloured	25	10
202		8d. multicoloured	1·25	60

1963 (4 Sept). Red Cross Centenary. As Nos. 226/7 of Bahamas.

203		2d. red and black	15	10
204		1s.6d. red and blue	50	1·50

1963–64. As Nos. 181/90, but wmk w **12**.

205	**67**	½d. black and deep orange-red (3.12.63*)	10	15
206	**68**	1d. black and emerald (3.4.64)	10	1·75
207	**70**	2½d. black and deep bright blue (3.4.64)	25	2·75
208	**71**	3d. emerald and red-brown (17.12.63*)	15	15
209	**73**	5d. scarlet and bronze-green (3.4.64)	40	2·75
210	**75**	8d. ultramarine and red-orange (3.4.64)	20	75
211	**76**	1s. yellow-green and blue (21.12.63*)	35	75
212	**78**	2s. dp blue & dp bronze-green (3.4.64)	60	7·00
213	**79**	3s. black and blue (5.2.64)	2·75	5·00
205/13 *Set of 9*			4·25	19·00

The overprint on the 8d., 1s. and 2s. is at lower left, the others as before.
*These are the earliest known dates recorded in Jamaica.

95 Carole Joan Crawford ("Miss World 1963")

(Des and photo D.L.R.)

1964 (14 Feb–25 May). "Miss World 1963" Commemoration. P 13.

214	**95**	3d. multicoloured	10	10
215		1s. multicoloured	15	10
216		1s.6d. multicoloured	20	50
214/16 *Set of 3*			40	60
MS216*a* 153×101 mm. Nos. 214/16. Imperf (25.5.64)			1·40	2·75

96 Lignum Vitae

97 Blue Mahoe

103 Gypsum Industry

109 Arms of Jamaica

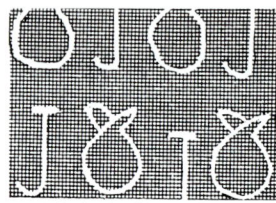

111 Multiple "J" and Pineapple

(Des V. Whiteley. Photo Harrison)

1964 (4 May)–**68**. T **96**/**7**, **103**, **109** and similar designs. W **111**. P 14½ (1d., 2d., 2½d., 6d., 8d.), 14×14½ (1½d., 3d., 4d., 10s.), 14½×14 (9d., 1s., 3s., 5s., £1) or 13½×14½ (1s.6d., 2s.).

217		1d. violet-blue, deep green and light brown (shades)	10	10
218		1½d. multicoloured	15	10
219		2d. red, yellow and grey-green	15	10
		w. Wmk inverted	9·50	
220		2½d. multicoloured	1·00	60
221		3d. yellow, black and emerald	15	10
222		4d. ochre and violet	50	10
223		6d. multicoloured	2·25	10
		a. Blue omitted	95·00	
		b. Value omitted	£2000	
		w. Wmk inverted	17·00	
224		8d. mult (yellowish green background)	2·50	1·50
		a. Red (beak) omitted	£200	
		b. Greyish green background (16.7.68)	9·00	8·00
225		9d. blue and yellow-bistre	1·50	10
226		1s. black and light brown	20	10
		a. Light brown omitted	£3000	£3000
		ab. Value only omitted	£1600	
		b. Black omitted	£2250	
		ba. "NATIONAL STADIUM" etc omitted	£1100	£1100
227		1s.6d. black, light blue and buff	4·00	15
228		2s. red-brown, black and light blue	2·75	15
229		3s. blue and dull green	1·00	80
		aw. Wmk inverted	13·00	
		b. Perf 13½×14½	35	65
230		5s. black, ochre and blue	1·25	1·00
		w. Wmk inverted	£100	
231		10s. multicoloured	1·25	1·25
		a. Blue ("JAMAICA", etc) omitted	£450	
232		£1 multicoloured	2·50	1·00
217/32 *Set of 16*			18·00	6·00

Designs: *Horiz*. (As T **96**)—1½d. Ackee; 2½d. Land shells; 3d. National flag over Jamaica; 4d. Antillean Murex (*Murex formosus*) (shell); 6d. *Papilio homerus* (butterfly); 8d. Streamertail. As T **103**—1s. National Stadium; 1s.6d. Palisadoes International Airport; 2s. Bauxite mining; 3s. Blue Marlin (sport fishing); 5s. Exploration of sunken city, Port Royal; £1 Queen Elizabeth II and national flag.

No. 223*b*. Two left half sheets are known with the black printing shifted downwards to such an extent that the value is omitted from the top row.

Nos. 226*a*/*ab* came from a sheet on which the two bottom rows had the colour omitted with the next row showing it missing from the lower third of the stamps.

No. 226*b* comes from the bottom row of one sheet and rows seven and eight of a second sheet; the latter also being the source of No. 226*ba*.

For a full range of Stanley Gibbons catalogues, please visit **www.stanleygibbons.com**

112

JAMAICA

112 Scout Belt
113 Globe, Scout Hat and Scarf 
114 Scout Badge and Alligator 

(Photo Harrison)

1964 (27 Aug). Sixth Inter-American Scout Conference, Kingston. W **111**. P 14 (1s.) or 14½×14 (others).

233	112	3d. red, black and pink	10	10
234	113	8d. bright blue, olive and black	15	25
		w. Wmk inverted	38·00	
235	114	1s. gold, deep blue and light blue	20	45
		w. Wmk inverted	20	45
233/5 Set of 3			40	70

115 Gordon House, Kingston
118 Eleanor Roosevelt 

(Des V. Whiteley. Photo Harrison)

1964 (16 Nov). Tenth Commonwealth Parliamentary Conference, Kingston. T **115** and similar horiz designs. W **111**. P 14½×14.

236		3d. black and yellow-green	10	10
237		6d. black and carmine-red	30	10
238		1s.6d. black and bright blue	50	30
236/8 Set of 3			80	40

Designs:—6d. Headquarters House, Kingston; 1s.6d. House of Assembly, Spanish Town.

(Des V. Whiteley. Photo Harrison)

1964 (10 Dec). 16th Anniv of Declaration of Human Rights. W **111**. P 14½×14.

239	118	1s. black, red and light green	10	10

119 Guides' Emblem on Map
120 Guide Emblems 

(Photo Harrison)

1965 (17 May). Golden Jubilee of Jamaica Girl Guides Association. W **111** (sideways on 3d.). P 14×14½ (3d.) or 14 (1s.).

240	119	3d. yellow, green and light blue	10	10
241	120	1s. yellow, black and apple-green	20	40
		w. Wmk inverted	20	40

121 Uniform Cap
122 Flag-bearer and Drummer 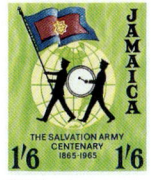

(Photo Harrison)

1965 (23 Aug). Salvation Army Centenary. W **111**. P 14×14½ (3d.) or 14½×14 (1s.6d.).

242	121	3d. multicoloured	30	10
		w. Wmk inverted	17·00	
243	122	1s.6d. multicoloured	70	50
		w. Wmk inverted	38·00	

123 Paul Bogle, William Gordon and Morant Bay Court House
124 Abeng-blower, "Telstar", Morse Key and I.T.U. Emblem 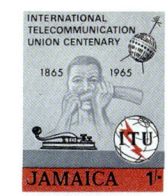

(Photo Enschedé)

1965 (29 Dec). Centenary of Morant Bay Rebellion. No wmk. P 14×13.

244	123	3d. light brown, ultramarine and black	10	10
245		1s.6d. light brown, yellow-green and black	20	10
246		3s. light brown, rose and black	30	95
244/6 Set of 3			55	1·00

(Photo Harrison)

1965 (29 Dec). I.T.U. Centenary. W **111**. P 14×14½.

247	124	1s. black, grey-blue and red	40	20

(125) 
126 Sir Winston Churchill

1966 (3 Mar). Royal Visit. Nos. 221, 223, 226/7 optd with T **125**.

248		3d. yellow, black and emerald	15	10
249		6d. multicoloured	2·25	50
250		1s. black and light brown	55	10
251		1s.6d. black, light blue and buff	2·50	2·75
248/51 Set of 4			5·00	3·00

(Des Jennifer Toombs. Photo Harrison)

1966 (18 April). Churchill Commemoration. W **111**. P 14.

252	126	6d. black and olive-green	65	30
253		1s. bistre-brown and deep violet-blue	85	80

127 Statue of Athlete and Flags
131 Bolivar's Statue and Flags of Jamaica and Venezuela 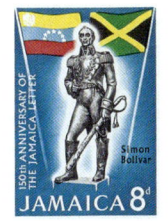

(Des V. Whiteley. Photo Harrison)

1966 (4 Aug). Eighth British Empire and Commonwealth Games. T **127** and similar horiz designs. W **111**. P 14½×14.

254		3d. multicoloured	10	10

113

JAMAICA

255		6d. multicoloured	60	10
		w. Wmk inverted	32·00	
256		1s. multicoloured	10	10
257		3s. bright gold and deep blue	35	45
		w. Wmk inverted	32·00	
254/7	*Set of 4*		1·00	55
MS258	128×103 mm. Nos. 254/7. Imperf		4·00	8·00

Designs:—6d. Racing cyclists; 1s. National Stadium, Kingston; 3s. Games emblem.

No. **MS**258 has been seen with the whole printing inverted except for the brown background.

(Des and photo Harrison)

1966 (5 Dec). 150th Anniv of "Jamaica Letter". W **111**. P 14×15.

259	**131**	8d. multicoloured	20	10
		w. Wmk inverted	32·00	

132 Jamaican Pavilion

133 Sir Donald Sangster (Prime Minister)

(Des V. Whiteley. Photo Harrison)

1967 (28 Apr). World Fair, Montreal. W **111**. P 14½.

260	**132**	6d. multicoloured	10	15
261		1s. multicoloured	10	15
		w. Wmk inverted	10·00	

(Des and photo Enschedé)

1967 (28 Aug). Sangster Memorial Issue. P 13½.

262	**133**	3d. multicoloured	10	10
263		1s.6d. multicoloured	20	20

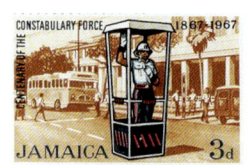

134 Traffic Duty

135 Personnel of the Force

(Des V. Whiteley. Photo Enschedé)

1967 (28 Nov). Centenary of the Constabulary Force. T **134**/5 and similar horiz design. Multicoloured. W **111**. P 13½×14.

264		3d. Type **134**	40	10
		a. Wmk sideways	1·50	2·75
265		1s. Type **135**	40	10
266		1s.6d. Badge and Constables of 1867 and 1967 (as T **134**)	50	75
264/6	*Set of 3*		1·10	85

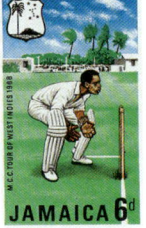

136 Wicket-keeping

137 Sir Alexander and Lady Bustamante

(Des V. Whiteley. Photo Harrison)

1968 (8 Feb). M.C.C.'s West Indian Tour. T **136** and similar vert designs. Multicoloured. W **111** (sideways*). P 14.

267		6d. Type **136**	50	65
		a. Horiz strip of 3. Nos. 267/9	1·25	1·75
		w. Wmk top of J to right	50	65
268		6d. Batting	50	65
		w. Wmk top of J to right	50	65
269		6d. Bowling	50	65
		w. Wmk top of J to right	50	65
267/9	*Set of 3*		1·25	1·75

*The normal sideways watermark shows the top of the "J" to left, *as seen from the back of the stamp.*

Nos. 267/9 were issued in small sheets of 9 comprising three *se-tenant* strips as No. 267a.

Nos. 267/9 exist on PVA gum as well as on gum arabic.

(Des and photo Harrison)

1968 (23 May). Labour Day. W **111**. P 14.

270	**137**	3d. rose and black	10	15
271		1s. olive and black	10	15

138 Human Rights Emblem over Map of Jamaica

(Photo Harrison)

1968 (3 Dec). Human Rights Year. T **138** and similar multicoloured designs. W **111**. P 14.

272		3d. Type **138**	10	10
		a. Gold (flame) omitted	£150	
		w. Wmk inverted	6·50	
273		1s. Hands cupping Human Rights emblem (vert)	20	10
274		3s. Jamaican holding "Human Rights"	60	1·25
		a. Gold (flame) omitted	£170	
272/4	*Set of 3*		75	1·25

Three designs, showing 3d. Bowls of Grain, 1s. Abacus, 3s. Hands in Prayer, were prepared but not issued (*Price for set of 3 mint £200*).

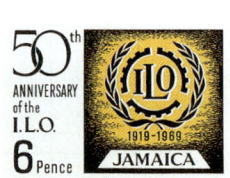

141 I.L.O. Emblem

142 Nurse, and Children being weighed and measured

(Des V. Whiteley. Litho Format)

1969 (23 May). 50th Anniv of International Labour Organization. P 14.

275	**141**	6d. orange-yellow and blackish brown	10	10
276		3s. bright emerald and blackish brown	30	45

(Des and photo Harrison)

1969 (30 May). 20th Anniv of W.H.O. T **142** and similar designs. W **111**. P 14.

277		6d. grey, brown and orange	10	15
278		1s. black, sepia and blue-green	10	15
279		3s. grey-black, brown and pale bright blue	20	1·25
277/9	*Set of 3*		30	1·40

Designs: *Horiz*—1s. Malaria eradication. *Vert*—3s. Trainee nurse.

(New Currency. 100 cents = 1 Jamaica dollar)

C-DAY
8th September 1969
1c

(145)

114

JAMAICA

1969 (8 Sept). Decimal currency. Nos. 217, 219, 221/3 and 225/32 surch as T **145**. Sterling values unobliterated except 1c. to 4c. and 8c.

280	1c. on 1d. violet-blue, deep green & light brown	10	10
281	2c. on 2d. red, yellow and grey-green	10	10
	w. Wmk inverted	3·00	
282	3c. on 3d. yellow, black and emerald	10	10
283	4c. on 4d. ochre and violet	1·25	10
	a. "8t" of "8th" omitted (R. 10/1)	65·00	
284	5c. on 6d. multicoloured	1·25	10
	a. Blue omitted	£100	
285	8c. on 9d. blue and yellow-bistre	10	10
286	10c. on 1s. black and light brown	10	10
287	15c. on 1s.6d. black, light blue and buff	50	90
288	20c. on 2s. red-brown, black and light blue	1·50	1·50
	a. "8th" omitted	£1700	
289	30c. on 3s. blue and dull green	2·50	3·00
290	50c. on 5s. black, ochre and blue	1·25	3·00
291	$1 on 10s. multicoloured	1·25	6·50
	w. Wmk inverted	£130	
292	$2 on £1 multicoloured	2·25	6·50
280/92 Set of 13		10·50	19·00

No. 281 exists with PVA gum as well as gum arabic.
Unlike the positional No. 283a the similar variety on the 20c. on 2s. was caused by a paper fold.

146 "The Adoration of the Kings" (detail, Foppa)

149 Half Penny, 1869

(Des J. Cooter. Litho D.L.R.)

1969 (25 Oct). Christmas. Paintings. T **146** and similar vert designs. Multicoloured. W **111**. P 13.

293	2c. Type **146**	20	40
294	5c. "Madonna, Child and St. John" (Raphael)	25	40
295	8c. "The Adoration of the Kings" (detail, Dosso Dossi)	25	40
293/5 Set of 3		65	1·10

(Des G. Drummond. Litho P.B.)

1969 (27 Oct). Centenary of First Jamaican Coins. T **149** and similar horiz design. W **111**. P 12½.

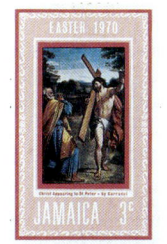

296	3c. silver, black and mauve	15	25
	b. Wmk sideways	1·25	1·75
297	15c. silver, black and light emerald	10	10

Design:—15c. One penny, 1869.

151 George William Gordon

156 "Christ appearing to St. Peter" (Carracci)

(Des G. Vasarhelyi. Litho Enschedé)

1970 (11 Mar). National Heroes. T **151** and similar vert designs. Multicoloured. P 12×12½.

298	1c. Type **151**	10	10
	a. Yellow (from flags) omitted	£400	
299	3c. Sir Alexander Bustamante	10	10
300	5c. Norman Manley	10	10
301	10c. Marcus Garvey	15	10
302	15c. Paul Bogle	30	25
298/302 Set of 5		50	40

(Des G. Drummond. Photo Enschedé)

1970 (23 Mar). Easter. T **156** and similar vert designs. Multicoloured. W **111**. P 12×12½.

303	3c. Type **156**	10	10
	w. Wmk inverted		

304	10c. "Christ Crucified" (Antonello da Messina)	10	10
	w. Wmk inverted		
305	20c. Easter Lily	20	60
303/5 Set of 3		30	70

(**159**)

1970 (16 July). No. 219 surch with T **159**.

| 306 | 2c. on 2d. red, yellow and grey-green | 20 | 20 |

160 Lignum Vitae

1970 (7 Sept–2 Nov). Decimal Currency. Designs as Nos. 217/32 but inscr as T **160** in new currency. W **111** (sideways on 2, 4, 15, 20c. and $1). P 14½ (1, 5c.), 14×14½ (4c., $1), 13½×14½ (15, 20c.) or 14½×14 (others).

307	1c. violet-blue, deep green & light brown	75	2·00
308	2c. red, yellow and grey-green (as 2d.)	30	10
309	3c. yellow, black and emerald (as 3d.)	50	1·00
310	4c. ochre and violet (as 4d.)	2·75	30
311	5c. multicoloured (as 6d.)	3·00	65
312	8c. blue and yellow-bistre (as 9d.)	2·25	10
	a. Wmk sideways	2·00	45
313	10c. black and light brown (as 1s.)	60	20
314	15c. light blue and buff (as 1s.6d.) (2.11)	2·75	3·00
315	20c. red-brown, black and lt blue (as 2s.) (2.11)	1·25	3·00
316	30c. blue and dull green (as 3s.) (2.11)	4·00	6·50
317	50c. black, ochre and blue (as 5s.) (2.11)	1·75	3·75
318	$1 multicoloured (as 10s.) (2.11)	1·00	5·50
319	$2 multicoloured (as £1) (2.11)	1·50	4·00
307/19 Set of 13		19·00	26·00

161 Cable Ship *Dacia*

(Des G. Drummond. Litho J.W.)

1970 (12 Oct). Centenary of Telegraph Service. T **161** and similar horiz designs. W **111** (sideways). P 14½×14.

320	3c. yellow, red and black	25	10
321	10c. black and turquoise	35	10
322	50c. multicoloured	80	1·00
320/2 Set of 3		1·25	1·10

Designs:—10c. Bright's cable gear aboard *Dacia*; 50c. Morse key and chart.

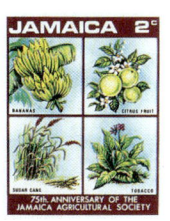

164 Bananas, Citrus, Sugar-Cane and Tobacco

165 Locomotive *Projector* (1845)

(Des G. Drummond. Litho Questa)

1970 (2 Nov). 75th Anniv of Jamaican Agricultural Society. W **111**. P 14.

323	**164**	2c. multicoloured	25	60
		w. Wmk inverted	8·50	
324		10c. multicoloured	45	10

(Des V. Whiteley. Litho Format)

1970 (21 Nov). 125th Anniv of Jamaican Railways. T **165** and similar horiz designs. Multicoloured. W **111** (sideways). P 13½.

325	3c. Type **165**	30	10
326	15c. Steam locomotive No. 54 (1944)	65	30
327	50c. Diesel locomotive No. 102 (1967)	1·25	1·75
325/7 Set of 3		2·00	2·00

JAMAICA

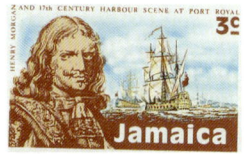

168 Church of St. Jago de la Vega

169 Henry Morgan and Ships

(Des R. Granger Barrett. Litho J.W.)

1971 (22 Feb). Centenary of Disestablishment of the Church of England in Jamaica. T **168** and similar vert design. Multicoloured. W **111**. P 14½.

328	3c. Type **168**	10	10
329	10c. Type **168**	10	10
	w. Wmk inverted		
330	20c. Type **168**	30	30
	w. Wmk inverted	50·00	
331	30c. Emblem of Church of England in Jamaica	30	1·25
	w. Wmk inverted		
328/31 Set of 4		60	1·50

(Des J.W. Litho Questa)

1971 (10 May). Pirates and Buccaneers. T **169** and similar horiz designs. Multicoloured. W **111** (sideways*). P 14.

332	3c. Type **169**	1·00	10
	w. Wmk top of J to right	14·00	
333	15c. Mary Read, Anne Bonny and trial pamphlet	1·25	15
334	30c. Pirate schooner attacking merchantman	2·00	1·25
332/4 Set of 3		3·75	1·40

*The normal sideways watermark shows the top of the "J" to left, *as seen from the back of the stamp.*

170 1s. Stamp, of 1919 with Frame Inverted

171 Satellite and Dish Aerial

(Des Jennifer Toombs. Litho J. W.)

1971 (30 Oct). Tercentenary of Post Office Establishment. T **170** and similar designs. W **111** (sideways* except 50c.). P 13½.

335	3c. black and lake	15	20
336	5c. grey-black and bright green	20	20
337	8c. black and violet	20	10
	w. Wmk top of J to right		
338	10c. brown, black and indigo	20	10
339	20c. multicoloured	35	45
340	50c. ochre, black and slate	50	2·00
335/40 Set of 6		1·40	2·75

Designs: *Horiz*—3c. Dummer packet letter, 1705; 5c. Pre-stamp inland letter, 1793; 8c. Harbour St. P.O., Kingston, 1820; 10c. Modern stamp and cancellation; 20c. British stamps used in Jamaica, 1859.

*The normal sideways watermark shows top of J to left, *as seen from the back of the stamp.*

(Des Cable & Wireless Ltd. Litho J.W.)

1972 (17 Feb). Opening of Jamaican Earth Satellite Station. W **111**. P 14×13½.

341	**171**	3c. multicoloured	15	10
		w. Wmk inverted	†	—
342		15c. multicoloured	30	15
343		50c. multicoloured	65	1·25
341/3 Set of 3			1·00	1·25

172 Causeway, Kingston Harbour

173 Air Jamaica Hostess and Vickers VC-10

(Des J.W. Litho Format)

1972 (17 Apr–2 Oct). Multicoloured designs as T **172** (1 to 6c.) or **173** (8c. to $2). W **111** (sideways* on horiz designs). P 14½×14 (1, 2c.), 14×14½ (3, 4, 5, 6c.) or 13½ (others).

344	1c. Pimento (*vert*) (5.6)	10	10
345	2c. Red Ginger (5.6)	10	10
346	3c. Bauxite Industry (5.6)	10	10
	w. Wmk top of J to right	6·50	
347	4c. Type **172**	10	10
	w. Wmk top of J to right	10	10
348	5c. Oil Refinery (5.6)	10	10
	w. Wmk top of J to right	28·00	
349	6c. Senate Building, University of the West Indies (5.6)	10	10
350	8c. National Stadium (5.6)	30	10
	w. Wmk top of J to right		
351	9c. Devon House (5.6)	10	10
352	10c. Type **173**	20	10
	w. Wmk top of J to right	38·00	
353	15c. Old Iron Bridge, Spanish Town (*vert*) (2.10)	2·00	10
354	20c. College of Arts, Science and Technology (2.10)	30	15
355	30c. Dunn's River Falls (*vert*) (2.10)	65	15
356	50c. River rafting (5.6)	1·75	40
357	$1 Jamaica House (2.10)	75	1·50
	w. Wmk top of J to right	40·00	
358	$2 Kings House (2.10)	1·00	1·50
344/58 Set of 15		6·50	3·75

*The normal sideways watermark shows the top of the J to the left, *as seen from the back of the stamp.*

TENTH ANNIVERSARY INDEPENDENCE 1962-1972
(174)

1972 (8 Aug). Tenth Anniv of Independence. Nos. 346, 352 and 356 optd as T **174**.

359	3c. Bauxite Industry	30	30
	w. Wmk top of J to right	19·00	
360	10c. Type **173**	30	10
	w. Wmk top of J to right		
361	50c. River rafting	75	2·25
359/61 Set of 3		1·25	2·25

*The normal sideways watermark shows top of J to left, *as seen from the back of the stamp.*

175 Arms of Kingston

176 Small Indian Mongoose on Map

(Des R. Granger Barrett. Litho J.W.)

1972 (4 Dec). Centenary of Kingston as Capital. W **111** (sideways on 50c.). P 13½×14 (5 and 30c.) or 14×13½ (50c.).

362	**175**	5c. multicoloured	15	10
363		30c. multicoloured	35	35
364	—	50c. multicoloured	60	2·25
362/4 Set of 3			1·00	2·40

The 50c. is as T **175**, but horiz.

JAMAICA

(Des R. Granger Barrett. Litho Questa)

1973 (9 Apr). Centenary of Introduction of the Mongoose. T **176** and similar horiz designs. W **111** (sideways). P 14×14½.

365	8c. light apple-green, yellow-green and black .	15	10
366	40c. light cobalt, light blue and black................	35	65
367	60c. salmon-pink, brownish salmon and black.	60	1·25
365/7 *Set of 3*		1·00	1·75
MS368 165×95 mm. Nos. 365/7		1·10	4·00

Designs:—10c. Mongoose and rat; 60c. Mongoose and chicken.

177 *Euphorbia punicea*

(Des Sylvia Goaman. Litho Questa)

1973 (9 July). Flora. T **177** and similar diamond-shaped designs. Multicoloured. W **111**. P 14.

369	1c. Type **177**...	10	30
370	6c. *Hylocereus triangularis*	15	20
371	9c. *Columnea argentea*	15	20
372	15c. *Portlandia grandiflora*	25	20
373	30c. *Samyda pubescens*	40	60
374	50c. *Cordia sebestena*	60	1·40
369/74 *Set of 6*		1·50	2·50

178 *Broughtonia sanguinea*

(Des Sylvia Goaman. Litho B.W.)

1973 (8 Oct). Orchids. T **178** and similar multicoloured designs. W **111** (sideways on 5c., $1). P 14×13½ (5c., $1) or 13½×14 (others).

375	5c. Type **178**...	40	10
376	10c. *Arpophyllum jamaicense* (vert)..................	50	10
	w. Wmk inverted	18·00	
377	20c. *Oncidium pulchellum* (vert)	1·00	25
378	$1 *Brassia maculata*	2·50	3·25
375/8 *Set of 4*		4·00	6·00
MS379 161×95 mm. Nos. 375/8. Wmk sideways. P 12 ...		4·00	5·50
	a. Printed on the gummed side (blue and brown plates only)..		

No. **MS**379a has positive impressions of the blue and brown plates printed on the reverse in addition to the normal design on the front.

179 *Mary*, 1808–15

(Des J. Cooter. Litho J.W.)

1974 (8 Apr). Mail Packet Boats. T **179** and similar horiz designs. Multicoloured. W **111** (sideways on Nos. 380/3, upright on **MS**384). P 13½ (5c., 50c.) or 14½ (others).

380	5c. Type **179**...	75	10
	a. Perf 14½	1·00	3·50
381	10c. *Queensbury*, 1814–27................................	75	10
382	15c. *Sheldrake*, 1829–34	1·00	40
383	50c. *Thames I*, 1842	2·00	2·50
380/3 *Set of 4*		4·00	2·75
MS384 133×159 mm. Nos. 380/3. P 13½ (*sold at 90c.*) ..		2·75	5·00

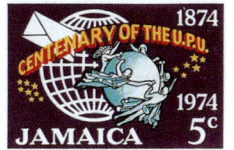

180 "Journeys"

181 U.P.U. Emblem and Globe

(Des R. Granger Barrett. Litho Questa)

1974 (1 Aug). National Dance Theatre Company. T **180** and similar vert designs showing dance-works. Multicoloured. W **111**. P 13½.

385	5c. Type **180**...	10	10
386	10c. "Jamaican Promenade".............................	10	10
387	30c. "Jamaican Promenade".............................	30	30
388	50c. "Miss Criolla"...	50	80
385/8 *Set of 4*		80	1·10
MS389 161×102 mm. Nos. 385/8 (*sold at $1*)		1·50	2·50

(Des V. Whiteley. Litho J.W.)

1974 (9 Oct). Centenary of Universal Postal Union. W **111** (sideways*). P 14.

390	**181** 5c. multicoloured	10	10
391	9c. multicoloured	10	10
392	50c. multicoloured	35	80
	w. Wmk top of J to right	50·00	
390/2 *Set of 3*		50	80

*The normal sideways watermark shows the top of the J to left, *as seen from the back of the stamp*.

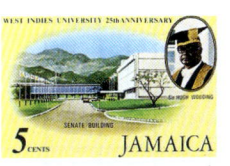

182 Senate Building and Sir Hugh Wooding

183 Commonwealth Symbol

(Des R. Granger Barrett. Litho Questa)

1975 (13 Jan). 25th Anniv of University of West Indies. T **182** and similar horiz design. Multicoloured. W **111** (sideways). P 14.

393	5c. Type **182**...	10	10
394	10c. University Chapel and H.R.H. Princess Alice	10	10
395	30c. Type **182**...	20	25
396	50c. As 10c.	35	60
393/6 *Set of 4*		60	80

(Des C. Abbott. Litho Questa)

1975 (29 Apr). Heads of Commonwealth Conference. T **183** and similar square designs. Multicoloured. W **111**. P 13½.

397	5c. Type **183**...	10	10
398	10c. Jamaican coat of arms	10	10
399	30c. Dove of Peace	15	30
400	50c. Jamaican flag	30	2·25
397/400 *Set of 4*		50	2·40

184 Jamaican Kite Swallowtail (*Eurytides marcellinus*)

185 Koo Koo or Actor Boy

117

JAMAICA

(Des J. Cooter. Litho Questa)

1975 (25 Aug). Butterflies (1st series). T **184** and similar vert designs showing the family Papilionidae. Multicoloured. W **111**. P 14.
401	10c. Type **184**...	55	20
402	20c. Orange Swallowtail (*Papilo thoas*)	1·10	1·10
403	25c. False Androgeus Swallowtail (*Papilo thersites*)	1·25	2·00
404	30c. Homerus Swallowtail (*Papilo homerus*)...	1·40	2·75
401/4 Set of 4		4·00	5·50
MS405 134×179 mm. Nos. 401/4 (sold at 95c.)		5·50	7·50

See also Nos. 429/33 and 443/47.

(Des C. Abbott. Litho J.W.)

1975 (3 Nov). Christmas. T **185** and similar vert designs showing Belisario prints of "John Canoe" (Christmas) Festival (1st series). Multicoloured. W **111**. P 14.
406	8c. Type **185**...	15	10
407	10c. Red Set-girls	15	10
408	20c. French Set-girls	50	20
409	50c. Jaw-bone or House John Canoe	95	2·50
	w. Wmk inverted		
406/9 Set of 4		1·60	2·50
MS410 138×141 mm. Nos. 406/9. P 13½ (sold at $1)........		2·00	3·75

See also Nos. 421/4.

186 Bordone Map, 1528

(Des L. Curtis. Litho Questa)

1976 (12 Mar). 16th-century Maps of Jamaica. T **186** and similar horiz designs. W **111** (sideways*). P 13½.
411	10c. brown, light stone and light vermilion....	25	10
412	20c. multicoloured	45	25
	w. Wmk top of J to right	22·00	
413	30c. multicoloured	70	85
414	50c. multicoloured	95	2·75
411/14 Set of 4		2·10	3·50

Designs:—20c. Porcacchi map, 1576; 30c. DeBry map, 1594; 50c. Langenes map, 1598.

*The normal sideways watermark shows the top of the J to left, *as seen from the back of the stamp*.

See also Nos. 425/8.

187 Olympic Rings

(Des Sir H. McDonald: adapted V. Whiteley Studio. Litho Walsall)

1976 (14 June). Olympic Games, Montreal. W **111** (sideways). P 13½.
415	**187**	10c. multicoloured	15	10
416		20c. multicoloured	30	20
417		25c. multicoloured	30	25
418		50c. multicoloured	45	2·25
415/18 Set of 4			1·10	2·50

187a Map of the Caribbean

(Des PAD Studio. Litho Questa)

1976 (9 Aug). West Indian Victory in World Cricket Cup. T **187a** and similar design. No wmk. P 14.
419	10c. multicoloured	50	50
420	25c. black and magenta............................	75	1·75

Design: *Vert*—25c. Prudential Cup.

(Des C. Abbott. Litho J.W.)

1976 (8 Nov). Christmas. Belisario Prints (2nd series). Multicoloured designs as T **185**. W **111**. P 13½.
421	10c. Queen of the set-girls	10	10
422	20c. Band of the Jaw-bone John Canoe..........	25	10
423	50c. Koo Koo (actor-boy)...........................	45	2·00
	w. Wmk inverted	7·00	
421/3 Set of 3		70	1·75
MS424 110×140 mm. Nos. 421/3. P 14×14½ (sold at 90c.)		70	2·00

(Des L. Curtis. Litho J.W.)

1977 (28 Feb). 17th Century Maps of Jamaica. Designs as T **186**. W **111** (sideways). P 13.
425	9c. multicoloured	30	40
426	10c. multicoloured	30	10
427	25c. grey-black, pale blue and bright blue.....	70	60
428	40c. grey-black, light turquoise and grey-blue.	80	2·25
425/8 Set of 4		1·90	3·00

Designs:—9c. Hickeringill map, 1661; 10c. Ogilby map, 1671; 25c. Visscher map, 1680; 40c. Thornton map, 1689.

(Des J. Cooter. Litho J.W.)

1977 (9 May). Butterflies (2nd series). Multicoloured designs as T **184**. W **111**. P 13½.
429	10c. False Barred Sulphur (*Eurema elathea*)....	35	10
430	20c. Bronze Wing (*Dynamine egaea*).............	75	55
431	25c. Jamaican Harlequin (*Chlosyne pantoni*)..	1·00	1·50
	w. Wmk inverted	24·00	
432	40c. Mimic (*Hypolimnas misippus*)	1·50	5·00
	w. Wmk inverted	60·00	
429/32 Set of 4		3·25	6·50
MS433 139×120 mm. Nos. 429/32. P 14½ (sold at $1.05)		4·50	7·00

188 Map, Scout Emblem and Streamertail

189 Trumpeter

(Des Daphne Padden. Litho Questa)

1977 (5 Aug). Sixth Caribbean Jamboree, Jamaica. Multicoloured; background colours given. W **111** (sideways). P 13½.
434	**188**	10c. new blue	65	10
435		20c. light yellow-green	1·00	25
436		25c. orange	1·00	35
437		50c. light magenta	1·50	1·75
434/7 Set of 4			3·75	2·25

(Des C. Abbott, Litho Questa)

1977 (19 Dec). 50th Anniv of Jamaica Military Band. T **189** and similar multicoloured designs. W **111** (sideways on horiz designs). P 14.
438	9c. Type **189**...	15	10
439	10c. Clarinet players and oboe player............	15	10
440	20c. Kettle drummer and clarinetist (*vert*)	40	35
441	25c. Double-bass player and trumpeter (*vert*)	55	65
438/41 Set of 4		1·10	1·00
MS442 120×137 mm. Nos. 438/41. Wmk sideways (sold at 75c.)		2·50	4·50

(Des J. Cooter. Litho Walsall)

1978 (17 Apr). Butterflies (3rd series). Multicoloured designs as T **184**. W **111**. P 14.
443	10c. Jamaican Hairstreak (*Callophrys crethona*)	50	10
444	20c. Malachite (*Siproeta stelenes*)	85	20
445	25c. Common Long-tailed Skipper (*Urbanus proteus*)...	95	65
446	50c. Troglodyte (*Anaea troglodyta*).............	2·00	3·25
443/6 Set of 4		3·75	3·75
MS447 100×125 mm. Nos. 443/6 (sold at $1.15)		4·50	6·00
	a. Error. Imperf	£200	

NEW INFORMATION

The editor is always interested to correspond with people who have new information that will improve or correct this catalogue

118

JAMAICA

190 Half-figure with Canopy

191 Norman Manley (statue)

(Des J. Cooter. Litho J.W.)

1978 (10 July). Arawak Artefacts (1st series). T **190** and similar vert designs. W **111**. P 13½×13.

448	10c. deep brown, yellow and black	10	10
449	20c. deep brown, mauve and black	15	10
450	50c. deep brown, apple-green and black	35	35
448/50 Set of 3		50	45
MS451 135×90 mm. Nos. 448/50. P 14 (*sold at* 90c.)		60	1·25

Designs:—20c. Standing figure; 50c. Birdman.
See also Nos. 479/83.

(Des and litho J.W.)

1978 (25 Sept). 24th Commonwealth Parliamentary Conference. T **191** and similar vert designs. Multicoloured. W **111**. P 13.

452	10c. Type **191**	15	10
453	20c. Sir Alexander Bustamante (statue)	25	15
454	25c. City of Kingston Crest	35	20
455	40c. Gordon House Chamber, House of Representatives	35	65
452/5 Set of 4		1·00	1·00

192 Band and Banner

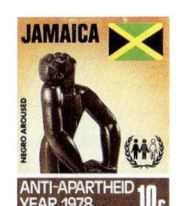

193 "Negro Aroused" (sculpture by Edna Manley)

(Des V. Whiteley. Litho J. W.)

1978 (4 Dec). Christmas. Centenary of Salvation Army. T **192** and similar horiz designs. Multicoloured. W **111** (sideways). P 14.

456	10c. Type **192**	30	10
457	20c. Trumpeter	35	20
458	25c. Banner	35	30
459	50c. William Booth (founder)	60	2·00
456/9 Set of 4		1·40	2·25

(Des G. Hutchins. Litho J.W.)

1978 (11 Dec). International Anti-Apartheid Year. W **111**. P 13.

460	**193**	10c. multicoloured	30	20

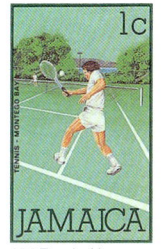

194 Tennis, Montego Bay

195 Arms and Map of Jamaica

(Des and litho Harrison ($5). Des Walsall. Litho J.W. (others))

1979 (15 Jan)–**84**. Vert designs as T **194**, and T **195**. Multicoloured. White ordinary paper (15, 65, 75c., $5) or cream chalk-surfaced paper (others). W **111** (sideways on $5). P 14½×14 ($5) or 13½ (others).

461	1c. Type **194** (26.11.79)	70	1·00
462	2c. Golf, Tryall, Hanover (26.11.79)	2·25	3·00
	a. White ordinary paper (8.84)	3·50	3·50
463	4c. Horse riding, Negril Beach (26.11.79)	1·00	2·50
	a. White ordinary paper (8.84)	3·50	3·50
464	5c. Old waterwheel, Tryall, Hanover (26.11.79)	1·25	30
	a. White ordinary paper (27.8.82)	3·50	3·00
465	6c. Fern Gully, Ocho Rios (26.11.79)	1·50	2·75
466	7c. Dunn's River Falls, Ocho Rios (26.11.79)	70	30
467	8c. Jamaican Tody (bird) (28.4.80)	1·00	1·25
468	10c. Jamaican Mango (bird) (28.4.80)	1·00	20
	a. White ordinary paper (27.8.82)	3·50	1·00
469	12c. Yellow-billed Amazon (28.4.80)	1·00	2·00
470	15c. Streamertail (bird) (28.4.80)	1·00	30
471	35c. White-chinned Thrush (28.4.80)	1·50	30
472	50c. Jamaican Woodpecker (28.4.80)	1·75	30
473	65c. Rafting, Martha Brae Trelawny (28.4.80)	1·75	3·25
474	75c. Blue Marlin Fleet, Port Antonio (28.4.80)	2·00	2·75
475	$1 Scuba Diving, Ocho Rios (28.4.80)	2·50	2·75
	a. White ordinary paper (27.8.82)	6·00	4·75
476	$2 Sailing boats, Montego Bay (28.4.80)	2·50	1·00
	a. White ordinary paper (27.8.82)	6·00	5·00
477	$5 Type **195**	1·00	1·75
461/77 Set of 17		22·00	23·00

TENTH ANNIVERSARY AIR JAMAICA 1st APRIL 1979
(**196**)

197 Grinding Stone, *circa* 400 BC.

1979 (2 Apr). 10th Anniv of Air Jamaica. No. 352 optd with T **196**.

478	10c. Type **173**	50	50

(Des D. Bowen. Litho Questa)

1979 (23 Apr). Arawak Artefacts (2nd series). T **197** and similar multicoloured designs. W **111** (sideways on 10, 20 and 25c.). P 14.

479	5c. Type **197**	10	10
480	10c. Stone implements, *c*. 500 AD (*horiz*)	10	10
481	20c. Cooking pot, *c*. 300 AD (*horiz*)	10	15
482	25c. Serving boat, *c*. 300 AD (*horiz*)	10	20
483	50c. Storage jar fragment, *c*. 300 AD	25	60
479/83 Set of 5		55	1·00

198 1962 1s.6d. Independence Commemorative Stamp

(Des J. W. from a local design by J. Mahfood. Litho Walsall)

1979 (13 Aug). Death Centenary of Sir Rowland Hill. T **198** and similar horiz designs showing stamps and Sir Rowland Hill. W **111** (sideways*). P 14.

484	10c. black, scarlet–vermilion and brt scarlet	15	10
	w. Wmk top of J to right	5·00	
485	20c. orange–yellow and yellowish brown	15	15
486	25c. mauve and blue	20	20
487	50c. multicoloured	25	70
484/7 Set of 4		65	1·00
MS488 146×94 mm. No. 485 (*sold at* 30c.)		30	85

Designs:—20c. 1920 1s. with frame inverted; 25c. 1860 6d.; 50c. 1968 3d. Human Rights Year commemorative.

*The normal sideways watermark has top of J to left, *when seen from the back of the stamp.*

199 Group of Children

119

JAMAICA

(Des J.W. Litho Harrison)

1979 (1 Oct). Christmas. International Year of the Child. T **199** and similar multicoloured designs. W **111** (sideways on 10, 25 and 50c.). P. 14.

489	10c. Type **199**	10	10
490	20c. Doll (*vert*)	10	10
491	25c. "The Family" (painting by child)	15	15
492	50c. "House on the Hill" (painting by child)	25	40
489/92	Set of 4	50	60

200 Date Tree Hall, 1886 (original home of Institute)

(Des G. Drummond. Litho Walsall)

1980 (25 Feb). Centenary of Institute of Jamaica. T **200** and similar multicoloured designs. W **111** (sideways on 5, 15 and 50c.). P 13½.

493	5c. Type **200**	10	10
494	15c. Institute building, 1980	15	10
495	35c. Microfilm reader (*vert*)	25	20
496	50c. Hawksbill Turtle and Green Turtle	45	85
497	75c. Jamaican Owl (*vert*)	1·75	3·00
493/7	Set of 5	2·50	3·75

201 Don Quarrie (200 Metres, 1976)

(Des BG Studio. Litho J.W.)

1980 (21 July). Olympic Games, Moscow. Jamaican Olympic Athletics Gold Medal Winners. T **201** and similar horiz designs. Multicoloured. W **111** (sideways*). P. 13.

498	15c. Type **201**	40	15
	w. Wmk top of J to left	11·00	
499	35c. Arthur Wint (4×400 Metres Relay, 1952)	45	80
	a. Horiz strip of 4. Nos. 499/502	1·60	3·00
500	35c. Leslie Laing (4×400 Metres Relay, 1952)	45	80
501	35c. Herbert McKenley (4×400 Metres Relay, 1952)	45	80
502	35c. George Rhoden (4×400 Metres Relay, 1952)	45	80
498/502	Set of 5	2·00	3·00

*The normal sideways watermark shows the top of J to right, *as seen from the back of the stamp*.

Nos. 499/502 were printed together, *se-tenant*, in horizontal strips of 4 throughout the sheet.

202 Parish Church    **203** Blood Cup Sponge

(Des J.W. Litho Harrison)

1980 (24 Nov). Christmas. Churches (1st series). T **202** and similar horiz designs. Multicoloured. W **111** (sideways). P. 14.

503	15c. Type **202**	10	10
504	20c. Coke Memorial Church	10	10
505	25c. Church of the Redeemer	15	10
506	$5 Holy Trinity Cathedral	1·00	2·00
503/6	Set of 4	1·10	2·10
MS507	120×139 mm. Nos. 503/6. P 14½ (*sold at $5.70*)	1·25	3·25

See also Nos. 537/40 and 570/2.

(Des J. Mahfood. Litho Walsall)

1981 (27 Feb). Marine Life (1st series). T **203** and similar multicoloured designs. W **111** (sideways on 45 and 75c.). P. 14.

508	20c. Type **203**	15	10
509	45c. Tube Sponge (*horiz*)	25	35
510	60c. Black Coral	35	45
511	75c. Tyre Reef (*horiz*)	40	75
508/11	Set of 4	1·00	1·50

See also Nos. 541/5.

204 Brown's Hutia (or Indian Coney) 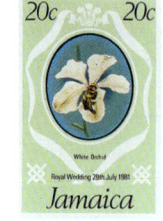   **205** White Orchid

(Des D. Bowen. Litho Questa)

1981 (25 May). Brown's Hutia (or Indian Coney). T **204** and similar horiz designs. Multicoloured. W **111**. P. 14.

512	20c. Hutia facing right	20	30
	a. Horiz strip of 4. Nos. 512/15	70	1·10
513	20c. Type **204**	20	30
514	20c. Hutia facing left and eating	20	30
515	20c. Hutia family	20	30
512/15	Set of 4	70	1·10

Nos. 512/15 were printed together, *se-tenant*, in horizontal strips of 4 throughout the sheet.

(Des J.W. Litho Format)

1981 (29 July). Royal Wedding. T **205** and similar vert designs. Multicoloured. W w **14** (sideways*). P 13½ ($5) or 15 (others).

516	20c. Type **205**	10	10
	aw. Wmk Crown to right of CA	35	
	b. Perf 15×14½	25	25
	ba. Booklet pane. Nos. 516b/19b	3·50	
517	45c. Royal Coach	10	10
	aw. Wmk Crown to right of CA	55	
	b. Perf 15×14½	50	50
518	60c. Prince Charles and Lady Diana Spencer	25	20
	aw. Wmk Crown to right of CA	60	
	b. Perf 15×14½	60	60
519	$5 St. James' Palace	70	85
	aw. Wmk Crown to right of CA	2·50	
	b. Perf 15×14½	2·50	3·50
	bw. Wmk Crown to right of CA	2·50	
516/19	Set of 4	1·00	1·00
MS520	98×85 mm. No. 519. Wmk upright. P 13½	1·00	1·75
	w. Wmk inverted	2·75	

*The normal sideways watermark shows Crown to left of CA, *as seen from the back of the stamp*.

Nos. 516/18 also exist perforated 13½ (*price for set of 3 70p. mint or used*) from additional sheetlets of 5 stamps and one label. No. 519 exists from both normal sheets and sheetlets.

Nos. 516b/19b are from $6.25 stamp booklets.

206 Blind Man at Work    **207** W.F.D. Emblem on 1964 1½d. Definitive

(Des G. Vasarhelyi. Litho J.W.)

1981 (14 Sept). International Year for Disabled Persons. T **206** and similar horiz designs. Multicoloured. W **111** (sideways). P. 13.

521	20c. Type **206**	20	15
522	45c. Painting with the mouth	40	40
523	60c. Deaf student communicating with sign language	50	75
524	$1.50 Basketball players	2·25	2·50
521/4	Set of 4	3·00	3·50

120

JAMAICA

(Des J. Mahfood. Litho J. W.)

1981 (16 Oct). World Food Day. Stamps on Stamps. T **207** and similar designs showing W.F.D. emblems on various definitives. W **111** (sideways on 20c., $2 and $4). P. 13.

525	20c. multicoloured	45	15
526	45c. black, rose and orange	80	40
527	$2 black, violet-blue and green	2·25	1·40
528	$4 black, green and light brown	3·25	2·50
525/8 Set of 4		6·00	4·00

Designs: Vert as T **207**—45c. 1922 1d. (40×26 mm.)—$2 As 1938 3d. but with W.F.D. emblem replacing King's head; $4 As 1938 1s. but with W.F.D. emblem replacing King's head.

Nos. 525/8 were so designed that the face values obliterated those on the stamps depicted.

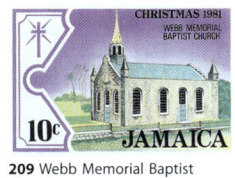

208 "Survival" (song title)

209 Webb Memorial Baptist Church

(Litho Format)

1981 (20 Oct). Bob Marley (musician) Commemoration. T **208** and similar vert designs inscribed with song titles. In black and vermilion ($5.25) or multicoloured (others). W w **14** (sideways). P. 15.

529	1c. Type **208**	70	1·10
530	2c. "Exodus"	70	1·10
531	3c. "Is this Love"	70	1·10
532	15c. "Coming in from the Cold"*	3·25	30
533	20c. "Positive Vibration"†	3·25	30
534	60c. "War"	4·00	3·00
535	$3 "Could you be Loved"	6·50	12·00
529/35 Set of 7		17·00	17·00
MS536 134×110 mm. $5.25, Bob Marley (wmk upright)		8·50	4·75

*Part of initial "C" of song title inscription does not show on the design.
†Incorrectly inscribed "OSITIVE VIBRATION".

(Des J.W. Litho Questa)

1981 (11 Dec). Christmas. Churches (2nd series). T **209** and similar horiz designs. Multicoloured. W **111** (sideways). P. 14.

537	10c. Type **209**	10	10
538	45c. Church of God in Jamaica	30	15
539	$5 Bryce United Church	1·75	2·50
537/9 Set of 3		1·90	2·50
MS540 120×168 mm. Nos. 537/9 (wmk upright). P 12		3·50	3·50

210 Gorgonian Coral

211 Cub Scout

(Des J. Mahfood; adapted PAD Studio. Litho Questa)

1982 (22 Feb). Marine Life (2nd series). T **210** and similar multicoloured designs. W **111** (sideways on 45, 60, 75c. and $3). P. 14.

541	20c. Type **210**	45	10
542	45c. Hard Sponge and diver (horiz)	65	25
543	60c. American Manatee (horiz)	90	55
544	75c. Plume Worm (horiz)	1·00	65
545	$3 Coral Banded Shrimp (horiz)	2·50	1·75
541/5 Set of 5		5·00	3·00

(Des L. Curtis. Litho J.W.)

1982 (12 July). 75th Anniv of Boy Scout Movement. T **211** and similar vert designs. Multicoloured. W **111**. P 13½×13.

546	20c. Type **211**	50	15
547	45c. Scout camp	85	40
548	60c. "Out of Many, One People"	1·10	90
549	$2 Lord Baden-Powell	1·75	2·50
546/9 Set of 4		3·75	3·50
MS550 80×130 mm. Nos. 546/9		5·00	6·00

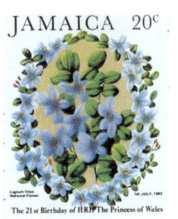

212 Lignum vitae (national flower)

(**212**a)

(Des R. Sauer. Litho Questa)

1982 (30 Aug). 21st Birthday of Princess of Wales. T **212** and similar vert designs. W **111**. P 14½×14.

551	20c. Type **212**	35	20
	a. Booklet pane. Nos. 551/3	2·00	
552	45c. Carriage ride	50	35
553	60c. Wedding	70	60
554	75c. Saxifraga longifolia	1·25	2·75
	a. Booklet pane. Nos. 554/6	3·50	
555	$2 Princess of Wales	1·60	3·00
556	$3 Viola gracilis major	1·60	3·50
551/6 Set of 6		5·50	9·50
MS557 106×75 mm. $5 Honeymoon photograph		1·40	2·50

Nos. 554 and 556 were printed in small sheets of 6 including one se-tenant, stamp-size, label. The other values were printed in sheets of 40.

1982 (13 Sept). Birth of Prince William of Wales. Nos. 551/7 optd with T **212**a.

558	20c. Type **212**	20	20
	a. Booklet pane. Nos. 558/60	80	
559	45c. Carriage ride	30	35
560	60c. Wedding	40	60
561	75c. Saxifraga longifolia	70	2·25
	a. Booklet pane. Nos. 561/3	2·25	
562	$2 Princess of Wales	75	2·75
563	$3 Viola gracilis major	1·00	2·50
558/63 Set of 6		3·25	8·50
MS564 106×75 mm. $5 Honeymoon photograph		1·50	3·50

213 Prey Captured

214 Queen Elizabeth II

(Des N. Arlott. Litho Questa)

1982 (25 Oct). Jamaican Birds (1st series). Jamaican Lizard Cuckoo. T **213** and similar vert designs. Multicoloured. W **111**. P 14½.

565	$1 Type **213**	1·40	1·60
	a. Horiz strip of 5. Nos. 565/9	6·00	7·00
566	$1 Searching for prey	1·40	1·60
567	$1 Calling prior to prey search	1·40	1·60
568	$1 Adult landing	1·40	1·60
569	$1 Adult flying in	1·40	1·60
565/9 Set of 5		6·00	7·00

Nos. 565/9 were printed in horizontal se-tenant strips of 5 throughout the sheet.

See also Nos. 642/5 and 707/10.

(Des and litho J.W.)

1982 (8 Dec). Christmas. Churches (3rd series). Horiz designs as T **209**. Multicoloured. W **111** (sideways). P. 13.

570	20c. United Pentecostal Church	70	10
571	45c. Disciples of Christ Church	1·25	25
572	75c. Open Bible Church	2·00	3·75
570/2 Set of 3		3·50	3·75

(Des D. Miller. Litho Walsall)

1983 (14 Feb). Royal Visit. T **214** and similar vert design. Multicoloured. W **111**. P. 14.

573	$2 Type **214**	3·00	3·50
574	$3 Coat of Arms	4·00	6·00

121

JAMAICA

215 Folk Dancing

(Des Walsall. Litho Format)

1983 (14 Mar). Commonwealth Day. T **215** and similar horiz designs. Multicoloured. W **111** (sideways*). P 14.

575	20c. Type **215**	15	15
576	45c. Bauxite mining	35	35
577	75c. World map showing position of Jamaica	45	45
578	$2 Coat of arms and family	60	1·40
	w. Wmk top of J to right	14·00	
575/8 Set of 4		1·40	2·10

*The normal sideways watermark has top of "J" to left, *as seen from the back of the stamp.*

216 General Cargo Ship at Wharf

217 Norman Manley and Sir Alexander Bustamante

(Des A. Theobald. Litho Format)

1983 (17 Mar). 25th Anniv of International Maritime Organization. T **216** and similar horiz designs. Multicoloured. P 14.

579	15c. Type **216**	75	40
580	20c. *Veendam* (cruise liner) at Kingston	1·00	40
581	45c. *Astronomer* (container ship) entering port	1·75	85
582	$1 Tanker passing International Seabed Headquarters Building	2·75	5·50
579/82 Set of 4		5·50	6·50

(Des D. Miller. Litho Harrison)

1983 (25 July). 21st Anniv of Independence. W **111**. P 14.

583	**217**	15c. multicoloured	15	50
584		20c. multicoloured	15	60
585		45c. multicoloured	30	85
583/5 Set of 3			55	1·75

218 Ship-to-Shore Radio

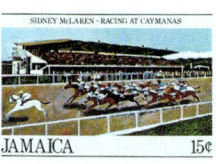

219 "Racing at Caymanas" (Sidney McLaren)

(Des Walsall. Litho Harrison)

1983 (18 Oct). World Communications Year. T **218** and similar horiz designs. Multicoloured. W **111** (sideways). P 14.

586	20c. Type **218**	90	15
587	45c. Postal services	1·75	40
588	75c. Telephone communications	1·90	3·50
589	$1 T.V. via satellite	2·00	4·00
586/9 Set of 4		6·00	7·25

(Des D. Miller. Litho J.W.)

1983 (12 Dec). Christmas. Paintings. T **219** and similar multicoloured designs. W **111** (sideways on 15c., 20c.). P 13½×13½ (15c., 20c.) or 13½×13 (others).

590	15c. Type **219**	15	10
591	20c. "Seated Figures" (Karl Parboosingh)	15	10
592	75c. "The Petitioner" (Henry Daley) (*vert*)	50	65
593	$2 "Banana Plantation" (John Dunkley) (*vert*)	1·25	4·00
590/3 Set of 4		1·90	4·25

220 Sir Alexander Bustamante

221 De Havilland D.H. 60G Gipsy Moth Seaplane

(Des D. Miller. Litho Questa)

1984 (24 Feb). Birth Centenary of Sir Alexander Bustamante. T **220** and similar vert design. Multicoloured. W **111**. P 14.

594	20c. Type **220**	90	1·60
	a. Horiz pair. Nos. 594/5	1·75	3·00
595	20c. Birthplace, Blenheim	90	1·60

Nos. 594/5 were printed together, *se-tenant*, in horizontal pairs throughout the sheet.

(Des A. Theobald. Litho Questa)

1984 (11 June). Seaplanes and Flying Boats. T **221** and similar horiz designs. Multicoloured. W **111** (sideways). P 14.

596	25c. Type **221**	1·50	20
597	55c. Consolidated Commodore flying boat	2·00	85
598	$1.50 Sikorsky S-38A flying boat	3·25	4·00
599	$3 Sikorsky S-40 flying boat *American Clipper*	4·00	6·00
596/9 Set of 4		9·50	10·00

222 Cycling

(Des G. Vasarhelyi. Litho J.W.)

1984 (11 July). Olympic Games, Los Angeles. T **222** and similar horiz designs. Multicoloured. W **111** (sideways). P 14.

600	25c. Type **222**	2·00	50
601	55c. Relay running	60	30
602	$1.50 Start of race	1·75	4·50
603	$3 Finish of race	2·25	5·00
600/3 Set of 4		6·00	9·25
MS604 135×105 mm. Nos. 600/3 (*sold at $5.40*). P 13×13½		7·50	8·50

223

1984 (7 Aug). Nos. 465 and 469 surch as T **223**.

605	5c. on 6c. Fern Gully, Ocho Rios	15	40
606	10c. on 12c. Yellow-billed Amazon	1·10	60

224 Head of Jamaican Boa Snake

(Des I. Loe. Litho Questa)

1984 (22 Oct). Endangered Species. Jamaican Boa Snake. T **224** and similar horiz designs. Multicoloured. W **111** (sideways). P 14½.

607	25c. Type **224**	6·00	40
608	55c. Boa snake on branch over stream	7·00	80
609	70c. Snake with young	8·00	4·00
610	$1 Snake on log	9·00	5·00
607/10 Set of 4		27·00	9·25
MS611 133×97 mm. As Nos. 607/10 but without W.W.F. emblem (*sold at $2.60*)		6·00	7·00

JAMAICA

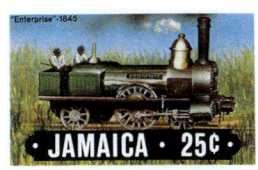

225 Locomotive *Enterprise* (1845)

(Des D. Hartley–Marjoram. Litho Enschedé)

1984 (16 Nov). Railway Locomotives (1st series). T **225** and similar horiz designs. Multicoloured. W **111** (sideways). P 13½×13.
612	25c. Type **225**...	1·50	30
613	55c. Tank locomotive (1880)	1·75	70
614	$1.50 Kitson-Meyer tank locomotive (1904).....	2·75	3·00
615	$3 Super-heated locomotive No. 40 (1916)	4·00	5·50
612/15 *Set of 4*...		9·00	8·50

See also Nos. 634/7.

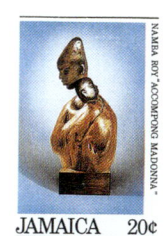

226 "Accompong Madonna" (Namba Roy)

227 Brown Pelicans flying

(Des G. Vasarhelyi. Litho Harrison)

1984 (6 Dec). Christmas. Sculptures. T **226** and similar vert designs. Multicoloured. W **111**. P 14.
616	20c. Type **226**...	30	10
617	25c. "Head (Alvin Marriott)	35	10
618	55c. "Moon" (Edna Manley)	70	65
619	$1.50 "All Women are Five Women" (Mallica Reynolds (Kapo))	1·50	4·00
616/19 *Set of 4*...		2·50	4·25

(Des N. Arlott. Litho Walsall)

1985 (15 Apr). Birth Bicentenary of John J. Audubon (ornithologist). Brown Pelican. T **227** and similar vert designs. Multicoloured. W **111**. P 13½×13.
620	20c. Type **227**...	1·00	20
621	55c. Diving for fish	1·50	40
622	$2 Young pelican taking food from adult.....	2·50	3·25
623	$5 "Brown Pelican" (John J. Audubon)..........	3·75	6·50
620/3 *Set of 4*...		8·00	9·25
MS624 100×100 mm. Nos. 620/3 (*sold at $7.85*)		6·00	8·00

228 The Queen Mother at Belfast University

229 Maps and Emblems

(Des A. Theobald ($5), C. Abbott (others). Litho Questa)

1985 (7 June). Life and Times of Queen Elizabeth the Queen Mother. T **228** and similar vert designs. Multicoloured. W **111**. P 14½×14.
625	25c. With photograph album, 1963	50	10
626	55c. With Prince Charles at Garter Ceremony, Windsor Castle, 1983	70	15
	w. Wmk inverted	50	
627	$1.50 Type **228**...	1·25	1·75
628	$3 With Prince Henry at his christening (from photo by Lord Snowdon).................	2·25	3·25
625/8 *Set of 4*...		4·00	4·75
MS629 91×74 mm. $5 With the Queen, Prince Philip and Princess Anne at Ascot. Wmk sideways		2·75	1·75

(Des D. Miller. Litho Harrison)

1985 (30 July). International Youth Year and 5th Pan-American Scout Jamboree. W **111** (sideways). P 14.
630	**229** 25c. multicoloured	1·50	10
631	55c. multicoloured	1·75	25
632	70c. multicoloured	2·00	1·50
633	$4 multicoloured	4·00	10·00
630/3 *Set of 4*...		8·25	10·50

(Des D. Hartley. Litho Harrison)

1985 (30 Sept). Railway Locomotives (2nd series). Horiz designs as T **225**. Multicoloured. W **111** (sideways). P 14.
634	25c. Baldwin steam locomotive No. 16...........	1·25	30
635	55c. Rogers locomotive................................	1·75	35
636	$1.50 Locomotive *Projector*, 1845.......................	2·75	3·50
637	$4 Diesel locomotive No. 102.......................	3·75	6·50
634/7 *Set of 4*...		8·50	9·50

230 "The Old Settlement" (Ralph Campbell)

(Litho Format)

1985 (9 Dec). Christmas. Jamaican Paintings. T **230** and similar multicoloured designs. W **111** (sideways on 20, 75c.). P 14.
638	20c. Type **230**...	10	10
639	55c. "The Vendor" (Albert Huie) (*vert*)........	15	15
640	75c. "Road Menders" (Gaston Tabois)	20	35
641	$4 "Woman, must I not be about my Father's business?" (Carl Abrahams) (*vert*)...............	1·10	2·25
638/41 *Set of 4*...		1·40	2·50

(Des N. Arlott. Litho B.D.T.)

1986 (10 Feb). Jamaican Birds (2nd series). Vert designs as T **213**. Multicoloured. W **111**. P 14.
642	25c. Chestnut-bellied Cuckoo.....................	50	10
643	55c. Jamaican Becard..................................	65	30
644	$1.50 White-eyed Thrush	85	2·00
645	$5 Rufous-tailed Flycatcher........................	1·75	4·75
642/5 *Set of 4*...		3·25	6·25

230a Princess Elizabeth and Princess Margaret, 1939

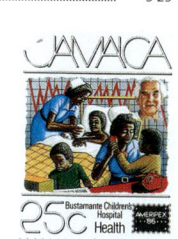

231 Bustamante Children's Hospital

(Des A. Theobald. Litho Harrison)

1986 (21 Apr). 60th Birthday of Queen Elizabeth II. T **230a** and similar vert designs. Multicoloured. W **111**. P 14½×14.
646	20c. Type **230a**...	35	10
647	25c. With Prince Charles and Prince Andrew, 1962..	35	10
648	70c. Queen visiting War Memorial, Montego Bay, 1983	40	30
649	$3 On state visit to Luxembourg, 1976.........	60	1·50
650	$5 At Crown Agents Head Office, London, 1983..	75	2·25
646/50 *Set of 5*...		2·25	3·75

(Des D. Miller. Litho Questa)

1986 (19 May). "Ameripex '86" International Stamp Exhibition, Chicago. T **231** and similar vert designs. Multicoloured. W **111**. P 14½×14.
651	25c. Type **231**...	70	15
652	55c. Air Jamaica Boeing 737 airliner and map of holiday resorts	2·25	40
653	$3 Norman Manley Law School.......................	1·25	4·00
654	$5 Bauxite and agricultural exports...............	7·50	9·50
651/4 *Set of 4*...		10·50	12·50
MS655 85×106 mm. Nos. 651/4 (*sold at $8.90*).................		12·00	13·00

123

JAMAICA

231a Prince Andrew and Miss Sarah Ferguson, Ascot, 1985

236 Norman Manley

237 Arms of Jamaica

(Des D. Miller. Litho Walsall)

1986 (23 July). Royal Wedding. T **231a** and similar square design. Multicoloured. W **111**. P 14½×14.

656	20c. Type **231a**	15	10
657	$5 Prince Andrew making speech, Fredericton, Canada, 1985	1·00	2·25

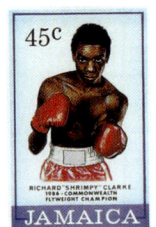

232 Richard "Shrimpy" Clarke

(233)

(Des G. Vasarhelyi. Litho Questa)

1986 (27 Oct). Jamaican Boxing Champions. T **232** and similar vert designs. Multicoloured. W **111**. P 14.

658	45c. Type **232**	20	15
659	70c. Michael McCallum	30	30
660	$2 Trevor Berbick	70	1·75
661	$4 Richard "Shrimpy" Clarke, Michael McCallum and Trevor Berbick	1·25	3·00
658/61	Set of 4	2·25	4·75

1986 (3 Nov). Nos. 472/3 surch as T **233**.

662	5c. on 50c. Jamaican Woodpecker	3·00	3·00
663	10c. on 65c. Rafting, Martha Brae Trelawny	1·75	2·50

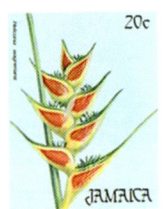

234 Heliconia wagneriana

235 Crown Cone (*Conus regius*)

(Des Annette Robinson. Litho B.D.T.)

1986 (1 Dec). Christmas. Flowers (1st series). T **234** and similar multicoloured designs. W **111** (sideways on 25c., $5). P 13½.

664	20c. Type **234**	10	10
665	25c. *Heliconia psittacorum* (horiz)	10	10
666	55c. *Heliconia rostrata*	20	30
667	$5 *Strelitzia reginae* (horiz)	1·60	5·00
664/7	Set of 4	1·75	5·00

See also Nos. 703/6 and 739/42.

(Des A. Riley. Litho Format)

1987 (23 Feb). Sea Shells. T **235** and similar vert designs. Multicoloured. W **111**. P 15.

668	35c. Type **235**	45	15
669	75c. Measled Cowrie (*Cypraea zebra*)	65	60
670	$1 Atlantic Trumpet Triton (*Charonia variegata*)	75	90
671	$5 Rooster-tail Conch (*Strombus gallus*)	1·50	4·50
668/71	Set of 4	3·00	5·50

(Des C. Slania (1c. to 90c.). Litho Enschedé)

1987 (18 May)–**97**. Vert portraits as T **236** and T **237**. W **111** (sideways on $1 to $50). Cream paper (2c. to 9c. Nos. 673A/80A). P 12½×13 (1 to 90c.) or 13×13½ ($1 to $50).

A. Without imprint

672A	**236**	1c. scarlet and pale pink	10	1·25
673A		2c. bright carmine and pale rose-pink	10	1·25
674A		3c. yellow-olive and pale stone	15	1·25
675A		4c. myrtle-green and pale green	15	1·25
676A		5c. slate-blue and pale bluish grey	45	1·00
677A		6c. dull ultram and pale lavender-grey	30	1·00
678A		7c. reddish violet and pale mauve	60	1·00
679A		8c. deep magenta and pale rose-pink	30	15
680A		9c. olive-sepia and pale brown	60	20
681A	–	10c. deep rose-red and pale pink	40	10
682A	–	20c. reddish orange and flesh	60	40
683A	–	30c. bright green and pale green	50	15
684A	–	40c. dp turquoise-grn and pale turq-grn	60	40
685A	–	50c. grey-olive and pale olive-grey	70	40
686A	–	60c. bright blue and pale azure	40	40
687A	–	70c. bluish violet and pale violet	40	30
688A	–	80c. reddish violet and pale rose-lilac	50	40
689A	–	90c. lt reddish brown and pale grey-brn	50	50
690A	**237**	$1 olive-sepia and cream	50	30
691A		$2 bright orange and cream	50	70
692A		$5 brown-olive and pale stone	60	1·25
693A		$10 deep turquoise-blue and pale azure	70	1·75
672A/93A	Set of 22		8·50	13·50

B. With imprint date at foot

676B	**236**	5c. slate-blue and pale bluish grey (6.6.88)	50	1·00
681B	–	10c. dp rose-red and pale pk (11.93)	1·25	1·00
		a. Chalk-surface paper (10.10.94)	2·50	1·00
682B	–	20c. reddish orange and flesh (6.6.88)	50	10
		a. Chalk-surfaced paper (5.92)	20	30
683aB	–	30c. bright green and pale green (*chalk-surfaced paper*) (10.10.94)	1·25	1·75
684B	–	40c. dp turquoise-green and pale turq-green (12.2.91)	1·00	1·00
		a. Chalk-surfaced paper (5.92)	60	1·00
685B	–	50c. grey-ol and pale ol-grey (12.2.91)	1·50	1·00
		a. Chalk-surfaced paper (5.92)	60	1·00
685cB	–	55c. brown-bistre and cream (*chalk-surfaced paper*) (10.10.94)	1·50	1·25
689B	–	90c. light reddish brown and pale grey-brown (11.93)	2·25	1·00
		a. Chalk-surfaced paper (5.92)	1·00	1·50
690B	**237**	$1 olive-sepia and cream (6.6.91)	70	50
		a. Chalk-surfaced paper (30.4.97)	50	40
690cB		$1.10 olive-sepia and cream (*chalk-surfaced paper*) (10.10.94)	1·00	40
691aB		$2 bright orange and cream (*chalk-surfaced paper*) (30.4.97)	1·50	1·25
692aB		$5 brown-olive and pale stone (*chalk-surfaced paper*) (30.4.97)	1·50	1·50
693cB		$25 bluish violet and pale lavender (9.10.91)	1·50	2·00
693dB		$50 deep mauve and pale rose-lilac (9.10.91)	2·50	3·25
676B/93dB	Set of 13		14·00	15·00

Designs:—10c. to 90c. Sir Alexander Bustamante.
Imprint dates: "1988", Nos. 676B, 682B; "1989", No. 682B; "1991", Nos. 684B/5/B, 690B, 693cB/dB; "1992", Nos. 682Ba, 684Ba, 685Ba, 689Ba, 690B; "1993", Nos. 681B/2B, 685B, 689B/90B; "1994", Nos. 681Ba, 682Ba, 683aB, 684Ba, 685Ba, 685cB, 690cB; "1997", Nos. 690Ba, 691aB, 692aB.

The background colour on printings of Type **237** from 1992 onwards is fluorescent.

JAMAICA

238 Jamaican Flag and Coast at Sunset

239 Marcus Garvey

(Des D. Miller. Litho Walsall)

1987 (27 July). 25th Anniv of Independence. T **238** and similar multicoloured design. W **111** (sideways on 70c.). P 14.
694	55c. Type **238**	1·50	60
695	70c. Jamaican flag and inscription (*horiz*)	1·50	2·75

(Des D. Miller. Litho Walsall)

1987 (17 Aug). Birth Centenary of Marcus Garvey (founder of Universal Negro Improvement Association). T **239** and similar vert design, both black, emerald and lemon. W **111**. P 14.
696	25c. Type **239**	1·25	2·00
	a. Horiz pair. Nos. 696/7	2·50	4·00
697	25c. Statue of Marcus Garvey	1·25	2·00

Nos. 696/7 were printed together, *se-tenant*, in horizontal pairs throughout the sheet.

240 Salvation Army School for the Blind

241 Hibiscus Hybrid

(Des L. Curtis. Litho Walsall)

1987 (8 Oct). Centenary of Salvation Army in Jamaica. T **240** and similar horiz designs. Multicoloured. W **111** (sideways). P 13×13½.
698	25c. Type **240**	1·50	30
699	55c. Col. Mary Booth and Bramwell Booth Memorial Hall	1·50	30
700	$3 Welfare Service lorry, 1929	4·75	5·50
701	$5 Col. Abram Davey and S.S. *Alene*, 1887	6·00	8·50
698/701 Set of 4		12·50	13·00
MS702 100×80 mm. Nos. 698/701 (*sold at $8.90*)		15·00	15·00

(Des Annette Robinson. Litho Harrison)

1987 (30 Nov). Christmas. Flowers (2nd series). T **241** and similar vert designs. Multicoloured. W **111**. P 14½×14.
703	20c. Type **241**	15	10
704	25c. *Hibiscus elatus*	15	10
705	$4 *Hibiscus cannabinus*	2·00	3·75
706	$5 *Hibiscus rosasinensis*	2·25	3·75
703/6 Set of 4		4·00	7·00

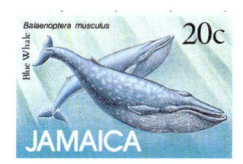

242 Chestnut-bellied Cuckoo, Black-billed Amazon and Jamaican Euphonia

243 Blue Whales

(Des N. Arlott. Litho Walsall)

1988 (22 Jan). Jamaican Birds (3rd series). T **242** and similar vert designs. Multicoloured. W **111**. P 14.
707	45c. Type **242**	1·75	2·50
	a. Horiz pair. Nos. 707/8	3·50	5·00
708	45c. Black-billed Amazon, Jamaican White-eyed Vireo, Rufous-throated Solitaire and Yellow Elaenia	1·75	2·50
709	$5 Snowy Plover, Little Blue Heron and Great Blue Heron (white phase)	4·25	5·50
	a. Horiz pair. Nos. 709/10	8·50	11·00
710	$5 Black-necked Stilt, Snowy Egret, Snowy Plover and Black-crowned Night Heron	4·25	5·50
707/10 Set of 4		11·00	14·50

The two designs of each value were printed together, *se-tenant*, in horizontal pairs throughout the sheets, each pair forming a composite design.

(Des A. Riley. Litho Harrison)

1988 (14 Apr). Marine Mammals. T **243** and similar horiz designs. Multicoloured. W **111** (sideways). P 14.
711	20c. Type **243**	2·00	70
712	25c. Gervais's Whales	2·00	70
713	55c. Killer Whales	3·00	80
714	$5 Common Dolphins	5·00	10·00
711/14 Set of 4		11·00	11·00

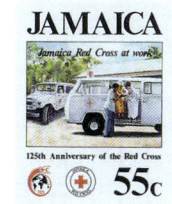

243a Jackie Hendriks

244 Jamaican Red Cross Workers with Ambulance

(Des D. Hartley. Litho Walsall)

1988 (6 June). West Indian Cricket. T **243a** and similar horiz designs, each showing portrait, cricket equipment and early belt buckle. Multicoloured. W **111** (sideways). P 14.
715	25c. Type **243a**	1·50	40
716	55c. George Headley	1·60	80
717	$2 Michael Holding	3·50	3·00
718	$3 R.K. Nunes	3·75	4·75
719	$4 Allan Rae	4·00	5·00
715/19 Set of 5		13·00	12·00

(Des S. Noon. Litho Walsall)

1988 (8 Aug). 125th Anniv of International Red Cross. T **244** and similar vert design. Multicoloured. W **111**. P 14½×14.
720	55c. Type **244**	75	30
721	$5 Henri Dunant (founder) in field hospital	2·75	4·25

245 Boxing

(Des P. Broadbent. Litho B.D.T.)

1988 (24 Aug). Olympic Games, Seoul. T **245** and similar horiz designs. Multicoloured. W **111** (sideways). P 14.
722	25c. Type **245**	40	10
723	45c. Cycling	2·50	70
724	$4 Athletics	2·50	3·25
725	$5 Hurdling	2·50	3·25
722/5 Set of 4		7·00	6·50
MS726 127×87 mm. Nos. 722/5 (*sold at $9.90*)		7·00	7·00

246 Bobsled Team Members and Logo

JAMAICA

(Des D. Miller. Litho B.D.T.)

1988 (4 Nov). Jamaican Olympic Bobsled Team. T **246** and similar horiz designs. Multicoloured. W **111** (sideways*). P 14.

727	25c. Type **246**	50	1·25
	a. Horiz pair. Nos. 727/8	1·00	2·50
728	25c. Two-man bobsled	50	1·25
729	$5 Bobsled team members (*different*) and logo	2·50	4·00
	a. Horiz pair. Nos. 729/30	5·00	8·00
	aw. Wmk top of J to right	5·50	9·00
730	$5 Four-man bobsled	2·50	4·00
727/30 Set of 4		5·50	9·50

*The normal sideways watermark has top of "J" to left, *as seen from the back of the stamp*.

Nos. 727/8 and 729/30 were printed together, *se-tenant*, in horizontal pairs throughout the sheets.

+25c

HURRICANE GILBERT RELIEF FUND
(**247**)

1988 (11 Nov). Hurricane Gilbert Relief Fund. Nos. 722/5 surch as T **247** by Format in red or black (same price either colour).

731	25c. +25c. Type **245**	10	20
732	45c. +45c. Cycling	50	30
733	$4 +$4 Athletics	1·10	2·25
734	$5 +$5 Hurdling	1·10	2·50
731/4 Set of 4		2·50	4·75

248 Nurses and Firemen

(Des S. Noon. Litho Format)

1988 (24 Nov). Year of the Worker. T **248** and similar horiz designs. Multicoloured. W **111** (sideways). P 14.

735	25c. Type **248**	2·00	30
736	55c. Woodcarver	45	30
737	$3 Textile workers	1·00	3·00
738	$5 Workers on fish farm	1·25	3·50
735/8 Set of 4		4·25	6·25

(Des Annette Robinson. Litho Format)

1988 (15 Dec). Christmas. Flowers (3rd series). Multicoloured designs as T **241**. W **111** (sideways on 55c., $4). P 14.

739	25c. *Euphorbia pulcherrima*	70	10
740	55c. *Spathodea campanulata* (horiz)	85	15
741	$3 *Hylocereus triangularis*	2·00	2·25
742	$4 *Broughtonia sanguinea* (horiz)	2·00	2·25
739/42 Set of 4		5·00	4·25

249 Old York Castle School

250 *Syntomidopsis variegata*

(Des A. Theobald. Litho B.D.T.)

1989 (19 Jan). Bicentenary of Methodist Church in Jamaica. T **249** and similar horiz designs. Multicoloured. W **111** (sideways). P 14.

743	25c. black and bright blue	30	10
744	45c. black and rosine	35	10
745	$5 black and yellow-green	3·00	5·50
743/5 Set of 3		3·25	5·50

Designs:—45c. Revd. Thomas Coke and Parade Chapel, Kingston; $5 Father Hugh Sherlock and St. John's Church.

(Des I. Loe. Litho B.D.T.)

1989 (30 Aug). Jamaican Moths (1st series). T **250** and similar vert designs. Multicoloured. W **111**. P 13½.

746	25c. Type **250**	50	10
747	55c. *Himantoides perkinsae*	80	30
748	$3 *Arctia nigriplaga*	1·50	3·50
749	$5 *Sthenognatha toddi*	1·90	4·25
746/9 Set of 4		4·25	7·25

See also Nos. 758/61 and 790/3.

251 Arawak Fisherman with Catch

252 Girl Guide

(Des Josephine Martin. Litho Cartor)

1989 (22 Dec). 500th Anniv of Discovery of America by Columbus (1992) (1st issue). T **251** and similar vert designs. Multicoloured. W **111**. P 13½.

750	25c. Type **251**	20	10
751	70c. Arawak man smoking	45	30
752	$5 King Ferdinand and Queen Isabella inspecting caravels	3·25	4·50
753	$10 Columbus with chart	6·50	9·50
750/3 Set of 4		9·25	13·00
MS754 150×200 mm. Nos. 750/3. Wmk sideways. P 12½ (sold at $16.75)		17·00	17·00

No. **MS**754 also exists imperforate from a limited printing used in Presentation Packs.

See also Nos. 774/9 and 802/7.

(Des J. Sayer. Litho B.D.T.)

1990 (28 June). 75th Anniv of Girl Guide Movement in Jamaica. T **252** and similar vert designs. Multicoloured. W **111** (inverted on $5). P 14.

755	45c. Type **252**	1·50	30
756	55c. Guide leader	1·50	30
757	$5 Brownie, guide and ranger	6·00	9·00
755/7 Set of 3		8·00	9·00

(Des I. Loe. Litho B.D.T.)

1990 (12 Sept). Jamaican Moths (2nd series). Vert designs as T **250**. Multicoloured. W **111**. P 13½.

758	25c. *Eunomia rubripunctata*	85	35
759	55c. *Perigonia jamaicensis*	1·25	35
760	$4 *Uraga haemorrhoa*	2·50	4·50
761	$5 *Empyreuma pugione*	2·50	4·50
758/61 Set of 4		6·25	9·00

(**253**)   **254** Teaching English

1990 (12 Sept). "EXPO 90" International Garden and Greenery Exhibition, Osaka. Nos. 758/61 optd with T **253**.

762	25c. *Eunomia rubripunctata*	85	35
763	55c. *Perigonia jamaicensis*	1·25	35
764	$4 *Uraga haemorrhoa*	2·50	4·50
765	$5 *Empyreuma pugione*	2·50	4·50
762/5 Set of 4		6·25	9·00

(Des G. Vasarhelyi. Litho B.D.T.)

1990 (10 Oct). International Literacy Year. T **254** and similar horiz design. Multicoloured. W **111** (sideways). P 14.

766	55c. Type **254**	75	25
767	$5 Teaching maths	4·75	6·50

255 "To the Market"

(Adapted J. Mahfood and D. Miller. Litho Walsall)

1990 (7 Dec). Christmas. Children's Paintings. T **255** and similar multicoloured designs. W **111** (sideways on horiz designs). P 14×13½ ($5) or, 13½×14 (others).

768	20c. Type **255**	60	10
769	25c. "House and Garden"	60	10
770	55c. "Jack and Jill"	80	15
771	70c. "Market"	1·00	40
772	$1.50 "Lonely"	1·75	3·50
773	$5 "Market Woman" (vert)	3·50	7·00
768/73 Set of 6		7·50	10·00

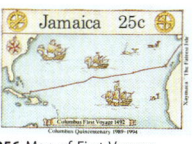

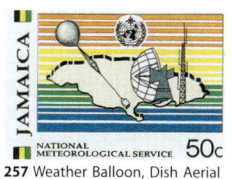

256 Map of First Voyage, 1492

257 Weather Balloon, Dish Aerial and Map of Jamaica

(Des Josephine Martin. Litho Questa)

1990 (19 Dec). 500th Anniv of Discovery of America by Columbus (1992) (2nd issue). T **256** and similar horiz designs. Multicoloured. W **111** (sideways). P 14.

774	25c. Type **256**	1·50	40
775	45c. Map of second voyage, 1493	1·75	40
776	$5 Map of third voyage, 1498	5·50	6·00
777	$10 Map of fourth voyage, 1502	8·00	10·00
774/7 Set of 4		15·00	15·00
MS778 126×99 mm. 25, 45c., $5, $10 Composite map of Caribbean showing routes of voyages		16·00	19·00
MS779 148×207 mm. Nos. 774/7. Imperf		18·00	20·00

Unlike the imperforate version of No. **MS**754, No. **MS**779 was freely available at face value.

(Adapted G. Vasarhelyi. Litho B.D.T.)

1991 (20 May). 11th World Meteorological Congress, Kingston. W **111** (sideways). P 14.

780	**257**	50c. multicoloured	50	20
781		$10 multicoloured	6·50	9·50

258 Bust of Mary Seacole

259 Jamaican Iguana

(Des Jennifer Toombs. Litho B.D.T.)

1991 (24 June). International Council of Nurses Meeting of National Representatives. T **258** and similar horiz designs. W **111** (sideways). P 13½.

782	50c. multicoloured	85	30
783	$1.10 multicoloured	1·75	2·25
MS784 89×60 mm. $8 agate, pale orange-brown and yellow-ochre (sold at $8.20)		3·75	7·50

Designs:—$1.10, Mary Seacole House; $8 Hospital at Scutari, 1854.

(Des I. Loe. Litho Cartor)

1991 (29 July). 50th Anniv of Natural History Society of Jamaica. Jamaican Iguana. T **259** and similar vert designs. Multicoloured. W **111**. P 13.

785	$1.10 Type **259**	90	1·00
	a. Horiz strip of 5. Nos. 785/9	4·00	4·50
786	$1.10 Head of iguana looking right	90	1·00
787	$1.10 Iguana climbing	90	1·00
788	$1.10 Iguana on rock looking left	90	1·00
789	$1.10 Close-up of iguana's head	90	1·00
785/9 Set of 5		4·00	4·50

Nos. 785/9 were printed together, se-tenant, in horizontal strips of 5 throughout the sheet.

(Des I. Loe. Litho B.D.T.)

1991 (12 Aug). Jamaican Moths (3rd series). Multicoloured designs as T **250**. W **111**. P 13½.

790	50c. *Urania sloanus*	65	20
791	$1.10 *Phoenioprocta jamaicensis*	90	60
792	$1.40 *Horama grotei*	1·10	90
793	$8 *Amplypterus gannascus*	3·25	6·50
790/3 Set of 4		5·50	7·50

(**260**) **261** "Doctor Bird"

1991 (23 Sept). "Phila Nippon '91" International Stamp Exhibition, Tokyo. Nos. 790/3 optd with T **260**.

794	50c. *Urania sloanus*	1·00	20
795	$1.10 *Phoenioprocta jamaicensis*	1·40	65
796	$1.40 *Horama grotei*	1·50	1·25
797	$8 *Amplypterus gannascus*	5·00	9·00
794/7 Set of 4		8·00	10·00

(Adapted J. Mahfood. Litho Enschedé)

1991 (27 Nov). Christmas. Children's Paintings. T **261** and similar horiz designs. Multicoloured. W **111** (sideways). P 14×15.

798	50c. Type **261**	80	10
799	$1.10 "Road scene"	1·25	25
800	$5 "Children and house"	4·00	3·75
801	$10 "Cows grazing"	7·00	10·00
798/801 Set of 4		11·50	12·50

262 Indians threatening Ships

263 Compasses and Square Symbol

(Des Josephine Martin. Litho B.D.T.)

1991 (16 Dec). 500th Anniv of Discovery of America by Columbus (1992) (3rd issue). T **262** and similar horiz designs. Multicoloured. W **111** (sideways). P 13½.

802	50c. Type **262**	65	15
803	$1.10 Spaniards setting dog on Indians	75	30
804	$1.40 Indian with gift of pineapple	75	30
805	$25 Columbus describes Jamaica with crumpled paper	8·50	12·00
802/5 Set of 4		9·50	12·00
MS806 125×102 mm. Nos. 802/5 (sold at $28.20)		9·00	12·00
MS807 210×150 mm. Nos. 802/5. Imperf		11·00	13·00

(Litho Cartor)

1992 (1 May). 250th Anniv of First Provisional Grand Master of English Freemasonry in Jamaica. T **263** and similar vert designs. Multicoloured. W **111**. P 13½.

808	50c. Type **263**	80	30
809	$1.10 Symbol in stained glass window	1·10	40
810	$1.40 Compasses and square on book	1·10	40
811	$25 Eye in triangle symbol	10·00	13·00
808/11 Set of 4		11·50	13·00
MS812 140×80 mm. Nos. 808/11 (sold at $28.50)		15·00	16·00

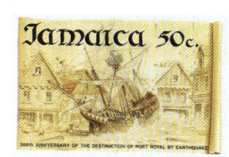

264 Ship in Flooded Street

(Des J. Batchelor. Litho Cartor)

1992 (1 June). 300th Anniv of Destruction of Port Royal. T **264** and similar horiz designs. Multicoloured. W **111** (sideways). P 14×13½.

813	50c. Type **264**	55	40
814	$1.10 Church tower falling	70	45
815	$1.40 Houses collapsing	70	45
816	$25 Inhabitants falling into fissure	9·00	12·00
813/16 Set of 4		10·00	12·00

JAMAICA

MS817 116×75 mm. $5 Contemporary broadsheet of earthquake. Wmk upright. P 13×12 .... 7·00 8·00

No. **MS**817 has a description of the broadsheet printed on the reverse under the gum.

265 Credit Union Symbol

(Des G. Vasarhelyi. Litho Enschedé)

1992 (24 Aug). 50th Anniv of Credit Union Movement. T **265** and similar horiz design. W **111** (sideways). P 14×15.

| 818 | 50c. dp dull bl, emer and pale turquoise-green | 1·00 | 50 |
| 819 | $1.40 multicoloured | 1·75 | 1·75 |

Design:—$1.40, O'Hare Hall.

266 Jamaican Flag and Beach Scene   **267** "Rainbow" (Cecil Baugh)

(Des G. Vasarhelyi. Litho Cartor)

1992 (26 Oct). 30th Anniv of Independence. W **111** (sideways). P 13½.

820	**266**	50c. multicoloured	10	10
821		$1.10 multicoloured	20	20
822		$25 multicoloured	2·75	6·50
820/2 Set of 3			2·75	6·50

(Des D. Bowen. Litho Cartor)

1993 (26 Apr). Art Ceramics and Pottery. T **267** and similar vert designs. Multicoloured. W **111**. P 13½.

823	50c. Type **267**	20	10
824	$1.10 "Yabba Pot" (Louisa Jones)	30	20
825	$1.40 "Sculptured Vase" (Gene Pearson)	30	20
826	$25 "Lidded Form" (Norma Harrack)	4·00	6·50
823/6 Set of 4		4·25	6·50

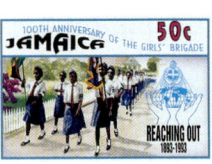

268 Girls' Brigade Parade   **269** Cadet, Armoured Car and Emblem

(Des G. Vasarhelyi. Litho Cartor)

1993 (9 Aug). Centenary of Girls' Brigade. T **268** and similar horiz design. Multicoloured. W **111** (sideways). P 14×13½.

| 827 | 50c. Type **268** | 90 | 50 |
| 828 | $1.10 Brigade members | 1·00 | 1·10 |

(Des D. Miller. Litho B.D.T.)

1993 (8 Nov). 50th Anniv of Jamaica Combined Cadet Force. T **269** and similar multicoloured designs. W **111** (sideways on $1.10, $3). P 14.

829	50c. Type **269**	50	20
830	$1.10 Cadet and Britten Norman Islander light aircraft (*horiz*)	80	40
831	$1.40 Cadet and patrol boats	80	40
832	$3 Cadet and emblem (*horiz*)	1·00	2·25
829/32 Set of 4		2·75	3·00

270 Constant Spring Golf Course   **271** Norman Manley

(Des D. Miller. Litho B.D.T.)

1993 (16 Dec). Golf Courses. T **270** and similar multicoloured designs. W **111** (sideways). P 14.

833	50c. Type **270** (21 Dec)	45	10
834	$1.10 Type **270** (21 Dec)	65	20
835	$1.40 Half Moon (21 Dec)	70	20
836	$2 As $1.40 (21 Dec)	1·00	90
837	$3 Jamaica Jamaica (21 Dec)	1·10	1·25
838	$10 As $3 (21 Dec)	2·50	3·50
833/8 Set of 6		4·50	6·50

MS839 66×71 mm. $25 Tryall (*vert*). Wmk upright (*sold at $28*) .... 5·75 6·00

(Des R. Larson. Litho B.D.T.)

1994 (12 Jan). Birth Centenary of Norman Manley. T **271** and similar vert portrait. W **111**. P 14×15.

840	$25 multicoloured	2·00	2·75
	a. Horiz pair. Nos. 840/1	4·50	7·00
841	$50 multicoloured	2·50	4·25

Nos. 840/1 were printed together, *se-tenant*, in horizontal pairs throughout the sheet.

(**272**)   **273** Flags of Great Britain and Jamaica

1994 (18 Feb). "Hong Kong '94" International Stamp Exhibition. No. **MS**839 optd with T **272**.

MS842 66×71 mm. $25 Tryall .... 6·00 6·50

(Des D. Miller. Litho B.D.T.)

1994 (1 Mar). Royal Visit. T **273** and similar vert designs. Multicoloured. W **111**. P 14×13½.

843	$1.10 Type **273**	65	10
844	$1.40 Royal Yacht *Britannia*	1·75	30
845	$25 Queen Elizabeth II	3·25	4·00
846	$50 Queen Elizabeth and Prince Philip	5·50	8·00
843/6 Set of 4		10·00	11·00

274 Douglas DC-9   **275** Giant Swallowtail

(Des E. Nisbet. Litho Walsall)

1994 (26 Apr). 25th Anniv of Air Jamaica. T **274** and similar horiz designs. Multicoloured. W **111** (sideways). P 14.

847	50c. Type **274**	35	25
848	$1.10 Douglas DC-8	35	25
849	$5 Boeing 727	75	75
850	$50 Airbus A300	3·50	6·50
847/50 Set of 4		4·50	7·00

JAMAICA

(Des N. Shewring. Litho B.D.T.)

1994 (18 Aug). Giant Swallowtail Butterfly Conservation. T **275** and similar vert designs. Multicoloured. W **111**. P 13½.
851	50c. Type **275**		40	25
852	$1.10 With wings closed		40	25
853	$10 On flower		1·60	2·25
854	$25 With wings spread		2·75	5·00
851/4 Set of 4			4·75	7·00
MS855 56×61 mm. $50 Pair of butterflies			5·50	7·00

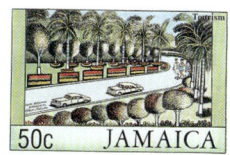

276 "Royal Botanical Gardens" (Sidney McLaren)

(Des G. Vasarhelyi. Litho Questa)

1994 (7 Sept). Tourism. T **276** and similar horiz designs. Multicoloured. W **111** (sideways). P 14.
856	50c. Type **276**		55	20
857	$1.10 Blue Mountains		85	30
858	$5 Tourist in hammock and water sports		3·00	3·75
856/8 Set of 3			4·00	3·75
MS859 105×80 mm. $25 Carolina Parakeets; $25 Silhouetted scuba diver; $25 Carolina Parakeet and foliage; $25 Tourist raft			6·00	7·50

277 Jamaican Red Poll Calf

(Des R. Watton. Litho Cartor)

1994 (16 Nov). Jamaican Red Poll Cattle. T **277** and similar horiz designs. Multicoloured. W **111** (sideways). P 13.
860	50c. Type **277**		10	10
861	$1.10 Red Poll heifer		10	10
862	$25 Red Poll cow		1·25	2·25
863	$50 Red Poll bull		2·50	4·50
860/3 Set of 4			3·75	6·00

278 Refuse Collectors

279 Jamaican Band-tailed Pigeon ("Ring-tailed Pigeon")

(Des D. Miller. Litho Enschedé)

1994 (1 Dec). Christmas. Children's Paintings. T **278** and similar horiz designs. Multicoloured. W **111** (sideways). P 14×15.
864	50c. Type **278**		10	10
865	90c. Hospital ward		10	10
866	$1.10 House		10	10
867	$50 Landscape		3·75	6·00
864/7 Set of 4			3·75	6·00

(Des N. Arlott. Litho B.D.T.)

1995 (24 Apr). Jamaican Wild Birds. T **279** and similar vert designs. Multicoloured. W w **16**. P 14.
868	50c. Type **279**		65	40
869	90c. Yellow-billed Amazon ("Yellow-billed Parrot")		80	40
870	$1.10 Black-billed Amazon ("Black-billed Parrot")		80	40
871	$50 Jamaican Owl ("Brown Owl")		5·50	7·00
868/71 Set of 4			7·00	7·50
MS872 47×62 mm. $50 Streamertail			4·75	7·00

For No. **MS**872 additionally inscribed for "Singapore '95" see No. **MS**888.

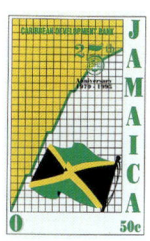

280 Graph, National Flag and Logo

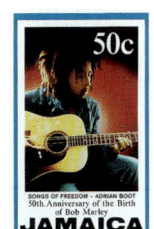

281 "Song of Freedom"

(Litho Cartor)

1995 (11 May). 25th Anniv of Caribbean Development Bank. T **280** and similar designs. W **111** (sideways on horiz designs). P 13½.
873	**280**	50c. blue-green, black and chrome-yellow	10	10
874		$1 blue-green, black and chrome-yellow	10	10
875		– $1.10 multicoloured	10	10
876		– $50 multicoloured	2·75	6·00
873/6 Set of 4			2·75	6·00

Designs: Horiz–$1.10, Industry, agriculture and commerce; $50 Jamaican currency.

(Des D. Miller. Litho Questa)

1995 (31 July). 50th Birth Anniv of Bob Marley (reggae singer). T **281** and similar vert designs showing record covers. Multicoloured. W **111**. P 14.
877	50c. Type **281**		50	15
878	$1.10 "Fire"		65	20
879	$1.40 "Time will Tell"		75	25
880	$3 "Natural Mystic"		1·10	1·00
881	$10 "Live at Lyceum"		2·00	3·00
877/81 Set of 5			4·50	4·25
MS882 105×57 mm. $100 "Legend". Wmk sideways			8·00	10·00

282 Queen Elizabeth the Queen Mother

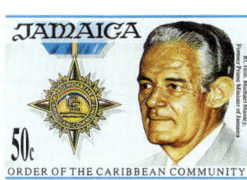

283 Michael Manley

(Des Jennifer Toombs. Litho B.D.T.)

1995 (4 Aug). 95th Birthday of Queen Elizabeth the Queen Mother. Sheet 81×95 mm. W **111**. P 13½.
MS883 **282** $75 multicoloured		4·50	5·50

(Des G. Vasarhelyi. Litho B.D.T.)

1995 (23 Aug). Recipients of the Order of the Caribbean Community. T **283** and similar horiz designs. Multicoloured. W **111** (sideways). P 14×15.
884	50c. Type **283**		15	15
885	$1.10 Sir Alister McIntyre		20	10
886	$1.40 Justice P. Telford Georges		20	10
887	$50 Dame Nita Barrow		5·50	8·50
884/7 Set of 4			5·50	8·50

1995 (1 Sept). "Singapore '95" International Stamp Exhibition. No. **MS**872 additionally inscr with exhibition emblem on sheet margin.
MS888 47×62 mm. $50 Streamertail		3·75	5·00

284 Dish Aerial and Landrover, Balkans

(Des A. Theobald. Litho B.D.T.)

1995 (24 Oct). 50th Anniv of United Nations. T **284** and similar horiz designs. Multicoloured. W **111** (sideways). P 14.
889	50c. Type **284**		30	20

129

JAMAICA

890	$1.10 Antonov An-32 aircraft, Balkans	55	25
891	$3 Bedford articulated road tanker, Balkans	70	90
892	$5 Fairchild C-119 Flying Boxcar, Korea	80	1·40
889/92	Set of 4	2·10	2·50
MS893	100×70 mm. $50 U.N.T.A.G. vehicles, Namibia	2·25	3·50

285 Landing of Indian Immigrants

286 Jamaican Flag and U.N.I.C.E.F. Emblem

(Des K. Reece. Litho Cot Printery Ltd, Barbados)

1996 (22 May). 150th Anniv of Indian Immigration to Jamaica. T **285** and similar horiz design. Multicoloured. W **111** (sideways). P 14.

894	$2.50 Type **285**	25	15
895	$10 Indian musicians and traditional dancers	75	1·25

(Des K. Reece. Litho Cot Printery Ltd. Barbados)

1996 (2 Sept). 50th Anniv of U.N.I.C.E.F. W **111**. P 14½×14.

896	**286**	$2.50 multicoloured	65	20
897		$8 multicoloured	1·25	1·25
898		$10 multicoloured	1·25	1·50
896/8		Set of 3	2·75	2·75

287 Brown's Hutia

(Des W. Oliver. Litho Enschedé)

1996 (23 Sept). Endangered Species. Brown's Hutia ("Jamaican Hutia"). T **287** and similar horiz designs. Multicoloured. W **111** (sideways). P 13½.

899	$2.50 Type **287**	15	10
900	$10 Hutia on rock	50	65
901	$12.50 Female with young	60	1·00
902	$25 Head of Hutia	1·25	2·25
899/902	Set of 4	2·25	3·50

288 High Altar, Church of St. Thomas the Apostle

(Des W. Wright. Litho Questa)

1997 (7 Feb). 300th Anniv of the Kingston Parish Church. T **288** and similar multicoloured designs. P 14.

903	$2 Type **288**	35	10
904	$8 Church of St. Thomas the Apostle	1·10	80
905	$12.50 "The Angel" (wood carving by Edna Manley) (vert)	1·75	2·25
903/5	Set of 3	2·75	2·75
MS906	106×76 mm. $60 St. Thomas the Apostle at sunset (42×56 mm)	3·50	4·50

No. 903 is inscribed "ALTER" in error.

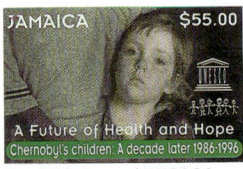

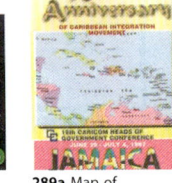

289 Child's Face and U.N.E.S.C.O. Emblem

289a Map of Caribbean

(Litho Questa)

1997 (7 Apr). 10th Anniv of Chernobyl Nuclear Disaster. P 13½×14.

907	**289**	$55 multicoloured	3·50	3·75

(Litho Cot Printery Ltd, Barbados)

1997 (30 June). 50th Anniv of Caribbean Integration Movement and 18th CARICOM Heads of Government Conference. T **289a** and similar vert design. W **111**. P 14½×14.

907a	$2.50 Type **289a**	5·50	5·50
907b	$8 Coastal scenery	6·50	2·25
907c	$10 As $8	7·00	2·25
907a/c	Set of 3	17·00	9·00

290 Coelia triptera

291 Diana, Princess of Wales

(Litho Questa)

1997 (9 Oct)–**99**. Orchids. T **290** and similar multicoloured designs. W **111** (sideways on horiz designs). P 14.

A. Without imprint date

908A	$1 Type **290**	45	1·00
909A	$2 Oncidium pulchellum (horiz)	60	1·00
910A	$2.50 Oncidium triquetum	60	1·00
911A	$3 Broughtonia negrilensis	75	1·25
912A	$4.50 Oncidium gauntlettii (horiz) (1.12.97)	1·00	1·25
913A	$5 Encyclia fragans (horiz)	1·00	1·00
914A	$8 Broughtonia sanguinea (horiz) (1.12.97)	1·25	1·25
915A	$12 Phaius tankervilleae (1.12.97)	1·75	1·75
916A	$25 Cochleanthes flabelliformis (horiz) (1.12.97)	3·25	4·25
917A	$50 Broughtonia sanguinea (three varieties) (horiz) (1.12.97)	2·75	3·00
908A/17A	Set of 10	12·00	15·00

B. Imprint date ("1999") at foot

916B	$25 Cochleanthes flabelliformis (horiz) (1.2.99)	3·25	3·00

(Des M. Friedman. Litho Questa)

1998 (24 Feb). Diana, Princess of Wales Commemoration. T **291** and similar vert design. Multicoloured. P 14.

918	$20 Type **291**	1·00	1·25
	a. Sheetlet. No. 918×6	5·50	
MS919	70×100 mm. $80 Princess Diana and Mother Theresa (42×55 mm)	4·50	5·50

No. 918 was issued in sheetlets of 6 with illustrated margins.

292 University Chapel, Mona

(Litho B.D.T.)

1998 (31 July). 50th Anniv of University of West Indies. T **292** and similar multicoloured designs. W **111** (sideways on horiz designs). P 13½.

920	$8 Type **292**	40	40
921	$10 Philip Sherlock Centre for Creative Arts, Mona	40	40
922	$50 University arms (vert)	2·25	3·75
920/2	Set of 3	2·75	4·00

293 Flags of Jamaica and CARICOM

130

(Des R. Sauber. Litho Cartor)

1998 (17 Sept). 25th Anniv of Caribbean Community. P 13½.
| 923 | **293** | $30 multicoloured | 2·50 | 2·50 |

294 Jamaican Footballer

(Des D. Bowen. Litho Cartor)

1998 (25 Sept). World Cup Football Championship, France. T **294** and similar multicoloured designs. W w **14** (sideways on horiz designs). P 13½.
924	$10 Type **294**	65	40
925	$25 Jamaican team (*horiz*)	1·50	1·50
926	$100 As $25	5·00	7·00
924/6 Set of 3		6·50	8·00

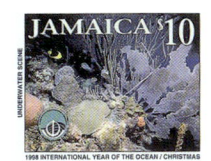

295 Coral Reef

(Litho Cot Printery Ltd, Barbados)

1998 (23 Dec). Christmas. International Year of the Ocean. T **295** and similar multicoloured designs. W **111** (sideways on horiz designs). P 14 ($100) or 14×14½ (others).
927	$10 Type **295**	1·25	40
928	$30 Fishing boats, Negril	2·75	1·25
929	$50 Black Spiny Sea Urchin	3·75	4·00
930	$100 Composite design as Nos. 927/9 (22×41 *mm*)	7·25	11·00
927/30 Set of 4		13·50	15·00

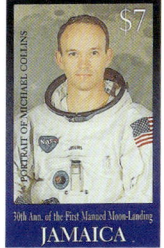

296 Michael Collins (astronaut)

297 Lesley Ann Masterton and Fong-Yee (polo)

(Des N. Shewring. Litho Walsall)

1999 (20 July). 30th Anniv of First Manned Landing on Moon. T **296** and similar multicoloured designs. W **111**. P 14×13½.
931	$7 Type **296**	40	25
932	$10 Service module docking with lunar module	50	40
933	$25 Buzz Aldrin on Moon's surface	1·00	1·40
934	$30 Command module in Earth orbit	1·10	1·50
931/4 Set of 4		2·75	3·25
MS935 90×80 mm. $100 Earth as seen from Moon (*circular*, 40 *mm* diam). Wmk sideways. P 14		3·50	4·75

(Des J. Batchelor. Litho B.D.T.)

1999 (3 Aug). Jamaican Sporting Personalities. T **297** and similar multicoloured designs. W **111** (sideways on horiz designs). P 13½.
936	$5 Type **297**	75	50
937	$10 Lawrence Rowe, Collie Smith and Alfred Valentine (cricket)	1·25	55
938	$20 Vivalyn Latty-Scott (women's cricket) (*vert*)	1·75	1·50
939	$25 Lindy Delapenha (football) (*vert*)	1·75	1·25
940	$30 Joy Grant-Charles (netball) (*vert*)	1·75	1·75
941	$50 Percy Hayles, Gerald Gray and Bunny Grant (boxing)	1·90	4·25
936/41 Set of 6		8·25	9·00
MS942 110×90 mm. $100 Lindy Delapenha and Joy Grant-Charles (56×42 *mm*). Wmk upright		4·50	6·00

298 *Spey* (mail ship), 1891

(Des J. Batchelor. Litho B.D.T.)

1999 (8 Oct). 125th Anniv of Universal Postal Union. T **298** and similar horiz designs. Multicoloured. W **111** (sideways). P 14.
943	$7 Type **298**	1·25	50
944	$10 *Jamaica Planter* (mail ship), 1936	1·50	50
945	$25 Lockheed Constellation (aircraft), 1950	2·75	3·00
946	$30 Airbus A-310 (aircraft), 1999	2·75	3·25
943/6 Set of 4		7·50	6·50

299 Airbus A-310

300 Shih Tzu

(Litho B.D.T.)

1999 (1 Nov). 30th Anniv of Air Jamaica. T **299** and similar horiz designs. Multicoloured. W **111** (sideways). P 14.
947	$10 Type **299**	1·50	50
948	$25 A-320	2·25	2·50
949	$30 A-340	2·50	2·75
947/9 Set of 3		5·50	5·25

(Litho Questa)

1999 (25 Nov). Dogs. T **300** and similar vert designs. Multicoloured. W **111**. P 14½.
950	$7 Type **300**	1·50	75
951	$10 German Shepherd	1·75	75
952	$30 Doberman Pinscher	3·50	3·75
950/2 Set of 3		6·00	4·75

301 Nelson Mandela Park

302 "The Prophet" (sculpture)

(Litho Questa)

1999 (15 Dec). Parks and Gardens. T **301** and similar horiz designs. Multicoloured. W **111** (sideways). P 14.
953	$7 Type **301**	40	40
954	$10 St. William Grant Park	50	40
955	$25 Seaview Park	1·25	1·50
956	$30 Holruth Park	1·50	2·25
953/6 Set of 4		3·25	4·00

(Litho Questa)

2000 (1 Mar). Birth Centenary of Edna Manley (artist). T **302** and similar vert designs. Multicoloured. W **111**. P 13½×14.
| 957 | $10 Type **302** | 45 | 35 |

JAMAICA

131

JAMAICA

958	$25 "Horse of the Morning"...................	1·10	90
959	$30 "The Angel"...................................	1·40	1·25
960	$100 Edna Manley...............................	4·50	7·50
957/60 Set of 4..		6·75	9·00
MS961 128×159 mm. Nos. 957/60.....................		7·00	10·00

303 Lennox Lewis

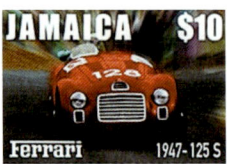

304 Ferrari 125S Racing Car, 1947

(Litho Questa)

2000 (24 Mar). Lennox Lewis, World Heavyweight Boxing Champion. T **303** and similar vert designs. Multicoloured. W **111** (sideways). P 14.

962	$10 Holding WBC Championship belt............	30	45
	a. Sheetlet. Nos. 962/70...........................	6·00	7·00
963	$10 In ring with right arm raised....................	30	45
964	$10 Holding WBC belt above head.................	30	45
965	$25 Taking punch on chin...............................	75	1·00
966	$25 Type **303**..	75	1·00
967	$25 In corner...	75	1·00
968	$30 With WBC belt after fight..........................	95	1·10
969	$30 Holding all four belts.................................	95	1·10
970	$30 With belts in front of skyscraper..............	95	1·10
962/70 Set of 9..		6·00	7·00

Nos. 962/70 were printed together, *se-tenant*, in sheetlets of 9.

(Litho Questa)

2000 (26 May). Birth Centenary of Enzo Ferrari (car designer) (1998). T **304** and similar horiz designs showing racing cars. Multicoloured. P 14.

971	$10 Type **304**..	60	70
972	$10 375 F1, 1950..	60	70
973	$10 312 F1, 1966..	60	70
974	$25 DINO 166 P, 1965......................................	1·10	1·50
975	$25 312 P, 1971..	1·10	1·50
976	$25 F1 90, 1990..	1·10	1·50
971/6 Set of 6...		4·50	6·00

305 Queen Elizabeth the Queen Mother

306 "The Runner", Jamaican Flag and Olympic Rings

(Litho Questa)

2000 (4 Aug). Queen Elizabeth the Queen Mother's 100th Birthday. T **305** and similar vert designs showing various recent photographs. Multicoloured. Background colours given. W **111**. P 14.

977	$10 lavender..	70	35
978	$25 light turquoise-green...............................	90	90
979	$30 light mauve...	1·60	1·40
980	$50 pale blue...	2·50	4·00
977/80 Set of 4...		5·50	6·00

(Litho Questa)

2000 (1 Sept). Olympic Games, Sydney. T **306** and similar multicoloured designs, each showing "The Runner" (sculpture by Alvin Marriot), Jamaican flag and Olympic Rings. W **111** (sideways on $10 and $25). P 14.

981	$10 Type **306**..	80	35
982	$25 Head and shoulders..................................	1·40	90
983	$30 With flag at top (*vert*)...............................	1·75	1·40
984	$50 With flag in centre (*vert*).........................	2·75	4·00
981/4 Set of 4...		6·00	6·00

307 Bull Thatch Palm

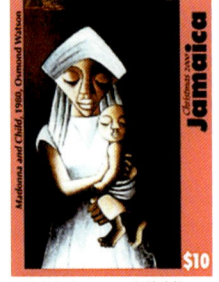

308 "Madonna and Child" (Osmond Watson)

(Litho Enschedé)

2000 (6 Oct). Native Trees. T **307** and similar multicoloured designs. W **111**. P 14.

985	$10 Type **307**...	80	35
986	$25 Blue Mahoe..	1·75	1·25
987	$30 Silk Cotton..	2·00	1·75
988	$50 Yellow Poui...	3·00	5·00
985/8 Set of 4...		6·50	7·50
MS989 112×70 mm. $100 Lignum Vitae (*horiz*). Wmk sideways...		8·00	9·00

(Litho Questa)

2000 (6 Dec). Christmas. Jamaican Religious Paintings. T **308** and similar multicoloured designs. W **111** (sideways on $20). P 13½.

990	$10 Type **308**...	55	35
991	$20 "Boy in the Temple" (Carl Abrahams) (*horiz*)...	90	90
992	$25 "Ascension" (Carl Abrahams)..................	1·10	1·10
993	$30 "Jah Lives" (Osmond Watson)..................	1·25	1·40
990/3 Set of 4...		3·50	3·25

309 Children of the Commonwealth

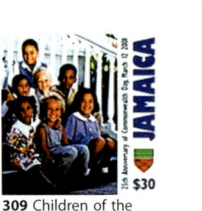

310 Andrew Mowatt (founder)

(Des D. McLeod. Litho Cartor)

2001 (12 Mar). 25th Anniv of Commonwealth Day. W **111**. P 12½.

994	**309** $30 multicoloured...........................	1·50	1·75

(Des D. McCloud. Litho BDT)

2001 (12 Oct). Centenary of Jamaica Burial Scheme Society. W **111** (inverted). P 13.

995	**310** $15 multicoloured............................	1·25	1·25

311 "Falmouth Market" (lithograph)

(Des D. McLeod. Litho Cartor)

2001 (14 Nov). Birth Bicentenary of Adolphe Duperly (pioneer photographer). T **311** and similar horiz designs. Multicoloured. W **111**. P 13.

996	$15 Type **311**...	1·00	50
997	$40 "Ferry Inn, Spanish Town Road" (lithograph)..	2·25	2·50
998	$45 "Coke Chapel, Kingston" (lithograph)......	2·25	2·50

132

JAMAICA

999	$60 "King Street, Kingston" (lithograph)	3·00	4·00
996/9	Set of 4	7·75	8·50
MS1000	103×70 mm. Nos. 996/9	9·00	11·00

312 Poinsettia in Church Window

313 Queen Elizabeth and Jamaican Royal Standard

(Des N. Shewring. Litho Cartor)

2001 (10 Dec). Christmas. W **111**. P 13½.

1001	**312**	$15 multicoloured	1·00	50
1002		$30 multicoloured	2·00	1·40
1003		$40 multicoloured	2·25	2·25
1001/3	Set of 3		4·75	3·75

(Des A. Robinson. Litho Questa)

2002 (6 Feb). Golden Jubilee. Designs as T **253a** of Bahamas. W w **14** (sideways). P 14½.

1004	$15 agate, deep blue and gold	1·00	50
1005	$40 multicoloured	2·25	2·25
1006	$45 grey-black, deep blue and gold	2·25	2·25
1007	$60 multicoloured	3·00	3·50
1004/7	Set of 4	7·75	7·75
MS1008	162×95 mm. Nos. 1004/7 and $30 multicoloured. P 13½ ($30) or 14½ (others)	8·00	8·50

Designs: *Horiz (as Type **253a** of Bahamas)*—$15 Princess Elizabeth, in orchard, 1941; $40 Queen Elizabeth wearing pearls and striped dress; $45 Queen Elizabeth in evening dress, 1953; $60 Queen Elizabeth visiting, Gloucester, 1995. *Vert (38×51 mm)*—$2 Queen Elizabeth after Annigoni. Designs as Nos. 1004/7 in No. **MS**1008 omit the gold frame around each stamp and the "Golden Jubilee 1952–2002" inscription.

(Des N. Shewring. Litho Cartor)

2002 (18 Feb). Royal Visit. T **313** and and similar horiz design. Multicoloured. W **111** (sideways). P 13½.

| 1009 | $15 Type **313** | 1·25 | 50 |
| 1010 | $45 Queen Elizabeth in evening dress and Jamaican coat of arms | 3·25 | 3·25 |

314 Sir Philip Sherlock

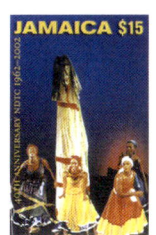

315 Female Dancers

(Des D. McLeod. Litho Walsall)

2002 (11 Mar). Birth Centenary of Sir Philip Sherlock (historian). W **111**. P 14.

| 1011 | **314** | $40 bright magenta, deep magenta and new blue | 1·50 | 1·60 |

(Des D. McLeod. Litho B.D.T.)

2002 (31 Oct). 40th Anniv of National Dance Theatre Company. W **111**. P 14.

| 1012 | **315** | $15 multicoloured | 1·25 | 1·00 |

316 PAHO Centenary Logo

(Des D. Boxer. Litho B.D.T.)

2002 (2 Dec). Centenary of Pan American Health Organization. W **111** (sideways). P 13½.

| 1013 | **316** | $40 multicoloured | 2·25 | 1·75 |

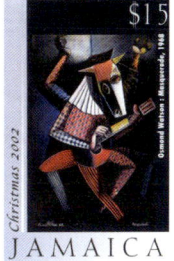

317 "Masquerade" (Osmond Watson)

318 Dancers

(Litho Questa)

2002 (6 Dec). Christmas. Local Works of Art. T **317** and similar multicoloured designs. W **111** (sideways on horiz designs). P 14.

1014	$15 Type **317**	1·00	45
1015	$40 "John Canoe in Guanaboa Vale" (Gaston Tabois) (*horiz*)	2·00	1·50
1016	$45 "Mother and Child" (carving by Kapo)	2·00	1·75
1017	$60 "Hills of Papine", (carving by Edna Manley) (*horiz*)	2·75	3·25
1014/17	Set of 4	7·00	6·25

(Litho Questa)

2002 (20 Dec). 40th Anniv of Independence. T **318** and similar horiz designs. Multicoloured. W **111** (sideways). P 14.

1018	$15 Type **318**	1·00	45
1019	$40 Independence Day celebrations	2·25	1·75
1020	$60 Welder and fish processing worker	3·50	5·00
1018/20	Set of 3	6·00	6·50

319 Kingston in Early 1800s

(Litho Questa)

2002 (20 Dec). Bicentenary of Kingston. T **319** and similar horiz designs. Multicoloured. W **111** (sideways). P 13½×14.

1021	$15 Type **319**	1·00	1·25
	a. Horiz strip of 3. Nos. 1021/3	2·75	3·25
1022	$15 Wharf and statue of Queen Victoria, early 1900s	1·00	1·25
1023	$15 Horse-drawn cab, early 1900s and modern street scene	1·00	1·25
1021/3	Set of 3	2·75	3·25

Nos. 1021/3 were printed together, *se-tenant*, as horizontal strips of 3 throughout the sheet, forming a montage.

320 Queen Elizabeth II in St. Edward's Chair flanked by Bishops of Durham and Bath & Wells

321 "30" as Key

(Des A. Robinson. Litho DLR)

2003 (2 June). 50th Anniv of Coronation. T **320** and similar horiz design. Multicoloured. W **111** (sideways). P 14×14½.

1024	$15 Type **320**	1·00	45
1025	$45 Coronation Coach in procession	2·50	3·00
MS1026	95×115 mm. $50 As $45; $100 As Type **320**	6·00	7·50

Nos. 1024/5 have scarlet frame; stamps from **MS**1026 have no frame and country name in mauve panel.

133

JAMAICA

(Litho BDT)
2003 (4 July). 30th Anniv of CARICOM. W **111** (sideways). P 14.
| 1027 | **321** | $40 multicoloured | 2·25 | 2·00 |

322 Jamaican Stripe-headed Tanager

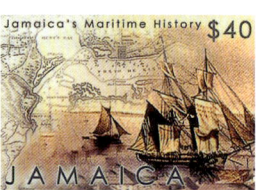

323 Sailing ships and Map of Kingston Harbour

(Des N. Arlott. Litho DLR)
2003 (19 Sept). Bird Life International (1st series). Jamaican Birds. T **322** and similar multicoloured designs. W **111** (sideways on horiz designs). P 14.
1028	$15 Type **322**	1·25	65
1029	$40 Crested Quail Dove (horiz)	2·00	1·75
1030	$45 Jamaican Tody (horiz)	2·00	1·75
1031	$60 Blue Mountain Vireo	2·75	3·50
1028/31 Set of 4		7·25	7·00

MS1032 175×80 mm. $30 Jamaican Blackbird nestlings (34×30 mm); $30 Searching for food in bromeliad (30×34 mm); $30 Singing from perch (30×34 mm); $30 Singing from perch (34×30 mm); $30 With insect in beak (34×30 mm). Wmk sideways. P 14½ .... 8·50 9·00
See also Nos. 1040/9.

(Litho BDT)
2003 (25 Sept). Maritime History. T **323** and similar horiz designs. Multicoloured. W **111** (sideways). P 14×15.
1033	$40 Type **323**	2·50	2·50
	a. Horiz strip of 3. Nos. 1033/5	6·75	6·75
1034	$40 Passengers on cruise ship and sailing ships	2·50	2·50
1035	$40 Sugar Refiner (cargo ship)	2·50	2·50
1033/5 Set of 3		6·75	6·75

Nos. 1033/5 were printed together, *se-tenant*, in horizontal strips of three, each strip forming a composite design.

324 Baby Jesus

(Des D. Miller. Litho BDT)
2003 (15 Dec). Christmas. T **324** and similar horiz designs. Multicoloured. W **111** (sideways). P 13.
1036	$15 Type **324**	85	35
1037	$30 Close-up of Baby Jesus	1·60	65
1038	$60 Holy Family	2·75	3·50
1036/8 Set of 3		4·75	4·00

325 Toussaint L'Ouverture

326 Yellow-billed Amazon

(Litho BDT)
2004 (31 Jan). Bicentenary of Haitian Revolution. W **111**. P 13½.
| 1039 | **325** | $40 multicoloured | 2·25 | 1·75 |

(Des A. Robinson. Litho BDT)
2004 (17 May). Bird Life International (2nd series). Caribbean Endemic Birds Festival. T **326** and similar horiz designs. Multicoloured. W **111** (sideways). P 13½.
1040	$10 Type **326**	1·00	1·00
	a. Block of 10. Nos. 1040/9	9·00	9·00
1041	$10 Jamaican Oriole	1·00	1·00
1042	$10 Orangequit	1·00	1·00
1043	$10 Yellow-shouldered Grassquit	1·00	1·00
1044	$10 Jamaican Woodpecker	1·00	1·00
1045	$10 Streamertail ("Red-billed Streamertail")	1·00	1·00
1046	$10 Jamaican Mango	1·00	1·00
1047	$10 White-eyed Thrush	1·00	1·00
1048	$10 Jamaican Lizard Cuckoo	1·00	1·00
1049	$10 Arrow-headed Warbler	1·00	1·00
1040/9 Set of 10		9·00	9·00

Nos. 1040/9 were printed together, *se-tenant*, in blocks of ten in sheets of 40.

327 Water Lilies

328 Hurdling

(Litho Cartor)
2004 (5 June). World Environment Day. Sheet 195×85 mm containing T **327** and similar horiz designs. Multicoloured. W **111** (sideways). P 14.

MS1050 $10 Type **327**; $10 Hawksbill Turtle; $10 Tube Sponge; $10 Man in canoe, Parottee Pond; $40 Vase Sponge and Star Coral; $40 Sea Fan and Black and White Crinoid; $40 Glassy Sweeper; $40 Giant Sea Anemone .... 6·50 8·00

(Des J. Vasarhelyi. Litho BDT)
2004 (24 Aug). Olympic Games, Athens. T **328** and similar vert designs. Multicoloured. W **111**. P 14.
1051	$30 Type **328**	1·25	65
1052	$60 Running	2·25	1·75
1053	$70 Swimming	2·25	2·25
1054	$90 Badminton and shooting	3·00	4·25
1051/4 Set of 4		8·00	8·00

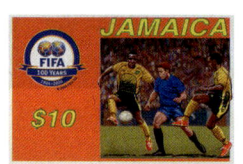

329 Two Jamaican Players and Opponent (blue strip)

(Des R. Watton. Litho Enschedé)
2004 (13 Oct). Centenary of FIFA (Fédération Internationale de Football Association). T **329** and similar horiz designs. Multicoloured. W **111** (sideways). P 14.
1055	$10 Type **329**	55	30
1056	$30 Two Jamaican players and opponent (white top)	1·25	70
1057	$45 Two Jamaican players and opponent (blue top)	1·75	1·50
1058	$50 Two Jamaican players and opponent (white strip)	1·75	3·00
1055/8 Set of 4		4·75	5·00

330 Ambassador John Pringle and Round Hill Hotel

331 White Sorrel

JAMAICA

(Litho Cartor)

2004 (12 Nov). Centenary of the Jamaica Hotel Law. T **330** and similar horiz designs. Multicoloured. P 13½×14.

MS1059	152×114 mm. $40 Type **330** (bottom left panel in pink or violet-blue, three of each)	9·00	11·00
MS1060	152×114 mm. $40 Abe Issa and Tower Isle Hotel; $40 John Issa and Tower Isle Hotel (both with bottom right panels in bright yellow-green, light green or carmine, two of each)	9·00	11·00
MS1061	152×114 mm. $40 Ralph Lauren and Doctors Cave Beach, Montego Bay (with left-hand panel in dark blue, violet-blue or azure, two of each) (19 Nov)	9·00	11·00

(Litho BDT)

2004 (22 Nov). Christmas. T **331** and similar designs showing white sorrel. W **111** (sideways on horiz designs). P 14½.

1062	**331**	$10 multicoloured	65	20
1063	–	$20 multicoloured	1·25	40
1064	–	$50 multicoloured (*horiz*)	2·75	3·00
1065	–	$60 multicoloured (*horiz*)	2·75	3·00
1062/5 Set of 4			6·75	6·00

332 Mary Morris Knibb and Mizpah Moravian Church

(Litho BDT)

2004 (14 Dec). 250th Anniv of the Moravian Church in Jamaica. T **332** and similar horiz designs. Multicoloured. W **111** (sideways). P 14×14½.

1066	90c. Type **332**	10	40
1067	$10 Reverend W. O'Meally and Mizpah Moravian Church	65	30
1068	$50 Bishop S. U. Hastings and Redeemer Moravian Church	3·25	3·75
1066/8 Set of 3		3·50	4·00

333 Ackee, Lychee and Pak Choy

(Litho BDT)

2005 (2 Feb). 150th Anniv of Chinese Population in Jamaica. T **333** and similar horiz designs. Multicoloured. W **111** (sideways). P 14.

1069	$30 Type **333**	1·25	60
1070	$60 Old Chinatown	2·50	2·00
1071	$90 Entrance to Chinese Benevolent Association Headquarters, Kingston	4·00	5·50
1069/71 Set of 3		7·00	7·25

334 Rose Hall Great House, St James

335 CEPT Emblem

(Litho Cartor)

2005 (25 Feb)–**08**. Buildings (1st series). T **334** and similar horiz designs. Multicoloured.

(a) PVA gum. W111 (sideways). P 13½

A. Without imprint date

1072A	90c. Type **334**	10	20
1073A	$5 Holy Trinity Cathedral (11.05.05)	20	20
1074A	$30 Atrium of the National Commercial Bank, New Kingston	1·40	90
1075A	$60 The Court House, Falmouth	2·75	2·50
1072A/5A Set of 4		4·00	3·50

B. With imprint date "2008"

1074B	$30 Atrium of the National Commercial Bank, New Kingston (2008)	85	60
1075B	$60 The Court House, Falmouth	1·75	1·25

(b) Self-adhesive. Die-cut perf 12½

1076	$5 Holy Trinity Cathedral	20	30
1077	$30 As No. 1074	1·10	1·10
	a. Booklet pane. No. 1077×10	10·00	
1078	$60 As No. 1075	2·25	2·75
1076/8 Set of 3		3·25	3·75

No. 1077 was available from $300 booklets (No. SB19).

(Litho BDT)

2005 (1 June). 50th Anniv of the European Philatelic Corporation (Europa). T **335** and similar vert designs showing the CEPT emblem, each with a different colour "stamp frame". Multicoloured. P 14.

1079	$60 Type **335**	1·60	1·25
1080	$70 Yellow frame	1·75	2·00
1081	$100 Blue frame	2·50	4·00
1079/81 Set of 3		5·25	6·50
MS1082 120×70 mm. Nos. 1079/81		5·25	6·50

336 Gun Captain holding Powder Cartridge

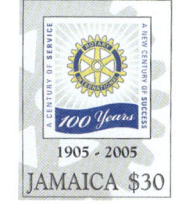

337 Rotary Emblem

(Des J. Batchelor. Litho and thermograph ($90) Cartor)

2005 (23 June). Bicentenary of the Battle of Trafalgar (1st issue). T **336** and similar multicoloured designs. No wmk ($90) or W **111** (sideways on $20 and $50). P 13½.

1083	$20 Type **336**	1·10	1·00
1084	$30 Admiral Nelson (*vert*)	1·50	1·00
1085	$50 British 12 Pounder cannon	1·75	1·50
1086	$60 HMS *Africa* (*vert*)	2·50	1·75
1087	$70 HMS *Leviathan* (*vert*)	2·75	2·75
1088	$90 HMS *Victory*	3·50	5·00
1083/8 Set of 6		12·00	12·00
MS1089 120×79 mm. $200 HMS *Africa* at Port Royal (44×44 *mm*)		9·00	11·00

Nos. 1083/8 were each printed in sheets of six stamps with decorative margins and with the Trafalgar Festival 2005 logo at foot. No. 1088 contains traces of powdered wood from HMS *Victory*. See also Nos. 1092/4.

2005 (30 June). Centenary of Rotary International. Litho. W **111**. P 14.

1090	**337**	$30 multicoloured	1·50	1·50

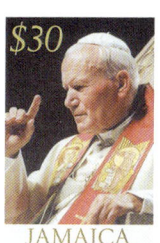

338 Pope John Paul II

339 H.M.S. *Victory*

(Des A. Robinson. Litho BDT)

2005 (18 Aug). Pope John Paul II Commemoration. P 14.

1091	**338**	$30 multicoloured	1·50	1·50

No. 1091 was printed in sheetlets of eight stamps with an enlarged, illustrated right margin.

(Des J. Batchelor ($50) or Pauline Gyles ($100). Litho Cartor)

2005 (18 Oct). Bicentenary of the Battle of Trafalgar (2nd issue). T **339** and similar multicoloured designs. P 13½.

1092	$50 Type **339**	2·75	1·40
1093	$90 Ships engaged in battle (*horiz*)	4·00	4·25
1094	$100 Admiral Lord Nelson	4·00	4·25
1092/4 Set of 3		9·75	9·00

135

JAMAICA

340 Mary Seacole and Herbal Remedies and Medicines

(Des D. Miller. Litho BDT)

2005 (21 Nov). Birth Bicentenary of Mary Seacole (nursing pioneer). T **340** and similar horiz designs. Multicoloured. W **111** (sideways). P 13½.

1095	$30 Type **340**...	1·00	65
1096	$50 Mary Seacole and Seacole Hall, Mona Campus, University of the West Indies ...	1·40	1·25
1097	$60 Mary Seacole and Crimean War soldiers, 1854–6...........................	2·00	1·50
1098	$70 Mary Seacole and her British Crimean, Turkish Medjidie, French Legion of Honour and Jamaican Order of Merit medals.........	2·00	2·50
1095/8 Set of 4..		5·75	5·50

341 AIDS Emblem and Montage of Faces

342 Poinsettia Flowers and Star

(Litho BDT)

2005 (1 Dec). World AIDS Day. W **111**. P 15×14.

1099	**341**	$30 multicoloured.............................	1·00	1·00

(Litho BDT)

2005 (1 Dec). Christmas. Multicoloured (background colours given). W **111**. P 15×14.

1100	**342**	$20 deep claret and bright scarlet.........	70	40
1101		$30 violet and bright scarlet...................	95	55
1102		$50 bright scarlet and emerald..............	1·50	1·00
1103		$80 deep bluish-green and bright scarlet	2·50	4·00
1100/3 Set of 4...			5·00	5·50

343 Jessie Ripoll (Mother Claver) (founder)

344 Nestlings

(Litho BDT)

2005 (12 Dec). 12th Anniv of Alpha. W **111**. P 14×13½.

1104	**343**	$30 multicoloured.............................	75	75

(Litho Enschede)

2006 (12 May). Buildings (2nd series). Horiz designs as T **334**. Multicoloured.

(a) PVA gum. W **111** (sideways). P 14×13½

A. Without imprint date

1105A	$10 Courthouse, Morant Bay............................	75	45
1106A	$15 Spanish Town Square, St. Catherine.........	65	40
1107A	$20 Mico College..	1·50	1·00
1108A	$25 Jamaica College..	90	60
1109A	$50 Devon House, St. Andrew	2·75	1·75
1110A	$70 Ward Theatre...	3·50	3·25
1111A	$90 Vale Royal, St. Andrew.............................	4·50	5·00
1112A	$100 Falmouth Post Office	2·75	3·25
1105A/12A Set of 8...		15·00	14·00

B. With imprint date "2008"

1105B	$10 Courthouse, Morant Bay (2008).................	35	30
1107B	$20 Mico College (2008)..................................	70	40
1109B	$50 Devon House, St. Andrew (2008)..............	1·75	1·00
1110B	$70 Ward Theatre (2008).................................	2·25	1·75
1111B	$90 Vale Royal, St. Andrew (2008)..................	2·75	2·75
1105B/11B Set of 5...		7·00	5·25

(b) Self-adhesive. Die-cut perf 13½×14

1113	$10 As No. 1105...	35	45
1114	$15 As No. 1106...	60	65
1115	$20 As No. 1107...	70	75
1116	$25 As No. 1108...	85	90
1117	$50 As No. 1109...	1·75	2·00
1118	$70 As No. 1110...	2·25	2·75
1119	$90 As No. 1111...	2·75	3·25
1120	$100 As No. 1112...	2·75	3·25
1113/20 Set of 8...		10·50	12·50

(Des D. Miller. Litho BDT)

2006 (30 Nov). Endangered Species. Black-billed Amazon (*Amazona agilis*). T **344** and similar square designs. Multicoloured. W **111** (sideways). P 13½.

1121	$5 Type **344**..	75	75
	a. Strip of 4. Nos. 1121/4............................	7·75	7·75
1122	$10 In close-up...	1·00	75
1123	$30 In captivity...	2·75	1·75
1124	$50 Pair in native forest...................................	4·00	4·25
1121/4 Set of 4..		7·75	6·75

Nos. 1121/4 were printed together, *se-tenant*, as horizontal and vertical strips of four stamps in sheets of 16, and also in separate sheets of 50 (2 panes of 25).

345 *Blakea trinervia* (cup and saucer)

346 Courtney Walsh (fast bowler 1984–2001)

(Litho Cartor)

2006 (30 Nov). Christmas. Flowers. T **345** and similar multicoloured designs. W **111** (sideways on horiz designs). P 13½.

1125	$20 Type **345**..	1·25	70
1126	$30 *Guaiacum officinale* (Lignum Vitae).........	1·75	90
1127	$50 *Neocogniauxia monophylla* (*vert*).............	2·25	2·00
1128	$60 *Dendrophylax funalis* (ghost orchid) (*vert*)..	2·50	3·50
1125/8 Set of 4..		7·00	6·25

(Des A. Melville-Brown. Litho BDT)

2007 (28 Feb). ICC Cricket World Cup. T **346** and similar multicoloured designs. W **111** (sideways on horiz designs). P 14.

1129	$30 Type **346**..	2·00	1·40
1130	$30 Collie Smith (cricketer 1955–9).................	2·00	1·40
1131	$40 New Sabina Park Stadium, Kingston (*horiz*)..	2·25	1·50
1132	$50 Type **346**..	2·50	2·00
1133	$60 Trelawny Multi-purpose Sports Complex (*horiz*)..	2·75	3·25
1129/33 Set of 5..		10·50	8·50
MS1134 118×92 mm. $200 ICC Cricket World Cup trophy		11·00	13·00

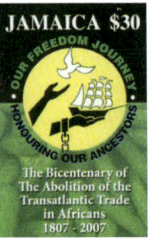

347 Emblem

348 Scout and Jamaican Flag

(Litho BDT)

2007 (7 June). Bicentenary of the Abolition of the Transatlantic Trade in Africans. W **111**. P 14.

| 1135 | 347 | $30 multicoloured | 1·00 | 75 |

(Des Andrew Robinson. Litho BDT)

2007 (9 July). Centenary of Scouting. T **348** and similar multicoloured designs. W **111** (sideways). P 14.

1136	$5 Type **348**	35	35
1137	$10 Early Jamaican scouts	50	35
1138	$30 Scout leaders	1·25	75
1139	$70 Scouts with Jamaican flag	2·75	4·25
1136/9 Set of 4		4·25	5·00
MS1140 90×65 mm. $50 Scout parade (vert); $100 Lord Baden-Powell (vert)		7·00	8·00

349 *Tolumnia triquetra*

350 Asafa Powell

(Litho BDT)

2007 (9 Nov). "The Christmas Collection 2007". Flowers. T **349** and similar multicoloured designs. W **111**. P 14.

1141	$20 Type **349**	80	35
1142	$30 *Broughtonia negrilensis* (horiz)	1·25	50
1143	$50 *Broughtonia sanguinea* (horiz)	2·00	1·75
1144	$60 *Spathelia sorbifolia*	2·25	2·75
1141/4 Set of 4		5·75	4·75

(Des Richard Allen. Litho BDT)

2008 (30 Apr). Olympic Games, Beijing. T **350** and similar square designs showing athletes. Multicoloured. W **111** (inverted on $60). P 13½.

1145	$20 Type **350**	1·00	40
1146	$30 Aleen Bailey and Veronica Campbell-Brown	1·50	1·75
	a. Horiz pair. Nos. 1146/7	3·00	3·50
1147	$30 Sherone Simpson and Tayna Lawrence	1·50	1·75
1148	$60 Veronica Campbell-Brown	2·75	3·00
1145/8 Set of 4		6·00	6·25

Nos. 1146/7 were printed together, se-tenant, as horizontal pairs in sheets of 50, each pair forming a composite design showing athletes with medals.

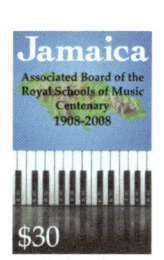

351 Anniversary Emblem

352 Keyboard

(Litho Enschedé)

2008 (26 May). 50th Anniv of University of Technology, Jamaica. W **111**. P 14.

| 1149 | **351** | $30 multicoloured | 1·50 | 1·00 |
| MS1150 95×70 mm. **351** $30 multicoloured | | 1·50 | 1·75 |

(Litho BDT)

2008 (30 Oct). Centenary of ABRSM (Associated Board of the Royal Schools of Music) Examinations in Jamaica. T **352** and similar vert design. Multicoloured. W **111**. P 14.

| 1151 | $30 Type **352** | 1·25 | 60 |
| 1152 | $70 Violin | 2·50 | 3·00 |

353 Fern Fronds

(Litho BDT)

2008 (21 Nov). Christmas. Ferns. T **353** and similar horiz designs. Multicoloured. W **111** (sideways). P 13½.

1153	$20 Type **353**	80	50
1154	$30 Curled single fern leaf	1·25	60
1155	$50 Close-up of fern frond	2·00	1·75
1156	$60 Fern frond	2·25	2·75
1153/6 Set of 4		5·75	5·00

354 George Headley

355 Angel and Two Children

(Litho BDT)

2009 (25 Sept). Birth Centenary of George Headley (cricketer). T **354** and similar vert designs. Multicoloured. W **111**. P 14.

1157	$10 Type **354**	50	30
1158	$30 George Headley at wicket	1·00	40
1159	$200 Statue of George Headley	6·00	6·75
1157/9 Set of 3		6·75	6·75
MS1160 110×95 mm. $250 Statue of George Headley at Sabina Park, Kingston (42×56 *mm*). Wmk sideways		7·00	8·00

(Litho BDT)

2009 (20 Nov). Christmas. T **355** and similar multicoloured designs. W **111** (sideways on $50). P 13½.

1161	$20 Type **355**	60	25
1162	$30 Madonna and infant Jesus	75	30
1163	$50 Madonna (*horiz*)	1·25	1·50
1161/3 Set of 3		2·40	1·90

356 NDTC Singers

356a Prince William and Miss Catherine Middleton

(Des Kevin Reittie. Litho B.D.T)

2010 (15 Dec). Christmas. Choirs. T **356** and similar horiz designs. Multicoloured. W **111** (sideways). P 13½.

1164	$40 Type **356**	1·25	50
1165	$60 Kingston College Chapel Choir	1·75	1·00
1166	$120 The University Singers	3·25	3·50
1167	$160 The Jamaican Folk Singers	4·25	4·50
1164/7 Set of 4		9·50	8·50

(Litho BDT)

2011 (29 Apr). Royal Wedding. Sheet 118×90 mm. W **111** (sideways). P 14½×14.

| MS1168 **356a** $400 multicoloured | 9·00 | 9·50 |

JAMAICA

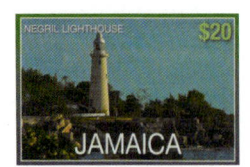

357 Negril Lighthouse

(Litho BDT)

2011 (4 July). Lighthouses. T **357** and similar multicoloured designs. W **111** (sideways on horiz designs). P 14.

1169	$20 Type **357**	1·25	65
1170	$50 Morant Point Lighthouse	1·75	1·25
1171	$60 Lover's Leap Lighthouse (vert)	2·00	1·50
1172	$200 Galina Lighthouse (vert)	4·75	6·00
1169/72	Set of 4	8·75	8·50

358 Hummingbird Emblem

(Litho BDT)

2012 (31 Aug). 50th Anniv of Independence. T **358** and similar multicoloured design. W **111** (sideways on $60). P 14×14½ ($60) or 14½×14 ($120).

1173	$60 Type **358**	1·50	1·00
1174	$120 Arms of Jamaica (vert)	2·75	3·25

STAMP BOOKLETS

1912. Black on red covers. Stapled.
SB1 2s. booklet containing twenty-four 1d. (No. 40) in blocks of 6 (9 Mar)
SB2 2s. booklet containing twelve ½d. and eighteen 1d. (Nos. 38, 58), each in blocks of 6 (5 Dec) £1500

1923 (Dec). Black on red cover. Stapled.
SB3 2s. booklet containing twelve ½d. (No. 94) in blocks of 4 and eighteen 1d. (No. 95) in blocks of 6 .... £1000

1928. Black on red cover. Stapled.
SB4 2s. booklet containing twelve ½d. and eighteen 1d. (Nos. 92a, 95) in blocks of 6 .... £1700

1928 (5 Sept). Black on red cover. Stapled.
SB5 1s.6d. booklet containing twelve ½d. and 1d. (Nos. 92a, 95), each in blocks of 6 ....

1929 (July)–**32**. Black on red cover. Stapled.
SB6 2s. booklet containing six ½d., twelve 1d. and six 1½d. (Nos. 92a, 108/9) in blocks of 6 .... £1300
  a. With 1d. Die II (No. 108a) (1932) ....

1930–33. Black on red cover. Stapled.
SB7 2s. booklet containing twelve ½d. and eighteen 1d. (Nos. 92a, 108), each in blocks of 6 ....
  a. With 1d. Die II (No. 108a) (1933) £1100
  b. Black on blue cover (1933) £1700

1935. Silver Jubilee. Black on pink cover. Stapled.
SB8 2s. booklet containing twenty-four 1d. (No. 114) in blocks of 6 .... £1500
  a. In blocks of 4 .... £2250

1938–40. Black on green cover inscr "JAMAICA POSTAGE STAMPS" in one line. Inland Postage Rates on interleaf. Stapled.
SB9 2s. booklet containing twelve ½d. and eighteen 1d. (Nos. 121/2), each in blocks of 6 (inland letter rate 1d. per oz) £475
  a. Inland letter rate 1½d. for first 2 oz (1940) £500

1942–47. Black on blue cover inscr "JAMAICA POSTAGE STAMPS" in three lines. Inland Postage Rates on inside front cover. Stapled.
SB10 2s. booklet containing twelve ½d. and eighteen 1d. (Nos. 121/2), each in blocks of 6 (Inland letter rate 1½d. for first 2 oz) £250
  a. Black on yellow cover (1947) £110

1946. New Constitution. Black on blue cover. Stapled.
SB12 2s. booklet containing sixteen 1½d. (No. 134a) in blocks of 4 .... £225

1952. Black on yellow cover. Stapled.
SB13 2s. booklet containing twelve ½d. and eighteen 1d. (Nos. 121b, 122a), each in blocks of 6 .... 25·00

1956. Black on green cover, 83×59 mm. Stitched.
SB14 3s. booklet containing ½d., 1d., 2d. and 2½d. (Nos. 159/62) in blocks of 6 .... 11·00

1965 (15 Nov). Black on green cover, 93×50 mm. Stitched.
SB15 3s. booklet containing 1d., 2d. and 3d. (Nos. 217, 219, 221) in blocks of 6 .... 5·00

1981 (29 July). Royal Wedding. Multicoloured cover, 155×85 mm, showing Prince Charles, Lady Diana Spencer and St. Paul's Cathedral. Stitched.
SB16 $6.25 booklet containing se-tenant pane of 4 (No. 516ba) .... 3·50

1982 (30 Aug). 21st Birthday of Princess of Wales. Multicoloured cover, 155×85 mm, showing Princess of Wales and Highgrove House. Stitched.
SB17 $7.50 booklet containing two different se-tenant panes of 3 (Nos. 551a, 554a) .... 5·50

1982 (13 Sept). Birth of Prince William of Wales. No. SB17 optd "ROYAL BABY 21.6.82".
SB18 $7.50 booklet containing two different se-tenant panes of 3 (Nos. 558a, 561a) .... 3·00

2005 (25 Feb). Buildings. Multicoloured cover, 159×61 mm, showing stamps from set. Self-adhesive.
SB19 $300 booklet containing pane of ten $30 (No. 1077a).   10·00

POSTAL FISCALS

Revenue stamps were authorised for postal use by Post Office notice of 12 October 1887.

F **1**

(Typo D.L.R.)

1865–73. P 14.

*(a) Wmk Pineapple (T **7**)*
F1 F **1** 1d. rose (1865) .... 95·00 £100
    a. Imperf (pair) £550

(b) Wmk Crown CC
F2 F **1** 1d. rose (1871) .... 65·00 55·00

(c) Wmk CA over Crown (Type w 7 sideways, covering two stamps)
F3 F **1** 1d. rose (1873) .... 45·00 7·00
    a. Imperf

F **2**   F **3**

(Typo D.L.R.)

1855–74. (Issued). Glazed paper. P 14.

(a) No wmk
F4 F **2** 1½d. blue/blue (1857) .... 65·00 50·00
    a. Imperf (1855) ....
    b. Blue on white .... 80·00 60·00
F5   3d. purple/blue (1857) .... 65·00 55·00
    a. Imperf (1855) ....
    b. Purple on lilac (1857) .... 65·00 55·00
    ba. Imperf (1855) £700
    c. Purple on white (1857) .... 85·00 55·00

(b) Wmk Crown CC
F6 F **2** 3d. purple/blue (1874) .... 26·00 26·00
All the above stamps *imperf* are exceedingly rare postally used.

1858 (1 Jan). (Issued). No wmk. P 15½×15.
F7 F **3** 1s. rose/bluish .... £110 90·00
F8   5s. lilac/bluish £500 £500
F9   10s. green/bluish £650 £650
Telegraph stamps were also used postally, but no authority was given for such use.

OFFICIAL STAMPS

OFFICIAL (O **1**)   **OFFICIAL** (O **2**)

1890 (1 Apr)–**91**. No. 16a optd with Type O **1** by C. Vendryes, Kingston.

(a) "OFFICIAL" 17 to 17½ mm long

O1	8	½d. green	18·00	2·25
		a. "O" omitted	£800	
		b. One "I" omitted	£800	
		c. Both "I"s omitted	£900	£900
		d. "L" omitted	£950	£950
		e. Opt inverted	£100	£110
		f. Opt double	£100	£110
		g. Opt double, one inverted	£550	£550
		h. Opt double, one vertical	£900	
		j. Pair, overprints *tête-bêche*		

(b) "OFFICIAL" 15 to 16 mm long

O2	8	½d. green (3.91)	42·00	28·00
		a. Opt double	£800	

There were five settings of the locally-overprinted Officials. No. O1 occurred from settings I (2×10), II (3×6), IV and V (horizontal row of 6 each). No. O2 came from setting III (2×6). There are numerous minor varieties, due to broken type, etc. (*e.g.* a broken "E" used for "F").

Stamps with the 17–17½ mm opt were reissued in 1894 during a temporary shortage of No. O3.

1890 (1 Apr)–**91**. Optd with Type O **2** by D.L.R. Wmk Crown CA. P 14.

O3	8	½d. green (1891)	10·00	1·75
O4	11	1d. rose	8·00	1·25
O5		2d. grey	24·00	1·25
O3/5	*Set of 3*		38·00	3·75
O3s/5s	Optd "SPECIMEN" *Set of 3*		£150	

Nos. O4/5 were not issued without overprint.

The use of Official stamps ceased from 1 January 1898.

TELEGRAPH STAMPS

T **1**   T **2**

(Typo D.L.R.)

1879 (Oct). Wmk Crown CC (sideways on 3d.). P 14.

T1	T **1**	3d. lilac (shades)	42·00	10·00
T2	T **2**	1s. purple-brown (shades)	22·00	2·50
		s. Optd "SPECIMEN"	65·00	

1889. Wmk Crown CA (sideways). P14.

T3	T **1**	3d. lilac (shades)	11·00	3·50
		s. Optd "SPECIMEN"	65·00	

Nos. T2s and T3s were distributed to UPU member countries in March 1892.

1904. Wmk Mult Crown CA (sideways). P. 14.

T4	T **1**	3d. lilac	32·00	22·00

Give your collection the home it deserves

Frank Godden albums are a labour of love, with each individual album beautifully handmade to an unmistakable and unmatchable quality.

All leaves are now made to the internationally recognised standard for archival paper, the type that is used and recommended by all major museums.

Revered throughout the philatelic world for their supreme quality and craftsmanship, Frank Godden albums are built to last a lifetime and to offer you a lifetime of enjoyment.

If you are passionate about your collection, then Frank Godden provides the home it deserves.

Whether you are looking for the best quality albums, exhibition cases, protectors, leaves or interleaving, you can find whatever you are looking for at Stanley Gibbons, the new home of Frank Godden.

To order, call **0800 611 622** (UK only) or email **order@stanleygibbons.com**

Est 1856
STANLEY GIBBONS

Stanley Gibbons Limited
7 Parkside, Christchurch Road,
Ringwood, Hants, BH24 3SH
+44 (0)1425 472 363
www.stanleygibbons.com

Turks and Caicos Islands

TURKS ISLANDS
DEPENDENCY OF JAMAICA

A branch of the British Post Office opened at Grand Turk on 11 December 1854 replacing an earlier arrangement under which mail for the islands was sorted by local R.M.S.P. agents.

No. CC 1 is known used between 22 October 1857 and 20 April 1862.

GRAND TURK
CROWNED-CIRCLE HANDSTAMPS

CC 1

| CC1 | CC **1** TURKS-ISLANDS (Oct 1857) | *Price on cover* | £5500 |

PRICES FOR STAMPS ON COVER TO 1945	
Nos. 1/5	from × 30
No. 6	—
Nos. 7/20	from × 50
Nos. 20a/48	—
Nos. 49/52	from × 12
Nos. 53/7	from × 10
Nos. 58/65	from × 20
Nos. 66/9	from × 5
Nos. 70/2	from × 10
Nos. 101/9	from × 8
Nos. 110/26	from × 6
Nos. 129/39	from × 4
Nos. 140/53	from × 12
Nos. 154/90	from × 3
Nos. 191/3	from × 10
Nos. 194/205	from × 2

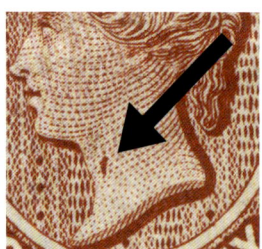

1

Throat flaw (R. 3/4)

(Recess P.B.)

1867 (4 Apr). No wmk. P 11–12½.

1	1	1d. dull rose	65·00	60·00
		a. Throat flaw	£250	£250
2		6d. black	£110	£130
3		1s. dull blue	95·00	60·00

1873–79. Wmk Small Star. W **w 2** (sideways on Nos. 5 and 6). P 11–12½×14½–15½.

4	1	1d. dull rose-lake (7.73)	55·00	50·00
		a. Throat flaw	£225	£225

5		b. Wmk sideways	90·00	90·00
		ba. Throat flaw	£325	£350
		1d. dull red (1.79)	60·00	60·00
		a. Imperf between (horiz pair)	£26000	
		b. Throat flaw	£250	£250
		c. Wmk upright		
6		1s. lilac (1.79)	£5000	£2000

1881 (1 Jan). Stamps of the preceding issues surcharged locally, in black. Sheets of 30 (10×3).
There are twelve different settings of the ½d., nine settings of the 2½d., and six settings of the 4d.

$\frac{1}{2}$ (2) $\frac{1}{2}$ (3)

Setting 1. T **2**. Long fraction bar. Two varieties in a horizontal pair repeated fifteen times in the sheet.

| 7 | | ½ on 6d black | £100 | £170 |

Setting 2. T **3**. Short fraction bar. Three varieties in a vertical strip repeated ten times in sheet.

Setting 3. Similar to setting 2, but the middle stamp of the three varieties has a longer bar.

8		½ on 6d. black (*setting* 2 *only*)	£100	£150
9		½ on 1s. dull blue	£140	£200
		a. Surch double	£8000	

$\frac{1}{2}$ (4) $\frac{1}{2}$ (5) $\frac{1}{2}$ (6)

Three varieties in a vertical strip repeated ten times in sheet.
Setting 4. Types **4**, **5**, **6**.
Setting 5. Types **4** (without bar), **5**, **6**.
Setting 6. Types **4**, **5**, **6** (without bar).
Setting 7. Types **4** (shorter thick bar), **6**, **6**.

10		½ on 1d. dull red (*setting* 7 *only*) (T **6**)		
		a. Type **4** (shorter thick bar)	£16000	
11		½ on 1s. dull blue (*setting* 6 *and* 7) (T **4**)	£2000	
		a. Type **4** (shorter thick bar)	£3000	
		b. Type **5**	£1500	
		c. Type **6**	£1200	
		d. Type **6** (without bar)	£2500	
		e. Surch double (T **4**)	£13000	
		f. Surch double (T **5**)	£13000	
		g. Surch double (T **6** without bar)		
12		½ on 1s. lilac (T **4**)	£275	£425
		a. Without bar	£600	
		b. With short thick bar	£550	
		c. Surch double	£4000	
		cb. Surch double and short thick bar	£13000	
13		½ on 1s. lilac (T **5**)	£160	£300
		a. Surch double	£3750	
14		½ on 1s. lilac (T **6**)	£150	£275
		a. Without bar	£700	
		b. Surch double	£8000	
		ba. Surch double and without bar	£13000	

Care should be taken in the identification of Types **6** and **7** which are very similar. For the 1s. value some varieties of No. 9 are often confused with Nos. 11b/c.

$\frac{1}{2}$ (7) $\frac{1}{2}$ (8) $\frac{1}{2}$ (9) $\frac{1}{2}$ (10)

Setting 8. T **7**. Three varieties in a vertical strip. All have a very short bar.

15		½. on 1d dull red	85·00	£150
		a. Throat flaw	£350	
		b. Surch double	£7500	

Setting 9. T **8**. Three varieties in a vertical strip. Bars long and thick and "1" leaning a little to left.

16		½ on 1d. dull red	£200	£350
		a. Surch double	£6000	
		b. Throat flaw	£700	

Setting 10. T **9** and **10**. Fifteen varieties repeated twice in a sheet. Ten are of T **9** (Rows 1 and 2), five of T **10** (Row 3).

17		½ on 1d. dull red (T **9**)	60·00	£150
		a. Surch double	£6500	

140

18	½ on 1d. dull red (T **10**)		95·00	£200
	a. Surch double		£11000	
	b. Throat flaw		£350	
19	½ on 1s. lilac (T **9**)		£100	£225
20	½ on 1s. lilac (T **10**)		£180	£400
20*a*	½. on 1s. dull blue (T **9**)		£12000	
20*b*	½ on 1s. dull blue (T **10**)		£22000	

Types **9** and **11**. The difference is in the position of the "2" in relation to the "1". In setting 10 the "2" is to the left of the "1" except on No. 10 (where it is directly below the "1") and in setting 11 it is to the right except on No. 2 (where it is to the left, as in setting 10).

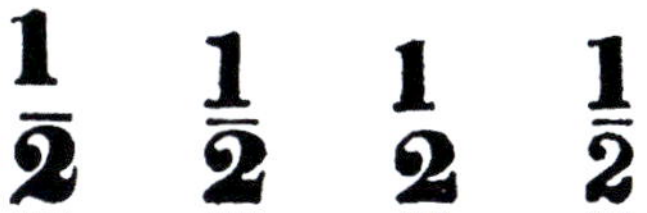

(11) (12) (13) (14)

Setting 11. T **9** and **11** to **14**. Fifteen varieties repeated twice in a sheet. Nine of T **11**, three of T **12**, and one each of T **9**, **13** and **14**.

Setting 12. Similar to last, but T **13** replaced by another T **12**.

21	½ on 1d. dull red (T **11**)		£120	£225
22	½ on 1d. dull red (T **12**)		£325	
	a. Throat flaw		£1300	
23	½ on 1d. dull red (T **13**)		£1100	
	a. Throat flaw		£1100	
24	½ on 1d. dull red (T **14**)		£700	
24*a*	½ on 1s. dull blue (T **11**)		£22000	

Type **9** from these settings, where it occurs on position 2, can only be distinguished from similar stamps from setting 10 when *se-tenant* with Type **11**.

In setting 11 Type **13** occupied R. 3/4 in the setting (5×3), corresponding to the position of the "Throat flaw" on the left half of each sheet of 30 (10×3). Nos. 23 and 23a therefore exist in equal quantities.

(15) (16)

Setting 1. T **15**. Fraction in very small type.
25   2½ on 6d. black £16000

Setting 2. T **16**. Two varieties repeated fifteen times in a sheet. Large "2" on level with top of the "1", long thin bar.

26	2½ on 6d. black		£400	£600
	a. Imperf between (horiz pair)		£40000	
	b. Surch double		£17000	

(17) (18) (19)

Setting 3. T **17**. As T **16**, but large "2" not so high up.
27   2½ on 1s. lilac £4000

Setting 4. T **18**. Three varieties in a vertical strip repeated ten times in sheet. Large "2" placed lower and small bar.

28	2½ on 1s. lilac		£250	£425
	a. Surch double		£16000	

Setting 5. T **19**. Three varieties in a vertical strip repeated ten times in sheet "2" further from "½", small fraction bar.

29	2½ on 1s. lilac		£550	£1000

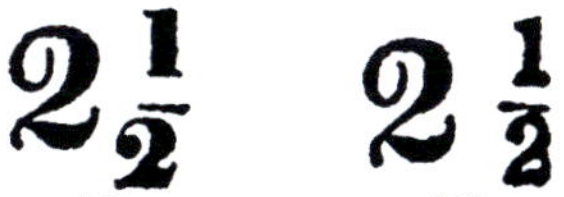

(20) (21)

Setting 6. T **20** and **21**. Fifteen varieties. Ten of T **20** and five of T **21**, repeated twice in a sheet.

30	2½ on 1s. lilac (T **20**)	£13000	
31	2½ on 1s. lilac (T **21**)	£24000	

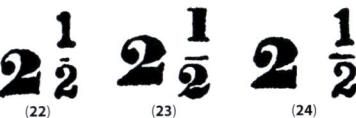

(22) (23) (24)

Setting 7. T **22**. Three varieties in a vertical strip, repeated ten times in a sheet.

32	2½ on 6d. black	£9500
33	2½ on 1s. dull blue	£27000

Setting 8. T **23** and **24**. Fifteen varieties. Ten of T **23** and five of T **24** repeated twice in a sheet.

34	2½ on 1d. dull red (T **23**)	£750	
35	2½ on 1d. dull red (T **24**)	£1500	
	a. Throat flaw	£4750	
36	2½ on 1s. lilac (T **23**)	£600	£850
	a. Surch "½" double	£4750	
37	2½ on 1s. lilac (T **24**)	£1200	
	a. Surch "½" double	£9000	

(25) (26) (27)

Setting 9. T **25**, **26**, and **27**. Fifteen varieties. Ten of T **25**, three of T **26**, one of T **26** without bar, and one of T **27**, repeated twice in a sheet.

38	2½ on 1s. dull blue (T **25**)	£1100
39	2½ on 1s. dull blue (T **26**)	£3750
40	2½ on 1s. dull blue (T **26**) (without bar)	£15000
41	2½ on 1s. dull blue (T **27**)	£15000

(28) (29) (30)

Setting 1. T **28**. "4" 8 mm high, pointed top.
42   4 on 6d. black £750   £350

Settings 2-6. T **29** and **30**.

43	4 on 6d. black (T **29**)	£110	£150
44	4 on 6d. black (T **30**)	£400	£500
45	4 on 1s. lilac (T **29**)	£475	£750
	a. Surch double		
46	4 on 1s. lilac (T **30**)	£2500	
	a. Surch double		
47	4 on 1d. dull red (T **29**)	£750	£475
48	4 on 1d. dull red (T **28**)	£850	£550

The components of these settings can only be distinguished when in blocks. Details are given in the handbook by John J. Challis.

31 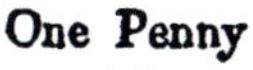 (32)

1881 (Typo (No. 50) or recess D.L.R.). Wmk Crown CC (sideways* on T **1**). P 14.

49	**1**	1d. brown-red (Oct)	85·00	£100
		a. Throat flaw	£300	£375
50	**31**	4d. ultramarine (Die I) (Aug)	£170	60·00
		w. Wmk inverted	—	£400
51	**1**	6d. olive-black (Oct)	£160	£200
52		1s. slate-green (Oct)	£200	£150

*The normal sideways watermark shows Crown to right of CC, *as seen from the back of the stamp*.

Nos. 49 and 51/2 also exist showing Crown to left of CC, but due to the position of the watermark such varieties are difficult to detect on single stamps. Reversed watermarks are also known.

Top left triangle detached
(Pl 2 R. 3/3 of right panel)

1882–85. Wmk Crown CA (reversed on 1d.). P 14.

53	**31**	½d. blue-green (Die I) (2.82)	24·00	29·00
		a. Pale green (12.85)	6·50	6·00
		b. Top left triangle detached	£375	
		w. Wmk inverted	£225	

55	1	1d. orange-brown (10.83)	£100	38·00
		a. Bisected (½d.) (on cover)	†	£5000
		b. Throat flaw	£375	£150
		x. Wmk normal (not reversed)	£190	£110
56	31	2½d. red-brown (Die I) (2.82)	40·00	16·00
57		4d. grey (Die I) (10.84)	38·00	4·00
		a. Bisected (2d.) (on cover)	†	£5000

1887 (July)–**89**. Wmk Crown CA.

(a) P 12

58	1	1d. crimson-lake	32·00	8·00
		a. Imperf between (horiz pair)	£27000	
		b. Throat flaw	85·00	21·00
		x. Wmk reversed	21·00	5·00

(b) P 14

59	1	6d. yellow-brown (2.89)	4·50	5·00
		s. Optd "SPECIMEN"	50·00	
60		1s. sepia	6·00	4·50

During a shortage of 1d. stamps a supply of JAMAICA No. 27 was sent to the Turks and Caicos Islands in April 1889 and used until replaced by No. 61. *Price from* £250 *used.*

1889 (May). Surch at Grand Turk with T **32**.

61	31	1d. on 2½d. red-brown	22·00	19·00
		a. "One" omitted	£1600	
		b. Bisected (½d.) (on cover)	†	£5000

No. 61a was caused by misplacement of the surcharge. Stamps from the same sheet can be found with the surcharge reading "Penny One".

Neck flaw (R. 3/2)

1889–93. Wmk Crown CA. P 14.

62	1	1d. crimson-lake (7.89)	8·00	6·00
		a. Bisected (½d.) (on cover)	†	£4750
		b. Throat flaw	26·00	26·00
		c. Neck flaw	42·00	42·00
		x. Wmk reversed	75·00	
63		1d. lake	6·50	4·25
		a. Bisected (½d.) (on cover)	†	£4750
		b. Throat flaw	20·00	20·00
		c. Neck flaw	35·00	35·00
64		1d. pale rosy lake	6·50	8·00
		b. Throat flaw	20·00	32·00
		c. Neck flaw	35·00	45·00
65	31	2½d. ultramarine (Die II) (4.93)	6·00	4·25
		s. Optd "SPECIMEN"	50·00	

(33)   34

1893 (10 June). No. 57 surch at Grand Turk with T **33**.

Setting 1. Bars between "1d." and "2" separate, instead of continuous across the rows of stamps.

66		½d. on 4d. grey	£3250	£1400

Setting 2. Continuous bars. Thin and thick bar 10¾ mm apart. "2" under the "1".

67		½d. on 4d. grey	£200	£140

Setting 3. As last, but bars 11¾ mm apart.

68		½d. on 4d. grey	£180	£190

Setting 4. Bars 11 mm apart. Five out of the six varieties in the strip have the "2" below the space between the "1" and "d".

69		½d. on 4d. grey	£225	£180

There is a fifth setting, but the variation is slight.

(Typo D.L.R.)

1893–95. Wmk Crown CA. P 14.

70	31	½d. dull green (Die II) (12.93)	6·00	4·00
71		4d. dull purple & ultramarine (Die II) (5.95)	22·00	24·00
72	34	5d. olive-green and carmine (6.94)	10·00	25·00
		a. Bisected (2½d.) (on cover)	†	£4750
70/2 Set of 3			35·00	48·00
71s/2s Optd "SPECIMEN" Set of 2			£100	

TURKS AND CAICOS ISLANDS

35 Badge of the Islands   **36** Badge of the Islands

The dates on the stamps have reference to the political separation from Bahamas.

(Recess D.L.R.)

1900 (10 Nov)–**04**. Wmk Crown CA (½d. to 1s.) or Wmk Crown CC (2s., 3s.). P 14.

101	35	½d. green	2·75	4·00
		x. Wmk reversed	£170	
102		1d. red	3·50	75
		w. Wmk inverted	£110	
103		2d. sepia	1·00	1·25
		w. Wmk inverted	£130	
		x. Wmk reversed	£130	
104		2½d. blue	10·00	16·00
		a. Greyish blue (1904)	1·75	1·00
		aw. Wmk inverted	£110	
		ay. Wmk inverted and reversed	—	£200
105		4d. orange	3·75	7·00
106		6d. dull mauve	2·50	6·50
107		1s. purple-brown	3·25	21·00
108	36	2s. purple	50·00	80·00
109		3s. lake	80·00	£110
101/9 Set of 9			£130	£200
101s/9s Optd "SPECIMEN" Set of 9			£250	

Nos. 101/7 exist without watermark or with double-lined lettering from the marginal watermark due to the way in which full sheets were cut for printing.

1905–08. Wmk Mult Crown CA. P 14.

110	35	½d. green	5·00	15
		x. Wmk reversed	—	£200
111		1d. red	19·00	50
		w. Wmk inverted	£200	
		x. Wmk reversed	£200	
112		3d. purple/*yellow* (1908)	2·25	6·00
		s. Optd "SPECIMEN"	50·00	
		w. Wmk inverted	£200	
110/12 Set of 3			24·00	6·00

37 Turk's-head Cactus   **38**

(Recess D.L.R.)

1909 (2 Sept)–**11**. Wmk Mult Crown CA. P 14.

115	37	¼d. rosy mauve (1910)	1·75	1·00
		w. Wmk inverted		
116		¼d. red (1911)	60	40
		w. Wmk inverted		
117	38	½d. yellow-green	75	40
		w. Wmk inverted		
		x. Wmk reversed	65·00	
		y. Wmk inverted and reversed	£170	
118		1d. red	1·25	40
119		2d. greyish slate	5·50	1·40
120		2½d. blue	8·00	2·25
		w. Wmk inverted		
		x. Wmk reversed	80·00	90·00
		xs. Ditto opt "SPECIMEN"	£110	
121		3d. purple/*yellow*	2·50	2·00
122		4d. red/*yellow*	3·25	7·00

123		6d. purple	7·00	3·50
124		1s. black/green	7·50	6·50
		w. Wmk inverted	£275	
125		2s. red/green	45·00	60·00
126		3s. black/red	48·00	40·00
115/26 Set of 12			£110	£110
115s/26s Optd "SPECIMEN" Set of 12			£275	

See also Nos. 154 and 162.

WAR TAX
39 (40)

1913 (1 Apr)–**21**. Wmk Mult Crown CA. P 14.

129	39	½d. green	50	1·75
		w. Wmk inverted		
130		1d. red	1·00	2·25
		a. Bright rose-scarlet	1·10	2·00
		ax. Wmk reversed	80·00	
		b. Rose-carmine (1918)	3·75	7·00
131		2d. greyish slate	2·25	3·50
132		2½d. ultramarine	2·25	3·00
		aw. Wmk inverted		
		b. Bright blue (1918)	4·25	2·75
133		3d. purple/yellow	2·25	11·00
		a. On lemon	16·00	
		b. On yellow-buff	4·00	11·00
		c. On orange-buff	1·75	
		cx. Wmk reversed	£100	
		d. On pale yellow	2·75	11·00
134		4d. red/yellow	1·00	9·50
		a. On orange-buff	1·60	7·50
		ab. "A" of "CA" missing from wmk		
		as. Optd "SPECIMEN"	48·00	
		b. Carmine on pale yellow	7·50	16·00
135		5d. pale olive-green (18.5.16)	6·50	22·00
136		6d. dull purple	2·50	3·50
		w. Wmk inverted		
		x. Wmk reversed		
137		1s. brown-orange	1·50	5·00
		w. Wmk inverted		
138		2s. red/blue-green	18·00	42·00
		a. On greenish white (1919)	29·00	70·00
		b. On emerald (3.21)	48·00	75·00
		bs. Optd "SPECIMEN"	55·00	
		bx. Wmk reversed	£250	
139		3s. black/red	15·00	26·00
129/39 Set of 11			48·00	£110
129s/39s Optd "SPECIMEN" Set of 11			£200	

1917 (3 Jan). Optd locally with T **40** at bottom of stamp.

140	39	1d. red	10	1·50
		a. Opt double	£180	£250
		ab. Opt double (in horiz pair with normal)	£400	
		b. "TAX" omitted		
		c. "WAR TAX" omitted in vert pair with normal	£700	
		d. Opt inverted at top	65·00	85·00
		e. Opt double, one inverted	£110	
		f. Opt inverted only, in pair with No. 140e	£600	
141		3d. purple/yellow-buff	1·25	8·50
		a. Opt double	£100	
		b. On lemon	3·50	12·00
		ba. Opt double	£100	£130
		bb. Opt double, one inverted	£325	

The overprint was in a setting of 60, using a plate supplied by De La Rue, applied twice to the sheets of 120. One sheet of the 1d. exists with the right-hand impression of the setting misplaced one row to the left so that stamps in vertical row 6 show a double overprint (No. 140ab). It appears that the right-hand vertical row on this sheet had the overprint applied at a third operation.

In Nos. 140e/f the inverted overprint is at foot and reads "TAX WAR" owing to displacement. No. 140e also exists with "WAR" omitted from the inverted overprint.

In both values of the first printings the stamp in the bottom left-hand corner of the sheet has a long "T" in "TAX", and on the first stamp of the sixth row the "X" is damaged and looks like a reversed "K". The long "T" was subsequently converted.

1917 (Oct). Second printing with overprint at top or in middle of stamp.

143	39	1d. red	10	1·25
		a. Inverted opt at bottom or centre	50·00	
		c. Opt omitted (in pair with normal)	£650	
		d. Opt double, one at top, one at bottom	65·00	
		e. As d., but additional opt in top margin	£120	
		f. Pair, one as d., the other normal	£325	
		g. Pair, one opt inverted, one normal	£650	
		h. Double opt at top (in pair with normal)	£275	
		i. Opt double	48·00	60·00
144		3d. purple/yellow	60	1·75
		a. Opt double	50·00	
		b. Opt double, one inverted	£350	
		c. On lemon	4·50	

1918 (18 Dec). Overprinted with T **40**.

145	39	3d. purple/yellow (R.)	20·00	55·00
		a. Opt double	£325	

WAR TAX (41)　**WAR TAX** (42)　**WAR TAX** (43)

1918 (26 June). Optd with T **41** in London by D.L.R.

146	39	1d. rose-carmine	20	2·25
		a. Bright rose-scarlet	15	1·75
		aw. Wmk inverted	75·00	
147		3d. purple/yellow	5·50	6·00
146s/7s Optd "SPECIMEN" Set of 2			85·00	

1919 (14 Apr). Optd with T **41** in London by D.L.R.

148	39	3d. purple/orange-buff (R.)	20	5·50
		s. Optd "SPECIMEN"	45·00	

1919 (17 Apr). Local overprint. T **40**, in violet.

149	39	1d. bright rose-scarlet	1·00	6·00
		a. "WAR" omitted (in pair with normal)	£200	
		b. Opt double	21·00	
		c. Opt double in pair with normal	£120	
		d. Opt double, one inverted		
		e. Opt triple		
		f. Rose-carmine	9·00	19·00
		fa. Opt double		
		w. Wmk inverted	32·00	

1919 (20 Aug). Optd locally with T **42**.

150	39	1d. scarlet	10	1·75
		a. Opt double	£150	£180
151		3d. purple/orange-buff	30	2·75
		w. Wmk inverted	40·00	
		x. Wmk reversed	40·00	

1919 (17 Dec). Optd locally with T **43**.

152	39	1d. scarlet	20	3·50
		a. Opt inverted		
153		3d. purple/orange-buff	1·50	3·50
		w. Wmk inverted	38·00	
		x. Wmk reversed	25·00	
		y. Wmk inverted and reversed	12·00	

The two bottom rows of this setting have the words "WAR" and "TAX" about 1 mm further apart.

1921 (23 Apr). Wmk Mult Script CA. P 14.

154	37	¼d. rose-red	4·75	24·00
155	39	½d. green	2·75	5·50
156		1d. carmine-red	1·00	5·50
157		2d. slate-grey	1·00	20·00
		y. Wmk inverted and reversed	90·00	
158		2½d. bright blue	1·75	7·50
		x. Wmk reversed	£130	
159		5d. sage-green	10·00	65·00
160		6d. purple	6·50	65·00
		w. Wmk inverted		
		x. Wmk reversed	£100	
161		1s. brown-orange	12·00	42·00
154/61 Set of 8			35·00	£200
154s/61s Optd "SPECIMEN" Set of 8			£150	

44　45

TURKS AND CAICOS ISLANDS

(Recess D.L.R.)
1922 (20 Nov)–**26**. P 14.

(a) Wmk Mult Script CA

162	37	¼d. black (11.10.26)	80	1·00
163	44	½d. yellow-green	4·75	4·25
		a. Bright green	4·75	4·25
		b. Apple-green	7·00	11·00
164		1d. brown	50	3·25
165		1½d. scarlet (24.11.25)	8·00	17·00
166		2d. slate	50	5·00
167		2½d. purple/*pale yellow*	50	1·75
168		3d. bright blue	50	5·00
169		4d. red/*pale yellow*	1·25	18·00
		ax. Wmk reversed	95·00	
		b. Carmine/*pale yellow*	4·50	16·00
170		5d. sage-green	85	22·00
		y. Wmk inverted and reversed	£110	
171		6d. purple	70	12·00
		x. Wmk reversed	£110	
172		1s. brown-orange	80	23·00
173		2s. red/*emerald* (24.11.25)	2·00	9·50

(b) Wmk Mult Crown CA

174	44	2s. red/*emerald*	25·00	95·00
175		3s. black/*red*	5·00	35·00
162/75 Set of 14			45·00	£225
162s/75s Optd "SPECIMEN" Set of 14			£250	

1928 (1 Mar). Inscr "POSTAGE & REVENUE". Wmk Mult Script CA. P 14.

176	45	½d. green	75	50
177		1d. brown	75	70
178		1½d. scarlet	75	4·50
179		2d. grey	75	50
180		2½d. purple/*yellow*	75	5·00
181		3d. bright blue	75	9·50
182		6d. purple	75	7·50
183		1s. brown-orange	3·75	7·50
184		2s. red/*emerald*	6·50	38·00
185		5s. green/*yellow*	12·00	35·00
186		10s. purple/*blue*	60·00	£120
176/86 Set of 11			80·00	£200
176s/86s Optd "SPECIMEN" Set of 11			£190	

1935 (6 May). Silver Jubilee. As Nos. 141/4 of Bahamas, but ptd by Waterlow. P 11×12.

187		½d. black and green	30	1·00
		k. Kite and vertical log	45·00	
		l. Kite and horizontal log	48·00	70·00
188		3d. brown and deep blue	5·00	4·00
		k. Kite and vertical log	£120	£150
189		6d. light blue and olive-green	1·75	5·50
		k. Kite and vertical log	£100	£150
190		1s. slate and purple	1·75	4·00
		k. Kite and vertical log	£100	£150
187/90 Set of 4			8·00	14·00
187s/90s Perf "SPECIMEN" Set of 4			£100	

For illustrations of plate varieties see Omnibus section following Zanzibar.

1937 (12 May). Coronation. As Nos. 146/8 of Bahamas, but ptd by D.L.R. P 14.

191		½d. myrtle-green	10	10
		a. Deep green	40·00	
192		2d. grey-black	80	65
193		3d. bright blue	80	65
191/3 Set of 3			1·50	1·25
191s/3s Perf "SPECIMEN" Set of 3			90·00	

46 Raking Salt

47 Salt Industry

(Recess Waterlow)
1938 (18 June)–**45**. Wmk Mult Script CA. P 12½.

194	46	¼d. black	20	10
195		½d. yellowish green	7·00	15
		a. Deep green (6.11.44)	2·75	70
196		1d. red-brown	75	10
197		1½d. scarlet	75	15
198		2d. grey	1·00	30
199		2½d. yellow-orange	9·00	80
		a. Orange (6.11.44)	5·50	3·00
200		3d. bright blue	70	30
201		6d. mauve	22·00	3·25
201a		6d. sepia (9.2.45)	50	20
202		1s. yellow-bistre	5·00	13·00
202a		1s. grey-olive (9.2.45)	50	20
203	47	2s. deep rose-carmine	45·00	19·00
		a. Bright rose-carmine (6.11.44)	21·00	20·00
204		5s. yellowish green	55·00	27·00
		a. Deep green (6.11.44)	50·00	27·00
205		10s. bright violet	29·00	7·50
194/205 Set of 14			£120	60·00
194s/205s Perf "SPECIMEN" Set of 14			£350	

1946 (4 Nov). Victory. As Nos. 176/7 of Bahamas.

206		2d. black	10	15
207		3d. blue	15	20
206s/7s Perf "SPECIMEN" Set of 2			80·00	

1948 (13 Sept). Royal Silver Wedding. As Nos. 194/5 of Bahamas.

208		1d. red-brown	15	10
209		10s. mauve	14·00	20·00

50 Badge of the Islands

51 Flag of Turks and Caicos Islands

52 Map of islands

53 Queen Victoria and King George VI

(Recess Waterlow)
1948 (14 Dec). Centenary of Separation from Bahamas. T **50**/**53**. Wmk Mult Script CA. P 12½.

210	50	½d. blue-green	2·00	15
211		2d. carmine	2·00	15
212	51	3d. blue	1·75	15
213	52	6d. violet	1·75	30
214	53	2s. black and bright blue	1·25	2·25
215		5s. black and green	1·50	7·50
216		10s. black and brown	4·25	7·50
210/16 Set of 7			13·00	16·00

1949 (10 Oct). 75th Anniv of U.P.U. As Nos. 196/9 of Bahamas.

217		2½d. red-orange	20	2·00
218		3d. deep blue	2·25	60
219		6d. brown	30	75
220		1s. olive	20	35
217/20 Set of 4			2·75	3·25

54 Bulk Salt Loading

55 Salt Cay

56 Caicos mail

57 Grand Turk

58 Sponge diving

59 South Creek

TURKS AND CAICOS ISLANDS

60 Map
61 Grand Turk Light 
62 Government House 
63 Cockburn Harbour 
64 Government offices 
65 Loading salt 
66 Dependency's Badge 

(Recess Waterlow)

1950 (1 Aug). T **54/66**. Wmk Mult Script CA. P 12½.

221	54	½d. green	85	40
222	55	1d. red-brown	80	75
223	56	1½d. deep carmine	1·25	55
224	57	2d. red-orange	1·00	40
225	58	2½d. grey-olive	1·25	50
226	59	3d. bright blue	60	40
227	60	4d. black and rose	3·50	70
228	61	6d. black and blue	3·00	50
229	62	1s. black and blue-green	2·75	40
230	63	1s.6d. black and scarlet	15·00	3·25
231	64	2s. emerald and ultramarine	6·50	4·50
232	65	5s. blue and black	25·00	8·50
233	66	10s. black and violet	27·00	25·00
221/33 Set of 13			80·00	42·00

1953 (2 June). Coronation. As No. 200 of Bahamas, but ptd by B.W. & Co. P 13½×13.

234		2d. black and orange-red	60	1·25

67 M.V. *Kirksons*

(Recess Waterlow)

1955 (1 Feb). T **67** and similar horiz design. Wmk Mult Script CA. P 12½.

235		5d. black and bright green	1·50	70
236		8d. black and brown	2·75	70

Design:—8d. Greater Flamingoes in flight.

69 Queen Elizabeth II (after Annigoni) 
70 Bonefish

82 Dependency's Badge

(Recess B.W.)

1957 (25 Nov). T **69/70**, **82** and similar horiz designs as T **70**. W w **12**. P 13½×14 (1d.), 14 (10s.) or 13½ (others).

237	1d. deep blue and carmine	30	20
238	1½d. grey-green and orange	20	30
239	2d. red-brown and olive	20	15
240	2½d. carmine and green	20	15
241	3d. turquoise-blue and purple	20	15
242	4d. lake and black	1·25	15
243	5d. slate-green and brown	1·25	40
244	6d. carmine-rose and blue	2·00	55
245	8d. vermilion and black	3·25	20
246	1s. deep blue and black	1·25	10
247	1s.6d. sepia and deep ultramarine	18·00	1·50
248	2s. deep ultramarine and brown	16·00	2·50
249	5s. black and carmine	8·00	2·00
250	10s. black and purple	24·00	9·00
237/250 *and* 253 Set of 15		£110	29·00

Designs:—2d. Red Grouper; 2½d. Spiny Lobster; 3d. Albacore; 4d. Mutton Snapper; 5d. Permit; 6d. Queen or Pink Conch; 8d. Greater Flamingoes; 1s. Spanish Mackerel; 1s.6d. Salt Cay; 2s. *Uakon* (Caicos sloop); 5s. Cable Office.

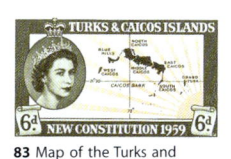

83 Map of the Turks and Caicos Islands

(Photo D.L.R.)

1959 (4 July). New Constitution. Wmk Mult Script CA. P 13½×14.

251	**83**	6d. deep olive and light orange	80	70
252		8d. violet and light orange	80	40

84 Brown Pelican

(Des Mrs. S. Hurd. Photo Harrison)

1960 (1 Nov). W w **12**. P 14×14½.

253	**84**	£1 sepia and deep red	45·00	16·00

CROWN COLONY

1963 (4 June). Freedom from Hunger. As No. 223 of Bahamas.

254		8d. carmine	30	15

1963 (2 Sept). Red Cross Centenary. As Nos. 226/7 of Bahamas.

255		2d. red and black	15	50
256		8d. red and blue	30	50

1964 (23 Apr). 400th Birth Anniv of William Shakespeare. As No. 244 of Bahamas

257		8d. green	30	10

1965 (17 May). I.T.U. Centenary. As Nos. 262/3 of Bahamas.

258		1d. vermilion and brown	10	10
259		2s. light emerald and turquoise-blue	20	20

1965 (25 Oct). International Co-operation Year. As Nos. 265/6 of Bahamas

260		1d. reddish purple and turquoise-green	10	15
261		8d. deep bluish green and lavender	20	15

1966 (24 Jan). Churchill Commemoration. As Nos. 267/70 of Bahamas.

262		1d. new blue	10	10
263		2d. deep green	20	10
264		8d. brown	35	10
		a. Gold ptg double	£160	

TURKS AND CAICOS ISLANDS

265	1s.6d. bluish violet	50	1·10
262/5 Set of 4		1·00	1·25

The price quoted for No. 264a is for examples with the two impressions clearly separated. Examples with the two impressions nearly co-incident are worth much less.

1966 (4 Feb). Royal Visit. As Nos. 271/2 of Bahamas.

266	8d. black and ultramarine	40	10
267	1s. 6d. black and magenta	60	20

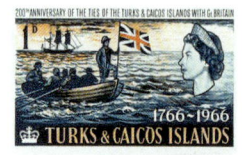

85 Andrew Symmer going ashore

(Des V. Whiteley. Photo D.L.R.)

1966 (1 Oct). Bicentenary of "Ties with Britain" T **85** and similar horiz designs. P 13½.

268	1d. deep blue and orange	10	10
269	8d. red, blue and orange-yellow	20	15
270	1s.6d. multicoloured	25	20
268/70 Set of 3		50	40

Designs:—8d. Andrew Symmer and Royal Warrant; 1s.6d. Arms and Royal Cypher.

1966 (1 Dec). 20th Anniv of U.N.E.S.C.O. As Nos. 292/4 of Bahamas.

271	1d. slate-violet, red, yellow and orange	10	10
272	8d. orange-yellow, violet and deep olive	40	10
273	1s.6d. black, bright purple and orange	65	40
271/3 Set of 3		1·00	50

88 Turk's-head Cactus   **89** Boat-building

90 Arms of Turks and Caicos Islands   **91** Queen Elizabeth II

(Des V. Whiteley. Photo Harrison)

1967 (1 Feb). Designs as T **88**/**91**. W w **12**. P 14½×14 (vert) or 14×14½ (horiz).

274	1d. olive-yellow, vermilion and bright bluish violet	10	10
275	1½d. brown and orange-yellow	1·50	10
276	2d. deep slate and deep orange-yellow	20	10
277	3d. agate and dull green	20	10
278	4d. bright mauve, black and turquoise	2·75	10
279	6d. sepia and new blue	2·25	10
280	8d. yellow, turquoise-blue and deep blue	55	10
281	1s. maroon and turquoise	20	10
282	1s.6d. orange-yellow, lake-brown and deep turquoise-blue	50	20
283	2s. multicoloured	1·25	2·00
284	3s. maroon and turquoise-blue	2·25	40
285	5s. ochre, blue and new blue	2·00	2·75
286	10s. multicoloured	3·50	3·00
287	£1 Prussian blue, silver and crimson	4·25	9·50
274/287 Set of 14		19·00	16·00

Designs: *Vert* as T **88**—2d. Donkey; 3d. Sisal industry 6d. Salt industry; 8d. Skin-diving; 1s.6d. Water-skiing. *Horiz* as T **89**—4d. Conch industry; 1s. Fishing; 2s. Crawfish industry; 3s. Maps of Turks and Caicos Islands and West Indies; 5s. Fishing industry.

102 Turks Islands 1d. Stamp of 1867

(Des R. Granger Barrett. Photo Harrison)

1967 (1 May). Stamp Centenary. T **102** and similar horiz designs. W w **12**. P 14½.

288	1d. black and light magenta	15	10
	w. Wmk inverted	50·00	
289	6d. black and bluish grey	25	15
290	1s. black and turquoise-blue	25	15
288/90 Set of 3		60	30

Designs:—6d. Queen Elizabeth "stamp" and Turks Islands 6d. stamp of 1867; 1s. Turks Islands 1s. stamp of 1867.

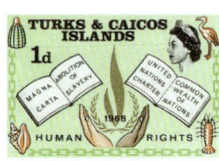

104 Human Rights Emblem and Charter

(Des R. Granger Barrett. Photo Harrison)

1968 (1 Apr). Human Rights Year. W w **12**. P 14×14½.

291	**104**	1d. multicoloured	10	10
292		8d. multicoloured	15	15
293		1s.6d. multicoloured	15	15
291/3 Set of 3			30	30

105 Dr Martin Luther King and "Freedom March"

(Des V. Whiteley. Photo Harrison)

1968 (1 Oct). Martin Luther King Commemoration. W w **12**. P 14×14½.

294	**105**	2d. yellow-brown, blackish brown and deep blue	10	10
295		8d. yellow-brown, blackish brown and lake	15	15
296		1s.6d. yellow-brown, blackish brown and violet	15	15
294/6 Set of 3			30	30

(New Currency. 100 cents = 1 dollar)

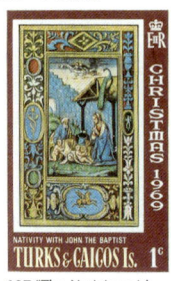

(**106**)   **107** "The Nativity with John the Baptist"

1969 (8 Sept)–**71**. Decimal currency. Nos. 274/87 surch as T **106** by Harrison & Sons, and new value (¼c.) as T **90**.

297	¼c. pale greenish grey and multicoloured	10	10
	a. Bronze-green and multicoloured (2.2.71)	1·75	30
298	1c. on 1d.olive-yellow, vermilion and bright bluish violet	10	10
	a. Wmk sideways	10	10
299	2c. on 2d. deep slate and deep orange-yellow	10	10

TURKS AND CAICOS ISLANDS

	a. Wmk sideways	10	10
300	3c. on 3d. agate and dull green	10	10
	a. Wmk sideways	10	10
301	4c. on 4d. bright mauve, black and turquoise	2·50	10
302	5c. on 6d. sepia and new blue	10	10
	a. Wmk sideways	10	10
303	7c. on 8d. yellow, turquoise-blue and deep blue	10	10
	a. Wmk sideways	10	40
304	8c. on 1½d. brown and orange-yellow	10	10
	w. Wmk inverted	28·00	
305	10c. on 1s. maroon and turquoise	20	10
306	15c. on 1s.6d. orange-yellow, lake-brown and deep turquoise-blue	25	10
	a. Wmk sideways	20	25
307	20c. on 2s. multicoloured	30	25
308	30c. on 3s. maroon and turquoise-blue	55	35
309	50c. on 5s. ochre, blue and new blue	1·25	45
310	$1 on 10s. mulicoloured	2·50	1·00
311	$2 on £1 Prussian blue, silver and crimson	2·75	14·00
	a. Wmk sideways	2·00	6·00
297/311 Set of 15		9·50	15·00
298a/311a Set of 7		2·25	6·25

The 4, 8, 10, 20, 30, 50c., and $1 exist with PVA gum as well as gum arabic.

No. 311 was only on sale through the Crown Agents.

(Des adapted by V. Whiteley. Litho D.L.R.)

1969 (20 Oct). Christmas. Scenes from 16th-cent Book of Hours. T **107** and similar vert design. Multicoloured. W w **12**. P 13×12½.

312	1c. Type **107**	10	10
313	3c. "The Flight into Egypt"	10	10
314	15c. Type **107**	15	10
315	30c. As 3c.	25	20
312/15 Set of 4		40	40

109 Coat of Arms  **110** "Christ bearing the Cross"

(Des L. Curtis. Litho B.W.)

1970 (2 Feb). New Constitution. Multicoloured; background colours given. W w **12** (sideways). P 13×12½.

316	**109**	7c. brown	20	25
317		35c. deep violet-blue	35	25

(Des, recess and litho Enschedé)

1970 (17 Mar). Easter. Details from the *Small Engraved Passion* by Dürer. T **110** and similar vert designs. W w **12** (sideways). P 13×13½.

318	5c. olive-grey and blue	10	10
319	7c. olive-grey and vermilion	10	10
320	50c. olive-grey and red-brown	60	1·00
318/20 Set of 3		70	1·10

Designs:—7c. "Christ on the Cross"; 50c. "The Lamentation of Christ".

113 Dickens and Scene from *Oliver Twist*

(Des Sylvia Goaman. Recess and litho D.L.R.)

1970 (17 June). Death Centenary of Charles Dickens. T **113** and similar horiz designs. W w **12** (sideways). P 13.

321	1c. black and yellow-brown/*yellow*	10	50
322	3c. black and Prussian blue/*flesh*	20	40
323	15c. black and grey/*flesh*	60	20
324	30c. black and drab/*blue*	80	40
321/4 Set of 4		1·50	1·40

Designs (each incorporating portrait of Dickens as in T **113**, and a scene from one of his novels):—3c. *A Christmas Carol*; 15c. *Pickwick Papers*; 30c. *The Old Curiosity Shop*.

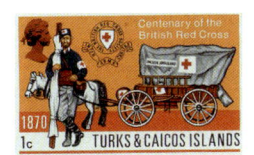

114 Ambulance—1870

(Des Harrison. Litho B.W.)

1970 (4 Aug). Centenary of British Red Cross. T **114** and similar horiz design. Multicoloured. W w **12**. P 13½×14.

325	1c. Type **114**	10	20
326	5c. Ambulance—1970	20	10
	a. Wmk sideways	30	10
	ab. Grey omitted	£350	
327	15c. Type **114**	40	15
	a. Wmk sideways	50	10
328	30c. As 5c.	50	20
	a. Wmk sideways	60	40
325/8 Set of 4		1·00	55

115 Duke of Albemarle and Coat of Arms

(Des V. Whiteley. Litho Enschedé)

1970 (1 Dec). Tercentenary of Issue of Letters Patent. T **115** and similar horiz design. Multicoloured. W w **12**. P 12½×13½.

329	1c. Type **115**	10	30
330	8c. Arms of Charles II and Elizabeth II	25	40
331	10c. Type **115**	25	15
332	35c. As 8c.	55	75
329/32 Set of 4		1·00	1·40

116 Boat-building  **117** Lined Seahorse

1971 (2 Feb). Designs as T **88/91** etc., but inscr in decimal currency as in T **116**. W w **12** (sideways on 1c., 2c., 3c., 5c., 7c., 15c. and $2).

333	1c. olive-yell, verve & brt bluish vio (as 1d.)	10	10
334	2c. deep slate & deep orange-yell (as 2d.)	10	10
335	3c. agate and dull green (as 3d.)	15	10
336	4c. brt mauve, black & turquoise (as 4d.)	1·25	10
337	5c. sepia and new blue (as 6d.)	40	10
338	7c. yellow, turquoise-blue & dp bl (as 8d.)	30	10
339	8c. brown and orange-yellow	1·25	10
340	10c. maroon and turquoise (as 1s.)	75	10
341	15c. orange-yellow, lake-brown and deep turquoise-blue (as 1s.6d.)	1·00	65
342	20c. multicoloured (as 2s.)	1·50	2·50
343	30c. maroon and turquoise-blue (as 3s.)	25	1·25
344	50c. ochre, blue and new blue (as 5s.)	3·25	2·00
345	$1 multicoloured (as 10s.)	3·00	3·00
	a. Green omitted	£1000	
	w. Wmk inverted	4·00	5·00
346	$2 Prussian blue, silver & crimson (as £1)	4·00	8·00
333/46 Set of 14		17·00	16·00

The ¼c. value was also re-issued and is listed as No. 297a.

(Des G. Vasarhelyi. Litho J.W.)

1971 (4 May). Tourist Development. T **117** and similar multicoloured designs. W w **12** (sideways on Nos. 348/50). P 14×14½ (1c.) or 14½×14 (others).

347	1c. Type **117**	10	10
348	3c. Queen or Pink Conch Shell (*horiz*)	15	10

147

TURKS AND CAICOS ISLANDS

349	15c. Oystercatcher (*horiz*)	50	20
350	30c. Sailfish ("Blue Marlin") (*horiz*)	35	25
347/50	Set of 4	1·00	55

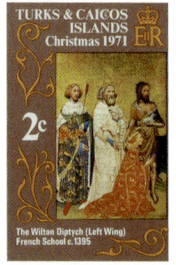

118 Pirate Sloop

119 The Wilton Diptych (Left Wing)

(Des and litho J.W.)

1971 (27 July). Pirates. T **118** and similar horiz designs. Multicoloured. W w **12** (sideways). P 14.

351	2c. Type **118**	10	10
352	3c. Pirate treasure	10	10
353	15c. Marooned sailor	45	15
354	30c. Buccaneers	70	45
351/4	Set of 4	1·25	70

(Des J.W. Litho Questa)

1971 (12 Oct). Christmas. T **119** and similar vert design. Multicoloured. W w **12**. P 13½.

355	2c. Type **119**	10	10
	a. Horiz pair. Nos. 355/6	10	10
356	2c. The Wilton Diptych (Right Wing)	10	10
357	8c. Type **119**	10	10
	a. Horiz pair. Nos. 357/8	20	20
358	8c. As No. 356	10	10
359	15c. Type **119**	20	10
	a. Horiz pair. Nos. 359/60	40	20
360	15c. As No. 356	20	10
355/60	Set of 6	65	45

The two stamps of each denomination were printed in horizontal *se-tenant* pairs throughout the sheet.

120 Cape Kennedy Launching Area

121 "Christ before Pilate" (Rembrandt)

(Des V. Whiteley. Litho A. & M.)

1972 (21 Feb). Tenth Anniv of Colonel Glenn's Splashdown. T **120** and similar multicoloured designs. W w **12** (sideways* on 5, 10 and 15c.). P 13½.

361	5c. Type **120**	10	10
	w. Wmk Crown to right of CA	20	20
362	10c. "Friendship 7" space capsule	10	10
	w. Wmk Crown to right of CA	30	30
363	15c. Map of Islands and splashdown	15	10
	w. Wmk Crown to right of CA	30	30
364	20c. N.A.S.A. Space Medal (*vert*)	15	10
	w. Wmk inverted	30	30
361/4	Set of 4	40	30

*The normal sideways watermark shows Crown to left of CA, *as seen from the back of the stamp*.

(Des and litho J.W.)

1972 (21 Mar). Easter. T **121** and similar designs. W w **12** (sideways on 15c.). P 13½.

365	2c. black and lilac	10	10
366	15c. black and rose-pink	20	10
367	30c. black and greenish yellow	30	15
365/7	Set of 3	50	30

Designs: *Horiz*—15c. "The Three Crosses" (Rembrandt). *Vert*—30c. "The Descent from the Cross" (Rembrandt).

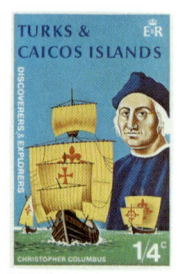

122 Christopher Columbus

123 Turk's-head Cactus and Spiny Lobster

(Des P. Powell. Litho J.W.)

1972 (28 July*). Discoverers and Explorers. T **122** and similar multicoloured designs. W w **12** (sideways on 8 and 30c.). P 13½.

368	¼c. Type **122**	20	75
369	8c. Sir Richard Grenville (*horiz*)	1·00	30
370	10c. Capt. John Smith	1·00	10
371	30c. Juan Ponce de Leon (*horiz*)	1·75	90
368/71	Set of 4	3·50	1·75

*This was the local date of issue; the Crown Agents released the stamps on 4 July.

(Des (from photograph by D. Groves) and photo Harrison)

1972 (20 Nov). Royal Silver Wedding. Multicoloured; background colour given. W w **12**. P 14×14½.

372	**123** 10c. dull ultramarine	15	10
373	20c. myrtle-green	15	10
	w. Wmk inverted	£275	

124 Treasure Hunting, circa 1700

125 Arms of Jamaica and Turks & Caicos Islands

(Des C. Abbott. Litho Questa)

1973 (18 Jan). Treasure. T **124** and similar vert designs. W w **12** (sideways*). P 14×14½.

374	3c. multicoloured	10	10
375	5c. reddish purple, silver and black	10	10
376	10c. magenta, silver and black	20	10
	w. Wmk Crown to right of CA		
377	30c. multicoloured	60	30
374/7	Set of 4	85	35
MS378	127×108 mm. Nos. 374/7	1·10	2·25

Designs:—5c. Silver Bank medallion (obverse); 10c. Silver Bank medallion (reverse); 30c. Treasure hunting, 1973.

*The normal sideways watermark shows Crown to left of CA, *as seen from the back of the stamp*.

(Des PAD Studio. Litho Walsall)

1973 (16 Apr). Centenary of Annexation to Jamaica. W w **12** (sideways). P 13½×14.

379	**125** 15c. multicoloured	25	10
380	35c. multicoloured	45	20

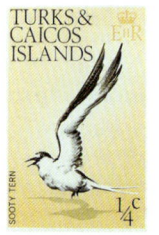

126 Sooty Tern

127 Bermuda Sloop

TURKS AND CAICOS ISLANDS

(Des R. Granger, Barrett. Litho Questa)

1973 (1 Aug). Birds. T **126** and similar vert designs. W w **12** (sideways*). P 14.

381	¼c. Type **126**		10	40
382	1c. Magnificent Frigate Bird		30	60
383	2c. Common Noddy		30	60
	w. Wmk Crown to right of CA		65·00	
384	3c. Blue-grey Gnatcatcher		85	50
385	4c. Little Blue Heron		35	1·50
	w. Wmk Crown to right of CA		£100	
386	5c. Catbird		30	30
	w. Wmk Crown to right of CA		1·00	
387	7c. Black-whiskered Vireo		5·00	30
	w. Wmk Crown to right of CA		£110	
388	8c. Osprey		5·50	3·25
389	10c. Greater Flamingo		70	1·25
390	15c. Brown Pelican		1·25	50
	w. Wmk Crown to right of CA		£120	
391	20c. Parula Warbler		3·50	1·25
392	30c. Northern Mockingbird		1·75	90
393	50c. Ruby-throated Hummingbird		3·50	3·75
394	$1 Bananaquit		3·50	4·00
	w. Wmk Crown to right of CA		8·00	
395	$2 Cedar Waxwing		4·50	5·50
381/95 Set of 15			28·00	22·00

*The normal sideways watermark shows Crown to left of CA, *as seen from the back of the stamp.*
See also Nos. 411/14 and 451/64.

(Des R. Granger Barrett. Litho Questa)

1973 (14 Aug). Vessels. T **127** and similar horiz designs. Multicoloured. W w **12**. P 13½.

396	2c. Type **127**		15	1·00
397	5c. H.M.S. *Blanche* (screw sloop)		20	10
398	8c. *Grand Turk* (American privateer) and *Hinchinbrook II* (British packet), 1813		25	1·00
399	10c. H.M.S. *Endymion* (frigate), 1790		25	15
400	15c. *Medina* (paddle-steamer)		25	80
401	20c. H.M.S. *Daring* (brig), 1804		30	1·25
396/401 Set of 6			1·25	3·75
MS402 198×101 mm. Nos. 396/401			1·10	3·75

1973 (14 Nov). Royal Wedding. As Nos. 297/8 of Bermuda.

403	12c. light turquoise-blue		10	10
	w. Wmk Crown to right of CA		50·00	
404	18c. dull indigo		10	10

*The normal sideways watermark shows Crown to left of CA, *as seen from the back of the stamp.*

128 Dubo (stool)

(Des Jennifer Toombs. Litho Questa)

1974 (17 July). Lucayan Remains. T **128** and similar horiz designs. Multicoloured. W w **12** (sideways*). P 14½×14.

405	6c. Type **128**		10	10
406	10c. Broken wood bowl		15	10
	w. Wmk Crown to right of CA		1·75	
407	12c. Greenstone axe		15	10
408	18c. Wood bowl		15	10
409	35c. Fragment of duho		20	20
405/9 Set of 5			65	40
MS410 240×90 mm. Nos. 405/9			1·10	1·75

*The normal sideways watermark shows Crown to left of CA, *as seen from the back of the stamp.*

1974–75. As Nos. 381 etc, but W w **12** (upright).

411	1c. Magnificent Frigate Bird (11.6.75)		1·00	2·50
412	2c. Common Noddy (27.9.74)		1·50	1·00
413	3c. Blue-grey Gnatcatcher (19.3.75)		2·25	1·00
	w. Wmk inverted		11·00	
414	20c. Parula Warbler (11.6.75)		1·75	3·75
411/14 Set of 4			6·00	7·50

Nos. 415/25 are vacant.

When you buy an album look for the name STANLEY GIBBONS, it means quality combined with value for money

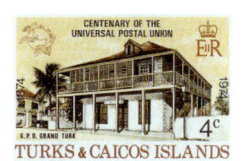

---

129 G.P.O., Grand Turk

(Des G. Drummond. Litho Questa)

1974 (9 Oct). Centenary of Universal Postal Union. T **129** and similar horiz designs. Multicoloured. W w **12**. P 14.

426	4c. Type **129**		10	10
427	12c. Sloop and island map		20	10
428	18c. "U.P.U." and globe		20	10
429	55c. Posthorn and emblem		35	35
426/9 Set of 4			75	55

130 Churchill and Roosevelt   **131** Spanish Captain, *circa* 1492

(Des V. Whiteley. Litho Questa)

1974 (30 Nov). Birth Centenary of Sir Winston Churchill. T **130** and similar horiz design. Multicoloured. W w **14** (sideways). P 14.

430	12c. Type **130**		15	15
431	18c. Churchill and vapour-trails		15	15
MS432 85×85 mm. Nos. 430/1			40	45

(Des J.W. Litho Questa)

1975 (26 Mar). Military Uniforms. T **131** and similar vert designs. Multicoloured. W w **14**. P 14.

433	5c. Type **131**		10	10
434	20c. Officer, Royal Artillery, 1783		20	15
435	25c. Officer, 67th Foot, 1798		25	15
436	35c. Private, 1st West India Regt, 1833		35	25
433/6 Set of 4			80	50
MS437 145×88 mm. Nos. 433/6			1·00	2·00

132 Ancient Windmill, Salt Cay   **133** Star Coral

(Des P. Powell. Litho Questa)

1975 (16 Oct). Salt-raking Industry. T **132** and similar multicoloured designs. W w **12** (sideways on 10 and 20c.). P 14.

438	6c. Type **132**		15	10
439	10c. Salt pans drying in sun (*horiz*)		15	10
440	20c. Salt-raking (*horiz*)		25	25
441	25c. Unprocessed salt heaps		30	30
	w. Wmk inverted		42·00	
438/41 Set of 4			75	60

(Des C. Abbott. Litho Questa)

1975 (4 Dec). Island Coral. T **133** and similar horiz designs. Multicoloured. W w **14** (sideways). P 14.

442	6c. Type **133**		15	10
443	10c. Elkhorn Coral		20	10
444	20c. Brain Coral		35	15
	w. Wmk Crown to right of CA		65·00	

TURKS AND CAICOS ISLANDS

445	25c. Staghorn Coral	40	20
442/5 Set of 4		1·00	40

*The normal sideways watermark shows Crown to left of CA, *as seen from the back of the stamp*.

134 American Schooner

135 1s.6d. Royal Visit Stamp of 1966

(Des J.W. Litho Questa)

1976 (28 May). Bicentenary of American Revolution. T **134** and similar vert designs. Multicoloured. W w **14**. P 13½.

446	6c. Type **134**..	25	15
447	20c. British ship of the line	30	20
448	25c. American privateer *Grand Turk*	30	25
	w. Wmk inverted	85·00	
449	55c. British ketch..	40	65
	w. Wmk inverted	4·25	
446/9 Set of 4		1·10	1·10
MS450 95×151 mm. Nos. 446/9		1·00	4·00

Each value depicts, at the top, the engagement between the *Grand Turk* and the P.O. Packet *Hinchinbrooke*, as in T **134**.

1976–77. As Nos. 381/95, and new value ($5), but W w **14** (upright).

451	¼c. Type **126** (12.77)	75	3·50
452	1c. Magnificent Frigate Bird (12.77)	75	2·75
453	2c. Common Noddy (12.77)	75	4·50
454	3c. Blue-grey Gnatcatcher (14.6.76)	90	70
455	4c. Little Blue Heron (12.77)	1·75	2·75
456	5c. Catbird (12.77)	1·25	4·50
457	10c. Greater Flamingo (12.77)	1·25	3·50
458	15c. Brown Pelican (12.77)	1·50	2·50
459	20c. Parula Warbler (30.11.76)	1·50	75
460	30c. Northern Mockingbird (12.77)	1·25	2·25
461	50c. Ruby-throated Hummingbird (12.77)...	1·50	2·25
462	$1 Bananaquit (12.77)	2·50	2·75
463	$2 Cedar Waxwing (12.77)	6·00	4·50
464	$5 Painted Bunting (24.11.76)	1·75	1·75
451/64 Set of 14		19·00	35·00

No. 465 is vacant.

(Des V. Whiteley Studio. Litho Walsall)

1976 (14 July). Tenth Anniv of Royal Visit. T **135** and similar horiz design. Multicoloured. W w **14** (sideways). P 14½×14.

466	20c. Type **135**...	30	30
467	25c. 8d. Royal Visit stamp	40	30

136 "The Virgin and Child with Flowers" (C. Dolci)

137 Balcony Scene, Buckingham Palace

(Des G. Drummond. Litho Questa)

1976 (10 Nov). Christmas. T **136** and similar vert designs. Multicoloured. W w **14**. P 13½.

468	6c. Type **136**	10	10
469	10c. "Virgin and Child with St. John and an Angel" (Studio of Botticelli)	10	10
470	20c. "Adoration of the Magi" (Master of Paraiso)	30	15
471	25c. "Adoration of the Magi" (French miniature)	30	20
468/71 Set of 4		65	35

(Des J.W. (**MS**475), C. Abbott (others) Litho Questa)

1977 (7 Feb–6 Dec). Silver Jubilee. T **137** and similar vert designs. Multicoloured. W w **14**. P 14×13½ (**MS**475) or 13½ (others).

472	6c. Queen presenting O.B.E. to E. T. Wood....	10	10
	w. Wmk inverted	12·00	
473	25c. The Queen with regalia	15	20
474	55c. Type **137**...	30	45
472/4 Set of 3		40	60
MS475 120×97 mm. $5 Queen Elizabeth II (6.12.77)		1·00	80

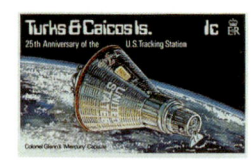

138 Col. Glenn's "Mercury" Capsule

(Des and litho J.W.)

1977 (20 June). 25th Anniv of U.S. Tracking Station. T **138** and similar multicoloured designs. W w **14** (sideways on horiz designs). P 13½.

476	1c. Type **138**...	10	10
477	3c. Moon buggy "Rover" (*vert*)	10	10
478	6c. Tracking Station, Grand Turk...............	10	10
479	6c. Moon landing craft (*vert*)	15	15
480	25c. Col. Glenn's rocket launch (*vert*)	20	20
481	50c. "Telstar 1" satellite	30	40
476/81 Set of 6		70	80

139 "Flight of the Holy Family" (Rubens)

(Des J.W. Litho Questa)

1977 (23 Dec). Christmas and 400th Birth Anniv of Rubens. T **139** and similar vert designs. Multicoloured. P 14.

482	¼c. Type **139**..	10	10
483	½c. "Adoration of the Magi" (1634)	10	10
484	1c. "Adoration of the Magi" (1624)	10	10
485	6c. "Virgin within Garland"	10	10
486	20c. "Madonna and Child Adored by Angels"	15	10
487	$2 "Adoration of the Magi" (1618)	1·25	1·25
482/7 Set of 6		1·40	1·25
MS488 100×81 mm. $1 detail of 20c.		1·10	1·40

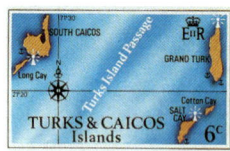

140 Map of Passage

(Des R. Granger Barrett. Litho J.W.)

1978 (2 Feb). Turks Islands Passage. T **140** and similar horiz designs. Multicoloured. P 13½.

A. No wmk

489A	6c. Type **140**...	15	20
490A	20c. Caicos sloop passing Grand Turk Lighthouse..	45	75
491A	25c. Motor cruiser.....................................	45	85
492A	55c. *Jamaica Planter* (freighter)	95	2·25
489A/92A Set of 4		1·75	3·50
MS493A 136×88 mm. Nos. 489A/92A. P 14½		1·10	2·75

*B. W w***14** *(sideways)*

489B	6c. Type **140**...	15	15
490B	20c. Caicos sloop passing Grand Turk Lighthouse..	45	65
491B	25c. Motor cruiser.....................................	45	75
492B	55c. *Jamaica Planter* (freighter)	95	2·00
489B/92B Set of 4		1·75	3·25
MS493B 136×88 mm. Nos. 489B/92B. P 14½		25·00	27·00

150

TURKS AND CAICOS ISLANDS

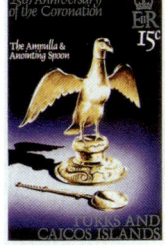

141 "Queen Victoria" (Sir George Hayter)

142 Ampulla and Anointing Spoon

(Manufactured by Walsall (Nos. 499/501). Des PAD Studio. Litho Questa (others))

1978 (2 June–July). 25th Anniv of Coronation. Multicoloured.

(a) Sheet stamps. Vert designs as T 141 showing British monarchs in coronation robes. P 14

494	6c. Type **141**	10	10
495	10c. "King Edward VII" (Sir Samuel Fildes)	10	10
496	25c. King George V	20	10
497	$2 King George VI	50	70
494/7 Set of 4		75	75
MS498 161×113 mm. $2.50, Queen Elizabeth II		75	75

(b) Booklet stamps. Vert designs as T 142. Imperf×roul 5*. Self-adhesive (July)

499	15c. Type **142**	15	30
	a. Booklet pane. Nos. 499/501	1·10	
	b. Booklet pane. Nos. 499/500, each×3	80	
500	25c. St. Edward's Crown	15	30
501	$2 Queen Elizabeth II in coronation robes	1·00	2·25
499/501 Set of 3		1·10	2·50

Nos. 494/7 also exist perf 12 (*Price for set of 4 75p mint or used*) from additional sheetlets of 3 stamps and 1 label. Stamps perforated 14 are from normal sheets of 50.

Nos. 499/501 are separated by various combinations of rotary-knife (giving a straight edge) and roulette.

143 Wilbur Wright and Wright Type A

(Des Curtis Design. Litho Format)

1978 (29 June). 75th Anniv of Powered Flight. T **143** and similar horiz designs. Multicoloured. P 14½.

502	1c. Type **143**	10	10
503	6c. Wright brothers and Cessna 337 Super Skymaster	10	10
504	10c. Orville Wright and Lockheed L.188 Electra	10	10
505	15c. Wilbur Wright and Douglas C-47 Skytrain	15	15
506	35c. Wilbur Wright and Britten Norman Islander	35	35
507	$2 Wilbur Wright and Wright Type A	1·00	1·75
502/7 Set of 6		1·50	2·25
MS508 111×84 mm. $1 Orville Wright and Wright glider No. III		60	1·60

No. 502 is inscribed "FLYER III" in error.

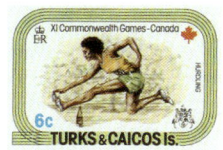

144 Hurdling

(Des J.W. Litho Format)

1978 (3 Aug). Commonwealth Games, Edmonton. T **144** and similar horiz designs. Multicoloured. P 14½.

509	6c. Type **144**	10	10
510	20c. Weightlifting	15	15
511	55c. Boxing	20	30
512	$2 Cycling	50	1·25
509/12 Set of 4		75	1·50
MS513 105×79 mm. $1 Sprinting		55	1·50

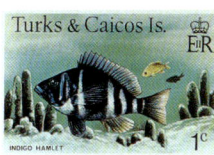

145 Indigo Hamlet

146 "Madonna of the Siskin"

(Des G. Drummond. Litho Questa)

1978 (17 Nov)–**83**. Fishes. Horiz designs as T **145**. Multicoloured.

A. No imprint date. P 14

514A	1c. Type **145**	15	50
515A	2c. Tobacco Fish (19.1.79)	75	1·00
516A	3c. Bar Jack	50	30
517A	4c. Porkfish (19.1.79)	75	1·00
518A	5c. Spanish Grunt	50	40
519A	7c. Yellow-tailed Snapper (19.1.79)	1·00	1·75
520A	8c. Four-eyed Butterflyfish (19.1.79)	1·00	15
521A	10c. Yellow-finned Grouper	50	15
522A	15c. Beau Gregory	1·50	30
523A	20c. Queen Angelfish	50	30
524A	30c. Hagfish (19.1.79)	1·75	40
525A	50c. Royal Gramma ("Fairy Basslet") (19.1.79)	1·00	65
526A	$1 Fin-spot Wrasse (19.1.79)	1·50	1·60
527A	$2 Stoplight Parrotfish (19.1.79)	1·50	2·50
528A	$5 Queen Triggerfish (19.1.79)	1·50	6·50
514A/28A Set of 15		12·00	15·00

B. With imprint date at foot of design. P 14 (15c.) or 12 (others)

514B	1c. Type **145** (15.12.81)	2·25	2·25
518B	5c. Spanish Grunt (15.12.81)	2·75	2·75
521B	10c. Yellow-finned Grouper (15.12.81)	2·75	2·75
522B	15c. Beau Gregory (25.1.83)	2·50	2·25
523B	20c. Queen Angelfish (15.12.81)	1·25	1·00
	a. Perf 14 (25.1.83)	85	1·25
525B	50c. Royal Gramma ("Fairy Basslet") (15.12.81)	7·00	6·00
526B	$1 Fin-spot Wrasse (15.12.81)	3·25	3·00
	a. Perf 14 (25.1.83)	2·00	3·00
527B	$2 Stoplight Parrotfish (15.12.81)	5·50	5·00
	a. Perf 14 (25.1.83)	2·50	4·50
528B	$5 Queen Triggerfish (15.12.81)	9·50	11·00
	a. Perf 14 (25.1.83)	5·50	9·00
514B/28B Set of 9		25·00	30·00

Imprint dates: "1981", Nos. 514B, 518B, 521B, 523B, 525B/8B; "1983", Nos. 522B, 523Ba, 526Ba, 527Ba, 528Ba.

(Des BG Studio. Litho Questa)

1978 (11 Dec). Christmas. Paintings by Dürer. T **146** and similar multicoloured designs. P 14.

529	6c. Type **146**	15	10
530	20c. "The Virgin and Child with St. Anne"	20	15
531	35c. "Paumgartner Nativity" (*horiz*)	35	25
532	$2 "Praying Hands"	85	1·60
529/32 Set of 4		1·40	1·90
MS533 137×124 mm. $1 "Adoration of the Magi" (*horiz*)		1·75	2·75

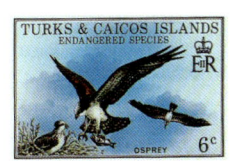

147 Osprey

(Des G. Drummond. Litho Questa)

1979 (29 May). Endangered Wildlife. T **147** and similar horiz designs. Multicoloured. P 14.

534	6c. Type **147**	75	20
535	20c. Green Turtle	65	20
536	25c. Queen or Pink Conch	75	25
537	55c. Rough-toothed Dolphin	90	50
538	$1 Humpback Whale	2·00	2·50
534/8 Set of 5		4·50	3·25
MS539 117×85 mm. $2 Iguana		2·50	4·25

151

TURKS AND CAICOS ISLANDS

148 "The Beloved" (painting by D. G. Rossetti)

(Des G. Vasarhelyi. Litho Questa)

1979 (2 July). International Year of the Child. T **148** and similar horiz designs showing paintings and I.Y.C. emblem. Multicoloured. P 14.

540	6c. Type **148**	10	10
541	25c. "Tahitian Girl" (P. Gauguin)	15	10
542	55c. "Calmady Children" (Sir Thomas Lawrence)	25	20
543	$1 Mother and Daughter" (detail, P. Gauguin)	45	45
540/3 Set of 4		80	70
MS544 112×85 mm. $2 "Marchesa Elena Grimaldi" (A. van Dyck)		55	1·50

149 Medina (paddle-steamer) and Handstamped Cover

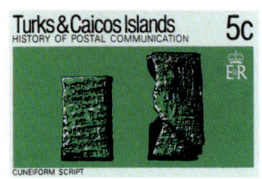

150 Cuneiform Script

(Des J.W. Litho Questa (Nos. 545/51). Des and litho Walsall (Nos. 552/64))

1979 (27 Aug)–**80**. Death Centenary of Sir Rowland Hill.

*(a) Sheet stamps. Horiz designs as T **149**. Multicoloured. P 12 ($2) or 14 (others)*

545	6c. Type **149**	10	10
546	20c. Sir Rowland Hill and map of Caribbean	15	15
547	45c. *Orinoco I* (mail paddle-steamer) and cover bearing Penny Black stamp	20	20
548	75c. *Shannon* (screw steamer) and letter to Grand Turk	30	30
549	$1 *Trent I* (paddle-steamer) and map of Caribbean	35	35
550	$2 Turks Islands 1867 and Turks and Caicos Islands 1900 1d. stamps (6.5.80)	3·50	4·00
545/50 Set of 6		4·00	4·50
MS551 170×113 mm. As No. 550. P 14		70	1·50

Nos. 545/9 also exist perf 12 (*Price for set of 5 £1.10 mint or used*) from additional sheetlets of 5 stamps and 1 label. No. 550 only exists in this format and has the inscription "International Stamp Exhibition Earls Court—London 6–14 May 1980" overprinted on the sheet margin. The individual stamps are not overprinted. Stamps perforated 14 are from normal sheets of 40.

*(b) Booklet stamps. Designs as T**150**. Imperf×roul 5*.*
Self adhesive (27.9.79)

552	5c. black and bright emerald	10	10
	a. Booklet pane. Nos. 552/7	80	80
553	5c. black and bright emerald	10	10
554	5c. black and bright emerald	10	10
555	15c. black and light blue	20	20
556	15c. black and light blue	20	20
557	15c. black and light blue	20	20
558	25c. black and light blue	30	30
	a. Booklet pane. Nos. 558/63	2·25	2·25
559	25c. black and light blue	60	45
560	25c. black and light blue	30	30
561	40c. black and bright rosine	45	45
562	40c. black and bright rosine	45	45
563	40c. black and bright rosine	45	45
564	$1 black and lemon	70	1·25
	a. Booklet pane of 1	70	1·25

Designs: *Horiz*—No. 552, Type **150**; No. 553, Egyptian papyrus; No. 554, Chinese paper; No. 555, Greek runner; No. 556, Roman post horse; No. 557, Roman post ship; No. 558, Pigeon post; No. 559, Railway post; No. 560, Packet paddle-steamer; No. 561, Balloon post; No. 562, First airmail; No. 563, Supersonic airmail. *Vert*—No. 564, Original stamp press.

*Nos. 552/63 are separated by various combinations of rotary knife (giving a straight edge) and roulette. No. 564 exists only with straight edges.

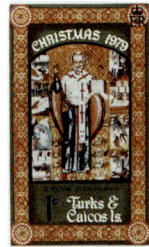

BRASILIANA 79
(151)

152 "St. Nicholas", Prikra, Ukraine

1979 (10 Sept). "Brosiliana 79" International Stamp Exhibition, Rio de Janeiro. No. **MS**551 optd with T **151**.
MS565 170×113 mm. $2 Turks Islands 1867 and Turks and Caicos Islands 1900 1d. stamps .... 65 1·50

Stamps from Nos. **MS**551 and **MS**565 are identical as the overprint on **MS**565 appears on the margin of the sheet.

(Des M. Diamond. Litho Questa)

1979 (19 Oct). Christmas. Art. T **152** and similar vert designs. Multicoloured. P 13½×14.

566	1c. Type **152**	10	20
567	3c. "Emperor Otto II with Symbols of Empire" (Master of the Registrum Gregorii)	10	20
568	6c. Portrait of St. John" (Book of Lindisfarne)	10	10
569	15c. Adoration of the Majestas Domini" (Prayer Book of Otto II)	10	10
570	20c. "Christ attended by Angels" (Book of Kells)	15	15
571	25c. "St. John the Evangelist" (Gospels of St. Medard of Soissons), Charlemagne	20	15
572	65c. "Christ Pantocrator", Trocany, Ukraine	30	25
573	$1 "Portrait of St. John" (Canterbury Codex Aureus)	45	60
566/73 Set of 8		1·10	1·50
MS574 106×133 mm. $2 "Portrait of St. Matthew" (Book of Lindisfarne)		70	1·50

153 Pluto and Starfish

(Litho Format)

1979 (2 Nov). International Year of the Child. Walt Disney Cartoon Characters. T **153** and similar vert designs showing characters at the seaside. Multicoloured. P 11.

575	¼c. Type **153**	10	10
576	½c. Minnie Mouse in summer outfit	10	10
577	1c. Mickey Mouse underwater	10	10
578	2c. Goofy and turtle	10	10
579	3c. Donald Duck and dolphin	10	10
580	4c. Mickey Mouse fishing	10	10
581	5c. Goofy surfing	10	10
582	25c. Pluto and crab	45	20
583	$1 Daisy water-skiing	75	2·25
575/83 Set of 9		1·25	2·50
MS584 126×96 mm. $1.50, Goofy after water-skiing accident. P 13½		1·00	1·60
	a. Error. Imperf	£190	

TURKS AND CAICOS ISLANDS

154 "Christina's World" (painting by Andrew Wyeth)

(Des J.W. Litho Format)

1979 (19 Dec). Works of Art. T **154** and similar multicoloured designs. P 13½.

585	6c. Type **154**	10	10
586	10c. Ivory Leopards, Benin (19th-cent)	10	10
587	20c. "The Kiss" (painting by Gustav Klimt) (*vert*)	15	15
588	25c. "Portrait of a Lady" (painting by R. van der Weyden) (*vert*)	15	15
589	80c. Bull's head harp, Sumer, c. 2600 B.C. (*vert*)	20	30
590	$1 The Wave" (painting by Hokusai)	25	50
585/90	Set of 6	70	1·00
MS591	110×140 mm. $2 "Holy Family" (painting by Rembrandt) (*vert*)	70	1·25

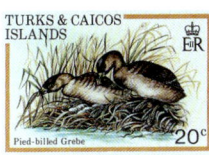

155 Pied-billed Grebe

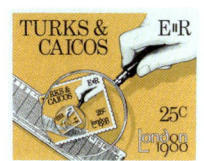

156 Stamp, Magnifying Glass and Perforation Gauge

(Des G. Drummond. Litho Questa)

1980 (20 Feb). Birds. T **155** and similar horiz designs. Multicoloured. P 14.

592	20c. Type **155**	70	55
593	25c. Ovenbirds at nest	75	55
594	35c. Hen Harrier	1·00	60
595	55c. Yellow-bellied Sapsucker	1·25	65
596	$1 Blue-winged Teal	1·50	3·00
592/6	Set of 5	4·75	4·75
MS597	107×81 mm. $2 Glossy Ibis	2·75	2·25

(Des BG Studio. Litho Questa)

1980 (6 May). "London 1980" International Stamp Exhibition. T **156** and similar horiz designs. P 14.

598	25c. black and chrome-yellow	15	15
599	40c. black and bright green	15	25
MS600	76×97 mm. $2 vermilion, black and blue	70	1·10

Designs:—40c. Stamp, tweezers and perforation gauge; $2, Earls Court Exhibition Centre.

157 Atlantic Trumpet Triton (*Charonia variegata*)

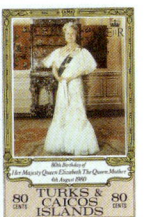

158 Queen Elizabeth the Queen Mother

(Des G. Drummond. Litho Questa)

1980 (26 June). Shells. T **157** and similar horiz designs. Multicoloured. P 14.

601	15c. Type **157**	15	20
602	20c. Measled Cowrie (*Cypraea zebra*)	15	25
603	30c. True Tulip (*Fasciolaria tulipa*)	20	35
604	45c. Lion's-paw Scallop (*Lyropecten nodosa*)	25	45
605	55c. Sunrise Tellin (*Tellina radiata*)	30	55
606	70c. Crown Cone (*Conus regius*)	35	70
601/6	Set of 6	1·25	2·25

(Des G. Vasarhelyi. Litho Questa)

1980 (4 Aug). 80th Birthday of Queen Elizabeth the Queen Mother. P 14.

607	**158**	80c. multicoloured	50	1·40
MS608	57×80 mm. **158** $1.50, multicoloured. P 12		80	2·00

159 Doctor examining Child and Lions International Emblem

(Des Design Images. Litho Questa)

1980 (29 Aug). "Serving the Community". T **159** and similar horiz designs. Multicoloured. P 14.

609	10c. Type **159**	15	10
610	15c. Students receiving scholarships and Kiwanis International emblem	20	10
611	45c. Teacher with students and Soroptimist emblem	40	35
612	$1 Lobster trawler and Rotary International emblem	75	80
609/12	Set of 4	1·40	1·25
MS613	101×74 mm. $2 School receiving funds and Rotary International emblem	1·00	2·00

No. **MS**613 also commemorates the 75th anniversary of Rotary International.

(Litho Walsall)

1980 (30 Sept). Christmas. Scenes from Walt Disney's Cartoon Film "Pinocchio". Horiz designs as T **153**. Multicoloured. P 11.

614	¼c. Scene from *Pinocchio*	10	10
615	½c. As puppet	10	10
616	1c. Pinocchio changed into a boy	10	10
617	2c. Captured by fox	10	10
618	3c. Pinocchio and puppeteer	10	10
619	4c. Pinocchio and bird's nest nose	10	10
620	5c. Pinocchio eating	10	10
621	75c. Pinocchio with ass ears	1·00	90
622	$1 Pinocchio underwater	1·25	1·00
614/22	Set of 9	2·25	2·00
MS623	127×102 mm. $2 Pinocchio dancing (*vert*)	2·50	2·50

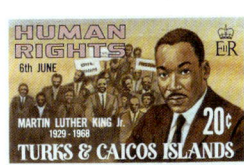

160 Martin Luther King Jr

(Des Design Images. Litho Questa)

1980 (22 Dec). Human Rights. Personalities. T **160** and similar horiz designs. Multicoloured. P 14×13½.

624	20c. Type **160**	15	10
625	30c. John F. Kennedy	30	25
626	45c. Roberto Clemente (baseball player)	45	35
627	70c. Sir Frank Worrel (cricketer)	2·00	1·50
628	$1 Harriet Tubman	1·10	1·25
624/8	Set of 5	3·50	3·00
MS629	103×80 mm. $2 Marcus Garvey	1·10	1·25

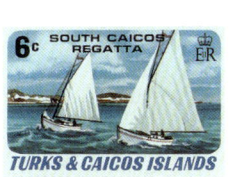

161 Yachts

162 Night Queen Cactus

(Litho Questa)

1981 (29 Jan). South Caicos Regatta. T **161** and similar horiz designs. Multicoloured. P 14.

630	6c. Type **161**	10	10
631	15c. Trophy and yachts	15	15
632	35c. Spectators watching speedboat race	25	20

TURKS AND CAICOS ISLANDS

633	$1 Caicos sloops	60	65
630/3	Set of 4	1·00	1·00
MS634	113×85 mm. $2 Queen Elizabeth II and map of South Caicos (*vert*)	80	1·75

(Des J. Cooter. Litho Questa)

1981 (10 Feb). Flowering Cacti. T **162** and similar vert designs. Multicoloured. P 13½×14.

635	25c. Type **162**	20	25
636	35c. Ripsaw Cactus	25	35
637	55c. Royal Strawberry Cactus	30	60
638	80c. Caicos Cactus	40	1·00
635/8	Set of 4	1·00	2·00
MS639	72×86 mm. $2 Turks Head Cactus. P 14½	1·00	2·00

(Litho Format)

1981 (16 Feb). 50th Anniv of Walt Disney's Cartoon Character, Pluto. Vert designs as T **153**. Multicoloured. P 13½.

640	10c. Pluto playing on beach with Queen or Pink Conch shell	10	10
641	75c. Pluto on raft, and porpoise	50	90
MS642	127×101 mm. $1.50 Pluto in scene from film *Simple Things*	1·00	2·25

(Litho Format)

1981 (20 Mar). Easter. Walt Disney Cartoon Characters. Vert designs as T **153**. Multicoloured. P 11.

643	10c. Donald Duck and Louie	20	20
644	25c. Goofy and Donald Duck	25	40
645	60c. Chip and Dale	30	1·00
646	80c. Scrooge McDuck and Huey	35	1·40
643/6	Set of 4	1·00	2·75
MS647	126×101 mm. $4 Chip (or Dale). P 13½	4·00	3·50

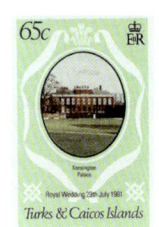

163 "Woman with Fan"   **164** Kensington Palace

(Des J.W. Litho Questa)

1981 (28 May). Birth Centenary of Picasso. T **163** and similar vert designs. Multicoloured. P 13½×14.

648	20c. Type **163**	15	15
649	45c. "Woman with Pears"	20	15
650	80c. "The Accordionist"	30	40
651	$1 "The Aficionado"	45	60
648/51	Set of 4	1·00	1·10
MS652	102×127 mm. $2 "Girl with a Mandolin"	1·00	1·00

(Des J.W. Litho Questa)

1981 (23 June). Royal Wedding. T **164** and similar vert designs. Multicoloured. P 14.

653	35c. Prince Charles and Lady Diana Spencer	15	10
654	65c. Type **164**	20	20
655	90c. Prince Charles as Colonel of the Welsh Guards	25	30
653/5	Set of 3	50	50
MS656	96×82 mm. $2 Glass Coach	50	55

Nos. 653/5 also exist perforated 12 (*price for set of 3 50p. mint or used*) from additional sheetlets of five stamps and one label. The 65c. and 90c. values from these sheetlets have changed background colours.

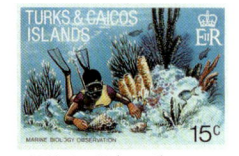

165 Lady Diana Spencer   **166** Marine Biology Observation

(Manufactured by Walsall)

1981 (7 July). Royal Wedding. T **165** and similar vert designs. Multicoloured. Roul 5×*imperf**. Self-adhesive.

657	20c. Type **165**	25	30
	a. Booklet pane. Nos. 657/8, each×3	1·60	
658	$1 Prince Charles	35	70
659	$2 Prince Charles and Lady Diana Spencer	1·10	2·25
	a. Booklet pane of 1	1·10	
657/9	Set of 3	1·50	3·00

*The 20c. and $1 values were each separated by various combinations of rotary knife (giving a straight edge) and roulette. The $2 value exists only with straight edges.

Nos. 657/9 were only issued in $5.60 stamp booklets.

(Des G. Drummond. Litho Questa)

1981 (21 Aug). Diving. T **166** and similar horiz designs. Multicoloured. P 14.

660	15c. Type **166**	20	15
661	40c. Underwater photography	35	35
662	75c. Wreck diving	60	70
663	$1 Diving with dolphins	80	1·00
660/3	Set of 4	1·75	2·00
MS664	91×75 mm. $2 Diving flag	1·50	2·25

(Litho Questa)

1981 (2 Nov). Christmas. Horiz designs as T **153** showing scenes from Walt Disney's cartoon film "Uncle Remus". P 13½.

665	¼c. multicoloured	10	10
666	½c. multicoloured	10	10
667	1c. multicoloured	10	10
668	2c. multicoloured	10	10
669	3c. multicoloured	10	10
670	4c. multicoloured	10	10
671	5c. multicoloured	10	10
672	75c. multicoloured	1·00	80
673	$1 multicoloured	1·25	1·00
665/73	Set of 9	2·25	1·90
MS674	128×103 mm. $2 multicoloured	1·75	2·25

167 Map of Grand Turk, and Lighthouse   **168** *Junonia evarete*

(Des J.W. Litho Questa)

1981 (1 Dec). Tourism. T **167** and similar horiz designs. Multicoloured. P 14.

675	20c. Type **167**	70	50
	a. Vert strip of 10. Nos. 675/84	6·25	4·50
676	20c. Map of Salt Cay, and "industrial archaeology"	70	50
677	20c. Map of South Caicos, and "island flying"	70	50
678	20c. Map of East Caicos, and "beach combing"	70	50
679	20c. May, of Grand Caicos (middle), and cave exploring	70	50
680	20c. Map of North Caicos, and camping and hiking	70	50
681	20c. Map of North Caicos, Parrot Cay, Dellis Cay, Fort George Cay, Pine Cay and Water Cay, and environmental studies"	70	50
682	20c. Map of Providenciales, and scuba diving	70	50
683	20c. Map of West Caicos, and "cruising and bird sanctuary"	70	50
684	20c. Turks and Caicos Islands flag	70	50
675/84	Set of 10	6·25	4·50

Nos. 675/84 were printed together, *se-tenant*, in vertical strips of 10 throughout the sheet of 40, the two panes (2×10), separated by a gutter margin, being *tête-bêche*.

(Des J. Cooter. Litho Questa)

1982 (21 Jan). Butterflies. T **168** and similar vert designs. Multicoloured. P 14.

685	20c. Type **168**	30	30
686	35c. *Strymon maesites*	45	55
687	65c. *Agraulis vanillae*	70	1·25
688	$1 *Eurema dina*	1·00	2·00
685/8	Set of 4	2·50	3·75
MS689	72×56 mm. $2 *Anaea intermedia*	2·25	3·75

TURKS AND CAICOS ISLANDS

169 Flag Salute on Queen's Birthday

170 Footballer

(Litho Questa)

1982 (17 Feb). 75th Anniv of Boy Scout Movement. T **169** and similar vert designs. Multicoloured. P 14.

690	40c. Type **169**.	50	50
691	50c. Raft building	60	60
692	75c. Sea scout cricket match	1·10	1·60
693	$1 Nature study	1·50	1·75
690/3 Set of 4		3·25	4·00
MS694 100×70 mm. $2 Lord Baden-Powell and scout salute		1·50	3·00

(Des G. Vasarhelyi. Litho Questa)

1982 (30 Apr). World Cup Football Championship, Spain. T **170** and similar designs showing footballers. P 14.

695	10c. multicoloured	15	15
696	25c. multicoloured	20	20
697	45c. multicoloured	25	25
698	$1 multicoloured	80	80
695/8 Set of 4		1·25	1·25
MS699 117×83 mm. $2 multicoloured (*horiz*)		1·25	2·00

171 Washington crossing the Delaware and Phillis Wheatley (poetess)

(Des Design Images. Litho Questa)

1982 (3 May). 250th Birth Anniv of George Washington (20, 35 c.) and Birth Centenary of Franklin D. Roosevelt (65, 80 c.). T **171** and similar horiz designs. Multicoloured. P 14.

700	20c. Type **171**.	20	30
701	35c. George Washington and Benjamin Banneker (surveyor)	30	45
702	65c. Franklin D. Roosevelt meeting George Washington Carver (agricultural researcher)	35	80
703	80c. Roosevelt as stamp collector	45	1·00
700/3 Set of 4		1·10	2·25
MS704 100×70 mm. $2 Roosevelt with stamp showing profile of Washington		1·00	2·50

172 "Second Thoughts"

173 Princess of Wales

(Litho Questa)

1982 (23 June). Norman Rockwell (painter) Commemoration. T **172** and similar vert designs. Multicoloured. P 14×13½.

705	8c. Type **172**.	15	10
706	15c. "The Proper Gratuity"	20	20
707	20c. "Doctor's Office" (inscr "Before the Shot")	25	30
708	25c. Bottom of the Sixth" (inscr "The Three Umpires")	25	30
705/8 Set of 4		75	80

(Des PAD Studio. Litho Questa)

1982 (1 July—18 Nov). 21st Birthday of Princess of Wales. T **173** and similar vert designs. Multicoloured. P 14½×14.

(a) Sheet stamps. Pale green frames

709	55c. Sandringham	35	45
710	70c. Prince and Princess of Wales	60	55
711	$1 Type **173**	90	80
709/11 Set of 3		1·75	1·75
MS712 102×76 mm. $2 Princess Diana (*different*)		1·50	1·75

(b) Booklet stamps. As Nos. 709/11 but printed with new values and blue frame (18.11.82)

713	8c. Sandringham	15	35
714	35c. Prince and Princess of Wales	55	1·00
715	$1.10 Type **173**	80	2·00
713/15 Set of 3		1·40	3·00

Nos. 713/15 also exist from sheets printed in horizontal *tête-bêche* pairs throughout.

174 Cessna 337 Super Skymaster over Caicos Cays

(Des MBI Studios. Litho Questa)

1982 (23 Aug). Aircraft. T **174** and similar horiz designs. Multicoloured. P 14.

716	8c. Type **174**.	15	15
717	15c. Lockheed JetStar II over Grand Turk	20	25
718	65c. Sikorsky S.58 helicopter over South Caicos	65	80
719	$1.10 Cessna 182 Skylane seaplane over Providenciales	1·10	1·25
716/19 Set of 4		1·90	2·25
MS720 99×69 mm. $2 Boeing 727-200 over Turks and Caicos Islands		2·00	2·50

(Litho Questa)

1982 (1 Dec). Christmas. Scenes from Walt Disney's Cartoon Film "Mickey's Christmas Carol". Horiz designs as T **153**. Multicoloured. P 13½.

721	1c. Donald Duck, Mickey Mouse and Scrooge	10	10
722	1c. Goofy (Marley's ghost) and Scrooge	10	10
723	2c. Jimmy Cricket and Scrooge	10	10
724	2c. Huey, Dewey and Louie	10	10
725	3c. Daisy Duck and youthful Scrooge	10	10
726	3c. Giant and Scrooge	10	10
727	4c. Two bad wolves, a wise pig and a reformed Scrooge	10	10
728	65c. Donald Duck and Scrooge	1·00	75
729	$1.10 Mortis and Scrooge	1·60	1·25
721/9 Set of 9		2·50	2·00
MS730 126×101 mm. $2 Mickey and Minnie Mouse with Mortie		2·75	2·50

175 West Caicos Mule-drawn Wagon

(Des N. Waldman. Litho Questa)

1983 (18 Jan). Trams and Locomotives. T **175** and similar horiz designs. Multicoloured. P 14.

731	15c. Type **175**.	20	25
732	55c. West Caicos steam locomotive	65	70
733	90c. East Caicos mule-drawn sisal train	90	1·00
734	$1.60 East Caicos steam locomotive	1·75	1·90
731/4 Set of 4		3·25	3·50
MS735 99×69 mm. $2.50, Steam sisal train		2·25	2·25

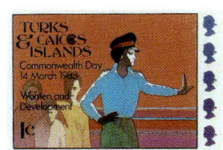

176 Policewoman on Traffic Duty

155

TURKS AND CAICOS ISLANDS

(Des N. Waldman. Litho Questa)

1983 (14 Mar). Commonwealth Day. T **176** and similar horiz designs. Multicoloured. P 14.

736	1c. Type **176**..	85	50
	a. Vert strip of 4. Nos. 736/9	3·50	3·25
737	8c. Stylized sun and weather vane................	30	20
738	65c. Yacht..	85	1·00
739	$1 Cricket..	2·00	2·00
736/9 Set of 4		3·50	3·25

Nos. 736/9 were printed together, *se-tenant*, in vertical strips of four throughout the sheet.

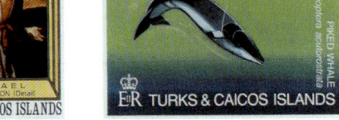

177 "St. John and the Virgin Mary" (detail)

178 Minke Whale

(Des Design Images. Litho Questa)

1983 (7 Apr). Easter. T **177** and similar vert designs showing details from the "Mond Crucifixion" by Raphael. Multicoloured. P 13½×14.

740	35c. Type **177**..	20	25
741	50c. Women..	30	35
742	95c. "Angel with two jars"............................	40	60
743	$1.10 "Angel with one jar"...........................	60	80
740/3 Set of 4		1·40	2·00
MS744 100×130 mm. $2.50, "Christ on the Cross"........		1·50	2·00

(Des D. Hamilton. Litho Questa)

1983 (16 May—11 July). Whales. T **178** and similar horiz designs. Multicoloured. P 13½.

745	50c. Type **178**..	2·00	2·00
746	65c. Black Right Whale (11.7.83)..................	2·25	2·25
747	70c. Killer Whale (13.6.83)..........................	2·50	2·50
748	95c. Sperm Whale (13.6.83)........................	2·75	2·75
749	$1.10 Cuvier's Beaked Whale (11.7.83)........	3·00	3·00
750	$2 Blue Whale (13.6.83)..........................	5·00	5·00
751	$2.20 Humpback Whale	5·50	5·50
752	$3 Long-finned Pilot Whale....................	6·25	6·25
745/52 Set of 8		26·00	26·00
MS753 112×82 mm. $3 Fin Whale (11.7.83)...........		7·00	5·00

Nos. 745/52 were each issued in sheetlets of four.

179 First Hydrogen Balloon *The Globe*, 1783

180 Fiddler Pig

(Des BG Studio. Litho Questa)

1983 (30 Aug). Bicentenary of Manned Flight. T **179** and similar vert designs. Multicoloured. P 14.

754	25c. Type **179**..	20	25
755	35c. *Friendship 7*	25	35
756	70c. First hot air balloon *Le Martial*, 1783	40	70
757	95c. Space shuttle *Columbia*	55	90
754/7 Set of 4		1·25	2·00
MS758 112×76 mm. $2 Montgolfier balloon and Space shuttle..		1·25	2·00

(Litho Format)

1983 (4 Oct). Christmas. Walt Disney Cartoon Characters. T **180** and similar vert designs. Multicoloured. P 11.

759	1c. Type **180**...	10	10
760	1c. Fifer Pig..	10	10
761	2c. Practical Pig......................................	10	10
762	2c. Pluto...	10	10
763	3c. Goofy...	10	10
764	3c. Mickey Mouse...................................	10	10
765	35c. Gyro Gearloose.................................	70	35
766	50c. Ludwig von Drake..............................	70	60
767	$1.10 Huey, Dewey and Louie....................	1·40	1·25
759/67 Set of 9		2·50	2·00
MS768 127×102 mm. $2.50, Mickey and Minnie Mouse with Huey, Dewey and Louie. P 13½		3·25	4·00

181 Bermuda Sloop

(Des G. Drummond. Litho Questa)

1983 (5 Oct)–**85**. Ships. T **181** and similar horiz designs. Multicoloured. P 14.

769	4c. Arawak dug-out canoe (9.1.84)	1·50	3·75
	a. Perf 12½×12 (3.85)	2·75	3·75
770	5c. *Santa Maria* (9.1.84)	2·00	3·75
	a. Perf 12½×12 (12.8.85)	1·00	2·75
771	8c. British and Spanish ships in battle (16.12.83)	2·25	3·75
	a. Perf 12½×12 (3.85)	3·50	3·25
772	10c. Type **181**..	2·25	1·50
	a. Perf 12½×12 (3.85)	3·50	2·00
773	20c. U.S. privateer *Grand Turk* (9.1.84)	1·75	2·25
	a. Perf 12½×12 (12.8.85)	50	3·00
774	25c. H.M.S. *Boreas* (frigate) (16.12.83)	3·00	1·75
	a. Perf 12½×12 (12.8.85)	60	3·00
775	30c. H.M.S. *Endymion* (frigate) attacking French ship, 1790s	3·00	1·50
	a. Perf 12½×12 (3.85)	3·00	2·00
776	35c. *Caesar* (barque) (9.1.84)	2·00	3·25
	a. Perf 12½×12 (12.8.85)	60	3·25
777	50c. *Grapeshot* (American schooner) (16.12.83)	3·50	1·25
	a. Perf 12½×12 (12.8.85)	60	2·50
778	65c. H.M.S. *Invincible* (battle cruiser)............	4·50	2·50
	a. Perf 12½×12 (12.8.85)	2·50	3·75
779	95c. H.M.S. *Magicienne* (cruiser) (16.12.83)	4·50	3·75
	a. Perf 12½×12 (12.8.85)	2·50	3·75
780	$1.10 H.M.S. *Durban* (cruiser).....................	6·00	3·75
	a. Perf 12½×12 (3.85)	10·00	5·00
781	$2 *Sentinel* (cable ship).........................	7·00	4·00
	a. Perf 12½×12 (12.8.85)	2·50	6·50
782	$3 H.M.S. *Minerva* (frigate)....................	7·50	7·50
	a. Perf 12½×12 (12.8.85)	8·00	15·00
783	$5 Caicos sloop (9.1.84)........................	8·50	14·00
	a. Perf 12½×12 (3.85)	17·00	18·00
769/83 Set of 15		50·00	50·00
769a/83a Set of 15		50·00	65·00

182 President Kennedy and Signing of Civil Rights Legislation

(Des Design Images. Litho Questa)

1983 (22 Dec). 20th Death Anniv of President J. F. Kennedy. P 14.

784	**182** 20c. multicoloured................................	20	15
785	$1 multicoloured.................................	50	1·25

183 Clarabelle Cow Diving

156

TURKS AND CAICOS ISLANDS

(Litho Questa)

1984 (21 Feb–Apr). Olympic Games, Los Angeles. T **183** and similar horiz designs showing Disney cartoon characters in Olympic events. Multicoloured. P 14×13½.

A. Inscr "1984 LOS ANGELES"

786A	1c. Type **183**	10	10
787A	1c. Donald Duck in 500 m kayak race	10	10
788A	2c. Huey, Dewey and Louie in 1000 m kayak race	10	10
789A	2c. Mickey Mouse in single kayak	10	10
790A	3c. Donald Duck highboard diving	10	10
791A	3c. Minnie Mouse in kayak slalom	10	10
792A	25c. Mickey Mouse freestyle swimming	85	45
793A	75c. Donald Duck playing water-polo	2·25	2·00
794A	$1 Uncle Scrooge and Donald Duck yachting	2·25	2·00
786A/94A	*Set of 9*	5·00	4·25
MS795A	117×90 mm. $2 Pluto platform diving	4·00	4·50

B. Inscr "1984 OLYMPICS LOS ANGELES" and Olympic emblem. P 12 (4.84)

786B	1c. Type **183**	10	10
787B	1c. Donald Duck in 500 m kayak race	10	10
788B	2c. Huey, Dewey and Louie in 1000 m kayak race	10	10
789B	2c. Mickey Mouse in single kayak	10	10
790B	3c. Donald Duck highboard diving	10	10
791B	3c. Minnie Mouse in kayak slalom	10	10
792B	25c. Mickey Mouse freestyle swimming	70	45
793B	75c. Donald Duck playing water-polo	2·00	2·00
794B	$1 Uncle Scrooge and Donald Duck yachting	2·00	2·00
786B/94B	*Set of 9*	4·50	4·25
MS795B	117×90 mm. $2 Pluto platform diving. P 14×13½	4·00	6·00

184 "Cadillac V-16", 1933

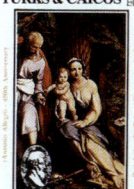

185 "Rest during the Flight to Egypt, with St. Francis"

(Des N. Waldman. Litho Questa)

1984 (15 Mar). Classic Cars and 125th Anniv of first Commercial Oil Well. T **184** and similar horiz designs. Multicoloured. P 14.

796	4c. Type **184**	30	10
797	8c. Rolls-Royce "Phantom III", 1937	40	15
798	10c. Saab "99", 1969	40	15
799	25c. Maserati "Bora", 1973	90	40
800	40c. Datsun "260Z", 1970	1·25	65
801	55c. Porsche "917", 1971	1·40	80
802	80c. Lincoln "Continental", 1939	1·50	90
803	$1 Triumph "TR3A", 1957	1·60	1·25
796/803	*Set of 8*	7·00	4·00
MS804	70×100 mm. $2 Daimler, 1886	2·00	2·50

(Des S. Karp. Litho Walsall)

1984 (9 Apr). Easter. 450th Death Anniv of Correggio (painter). T **185** and similar vert designs. Multicoloured. P 14.

805	15c. Type **185**	20	15
806	40c. "St. Luke and St. Ambrose"	45	40
807	60c. "Diana and her Chariot"	65	65
808	95c. "The Deposition of Christ"	80	80
805/8	*Set of 4*	1·90	1·75
MS809	100×79 mm. $2 "The Nativity with Saints Elizabeth and John the younger" (*horiz*)	1·25	2·50

(186)

1984 (19 June). Universal Postal Union Congress, Hamburg. Nos. 748/9 and **MS**753 optd with T **186**.

810	95c. Sperm Whale	2·50	3·00
811	$1.10 Cuvier's Beaked Whale	2·50	3·00
MS812	112×82 mm. $3 Fin Whale	4·25	4·25

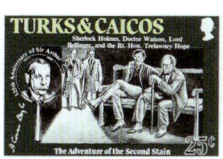

187 "The Adventure of the Second Stain"

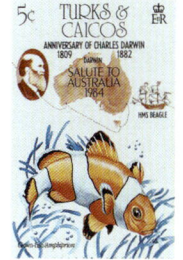

188 Orange Clownfish

(Des S. Karp. Litho Walsall)

1984 (16 July). 125th Birth Anniv of Sir Arthur Conan Doyle (author). T **187** and similar horiz designs showing scenes from Sherlock Holmes stories. Multicoloured. P 14.

813	25c. Type **187**	2·75	1·50
814	45c. "The Adventure of the Final Problem"	3·50	2·25
815	70c. "The Adventure of the Empty House"	5·50	3·50
816	85c. "The Adventure of the Greek Interpreter"	6·50	4·00
813/16	*Set of 4*	16·00	10·00
MS817	100×70 mm. $2 Sir Arthur Conan Doyle	13·00	11·00

(Des Susan David. Litho Walsall)

1984 (22 Aug). "Ausipex" International Stamp Exhibition, Melbourne. 175th Birth Anniv of Charles Darwin. T **188** and similar vert designs. Multicoloured. P 14×13½.

818	5c. Type **188**	60	50
819	35c. Monitor Lizard	2·25	1·75
820	50c. Rainbow Lory	3·50	3·25
821	$1.10 Koalas	3·75	4·25
818/21	*Set of 4*	9·00	8·75
MS822	100×70 mm. $2 Eastern Grey Kangaroo	2·50	4·50

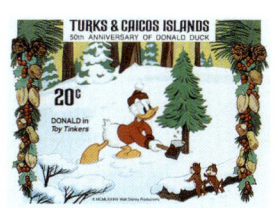

189 Donald Duck cutting down Christmas Tree

(Litho Questa)

1984 (8 Oct–26 Nov). Christmas. Walt Disney Cartoon Characters. T **189** and similar horiz designs showing scenes from "Toy Tinkers". Multicoloured. P 12 (75c.) or 14×13½ (others).

823	20c. Type **189**	85	45
824	35c. Donald Duck and Chip n'Dale playing with train set	1·10	75
825	50c. Donald Duck and Chip n'Dale playing with catapult	1·60	1·10
826	75c. Donald Duck, Chip n'Dale and Christmas tree (26.11)	2·25	1·75
827	$1.10 Donald Duck, toy soldier and Chip n'Dale	2·50	2·50
823/7	*Set of 5*	7·50	6·00
MS828	126×102 mm. $2 Donald Duck as Father Christmas	3·25	4·00

No. 826 was printed in sheetlets of 8 stamps.

190 Magnolia Warbler

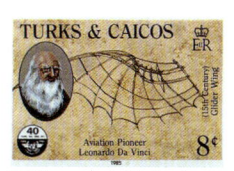

191 Leonardo da Vinci and Illustration of Glider Wing (15th century)

157

TURKS AND CAICOS ISLANDS

(Des Susan David. Litho Walsall)

1985 (28 Jan). Birth Bicentenary of John J. Audubon (ornithologist). T **190** and similar vert designs. Multicoloured. P 14.

829	25c. Type **190**	2·00	75
830	45c. Short-eared Owl	3·00	1·50
831	70c. Mourning Dove and eggs	3·50	2·75
832	85c. Caribbean Martin	3·50	3·00
829/32 Set of 4		11·00	7·25
MS833 100×70 mm. $2 Oystercatcher and chicks		4·50	4·50

(Des K. Gromol. Litho Walsall)

1985 (22 Feb). 40th Anniv of International Civil Aviation Organization. Aviation Pioneers. T **191** and similar horiz designs. Multicoloured. P 14.

834	8c. Type **191**	65	40
835	25c. Sir Alliott Verdon Roe and Avro (Canada) CF-102 jetliner (1949)	1·75	55
836	65c. Robert H. Goddard and first liquid fuel rocket (1926)	2·50	1·75
837	$1 Igor Sikorsky and Vought-Sikorsky VS-300 helicopter prototype (1939)	6·00	4·25
834/7 Set of 4		9·75	6·25
MS838 100×70 mm. $2 Amelia Earhart's Lockheed 10E Electra (1937)		2·75	3·25

192 Benjamin Franklin and Marquis de Lafayette

(Des Susan David. Litho Walsall)

1985 (28 Mar). Centenary of the Statue of Liberty's Arrival in New York. T **192** and similar horiz designs. Multicoloured. P 14.

839	20c. Type **192**	80	50
840	30c. Frederic Bartholdi (designer) and Gustave Eiffel (engineer)	1·10	80
841	65c. *Isere* (French screw warship) arriving in New York with statue, 1885	2·50	1·75
842	$1.10 United States fund raisers Louis Agassiz, Charles Sumner, H. W. Longfellow and Joseph Pulitzer	2·50	2·25
839/42 Set of 4		6·25	4·75
MS843 99×69 mm. $2 Dedication ceremony, 1886		3·00	3·50

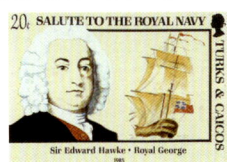

193 Sir Edward Hawke and H.M.S. *Royal George* (ship of the line), 1782

(Des Susan David. Litho Walsall)

1985 (17 Apr). Salute to the Royal Navy. T **193** and similar multicoloured designs. P 14.

844	20c. Type **193**	2·50	1·90
845	30c. Lord Nelson and H.M.S. *Victory* (ship of the line), 1805	3·00	2·25
846	65c. Admiral Sir George Cockburn and H.M.S. *Albion* (ship of the line), 1802	4·00	3·25
847	95c. Admiral Sir David Beatty and H.M.S. *Indefatigable* (battle cruiser), 1916	5·00	4·75
844/7 Set of 4		13·00	11·00
MS848 99×69 mm. $2 18th-century sailor and cannon (vert)		3·25	4·00

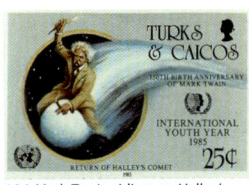

194 Mark Twain riding on Halley's Comet

195 The Queen Mother outside Clarence House

(Des J. Iskowitz. Litho Walsall)

1985 (17 May). International Youth Year. Birth Annivs of Mark Twain (150th) and Jakob Grimm (Bicentenary). T **194** and similar multicoloured designs. P 13½×14 (25, 35c., $2) or 14×13½ (50, 95c.).

849	25c. Type **194**	1·25	65
850	35c. *Grand Turk* (Mississippi river steamer)	2·25	90
851	50c. Hansel and Gretel and gingerbread house (vert)	2·25	1·75
852	95c. Rumpelstiltskin (vert)	3·00	3·25
849/52 Set of 4		8·00	6·00
MS853 99×68 mm. $2 Mark Twain and the Brothers Grimm		3·50	5·00

(Des J.W. Litho Questa)

1985 (15 July). Life and Times of Queen Elizabeth the Queen Mother. T **195** and similar multicoloured designs. P 14.

854	30c. Type **195**	70	45
855	50c. Visiting Biggin Hill airfield (*horiz*)	2·25	1·00
856	$1.10 80th birthday portrait	2·25	2·50
854/6 Set of 3		4·75	3·50
MS857 56×85 mm. $2 With Prince Charles at Garter ceremony, Windsor Castle, 1968		2·00	3·00

196 King George II and Score of "Zadok the Priest" (1727)

196a Bassoon

(Des Susan David. Litho Format)

1985 (17 July). 300th Birth Anniv of George Frederick Handel (composer). T **196** and similar vert designs. P 15.

858	4c. multicoloured	65	50
859	10c. multicoloured	1·00	50
860	25c. multicoloured	2·50	2·50
861	$1.10 multicoloured	3·00	5·50
858/61 Set of 4		6·50	8·00
MS862 101×76 mm. $2 black, deep dull purple and dull violet-blue		5·50	7·50

Designs:—10c. Queen Caroline and score of "Funeral Anthem"; 50c. King George I and score of "Water Music" (1714); $1.10, Queen Anne and score of "Or la Tromba" from *Rinaldo* (1711); $2 George Frederick Handel.

(Des Susan David. Litho Format)

1985 (17 July). 300th Birth Anniv of Johann Sebastian Bach (composer). T **196a** and similar vert designs. P 15.

863	15c. Type **196a**	1·00	40
864	40c. Natural Horn	1·50	85
865	60c. Viola D'Amore	2·00	1·25
866	95c. Clavichord	2·25	2·25
863/6 Set of 4		6·00	4·25
MS867 102×76 mm. $2 Johann Sebastian Bach		4·00	4·00

197 Harley-Davidson Dual Cylinder (1915) on Middle Caicos

(Des Mary Walters. Litho Questa)

1985 (4 Sept). Centenary of the Motor Cycle. T **197** and similar multicoloured designs. P 14.

868	8c. Type **197**	1·00	30
869	25c. Triumph "Thunderbird" (1950) on Grand Turk	2·00	70
870	55c. BMW "K100RS" (1985) on North Caicos	3·00	1·75
871	$1.20 Honda "1100 Shadow" (1985) on South Caicos	4·00	7·00
868/71 Set of 4		9·00	8·75
MS872 106×77 mm. $2 Daimler single track (1885) (vert)		5·00	5·00

158

TURKS AND CAICOS ISLANDS

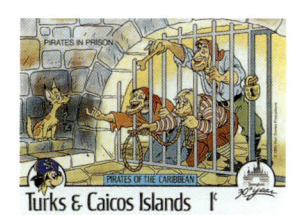

198 Pirates in Prison

(Des Walt Disney Productions. Litho Questa)

1985 (4 Oct). 30th Anniv of Disneyland, U.S.A. T **198** and similar horiz designs showing scenes from "Pirates of the Caribbean" exhibition. Multicoloured. P 14×13½.

873	1c. Type **198**...	10	10
874	1c. The fate of Captain William Kidd...............	10	10
875	2c. Bartholomew Roberts	10	10
876	2c. Two buccaneers	10	10
877	3c. Privateers looting.....................................	10	10
878	3c. Auction of captives..................................	10	10
879	35c. Singing pirates	1·50	80
880	75c. Edward Teach—"Blackbeard"...................	3·00	3·25
881	$1.10 Sir Henry Morgan...............................	3·50	4·00
873/81 Set of 9..		7·50	7·50
MS882 123×86 mm. $2.50, Mary Read and Anne Bonney		5·00	4·50

199 Brownies from China, Turks and Caicos and Papua New Guinea

(Des Mary Walters. Litho Questa)

1985 (4 Nov). 75th Anniv of Girl Guide Movement and 35th Anniv of Grand Turk Company. T **199** and similar horiz designs. Multicoloured. P 14.

883	10c. Type **199**...	75	40
884	40c. Brownies from Surinam, Turks and Caicos and Korea	1·75	1·25
885	70c. Guides from Australia, Turks and Caicos and Canada	2·50	3·00
886	80c. Guides from West Germany, Turks and Caicos and Israel	2·75	3·00
883/6 Set of 4..		7·00	7·00
MS887 107×76 mm. $2 75th anniversary emblem		3·00	3·50

200 Iguana and Log

201 Duke and Duchess of York after Wedding

(Des I. MacLaury. Litho Questa)

1986 (20 Nov). Turks and Caicos Ground Iguana. T **200** and similar horiz designs. Multicoloured. P 14.

888	8c. Type **200**...	2·25	1·25
889	10c. Iguana on beach.....................................	2·25	1·25
890	20c. Iguana at nest...	3·50	2·50
891	35c. Iguana eating flowers.............................	6·50	4·50
888/91 Set of 4..		13·00	8·50
MS892 105×76 mm. $2 Map showing habitat		13·00	14·00

(Litho Questa)

1986 (19 Dec). Royal Wedding. T **201** and similar vert designs. Multicoloured. P 14.

893	35c. Type **201**...	1·50	55
894	65c. Miss Sarah Ferguson in wedding carriage	2·50	1·40
895	$1.10 Duke and Duchess of York on Palace balcony after wedding..............................	3·00	2·75
893/5 Set of 3..		6·25	4·25
MS896 85×85 mm. $2 Duke and Duchess of York leaving Westminster Abbey		4·75	5·50

202 "The Prophecy of the Birth of Christ to King Achaz"

203 H.M.S. *Victoria* (ship of the line), 1859, and Victoria Cross

(Litho Questa)

1987 (9 Dec). Christmas. T **202** and similar vert designs, each showing illuminated illustration by Giorgio Clovio from "Farnese Book of Hours". Multicoloured. P 14.

897	35c. Type **202**...	1·25	85
898	50c. "The Annunciation"................................	1·75	1·75
899	65c. "The Circumcision".................................	2·25	2·25
900	95c. "Adoration of the Kings".......................	3·25	4·00
897/900 Set of 4...		7·75	8·00
MS901 76×106 mm. $2 "The Nativity"............................		5·50	7·00

(Litho Questa)

1987 (24 Dec). 150th Anniv of Accession of Queen Victoria. T **203** and similar horiz designs. Multicoloured. P 14.

902	8c. Type **203**...	1·75	1·00
903	35c. *Victoria* (paddle-steamer) and gold sovereign..	3·00	2·25
904	55c. Royal Yacht *Victoria and Albert I* and 1840 Penny Black stamp...................................	3·25	2·75
905	95c. Royal Yacht *Victoria and Albert II* and Victoria Public Library................................	5·00	5·00
902/5 Set of 4..		11·50	10·00
MS906 129×76 mm. $2 *Victoria* (barque)......................		6·00	7·00

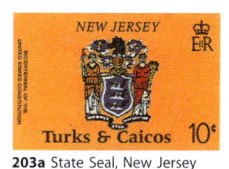

203a State Seal, New Jersey

(Des and litho Questa)

1987 (31 Dec). Bicentenary of U.S. Constitution. T **203a** and similar multicoloured designs. P 14.

907	10c. Type **203a**...	25	35
908	35c. 18th-century family going to church ("Freedom of Worship") (*vert*).................	75	75
909	65c. U.S. Supreme Court, Judicial Branch, Washington (*vert*).....................................	1·40	1·75
910	80c. John Adams (statesman) (*vert*)..............	1·60	2·50
907/10 Set of 4..		3·50	4·75
MS911 105×75 mm. $2 George Mason (Virginia delegate) (*vert*)...		1·75	4·00

Nos. 907/10 were each printed in sheetlets of five stamps and one stamp-size label, which appears in the centre of the bottom row.

204 Santa Maria

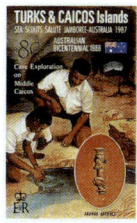

205 Arawak Artifact and Scouts in Cave, Middle Caicos

159

TURKS AND CAICOS ISLANDS

(Litho Questa)

1988 (20 Jan). 500th Anniv of Discovery of America by Columbus (1992) (1st issue). T **204** and similar horiz designs. Multicoloured. P 14.

912	4c. Type **204**	45	30
913	25c. Columbus meeting Tainos Indians	95	60
914	70c. *Santa Maria* anchored off Indian village	2·75	3·25
915	$1 Columbus in field of grain	2·75	3·25
912/15	Set of 4	6·25	6·75
MS916	105×76 mm. $2 *Santa Maria*, *Pinta* and *Nina*	3·50	4·50

See also Nos. 947/51, 1028/36, 1072/80 and 1166/76.

(Litho Questa)

1988 (12 Feb). World Scout Jamboree, Australia. T **205** and similar multicoloured designs. P 14.

917	8c. Type **205**	20	15
918	35c. *Santa Maria*, scouts and Hawks Nest Island (*horiz*)	55	55
919	65c. Scouts diving to wreck of galleon	95	1·25
920	95c. Visiting ruins of 19th-century sisal plantation (*horiz*)	1·40	1·75
917/20	Set of 4	2·75	3·25
MS921	118×82 mm. $2 Splashdown of John Glenn's "Mercury" capsule, 1962	3·25	5·00

No. **MS**921 is inscribed "Sight" in error.

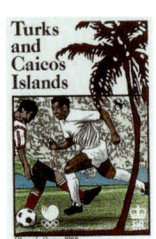

207 Football

1988 (14 Mar). Royal Ruby Wedding. Nos. 772A, 774A and 781A optd with T **206**.

922	10c. Type **181**	75	50
923	25c. H.M.S. *Boreas* (frigate)	1·25	55
924	$2 *Sentinel* (cable ship)	4·00	4·50
922/4	Set of 3	5·50	5·00

(Des L. Fried. Litho B.D.T.)

1988 (29 Aug). Olympic Games, Seoul. T **207** and similar vert designs. Multicoloured. P 14.

925	8c. Type **207**	45	15
926	30c. Yachting	80	50
927	70c. Cycling	5·50	2·00
928	$1 Athletics	1·75	2·25
925/8	Set of 4	7·75	4·50
MS929	102×71 mm. $2 Swimming	2·50	3·50

208 Game-fishing Launch and Swordfish

208a "Madonna and Child with Saint Catherine"

(Des L. Birmingham. Litho Questa)

1988 (5 Sept). Billfish Tournament. T **208** and similar multicoloured designs. P 14.

930	8c. Type **208**	55	30
931	10c. Competitors with swordfish catch	55	30
932	70c. Game-fishing launch	2·25	3·00
933	$1 Atlantic Blue Marlin	2·75	3·50
930/3	Set of 4	5·50	6·25
MS934	119×85 mm. $2 Stylized Sailfish (*horiz*)	3·00	5·50

(Litho Questa)

1988 (24 Oct). Christmas. 500th Birth Anniv of Titian (artist). T **208a** and similar vert designs. P 13½×14.

935	15c. Type **208a**	40	30

936	25c. "Madonna with a Rabbit"	50	40
937	35c. "Virgin and Child with Saints"	60	50
938	40c. "The Gypsy Madonna"	70	60
939	50c. "The Holy Family and a Shepherd"	80	70
940	65c. "Madonna and Child"	95	85
941	$3 "Madonna and Child with Saints"	4·25	6·00
935/41	Set of 7	7·50	8·50
MS942	Two sheets, each 110×95 mm. (a) $2 "Adoration of the Magi" (detail). (b) $2 "The Annunciation" (detail) Set of 2 sheets	6·50	7·50

209 Princess Alexandra and Government House

210 Coat of Arms

(Des and litho Questa)

1988 (14 Nov). Visit of Princess Alexandra. T **209** and similar multicoloured designs. P 14.

943	70c. Type **209**	2·50	1·50
944	$1.40 Princess Alexandra and map of islands	7·50	4·50
MS945	92×72 mm. $2 Princess Alexandra (*vert*)	12·00	10·00

(Des and litho Questa)

1988 (15 Dec). P 14½×15.

946	**210**	$10 multicoloured	11·00	13·00

210a Cutting Tree Bark for Canoe

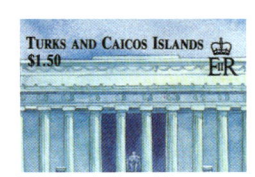

210b Lincoln Memorial

(Des D. Miller. Litho Questa)

1989 (15 May). 500th Anniv of Discovery of America by Columbus (1992) (2nd issue). Pre-Columbian Carib Society. T **210a** and similar multicoloured designs. P 14.

947	10c. Type **210a**	15	15
948	50c. Body painting (*horiz*)	80	80
949	65c. Religious ceremony (*horiz*)	95	1·10
950	$1 Canoeing	1·50	1·75
947/50	Set of 4	3·00	3·50
MS51	84×70 mm. $2 Cave pictograph (*horiz*)	3·50	5·00

(Des Design Element. Litho Questa)

1989 (17 Nov). "World Stamp Expo '89" International Stomp Exhibition, Washington (1st issue). Sheet 77×62 mm. Multicoloured. P 14.

MS952	**210b**	$1.50 multicoloured	2·50	3·50

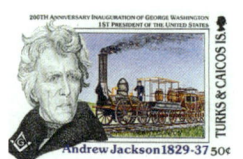

210c Andrew Jackson and Railway Locomotive *De Witt Clinton*

210d "Madonna and Child"

160

TURKS AND CAICOS ISLANDS

(Des W. Hanson Studio. Litho Questa)

1989 (19 Nov). "World Stamp Expo '89" International Stamp Exhibition, Washington (2nd issue). Bicentenary of the U.S. Presidency. T **210c** and similar horiz designs. Multicoloured. P 14.

953	50c. Type **210c**	1·40	1·40
	a. Sheetlet. Nos. 953/8	7·50	7·50
954	50c. Martin van Buren, Moses Walker and early baseball game	1·40	1·40
955	50c. William H. Harrison and campaign parade	1·40	1·40
956	50c. John Tyler, Davy Crockett and the Alamo, Texas	1·40	1·40
957	50c. James K. Polk, California gold miner and first U.S. postage stamp	1·40	1·40
958	50c. Zachary Taylor and Battle of Buena Vista, 1846	1·40	1·40
959	50c. Rutherford B. Hayes and end of Confederate Reconstruction	1·40	1·40
	a. Sheetlet. Nos. 959/64	7·50	7·50
960	50c. James A. Garfield and Battle of Shiloh	1·40	1·40
961	50c. Chester A. Arthur and opening of Brooklyn Bridge, 1883	1·40	1·40
962	50c. Grover Cleveland, Columbian Exposition, Chicago, 1893, and commemorative stamp	1·40	1·40
963	50c. Benjamin Harrison, Pan-American Union Building and map of Americas	1·40	1·40
964	50c. William McKinley and Rough Rider Monument	1·40	1·40
965	50c. Herbert Hoover, Sonya Heine (skater) and Ralph Metcalf (athlete)	1·40	1·40
	a. Sheetlet. Nos. 965/70	7·50	7·50
966	50c. Franklin D. Roosevelt with dog and in wheelchair	1·40	1·40
967	50c. Statue of Washington by Frazer and New York World's Fair, 1939	1·40	1·40
968	50c. Harry S. Truman, Veterans Memorial Building, San Francisco, and U.N. emblem	1·40	1·40
969	50c. Dwight D. Eisenhower and U.S. troops landing in Normandy, 1944	1·40	1·40
970	50c. John F. Kennedy and "Apollo 11" astronauts on Moon, 1969	1·40	1·40
953/70 *Set of 18*		21·00	21·00

Nos. 953/8, 959/64 and 965/70 were each printed together, *se-tenant*, in sheetlets of six stamps.

(Litho Questa)

1989 (18 Dec). Christmas. Paintings by Bellini. T **210d** and similar vert designs. Multicoloured. P 14.

971	15c. Type **210d**	85	50
972	25c. "The Madonna of the Shrubs"	95	50
973	35c. "The Virgin and Child"	1·10	60
974	40c. "The Virgin and Child with a Greek Inscription"	1·25	70
975	50c. "The Madonna of the Meadow"	1·40	80
976	65c. "The Madonna of the Pear"	2·50	1·75
977	70c. "The Virgin and Child" (*different*)	2·75	2·00
978	$1 "Madonna and Child" (*different*)	3·50	2·75
971/8 *Set of 8*		13·00	8·50

MS979 Two sheets, each 96×72 mm. (a) $2 "The Virgin and Child enthroned". (b) $2 "The Madonna with John the Baptist and another Saint" *Set of 2 sheets* .... 11·00 13·00

211 Lift-off of "Apollo 11"

212 *Zephyranthes rosea*

(Des W. Hanson Studio. Litho Questa)

1990 (8 Jan). 20th Anniv of First Manned Landing on Moon. T **211** and similar vert designs. Multicoloured. P 14.

980	50c. Type **211**	1·10	1·25
	a. Sheetlet. Nos. 980/4 and 5 labels	5·00	5·50
981	50c. Lunar module *Eagle* on Moon	1·10	1·25
982	50c. Aldrin gathering dust sample	1·10	1·25
983	50c. Neil Armstrong with camera	1·10	1·25
984	50c. *Eagle* re-united with command module *Columbia*	1·10	1·25
980/4 *Set of 5*		5·00	5·50

Nos. 980/4 were printed together, *se-tenant*, in sheetlets of five stamps, and five stamp-size labels, with Nos. 981/3 forming a composite design.

(Des C. Abbott. Litho Questa)

1990 (11 Jan)–**94**. Island Flowers. T **212** and similar vert designs. Multicoloured. P 14.

985	8c. Type **212**	70	20
	a. Perf 12 (1994)	70	20
986	10c. *Sophora tomentosa*	70	20
	a. Perf 12 (1994)	70	20
987	15c. *Coccoloba uvifera*	1·00	25
	a. Perf 12 (1994)	1·00	25
988	20c. *Encyclia gracilis*	1·00	30
	a. Perf 12 (1994)	1·00	30
989	25c. *Tillandsia streptophylla*	1·00	35
	a. Perf 12 (1994)	1·00	35
990	30c. *Maurandella antirrhiniflora*	1·25	70
	a. Perf 12 (1994)	1·25	60
991	35c. *Tillandsia balbisiana*	1·25	50
	a. Perf 12 (1994)	1·25	50
992	50c. *Encyclia rufa*	1·50	1·25
	a. Perf 12 (1994)	1·50	1·25
993	65c. *Aechmea lingulata*	1·75	1·50
	a. Perf 12 (1994)	1·75	1·50
994	80c. *Asclepias curassavica*	2·00	1·50
	a. Perf 12 (1994)	2·00	1·75
995	$1 *Caesalpinia bahamensis*	2·25	1·60
	a. Perf 12 (1994)	2·25	1·75
996	$1.10 *Capparis cynophallophora*	3·00	2·75
	a. Perf 12 (1994)	3·00	3·25
997	$1.25 *Stachytarpheta jamaicensis*	3·25	3·00
	a. Perf 12 (1994)	3·25	4·00
998	$2 *Cassia biflora*	4·00	4·00
	a. Perf 12 (1994)	4·00	5·00
999	$5 *Clusia rosea*	8·00	10·00
	a. Perf 12 (1994)	8·00	12·00
1000	$10 *Opuntia bahamana* (21.5.90)	16·00	18·00
	a. Perf 12 (1994)	16·00	22·00
985/1000 *Set of 16*		42·00	42·00
985a/1000a *Set of 16*		42·00	50·00

213 Queen Parrotfish

(Des J. Barbaris. Litho B.D.T.)

1990 (12 Feb). Fishes. T **213** and similar horiz designs. Multicoloured. P 14.

1001	8c. Type **213**	25	20
1002	10c. Queen Triggerfish	25	20
1003	25c. Sergeant Major	60	45
1004	40c. Spotted Goatfish	85	75
1005	50c. Neon Goby	1·00	85
1006	75c. Nassau Grouper	1·50	1·50
1007	80c. Yellow-headed Jawfish	1·75	2·00
1008	$1 Blue Tang	1·75	2·00
1001/8 *Set of 8*		7·00	7·00

MS1009 Two sheets, each 115×80 mm. (a) $2 Butter Hamlet. (b) $2 Queen Angelfish *Set of 2 sheets* .... 13·00 14·00

214 Yellow-billed Cuckoo

215 *Anartia jatrophae*

(Des W. Wright. Litho B.D.T.)

1990 (19 Feb). Birds (1st series). T **214** and similar horiz designs. Multicoloured. P 14.

1010	10c. Type **214**	1·40	80
1011	15c. White-tailed Tropic Bird	1·75	80
1012	20c. Kirtland's Warbler	2·50	1·25
1013	30c. Yellow-crowned Night Heron	2·50	1·25
1014	50c. Black-billed Whistling Duck ("West Indian Tree Duck")	3·00	1·75

161

TURKS AND CAICOS ISLANDS

1015	80c. Yellow-bellied Sapsucker	3·75	3·75
1016	$1 American Kestrel	3·75	3·75
1017	$1.40 Northern Mockingbird	4·00	5·00
1010/17	Set of 8	20·00	16·00

MS1018 Two sheets, each 104×78 mm. (a) $2 Yellow Warbler. (b) $2 Osprey *Set of 2 sheets* .... 18·00 11·50
See also Nos. 1050/8.

(Des Linda Vorovik. Litho Questa)

1990 (19 Mar). Butterflies (1st series). T **215** and similar multicoloured designs. P 14.

1019	15c. Type **215**	80	45
1020	25c. *Phoebis sennae* (horiz)	1·00	60
1021	35c. *Euptoieta hegesia* (horiz)	1·25	75
1022	40c. *Hylephila phylaeus* (horiz)	1·40	80
1023	50c. *Eurema chamberlaini* (horiz)	1·40	1·00
1024	60c. *Brephidium exilis*	1·60	1·40
1025	90c. *Papilio aristodemus* (horiz)	2·75	3·00
1026	$1 *Marpesia eleuchea*	2·75	3·00
1019/26	Set of 8	11·50	10·00

MS1027 Two sheets, each 106×76 mm. (a) $2 *Hemiargus thomasi* (horiz). (b) $2 *Danaus gilippus* (horiz) *Set of 2 sheets* .... 11·00 12·00
See also Nos. 1081/9.

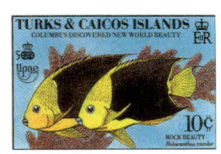

215a Rock Beauty

(Des Mary Walters. Litho Questa)

1990 (2 Apr). 500th Anniv of Discovery of America by Columbus (1992) (3rd issue). New World Natural History—Fishes. T **215a** and similar horiz designs. Multicoloured. P 14.

1028	10c. Type **215a**	60	40
1029	15c. Coney	70	45
1030	25c. Red Hind	1·00	60
1031	50c. Banded Butterflyfish	1·60	1·40
1032	60c. French Angelfish	1·90	1·75
1033	75c. Black-barred Soldierfish	2·25	2·25
1034	90c. Stoplight Parrotfish	2·50	2·50
1035	$1 French Grunt	2·50	2·75
1028/35	Set of 8	11·50	11·00

MS1036 Two sheets, each 109×75 mm. (a) $2 Blue Chromis. (b) $2 Grey Angelfish *Set of 2 sheets* .... 9·00 10·00

216 Penny "Rainbow Trial" in Blue

217 Pillar Box No. 1, 1855

(Des M. Pollard. Litho B.D.T.)

1990 (3 May). 150th Anniv of the Penny Black. T **216** and similar vert designs. P 14.

1037	25c. deep violet-blue	1·50	60
1038	75c. lake-brown	3·00	2·50
1039	$1 blue	3·75	3·75
1037/9	Set of 3	7·50	6·00

MS1040 144×111 mm. $2 brownish black .... 5·00 6·00
Designs:—75c. 1d. red-brown colour trial of December, 1840; $1 2d. blue of 1840; $2 Penny Black.

(Des M. Pollard. Litho B.D.T.)

1990 (3 May). "Stamp World London 90" International Stamp Exhibition. British Pillar Boxes. T **217** and similar vert designs. P 14.

1041	35c. purple-brown and brownish grey	1·25	65
1042	50c. deep violet-blue and brownish grey	1·60	1·10
1043	$1.25 dull ultramarine & brownish grey	3·50	4·00
1041/3	Set of 3	5·50	5·25

MS1044 143×111 mm. $2 brown-lake and black .... 6·50 6·50
Designs:—50c. Penfold box, 1866; $1.25, Air mail box, 1935; $2 "K" type box, 1979.

218 Queen Elizabeth the Queen Mother

219 Stripe-headed Tanager

(Des D. Miller. Litho Questa)

1990 (20 Aug). 90th Birthday of Queen Elizabeth the Queen Mother. T **218** and similar vert designs showing recent photographs of the Queen Mother. P 14.

1045	10c. multicoloured	35	15
1046	25c. multicoloured	75	50
1047	75c. multicoloured	1·40	1·60
1048	$1.25 multicoloured	2·00	2·50
1045/8	Set of 4	4·00	4·25

MS1049 70×73 mm. $2 multicoloured .... 4·00 5·00

(Des Tracy Pedersen. Litho Questa)

1990 (24 Sept). Birds (2nd series). T **219** and similar multicoloured designs. P 14.

1050	8c. Type **219**	1·00	55
1051	10c. Black-whiskered Vireo (horiz)	1·00	65
1052	25c. Blue-grey Gnatcatcher (horiz)	1·75	60
1053	40c. Lesser Scaup (horiz)	2·25	1·00
1054	50c. Bahama Pintail (horiz)	2·25	1·10
1055	75c. Black-necked Stilt (horiz)	2·75	2·75
1056	80c. Oystercatcher	2·75	3·00
1057	$1 Louisiana Heron (horiz)	3·75	4·00
1050/7	Set of 8	16·00	12·00

MS1058 Two sheets, each 98×69 mm. (a) $2 American Coot (horiz). (b) $2 Bahama Woodstar (horiz) *Set of 2 sheets* .... 7·50 8·50

220 "Triumph of Christ over Sin and Death" (detail, Rubens)

221 Canoeing

(Litho Questa)

1990 (17 Dec). Christmas. 350th Death Anniv of Rubens. T **220** and similar vert designs. Multicoloured. P 13½×14.

1059	10c. Type **220**	50	20
1060	35c. "St. Theresa Praying" (detail)	1·00	45
1061	45c. "St. Theresa Praying" (different detail)	1·10	60
1062	50c. "Triumph of Christ over Sin and Death" (different detail)	1·25	65
1063	65c. "St. Theresa Praying" (different detail)	1·75	1·10
1064	75c. "Triumph of Christ over Sin and Death" (different detail)	2·00	1·40
1065	$1.25 "St. Theresa Praying" (different detail)	2·50	3·75
1059/65	Set of 7	9·00	7·25

MS1066 Two sheets, each 70×100 mm. (a) $2 "Triumph of Christ over Sin and Death" (different detail). (b) $2 "St. Theresa Praying" (different detail) *Set of 2 sheets* .... 13·00 14·00

(Des D. Miller. Litho Questa)

1991 (7 Jan). Olympic Games, Barcelona (1992). T **221** and similar vert designs. Multicoloured. P 14.

1067	10c. Type **221**	35	25
1068	25c. 100 metre sprint	70	50
1069	75c. Pole vaulting	1·60	1·60
1070	$1.25 Javelin	2·25	3·00
1067/70	Set of 4	4·50	4·75

MS1071 109×70 mm. $2 Baseball .... 6·50 7·50

TURKS AND CAICOS ISLANDS

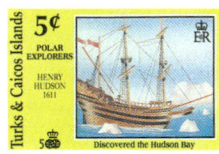

221a Henry Hudson in Hudson's Bay, 1611

(Des T. Agans. Litho Questa)

1991 (15 Apr). 500th Anniv of Discovery of America by Columbus (1992) (4th issue). History of Exploration. T **221a** and similar multicoloured designs. P 14.

1072	5c. Type **221a**	85	55
1073	10c. Roald Amundsen's airship N.1 *Norge*, 1926	85	55
1074	15c. Amundsen's *Gjoa* in the Northwest Passage, 1906	1·40	70
1075	50c. U.S.S. *Nautilus* (submarine) under North Pole, 1958	1·75	70
1076	75c. Robert Scott's *Terra Nova*, 1911	3·00	1·25
1077	$1 Byrd and Bennett's Fokker F.VIIIa/3m *Josephine Ford* aircraft over North Pole, 1926	3·25	2·00
1078	$1.25 Lincoln Ellsworth's Northrop Gamma *Polar Star* on trans-Antarctic flight, 1935	3·50	3·50
1079	$1.50 Capt. James Cook in the Antarctic, 1772–1775	4·50	5·00
1072/9	Set of 8	17·00	13·00

MS1080 Two sheets, each 116×76 mm. (a) $2 *Santa Maria* (vert). (b) $2 Bow of *Nina* (vert) Set of 2 sheets . 9·00 10·00

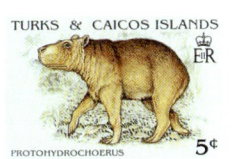

222 *Anartia jatrophae*   **223** Protohydrochoerus

(Des D. Miller. Litho Questa)

1991 (13 May). Butterflies (2nd series). T **222** and similar horiz designs. Multicoloured. P 14.

1081	5c. Type **222**	35	40
1082	25c. *Historis osius*	80	50
1083	35c. *Agraulis vanillae*	90	65
1084	45c. *Junonia evarete*	1·10	90
1085	55c. *Dryas julia*	1·25	1·25
1086	65c. *Siproeta stelenes*	1·60	1·60
1087	70c. *Appias drusilla*	1·75	1·75
1088	$1 *Ascia monuste*	1·90	2·00
1081/8	Set of 8	8·75	8·00

MS1089 Two sheets, each 114×72 mm. (a) $2 *Phoebis philea*. (b) $2 *Pseudolycaena marsyas* Set of 2 sheets ... 10·00 11·00

(Des R. Frank. Litho Questa)

1991 (3 June). Extinct Species of Fauna. T **223** and similar horiz designs. Multicoloured. P 14.

1090	5c. Type **223**	70	60
1091	10c. *Phororhacos*	70	60
1092	15c. *Prothylacynus*	85	60
1093	50c. *Borhyaena*	2·25	1·10
1094	75c. *Smilodon*	2·75	1·75
1095	$1 *Thoatherium*	3·00	2·00
1096	$1.25 *Cuvieronius*	3·25	3·75
1097	$1.50 *Toxodon*	3·25	4·00
1090/7	Set of 8	15·00	13·00

MS1098 Two sheets, each 79×59 mm. (a) $2 *Astrapotherium*. (b) $2 *Mesosaurus* Set of 2 sheets..... 12·00 13·00

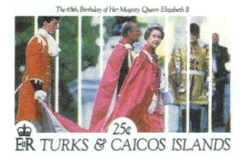

223a Queen and Prince Philip at St Paul's Cathedral, 1988

(Des D. Miller. Litho Walsall)

1991 (8 June). 65th Birthday of Queen Elizabeth II. T **223a** and similar horiz designs. Multicoloured. P 14.

1099	25c. Type **223a**	65	45
1100	35c. Queen and Prince Philip	80	60
1101	65c. Queen and Prince Philip at Garter Ceremony, 1988	1·40	1·40
1102	80c. Queen at Windsor, May 1988	1·75	2·00
1099/1102	Set of 4	4·25	4·00

MS1103 68×90 mm. $2 Separate photographs of Queen and Prince Philip 4·00 5·00

224 *Pluteus chrysophlebius*

(Des Wendy Smith-Griswold. Litho Questa)

1991 (24 June). Fungi. T **224** and similar multicoloured designs. P 14.

1104	10c. Type **224**	40	30
1105	15c. *Leucopaxillus gracillimus*	55	30
1106	20c. *Marasmius haematocephalus*	65	40
1107	35c. *Collybia subpruinosa*	85	45
1108	50c. *Marasmius atrorubens* (vert)	1·25	75
1109	65c. *Leucocoprinus birnbaumii* (vert)	1·50	1·25
1110	$1.10 *Trogia cantharelloides* (vert)	2·00	2·50
1111	$1.25 *Boletellus cubensis* (vert)	2·00	2·75
1104/11	Set of 8	8·25	8·00

MS1112 Two sheets, each 85×59 mm. (a) $2 *Pyrrhoglossum pyrrhum* (vert). (b) $2 *Gerronema citrinum* Set of 2 sheets 10·00 11·00

224a Prince and Princess of Wales, 1987

(Des D. Miller. Litho Walsall)

1991 (29 July). 10th Wedding Anniv of Prince and Princess of Wales. T **224a** and similar horiz designs. Multicoloured. P 14.

1113	10c. Type **224a**	80	25
1114	45c. Separate photographs of Prince, Princess and sons	2·50	90
1115	50c. Prince Henry in fire engine and Prince William applauding	3·50	1·50
1116	$1 Princess Diana in Derbyshire, 1990, and Prince Charles	3·25	3·00
1113/16	Set of 4	9·00	5·00

MS1117 68×90 mm. $2 Prince, Princess and family, Majorca, 1990 6·00 6·00

224b "Weaver with Spinning Wheel"

(Litho B.D.T.)

1991 (26 Aug). Death Centenary of Vincent van Gogh (artist) (1990). T **224b** and similar multicoloured designs. P 13.

1118	15c. Type **224b**	1·25	60
1119	25c. "Head of a Young Peasant with Pipe" (vert)	1·40	60
1120	35c. "Old Cemetery Tower at Nuenen" (vert)..	1·60	60
1121	45c. "Cottage at Nightfall" (vert)	1·75	70
1122	50c. "Still Life with Open Bible" (vert)	1·75	75
1123	65c. "Lane, Jardin du Luxembourg" (vert)	2·25	1·60
1124	80c. "Pont du Carrousel and Louvre, Paris" (vert)	2·75	3·25
1125	$1 "Vase with Poppies, Cornflowers, Peonies and Chrysanthemums" (vert)	3·00	3·25
1118/25	Set of 8	14·00	10·00

MS1126 Two sheets, each 117×80 mm. (a) $2 "Ploughed Field". (b) $2 "Entrance to the Public Park". Imperf Set of 2 sheets 12·00 13·00

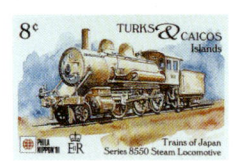

TURKS AND CAICOS ISLANDS

225 Series 8550 Steam Locomotive, 1899

1991 (4 Nov). "Phila Nippon '91" International Stamp Exhibition, Tokyo. Japanese Steam Locomotives. T **225** and similar horiz designs. Multicoloured. P 14.

1127	8c. Type **225**...	70	60
1128	10c. Class C57, 1937...	70	50
1129	45c. Series 4110, 1913...	1·50	70
1130	50c. Class C55, 1935...	1·50	70
1131	65c. Series 6250, 1915...	2·00	1·40
1132	80c. Class E10, 1948...	2·25	2·25
1133	$1 Series 4500,1902...	2·25	2·50
1134	$1.25 Class C11, 1932...	2·50	3·50
1127/34 Set of 8 ...		12·00	11·00

MS1135 Two sheets, each 112×80 mm. (a) $2 Class C58, 1938. (b) $2 Class C62, 1948 Set of 2 sheets .... 9·00 9·00

225a "Adoration of the Shepherds" (detail)

225c "St. Monica" (Luis Tristan)

225b Garden overlooking Sea

(Litho Walsall)

1991 (23 Dec). Christmas. Religious Paintings by Gerard David. T **225a** and similar vert designs. Multicoloured. P 12.

1136	8c. Type **225a**...	65	20
1137	15c. "Virgin and Child Enthroned with Two Angels"...	85	25
1138	35c. "The Annunciation" (outer wings)...	1·50	50
1139	45c. "The Rest on the Flight to Egypt"...	1·60	75
1140	50c. "The Rest on the Flight to Egypt" (different)...	1·60	90
1141	65c. "Virgin and Child with Angels"...	2·25	1·25
1142	80c. "Adoration of the Shepherds"...	2·75	3·00
1143	$1.25 " Perussis Altarpiece" (detail)...	3·25	4·50
1136/43 Set of 8 ...		13·00	10·00

MS1144 Two sheets, each 102×127 mm. (a) $2 "The Nativity". (b) $2 "Adoration of the Kings". P 14 Set of 2 sheets .... 10·00 11·00

(Des D. Miller. Litho Questa)

1992 (6 Feb). 40th Anniv of Queen Elizabeth II's Accession. T **225b** and similar horiz designs. Multicoloured. P 14.

1145	10c. Type **225b**...	75	40
1146	20c. Jetty...	1·25	55
1147	25c. Small bay...	1·40	60
1148	35c. Island road...	1·50	75
1149	50c. Grand Turk...	1·90	1·10
1150	65c. Beach...	2·25	1·60
1151	80c. Marina...	2·50	2·25
1152	$1.10 Grand Turk (different)...	2·75	2·75
1145/52 Set of 8 ...		13·00	9·00

MS1153 Two sheets, each 75×97 mm. (a) $2 Beach (different). (b) $2 Foreshore, Grand Turk Set of 2 sheets .... 12·00 12·00

(Litho B.D.T.)

1992 (26 May). "Granada '92" International Stamp Exhibition, Spain. Religious Paintings. T **225c** and similar vert designs. Multicoloured. P 13.

1154	8c. Type **225c**...	80	20
1155	20c. "The Vision of Ezekiel: The Resurrection of the Flesh" (detail) (Francisco Collantes)..	1·25	30
1156	45c. "The Vision of Ezekiel: The Resurrection of the Flesh" (different detail) (Collantes)...	1·75	65
1157	50c. "The Martyrdom of St. Phillip" (José de Ribera)...	1·75	65
1158	65c. "St. John the Evangelist" (Juan Ribalta)..	2·25	1·25
1159	80c. "Archimedes" (De Ribera)...	2·50	2·50
1160	$1 "St. John the Baptist in the Desert" (De Ribera)...	2·50	2·75
1161	$1.25 "The Martyrdom of St. Phillip" (detail) (De Ribera)...	2·75	3·25
1154/61 Set of 8 ...		14·00	10·50

MS1162 Two sheets, each 95×120 mm. (a) $2 "The Baptism of Christ" (Juan Fernández Navarrete). (b) $2 "Battle at El Sotillo" (Francisco Zurbarán). Imperf Set of 2 sheets............... 13·00 13·00

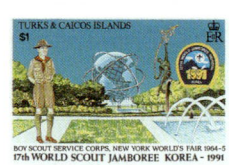

226 Boy Scout on Duty at New York World's Fair, 1964

(Des W. Hanson Studio. Litho Questa)

1992 (6 July). 17th World Scout Jamboree, Korea. T **226** and similar multicoloured designs. P 14.

1163	$1 Type **226**...	2·75	3·00
1164	$1 Lord Baden-Powell (vert)...	2·75	3·00

MS1165 117×89 mm. $2 Silver Buffalo award................ 6·50 8·00

227 Nina and Commemorative Coin

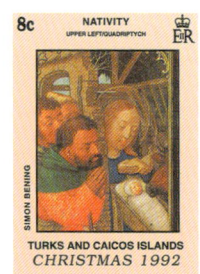

227a "Nativity" (detail) (Simon Bening)

(Litho Questa)

1992 (12 Oct). 500th Anniv of Discovery of America by Columbus (5th issue). T **227** and similar horiz designs, each showing a commemorative coin. Multicoloured. P 14.

1166	10c. Type **227**...	1·00	65
1167	15c. Departure from Palos...	1·10	65
1168	20c. Coat of Arms of Columbus...	1·10	80
1169	25c. Ships of Columbus...	1·75	80
1170	30c. *Pinta*...	1·75	80
1171	35c. Landfall in the New World...	1·75	85
1172	50c. Christopher Columbus...	2·00	1·25
1173	65c. *Santa Maria*...	2·25	1·50
1174	80c. Erecting commemorative cross...	2·25	2·50
1175	$1.10 Columbus meeting Amerindian...	2·50	3·50
1166/75 Set of 10 ...		15·00	12·00

MS1176 Two sheets, each 70×100 mm. (a) $2 Coins showing ships of Columbus. (b) $2 Coins showing landing in the New World Set of 2 sheets............ 14·00 11·00

(Litho Questa)

1992 (7 Dec). Christmas. Religious Paintings. T **227a** and similar vert designs. Multicoloured. P 13½×14.

1177	8c. Type **227a**...	80	15
1178	15c. "Circumcision" (detail) (Bening)...	1·25	30
1179	35c. "Flight to Egypt" (detail) (Bening)...	1·75	60
1180	50c. "Massacre of the Innocents" (detail) (Bening)...	2·00	80
1181	65c. "The Annunciation" (Dieric Bouts)...	2·50	1·25
1182	80c. "The Visitation" (Bouts)...	3·00	3·00
1183	$1.10 "Adoration of the Angels" (Bouts)...	3·25	3·50

TURKS AND CAICOS ISLANDS

1184	$1.25 "Adoration of the Wise Men" (Bouts)	3·25	4·75
1177/84	Set of 8	16·00	13·00

MS1185 Two sheets, each 77×102 mm. (a) $2 "The Virgin seated with the Child" (detail) (Bouts). (b) $2 "The Virgin and Child" (detail) (Bouts) Set of 2 sheets .... 12·00 13·00

228 American Astronaut repairing Satellite

Royal Visit HRH Duke of Edinburgh 20th March 1993 (229)

(Des W. Wright and L. Fried (Nos. 1186, 1191, **MS**1192a), W. Wright (others). Litho Questa)

1993 (8 Mar). Anniversaries and Events. T **228** and similar horiz designs. Multicoloured. P 14.

1186	25c. Type **228**	2·25	60
1187	50c. Dead and flourishing trees	2·50	90
1188	65c. Food and World map	3·00	1·60
1189	80c. Polluted and clean seas	3·50	3·25
1190	$1 Lions Club emblem	3·50	3·25
1191	$1.25 Projected orbiting quarantine modules.	4·00	5·00
1186/91	Set of 6	17·00	13·00

MS1192 Two sheets, each 107×80 mm. (a) $2 Projected orbital Martian vehicle. (b) $2 Industrialised town and clean beach Set of 2 sheets .... 15·00 16·00

Anniversaries and Events:—Nos. 1186, 1191, **MS**1192a, International Space Year; Nos. 1187, 1189, **MS**1192b, Earth Summit '92, Rio; No. 1188, International Conference on Nutrition, Rome; No. 1190, 75th anniv of International Association of Lions Clubs.

1993 (20 Mar). Visit of the Duke of Edinburgh. Nos. 1100/1 and **MS**1103 optd with T **229**.

1193	35c. Queen and Prince Philip (R.)	2·75	1·50
1194	65c. Queen and Prince Philip at Garter Ceremony, 1988 (R.)	4·00	2·50

MS1195 68×90 mm. $2 Separate photographs of Queen and Prince Philip .... 8·00 8·00

229a Communication Chalice and Plate

230a "Mary, Queen of the Angels" (detail) (Dürer)

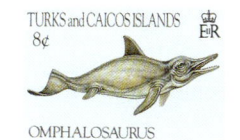

230 Omphalosaurus

(Des Kerri Schiff. Litho Questa)

1993 (2 June). 40th Anniv of Coronation. T **229a** and similar vert designs. P 13½×14.

1196	15c. multicoloured	50	50
	a. Sheetlet. Nos. 1196/9×2	8·50	9·50
1197	50c. multicoloured	1·25	1·40
1198	$1 deep emerald and black	1·60	1·75
1199	$1.25 multicoloured	1·60	1·75
1196/9	Set of 4	4·50	5·00

MS1200 70×100 mm. $2 multicoloured. P 14 .... 5·50 6·00

Designs: 50c. Queen Elizabeth II at Coronation (photograph by Cecil Beaton); $1 Queen Elizabeth during Coronation ceremony; $1.25, Queen Elizabeth and Prince Philip. (28½×42½ mm)—$2 "Queen Elizabeth II" (detail).

Nos. 1196/9 were printed together in sheetlets of 8, containing two se-tenant blocks of 4.

(Litho Questa)

1993 (15 Nov). Prehistoric Animals. T **230** and similar horiz designs. Multicoloured. P 14.

1201	8c. Type **230**	30	30
1202	15c. Coelophysis	40	30
1203	20c. Triceratops	45	30
1204	35c. Dilophosaurus	65	50
1205	50c. Pterodactylus	80	65
1206	65c. Elasmosaurus	1·10	1·00
1207	80c. Stegosaurus	1·25	1·40
1208	$1.25 Euoplocephalus	1·60	2·25
1201/8	Set of 8	6·00	6·00

MS1209 Two sheets, each 100×70 mm. (a) $2 As 20c. (b) $2 As 35c. Set of 2 sheets .... 12·00 12·00

(Litho Questa)

1993 (29 Nov). Christmas. Religious Paintings. T **230a** and similar designs. Black, pale lemon and red (Nos. 1210/12, 1217 and **MS**1218) or multicoloured (others). P 13½×14.

1210	8c. Type **230a**	70	20
1211	20c. "Mary, Queen of the Angels" (different detail) (Dürer)	1·10	30
1212	35c. "Mary, Queen of the Angels" (different detail) (Dürer)	1·40	50
1213	50c. "Virgin and Child with St. John the Baptist" (Raphael)	1·75	70
1214	65c. "The Canagiani Holy Family" (detail) (Raphael)	2·25	1·25
1215	80c. "The Holy Family with the Lamb" (detail) (Raphael)	2·50	2·50
1216	$1 "Virgin and Child with St. John the Baptist" (different detail) (Raphael)	2·75	2·75
1217	$1.25 "Mary, Queen of the Angels" (different detail) (Dürer)	3·25	4·00
1210/17	Set of 8	14·00	11·00

MS1218 Two sheets, each 102×127 mm. (a) $2 "Mary, Queen of the Angels" (different detail) (Dürer). P 13½×14. (b) $2 "The Canagiani Holy Family" (different detail) (Raphael) (horiz). P 14×13½ Set of 2 sheets .... 10·00 11·00

231 Blue-headed Wrasse

(Des J. Genzo. Litho Questa)

1993 (15 Dec). Fishes. T **231** and similar horiz designs. Multicoloured. P 14.

1219	10c. Type **231**	40	30
1220	20c. Honeycomb Cowfish	60	40
1221	25c. Glass-eyed Snapper	60	40
1222	35c. Spotted Drum	75	50
1223	50c. Jolt-headed Porgy	1·00	70
1224	65c. Small-mouthed Grunt	1·25	1·00
1225	80c. Candy Basslet ("Peppermint Bass")	1·40	1·75
1226	$1.10 Indigo Hamlet	1·75	2·75
1219/26	Set of 8	7·00	7·00

MS1227 Two sheets, each 106×75 mm. (a) $2 Bonnethead. (b) $2 Atlantic Sharp-nosed Shark Set of 2 sheets .... 7·50 8·50

The captions on No. **MS**1227 have been transposed in error.

232 Killdeer

(Des I. MacLaury. Litho Questa)

1993 (30 Dec). Birds. T **232** and similar multicoloured designs. P 14.

1228	10c. Type **232**	1·25	75
1229	15c. Yellow-crowned Night Heron (vert)	1·60	75
1230	35c. Northern Mockingbird	2·25	75
1231	50c. Eastern Kingbird (vert)	2·50	1·00
1232	65c. Magnolia Warbler	2·75	1·50
1233	80c. Cedar Waxwing (vert)	3·00	3·00
1234	$1.10 Ruby-throated Hummingbird	3·25	3·25
1235	$1.25 Painted Bunting (vert)	3·25	4·00
1228/35	Set of 8	18·00	13·50

MS1236 Two sheets, each 100×70 mm. (a) $2 Ruddy Duck. (b) $2 American Kestrel (vert) Set of 2 sheets .... 12·00 12·00

TURKS AND CAICOS ISLANDS

233 Sergio Goycoechea (Argentina)

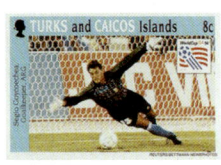

234 *Xerocomus guadelupae*

(Litho Questa)

1994 (26 Sept). World Cup Football Championship, U.S.A. T **233** and similar multicoloured designs. P 14.

1237	8c. Type **233**	50	20
1238	10c. Bodo Illgner (Germany)	50	20
1239	50c. Nico Claesen (Belgium), Bossis and Amoros (France)	1·75	70
1240	65c. German players celebrating	2·00	1·10
1241	80c. Cameroun players celebrating	2·25	2·00
1242	$1 Cuciuffo (Argentina), Santin and Francescoli (Uruguay)	2·25	2·25
1243	$1.10 Hugo Sanchez (Mexico)	2·25	2·50
1237/43 Set of 7		10·50	9·00

MS1244 Two sheets, each 100×70 mm. (a) $2 The Silverdome, Michigan. (b) $2 Michel Platini (France) (vert) *Set of 2 sheets* .... 6·50 7·50

No. 1237 is inscribed "Segio Goycoechea" and No. 1238 "Bado Illgner", both in error.

(Litho Questa)

1994 (10 Oct). Fungi. T **234** and similar multicoloured designs. P 14.

1245	5c. Type **234**	30	30
1246	10c. *Volvariella volvacea*	30	30
1247	35c. *Hygrocybe atrosquamosa* (horiz)	65	50
1248	50c. *Pleurotus ostreatus* (horiz)	90	65
1249	65c. *Marasmius pallescens* (horiz)	1·25	1·00
1250	80c. *Coprinus plicatilis*	1·40	1·50
1251	$1.10 *Bolbitius vitellinus* (horiz)	1·60	1·90
1252	$1.50 *Pyrrhoglossum lilaceipes*	2·00	2·50
1245/52 Set of 8		7·75	7·75

MS1253 Two sheets, each 102×72 mm. (a) $2 *Russula cremeolilacina*. (b) $2 *Lentinus edodes* (horiz) *Set of 2 sheets* .... 8·00 8·00

235 "The Annunciation"

236 *Dryas julia*

(Litho Questa)

1994 (5 Dec). Christmas. Illustrations from 15th-century French Book of Hours. T **235** and similar vert designs. P 14.

1254	25c. Type **235**	1·25	35
1255	50c. "The Visitation"	2·00	75
1256	65c. "Annunciation to the Shepherds"	2·50	1·25
1257	80c. "The Nativity"	2·75	2·75
1258	$1 "Flight into Egypt"	3·00	2·75
1254/8 Set of 5		10·50	7·00

MS1259 63×86 mm. $2 "The Adoration of the Magi" ...... 5·00 6·00

(Litho Questa)

1994 (12 Dec). Butterflies. T **236** and similar horiz designs. Multicoloured. P 14.

1260	15c. Type **236**	40	35
1261	20c. *Urbanus proteus*	45	40
1262	25c. *Colobura dirce*	50	40
1263	50c. *Papilio homerus*	90	65
1264	65c. *Chiodes catillus*	1·25	1·00
1265	80c. *Eurytides zonaria*	1·50	1·75
1266	$1 *Hypolymnas misippus*	1·60	1·75
1267	$1.25 *Phoebis avellaneda*	1·75	2·00
1260/7 Set of 8		7·50	7·50

MS1268 Two sheets, each 100×70 mm. (a) $2 *Eurema adamsi*. (b) $2 *Morpho peleides* *Set of 2 sheets* .... 6·50 7·00

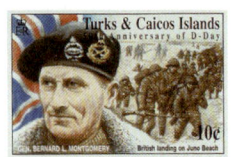

237 General Montgomery and British Troops landing on Juno Beach

(Des J. Iskowitz. Litho Questa)

1994 (19 Dec). 50th Anniv of D-Day. T **237** and similar horiz designs. Multicoloured. P 14.

1269	10c. Type **237**	30	30
1270	15c. Admiral Ramsay and British commandos at Sword Beach	45	35
1271	35c. Gun crew on H.M.S. *Belfast* (cruiser)	65	45
1272	50c. Montgomery and Eisenhower with Air Chief Marshal Tedder	90	65
1273	65c. General Eisenhower and men of U.S. 101st Airborne Division	1·25	1·00
1274	80c. Lt-Gen. Bradley and U.S. troops landing on Omaha Beach	1·40	1·50
1275	$1.10 Arrival of U.S. reinforcements	1·60	1·75
1276	$1.25 Eisenhower at briefing	1·75	1·90
1269/76 Set of 8		7·50	7·00

MS1277 Two sheets, each 100×70 mm. (a) $2 Landing craft and barrage balloon. (b) $2 Eisenhower and Montgomery *Set of 2 sheets* .... 6·50 7·00

238 *Cattleya deckeri*

(Des Dorothy Novak. Litho Questa)

1995 (5 Jan). Orchids. T **238** and similar horiz designs. Multicoloured. P 14.

1278	8c. Type **238**	50	20
1279	20c. *Epidendrum carpophorum*	70	30
1280	25c. *Epidendrum ciliare*	70	35
1281	50c. *Encyclia phoenicea*	95	70
1282	65c. *Bletia patula*	1·25	1·10
1283	80c. *Brassia caudata*	1·40	1·50
1284	$1 *Brassavola nodosa*	1·60	1·60
1285	$1.25 *Bletia purpurea*	1·90	2·25
1278/85 Set of 8		8·00	7·25

MS1286 Two sheets, each 100×70 mm. (a) $2 *Vanilla planifolia*. (b) $2 *Ionopsis utricularioides* *Set of 2 sheets* .... 7·50 8·00

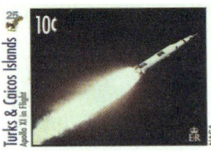

238a "Apollo 11"

(Des W. Hanson. Litho Questa)

1995 (9 Jan). 25th Anniv of First Moon Landing. T **238a** and similar multicoloured designs. P 14.

1287	10c. Type **238a**	35	30
1288	20c. Moon landing simulation	50	35
1289	25c. "Astronauts on the Moon" (detail) (Kovales)	55	35
1290	35c. First human foot on Moon	70	45
1291	50c. Astronaut Aldrin conducting solar wind experiment	1·00	65
1292	65c. Astronauts planting U.S.A. flag	1·40	1·00
1293	80c. Space module *Columbia* over lunar surface	1·50	1·50
1294	$1.10 "Apollo 11" after splashdown	1·75	1·90
1287/94 Set of 8		7·00	6·00

MS1295 Two sheets, each 104×84 mm. (a) $2 Sample of Moon rock. (b) $2 "Apollo 11" lift-off, Cape Canaveral (vert) *Set of 2 sheets* .... 7·00 7·50

TURKS AND CAICOS ISLANDS

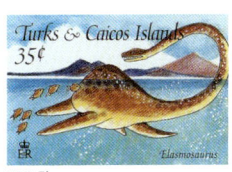

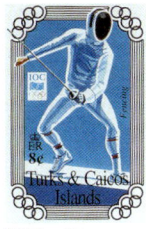

239 Elasmosaurus **240** Fencing

(Des Mary Walters. Litho Questa)

1995 (23 Jan). Jurassic Marine Reptiles. T **239** and similar horiz designs. Multicoloured. P 14.
1296	35c. Type **239**	65	65
	a. Sheetlet. Nos. 1296/307	7·00	7·00
1297	35c. Plesiosaurus	65	65
1298	35c. Ichthyosaurus	65	65
1299	35c. Archelon	65	65
1300	35c. Askeptosaurus	65	65
1301	35c. Macroplata	65	65
1302	35c. Ceresiosaurus	65	65
1303	35c. Liopleurodon	65	65
1304	35c. Henodus	65	65
1305	35c. Muraenosaurus	65	65
1306	35c. Placodus	65	65
1307	35c. Kronosaurus	65	65
1296/1307 Set of 12		7·00	7·00

Nos. 1296/1307 were printed together, se-tenant, in sheetlets of 12 forming a composite design.

No. 1303 is inscribed "Lipoleurodon" in error.

(Des D. Miller. Litho Questa)

1995 (6 Feb). Centenary of International Olympic Committee. T **240** and similar vert designs. Multicoloured. P 14.
1308	8c. Type **240**	50	40
1309	10c. Speed skating	50	40
1310	15c. Diving	70	40
1311	20c. Cycling	2·75	1·25
1312	25c. Ice hockey	2·75	1·25
1313	35c. Figure skating	1·50	70
1314	50c. Football	1·75	1·10
1315	65c. Bob-sleighing	1·75	1·40
1316	80c. Supergiant slalom	1·90	2·00
1317	$1.25 Show jumping	2·50	3·25
1308/17 Set of 10		15·00	11·00
MS1318 Two sheets, 89×110 mm. (a) $2 Downhill skiing. (b) $2 Gymnastics Set of 2 sheets		6·50	7·50

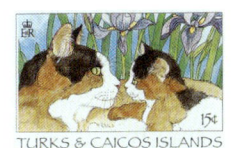

Both miniature sheets are incorrectly dated "1984–1994" on the margin.

241 Cat and Kitten

(Des Mary Walters. Litho Questa)

1995 (3 July). Cats. T **241** and similar horiz designs. Multicoloured. P 14.
1319	15c. Type **241**	1·10	60
1320	20c. Tabby on branch	1·25	60
1321	35c. Cat and ladybird	1·75	60
1322	50c. Black and white cat	2·25	1·10
1323	65c. Red cat with flower in paw	2·50	1·40
1324	80c. White cat on pink pillow	2·50	2·25
1325	$1 Siamese with flower in paws	2·50	2·50
1326	$1.25 Cats preening	2·75	3·50
1319/26 Set of 8		15·00	11·00
MS1327 Two sheets, each 106×76 mm. (a) $2 Kitten and ladybirds. (b) $2 Kittens asleep Set of 2 sheets		9·00	9·00

242 Belted Kingfisher

(Des Helen Bultfield. Litho B.D.T.)

1995 (2 Aug). Birds. T **242** and similar multicoloured designs. P 13½×13.
1328	10c. Type **242**	1·00	75
1329	15c. Clapper Rail	1·25	75
1330	20c. American Redstart	1·25	75
1331	25c. Roseate Tern	1·25	75
1332	35c. Purple Gallinule	1·50	75
1333	45c. Turnstone	1·75	80
1334	50c. Barn Owl	3·00	1·75
1335	60c. Brown Booby	2·00	1·40
1336	80c. Great Blue Heron	2·50	1·50
1337	$1 Antillean Nighthawk	3·00	2·25
1338	$1.25 Thick-billed Vireo	3·50	2·25
1339	$1.40 American Flamingo	4·00	3·50
1340	$2 Wilson's Plover	4·50	6·50
1341	$5 Blue-winged Teal	8·00	11·00
1342	$10 Pair of Reddish Egrets (50×28 mm)	14·00	19·00
1328/42 Set of 15		48·00	48·00

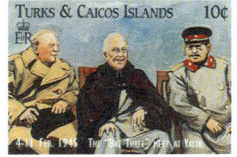

242a Queen Elizabeth the Queen Mother (pastel drawing) **242b** Churchill, Roosevelt and Stalin at Yalta Conference

(Des and litho Questa)

1995 (4 Aug). 95th Birthday of Queen Elizabeth the Queen Mother. T **242a** and similar vert designs. P 13½×14.
1344	50c. orange-brown, pale brown and black	1·75	1·75
	a. Sheetlet. Nos. 1344/7×2	12·00	12·00
1345	50c. multicoloured	1·75	1·75
1346	50c. multicoloured	1·75	1·75
1347	50c. multicoloured	1·75	1·75
1344/7 Set of 4		6·50	6·50
MS1348 102×127 mm. $2 multicoloured		6·50	6·50

Designs:—No. 1345, Wearing tiara; No. 1346, At desk (oil painting); No. 1347, Wearing blue dress; No. **MS**1348, Wearing pale blue dress and hat.

Nos. 1344/7 were printed together in sheetlets of 8, containing two se-tenant horizontal strips of 4.

(Des R. Sauber. Litho Questa)

1995 (14 Aug). 50th Anniv of End of Second World War in Europe. T **242b** and similar horiz designs. Multicoloured. P 14.
1349	10c. Type **242b**	80	60
1350	15c. Liberated Allied prisoners of war	70	50
1351	20c. Meeting of American and Soviet soldiers at River Elbe	80	50
1352	25c. Pres. Roosevelt's funeral cortege	80	35
1353	60c. U.S. bugler sounding cease-fire	1·50	1·25
1354	80c. U.S. sailor kissing nurse, New York	1·75	1·75
1355	$1 Nuremburg Trials	2·00	2·25
1349/55 Set of 7		7·50	6·50
MS1356 104×74 mm. $2 Fireworks over Allied capitals		3·50	4·00

243 William James Scuba, 1825

(Des L. Birmingham. Litho Questa)

1995 (1 Sept). "Singapore '95" International Stamp Exhibition. Deep Sea Diving T **243** and similar horiz designs. Multicoloured. P 14×14½.
1357	60c. Type **243**	1·50	1·50
	a. Sheetlet. Nos. 1357/65	12·00	12·00
1358	60c. Rouquayrol apparatus 1864	1·50	1·50
1359	60c. Fluess oxygen-rebreathing apparatus, 1878	1·50	1·50

TURKS AND CAICOS ISLANDS

1360	60c. Armoured diving suit, 1900	1·50	1·50
1361	60c. Diving on the *Lusiania* in Peress armoured diving suit, 1935	1·50	1·50
1362	60c. Cousteau Gagnan aqualung, 1943	1·50	1·50
1363	60c. Underwater camera, 1955	1·50	1·50
1364	60c. Sylvia Earle's record dive, 1979	1·50	1·50
1365	60c. Spider propeller-driven rigid suit, 1984	1·50	1·50
1357/65 Set of 9		12·00	12·00
MS1366 Two sheets, each 107×77 mm. (a) $2 Helmet diver, 1935. (b) $2 Jacques-Yves Cousteau (aqualung pioneer) *Set of 2 sheets*		6·00	6·50

Nos. 1357/65 were printed together, *se-tenant*, in sheetlets of 9.

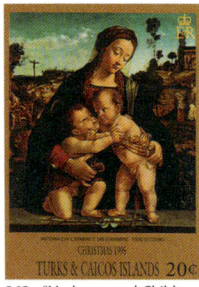

243a "Madonna and Child with St. Giovannino"

(Litho Questa)

1995 (29 Dec). Christmas. Religious Paintings by Piero di Cosimo. T **243a** and similar vert designs. Multicoloured. P 13½×14.

1367	20c. Type **243a**	1·25	50
1368	25c. "Adoration of the Child"	1·25	50
1369	60c. "Madonna and Child with St. Giovannino, St. Margherita and Angel"	2·50	1·25
1370	$1 "Madonna and Child with Angel"	2·75	3·25
1367/70 Set of 4		7·00	5·00
MS1371 76×106 mm. $2 "Madonna and Child with Angels and Saints" (detail)		7·50	8·50

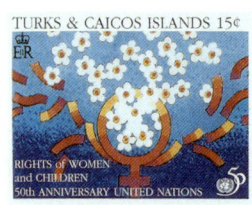

244 Daisies and Female Symbol ("Rights of Women and Children")

(Litho Questa)

1996 (26 Feb). 50th Anniv of the United Nations. T **244** and similar horiz designs. Multicoloured. P 14×13½.

1372	15c. Type **244**	40	25
1373	60c. Peace dove escaping from prison	1·10	1·00
1374	80c. Symbolic candles ("Human Rights")	1·40	1·60
1375	$1 People on open book	1·75	2·00
1372/5 Set of 4		4·25	4·25
MS1376 107×78 mm. $2 National flags forming "50"		3·25	4·25

245 Farmer on Tractor

(Litho Questa)

1996 (26 Feb). 50th Anniv of Food and Agriculture Organization. Sheet 111×80 mm. P 14×13½.
MS1377 **245** $2 multicoloured .... 2·40 3·00

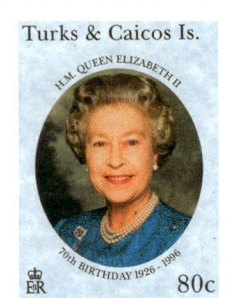

245a Queen Elizabeth II

(Litho Questa)

1996 (21 Apr). 70th Birthday of Queen Elizabeth II. T **245a** and similar vert designs. Multicoloured. P 13½×14.

1378	80c. Type **245a**	1·25	1·40
	a. Strip of 3. Nos. 1378/80	3·25	3·75
1379	80c. In blue coat and hat	1·25	1·40
1380	80c. At Trooping the Colour	1·25	1·40
1378/80 Set of 3		3·25	3·75
MS1381 125×104 mm. $2 In yellow dress and hat		3·75	4·00

Nos. 1378/80 were printed together, *se-tenant*, in horizontal or vertical strips of 3 throughout the sheet.

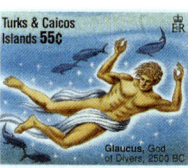

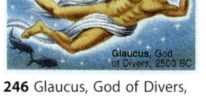

246 Glaucus, God of Divers, 2500 B.C.

247 Show Jumping

(Des L. Birmingham. Litho Questa)

1996 (13 May). "China '96" Asian International Philatelic Exhibition, Beijing. Underwater Exploration (1st series). T **246** and similar horiz designs. Multicoloured. P 14×14½.

1382	55c. Type **246**	1·40	1·40
	a. Sheetlet. Nos. 1382/90	11·00	11·00
1383	55c. Alexander the Great, 332 B.C	1·40	1·40
1384	55c. Salvage diver, 1430	1·40	1·40
1385	55c. Borelli's rebreathing device, 1680	1·40	1·40
1386	55c. Edmund Halley's diving bell, 1690	1·40	1·40
1387	55c. John Lethbridge's diving machine, 1715	1·40	1·40
1388	55c. Klingert's diving apparatus, 1789	1·40	1·40
1389	55c. Drieberg's triton, 1808	1·40	1·40
1390	55c. Seibe's diving helmet, 1819	1·40	1·40
1382/90 Set of 9		11·00	11·00
MS1391 Two sheets, each 102×77 mm. (a) $2 12th-century Arab diver. (b) $2 Caribbean pearl diver, 1498 *Set of 2 sheets*		8·00	8·50

Nos. 1382/90 were printed together, *se-tenant*, in sheetlets of 9. See also Nos. 1392/1401 and 1460/9.

(Des L. Birmingham. Litho Questa)

1996 (13 May). "Capex '96" World Stamp Exhibition, Toronto. Underwater Exploration (2nd series). Multicoloured designs as T **246**. P 14×14½.

1392	60c. Jim Jarrat exploring *Lusitania*, 1935	1·00	1·00
	a. Sheetlet. Nos. 1392/1400	8·00	8·00
1393	60c. Cousteau's first use of scuba gear for exploration, 1952	1·00	1·00
1394	60c. Discovery of oldest shipwreck, 1959	1·00	1·00
1395	60c. Raising of the *Vasa*, 1961	1·00	1·00
1396	60c. Mel Fisher discovering *Atocha*, 1971	1·00	1·00
1397	60c. Barry Clifford discovering *Whydah*, 1984	1·00	1·00
1398	60c. Argo robot over the *Bismarck*, 1989	1·00	1·00
1399	60c. Discovery of *Land Tortoise* in Lake George, New York, 1991	1·00	1·00
1400	60c. Nuclear submarine recovering artefacts from Roman shipwreck, 1994	1·00	1·00
1392/1400 Set of 9		8·00	8·00
MS1401 Two sheets, each 102×77 mm. (a) $2 Diver investigates the *Edmund Fitzgerald*. (b) $2 *Alvin* exploring the *Titanic Set of 2 sheets*		5·50	7·00

Nos. 1392/1400 were printed together, *se-tenant*, in sheetlets of 9.

168

TURKS AND CAICOS ISLANDS

(Litho Questa)

1996 (27 May). Olympic Games, Atlanta. T **247** and similar vert designs showing sports on medals. Multicoloured. P 13½×14.

1402	55c. Type **247**	90	1·00
	a. Sheetlet. Nos. 1402/11	8·00	9·00
1403	55c. Cycling	90	1·00
1404	55c. Fencing	90	1·00
1405	55c. Gymnastics	90	1·00
1406	55c. Pole vaulting	90	1·00
1407	55c. Sprinting	90	1·00
1408	55c. Swimming	90	1·00
1409	55c. Diving	90	1·00
1410	55c. Hurdling	90	1·00
1411	55c. Long-distance running	90	1·00
1402/11 Set of 10		8·00	9·00

Nos. 1402/11 were printed in individual sheets of each design and, *se-tenant*, as a sheetlet of 10.

248 James McCartney (First Chief Minister)

249 Space Dog

1996 (8 July). 20th Anniv of Ministerial Government. Litho. P 14.
1412 **248** 60c. multicoloured 70 75

No. 1412 was printed in sheetlets of 9 with a large illustrated margin at right.

(Des Mary Walters. Litho Questa)

1996 (8 Sept). Working Dogs. T **249** and similar vert designs. Multicoloured. P 14.

1413	25c. Type **249**	70	70
	a. Sheetlet. Nos. 1413/24	7·50	7·50
1414	25c. Greyhound	70	70
1415	25c. St. Bernard	70	70
1416	25c. Dog with medals	70	70
1417	25c. Retriever	70	70
1418	25c. Dog with bone	70	70
1419	25c. "Hearing ear" dog	70	70
1420	25c. Husky	70	70
1421	25c. Police Alsatian	70	70
1422	25c. Guard dog	70	70
1423	25c. Boxer	70	70
1424	25c. Sniffer dog	70	70
1413/24 Set of 12		7·50	7·50

MS1425 Two sheets, each 106×76 mm. (a) $2 Labrador guide dog. (b) $2 Border sheep dog *Set of 2 sheets* ... 11·00 11·00

Nos. 1413/24 were printed together, *se-tenant*, in sheetlets of 12.

250 Winnie the Pooh asleep in Chair

251 Giant Milkweed

1996 (25 Nov). Christmas. Winnie the Pooh. T **250** and similar vert designs. Multicoloured. Litho. P 13½×14.

1426	15c. Type **250**	80	40
1427	20c. Piglet holding star decoration	80	40
1428	35c. Tigger carrying presents	1·00	55
1429	50c. Pooh, Tigger and Piglet singing carols	1·40	80
1430	60c. Winnie and Rabbit	1·60	1·10
1431	80c. Tigger and Roo	2·25	1·75
1432	$1 Santa Pooh filling stockings	2·50	2·25
1433	$1.25 Christopher Robin and Winnie the Pooh	2·75	3·50
1426/33 Set of 8		12·00	9·75

MS1434 Two sheets. (a) 124×98 mm. $2 Piglet decorating biscuits. (b) 98×124 mm. $2.60, Piglet placing star on tree *Set of 2 sheets* .... 12·00 11·00

1997 (10 Feb). Flowers. T **251** and similar vert designs. Multicoloured. Litho. P 14.

1435	20c. Type **251**	55	65
	a. Sheetlet. Nos. 1435/8, each×2	4·00	4·75
1436	20c. Geiger Tree	55	65
1437	20c. Passion Flower	55	65
1438	20c. Hibiscus	55	65
1439	60c. Yellow Elder	80	90
	a. Sheetlet. Nos. 1439/42, each×2	6·00	6·50
1440	60c. Prickly Poppy	80	90
1441	60c. Frangipani	80	90
1442	60c. Seaside Mahoe	80	90
1435/42 Set of 8		4·75	5·50

MS1443 Two sheets, each 105×76 mm. (a) $2 Firecracker. (b) $2 Chain of Love *Set of 2 sheets* .... 5·50 6·50

Nos. 1435/8 and 1439/42 were each printed together, *se-tenant*, in sheetlets of 8 containing two of each design.

252 Canterbury Cathedral Tower

(Litho Questa)

1997 (24 Mar). 50th Anniv of U.N.E.S.C.O. Two sheets, each 127×102 mm, containing T **252** and similar horiz design. Multicoloured. P 14×13½.

MS1444 (a) $2 Type **252**; (b) $2 High Altar, Canterbury Cathedral *Set of 2 sheets* .... 5·50 6·50

The miniature sheets of No. **MS**1444 are inscribed "CATHREDRAL" in error.

253 White Dove (face value at right)

253a Queen Elizabeth II

1997 (24 Mar). 50th Anniv of U.N.I.C.E.F. T **253** and similar vert designs. Multicoloured. P 14.

1445	60c. Type **253**	1·50	1·75
	a. Sheetlet. Nos. 1445/8	5·50	6·25
1446	60c. White dove (with face value at left)	1·50	1·75
1447	60c. Three children	1·50	1·75
1448	60c. Two children with pets	1·50	1·75
1445/8 Set of 4		5·50	6·25

Nos. 1445/8 were printed together, *se-tenant*, in sheetlets of 4.

(Litho Questa)

1997 (21 Apr). Golden Wedding of Queen Elizabeth and Prince Philip. T **253a** and similar horiz designs. Multicoloured. P 14.

1449	60c. Type **253a**	1·75	1·50
	a. Sheetlet. Nos. 1449/54	9·50	8·00
1450	60c. Royal coat of arms	1·75	1·50
1451	60c. Queen Elizabeth and Prince Philip in carriage	1·75	1·50
1452	60c. Queen Elizabeth and Prince Philip on royal visit	1·75	1·50
1453	60c. Windsor Castle	1·75	1·50
1454	60c. Prince Philip	1·75	1·50
1449/54 Set of 6		9·50	8·00

MS1455 100×70 mm. $2 Princess Elizabeth and Duke of Edinburgh on wedding day .... 5·50 6·00

Nos. 1449/54 were printed together, *se-tenant*, in sheetlets of 6.

169

TURKS AND CAICOS ISLANDS

253b Britain Mail Coach, 1700s

(Des J. Iskowitz. Litho Questa)

1997 (1 July). "Pacific '97" International Stamp Exhibition, San Francisco. Death Centenary of Heinrich von Stephan (founder of the U.P.U.). T **253b** and similar horiz designs. P 14.

1456	50c. mauve	85	1·25
	a. Sheetlet. Nos. 1456/8	2·25	3·25
1457	50c. chestnut	85	1·25
1458	50c. deep blue	85	1·25
1456/8 Set of 3		2·25	3·25
MS1459 80×117 mm. $2 bright mauve and black		2·75	3·50

Designs:—No. 1457, Von Stephan and Mercury; No. 1458, Space Shuttle; No. **MS**1459, Von Stephan and Ancient Greek messenger.

Nos. 1456/8 were printed together, *se-tenant*, in sheets of 3 with enlarged right-hand margin.

1997 (21 Aug). "STAMPSHOW '97" 111th Annual A.P.S. Convention, Milwaukee. Underwater Exploration (3rd series). Horiz designs as T **246**. Multicoloured. Litho. P 14×13½.

1460	20c. Edgerton underwater camera, 1954	50	60
	a. Sheetlet. Nos. 1460/8	4·00	4·75
1461	20c. Conshelf Habitat, 1963	50	60
1462	20c. Sealab II, 1965	50	60
1463	20c. Research Habitat Tektite, 1970	50	60
1464	20c. Galapagos Volcanic rift, 1974	50	60
1465	20c. Epaulard robot survey craft, 1979	50	60
1466	20c. Underwater sealife, 1995	50	60
1467	20c. One-man research vessel, 1996	50	60
1468	20c. Okhotsk Tower, Japan, 1996	50	60
1460/8 Set of 9		4·00	4·75
MS1469 Two sheets, each 72×103 mm. (a) $2 Coelacanth. (b) $2 John Williamson making underwater movie. P 14×14½ Set of 2 sheets		6·00	7·00

Nos. 1460/8 were printed together, *se-tenant*, in sheetlets of 9.

254 "Adoration of an Angel" (detail) (studio of Fra Angelico)

255 Black-finned Snapper

(Litho Questa)

1997 (8 Dec). Christmas. Religious Paintings. T **254** and similar vert designs. Multicoloured. P 13½×14.

1470	15c. Type **254**	35	25
1471	20c. "Scenes from the life of St. John the Baptist" (detail) (Master of Saint Severin)	40	30
1472	35c. "Archangel Gabriel" (Masolino de Panicale)	65	45
1473	50c. "Jeremiah with two Angels" (detail) (Gherardo Starnina)	85	65
1474	60c. "Jeremiah with Two Angels" (different detail) (Starnina)	95	75
1475	80c. "The Annunciation" (detail) (Giovanni di Palo di Grazia)	1·25	1·40
1476	$1 "The Annunciation" (detail) (Carlo di Braccesco)	1·40	1·50
1477	$1.25 "The Nativity" (detail) (Benvenuto di Giovanni Guasta)	1·75	2·50
1470/7 Set of 8		7·00	7·00
MS1478 Two sheets. (a) 130×105 mm. $2 "The Journey of the Magi" (detail) (Benozzo Gozzoli). (b) 105×130 mm. $2 "The Wilton Diptych" (right panel) (anon) Set of 2 sheets		6·00	7·00

(Des H. Friedman. Litho)

1998 (24 Feb). Endangered Species. International Year of the Reef: Fishes. T **255** and similar horiz designs. Multicoloured. P 14.

1479	25c. Type **255**	55	65
	a. Block of 4. Nos. 1479/82	2·00	2·40
1480	25c. Dog Snapper	55	65
1481	25c. Cubera Snapper	55	65
1482	25c. Mahogany Snapper	55	65
1479/82 Set of 4		2·00	2·40

Nos. 1479/82 were printed together, *se-tenant*, in blocks of 4 throughout the sheet.

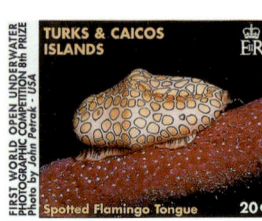

256 Spotted Flamingo Tongue (John Petrak)

257 Bird and Logo

(Litho B.D.T.)

1998 (1 May). First World Open Underwater Photographic Competition Prizewinners (1997). T **256** and similar horiz designs. Multicoloured. P 14.

1483	20c. Type **256**	40	35
1484	50c. Feather Duster (Dave Bothwell)	80	75
1485	60c. Squirrel Fish (Waldermar Seifert)	95	90
1486	80c. Queen Angelfish (Ralph Oberlander)	1·25	1·40
1487	$1 Barracuda (Steve Rosenburg)	1·50	1·60
1488	$1.25 Royal Gramma ("Fairy Basslet") (John Petrak)	1·90	2·25
1483/8 Set of 6		6·00	6·50
MS1489 Two sheets, each 148×85 mm. (a) $2 Spotted Cleaning Shrimp (Michael Boyer). (b) $2 Rough File Clam (Steve Rosenburg) Set of 2 sheets		6·00	7·00

1998 (30 July). International Year of the Ocean. T **257** and similar vert designs. Multicoloured. Litho. P 14.

1490	50c. Type **257**	1·00	1·10
	a. Sheetlet. Nos. 1490/3	3·50	4·00
1491	50c. Stylized crab	1·00	1·10
1492	50c. Fish	1·00	1·10
1493	50c. Logo in cloverleaf	1·00	1·10
1490/3 Set of 4		3·50	4·00
MS1494 102×71 mm. $2 Ocean and globe logo		3·50	4·00

Nos. 1490/3 were printed together, *se-tenant*, in sheetlets of 4.

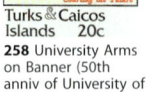

258 University Arms on Banner (50th anniv of University of West Indies)

259 S.E. 5A Aircraft

(Des L. Fried. Litho Questa)

1998 (30 July). Anniversaries and Events. T **258** and similar vert designs. Multicoloured. P 14.

1495	20c. Type **258**	40	35
1496	60c. Global logo (U.N.E.S.C.O. World Solar Energy Programme Summit)	1·00	1·00
1497	80c. Flame (50th anniv of Universal Declaration of Human Rights)	1·25	1·50
1498	$1 John Glenn (astronaut) (second space flight)	2·00	2·00
1495/8 Set of 4		4·25	4·25
MS1499 100×72 mm. $2 Space shuttle (John Glenn's second space flight)		3·50	3·75

(Des K. Gromell. Litho Questa)

1998 (18 Aug). 80th Anniv of Royal Air Force. T **259** and similar horiz designs. Multicoloured. P 14.

1500	20c. Type **259**	1·25	55

170

TURKS AND CAICOS ISLANDS

1501	50c. Sopwith Camel	1·75	1·10
1502	60c. Supermarine Spitfire	1·75	1·40
1503	80c. Avro Lancaster	2·25	2·00
1504	$1 Panavia Tornado	2·50	2·25
1505	$1.25 Hawker Hurricane	2·75	3·50
1500/5 Set of 6		11·00	9·75

MS1506 Two sheets, each 110×80 mm. (a) $2 Hawker Siddley Harrier. (b) $2 Avro Vulcan *Set of 2 sheets*...... 11·00 11·00

260 Diana, Princess of Wales

261 "Magi's Visit"

(Des D. Miller. Litho Questa)

1998 (31 Aug). 1st Death Anniv of Diana, Princess of Wales. P 14.

1507	**260**	60c. multicoloured	1·50	1·25
		a. Sheetlet of 6	8·00	

No. 1507 was printed in sheetlets of 6 with a large illustrated margin at right.

(Des Rosemary DeFiglio. Litho Questa)

1998 (30 Nov). Christmas. Paintings by Thomasita Fessler. T **261** and similar multicoloured designs. P 14.

1508	50c. Type **261**	1·10	1·25
	a. Sheetlet. Nos. 1508/13	6·00	6·50
1509	50c. "Flight into Egypt"	1·10	1·25
1510	50c. "Wedding Feast"	1·10	1·25
1511	50c. "Maria"	1·10	1·25
1512	50c. Annunciation and Visitation" (57×46 mm)	1·10	1·25
1513	50c. Nativity" (57×46 mm)	1·10	1·25
1508/13 Set of 6		6·00	6·50

MS1514 105×130 mm. $2 "Queen of Mothers"................ 3·25 3·75

Nos. 1508/13 were printed together, *se-tenant*, in sheetlets of 6.

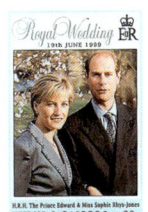

262 Flamingos

263 Prince Edward and Miss Sophie Rhys-Jones

(Des L. Birmingham. Litho)

1999 (7 June). Marine Life. T **262** and similar horiz designs. Multicoloured. P 14½.

1515	20c. Type **262**	80	80
	a. Sheetlet. Nos. 1515/38	17·00	17·00
1516	20c. Sailing dinghies	80	80
1517	20c. Seagulls and lighthouse	80	80
1518	20c. House on beach	80	80
1519	20c. Yellowtail Snapper and Pillar Coral	80	80
1520	20c. Yellowtail Snapper and Elliptical Star Coral	80	80
1521	20c. Porkfish	80	80
1522	20c. Spotted Eagle Ray	80	80
1523	20c. Large Ivory Coral	80	80
1524	20c. Shy Hamlet and Mustard Hill Coral	80	80
1525	20c. Blue Crust Coral	80	80
1526	20c. Fused Staghorn Coral	80	80
1527	20c. Queen Angelfish and Massive Starlet Coral	80	80
1528	20c. Pinnate Spiny Sea Fan	80	80
1529	20c. Knobby Star Coral	80	80
1530	20c. Lowridge Cactus Coral	80	80
1531	20c. Orange Telesto Coral	80	80
1532	20c. Spanish Hogfish and Knobby Ten-Ray Star Coral	80	80
1533	20c. Clown Wrasse and Boulder Brain Coral	80	80
1534	20c. Rainbow Parrotfish and Regal Sea Fan	80	80
1535	20c. Bluestriped Grunt and Great Star Coral	80	80
1536	20c. Blue Tang and Stinging Coral	80	80
1537	20c. Lavender Thin Finger Coral	80	80
1538	20c. Juvenile French Grunt and Brilliant Sea Fingers	80	80
1515/38 Set of 24		17·00	17·00

MS1539 Two sheets, each 100×70 mm. (a) $2 Elkhorn Coral. (b) $2 Sea Fan *Set of 2 sheets* .... 13·00 14·00

Nos. 1515/38 were printed together, *se-tenant*, in sheetlets of 24, with the backgrounds forming a composite design.

No. 1520 is inscribed "ELIPTICAL STAR CORAL" in error.

1999 (19 June). Royal Wedding. T **263** and similar vert designs. Multicoloured. Litho. P 14.

1540	60c. Type **263**	1·40	1·40
	a. Sheetlet. Nos. 1540/3	5·00	5·00
1541	60c. Prince Edward	1·40	1·40
1542	60c. Miss Sophie Rhys-Jones	1·40	1·40
1543	60c. Prince Edward and Miss Sophie Rhys-Jones (*different*)	1·40	1·40
1540/3 Set of 4		5·00	5·00

MS1544 Two sheets, each 76×60 mm. (a) $2 Prince Edward and Miss Sophie Rhys-Jones in front of building. (b) $2 Prince Edward and Miss Sophie Rhys-Jones in front of tree *Set of 2 sheets* .... 7·50 8·50

Nos. 1540/3 were printed together, *se-tenant*, in sheetlets of 4 with an enlarged illustrated left-hand margin.

264 Lady Elizabeth Bowes-Lyon, 1907

265 Peacock Flounder (M. Lynn)

(Litho Questa)

1999 (4 Aug)–**2002**. Queen Elizabeth the Queen Mothers's 99th Birthday. T **264** and similar vert designs. Multicoloured. P 13½×14.

1545	50c. Type **264**	1·40	1·40
	a. Sheetlet. Nos. 1545/54	12·00	12·00
	ab. Sheetlet. Nos. 1545/54 with additional marginal inscription (4.3.02)	12·00	12·00
1546	50c. Lady Elizabeth Bowes-Lyon, 1919	1·40	1·40
1547	50c. On wedding day, 1923	1·40	1·40
1548	50c. With Princess Elizabeth and Margaret, 1936	1·40	1·40
1549	50c. King George VI and Queen Elizabeth during Second World War	1·40	1·40
1550	50c. Queen Elizabeth the Queen Mother, 1958	1·40	1·40
1551	50c. Wearing blue outfit, 1960	1·40	1·40
1552	50c. Wearing floral dress, 1970	1·40	1·40
1553	50c. With prices Charles and William, 1983	1·40	1·40
1554	50c. Queen Mother, 1999	1·40	1·40
1545/54 Set of 10		12·00	12·00

Nos. 1545/54 were printed together, *se-tenant*, in sheetlets of 10 with illustrated margins. The sheetlet was re-issued in 2002 additionally inscribed "Good Health and Happiness to Her Majesty the Queen Mother on her 101st Birthday".

No. 1549 is inscribed "GEORGE IV" in error.

(Des J. Corbett. Litho Questa)

1999 (11 Nov)–**2000**. Winning Entries from Second World Open Underwater Photographic Competition. T **265** and similar horiz designs. Multicoloured. P 14½×14.

1555	10c. Type **265** (inscr "Painted Tunicates (S. Genkins)" in error)	40	60
	a. Sheetlet. Nos. 1555/60	7·00	8·25
1555b	10c. Painted Tunicates (S. Genkins) (6.11.00)	40	60
	ba. Sheetlet. Nos. 1555b/6b and 1557/60	7·00	8·25
1556	20c. Painted Tunicates (S. Genkins) (inscr "Peacock Flounder (M. Lynn)" in error)	60	70
1556b	20c. Type **265** (6.11.00)	60	70
1557	50c. Squat Anemone Shrimps (M. Boyer)	1·25	1·40
1558	60c. Juvenile Drum (N. Army)	1·40	1·50
1559	80c. Batwing Coral Crab (R. Jarnutowski)	1·60	1·75
1560	$1 Moon Jellyfish (R. Kaufman)	1·75	1·90
1555/60 Set of 8		7·00	8·25

TURKS AND CAICOS ISLANDS

MS1561 Two sheets, each 85×68 mm. (a) $2 Christmas Tree Worms (B. Joubert) (48½×36 mm). (b) $2 Longhorn Nudibranch (Trina Lochlear) (48½×36 mm). P 14×13½ Set of 2 sheets .... 12·00 12·00

Nos. 1555/60 were printed together, *se-tenant*, in sheetlets of 6. On the original printing the captions of the 10c. and 20c. were transposed in error. A further printing, issued 6 November 2000, showed them corrected.

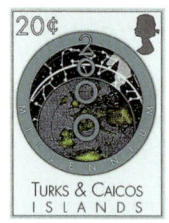

266 Constellations over Earth and "2000"

(Des A. Pichkhadze. Litho Questa)

1999 (15 Nov). New Millennium. T **266** and similar vert designs. Multicoloured. P 14½ (20c., $1) or 14×13½ (50c.).

1562	20c. Type **266**...	1·00	65
1563	50c. Big Ben, London (30×47 mm).............	2·25	2·00
	a. Sheetlet. Nos. 1563/8..........................	12·00	11·00
1564	50c. Flamingo, Turks and Caicos Islands (30×47 mm)...	2·25	2·00
1565	50c. Empire State Building, New York (30×47 mm)...	2·25	2·00
1566	50c. Coliseum, Rome (30×47 mm)............	2·25	2·00
1567	50c. Dome of the Rock, Jerusalem (30×47 mm)...	2·25	2·00
1568	50c. Eiffel Tower, Paris (30×47 mm)..........	2·25	2·00
1569	$1 Type **266**...	2·25	2·25
1552/9 Set of 8..	15·00	13·00

MS1570 Two sheets, each 106×86 mm. (a) $2 Part of globe and Turks and Caicos Islands flag (30×47 mm). (b) $2 Part of globe and Turks and Caicos Islands coat of arms (30×47 mm). P 14×13½ Set of 2 sheets............. 14·00 15·00

Nos. 1563/8 were printed together, *se-tenant*, in sheetlets of 6 with each design incorporating a clock face together with a map of the country depicted.

267 "The Mystic Marriage of St. Catherine" (Anthony Van Dyck)

(Litho Questa)

1999 (7 Dec). Christmas. T **267** and similar vert designs. Multicoloured. P 13½×14.

1571	20c. Type **267**...	1·00	35
1572	50c. "Rest on the Flight into Egypt".........	1·75	75
1573	$2 "Holy Family with Saints John and Elizabeth"...	5·50	6·50
1571/3 Set of 3...	7·50	7·00

MS1574 102×122 mm. $2 "The Madonna of the Rosary" ... 6·50 7·50
No. 1571 is inscribed "Marrige" in error.

268 *Pholiota squarroides*

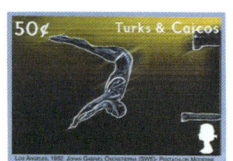

268a Johan Oxenstierna (Swedish swimmer), 1932

(Des Shelley Slick. Litho Questa)

2000 (6 July). Fungi. T **268** and similar multicoloured designs. P 14.

1575	50c. Type **268**...	1·40	1·40
	a. Sheetlet. Nos. 1565/70......................	7·50	7·50
1576	50c. *Psilocybe squmosa*.........................	1·40	1·40
1577	50c. *Spathularia velutipes*.....................	1·40	1·40
1578	50c. *Russula*..	1·40	1·40
1579	50c. *Clitocybe clavipes*..........................	1·40	1·40
1580	50c. *Boletus frostii*.................................	1·40	1·40
1575/80 Set of 6..	7·50	7·50

MS1581 Two sheets, each 108×71 mm. (a) $2 *Strobilurus conigenoides* (horiz). (b) $2 *Stereum astrea* (horiz) Set of 2 sheets.. 8·50 9·00

Nos. 1575/80 were printed together, *se-tenant*, in a sheetlet of 6 with the background forming a composite design and an enlarged illustrated right margin.

(Lithe B.D.T)

2000 (25 Sept). Olympic Games, Sydney. T **268a** and similar horiz designs. Multicoloured. P 14.

1582	50c. Type **268a**...	1·75	1·75
	a. Sheetlet. Nos. 1572/5.........................	6·25	6·25
1583	50c. Javelin...	1·75	1·75
1584	50c. Aztec Stadium, Mexico City, 1968, and Mexican flag....................................	1·75	1·75
1585	50c. Ancient Greek long-distance running..	1·75	1·75
1582/5 Set of 4..	6·25	6·25

Nos. 1572/5 were printed together, *se-tenant*, in sheetlets of 4 (2×2), with the horizontal rows separated by a gutter margin showing Sydney Opera House and athlete with Olympic Torch.

269 Scrub Turkey

(Litho Questa)

2000 (2 Oct). Caribbean Birds. T **269** and similar multicoloured designs. P 14.

1586	50c. Type **269**...	1·50	1·50
1587	50c. Sickle Bill Gull...................................	1·50	1·50
1588	50c. Chickadee...	1·50	1·50
1589	60c. Egret..	1·50	1·50
	a. Sheetlet. Nos. 1589/94......................	8·00	8·00
1590	60c. Tern...	1·50	1·50
1591	60c. Osprey...	1·50	1·50
1592	60c. Great Blue Heron..............................	1·50	1·50
1593	60c. Pelican..	1·50	1·50
1594	60c. Bahama Pintail.................................	1·50	1·50
1586/94 Set of 9...	12·00	12·00

MS1595 Two sheets, each 95×82 mm. (a) $2 Flamingo (vert). (b) $2 Macaw (vert) Set of 2 sheets................. 10·00 11·00

Nos. 1589/94 were printed together, *se-tenant*, in sheetlets of 6 with enlarged inscribed margins.

270 Airedale Terrier

(Litho Questa)

2000 (13 Nov). Cats and Dogs of the World. T **270** and similar horiz designs. Multicoloured. P 14.

1596	60c. Type **270**...	1·40	1·50
	a. Sheetlet. Nos. 1596/1601..................	7·50	8·00
1597	60c. Beagle...	1·40	1·50
1598	60c. Dalmatian...	1·40	1·50
1599	60c. Chow Chow......................................	1·40	1·50
1600	60c. Chihuahua..	1·40	1·50
1601	60c. Pug..	1·40	1·50
1602	80c. Egyptian Mau....................................	1·40	1·50
	a. Sheetlet. Nos. 1602/7.........................	8·00	8·50
1603	80c. Manx...	1·50	1·60
1604	80c. Burmese...	1·50	1·60

TURKS AND CAICOS ISLANDS

1605	80c. Korat	1·50	1·60
1606	80c. Maine Coon	1·50	1·60
1607	80c. American Shorthair	1·50	1·60
1596/1607	Set of 12	15·00	17·00

MS1608 Two sheets, each 95×82 mm. (a) $2 Collie. (b) $2 Devon Rex *Set of 2 sheets* .... 9·00 10·00

Nos. 15896/1601 (dogs) and 1602/7 (cats) were each printed together, *se-tenant*, in sheetlets of 6 with enlarged inscribed margins.

271 Sir Winston Churchill

(Des J. Iskowitz. Litho Questa)

2000 (4 Dec). 60th Anniv of Battle of Britain. T **271** and similar horiz designs. Multicoloured (except No. **MS**1625(a)). P 14.

1609	50c. Type **271**	1·75	1·50
	a. Sheetlet. Nos. 1609/1616	12·50	11·00
1610	50c. Barrage balloon	1·75	1·50
1611	50c. Heinkel He-III/Casa 2 IIIE (fighter)	1·75	1·50
1612	50c. Saying goodbye to young evacuee	1·75	1·50
1613	50c. Hawker Hurricane (fighter)	1·75	1·50
1614	50c. Dr. Jocelyn Peakins (clergyman) in Home Guard	1·75	1·50
1615	50c. R.A.F squadron scramble	1·75	1·50
1616	50c. Members of Royal Observer Corps watching sky	1·75	1·50
1617	50c. James "Ginger" Lacey	1·75	1·50
1618	50c. Douglas Bader	1·75	1·50
1619	50c. Edgar "Cobber" Kain	1·75	1·50
1620	50c. Air Vice-Marshal Keith Park (commander, No. 11 Group)	1·75	1·50
1621	50c. James "Johnny" Johnson	1·75	1·50
1622	50c. Adolph "Sailor" Malan	1·75	1·50
1623	50c. Alan "Al" Deere	1·75	1·50
1624	50c. Air Vice-Marshal, Trafford Leigh-Mallory (commander, No. 12 group)	1·75	1·50
1609/1624	Set of 16	25·00	22·00

MS1625 Two sheets. (a) 86×136 mm. $2 Child evacuees (salmon-pink, grey and black). (b) 118×85 mm. $2 Winston Churchill, Union Jack and pilots *Set of 2 sheets* .... 10·00 10·00

Nos. 1609/1616 were printed together, *se-tenant*, in sheetlets of 8 with the two horizontal rows separated by a gutter margin onto which some of the illustrations continue.

Nos. 1617/24 were printed in sheets with each stamp accompanied by a *se-tenant* label showing R.A.F squadron scramble.

272 Giant Swallowtail

(Des T. Wood. Litho Questa)

2000 (11 Dec). Caribbean Butterflies. T **272** and similar horiz designs. Multicoloured. P 14.

1626	50c. Type **272**	1·60	1·60
	a. Sheetlet. Nos. 1626/31	8·50	8·50
1627	50c. Common Morpho	1·60	1·60
1628	50c. Tiger Pierid	1·60	1·60
1629	50c. Banded King Shoemaker	1·60	1·60
1630	50c. Figure-of-Eight Butterfly	1·60	1·60
1631	50c. Polydamas Swallowtail	1·60	1·60
1632	50c. Clorinde	1·60	1·60
	a. Sheetlet. Nos. 1632/7	8·50	8·50
1633	50c. Blue Night Butterfly	1·60	1·60
1634	50c. Small Lace-wing	1·60	1·60
1635	50c. Mosaic	1·60	1·60
1636	50c. Monarch	1·60	1·60
1637	50c. Grecian Shoemaker	1·60	1·60
1626/37	Set of 12	17·00	17·00

MS1638 Two sheets, each 68×98 mm. (a) $2 Orange-barred Sulphur. (b) $2 White Peacock *Set of 2 sheets* . 10·00 10·00

Nos. 1626/31 and 1632/7 were each printed together, *se-tenant*, in sheetlets of 6 with the backgrounds forming composite designs.

273 *Neptune* (sailing packet)

(Des G. Capasso. Litho Questa)

2001 (15 May). Sailing Ships of the World. T **273** and similar multicoloured designs. P 14.

1639	60c. Type **273**	2·00	1·75
1640	60c. American clipper (*vert*)	2·00	1·75
1641	60c. USCG *Eagle* (cadet barque)	2·00	1·75
1642	60c. *Gloria* (Colombian cadet ship)	2·00	1·75
1643	60c. Viking longship	2·00	1·75
	a. Sheetlet. Nos. 1643/8	11·00	9·50
1644	60c. *Henri Grace a Dieu* (English galleon)	2·00	1·75
1645	60c. *Golden Hind* (Drake)	2·00	1·75
1646	60c. HMS *Endeavour* (Cook)	2·00	1·75
1647	60c. Anglo-Norman (British barque)	2·00	1·75
1648	60c. *Libertad* (Argentine full-rigged cadet ship)	2·00	1·75
1649	60c. Northern European cog	2·00	1·75
	a. Sheetlet Nos. 1649/54	11·00	9·50
1650	60c. 16th-century carrack	2·00	1·75
1651	60c. *Mayflower* (Pilgrim Fathers)	2·00	1·75
1652	60c. *Queen Anne's Revenge* (Blackbeard)	2·00	1·75
1653	60c. *Holkar* (British barque)	2·00	1·75
1654	60c. *Amerigo Vespucci* (Italian cadet ship)	2·00	1·75
1639/54	Set of 16	29·00	25·00

MS1655 Two sheets, each 48×67 mm. (a) $2 USS *Constitution* (frigate) (*vert*). (b) $2 *Danmark* (full-rigged Danish cadet ship) (*vert*) *Set of 2 sheets* .... 12·00 13·00

Nos. 1643/8 and 1649/54 were each printed together, se-tenant, in sheetlets of stamps containing two separate vertical strips of 3. No 1642 is inscribed "*Columbia*" and No. 1648 "*Liberated*", both in error.

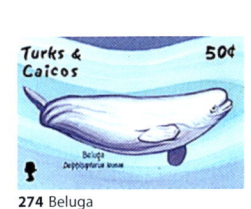

274 Beluga

274a "Caribbean Woman II"

(Des R. Martin. Litho Questa)

2001 (21 May). Whales and Dolphins. T **274** and similar horiz designs. Multicoloured. P 14.

1656	50c. Type **274**	1·75	1·75
1657	50c. Dwarf Sperm Whale	1·75	1·75
1658	50c. Killer Whale, swimming underwater	1·75	1·75
1659	50c. Shortfin Pilot Whale	1·75	1·75
1660	50c. Bowhead Whale	1·75	1·75
	a. Sheetlet. Nos. 1660/5	9·50	9·50
1661	50c. Two Killer Whales	1·75	1·75
1662	50c. Pygmy Sperm Whale	1·75	1·75
1663	50c. Right Whale	1·75	1·75
1664	50c. Sperm Whale with calf	1·75	1·75
1665	50c. California Grey Whale	1·75	1·75
1666	50c. Narwhal	1·75	1·75
	a. Sheetlet. Nos. 1666/71	9·50	9·50
1667	50c. Killer Whale leaping	1·75	1·75
1668	50c. Bryde's Whale	1·75	1·75
1669	50c. Two Belugas	1·75	1·75
1670	50c. Sperm Whale	1·75	1·75
1671	50c. Three Pilot Whales	1·75	1·75
1656/71	Set of 16	25·00	25·00

MS1672 Two sheets, each 92×69 mm. (a) $2 Humpback Whale and calf. (b) $2 Cuvier's Beaked Whale *Set of 2 sheets* .... 12·00 12·00

Nos. 1660/5 and 1666/71 were each printed together, *se-tenant*, in sheetlets of 6.

For a full range of Stanley Gibbons catalogues, please visit **www.stanleygibbons.com**

TURKS AND CAICOS ISLANDS

(Des Leisel Jobity. Litho Questa)
2001 (18 June). United Nations Women's Human Rights Campaign. T **274a** and similar vert designs. Multicoloured. P 14.
1673	60c. Type **274a**	2·00	2·00
1674	80c. Woman on beach	2·50	2·50

274b Queen Victoria

274c Queen Elizabeth

(Des R. Rundo. Litho Questa)
2001 (30 July). Death Centenary of Queen Victoria. T **274b** and similar vert designs. Multicoloured. P 14.
1675	60c. Type **274b**	1·90	1·90
	a. Sheetlet. Nos. 1675/8	7·00	7·00
1676	60c. As a girl in evening dress	1·90	1·90
1677	60c. Bare-headed	1·90	1·90
1678	60c. Wearing diadem	1·90	1·90
1679	60c. Holding fan	1·90	1·90
	a. Sheetlet. Nos. 1679/82	7·00	7·00
1680	60c. In Coronation robes (after Franz Winterhalter)	1·90	1·90
1681	60c. In carriage	1·90	1·90
1682	60c. As Empress of India	1·90	1·90
1675/82	*Set of 8*	14·00	14·00

MS1683 Two sheets, each 82×113 mm. (a) $2 Queen Victoria carrying umbrella. (b) $2 Wearing white hat and veil *Set of 2 sheets*............ 9·00 10·00

Nos. 1675/8 and 1679/82 were each printed together, *se-tenant*, in sheetlets of 4 with enlarged inscribed margins.

(Des J. Iskowitz. Litho Questa)
2001 (30 July). 75th Birthday of Queen Elizabeth II. T **274c** and similar vert designs. Multicoloured. P 14.
1684	60c. Type **274c**	1·75	1·60
	a. Sheetlet. Nos. 1684/9	9·50	8·50
1685	60c. Wearing tiara and evening dress	1·75	1·60
1686	60c. In green hat and coat	1·75	1·60
1687	60c. Wearing diadem and ruby necklace	1·75	1·60
1688	60c. In red hat and coat	1·75	1·60
1689	60c. Wearing tiara and veil	1·75	1·60
1684/9	*Set of 6*	9·50	8·50

MS1690 78×140 mm. $2 Queen Elizabeth in robes of the Order of the Bath........... 4·75 5·00

Nos. 1684/9 were printed together, *se-tenant*, in sheetlets of 6 with the two vertical rows of 3 separated by an enlarged gutter showing a further portrait.

275 "Rikaku II as a Fisherman" (Hirosada)

276 *Dismorphia cubana*

(Litho Walsall)
2001 (30 July). "Philanippon '01" International Stamp Exhibition, Tokyo. Japanese Art. T **275** and similar vert designs. Multicoloured. P 12×12½.
1691	60c. Type **275**	1·50	1·50
1692	60c. "Autumn Moon in Mirror" (Suzuki Harunobu)	1·50	1·50
1693	60c. "Musical Party" (Hishikawa Morunobu)	1·50	1·50
1694	60c. "Kannon and Four Farmers" (H. Gatto)	1·50	1·50
1695	60c. "Rain in Fifth Month" (I. Kunisada)	1·50	1·50
1696	60c. "The Lives of Women" (Utagawa Kuniyoshi)	1·50	1·50
1691/5	*Set of 6*	8·00	8·00

(Des R. Sauber)
2001 (27 Sept). Butterflies. T **276** and similar multicoloured designs. P 14½×15 (horiz) or 15×14½ (vert).

A. Litho Questa. Without imprint date
1697A	10c. Type **276**	65	65
1698A	15c. *Parides gundalachianus* (vert)	80	65
1699A	20c. *Graphium androcles*	1·00	75
1700A	25c. Eastern Black Swallowtail	2·50	1·00
1701A	35c. *Papilio velvois* (vert)	2·50	1·00
1702A	45c. Schaus Swallowtail (vert)	1·75	1·25
1703A	50c. Pipevine Swallowtail (vert)	1·75	1·25
1704A	60c. *Euploea mniszechii* (vert)	2·00	1·25
1705A	80c. *Papilio caiguanabus* (vert)	2·25	1·50
1706A	$1 *Graphium encelades* (vert)	2·75	2·75
1707A	$1.25 *Calisto zangis*	3·25	3·00
1708A	$1.40 Eastern Tiger Swallowtail	3·75	4·00
1709A	$2 *Graphium milon* (vert)	6·00	7·00
1710A	$5 Palamedes Swallowtail	12·00	14·00
1711A	$10 Zebra Swallowtail	20·00	23·00
1697A/711A	*Set of 15*	55·00	55·00

B. Litho DLR. With imprint date "2003" (15.7.03)
1700B	25c. Eastern Black Swallowtail	1·75	75
1701B	35c. *Papilio velvois* (vert)	1·75	75
1710B	$5 Palamedes Swallowtail	13·00	14·00
1711B	$10 Zebra Swallowtail	22·00	24·00
1700B/11B	*Set of 4*	35·00	35·00

No. 1704A is inscribed "MNISZECKI", in error.

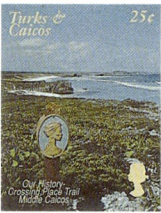

277 Crossing Place Trail Monument, Middle Caicos

2002 (1 June). Golden Jubilee. T **277** and similar designs. Multicoloured (except Nos. 1718/19). Litho. P 14½×14 (25c.), 14 (60c.) or 14×14½ (80c.).
1712	25c. Type **277**	80	80
	a. Sheetlet. Nos. 1712/17	4·25	4·25
1713	25c. Wades Green Plantation, North Caicos	80	80
1714	25c. Underwater scenery, Grand Turk	80	80
1715	25c. St. Thomas Anglican Church, Grand Turk	80	80
1716	25c. Ripsaw Band, Grand Turk	80	80
1717	25c. Basket weaving	80	80
1718	60c. Princess Mary with cannon, Grand Turk, 1960 (brownish black and gold)	1·75	1·75
	a. Sheetlet. Nos. 1718/22	8·00	8·00
1719	60c. Queen Elizabeth on South Caicos, 1966 (brownish black, gold and turquoise blue)	1·75	1·75
1720	60c. Princess Alexandra on Providenciales, 1988	1·75	1·75
1721	60c. Duke of Edinburgh on Grand Turk, 1998	1·75	1·75
1722	60c. Prince Andrew and aquarium, Grand Turk, 2000	1·75	1·75
1723	80c. Salt gathering, Salt Cay	2·00	2·00
	a. Sheetlet. Nos. 1723/7	9·00	9·00
1724	80c. Space capsule, Grand Turk	2·00	2·00
1725	80c. Legislative Council Chamber, Grand Turk	2·00	2·00
1726	80c. Map of Turks and Caicos Islands	2·00	2·00
1727	80c. National Museum, Grand Turk	2·00	2·00
1712/27	*Set of 16*	21·00	21·00

Nos. 1712/17 (29½×37 *mm*), 1718/22 (32×32 *mm*) and 1723/7 (29½×34 *mm*) were each printed together, *se-tenant*, in sheetlets of 5 or 6 with enlarged inscribed bottom margins.

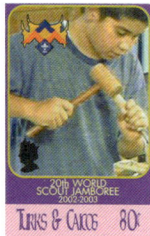

277a Scout Woodworking

277b Devil's Peak, South Africa

TURKS AND CAICOS ISLANDS

(Litho Questa)

2002 (15 July). 20th World Scout Jamboree, Thailand. T **277a** and similar vert designs. Multicoloured. P 14.

1728	80c. Type **277a**	1·75	1·75
	a. Sheetlet. Nos. 1728/31	6·25	6·25
1729	80c. Rifle shooting	1·75	1·75
1730	80c. Swinging over river	1·75	1·75
1731	80c. Scouts in tent at night	1·75	1·75
1728/31	*Set of 4*	6·25	6·25
MS1732	107×127 mm. $2 Disabled scouts playing football	4·25	4·50

Nos. 1728/31 were printed together, *se-tenant*, in sheetlets of 4 with enlarged illustrated left and bottom margins.

(Litho Questa)

2002 (27 July). International Year of Mountains. T **277b** and similar vert designs. Multicoloured. P 14.

1733	80c. Type **277b**	1·75	1·75
	a. Sheetlet. Nos. 1733/8	9·50	9·50
1734	80c. Drakensburg Mountains, South Africa	1·75	1·75
1735	80c. Mont Blanc, France	1·75	1·75
1736	80c. Roan Mountain, Tennessee, U.S.A.	1·75	1·75
1737	80c. Mount Sefton, New Zealand	1·75	1·75
1738	80c. Mount Cook, New Zealand	1·75	1·75
1733/8	*Set of 6*	9·50	9·50
MS1739	107×127 mm. $2 North-west Highlands, Scotland	4·25	4·50

Nos. 1733/8 were printed together, *se-tenant*, in sheetlets of 6 with an enlarged top margin.

277c Humpback Whale and Lighthouse

277d U.S. and Turks and Caicos Flags with Statue of Liberty's Torch

(Des R. Company. Litho Questa)

2002 (29 July). UN Year of Eco Tourism. T **277c** and similar multicoloured designs. P 14.

1740	60c. Type **277c**	1·75	1·75
	a. Sheetlet. Nos. 1740/5	9·50	9·50
1741	60c. Yacht	1·75	1·75
1742	60c. Two yachts racing	1·75	1·75
1743	60c. Queen Angelfish	1·75	1·75
1744	60c. Manta and tropical fish	1·75	1·75
1745	60c. Turtle with boy wearing snorkel	1·75	1·75
1740/5	*Set of 6*	9·50	9·50
MS1746	98×70 mm. $2 "Jojo" (Bottlenose Dolphin) (85×28 *mm*)	4·25	4·50

Nos. 1740/5 were printed together, *se-tenant*, in sheetlets of 6 forming a composite design.

2002 (5 Aug). "United We Stand". Support for Victims of 11 September 2001 Terrorist Attacks. Litho. P 14.

1747	**277d** 50c. multicoloured	1·60	1·60

No. 1747 was printed in sheetlets of four stamps with enlarged illustrated margins.

278 Sooty Tern

279 Duchess of York, 1923

(Des Dayna Elefant. Litho Questa)

2002 (12 Aug). Birds and Insects. T **278** and similar multicoloured designs. P 14.

1748	60c. Type **278**	2·00	1·75
	a. Sheetlet. Nos. 1748/53	11·00	9·50
1749	60c. Magnificent Frigatebird	2·00	1·75
1750	60c. American White Pelican	2·00	1·75
1751	60c. Northern Shoveler	2·00	1·75
1752	60c. Northern Oriole ("Baltimore Oriole")	2·00	1·75
1753	60c. Roseate Spoonbill	2·00	1·75
1754	60c. Hawk Moth	2·00	1·75
	a. Sheetlet. Nos. 1754/9	11·00	9·50
1755	60c. Burnet Moth	2·00	1·75
1756	60c. Mammoth Wasp	2·00	1·75
1757	60c. Branch-boring Beetle	2·00	1·75
1758	60c. Flower Mantid on leaf	2·00	1·75
1759	60c. Flower Mantid on tree trunk	2·00	1·75
1748/59	*Set of 12*	22·00	19·00
MS1760	Two sheets, each 95×93 mm. (a) $2 Greater Flamingo (*vert*). (b) $2 Tiphiid Wasp *Set of* 2 *sheets*	9·50	10·00

Nos. 1748/53 (birds) and 1754/9 (insects) were each printed together, *se-tenant*, in sheetlets of 6 with the backgrounds forming composite designs which extend onto the enlarged sheetlet margins. No. 1753 is inscribed "ROSTATE" in error.

(Des Akemi Etheridge. Litho Questa)

2002 (21 Oct). Queen Elizabeth the Queen Mother Commemoration. T **279** and similar vert design. Multicoloured. P 14.

1761	80c. Type **279**	2·00	1·75
	a. Sheetlet. Nos. 1761/2×2	7·25	6·25
1762	80c. Queen Elizabeth the Queen Mother on Remembrance Day	2·00	1·75

Nos. 1761/2 were printed together, *se-tenant*, in sheetlets of 4 containing two of each design with a further portrait in the enlarged left margin.

280 Charles Lindbergh as a Young Man

(Litho Questa)

2002 (18 Nov). 75th Anniv of First Solo Transatlantic Flight. T **280** and similar horiz designs. Multicoloured. P 14.

1763	60c. Type **280**	2·00	1·75
	a. Sheetlet. Nos. 1763/8	11·00	9·50
1764	60c. Lindbergh with *Spirit of St. Louis*	2·00	1·75
1765	60c. *Spirit of St. Louis*	2·00	1·75
1766	60c. *Spirit of St. Louis* taking off from Roosevelt Field	2·00	1·75
1767	60c. *Spirit of St. Louis* above Atlantic	2·00	1·75
1768	60c. Lindbergh in Paris	2·00	1·75
1763/8	*Set of 6*	11·00	9·50

Nos. 1763/8 were printed together, *se-tenant*, in sheetlets of 6, the two horizontal rows of three being separated by a large illustrated gutter.

281 John Kennedy as a Young Man

282 "Madonna and Child" (Giovanni Bellini)

(Litho Questa)

2002 (18 Nov). Pres John Kennedy Commemoration. T **281** and similar vert designs showing different portraits. Multicoloured, centre colours given. P 14.

1769	60c. chocolate (Type **281**)	1·75	1·75
	a. Sheetlet. Nos. 1769/74	9·50	9·50
1770	60c. deep mauve	1·75	1·75
1771	60c. olive-grey	1·75	1·75
1772	60c. deep ultramarine	1·75	1·75
1773	60c. bright violet	1·75	1·75
1774	60c. bistre-brown	1·75	1·75
1769/74	*Set of 6*	9·50	9·50

Nos. 1769/74 were printed together, *se-tenant*, in sheetlets of six, the two vertical rows of three being separated by a large gutter showing a further portrait.

TURKS AND CAICOS ISLANDS

(Litho Questa)

2002 (25 Nov). Christmas. Religious Paintings. T **282** and similar multicoloured designs. P 14.

1775	20c. Type **282**......................................	65	30
1776	25c. "Adoration of the Magi" (Antonio Correggio) (*horiz*)............................	70	35
1777	60c. "Transfiguration of Christ" (Bellini)......	1·75	1·00
1778	80c. "Polyptych of St. Vincent Ferrer" (Bellini)...	2·00	1·75
1779	$1 "Miraculous Mass" (Simone Martini)......	2·25	3·00
1775/9 Set of 5..		6·50	5·75
MS1780 90×125 $2 "Christ in Heaven with Four Saints" (Domenico Ghirlandaio) (*horiz*)....................		4·50	5·00

No. 1776 is inscribed "ADORATIO" in error.

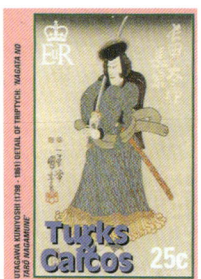

282a "Nagata no Tarō Nagamune" (detail) (Utagawa Kuniyoshi)

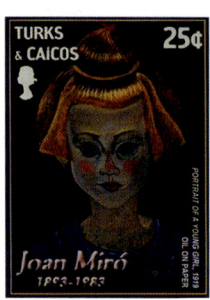

283 "Portrait of a Young Girl"

(Litho BDT)

2003 (16 June). Japanese Art. T **282a** and similar vert designs. Multicoloured. P 14.

1781	25c. Type **282a**.....................................	75	45
1782	35c. "Ichikawa Danjūro VII" (Utagawa Kunisada)...	85	45
1783	60c. "Nagata no Tarō Nagamune" (different detail) (Utagawa Kuniyoshi).............	1·60	1·25
1784	$1 "Nagata no Tarō Nagamune" (different detail) (Utagawa Kuniyoshi).............	2·25	3·00
1781/4 Set of 4..		5·00	4·75
MS1785 150×150 mm. 80c. Kabuki theatre actor (looking forwards); 80c. Actor with sword in mouth; 80c. Actor holding sword; 80c. Actor with red and yellow quilt..		6·00	7·00
MS1786 85×115 mm. $2 "Two Women by a River" (Hashimoto Chikanobu)......................................		4·25	4·50

Stamps from No. **MS**1785 all show details from "Scroll of Actors" by Toyohara Chikanobu et al.

(Litho BDT)

2003 (16 June). 20th Death Anniv of Joan Miró (artist). T **283** and similar multicoloured designs. P 14.

1787	25c. Type **283**......................................	75	50
1788	50c. "Table with Glove"............................	1·40	1·25
1789	60c. "Self-portrait, 1917".........................	1·60	1·40
1790	$1 "The Farmer's Wife"...........................	2·25	3·00
1787/90 Set of 4..		5·50	5·50
MS1791 200×135 mm. 80c. "Portrait of Ramon Sunyer"; 80c. "Self Portrait, 1919"; 80c. "Portrait of a Spanish Dancer"; 80c. "Portrait of Joana Obrador"..................		6·00	7·00
MS1792 Two sheets. (a) 83×104 mm. $2 "Flowers and Butterfly". Imperf. (b) 104×83 mm. $2 "Still Life of the Coffee Grinder". Imperf Set of 2 sheets....................		8·50	9·50

283a "Portrait of a Young Man resting his Chin on his Hand"

283b Union Flag, Flamingo and Emblem

(Litho BDT)

2003 (16 June). Rembrandt (artist) Commemoration. T **283a** and similar vert designs. Multicoloured. P 14.

1793	25c. Type **283a**......................................	75	40
1794	50c. "A Woman at an Open Door".............	1·25	75
1795	$1 "The Return of the Prodigal Son".........	2·25	3·00
1796	$1 "Portrait of an Elderly Man".................	2·25	3·00
1793/6 Set of 4..		6·00	6·25
MS1797 185×182 mm. 60c. "Nicolaas van Bambeeck"; 60c. "Agatha Bas, Wife of Nicolaas van Bambeeck"; 60c. "Portrait of a Man holding his Hat"; 60c. "Saskia in a Red Hat" (*all* 35×47 *mm*). P 13......................		4·50	5·00
MS1798 96×128 mm. $2 "Christ driving the Money-changers from the Temple". P 14........................		4·50	5·00

(Litho Questa)

2003 (4 July). 30th Anniv of CARICOM. P 14.

1799	**283b**	60c. multicoloured.................................	2·50	1·50

284 Tanya Streeter

284a Eddy Merckx

(1974)

2003 (15 July). Tanya Streeter's Freediving World Record (2002). T **284** and similar horiz designs. Multicoloured. Litho. P 14.

MS1800 98×179 mm. 20c. Type **284**; 20c. Tanya Streeter and practice dive; 20c. At seashore; 20c. With map of Turks and Caicos; 20c. Descending dive rope.............. 3·25 3·50

2003 (25 Aug). Centenary of Tour de France Cycle Race. T **284a** and similar vert designs. Multicoloured. P 14.

MS1801 160×100 mm. $1 Type **284a**; $1 Bernard Thévenet (1975); $1 Lucien van Impe (1976); $1 Bernard Thévenet (1977)................................. 10·00 11·00

MS1802 100×70 mm. $2 Bernard Hinault (1979)............ 5·50 6·00

285 Teddy Bear in Military Uniform

286 Prince William

2003 (25 Aug). Centenary of the Teddy Bear. German Teddy Bears. T **285** and similar vert designs. Multicoloured. Litho. P 12.

MS1803 184×129 mm. 50c. Type **285**; 50c. Teddy bear wearing blue dress, apron and headscarf; 50c. Musician bear carrying violin; 50c. Marching teddy bear wearing sword.. 3·50 4·00

MS1804 70×96 mm. $2 Beer mug with teddy bear pattern... 4·00 4·50

2003 (25 Aug). 21st Birthday of Prince William of Wales. T **286** and similar vert designs. Multicoloured. Litho. P 14.

MS1805 167×118 mm. $1 Type **286** (blue background); $1 Type **286** (pink background); $1 Prince William (head and shoulders).. 7·00 7·50

MS1806 76×101 mm. $2 Prince William .... 4·50 4·75

TURKS AND CAICOS ISLANDS

286a Vought F4U Corsair

287 Queen Elizabeth II wearing Imperial State Crown

2003 (25 Aug). Centenary of Powered Flight. T **286a** and similar horiz designs. Multicoloured. Litho. P 14.
MS1807 116×136 mm. 60c. Type **286a**; 60c. Messerschmitt Me 262; 60c. A6M; 60c. Hawker Hurricane .... 6·50   6·50
MS1808 101×76 mm. $2 Supermarine Spitfire Mk IX..... 5·50   5·50

2003 (25 Aug). 50th Anniv of Coronation. T **287** and similar vert designs. Multicoloured. Litho. P 14.
MS1809 147×91 mm. 80c. Type **287**; 80c. Wearing lilac dress; 80c Wearing Diadem .... 5·50   5·50
MS1810 Two sheets, each 76×101 mm. (a) $2 Queen in Garter robes. (b) $5 In profile .... 16·00   16·00

288 "Madonna of the Harpies" (detail, Andrea del Sarto)

(Litho BDT)

2003 (24 Nov). Christmas. T **288** and similar vert designs. Multicoloured. P 14.
1811   25c. Type **288**..   75   30
1812   60c. "Madonna and Child with St. Giovannino" (detail, del Sarto) ....   1·50   90
1813   80c. "Madonna and Child with St. Giuseppe and St. Pietro Martre" (detail, del Sarto) ....   1·75   1·60
1814 $1 "Madonna and Child with the Angels" (detail, del Sarto) ....   2·25   3·00
1811/14 Set of 4 ....   5·50   5·25
MS1815 81×115 mm. $2 Montefeltro Altarpiece (Piero della Francesca) ....   5·00   5·50

289 Beagle

(Litho BDT)

2003 (17 Dec). Dogs and Cats. T **289** and similar multicoloured designs. P 14.
1816   50c. Type **289**..   1·75   1·75
1817   50c. Persian ....   1·75   1·75
1818   60c. Sabueso Espagnol (dog) (vert) ....   1·75   1·75
1819   60c. Cymric (cat) ....   1·75   1·75
1820   80c. Basset Hound (vert) ....   2·00   2·00
1821   80c. Maine Coon (cat) (vert) ....   2·00   2·00
1822 $1 Jack Russell Terrier (vert) ....   2·50   2·50
1823 $1 Tiffany (cat) ....   2·50   2·50
1816/23 Set of 8 ....   14·50   14·50
MS1824 Two sheets. (a) 96×66 mm. $2 Dachshund. (b) 66×96 mm. $2 Kurile Island Bobtail (cat) (vert) Set of 2 sheets ....   11·00   12·00

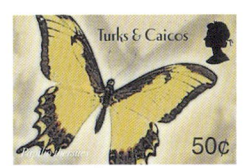

290 Papilio thersites

(Litho BDT)

2003 (17 Dec). Butterflies. T **290** and similar horiz designs. Multicoloured. P 14.
1825   50c. Type **290**..   2·00   1·40
1826   60c. Papilio andraemon ....   2·25   1·50
1827   80c. Papilio pelaus ....   2·75   2·50
1828 $1 Consul hippona ....   3·50   4·00
1825/8 Set of 4 ....   9·50   8·50
MS1829 96×66 mm. $2 Papilio pelaus ....   6·50   7·00

291 Laelia anceps

(Litho BDT)

2003 (17 Dec). Orchids. T **291** and similar horiz designs. Multicoloured. P 14.
1830   50c. Type **291**..   2·00   1·40
1831   60c. Laelia briegeri ....   2·25   1·50
1832   80c. Laelia fidelensis ....   2·75   2·50
1833 $1 Laelia cinnabarina ....   3·50   4·00
1830/3 Set of 4 ....   9·50   8·50
MS1834 96×66 mm. $2 Laelia rubescens ....   6·50   7·00

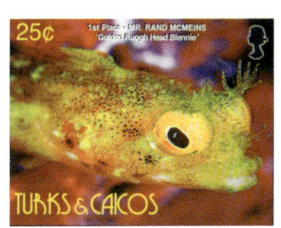

292 Golden Rough Head Blennie (Rand McMeins)

2006 (1 June). First Annual (2005) Turks and Caicos Underwater Photography Competition Entries. T **292** and similar multicoloured designs showing entries in photography competition. Litho. P 12.
1835   25c. Type **292**..   65   55
1836   50c. Octopus at night (Marc van Driessche) ..   1·25   1·00
1837   60c. Sea turtle (Mike Nebel) ....   1·40   1·25
1838   80c. Juvenile octopus (Amber Blecker) ....   1·75   1·75
1839 $1 School of horse eye jacks (Amber Blecker) ....   2·00   2·50
1835/9 Set of 5 ....   5·75   5·75
MS1840 261×102 mm. Nos. 1835/9. P 13 ....   6·50   6·50
MS1841 120×120 mm. $2 Coral reef (Keith Caplan) (vert). P 12 ....   4·25   4·50
Stamps from **MS**1840 have narrow blue borders.
No. 1835 is wrongly inscribed "Ruogh". The 25c. stamp from **MS**1840 is correctly spelled "Rough".

293 Young Queen Elizabeth II and Queen with Young Princess Anne

177

TURKS AND CAICOS ISLANDS

2006 (12 Sept). 80th Birthday of Queen Elizabeth II. T **293** and similar horiz designs. Multicoloured. Litho. P 13½.
MS1842 152×164 mm. 50c. Type **293**; 60c. Queen in recent years wearing white and wearing tiara; 80c. Queen in recent years wearing tiara and young Queen Elizabeth wearing white jacket and hat; $1 Painting of Princess Elizabeth in white dress and young Queen Elizabeth .... 7·50 7·50
MS1843 120×120 mm. $6 Young Queen Elizabeth II wearing diadem (*vert*) .... 14·00 14·00

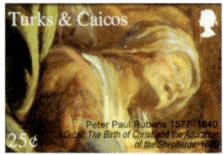

294 Shepherd

295 *Cymatium muricinum*

2006 (27 Dec). Christmas. Paintings by Peter Paul Rubens. T **294** and similar multicoloured designs. Litho. P 13½.

1844	25c. Type **294**...	70	40
1845	60c. Baby Jesus...	1·60	1·25
1846	80c. Two shepherds....................................	2·00	1·75
1847	$1 Virgin Mary..	2·25	3·00
1844/7 Set of 4...	6·00	5·75
MS1848 100×150 mm.As Nos. 1844/7.........................	6·00	6·00
MS1849 70×100 mm. $6 "Our Lady, the Christ Child and Saints" (detail) (*vert*)	13·00	14·00

Nos. 1844/7 show details from "The Birth of Christ and the Adoration of the Shepherds", and the margin of **MS**1849 shows the complete painting.
Nos. 1844/7 are inscribed with the title of the painting. Stamps from **MS**1848 omit this inscription.

2007 (11 June). Shells. T **295** and similar vert designs. Multicoloured. Litho. P 13.

1850	10c. Type **295**...	55	65
1851	15c. *Tellina radiata*	75	65
1852	20c. *Tonna maculosa*	1·00	50
1853	25c. *Leucozonia nassa*	1·00	50
1854	35c. *Trachycardium magnum*	1·25	70
1855	45c. *Papyridea soleniformis*	1·60	1·25
1856	50c. *Epitonium lamellosum*	1·75	1·25
1857	60c. *Astraea brevispina*	2·00	1·50
1858	80c. *Bulla striata*	2·50	2·00
1859	$1 *Murex margaritensis*	3·00	2·75
1860	$1.25 *Chama macerophylla*	3·50	3·00
1861	$1.40 *Vasum capitellum*	3·75	3·75
1862	$2 *Coralliophila abbreviata*	4·50	5·00
1863	$5 *Trachycardium isocardia*	8·00	8·50
1864	$10 *Oliva reticularis*	16·00	17·00
1850/63 Set of 15...	45·00	45·00

295a "The Virgin and Child" (Carlo Maratta)

296 Red-tailed Hawks

(Litho BDT)

2007 (10 Dec). Christmas. T **295a** and similar multicoloured designs. P 14×15 (*vert*) or 15×14 (*horiz*).

1865	25c. Type **295a**...	75	50
1866	60c. "The Adoration of the Magi" (detail) (Vincent Malo) (*horiz*)	1·60	1·25
1867	80c. "The Annunciation" (detail) (Robert Campin) (*horiz*)..	2·00	1·90
1868	$1 "The Adoration of the Magi" (detail) Giovanni di Paolo) (*horiz*)........................	2·25	3·00
1865/8 Set of 4...	6·00	6·00
MS1869 70×100 mm. $6 "The Adoration of the Magi" (Quentin Massys). P 14...	13·00	14·00

(Des Owen Bell. Litho)

2007 (24 Dec). Endangered Species. Red-tailed Hawk (*Buteo jamaicensis*). T **296** and similar horiz designs. Multicoloured. P 13½.

1870	50c. Type **296**...	1·75	1·75
	a. Horiz strip of 4. Nos. 1870/3...............	6·25	6·25
1871	50c. Adult at nest feeding young..............	1·75	1·75
1872	50c. Perched at edge of cliff, wings outstretched..	1·75	1·75
1873	50c. Close-up of head.................................	1·75	1·75
1870/3 Set of 4...	6·25	6·25
MS1874 115×168 mm. Nos. 1870/3, each ×2.................	12·00	13·00

Nos. 1870/3 were printed together, *se-tenant*, as horizontal strips of 4 in sheetlets of 16. No. **MS**1874 contains two blocks of the four different designs separated by a gutter.

297 Queen Elizabeth II and Prince Philip

298 Princess Diana

2007 (28 Dec). Diamond Wedding of Queen Elizabeth II and Prince Philip. T **297** and similar multicoloured designs. Litho. P 13½.

1875	$1 Type **297** (purple inscr).....................	2·75	2·50
	a. Sheetlet. Nos. 1875/80	15·00	13·50
1876	$1 Queen Elizabeth II (purple inscr).........	2·75	2·50
1877	$1 As No. 1876 (turquoise inscr)..............	2·75	2·50
1878	$1 As Type **297** (turquoise inscr)............	2·75	2·50
1879	$1 As Type **297** (black inscr)..................	2·75	2·50
1880	$1 As No. 1876 (black inscr)....................	2·75	2·50
1875/80 Set of 6...	15·00	13·50
MS1881 100×70 mm. $6 Queen Elizabeth II and Prince Philip on balcony (*horiz*)..	15·00	15·00

Nos. 1875/80 were printed together, *se-tenant*, in sheetlets of six stamps with enlarged illustrated margins.

2007 (28 Dec). Tenth Death Anniv of Princess Diana. T **298** and similar vert designs. Multicoloured. Litho. P 13½.

1882	$1 Type **298**..	2·25	2·25
	a. Sheetlet. Nos. 1882/5	8·00	8·00
1883	$1 Seen in profile, wearing red dress........	2·25	2·25
1884	$1 Seen in profile, wearing tiara..............	2·25	2·25
1885	$1 Wearing diamond and pearl drop earrings...	2·25	2·25
1882/5 Set of 4...	8·00	8·00
MS1886 101×70 mm. $6 Wearing fawn hat and pale sage-green jacket..	13·00	14·00

Nos. 1882/5 were printed together, *se-tenant*, in sheetlets of four stamps with enlarged illustrated margins.

299 Pope Benedict XVI

300 Silhouette of Lord Baden-Powell and National Flags

2008 (16 Sept). 80th Birthday of Pope Benedict XVI (2007). Litho. P 13½.
1887 **299** 75c. multicoloured... 2·25 2·25

No. 1887 was printed in sheetlets of eight stamps with enlarged illustrated margins.

(Des Michael Feigenbaum. Litho)

2008 (23 Sept). Centenary of World Scouting and 21st World Scout Jamboree, England (2007). T **300** and similar multicoloured designs. P 13½.

1888	80c. Type **300**...	1·50	1·50
	a. Sheetlet. Nos. 1888/93	8·00	8·00
1889	80c. Badge silhouette and jamboree emblems (peace dove emblem at bottom right)...	1·50	1·50
1890	80c. Badge silhouette and jamboree emblems (red and white chequered emblem at top right)..	1·50	1·50
1891	80c. Lord Baden-Powell silhouette and flags (white cross on red flag of Switzerland at bottom left)..	1·50	1·50
1892	80c. Lord Baden-Powell silhouette and flags (Philippines at top right, blue and red with sun in white triangle at left)	1·50	1·50

TURKS AND CAICOS ISLANDS

| 1893 | 80c. Badge silhouette and jamboree emblems (blue, white and red on green maple leaf badge at top right) | 1·50 | 1·50 |

1888/93 *Set of 6* .... 8·00 8·00
MS1894 110×80 mm. $6 Lord Baden-Powell (*vert*) .... 11·00 12·00

Nos. 1888/93 were printed together, *se-tenant*, in sheetlets of six stamps with enlarged illustrated margins.

301 International Space Station

302 "The Nativity" (Phillippe de Champaigne), 1643

2008 (23 Sept). 50 Years of Space Exploration and Satellites. International Space Station. T **301** and similar horiz designs. Multicoloured. Litho. P 13½.

1895	$1 Type **301**	2·40	2·40
	a. Sheetlet. Nos. 1895/8	8·50	8·50
1896	$1 Seen from above, over dry land	2·40	2·40
1897	$1 Seen from above, over clouds and ocean	2·40	2·40
1898	$1 Side view of International Space Station	2·40	2·40

1895/8 *Set of 4* .... 8·50 8·50
MS1899 100×70 mm. $6 International Space Station .... 13·00 14·00

Nos. 1895/8 were printed together, *se-tenant*, in sheetlets of four stamps with enlarged illustrated margins.

2008 (25 Nov). Christmas. T **302** and similar vert designs showing paintings. Multicoloured. Litho. P 14×14½.

1900	25c. Type **302**	65	45
1901	60c. "Mystic Nativity" (Sandro Botticelli), c. 1500	1·50	1·25
1902	80c. "The Virgin in a Rose Arbor" (Stefan Lochner), c. 1440	2·00	1·75
1903	$1 "The Adoration of the Shepherds" (Francisco Zurbáran), 1638–9	2·50	3·00

1900/3 *Set of 4* .... 6·00 5·75
MS1904 70×100 mm. $6 "The Virgin with Angels" (William Bouguereau) .... 13·00 14·00

303 Arrow Crab (Garin Bescoby)

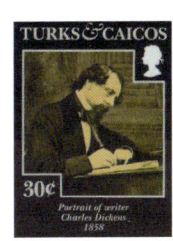

304 Charles Dickens, 1858

2008 (25 Nov). Third Annual (2007) Turks and Caicos Underwater Photography Competition. T **303** and similar horiz designs showing entries. Multicoloured. Litho. P 13.

1905	25c. Type **303**	60	45
1906	60c. Trumpet fish (Karin Nargis) (3rd)	1·40	1·25
1907	80c. Sting ray (Barbara Shively) (2nd)	1·75	1·75
1908	$1 Giant anemone (Roddy Mcleod) (1st)	2·25	2·75

1905/8 *Set of 4* .... 5·50 5·50
MS1909 130×100 mm. Nos. 1905/8 .... 5·50 6·00
MS1910 100×70 mm. $6 Red banded lobster (Jayne Baker) .... 13·00 14·00

(Litho)

2012 (12 July). Birth Bicentenary of Charles Dickens (writer). T **304** and similar multicoloured designs. P 14 (**MS**1911) or 12½ (**MS**1912).

MS1911 200×100 mm. 30c.×6 Type **304**; Illustration from *A Tale of Two Cities*; Charles Dickens, c. 1860; Statue of Charles Dickens in Philadelphia; Illustration from *OliverTwist*; Illustration from *A Christmas Carol* .. 3·00 3·00
MS1912 100×70 mm. $5 Portrait of Charles Dickens in his study (51×38 *mm*) .... 9·00 9·00

305 Titanic

306 Astronaut John Glenn

(Litho)

2012 (12 July). Centenary of Sinking of the *Titanic*. T **305** and similar horiz designs. Multicoloured. P 14.

MS1913 100×140 mm. $1×8 Type **305**; Bow of *Titanic*; Smokestacks of *Titanic* and crest of wave; Crest of wave and top of iceberg; *Titanic* (midsection with cabins); Iceberg; Survivors in lifeboat; *Titanic* sinking and survivors in lifeboat .... 13·00 13·00
MS1914 101×70 mm. $5 *Titanic* .... 9·00 9·00
MS1915 101×70 mm. $5 *Titanic* sinking and survivors in lifeboat .... 9·00 9·00

(Litho)

2012 (12 July). 50th Anniv of John Glenn's Orbit in Friendship 7. T **306** and similar vert designs. Multicoloured. P 14 (**MS**1916) or 12 (**MS**1917).

MS1916 150×110 mm. $1.25×4 Type **306**; Friendship 7 on launch pad; Blast off of Friendship 7; Friendship 7 splashdown .... 9·00 9·00
MS1917 100×70 mm. $6 Astronaut John Glenn and US flags .... 11·00 11·00

307 Dragon

(Litho)

2012 (12 July). Chinese New Year. Year of the Dragon. Sheet 130×70 mm. P 12.
MS1918 130×70 mm. **307** $3 multicoloured .... 5·00 6·00

308 Queen Elizabeth II

(Litho)

2012 (10 Oct). Diamond Jubilee. T **308** and similar diamond-shaped design. Multicoloured. P 13½.
MS1919 125×130 mm. $3.50 Type **308**×4 .... 20·00 20·00
MS1920 81×80 mm. $9 Queen Elizabeth II wearing tiara .. 14·00 14·00

309 Slave Cabin Replica, 2007, Cheshire Hall Plantation Ruins

TURKS AND CAICOS ISLANDS

(Litho)

2013 (7 Mar). 20th Anniv of Turks and Caicos National Trust. Sheet 65×65 mm. P 12½×13½.

| MS1921 | 309 | $3.50 multicoloured | 5·50 | 5·50 |

STAMP BOOKLETS

1977 (7 Feb). Silver Jubilee. Multicoloured cover, 80×55 mm. Stapled.
SB1 $1.60 booklet containing 25c. and 55c. (Nos. 473/4), each in pair .... 7·00

1978 (1 July). 25th Anniv of Coronation. Cover, 165×92 mm, black and purple on front showing Westminster Abbey and multicoloured on back. Stitched.
SB2 $3.60 booklet containing *se-tenant* panes of 3 and 6 (Nos. 499a/b) .... 1·90

1979 (27 Sept). Death Centenary of Sir Rowland Hill. Multicoloured cover, 165×92 mm, showing Penny Black stamp and Sir Rowland Hill. Stitched.
SB3 $3.55 booklet containing two different *se-tenant* panes of 6 and pane of 1 $1 (Nos. 552a, 558a, 564a).... 3·25

1981 (7 July). Royal Wedding. Cover, 165×90 mm; blue, gold and black on front showing Prince of Wales emblem and multicoloured on back. Stitched.
SB4 $5.60 booklet containing *se-tenant* pane of 6 and pane of 1 $2 (Nos. 657a, 659a) .... 2·40

1981 (1 Dec). Tourism. Multicoloured cover, 114×58 mm, showing tourist attractions. Stapled.
SB5 $4 booklet containing twenty 20c. (Nos. 675/84), in *se-tenant* blocks of 4 .... 9·00

1982 (18 Nov). 21st Birthday of Princess of Wales. Multicoloured cover, 101×49 mm, showing rainbow over South Caicos Harbour. Stapled.
SB6 $4.60 booklet containing 8c., 35c. and $1.10 (Nos. 713/15), each in strip of 3 .... 4·00

CAICOS ISLANDS

CAICOS ISLANDS
(1)

1981 (24 July). Nos. 514A, 518A 520A, 523A and 525A/7A of Turks and Caicos Islands optd with T **1**.

1	1c. Indigo Hamlet	15	30
2	5c. Spanish Grunt	20	40
3	8c. Four-eyed Butterflyfish	20	40
4	20c. Queen Angelfish	35	40
5	50c. Royal Gramma ("Fairy Basslet")	40	1·00
6	$1 Fin-spot Wrasse	60	1·75
7	$2 Stoplight Parrotfish	1·10	3·25
1/7	Set of 7	2·75	6·75

(2)   (3)

1981 (24 July). Royal Wedding. Nos. 653/6 of Turks and Caicos Islands optd.

A. With T **2** in London
8A	35c. Prince Charles and Lady Diana Spencer	20	25
9A	65c. Kensington Palace	30	40
10A	90c. Prince Charles as Colonel of the Welsh Guards	40	50
8A/10A	Set of 3	80	1·00
MS11A	96×82 mm. $2 Glass Coach	1·00	2·00

B. With T **3** in New York
8B	35c. Prince Charles and Lady Diana Spencer	30	70
	a. Opt inverted	£110	
9B	65c. Kensington Palace	40	1·00
	a. Opt inverted	80·00	
10B	90c. Prince Charles as Colonel of the Welsh Guards	50	1·50
	a. Opt inverted	90·00	
	b. Opt double	90·00	
8B/10B	Set of 3	1·10	3·00
MS11B	96×82 mm. $2 Glass Coach	1·00	2·50
	a. Opt inverted		

Nos. 8B/10 come either in sheets of 40 (2 panes 4×5) or in sheetlets of 5 stamps and one label. Examples of Nos. 8Ba, 9Ba and 10Ba are known from both formats, but No. 10Bb only exists from sheetlets.

Nos. 8B/10 also exist perforated 12 (*Price for set of 3 with London opt £2 or with New York opt £5, mint or used*) from additional sheetlets of five stamps and one label.

1981 (29 Oct). Royal Wedding. Booklet stamps. As Nos. 657/9 of Turks and Caicos Islands, but each inscr "Caicos Islands". Multicoloured. Roul 5×imperf*. Self-adhesive.

12	20c. Lady Diana Spencer	30	40
	a. Booklet pane. Nos. 12/13, each×3	3·00	
13	$1 Prince Charles	80	1·25
14	$2 Prince Charles and Lady Diana Spencer	4·00	5·50
	a. Booklet pane of 1	4·00	
12/14	Set of 3	4·50	6·50

*The 20c. and $1 values were each separated by various combinations of rotary knife (giving a straight edge) and roulette. The $2 value exists only with straight edges.

4 Queen or Pink Conch and Lobster Fishing, South Caicos

(Des J. Cooter (8c. to 20c.). Litho)

1983 (6 June)–84. T **4** and similar horiz designs. Multicoloured. P 14.

15	8c. Type **4**	2·00	
16	10c. Hawksbill Turtle, East Caicos	2·25	1·75
17	20c. Arawak Indians and idol, Middle Caicos	2·25	1·75
18	35c. Boat-building, North Caicos	2·25	2·25
19	50c. Marine biologist at work, Pine Cay	3·25	3·50
20	95c. Boeing 707 airliner at new airport, Providenciales	6·00	3·50
21	$1.10 Columbus' *Pinta*, West Caicos	6·00	3·50
22	$2 Fort George Cay (18.5.84)	4·00	5·00
23	$3 Pirates Anne Bonny and Calico Jack at Parrot Cay (18.5.84)	6·00	5·00
15/23	Set of 9	30·00	24·00

5 Goofy and Patch   **6** "Leda and the Swan"

(Litho Walsall)

1983 (7 Nov). Christmas. T **5** and similar vert designs showing Disney cartoon characters. Multicoloured. P 11.

30	1c. Type **5**	10	30
31	1c. Chip'n Dale	10	30
32	2c. Morty	10	30
33	2c. Morty and Ferdie	10	30
34	3c. Goofy and Louie	10	30
35	3c. Donald Duck, Huey, Dewey and Louie	10	30
36	50c. Uncle Scrooge	4·00	3·25
37	70c. Mickey Mouse and Ferdie	4·25	3·75
38	$1.10 Pinocchio, Jiminy Cricket and Figaro	5·00	4·50
30/8	Set of 9	12·00	12·00
MS39	126×101 mm. $2 Morty and Ferdie. P 13½×14	3·75	3·50

(Des and litho Questa)

1983 (15 Dec). 500th Birth Anniv of Raphael. T **6** and similar vert designs. Multicoloured. P 14.

| 40 | 35c. Type **6** | 75 | 50 |
| 41 | 50c. "Study of Apollo for Parnassus" | 1·00 | 70 |

TURKS AND CAICOS ISLANDS

42	95c. "Study of two figures for the battle of Ostia"	2·00	1·25
43	$1.10 "Study for the Madonna of the Goldfinch"	2·00	1·50
40/3 Set of 4		5·25	3·50
MS44 71×100 mm. $2.50, "The Garvagh Madonna"		3·00	3·25

7 High Jumping
8 Horace Horsecollar and Clarabelle Cow 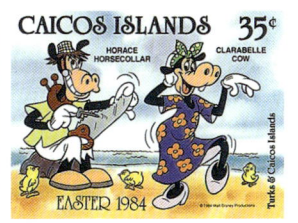

(Litho Questa)

1984 (1 Mar). Olympic Games, Los Angeles. T **7** and similar designs. P 14.

45	4c. multicoloured	10	20
46	25c. multicoloured	30	20
47	65c. black, deep grey-blue and new blue	2·25	75
48	$1.10 multicoloured	1·25	85
45/8 Set of 4		3·50	1·75
MS49 105×75 mm. $2 multicoloured		3·00	3·00

Designs: *Vert*—25c. Archery; 65c. Cycling; $1.10, Football. *Horiz*—$2 Showjumping.

(Des Walt Disney Productions. Litho Questa)

1984 (23 Apr). Easter. Walt Disney Cartoon Characters. T **8** and similar horiz designs. Multicoloured. P 14×13½.

50	35c. Type **8**	1·40	60
51	45c. Mickey and Minnie Mouse, and Chip	1·50	75
52	75c. Gyro Gearloose, Chip 'n Dale	1·90	1·25
53	85c. Mickey Mouse, Chip 'n Dale	1·90	1·40
50/3 Set of 4		6·00	3·50
MS54 127×101 mm. $2.20, Donald Duck		5·50	3·75

(9) **(10)**

1984 (19 June). Universal Postal Union Congress, Hamburg. Nos. 20/1 optd with T **9**.

| 55 | 95c. Boeing 707 airliner at new airport, Providenciales | 1·00 | 1·25 |
| 56 | $1.10 Columbus' *Pinta*, West Caicos | 1·25 | 1·50 |

1984 (22 Aug). "Ausipex" International Stamp Exhibition, Melbourne. No. 22 optd with T **10**.

| 57 | $2 Fort George Cay | 2·40 | 2·50 |

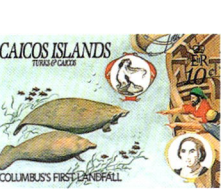

11 Seamen sighting American Manatees
12 Donald Duck and Mickey Mouse with Father Christmas 

(Des L. Lightbourne. Litho Walsall)

1984 (12 Sept). 492nd Anniv of Columbus' First Landfall. T **11** and similar horiz designs. Multicoloured. P 14.

58	10c. Type **11**	1·00	80
59	70c. Fleet of Columbus	3·75	3·25
60	$1 First landing in West Indies	4·25	3·25
58/60 Set of 3		8·00	6·50
MS61 99×69 mm. $2 Fleet of Columbus (*different*)		2·75	3·00

(Litho Questa)

1984 (26 Nov). Christmas. Walt Disney Cartoon Characters. T **12** and similar vert designs. Multicoloured. P 12 ($2) or 13½×14 (others).

62	20c. Type **12**	1·50	85
63	35c. Donald Duck opening refrigerator	1·75	1·00
64	50c. Mickey Mouse, Donald Duck and toy train	2·50	2·25
65	75c. Donald Duck and parcels	3·00	3·00
66	$1.10 Donald Duck and carol singers	3·25	3·25
62/6 Set of 5		11·00	9·25
MS67 127×102 mm. $2 Donald Duck as Christmas tree		3·75	4·00

No. 65 was printed in sheetlets of 8 stamps.

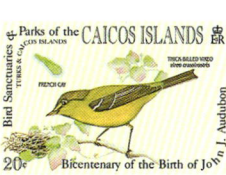

13 Thick-billed Vireo
14 Two Children learning to Read and Write (Education) 

(Des Susan David. Litho Walsall)

1985 (12 Feb). Birth Bicentenary of John J. Audubon (ornithologist). T **13** and similar horiz designs. Multicoloured. P 14.

68	20c. Type **13**	1·75	50
69	35c. Black-faced Grassquit	2·00	95
70	50c. Pearly-eyed Thrasher	2·25	1·50
71	$1 Greater Antillean Bullfinch	2·75	2·50
68/71 Set of 4		8·00	5·00
MS72 100×70 mm. $2 Stripe-headed Tanager		3·50	3·50

(Des C. Walters. Litho Walsall)

1985 (8 May). International Youth Year and 40th Anniv of United Nations. T **14** and similar vert designs. Multicoloured. P 14.

73	16c. Type **14**	20	25
74	35c. Two children on playground swings (Health)	50	55
75	70c. Boy and girl (Love)	1·00	1·10
76	90c. Three children (Peace)	1·25	1·40
73/6 Set of 4		2·75	3·00
MS77 101×71 mm. $2 Child, dove carrying ears of wheat and map of the Americas		2·75	3·75

15 Air Caicos Douglas DC-3 on Ground
16 The Queen Mother visiting Foundation for the Disabled, Leatherhead 

(Des K. Gromell. Litho Walsall)

1985 (23 May). 40th Anniv of International Civil Aviation Organization. T **15** and similar horiz designs. Multicoloured. P 14.

78	35c. Type **15**	3·50	55
79	75c. Air Caicos Convair CV 440 Metropolitan	4·50	1·40
80	90c. TCNA Britten Norman Islander	4·50	1·60
78/80 Set of 3		11·00	3·25
MS81 100×70 mm. $2.20, Hang-gliding over the Caicos Islands		3·00	3·25

(Des J.W. Litho Questa)

1985 (8 July). Life and Times of Queen Elizabeth the Queen Mother. T **16** and similar multicoloured designs. P 14.

82	35c. Type **16**	1·25	55
83	65c. With Princess Anne (*horiz*)	1·75	95
84	95c. At Epsom, 1961	2·25	1·60
82/4 Set of 3		4·75	2·75
MS85 56×85 mm. $2 Visiting Royal Hospital, Chelsea		5·00	3·00

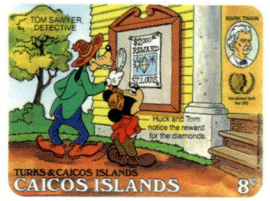

17

(Des Walt Disney Productions. Litho Questa)

1985 (5 Dec). 150th Birth Anniv of Mark Twain (author). Multicoloured designs as T **17** showing Walt Disney cartoon characters in scenes from "Tom Sawyer, Detective". P 14×13½.

86	8c. Huckleberry Finn (Goofy) and Tom Sawyer (Mickey Mouse) reading reward notice..	60	20
87	35c. Huck and Tom meeting Jake Dunlap	1·75	65
88	95c. Huck and Tom spying on Jubiter Dunlap..	3·25	2·00
89	$1.10 Huck and Tom with hound (Pluto)	3·25	2·25
86/9	Set of 4	8·00	4·75
MS90	127×101 mm. $2 Tom unmasking Jubiter Dunlap..	4·75	4·25

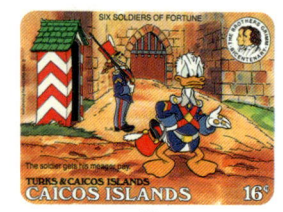

18

(Des Walt Disney Productions. Litho Questa)

1985 (5 Dec). Birth Bicentenaries of Grimm Brothers (folklorists). Multicoloured designs as T **18** horiz, showing Walt Disney cartoon characters in scenes from "Six Soldiers of Fortune". P 14×13½.

91	16c. The Soldier (Donald Duck) with his meagre pay...	1·70	30
92	25c. The Soldier meeting the Strong Man (Horace Horsecollar).............................	2·00	45
93	65c. The Soldier meeting the Marksman (Mickey Mouse).....................................	3·00	1·25
94	$1.35 The Fast Runner (Goofy) winning the race against the Princess (Daisy Duck)	3·50	2·25
91/4	Set of 4	10·50	3·75
MS95	126×101 mm. $2 The Soldier and the Strong Man with sack of gold	4·75	4·00

STAMP BOOKLET

1981 (29 Oct). Royal Wedding. As No. SB4 of Turks and Caicos Islands.

SB1	$5.60 booklet containing *se-tenant* pane of 6 and pane of 1 $2 (Nos. 12a, 14a)...................................	7·00

Commonwealth
Specialist Department

BY APPOINTMENT TO
HER MAJESTY THE QUEEN
STANLEY GIBBONS LTD
LONDON
PHILATELISTS

LOOKING FOR THAT ELUSIVE STAMP?

Send a copy of your wants list or call:

BRIAN LUCAS OR PAULINE MACBROOM

Tel: +44 (0)20 7557 4418 / 4450
Fax: +44 (0)20 7557 4499

email: blucas@stanleygibbons.com or pmacbroom@stanleygibbons.com

View our huge range of stock at **www.stanleygibbons.com**

STANLEY GIBBONS
Est 1856

Stanley Gibbons Limited
399 Strand, London, WC2R 0LX
+44 (0)20 7557 4444
www.stanleygibbons.com

Northern Caribbean Order Form

STANLEY GIBBONS Est 1856

YOUR ORDER

Stanley Gibbons account number ☐☐☐☐☐☐

Condition (mint/UM/ used)	Country	SG No.	Description	Price	Office use only
			POSTAGE & PACKING	£3.60	
			TOTAL		

The lowest price charged for individual stamps or sets purchased from Stanley Gibbons Ltd, is £1.

Payment & address details

Name

Address (We cannot deliver to PO Boxes)

Postcode

Tel No.

Email

PLEASE NOTE Overseas customers MUST quote a telephone number or the order cannot be dispatched. Please complete ALL sections of this form to allow us to process the order.

☐ Cheque (made payable to Stanley Gibbons)

☐ I authorise you to charge my

☐ Mastercard ☐ Visa ☐ Diners ☐ Amex ☐ Maestro

Card No. ☐☐☐☐ ☐☐☐☐ ☐☐☐☐ ☐☐☐☐ (Maestro only)

Valid from ☐☐ ☐☐ Expiry date ☐☐ ☐☐ Issue No. (Maestro only) ☐☐ CVC No. (4 if Amex) ☐☐☐☐

CVC No. is the last three digits on the back of your card (4 if Amex)

Signature

Date

4 EASY WAYS TO ORDER

Post to
Lesley Mourne,
Stamp Mail Order Department, Stanley Gibbons Ltd, 399 Strand, London, WC2R 0LX, England

Call
020 7836 8444
+44 (0)20 7836 8444

Fax
020 7557 4499
+44 (0)20 7557 4499

Click
lmourne@stanleygibbons.com/co.uk?

Did You Know You Can Buy
Northern Caribbean Till Sold or Given Away?

Plus All Other Countries of the World

By Using the Unique
UPA Reducing Estimate System

All Northern Caribbean Till Sold or Given Away:

Usually hundreds of Northern Caribbean lots offered each Quarter in our 20,000+ lot World auctions

Whatever You Collect Please

Request Your Free Catalogue Address Below / View Online at
www.UPAstampauctions.co.uk

Universal Philatelic Auctions (SG NCaribb)
4 The Old Coalyard, West End, Northleach, Glos. GL54 3HE, UK
T: 01451 861111 F: 01451 861297
e-mail: info@upastampauctions.co.uk

Because we sell more than most we always need to buy collections.
Northern Caribbean Stamps on Approval also available. Please ask.

Stanley Gibbons
Stamp Catalogues

We have catalogues to suit every aspect of stamp collecting

Our catalogues cover stamps issued from across the globe - from the Penny Black to the latest issues. Whether you're a specialist in a certain reign or a thematic collector, we should have something to suit your needs. All catalogues include the famous SG numbering system, making it as easy as possible to find the stamp you're looking for.

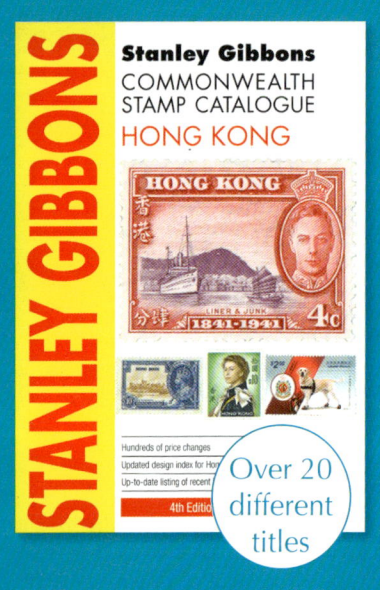

Over 20 different titles

Over 20 different titles

Over 5 different titles

Commonwealth Country Catalogues

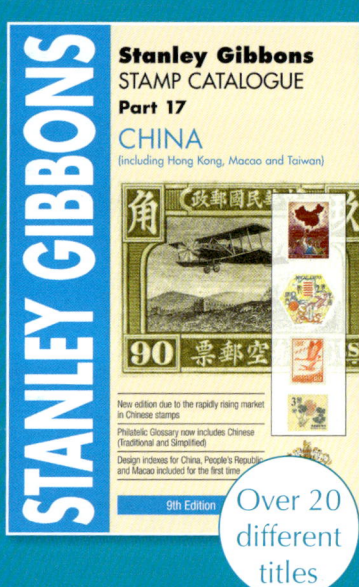

Foreign Countries

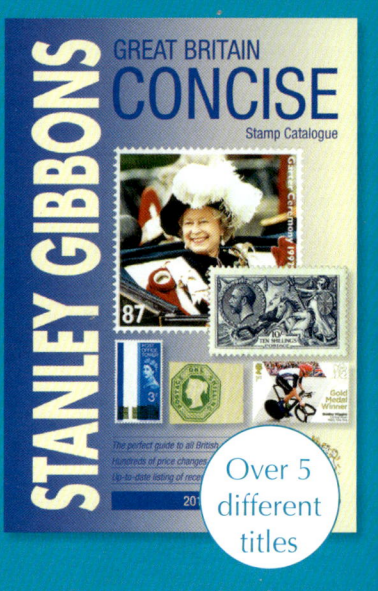

Great Britain Catalogues

For full details of our range of catalogues, call 01425 472 363
or visit www.stanleygibbons.com

Est 1856
STANLEY GIBBONS

Stanley Gibbons
7 Parkside, Christchurch Road, Ringwood, Hants, BH24 3SH
+44 (0)1425 472 363
www.stanleygibbons.com